BUSINESS/SCIENCE/TECHNOLOGY
CHICAGO PUBLIC LIBRARY
400 SOUTH STATE STREET
CHICAGO, IL 60605

Y0-DLD-005

REF

REF

TD   Environmental
169.3   regulatory
.E58   glossary.
1993

$68.00

DATE			

BUSINESS/SCIENCE/TECHNOLOGY DIVISION
CHICAGO PUBLIC LIBRARY
400 SOUTH STATE STREET
CHICAGO, IL 60605

BAKER & TAYLOR BOOKS

ENVIRONMENTAL REGULATORY GLOSSARY
Sixth Edition

Edited by

Thomas F. P. Sullivan

Government Institutes, Inc.

Government Institutes, Inc., Rockville, Maryland 20850

Copyright © 1993 by Government Institutes. All rights reserved.
Published June 1993.

98 97 96 95 94 93   5 4 3 2 1

No part of this work may be reproduced or transmitted in any form or by any means, electronic or mechanical, including photocopying, recording, or any information storage and retrieval system, without permission in writing from the publisher. All requests for permission to reproduce material from this work should be directed to Government Institutes, Inc., 4 Research Place, Suite 200, Rockville, Maryland 20850.

The editor and publisher make no representation or warranty, express or implied, as to the completeness, correctness or utility of the information in this publication. In addition, the editor and publisher assume no liability of any kind whatsoever resulting from the use of or reliance upon the contents of this book.

ISBN: 0-86587-353-4

Library of Congress Catalog Card Number: 92-43330

Printed in the United States of America.

PREFACE

The 1970s, 1980s, and now the 1990s have produced many new Federal statutes controlling pollution in the United States. Those statutes, in turn, have given rise to an even greater growth in regulations promulgated by the Environmental Protection Agency (EPA), the Occupational Safety and Health Administration (OSHA), and other Federal agencies implementing those statutes. As of 1993, the number of pages in the Code of Federal Regulations containing EPA's regulations totaled 11,722; OSHA's regulations covered 5,075 pages.

Because violations of the laws and regulations expose companies to fines and other penalties, clear and precise guidance on the scope of these requirements is crucial and places great emphasis on the numerous definitions used in the regulations and statutes.

While many regulations created new terminology to implement the statutory and regulatory provisions, many common terms and previously-used definitions assumed new meanings. The *Environmental Regulatory Glossary* collects these definitions and abbreviations in one convenient book. Definitions have been gathered from Federal agency regulations, from Federal statutes, and from government sources.

Users of this Glossary should be aware of what it is not. It is not a collection of absolute definitions but a resource to identify basic regulatory concepts. There may be other meanings for many of the terms but the definitions included in the Glossary often reflect use of the term in a specific regulatory or statutory context. Finally, the definitions are not static; use may vary and even the governmental interpretation may change.

Because the definitions are primarily drafted by the Federal government, there may be disagreement about the validity of a particular interpretation of a term included in the Glossary. Moreover, some definitions may only make sense with-in a particular framework. Explanatory statements have been added in brackets in an attempt to clarify the particular scope of the definition. Each definition also has a code letter indicating the source from which it came.

A glossary is a document that must be updated continuously. This is our sixth attempt at a compilation of the basic terms used in environmental regulations with which persons active in the field must be familiar. We welcome suggestions on future editions and sincerely hope that this will provide a useful tool to aid compliance with both the letter and spirit of the laws.

Thomas F. P. Sullivan, Editor

HOW TO USE THIS GLOSSARY

We have used key official sources for the definitions contained in this Glossary, namely the statutes and the *Code of Federal Regulations* plus U.S. EPA documents. The definitions have been compiled with editorial notes where needed.

Generally, at the end of each definition is a capital letter. This capital letter is a code (as shown) to designate the source.

Code	Source Material
A	Code of Federal Regulations, Title 40, Protection of Environment
B	Clean Air Act
C	Federal Insecticide, Fungicide, and Rodenticide Act
D	Federal Water Pollution Control Act (Clean Water Act)
E	Marine Protection, Research and Sanctuaries Act
F	National Environmental Policy Act
G	Noise Control Act
H	Occupational Health and Safety Act
I	Resource Conservation and Recovery Act
J	Safe Drinking Water Act
K	Toxic Substances Control Act
L	Comprehensive Environmental Response, Compensation, and Liability Act (Superfund or CERCLA)

Code	Source Material
<u>M</u>	Superfund Amendments and Reauthorization Act (SARA)
<u>N</u>	Official U.S. Environmental Protection Agency Documents
<u>O</u>	Code of Federal Regulations, Title 29, OSHA-Labor
<u>U</u>	Unpublished EPA documents

Acronyms and abbreviations also are included. An acronym is the first letter of each word in a series of words, while an abbreviation is a version of a word or phrase shortened by leaving out or substituting letters.

ABOUT THE EDITOR

Thomas F. P. Sullivan was an attorney in Washington, D.C. who has been in the forefront of the environmental field since the 1960s. He gained experience in industry before practicing law and representing clients in the environmental field. He has authored and edited numerous books such as *The Greening of American Business*, *Environmental Health and Safety Manager's Handbook*, and *Directory of Environmental Information Sources*. He is a regular lecturer internationally on environmental topics and currently serves as president of Government Institutes. Mr. Sullivan has undergraduate degrees from Cardinal Glennon College and St. Louis University, and a law degree from Catholic University.

ABOUT THE PUBLISHER

Government Institutes, now in its twentieth year, was one of the first organizations to provide practical and timely environmental information to the business community. Founded in 1973 when many of the nation's environmental laws were being enacted, Government Institutes has continued to be in the forefront as a source of compliance and regulatory information and has earned the reputation as the leader in the environmental, health and safety field. Its highly acclaimed reference materials provide authoritative guidance to engineers, managers, attorneys and professors in both federal and state environmental law, as well as environmental science and technology.

GI produces numerous vehicles of compliance information to help professionals interpret and implement the maze of government regulations. See the back of this book for more information on books, courses, subscriptions, videotapes and in-plant training capabilities.

ABOUT THE GI EDITORIAL TEAM

The GI editorial staff spent months combing through the regulations, reviewing the statutory amendments and collecting numerous documents from EPA. The 5th Edition had 449 pages while the 6th Edition has grown to 623 pages. Many contributed unselfishly to the successful completion of this project but special recognition must be given to Greg Balas as our project leader, Dave Williams, Cindy Adams, Charlene Ikonomou, and Diane Pacchione. To them and all of the GI staff contributors, thanks for a job well done.

A

A-scale sound level
A measurement of sound approximating the sensitivity of the human ear, used to note the intensity or annoyance of sounds. N

A&C
Abatement and control. U

AA
Adverse action. U

AAAS
American Association for the Advancement of Science. N

AAEE
American Academy of Environmental Engineers. N

AALACS
Ambient Aquatic Life Advisory Concentrations. A

AAP
Asbestos Action Program. U

AAQS
Ambient air quality standard. U

abandoned mine
A mine where mining operations have occurred in the past and (1) The applicable reclamation bond or financial assurance has been released or forfeited or (2) If no reclamation bond or other financial assurance has been posted, no mining operations have occurred for five years or more. A

abandoned well
A well whose use has been permanently discontinued or which is in a state of disrepair such that it cannot be used for its intended purpose or for observation purposes. A

abatement
Reducing the degree or intensity of, or eliminating, pollution. N

ABEL
EPA's computer model for analyzing a violator's ability to pay a civil penalty. N

ABES
Alliance for Balanced Environmental Solutions. U

abnormally treated vehicle
Any diesel light-duty vehicle or diesel light-duty truck that is operated for less than five miles in a 30-day period immediately prior to conducting a particulate emissions test. A

above ground storage facility
A tank or other container, the bottom of which is on a plane not more than 6 inches below the surrounding surface. A

above ground tank
A device meeting the definition of "tank" in 40 CFR 260.10 and that is situated in such a way that the entire surface area of the tank is completely above the plane of the adjacent surrounding surface and the entire surface area of the tank (including the tank bottom) is able to be visually inspected. A

abrasion
The wearing away of surface material, such as refractories in an incinerator or parts of solid waste handling equipment, by the scouring action of moving solids, liquids, or gases. U

abrasive wheel
A cutting tool consisting of abrasive grains held together by organic or inorganic bonds. Diamond and reinforced wheels are included. O

abs.
Abbreviation for absolute. A

ABS/SAN
Acrylonitrile - Butadiene - Styrene and Styrene-Acrylonitrile resin copolymers. A

absolute pressure (p.s.i.a.)
The sum of the atmospheric pressure and gauge pressure (p.s.i.g.). O

absorbed dose
The energy imparted to a unit mass of matter by ionizing radiation. The unit of absorbed dose is the rad. One rad equals 100 ergs per gram. U

absorption
The passage of one substance into or through another; e.g., an operation in which one or more soluble components of a gas mixture are dissolved in a liquid. N

ACBM
Asbestos-containing building material. A

accelerated erosion
The erosion of soil at a faster than natural rate. This occurs when vegetal cover is destroyed or is affected by some human activity. U

accelerator
(1) A device for increasing the kinetic energy of charged elementary particles, for example, electrons or protons, through the application of electrical and/or magnetic forces. (2) In radiation science, a device that speeds up charged particles such as electrons or protons. N

accelerator pump plunger
A device used to provide a supplemental supply of fuel during

increasing throttle opening as required. A

acceptable quality level
AQL. The maximum percentage of failings [regulated product] that, for purposes of sampling inspection, can be considered satisfactory as a process average. A

acceptance of a batch
The number of noncomplying vehicles in the batch sample is less than or equal to the acceptance number as determined by the appropriate sampling plan. A [ed. Part of certification procedures used to determine compliance with Federal emission limitations on new motor vehicles].

acceptance of a batch sequence
The number of rejected batches in the sequence is less than or equal to the sequence acceptance number as determined by the appropriate sampling plan. A [ed. Part of vehicle test certification procedures].

acceptance of a compressor
The measured noise emissions of the compressor, when measured in accordance with the applicable procedure, conforms to the applicable standard. A [ed. Part of noise standard certification procedures under Noise Control Act].

acceptance of a vehicle
The measured emissions of a vehicle when measured in accordance with the applicable procedure, conforms to the applicable standard. A [ed. Part of vehicle test verification procedures].

accepted
An installation that has been inspected and found by a nationally recognized testing laboratory to conform to specified plans or to procedures of applicable codes. O

accepted engineering practices
Those requirements which are compatible with standards of practice required by a registered professional engineer. O

access
A facility or practice shall not allow uncontrolled public access so as to expose the public to potential health and safety hazards at the disposal site. A

accessible
(1) As applied to equipment, admitting close approach; not guarded by locked doors, elevation, or other effective means. O (2) [As applied to wiring methods.] Capable of being removed or exposed without damaging the building structure or finish, or not permanently closed in by the structure or finish of the building. (See "concealed.") O

accessible environment
(1) The atmosphere; (2) land surfaces; (3) surface waters; (4) oceans; and (5) all of the lithosphere that is beyond the controlled area. A

accident
An unexpected, undesirable event, caused by the use or presence of a pesticide, that adversely affects man or the environment. A [ed. As used in connection with FIFRA].

accident site

The location of an unexpected occurrence, failure or loss, either at a plant or along a transportation route, resulting in a release of hazardous materials. N

accidental occurrence

An accident, including continuous or repeated exposure to conditions, which results in bodily injury or property damage neither expected nor intended from the standpoint of the insured. A

acclimation

(1) Physiological and behavioral adaptation to environmental conditions (e.g., housing and diet) associated with the test procedure. A (2) The physiological compensation by test organisms to new environmental conditions (e.g., temperature, hardness, pH). A

acclimatization

(1) The physiological and behavioral adjustments of an organism to changes in its environment. (2) The adaption over several generations of a species to a marked change in the environment. N

accredited

When referring to a person or laboratory means that such person or laboratory is accredited in accordance with section 206 of Title II of the TSCA Act. A

accumulated speculatively

A material is accumulated speculatively if it is accumulated before being recycled. A material is not accumulated speculatively, however, if the person accumulating it can show that the material is potentially recyclable and has a feasible means of being recycled; and that--during the calendar year (commencing on January (1)--the amount of material that is recycled, or transferred to a different site for recycling, equals at least 75 percent by weight or volume of the amount of that material accumulated at the beginning of the period. In calculating the percentage of turnover, the 75 percent requirement is to be applied to each material of the same type (e.g., slags from a single smelting process) that is recycled in the same way (i.e., from which the same material is recovered or that is used in the same way). Materials accumulating in units that would be exempt from regulation are not to be included in making the calculation. (Materials that are already defined as solid wastes also are not to be included in making the calculation). Materials are no longer in this category once they are removed from accumulation for recycling, however. A

accuracy

A measure of agreement between a measured value and an accepted or true value, expressed as the percentage difference between the true and measured values relative to the true value. A

ACEC

American Consulting Engineers Council. U

acetaldehyde (CH$_3$CHO)

A liquid sometimes found as an aerosol formed from gases in the

photochemical process; can be further oxidized to acetic acid. U

acetylcholine
A substance in the human body having important neurotransmitter effects on various internal systems; often used as a bronchoconstrictor. N

ACFM
Actual cubic feet per minute. O

ACGIH
American Conference of Governmental Industrial Hygienists. U

acid deposition
A complex chemical and atmospheric phenomenon that occurs when emissions of sulfur and nitrogen compounds and other substances are transformed by chemical processes in the atmosphere, often far from the original sources, and then deposited on earth in either a wet or dry form. The wet forms, popularly called "acid rain," can fall as rain, snow, or fog. The dry forms are acidic gases or particulates. N

acid or ferruginous mine drainage
Mine drainage which before any treatment either has a pH of less than 6.0 or a total iron concentration equal to or more than 10 mg/l. A

acid rain
See acid deposition. U

acidity
The quantitative capacity of aqueous solutions to react with hydroxyl ions. It is measured by titration with a standard solution of a base to a specified end point. Usually expressed as milligrams per liter of calcium carbonate. U

acidizing
Injection of acid through the borehole or "well" into a "formation" to increase permeability and porosity by dissolving the acid-soluble portion of the rock constituents. A

ACL
Alternate concentration limit, applicable in clean-up standards. N

ACM
Asbestos-containing material. A

active ingredient
Any substance (or group of structurally similar substances, if specified by EPA) that will prevent, destroy, repel or mitigate any pest, or that functions as a plant regulator, desiccant, or defoliant within the meaning of FIFRA sec. 2(a). A

acoustic descriptor
The numeric, symbolic, or narrative information describing a product's acoustic properties as they are determined according to the test methodology that the Agency prescribes. A

acoustical assurance period
AAP. A specified period of time or miles driven after sale to the ultimate purchaser during which a newly manufactured vehicle or exhaust system, properly used and maintained, must continue in compliance with the Federal standard. A

ACP
Air carcinogen policy. U

acquisition cost of purchased non-expendable personal property
The net invoice unit price of the property including the cost of modifications, attachments, accessories, or auxiliary apparatus necessary to make the property usable for the purpose for which it was acquired. Other charges such as the cost of installation, transportation, taxes, duty, or protective in-transit insurance, shall be included or excluded from the unit acquisition cost in accordance with the grantee's regular accounting practices. A

acrylic fiber
A manufactured synthetic fiber in which the fiber-forming substance is any long-chain synthetic polymer composed of at least 85 percent by weight of acrylonitrile units. A

ACS
American Chemical Society. N

act
The general term describing the legislative enactment which provides the authority for a particular regulatory action e.g., the Clean Air Act, the Clean Water Act. U

act of God
An unanticipated grave natural disaster or other natural phenomenon of an exceptional, inevitable, and irresistible character, the effects of which could not have been prevented or avoided by the exercise of due care or foresight. A, L

actinomycetes
A group of moldlike bacteria that give off an odor characteristic of rich earth and are the significant organisms in the stabilization of organic solid waste by composting. U

action level
(1) The exposure level at which OSHA regulations to protect employees take effect, e.g., workplace air analysis, employee training, medical monitoring, and recordkeeping. Exposure at or above the action level is termed occupational exposure. (2) Regulatory level recommended by EPA for enforcement by FDA and USDA when pesticide residues occur in food or feed commodities for reasons other than the direct application of the pesticide. As opposed to "tolerances" which are established for residues occurring as a direct result of proper usage, action levels are set for inadvertent residues resulting from previous legal use or accidental contamination. (3) In the Superfund program, the existence of a contaminant concentration in the environment high enough to warrant action or trigger a response under SARA and the National Oil and Hazardous Substances Contingency Plan. The term can be used similarly in other regulatory programs. (See: tolerances). N (4) A concentration designated in 29 CFR part 1910 for a specific substance, calculated as an eight (8)-hour time-weighted average, which initiates certain required activities such as exposure monitoring and medical surveillance. O

activated carbon
A highly adsorbent form of carbon used to remove odors and toxic

substances from liquid or gaseous emissions. In waste treatment, it is used to remove dissolved organic matter from waste water. It is also used in motor vehicle evaporative control systems. N

activated sludge
(1) Sludge that has been aerated and subjected to bacterial action; used to speed breakdown of organic matter in raw sewage during secondary waste treatment. N (2) Sludge that results when primary effluent is mixed with bacteria-laden sludge and then agitated and aerated to promote biological treatment. This speeds breakdown of organic matter in raw sewage undergoing secondary waste treatment. N

active grant
A project for which grant funds have been awarded, and the project period has not lapsed. U

active ingredient
(1) In the case of a pesticide other than a plant regulator, defoliant, or desiccant, an ingredient which will prevent, destroy, repel, or mitigate any pest; (2) In the case of a plant regulator, an ingredient which, through physiological action, will accelerate or retard the rate of growth or rate of maturation or otherwise alter the behavior of ornamental or crop plants or the product thereof; (3) In the case of a defoliant, an ingredient which will cause the leaves or foliage to drop from a plant; and (4) In the case of a desiccant, an ingredient which will artificially accelerate the drying of plant tissue. C

active institutional control
(1) Controlling access to a disposal site by any means other than passive institutional controls; (2) performing maintenance operations or remedial actions at a site; (3) controlling or cleaning up releases from a site; or (4) monitoring parameters related to disposal system performance. A

active life
(1) The period of operation beginning with the initial receipt of solid waste and ending at completion of closure activities in accordance with [40 CFR] § 258.60. A (2) Of a facility. The period from the initial receipt of hazardous waste at the facility until the Regional Administrator receives certification of final closure. A

active mine
An underground uranium mine which is being ventilated to allow workers to enter the mine for any purpose. A

active mining area
(1) A place where work or other activity related to the extraction, removal, or recovery of metal ore is being conducted, except, with respect to surface mines, any area of land on or in which grading has been completed to return the earth to desired contour and reclamation work has begun. (2) Areas, on and beneath land, used or disturbed in activity related to the extraction, removal, or recovery of coal from its natural deposits. This term excludes coal preparation plants, coal preparation plant associated areas and post-mining areas. A

active portion
(1) That part of a facility or unit that has received or is receiving wastes and that has not been closed in accordance with [40 CFR] § 258.60. A (2) That portion of a facility where treatment, storage, or disposal operations are being or have been conducted after the effective date of part 261 of [40 CFR] and which is not a closed portion. (See also "closed portion" and "inactive portion"). A

active waste disposal site
Any disposal site other than an inactive site. A

ACTS
Asbestos Contractor Tracking System. N

actual emissions
(1) The actual rate of emissions of a pollutant from an emissions unit. (2) In general, actual emissions as of a particular date shall equal the average rate, in tons per year, at which the unit actually emitted the pollutant during a two-year period which precedes the particular date and which is representative of normal source operation. The reviewing authority shall allow the use of a different time period upon a determination that it is more representative of normal source operation. Actual emissions shall be calculated using the unit's actual operating hours, production rates, and types of materials processed, stored, or combusted during the selected time period. (3) The reviewing authority may presume that the source-specific allowable emissions for the unit are equivalent to the actual emissions of the unit. (4) For any emissions unit which has not begun normal operations on the particular date, actual emissions shall equal the potential to emit of the unit on that date. A

actually be removed
The separation and isolation of discharged hazardous substances from the waters by chemical, physical, or biological means. A [ed. Used to determine application of requirements of 311 of FWPCA which hinge on the actual removability of the substance].

ACUS
Administrative Conference of the United States. U

acute
Occurring over a short period of time; used to describe brief exposures and effects which appear promptly after exposure. U

acute dermal LD$_{50}$
A statistically derived estimate of the single dermal dose of a substance that would cause 50 percent mortality to the test population under specified conditions. A

acute exposure
A single exposure to a toxic substance which results in severe biological harm or death. Acute exposures are usually characterized as lasting no longer than a day. N

acute health effect
An adverse effect on a human or animal body, with severe symptoms developing rapidly and coming quickly

to a crisis. Compare: chronic health effect. N

acute LC$_{50}$
A concentration of a substance, expressed as parts per million parts of medium, that is lethal to 50 percent of the test population of animals under specified test conditions. A [ed. Tests on live animals are used to determine degree of hazard as well as determine compliance with pollution control requirements].

acute lethal toxicity
The lethal effect produced on an organism within a short period of time of exposure to a chemical. A

acute oral LD$_{50}$
A single orally administered dose of a substance, expressed as milligrams per kilogram of body weight, that is lethal to 50 percent of the test population of animals under specified test conditions. A

acute oral toxicity
The adverse effects occurring within a short time of oral administration of a single dose of a substance or multiple doses given within 24 hours. A

acute respiratory disease
Respiratory infection, characterized by rapid onset and short duration. U

acute toxicity
(1) The discernible adverse effects induced in an organism within a short period of time (days) of exposure to a chemical. For aquatic animals this usually refers to continuous exposure to the chemical in water for a period of up to four days. The effects (lethal or sub-lethal) occurring may usually be observed within the period of exposure with aquatic organisms. A (2) A deleterious response (e.g., mortality, disorientation, immobilization) to a stimulus observed in 96 hours or less. A

acute toxicity test
A method used to determine the concentration of a substance that produces a toxic effect on a specified percentage of test organisms in a short period of time (e.g., 96 hours). In this guideline, death is used as the measure of toxicity. A

acutely toxic effects
A chemical substance produces acutely toxic effects if it kills within a short time period (usually 14 days): (1) At least 50 percent of the exposed mammalian test animals following oral administration of a single dose of the test substance at 25 milligrams or less per kilogram of body weight (LD$_{50}$). (2) At least 50 percent of the exposed mammalian test animals following dermal administration of a single dose of the test substance at 50 milligrams or less per kilogram of body weight (LD$_{50}$). (3) At least 50 percent of the exposed mammalian test animals following administration of the test substance for 8 hours or less by continuous inhalation at a steady concentration in air at 0.5 milligrams or less per liter of air (LC$_{50}$). A

ad valorem tax
A tax based upon the value of real property. A

adaptation
A change in structure or habit of an organism that produces a better adjustment to its surroundings. N

add-on control device
An air pollution control device such as carbon adsorber or incinerator which reduces the pollution in an exhaust gas. The control device usually does not affect the process being controlled and thus is "add-on" technology as opposed to a scheme to control pollution through making some alteration to the basic process. N

additions and alterations
The act of undertaking construction of any facility. A [ed. This type of physical change in a pollution source will often constitute a "modification" that will result in application of new source performance standards and certain new source review procedures under CAA and FWPCA].

additive
A chemical substance that is intentionally added to another chemical substance to improve its stability or impart some other desirable quality. A

additive manufacturer
Any person who produces or manufactures an additive for use as an additive and/or sells an additive under his own name. [ed. Used for § 211 of CAA]. A

additivity
A pharmacologic or toxicologic interaction in which the combined effect of two or more chemicals is approximately equal to the sum of the effect of each chemical alone. N

adenoma
A benign tumor originating in the covering tissue (epithelium) of a gland. N

adequate evidence
(1) More than mere accusation but less than substantial evidence. Consideration must be given to the amount of credible information available, reasonableness in view of surrounding circumstances, corroboration, and other inferences which may be drawn from the existence or absence of affirmative facts. A (2) Information sufficient to support the reasonable belief that a particular act or omission has occurred. A

adequate SO$_2$ emission limitation
An SIP stack emission limitation which was approved or promulgated by EPA as adequate to attain and maintain the NAAQS in the areas affected by the stack emissions without the use of any unauthorized dispersion technique. A

adequately wet
Sufficiently mixed or penetrated with liquid to prevent the release of particulates. If visible emissions are observed coming from asbestos-containing material, then that material has not been adequately wetted. However, the absence of visible emissions is not sufficient evidence of being adequately wet. A

adhesion
Molecular attraction which holds the

surfaces of two substances in contact, such as water and rock particles. N

adhesive
Any substance or mixture of substances intended to serve as a joining compound. A

ADI
Acceptable daily intake. N

adjacent
Bordering, contiguous, or neighboring. Wetlands separated from other waters of the United States by man-made dikes or barriers, natural river berms, beach dunes, and the like are "adjacent wetlands." O

adjusted configuration
[New Automobile] test configuration, after adjustment of engine calibrations to retrofit specifications, but excluding retrofit hardware installation. A [ed. Used for vehicle certification on test procedures under CAA].

adjusted loaded vehicle weight
The numerical average of vehicle curb weight and GVWR. A

administered dose
The amount of a substance given to a human or test animal in determining dose-response relationships, especially through ingestion or inhalation. Even though this term is frequently encountered in the literature, administered dose is actually a measure of exposure, because even though the substance is "inside" the organism once ingested or inhaled, administered dose does not account for absorption. N

administering agency
Any department, agency, and establishment in the Executive Branch of the Government, including any wholly owned Government corporation, which administers a program, including Federally assisted construction contracts. A

administration
Occupational Safety and Health Administration. [ed. Note: means EPA in 40 CFR.] O

administrative action
A nonjudicial enforcement action taken by the [EPA] Administrator (or designee) or a State. N

administrative amendment
An amendment to a [Federal] grant that does not involve additional costs to the government: e.g., rebudgeting of funds, extension of time without additional funds, changes in key personnel. U

administrative function
A nontechnical function individual in a Federal contract, sometimes referred to as a "business/fiscal" function. The clear separation of this from the technical area is often impossible. U

administrative law judge
Appointed pursuant to 5 U.S.C.3105 (see also 5 CFR Part 930, as amended by 37 FR 16787). Such term is synonymous with the term "Hearing Examiner" as used in the Act or in Title 5 of the United States Code. A [ed. Administrative Law Judges are given responsibility for conducting many adversary proceedings pursuant

to environmental statutes. They may be directed to make a final decision on the issue or make a recommendation to the head of the agency or department].

administrative order
AO. A legal document signed by EPA directing an individual, a business, or other entity to take corrective action or refrain from an activity. It describes the violations and actions to be taken, and can be enforced in court. Such orders may be issued, for example, as a result of an administrative complaint whereby the respondent is ordered to pay a penalty for violations of a statute. N

administrative order on consent
AOC. A legal agreement signed by EPA and an individual, business, or other entity through which the violator agrees to pay for correction of violations, take the required corrective or cleanup actions, or refrain from an activity. It describes the actions to be taken, may be subject to a comment period, applies to civil actions, and can be enforced in court. N

administrative procedure act
APA. A law that spells out procedures and requirements related to the promulgation of governmental regulations. N

administrator
The Administrator of the United States Environmental Protection Agency, or any employee of the Agency to whom the Administrator may either herein or by order delegate his authority to carry out his functions, or any person who shall by operation of law be authorized to carry out such functions. A, C, K, I, L

ADR
Alternative dispute resolution. N A term applied to mechanisms for resolving disputes other than litigation, e.g. arbitration, mediation, mini-trials. U

adsorption ratio
The amount of test chemical adsorbed by a sediment or soil (i.e., the solid phase) divided by the amount of test chemical in the solution phase, which is in equilibrium with the solid phase, at a fixed solid/solution ratio. A

ADSS
Air Data Screening System. N

adulterants
Chemical impurities or substances that by law do not belong in a food, plant, animal, or pesticide formulation. N

adulterated
Applies to any pesticide if: (1) its strength or purity falls below the professed standard of quality as expressed on its labeling under which it is sold; (2) any substance has been substituted wholly or in part for the pesticide; or (3) any valuable constituent of the pesticide has been wholly or in part abstracted. C

advance allowance
An allowance that may be used for purposes of compliance with a unit's sulfur dioxide emissions limitation requirements beginning no earlier than seven years following the year in

which the allowance is first offered for sale. A

advance auction
An auction of an advance allowance. A

advance sale
A sale of an advance allowance. A

advanced air emission control devices
Air pollution control equipment, such as electrostatic precipitators and high energy scrubbers, that are used to treat an air discharge which has been treated initially by equipment including knockout chambers and low energy scrubbers. U

advanced waste treatment
Any biological, chemical, or physical treatment process used during any stage of treatment that employs unconventional techniques. U

advanced waste water treatment
(1) Any treatment of sewage that goes beyond the secondary or biological water treatment stage and includes the removal of nutrients such as phosphorus and nitrogen and a high percentage of suspended solids. (2) The tertiary stage of sewage treatment. (See: primary, secondary treatment). N

adversary adjudication
An adjudication required by statute to be held pursuant to 5 U.S.C. 554 in which the position of the United States is represented by counsel or otherwise, but excludes an adjudication for the purpose of granting or renewing a license. A

adverse effect
A biochemical change, functional impairment, or pathological lesion that either singly or in combination adversely affects the performance of the whole organism, or reduces an organism's ability to respond to an additional environmental challenge. N

adverse impact on visibility
For purposes of [40 CFR] section 307, visibility impairment which interferes with the management, protection, preservation, or enjoyment of the visitor's visual experience of the Federal Class I area. This determination must be made on a case-by-case basis taking into account the geographic extent, intensity, duration, frequency and time of visibility impairments, and how these factors correlate with (1) times of visitor use of the Federal Class I area, and (2) the frequency and timing of natural conditions that reduce visibility. This term does not include effects on integral vistas. A

advertised engine displacement
The rounded off volumetric engine capacity used for marketing purposes by the motorcycle manufacturer. A

advisory
A non-regulatory document that communicates risk information to persons who may have to make risk management decisions. N

AEA
Atomic Energy Act. N

AEC
(1) Associate Enforcement Counsels.

C (2) U.S. Atomic Energy Commission. In 1975, the Atomic Energy Commission was divided into two new agencies. The regulatory portion became the Nuclear Regulatory Commission, and the reactor development portion became part of the Energy Research and Development Administration which in turn was absorbed into the U.S. Department of Energy. U

AECD
Auxiliary emission control device. A

AEE
Alliance for Environmental Education. U

AEM
Acoustic emission monitoring. N

aerated pond or lagoon
A natural or artificial wastewater treatment pond or basin in which mechanical or diffused air aeration is used to supplement oxygen supply. U

aeration
To circulate oxygen through a substance, as in waste water treatment where it aids in purification. N

aeration tank
A chamber used to inject air into water. N

aerobic
Life or processes that require, or are not destroyed by, the presence of oxygen. (ed. Compare: anaerobic). L

aerobic bacteria
Those bacteria that require free oxygen to live and grow. Used in certain types of waste water treatment processes. U

aerobic treatment
Process by which microbes decompose complex organic compounds in the presence of oxygen and use the liberated energy for reproduction and growth. Types of aerobic processes include extended aeration, trickling filtration, and rotating biological contactors. N

aerodynamic diameter
A measurement of the diameter of a particle expressed as the diameter of a unit density sphere with identical inertial properties. N

AEROS
Aerometric and Emissions Reporting System. A

aerosol
A particle of solid or liquid matter that can remain suspended in the air because of its small size. Particulates under 1 micron in diameter are generally called aerosols. U

aerosol propellant
A liquefied or compressed gas in a container where the purpose of the liquefied or compressed gas is to expel liquid or solid material from the container different from the aerosol propellant. A

AES
Augur electron spectometry. N

AFCA
Area fuel consumption allocation. N

affected employee
An employee who would be affected by the grant or denial of a variance, limitation, variation, tolerance, or exemption, or any one of his authorized representatives, such as his collective bargaining agent. O

affected facility
With reference to a stationary source, any apparatus to which a [air pollutant emission] standard is applicable. A

affiliate
(1) Persons are affiliates of each other if, directly or indirectly, either one controls or has the power to control the other, or, a third person controls or has the power to control both. Indicia of control include, but are not limited to: interlocking management or ownership, identity of interests among family members, shared facilities and equipment, common use of employees, or a business entity organized following the suspension or debarment of a person which has the same or similar management, ownership, or principal employees as the suspended, debarred, ineligible, or voluntarily excluded person. A (2) Any person whose governing instruments require it to be bound by the decision of another person or whose governing board includes enough voting representatives of the other person to cause or prevent action, whether or not the power is exercised. It may also include persons doing business under a variety of names, or where there is a parent/subsidiary relationship between persons. A

affiliated entity
A person who directly, or indirectly through one or more intermediaries, controls, is controlled by, or is under common control with the owner or operator of a source. A

after-flame
The time a test specimen continues to flame after the flame source has been removed. O

afterburner
(1) A/B. An exhaust gas incinerator used to control emissions of particulate matter. A (2) In incinerator technology, a burner located so that the combustion gases are made to pass through its flame in order to remove smoke and odors. It may be attached to or be separated from the incinerator proper. N

aftermarket part
Any part offered for sale for installation in or on a motor vehicle after such vehicle has left the vehicle manufacturer's production line. A

aftermarket part manufacturer
(1) A manufacturer of an aftermarket part or (2) A party that markets aftermarket parts under its own brand name, or (3) A rebuilder of original equipment or aftermarket parts, or (4) A party that licenses others to sell its parts. A

AGA
American Gas Association. U

aged catalytic converter
A converter that has been installed on a vehicle or engine stand designed

to chemically age, including exposure to representative lead concentrations, and mechanically stress the catalytic converter in a manner representative of in-use or engine conditions. A

Agency
(1) An Executive Department, as defined in 5 U.S.C. 101, or any employing unit or authority of the Executive Branch of the Government. O (2) The Environmental Protection Agency. J

agent orange
A toxic herbicide and defoliant which was used in the Vietnam conflict. It contains 2,4,5-trichlorophenoxyacitic acid (2,4,5-T) and 2-4 dichlorophenoxyacetic acid (2,4-D) with trace amounts of dioxin. N

agglomeration
The process by which precipitation particles grow larger by collision or contact with cloud particles or other precipitation particles. N

agglutination
The process of uniting solid particles coated with a thin layer of adhesive material or of arresting solid particles by impact on a surface coated with an adhesive. N

aggregate
Crushed rock or gravel screened to sizes for use in road surfaces, concrete, or bituminous mixes. U

aggregate risk
The sum of individual increased risks of an adverse health effect in an exposed population. U

AGI
Acute gastrointestinal illness. N

agreement states
Those states which, pursuant to Section 274 of the Atomic Energy Act of 1954, as amended, have entered into an agreement with the NRC for assumption of regulatory control of byproduct, source, and small quantities of special nuclear materials. Before approving an agreement state, NRC must determine that the state's radiation control program is compatible with NRC's regulatory program and is adequate to protect public health and safety. A

agricultural commodity
Any plant, or part thereof, or animal, or animal product, produced by a person (including farmers, ranchers, vineyardists, plant propagators, Christmas tree growers, aquaculturists, floriculturists, orchardists, foresters, or other comparable persons) primarily for sale, consumption, propagation, or other use by man or animals. A

agricultural pollution
The liquid and solid wastes from farming, including runoff and leaching from pesticides, fertilizers, and feedlots; erosion and dust from plowing; animal manure and carcasses; crop residues; and debris. N

agricultural solid waste
The solid waste that is generated by the rearing of animals, and the producing and harvesting of crops or trees. A

AHERA
Asbestos Hazard Emergency Response Act (1986). N

AIA
Asbestos Information Association. U

AICE
American Institute of Chemical Engineers. N

AIHA
American Industrial Hygiene Association. U

AIHC
American Industrial Health Council. N

air
So-called pure air is a mixture of gases containing about 78 percent nitrogen; 21 percent oxygen; less than 1 percent of carbon dioxide, argon, and other inert gases; and varying amounts of water vapor. U

Air Act
The Clean Air Act, as amended (42 U.S.C. 7401 et seq.). A

air bleed control device
A system or device (such as a modification to the engine's carburetor) that results in engine operation at an increased air-fuel ratio to achieve reduction in exhaust emissions of hydrocarbon and carbon monoxide from 1967 and earlier light-duty vehicles of at least 21 and 58 percent, respectively. A

air bleed to intake manifold retrofit
A system or device (such as a modification to the engine's carburetor) that results in engine operation at an increased airfuel ratio to achieve reduction in exhaust emissions of hydrocarbon and carbon monoxide from 1967 and earlier light-duty vehicles of at least 21 and 58 percent, respectively, and from 1973 and earlier medium-duty vehicles of at least 15 and 30 percent, respectively. A

air bleed/exhaust gas recirculation device
A system or device (such as modification of the engine's carburetor or positive crankcase ventilation system) that results in engine operation at an increased air-fuel ratio to achieve reductions of hydrocarbons and carbon monoxide of 25 percent and 40 percent, respectively, from light-duty vehicles of model years 1968 through 1971. A

air classifier
A system that uses a forced-air stream to separate mixed material according to size, density, and aerodynamic drag of the pieces. U

air cleaner filter element
A device to remove particulates from the primary air that enters the air induction system of the engine. A

air contaminant
(1) Any substance of either man-made or natural origin in the ambient air, such as dust, fly ash, gas, fumes, mist (other than H_2O), smoke, radiation, heat, noise, etc. (2) Any particulate matter, gas, or combination thereof, other than water vapor or

natural air. (See: air pollutant). N
(3) Any solid, liquid, or gaseous matter, any odor, or any form of energy, that is capable of being released into the atmosphere from an emissions source. A

air curtain
A method of containing oil spills. Air bubbling through a perforated pipe causes an upward water flow that slows the spread of oil. It can also be used to stop fish from entering polluted water. N

air emissions
The release or discharge of a pollutant (from a stationary source) by an owner or operator into the ambient air either (1) by means of a stack or (2) as a fugitive dust, mist or vapor as a result inherent to the manufacturing or formulating process. A [ed. Pollutants may also be discharged from mobile sources, from area sources such as roads and fields, and from non-manufacturing stationary sources]. U

air erosion
The passage of air over friable asbestos-containing building material (ACBM), which may result in the release of asbestos fibers. A

air flow controllers
Devices capable of maintaining constant air flows within ± 2% of the required flowrate. A

air flowmeters
Calibrated flowmeters capable of measuring and monitoring air flowrates with an accuracy of ± 2 percent of the measured flowrate. A

air heater
A heat exchanger through which air passes and is heated by a medium of a higher temperature, such as hot combustion gases in metal tubes. U

air jets
Streams of high-velocity air that issue from nozzles in an incinerator enclosure to provide turbulence, combustion air, or a cooling effect. U

air mass
A widespread body of air that gains certain meteorological or polluted characteristics--e.g., a heat inversion or smogginess-while set in one location. The characteristics can change as it moves away. N

air monitoring
The continuous sampling for, and measuring of, pollutants present in the atmosphere. N

air pollutant
(1) Dust, fumes, mist, smoke and other particulate matter, vapor, gas, odorous substances, or any combination thereof. A (2) Any air pollution agent or combination of such agents, including any physical, chemical, biological, radioactive (including source material, special nuclear material, and byproduct material) substance or matter which is emitted into or otherwise enters the ambient air. B (3) Any substance in air which could, if in high enough concentration, harm man, other animals, vegetation, or material. Pollutants may include almost any natural or artificial composition of matter capable of being airborne. They may be in the form of

solid particles, liquid droplets, gases, or in combinations of these forms. Generally, they fall into two main groups: (a) those emitted directly from identifiable sources and (b) those produced in the air by interaction between two or more primary pollutants, or by reaction with normal atmospheric constituents, with or without photoactivation. Exclusive of pollen, fog, and dust, which are of natural origin, about 100 contaminants have been identified and fall into the following categories; solids, sulfur compounds, volatile organic chemicals, nitrogen, compounds, oxygen compounds, halogen compounds, radioactive compounds, and odors. N

air pollution
The presence in the outdoor atmosphere of any dust, fumes, mist, smoke, other particulate matter, vapor, gas, odorous substances, or a combination thereof, in sufficient quantities and of such characteristics and duration as to be, or likely to be, injurious to health or welfare, animal or plant life, or property, or as to interfere with the enjoyment of life or property. A [ed. air pollution can occur in indoor locations, e.g. factories, but the EPA's authority under the Clean Air Act only extends to the outdoor atmosphere].

air pollution control agency
(1) A single State agency designated by the Governor of that State as the official State air pollution control agency for purposes of the Clean Air Act; (2) An agency established by two or more States and having substantial powers or duties pertaining to the prevention and control of air pollution; (3) A city, county, or other local government health authority, or, in the case of any city, county, or other local government in which there is an agency other than the health authority charged with responsibility for enforcing ordinances or laws relating to the prevention and control of air pollution, such other agency; or (4) An agency of two or more municipalities located in the same State or in different States and having substantial powers or duties pertaining to the prevention and control of air pollution. A, B

air pollution control equipment
Any equipment or facility of a type intended to eliminate, prevent, reduce or control the emission of specified air contaminants to the atmosphere. A

air pollution episode
A period of abnormally high concentration of air pollutants, often due to low winds and temperature inversion, that can cause illness and death. N

air pollution regulations
Legal constraints on pollutant emissions, production processes, or control systems. U

air pollution requirement
Any emission limitation, schedule or timetable for compliance, or other requirement, which is prescribed under any Federal, State, or local law or regulation, including the Clean Air Act (except for any requirement prescribed under section 119(c) or (d), section 110(a)(2)(F)(v), or section 303 of the [Clean Air] Act), and which limits

stationary source emissions resulting from combustion of fuels (including a prohibition on, or specification of, the use of any fuel of any type, grade, or pollution characteristic). A

air quality control region
An area designated by the Federal Government pursuant to § 107 of the Clean Air Act in which communities share a common air pollution problem, sometimes involving several States. N

air quality criteria
The levels of pollution and lengths of exposure above which adverse effects may occur on health and welfare. Also includes the compendia of data developed under 108 of the Clean Air Act as the basis for ambient air quality standards. L

air quality restricted operation of a spray tower
An operation utilizing formulations (e.g., those with high non-ionic content) which require a very high rate of wet scrubbing to maintain desirable quality of stack gases, and thus generate much greater quantities of waste water than can be recycled to process. A

air quality standards
The level of pollutants prescribed by law or regulation that cannot be exceeded during a specified time in a defined area. N

air toxics
Any air pollutant for which a national ambient air quality standard (NAAQS) does not exist (i.e. excluding ozone, carbon monoxide, PM-10, sulfur dioxide, nitrogen dioxide) that may reasonably be anticipated to cause cancer, developmental effects, reproductive dysfunctions, neurological disorders, heritable gene mutations or other serious or irreversible chronic or acute health effects in humans. N

air-cooled wall
A refractory wall with a lane directly behind it through which cool air flows. N

air/fuel control retrofit
A system or device (such as modification to the engine's carburetor or positive crankcase ventilation system) that results in engine operation at an increased air/fuel ratio to achieve reduction in exhaust emissions of hydrocarbon and carbon monoxide. A

airborne particulates
Total suspended particulate matter found in the atmosphere as solid particles or liquid droplets. Chemical composition of particulates varies widely, depending on location and time of year. Airborne particulates include: windblown dust, emissions from industrial processes, smoke from the burning of wood and coal, and the exhaust of motor vehicles. N

airborne pathogen
A disease-causing microorganism which travels in the air or on particles in the air. N

airborne release
Release of any chemical into the air. N

aircraft
Any airplane for which a U.S. standard airworthiness certificate or equivalent foreign airworthiness certificate is issued. A

aircraft engine
A propulsion engine which is installed in or which is manufactured for installation in an aircraft. A

aircraft exhaust emissions
Substances emitted to the atmosphere from the exhaust discharge nozzle of an aircraft or aircraft engine. A

aircraft gas turbine engine
A turboprop, turbofan, or turbojet aircraft engine. A

aircraft operation
An aircraft take-off or landing. A [ed. The number of aircraft operations influences air quality around an airport and may lead to regulation of the airport as an indirect source of air pollution].

aircraft power setting
The power or thrust output of an engine in terms of kilonewtons thrust for turbojet and turbofan engines and shaft power in terms of kilowatts for turboprop engines. A

airport
Public-use airport open to the public without prior permission and without restrictions within the physical capacities of available facilities. A

airshed
A term, denoting a geographical area, the whole of which, because of topography, meteorology, and climate, shares the same air mass. U

airway
Any conducting segment of the respiratory tract through which air passes during breathing. The bronchial tubes are examples of airways. N

airway resistance
The resistance to the passage of air exhibited by any part of the respiratory tract. U

AL
Acceptable level. U

ALAPO
Association of Local Air Pollution Control Officers. N

ALARA
As low as reasonably achievable. N

alcohol abuse
Any misuse of alcohol which demonstrably interferes with a person's health, interpersonal relations or working ability. A

aldehydes
A class of fast-reacting organic compounds containing oxygen, hydrogen, and carbon. U

Aldrin/Dieldrin formulator
A person who produces, prepares or processes a formulated product comprising a mixture of either aldrin or dieldrin and inert materials or other diluents, into a product intended for application in any use registered under the Federal Insecticide, Fungicide and

Rodenticide Act, as amended (7 U.S.C. 135, et seq.) A

Aldrin/Dieldrin manufacturer
A manufacturer, excluding any source which is exclusively an aldrin/ dieldrin formulator, who produces, prepares or processes technical aldrin or dieldrin or who uses aldrin or dieldrin as a material in the production, preparation or processing of another synthetic organic substance. A

alert level
That concentration of pollutants at which first stage control actions is to begin. An alert will be declared when any one of the following levels is reached at any monitoring site: (1) SO_2--ug/m^3, (0.3 ppm), 24-hour average. (2) Particulate--375 ug/m^3, 24-hour average. (3) SO_2 and particulate combined--product of SO ug/m^3, 24-hour average and particulate ug/m^3, 24-hour average equal to 65 x 10^3. (4) CO--17 mg/m^3 (15 ppm), 8-hour average. (5) Ozone (O_3)--200 ug/m^3 (0.1 ppm)--1-hour average. (6) NO_3--1130 ug/m^3 (0.6 ppm), 1-hour average, 282 ug/m^3 (0.15 ppm), 24-hour average and meteorological conditions are such that pollutant concentrations can be expected to remain at the above levels for twelve or more hours or increase, or in the case of ozone, the situation is likely to reoccur within the next 24 hours unless control actions are taken. (See "termination.") A

algae
Simple rootless plants that grow in bodies of water in relative proportion to the amounts of nutrients available. Algal blooms, or sudden growth spurts can affect water quality adversely. N [ed. Restrictions on discharges and other sources of pollutants are often intended to reduce nutrient loadings in the waters of the U.S.]

algal blooms
Sudden spurts of algal growth, which can affect water quality adversely and indicate potentially hazardous changes in local water chemistry. N

aliquot
A sample of specified volume used to make up a total composite sample. N

alive or live (energized)
Electrically connected to a source of potential difference, or electrically charged so as to have a potential significantly different from that of the earth in the vicinity. The term "live" is sometimes used in place of the term "current-carrying," where the intent is clear, to avoid repetition of the longer term. O

ALJ
Administrative Law Judge. N

alkali
Any chemical substance which forms soluble soaps with fatty acids. Alkalis are also referred to as bases. They may cause severe burns to the skin. Alkalis turn litmus paper blue and have pH values from 8 to 14. N

alkaline cleaning
Using a solution (bath), usually detergent, to remove lard, oil, and other such compounds from a metal surface. Alkaline cleaning is usually

followed by a water rinse. The rinse may consist of single or multiple stage rinsing. An alkaline cleaning operation is defined as a bath followed by a rinse, regardless of the number of rinse stages. Each alkaline cleaning bath and rinse combination is entitled to a discharge allowance. A

alkaline mine drainage
Mine drainage which, before any treatment, has a pH equal to or more than 6.0 and a total iron concentration of less than 10 mg/l. A

alkalinity
The measurable ability of solutions or aqueous suspensions to neutralize an acid. U

alkylation
The substitution of an alkyl radical for a hydrogen atom in a chemical molecule. An alkyl radical follows the general formula CnH2n+1. Alkylation is viewed as an event that may lead to toxicity. U

all-electric melter
A glass melting furnace in which all the heat required for melting is provided by electric current from electrodes submerged in the molten glass, although some fossil fuel may be charged to the furnace as raw material only. A

all-levels sample
One obtained by submerging a stoppered beaker or bottle to a point as near as possible to the draw-off level, then opening the sampler and raising it at a rate such that it is about 3/4 full (maximum 85 percent) as it emerges from the liquid. An all-levels sample is not necessarily an average sample because the tank volume may not be proportional to the depth and because the operator may not be able to raise the sampler at the variable rate required for proportionate filling. The rate of filling is proportional to the square root of the depth of immersion. A

allegation
A statement, made without formal proof or regard for evidence, that a chemical substance or mixture has caused a significant adverse reaction to health or the environment. A

allergen
Any of various sorts of material that, as a result of coming into contact with appropriate tissues of an animal body, after a latent period, induces a state of sensitivity and/or resistance to infection or toxic substances. U

alley collection
The collection of solid waste from containers placed adjacent to or in an alley. A

allocable costs
[In connection with Federal grants or contracts] those costs incurred specifically for the cost objectives of a particular project. For example, salary costs incurred on one project cannot be charged to another project. Note also, that an allowable cost may be unallocable, and an allocable cost may be ineligible or even unallowable. In order for a cost to be allocable to a grant or contract, it must: (1) be

incurred specifically for the grant or contract; (2) benefit both the grant or contract and other work, or both Government work and other work, and be distributable to them in reasonable proportion to the benefits received; or (3) be necessary to the overall operation of the business, although a direct relationship to any particular cost objective cannot be shown. Costs allocable to a specific cost objective, e.g., grant or contract, may not be shifted to other cost objectives in order to meet deficiencies covered by overruns or other fund considerations, to avoid restrictions imposed by law or the terms of the grant agreement, or for other reasons of convenience. U

allocable credits
[In connection with Federal grants or contracts] receipts or negative expenditure types of transactions which operate to offset or reduce expense items that are allocable to a grant project as direct or indirect costs are considered allocable credits. Typical examples of such credits are: purchase discounts, rebates, or allowances; recoveries or indemnities on losses; and adjustments of overpayments or erroneous charges. U

allotment
An amount representing a state's share of funds requested in the President's budget or appropriated by Congress for an environmental program, as EPA determines after considering any factors indicated by this regulation. The allotment is not an entitlement but rather the objective basis for determining the range for a state's planning target. A

allowable costs
Those eligible, reasonable, necessary, and allocable costs which are permitted under the appropriate Federal cost principles, in accordance with EPA policy, within the scope of the project and authorized for EPA participation. [ed. Applicable to Federal grants and establishing those items for which EPA will pay]. U

allowable emissions
The emissions rate of a stationary source calculated using the maximum rated capacity of the source (unless the source is subject to Federally enforceable limits which restrict the operating rate, or house of operation, or both) and the most stringent of the following: (a) The applicable standards set forth in 40 CFR Part 60 or 61; (b) Any applicable State Implementation Plan emissions limitation including those with a future compliance date; or (c) The emissions rate specified as a Federally enforceable permit condition, including those with a future compliance date. A [ed. The allowable emissions are the primary enforceable requirement imposed on stationary sources of air pollution]. U

allowance
An authorization, allocated by the [EPA] Administrator under the Acid Rain program, to emit up to one ton of sulfur dioxide during or after a specified calendar year. A

allowance tracking system
The system by which the Administrator allocates, records, and tracks allowances. A

allowance tracking system account
An account in the allowance tracking system established by the Administrator for purposes of allocating, holding, transferring, and using allowances. A

allowance transfer deadline
Midnight of January 30 or, if January 30 is not a business day, midnight of the first business day thereafter, and is the last day on which allowances may be submitted for recordation in an affected unit's compliance subaccount for the purposes of meeting sulfur dioxide emissions limitation requirements for the previous calendar year. A

alpha particle
The least penetrating type of radiation, usually not harmful to life. N

altered discharge
Any discharge other than a current discharge or improved discharge, as defined in 40 CFR § 125.58. A

altered growth
A change in offspring, organ, or body weight or size. Altered growth can be induced at any stage of development, may be reversible, or may result in a permanent change. N

alternative method
Any method of sampling and analyzing for an air pollutant which is not a reference method or an equivalent method but which has been demonstrated to the Administrator's satisfaction to produce, in specific cases, results adequate for his determination of compliance. A [ed. The administrator's prescribed "reference" method of sampling must normally be used by a source unless the administrator approves the source's request for an alternative method].

alternative technology
Proven wastewater treatment processes and techniques which provide for the reclaiming and reuse of water, productivity recycle wastewater constituents or otherwise eliminate the discharge of pollutants, or recover energy. Specifically, alternative technology includes land application of effluent and sludge; aquifer recharge; aquaculture; direct reuse (non-potable); horticulture; revegetation of disturbed land; containment ponds; sludge composting and drying prior to land application; self-sustaining incineration; methane recovery; co-disposal of sludge and solid waste and individual and on-site systems. A

alternative to conventional treatment works for a small community
For purposes of 40 CFR §§ 35.2020 and 35.2032, alternative technology used by treatment works in small communities include alternative technologies defined in paragraph (b)(4), as well as, individual and onsite systems; small diameter gravity, pressure or vacuum sewers conveying treated or partially treated wastewater. These systems can also include small diameter gravity sewers carrying raw wastewater to cluster systems. A

alternative wastewater treatment processes and techniques
Alternative waste water treatment processes and techniques are proven methods which provide for the re-

claiming and reuse of water, productively recycle waste water constituents or otherwise eliminate the discharge of pollutants, or recovery energy. (a) In the case of processes and techniques for the treatment of effluents, these include land treatment, aquifer recharge, aquaculture, silviculture, and direct reuse for industrial and other nonpotable purposes, horticulture and revegetation of disturbed land. Total containment ponds and ponds for the treatment and storage of waste water prior to land application and other processes necessary to provide minimum levels of reapplication treatment are considered to be part of alternative technology systems for the purpose of this section. (b) For sludges, these include land application for horticultural, silvicultural, or agricultural purposes (including supplemental processing by means such as composting or drying), and revegetation of disturbed lands. (c) Energy recovery facilities include codisposal measures for sludge and refuse which produce energy; anaerobic digestion facilities (Provided, That more than 90 percent of the methane gas is recovered and used as fuel); and equipment which provides for the use of digester gas within the treatment works. Self-sustaining incineration may also be included provided that the energy recovered and productively used is greater than the energy consumed to dewater the sludge to an autogenous state. (d) Also included are individual and other onsite treatment systems with subsurface or other means of effluent disposal and facilities constructed for the specific purpose of septage treatment. (e) The term "alternative" as used in this definition includes the terms "unconventional" and "alternative to conventional" as used in the FWPCA but not collector sewers, interceptors, storm or sanitary sewers or the separation thereof; or major sewer rehabilitation, except insofar as they are alternatives to conventional treatment works for small communities under 40 CFR § 35.915-1(e) or part of individual systems under 40 CFR § 35.918. A

alternative wastewater treatment works
A wastewater conveyance and/or treatment system other than a conventional system. Includes small diameter pressure and vacuum sewers and small diameter gravity sewers carrying partially or fully treated wastewater. A

altitude performance adjustments
Adjustments or modifications made to vehicle, engine, or emission control functions in order to improve emission control performance at altitudes other than those for which the vehicles were designed. A

alum tan
The process of converting animal skin into leather using a form of aluminum. A

aluminum basis material
Aluminum, aluminum alloys and aluminum coated steels which are processed in coil coating. A

aluminum equivalent
An amount of aluminum which can be produced from a Mg of anodes

produced by an anode bake plant as determined by 40 CFR § 60.195(g). A

aluminum forming
A set of manufacturing operations in which aluminum and aluminum alloys are made into semifinished products by hot or cold working. A

alveolar
Pertaining to the air sacs (alveoli) of the lung where gas exchange occurs. N

alveolar macrophage
A cell within the lung that contributes to immunological activities of the lung by phagocytosing (engulfing) and killing microbes, phagocytosing inhaled particles, secreting/excreting antimicrobial substances, and performing other activities. Under some conditions, it also can secrete/excrete enzymes capable of digesting lung tissue. N

alveolar ventilation
The volume of air entering the alveoli each minute. N

alveoli
The tiny air spaces at the end of the terminal bronchioles of the lungs, where the exchange with the blood of oxygen and carbon dioxide takes place. U

AMA
American Medical Association. N

AMBIENS
Atmospheric mass balance of industrially emitted and natural sulfur (experimental investigation by the MAP3S Community). N

ambient
Environmental or surrounding conditions. U

ambient air
(1) That portion of the atmosphere, external to buildings, to which the general public has access. A [ed. This is the area subject to jurisdiction of CAA]. (2) Any unconfined portion of the atmosphere: open air, surrounding air. N

ambient air quality standards
Those standards designed to protect the public health and welfare codified in 40 CFR part 50 and promulgated from time to time by the USEPA pursuant to authority contained in Section 108 of the Clean Air Act, 42 U.S.C. 7401 *et seq.*, as amended from time to time. A

ambient water criterion
That concentration of a toxic pollutant in a navigable water that, based upon available data, will not result in adverse impact on important aquatic life, or on consumers of such aquatic life, after exposure of that aquatic life for periods of time exceeding 96 hours and continuing at least through one reproductive cycle; and will not result in significant risk of adverse health effects in a large human population based on available information such as mammalian laboratory toxicity data, epidemiological studies of human occupational exposures, or human exposure data, or any other relevant data. A

amendment
Any change to a grant in terms of work scope, increase or decrease in funding level, changes in key personnel, site conditions, etc. U

amendment review
Review of any application requiring Agency approval to amend the registration of a currently registered product, or for which an application is pending Agency decision, not entailing a major change to the use pattern of an active ingredient. A

American Conference of Governmental Industrial Hygienists
ACGIH. An organization of professionals in governmental agencies or educational institutions engaged in occupational safety and health programs. ACGIH develops and publishes recommended occupational exposure limits for chemical substances and physical agents (see TLV). N

American Table of Distances
(Also known as Quantity Distance Tables). American Table of Distances for Storage of Explosives as revised and approved by the Institute of the Makers of Explosives, June 5, 1964. O

Ames test
An *in vitro* bacterial test for detecting point mutations in a group of histidine-requiring strains of *Salmonella typhimurium*. An Ames test is usually conducted with an exogenous source of metabolic activation by adding, for example, enzymes obtained from mammalian liver cells (S9 liver fraction), to the *S. typhimurium* assay system. N

ammonia stripping
The process in which ammonia is condensed from alkaline aqueous solutions after contact with steam at atmospheric pressure. It is commonly used in the treatment of hazardous waste. U

ammonia-N
Ammonia-Nitrogen. The value obtained by manual distillation (at pH 9.5) followed by the Nesslerization method specified in 40 CFR 136.3. A

ammonium sulfate dryer
A unit or vessel into which ammonium sulfate is charged for the purpose of reducing the moisture content of the product using a heated gas stream. The unit includes foundations, superstructure, material charger systems, exhaust systems, and integral control systems and instrumentation. A

ammonium sulfate feed material streams
(1) The sulfuric acid feed stream to the reactor/crystallizer for synthetic and coke oven byproduct ammonium sulfate manufacturing plants. (2) The total or combined feed streams (the oximation ammonium sulfate stream and the rearrangement reaction ammonium sulfate stream) to the crystallizer stage, prior to any recycle streams. A

amount of pesticide
The weight or volume of the pesticide, expressed as weight for solid or semi-solid products and as weight or volume for liquid products. A

ampacity
The current in amperes a conductor can carry continuously under the conditions of use without exceeding its temperature rating. O

amplitude
The voltage excursion recorded during the process of recording the compound nerve action potential. It is an indirect measure of the number of axons firing. A

AMPS
Automatic Mapping and Planning System. N

AMS
American Meteorological Society. N

AMSA
Association of Metropolitan Sewer Agencies. N

anadromous
(1) Fish that swim upriver to spawn, as do salmon. (2) Fish that spend their adult life in the sea but swim upriver to fresh-water spawning grounds to reproduce. N

anaerobic
A life or process that occurs in, or is not destroyed by, the absence of oxygen. N

anaerobic bacteria
Those bacteria that live and grow in the absence of free oxygen, to whom oxygen is lethal. U

analytical sensitivity
Airborne asbestos concentration represented by each fiber counted under the electron microscope. It is determined by the air volume collected and the proportion of the filter examined. This method requires that the analytical sensitivity be no greater than 0.005 structures/cm^3. A

anaphylaxis
An exaggerated reaction to an antigen to which an organism has been previously sensitized. N

anchorage
A secure point of attachment for lifelines, lanyards or deceleration devices, and which is independent of the means of supporting or suspending the employee. O

anemia
A condition characterized by a reduction in the number of circulating red blood cells and/or the number of hemoglobin molecules in red blood cells. N

anemometer
An instrument for measuring wind velocity. O

anergy
Diminished reactivity to specific antigens. U

aneuploidy
A condition in which the chromosome number is not an exact multiple of the usual number of chromosomes for that species. For example, a "normal" human has 46 chromosomes; an individual with 47 chromosomes would be described as aneuploid. N

angina pectoris
Severe constricting pain in the chest which may be caused by ischemia of the heart muscle; usually caused by coronary artery disease. U

anhydrous product
The theoretical product that would result if all water were removed from the actual product. A

animal
All vertebrate and invertebrate species, including but not limited to man and other mammals, birds, fish, and shellfish. C

animal feed
Any crop grown for consumption by animals, such as pasture crops, forage, and grain. A

animal feeding operation
A lot or facility (other than an aquatic animal production facility) where the following conditions are met: (i) Animals have been, are or will be stabled or confined and fed or maintained for a total of 45 days or more in any 12 month period, and (ii) Crops, vegetation, forage growth or post-harvest residues are not sustained in the normal growing season over any portion of the lot or facility. Two or more animal feeding operations under common ownership are deemed to be a single animal feeding operation if they are adjacent to each other or if they utilize a common area or system for the disposal of wastes. A

animal studies
Investigations using animals as surrogates for humans, on the expectation that results in animals are pertinent to humans. U

animal unit
A unit of measurement for any animal feeding operation calculated by adding the following numbers: The number of slaughter and feeder cattle multiplied by 1.0, plus the number of mature dairy cattle multiplied by 1.4, plus the number of swine weighing over 55 pounds multiplied by 0.4, plus the number of sheep multiplied by 0.1, plus the number of horses multiplied by 2.0. A [ed. The animal units determine whether the operation is a "concentrated" animal feeding operation that must have an NPDES permit if it discharges pollutants to the navigable waters].

animal waste
The high organic waste that is generated by the breeding, maintenance, use and slaughter of animals. U

animals
Appropriately sensitive living organisms which carry out respiration by means of a lung structure permitting gaseous exchange between air and the circulatory system. A

annual average
The maximum allowable discharge of BOD5 or TSS as calculated by multiplying the total mass (kkg or 1000 lb) of each raw commodity processed for

the entire processing season or calendar year by the applicable annual average limitation. A [ed. This period of measurement is one element of effluent limitations imposed on direct discharges].

annual capacity factor
The ratio between the actual heat input to a steam generating unit from the fuels listed in [40 CFR] § 60.42b(a), § 60.43b(a), or § 60.44b(a), as applicable, during a calendar year and the potential heat input to the steam generating unit had it been operated for 8,760 hours during a calendar year at the maximum steady state design heat input capacity. In the case of steam generating units that are rented or leased, the actual heat input shall be determined based on the combined heat input from all operations of the affected facility in a calendar year. A

annual document log (PCB)
The detailed information maintained at the facility on the PCB waste handling at the facility. A

annual incidence
The number of new cases of a disease occurring or predicted to occur in a population over a year. U

annual precipitation and annual evaporation
The mean annual precipitation and mean annual lake evaporation respectively, as established by the U.S. Department of Commerce, Environmental Science Services Administration, Environmental Data Services, or equivalent regional rainfall and evaporation data. A [ed. These measurements are used to determine the minimum size of some water treatment systems that utilize retention ponds].

annual report (PCB)
The written document submitted each year by each disposer and commercial storer of PCB waste to the appropriate EPA Regional Administrator. The annual report is a brief summary of the information included in the annual document log. A

annual research period
The time period from August 1 of a previous calendar year to July 31 of the given calendar year, e.g., the 1981 annual research period would be the time period from August 1, 1980 to July 31, 1981. A

anode bake plant
A facility which produces carbon anodes for use in a primary aluminum reduction plant. A

ANOVA
Analysis of variance. U

anoxia
Absence/lack of or significant reduction in oxygen. N

ANPR
Advance notice of proposed rulemaking. A preliminary notice that an agency is considering a regulatory action. It is issued before the agency develops a detailed proposed rule. It usually describes the general area that will be subject to the regulation, lists the alternatives that are under consideration, and asks for public comment

in developing a regulation. [ed. Often used by Federal agencies to stimulate data development and public discussion of a new program before a decision is made on the content of a proposed regulation]. N

ANSI
American National Standards Institute. A privately funded, voluntary membership organization that identifies industrial and public need for national consensus standards and coordinates the development. N

ANSI S3.19-1974
A revision of the ANSI Z24.22-1957 measurement procedure using one-third octave band stimuli presented under diffuse (reverberant) acoustic field conditions. A

ANSI Z24.22-1957
A measurement procedure published by the American National Standards Institute (ANSI) for obtaining hearing protector attenuation values at nine of the one-third octave band center frequencies by using pure tone stimuli presented to ten different test subjects under anechoic conditions. A

antagonism
A pharmacologic or toxicologic interaction in which the combined effect of two chemicals is less than the sum of the effect of each chemical alone; the chemicals either interfere with each other's actions, or one interferes with the action of the other. N

antarctic "ozone hole"
Refers to the seasonal depletion of ozone in a large area over Antarctica. N

anthracite
Coal that is classified as anthracite according to the American Society of Testing and Materials' (ASTM) Standard Specification for Classification of Coals by Rank D388-77. A

anti-degradation
Part of federal air quality and water quality requirements prohibiting deterioration where pollution levels are above the legal limit. N

anti-degradation clause
Regulatory concept that limits deterioration of existing air or water quality by restricting the addition of pollutants. N

antibodies
Proteins produced in the body by immune system cells in response to antigens, and capable of combining with antigens. N

anticoagulant
A chemical that interferes with blood clotting. N

antidote
A remedy to relieve, prevent, or counteract the affects of a poison. N

antigen
A substance that causes production of antibodies when introduced into animal or human tissue. N

antimicrobial agents
Includes all substances or mixtures of substances, except those defined as

fungicides and slimicides, intended for inhibiting the growth of, or destroying any bacteria, fungi pathogenic to man and other animals or viruses declared to be pests under 40 CFR 162.14 and existing in any environment except those specifically excluded: (i) Antimicrobial agents include, but are not limited to: (A) Disinfectants intended to destroy or irreversibly inactivate infectious or other undesirable bacteria, pathogenic fungi, or viruses on surfaces or inanimate objects. (B) Sanitizers intended to reduce the number of living bacteria or viable virus particles on inanimate surfaces, in water, or in air; (C) Bacteriostats intended to inhibit the growth of bacteria in the presence of moisture; (D) Sterilizers intended to destroy viruses and all living bacteria, fungi and their spores, on inanimate surfaces; (E) Fungicides and fungistats intended to inhibit the growth of, or destroy fungi (including yeasts), pathogenic to man or other animals on inanimate surfaces; and (F) Commodity preservatives and protectants intended to inhibit the growth of, or destroy bacteria in or on raw materials (such as adhesives and plastics) used in manufacturing, or manufactured products (such as fuel, textiles, lubricants, and paints). (ii) Antimicrobial agents do not include those antimicrobial substances or mixtures of substances subject to the provisions of the Federal Food, Drug and Cosmetic Act, as amended (21 U.S.C. 301 et seq.), such as: (A) Substances or mixtures of substances intended to inhibit the growth of, inactivate or destroy fungi, bacteria, or viruses in or on living man or other animals; and (B) Substances or mixtures of substances intended to inhibit the growth of, inactivate or destroy fungi, bacteria, or viruses in or on processed food, beverages, or pharmaceuticals including cosmetics. A

antimony
The total antimony present in the process wastewater stream exiting the wastewater treatment system. A

ANWR
Alaska Arctic National Wildlife Refuge. N

AO
Administrative Order. U

AOC
Administrative Order on Consent. U

APA
Administrative Procedure Act. U

APCA
Air Pollution Control Association. N

APCD
(1) Air pollution control device. U
(2) Air pollution control district. U

APCE
(1) Air pollution control equipment. U

APHA
American Public Health Association. N

API
American Petroleum Institute. A

API gravity
An empirical scale for measuring the density of liquid petroleum products, the unit being called the "degree API." A

apnea
Temporary cessation of breathing. N

appearance
A description of a substance at normal room temperature and normal atmospheric conditions. Appearance includes the color, size, and consistency of a material. N

appliances
Utilization equipment, generally other than industrial, normally built in standardized sizes or types, which is installed or connected as a unit to perform one or more functions such as clothes washing, air conditioning, food mixing, deep frying, etc. O

applicable effluent standards and limitations
All state and Federal effluent standards and limitations to which a discharge is subject under the [Clean Water] Act, including, but not limited to, effluent limitations, standards of performance, toxic effluent standards and prohibitions, and pretreatment standards. A

applicable legal requirements
(1) In the case of any major source, any emission limitation, emission standard, or compliance schedule under a EPA-approved state implementation plan (regardless of whether the source is subject to a Federal or state consent decree). (2) In the case of any source, any emission limitation, emission standard, standard of performance, or other requirement (including, but not limited to, work practice standards) established under Section 111 or 112 of the [Clean Air] Act. (3) In the case of a source that is subject to a Federal or Federally approved state judicial consent decree or EPA approved extension, order, or suspension, any interim emission control requirement or schedule of compliance under that consent decree, extension, order or suspension. (4) In the case of a nonferrous smelter which has received a primary nonferrous smelter order issued or approved by EPA under Section 119 of the [Clean Air] Act, any interim emission control requirement (including a requirement relating to the use of supplemental or intermittent controls) or schedule of compliance under that order. A

applicable standards and limitations (NPDES)
All state, interstate, and Federal standards and limitations to which a "discharge" or a related activity is subject under the CWA, including "effluent limitations," water quality standards, standards of performance, toxic effluent standards or prohibitions, "best management practices," and pretreatment standards under sections 301, 302, 303, 304, 306, 307, 308, 403, and 405 of CWA. A

applicable water quality standards
State water quality standards adopted by the state and approved by EPA pursuant to section 303 of the [Federal Water Pollution Control] Act

or promulgated by EPA pursuant to that section. A

applicant
(1) The person who requests a permit, grant, or other governmental authorization under Federal, state or local pollution laws. (2) Any person who has made application to have a pesticide registered or classified pursuant to the provisions of the FIFRA Act. A (3) A person who applies for a registration, amended registration, or reregistration, under FIFRA sec. 3. A

application
The EPA standard national forms for applying for a permit, including any additions, revisions or modifications to the forms; or forms approved by EPA for use in "approved States," including any approved modifications or revisions. A

application for research or marketing permit
Includes: (1) an application for registration, amended registration, or reregistration of a pesticide product under FIFRA sections 3, 4 or 24(c). (2) an application for an experimental use permit under FIFRA section 5. (3) an application for an exemption under FIFRA section 18. (4) a petition or other request for establishment or modification of a tolerance, for an exemption for the need for a tolerance, or for other clearance under FFDCA section 408. (5) a petition or other request for establishment or modification of a food additive regulation or other clearance by EPA under FFDCA section 409. (6) a submission of data in response to a notice issued by EPA under FIFRA section 3(c)(2)(B). (7) any other application, petition, or submission sent to EPA intended to persuade EPA to grant, modify, or leave unmodified a registration or other approval required as a condition of sale or distribution of a pesticide. A

application of a pesticide
The placement for effect of a pesticide at or on the site where the pest control or other response is desired. A

application, part A
That part of the Consolidated Permit Application forms which a RCRA permit applicant must complete to qualify for interim status under Section 3005(e) of RCRA and for consideration for a permit. Part A consists of Form 1 (General Information) and Form 3 (Hazardous Waste Application Form). N

application, part B
That part of the application which a RCRA permit applicant must complete to be issued a permit. (Note: EPA is not developing a specific form for Part B of the permit application, but an instruction booklet explaining what information must be supplied is available from the EPA Regional Office). N

applied coating solids
Volume of dried or cured coating solids which is deposited and remains on the surface of the automobile or light-duty truck body. A

applied dose
The amount of a substance given to

a human or test animal in determining dose-response relationships, esp. through dermal contact (see administered dose). Even though this term is encountered in the literature, applied dose is actually a measure of exposure, since it does not take absorption into account. N

approach angle
The smallest angle in a plan side view of an automobile, formed by the level surface on which the automobile is standing and a line tangent to the front tire static loaded radius arc and touching the underside of the automobile forward of the front tire. A

appropriate program official
The official at each decision level to whom the Assistant Administrator has delegated responsibility for carrying out the environmental review process. A

appropriate sensitive benthic marine organisms
At least one species each representing filter-feeding, deposit-feeding, and burrowing species chosen from among the most sensitive species accepted by EPA as being reliable test organisms to determine the anticipated impact on the site; provided, however, that until sufficient species are adequately tested and documented, interim guidance on appropriate organisms available for use will be provided by the Administrator, Regional Administrator, or the District Engineer, as the case may be. A [ed. Used to determine the acceptability of a site for ocean dumping of wastes].

appropriate sensitive marine organisms
At least one species each representative of phytoplankton or zooplankton, crustacean or mollusk, and fish species chosen from among the most sensitive species documented in the scientific literature or accepted by EPA as being reliable test organisms to determine the anticipated impact of the wastes on the ecosystem at the disposal site. Bioassays, except on phytoplankton or zooplankton, shall be run for a minimum of 96 hours under temperature, salinity, and dissolved oxygen conditions representing the extremes of environmental stress at the disposal site. Bioassays on phytoplankton or zooplankton may be run for shorter periods of time as appropriate for the organisms tested at the discretion of EPA, or EPA and the Corps of Engineers, as the case may be. A [ed. Used to determine the acceptability of a site for ocean dumping of wastes].

appropriations
Budget authority provided through the congressional appropriation process that permits Federal agencies to incur obligations and to make payments. U

approval authority
The Director in an NPDES State with an approved State pretreatment program and the appropriate Regional Administrator in a non-NPDES State or NPDES State without an approved State pretreatment program. A

approval of the facilities plan
Approval of the facilities plan for a proposed wastewater treatment works

pursuant to 40 CFR part 35, subpart E or I. A

approved
(1) Sanctioned, endorsed, accredited, certified, or accepted as satisfactory by a duly constituted and nationally recognized authority or agency. O (2) For the purpose of [29 CFR], means equipment that has been listed or approved by a nationally recognized testing laboratory such as Factory Mutual Engineering Corp., or Underwriters' Laboratories, Inc., or Federal agencies such as Bureau of Mines, or U.S. Coast Guard, which issue approvals for such equipment. O (3) Unless otherwise indicated, listed or approved by a nationally recognized testing laboratory. Refer to [20 CFR] § 1910.7 for definition of nationally recognized testing laboratory. O

approved for the purpose
Approved for a specific purpose, environment, or application described in a particular standard requirement. Suitability of equipment or materials for a specific purpose, environment or application may be determined by a nationally recognized testing laboratory, inspection agency or other organization concerned with product evaluation as part of its listing and labeling program. (See "labeled" or "listed.") O

approved POTW pretreatment program
A program administered by a POTW that meets the criteria established in [40 CFR] §§ 403.8 and 403.9 and which has been approved by a Regional Administrator or State Director in accordance with [40 CFR] § 403.11. A

[ed. Approval of a program allows the POTW to determine applicability of certain aspects of national pretreatment standards].

approved program or approved state
A state or interstate program which has been approved or authorized by EPA under 40 CFR Part 123. A, N

approved state program
A State program which has received EPA approval. A

apron
The area along the waterfront edge of the pier or wharf. O

APU
Auxiliary power unit. A

AQA
Air Quality Act. U

AQCCT
Air quality criteria and control techniques. N

AQCR
Air quality control region. [ed. Every area of every state is included in an AQCR. State implementation plans must provide for achievement of NAAQS in every AQCR]. B

AQDHS
Air Quality Data Handling System (OAR). N

AQDM
Air quality display model. N

AQL
Acceptable quality level. N

AQMA
Air quality maintenance area. N

AQMP
Air Quality Management Plan. N

AQSM
Air quality simulation model. N

AQTAD
Air Quality Technical Assistance Demonstration. N

aquaculture project
A defined managed water area which uses discharges of pollutants into that designated area for the maintenance or production of harvestable freshwater, estuarine, or marine plants or animals. A [ed. Regulated by § 318 of FWPCA]. "Designated area" means the portions of the waters of the United States within which the applicant plans to confine the cultivated species, using a method of plan or operation (including, but not limited to, physical confinement) which, on the basis of reliable scientific evidence, is expected to ensure that the specific individual organisms comprising an aquaculture crop will enjoy increased growth attributable to the discharge of pollutants and be harvested within a defined geographic area. N

aquatic animal production facility
A hatchery, fish farm, or other facility which contains, grows or holds: (1) Fish or other aquatic animals in ponds, raceways or other similar structures for purposes of production and from which there is a discharge on any 30 days or more per year, but does not include: (i) Closed ponds which discharge only during periods of excess runoff, or (ii) Facilities which produce less than 20,000 pounds of aquatic animals per year; (2) Any species of fish or other aquatic animal [other than carp (*Cyprinum carpio*), goldfish (*Carassius auratus*), or brown trout (*Salmo trutta*)] non-native to the United States (non-native fish are as defined in "Special Publication No. 6" of the American Fisheries Society entitled "A List of Common and Scientific Names of Fishes from the U.S. and Canada") and from which there is a discharge at any time. A

aquatic animals
Appropriately sensitive wholly aquatic animals which carry out respiration by means of a gill structure permitting gaseous exchange between the water and the circulatory system. A

aquatic ecosystem
See aquatic environment. A

aquatic environment
Waters of the United States, including wetlands, that serve as habitat for interrelated and interacting communities and populations of plants and animals. A

aquatic flora
Plant life associated with the aquatic eco-system including, but not limited to, algae and higher plants. A

aquepts
Soils with an aquic moisture regime and showing some soil development in the B-horizon; wet Inceptisols. N

aquic moisture regime
A moisture condition associated with a seasonal reducing environment that is virtually free of dissolved oxygen because the soil is saturated by ground water or by water of the capillary fringe, as in soils in Aquic suborders and Aquic subgroups. N

aquiclude
A saturated but poorly permeable underground bed, formation, or group of formations that impedes groundwater movement and does not yield water freely to a well or spring. However, an aquiclude may transmit appreciable water to or from adjacent aquifers, and where sufficiently thick, may constitute an important groundwater storage unit. U

aquifer
(1) An underground bed or layer of earth, gravel, or porous stone that contains water. (2) A geological "formation," group of formations, or part of a formation that is capable of yielding a significant amount of water to a well or spring. A

ARAR
Applicable or relevant and appropriate requirements. N

ARB
Air Resources Board. N

arbitration
A process for the resolution of disputes. Decisions are made by an impartial argitrator selected by the parties. These decisions are usually legally binding. (Compare: mediation). N

architectural coating
A coating used for buildings and their appurtenances. A

architectural or engineering (A/E) services
Consultation, investigation, reporting and design services offered within the scope of the practice of architecture or professional engineering as defined by the laws of a State or territory in which the recipient is located. A

area
The vertical projection of the pile upon the earth's surface. A

area director
The employee or officer regularly or temporarily in charge of an area office of the Occupational Safety and Health Administration, U.S. Department of Labor, or any other person or persons who are authorized to act for such employee or officer. The latter authorizations may include general delegations of the authority of an area director under this part to a Compliance Safety and Health Officer or delegations to such an officer for more limited purposes, such as the exercise of the area director's duties under [29 CFR] § 1903.14(a). The term also includes any employee or officer exercising supervisory responsibilities over an Area Director. A supervisory employee or officer is considered to exercise concurrent authority with the area director. O

area method
A sanitary landfilling method in which the waste is spread and compacted on the surface of the

ground and cover material is spread and compacted over it. A

area of review
The area surrounding an injection well described according to the criteria set forth in 40 CFR § 146.06 or in the case of an area permit, the project area plus a circumscribing area the width of which is either 1/4 of a mile or a number calculated according to the criteria set forth in 40 CFR § 146.06. A

area permit
A UIC permit applicable to all or certain wells within a geographic area, rather than to a specified well, under 40 CFR Section 122.37. N

area processed
The area actually exposed to process solutions. Usually this includes both sides of the metal strip. A

area source
Any small residential, governmental, institutional, commercial, or industrial fuel combustion operations [that contribute air pollutants to the ambient air but canot be modified as a point source]: onsite solid waste disposal facility; motor vehicles, aircraft, vessels, or other transportation facilities; or other miscellaneous sources as identified through inventory techniques similar to those described in: "A Rapid Survey Technique for Estimating Community Air Pollution Emissions," Public Health Service Publication No. 999-AP-29, October 1966. A [ed. Although emissions of pollutants from any one operation may be minimal, in the aggregate these small sources may be significant contributors to air pollution and require regulation on an area-wide basis].

areal cover
A measure of dominance that defines the degree to which above ground portions of plants cover the ground surface; it is possible for the total areal cover for all strata combined in a community or for single stratum to exceed 100 percent because: (1) most plant communities consist of two or more vegetative strata; (2) areal cover is estimated by vegetative layer; and (3) foliage within a single layer may overlap. N

areawide agency
An areawide management agency designated under section 208(c)(1) of the [Clean Water] Act. A

armored cable
Type AC armored cable is a fabricated assembly of insulated conductors in a flexible metallic enclosure. O

ARO
Alternate regulatory option. N

aromatic content
The aromatic hydrocarbon content in volume percent as determined by ASTM standard test method D 1319-88, entitled "Standard Test Method for Hydrocarbon Types in Liquid Petroleum Products by Fluorescent Indicator Adsorption." ASTM test method D 1319-88 is incorporated by reference. A

aromatics
A type of hydrocarbon, such as

benzene or toluene, added to gasoline in order to increase octane. Some aromatics are toxic. N

arrhythmia
Any variation from the normal rhythm of the heartbeat. U

ARRP
Acid Rain Research Program. N

arsenic-containing glass type
Any glass that is distinguished from other glass solely by the weight percent of arsenic added as a raw material and by the weight percent of arsenic in the glass produced. Any two or more glasses that have the same weight percent of arsenic in the raw materials as well as in the glass produced shall be considered to belong to one arsenic-containing glass type, without regard to the recipe used or any other characteristics of the glass or the method of production. A

artesian aquifer
An aquifer which is under pressure. When accessed, the water will rise above the water table to the piezometric surface. N

article
A manufactured item (1) which is formed to a specific shape or design during manufacture, (2) which has end use function(s) dependent in whole or in part upon its shape or design during end use, and (3) which has either no change of chemical composition during its end use or only those changes of composition which have no commercial purpose separate from that of the article and that result from a chemical reaction that occurs upon end use of other chemical substances, mixtures, or articles, as described in 40 CFR, 720.3 and 723.175, except that fluids and particles are not considered articles regardless of shape or design as described in 710.2. A

as expeditiously as practicable
As expeditiously as practicable but in no event later than three years after the date of approval of a plan revision under this section (§ 110) (or the date of promulgation of such a plan revision in the case of action by the Administrator under section 110(c) [of the Clean Air Act]). B [ed. The congressional time limit imposed on states for achievement of NAAQS under the CAA].

ASA
American Standards Association. U

asbestiform
A specific type of mineral fibrosity in which the fibers and fibrils possess high tensile strength and flexibility. A

asbestos
The asbestiform varieties of: chrysotile (serpentine); crocidolite (riebeckite); amosite (cummingtonite-grunerite); anthophyllite; tremolite; and actinolite. A

asbestos abatement project
Any activity involving the removal, enclosure, or encapsulation of friable asbestos material. A

asbestos debris
Pieces of ACBM that can be identified by color, texture, composition; or

dust, if the dust is determined by an accredited inspector to be ACM. A

asbestos material
Asbestos or any material containing asbestos. A

asbestos mill
Any facility engaged in the conversion of any intermediate step in the conversion of asbestos or into commercial asbestos. Outside storage of asbestos materials is not considered a part of such facility. A

asbestos mixture
A mixture which contains bulk asbestos or another asbestos mixture as an intentional component. An asbestos mixture may be either amorphuous or a sheet, cloth fabric, or other structure. This term does not include mixtures which contain asbestos as a contaminant impurity. A

asbestos sampling area
Any area, whether contiguous or not, within a school building which contains friable material that is homogeneous in texture and appearance. A

asbestos tailings
Any solid waste product of asbestos mining or milling operations which contains asbestos. A

asbestos waste from control devices
Any waste material that contains asbestos and is collected by a pollution control device. A

asbestos-containing building material
ACBM. Surfacing ACM, thermal system insulation asbestos-containing material (ACM), or miscellaneous ACM that is found in or on interior structural members or other parts of a school building. A

asbestos-containing material
ACM. When referring to school buildings means any material or product which contains more than 1 percent asbestos. A

asbestos-containing waste materials
(1) Any waste which contains commercial asbestos including asbestos mill tailings, control device asbestos waste, friable asbestos waste material, and bags or containers that previously contained commercial asbestos. A (2) Any waste that contains commercial asbestos. This term includes asbestos mill tailings, asbestos waste from control devices, friable asbestos waste material, and bags or containers that previously contained commercial asbestos. However, as applied to demolition and renovation operations, this term includes only friable asbestos waste and asbestos waste from control devices. K (3) This term includes filters from control devices, friable asbestos waste material, and bags or other similar packaging contaminated with commercial asbestos. As applied to demolition and renovation operations, this term also includes regulated asbestos-containing material waste and materials contaminated with asbestos including disposable equipment and clothing. A

asbestosis
A disease associated with chronic exposure to and inhalation of asbestos

fibers. The disease makes breathing progressively more difficult and can lead to death. N

ASCE
American Society of Civil Engineers.

ASCII
American Standard Code for Information Interchange. N

ASDWA
Association of State Drinking Water Administrators. N

ash
Inorganic residue remaining after ignition of combustible substances determined by definite prescribed methods. A

ash pit
A pit or hopper located below a furnace in which residue is accumulated and from which it is removed. U

ash sluice
A trench or channel in which water transports residue from an ash pit to a disposal or collection point. U

ash transport water
Water used in the hydraulic transport of either fly ash or bottom ash. A

ash-free basis
The method whereby the weight of ash in a fuel sample is subtracted from its total weight and the adjusted weight is used to calculate the percentages of certain constituents present. For example, the percentage of fixed carbon (FC) on an ash-free basis is computed as follows: A

$$\frac{FC(weight) \times 100}{fuel\ sample(weight) - ash(weight)}$$
= percentage of ash-free FC.

ASHAA
Asbestos in Schools Hazard Abatement Act. N

ASIWCPA
Association of State and Interstate Water Pollution Control Administrators. N

askarel
A generic term for a group of non-flammable synthetic chlorinated hydrocarbons used as electrical insulating media. Askarels of various compositional types are used. Under arcing conditions the gases produced, while consisting predominantly of noncombustible hydrogen chloride, can include varying amounts of combustible gases depending upon the askarel type. O

ASMDHS
Airshed Model Data Handling System. N

ASME Code
ASME (American Society of Mechanical Engineers) Boiler and Pressure Vessel Code, Section VIII, or an equivalent code which the employer can demonstrate to be equally effective. O

aspect ratio
A ratio of the length to the width of a particle. Minimum aspect ratio as defined by this method is equal to or greater than 5:1. A

asphalt catalyst
A substance which, when added to asphalt flux in a blowing still, alters the penetrating softening point relationship or increases the rate of oxidation of the flux. A

asphalt concrete plant
Any facility used to manufacture asphalt concrete by heating and drying aggregate and mixing with asphalt cements. For the purpose of 40 CFR § 60.90, an asphalt concrete plant is comprised only of any combination of the following: dryers; systems for screening, handling, storing, and weighing hot aggregate; systems for loading, transferring, and storing mineral filler; systems for mixing asphalt concrete; and the loading, transfer, and storage systems associated with emission control systems. A

asphalt processing plant
A plant which blows asphalt for use in the manufacture of asphalt products. A

asphalt storage tank
Any tank used to store asphalt at asphalt roofing plants, petroleum refineries, and asphalt processing plants. [ed. See also "cutback asphalts" and "emulsified asphalts"]. A

asphalts
Black, solid or semisolid bitumens which occur in nature or are obtained as residues during petroleum refining. A

asphyxiant
A vapor of gas that can cause unconsciousness or death by suffocation (lack of oxygen). Most simple asphyxiants are harmful to the body only when they become so concentrated that they reduce oxygen in the air (normally about 21 percent) to dangerous levels (18 percent or lower). Asphyxiation is one of the principal potential hazards of working in confined and enclosed spaces. N

ASRL
Atmospheric Sciences Research Laboratory. N

assay
A test for a particular chemical or effect. U

assets
All existing and all probable future economic benefits obtained or controlled by a particular entity. A

assimilation
The ability of a body of water to purify itself of pollutants. N

assimilative capacity
The capacity of a natural body of water to receive: (a) wastewaters, without deleterious effects; (b) toxic materials, without damage to aquatic life or humans who consume the water; (c) BOD, within prescribed dissolved oxygen limits. U

assistance agreement
The legal instrument EPA uses to transfer money, property, services, or anything of value to a recipient to accomplish a public purpose. It is either a grant or a cooperative agreement and will specify: budget and project periods; the Federal share of

eligible project costs; a description of the work to be accomplished; and any special conditions. A

assistant regional director
The employee or officer regularly or temporarily in charge of a Region of the Occupational Safety and Health Administration, U.S. Department of Labor, or any other person or persons who are specifically designated to act for such employee or officer in his absence. The term also includes any employee or officer in the Occupational Safety and Health Administration exercising supervisory responsibilities over the Assistant Regional Director. Such supervisory employee or officer is considered to exercise concurrent authority with the Assistant Regional Director. No delegation of authority under this paragraph shall adversely affect the procedures for independent informal review of investigative determinations prescribed under § 1903.12 of [40 CFR]. O

associate enforcement counsels
Senior managers in EPA's office of enforcement. U

associated parking area
A parking facility or facilities owned and/or operated in conjunction with an indirect source. A

asthma
A term currently used in the context of bronchial asthma in which there is widespread narrowing of the airways of the lung which leads to "wheezing" and shortness of breath. Abnormal responsiveness of the air passages to certain substances including air pollutants is common. An attack consists of a widespread narrowing of the bronchioles by muscle spasm, swelling of the mucous membrane, or thickening and increase of mucous secretions, accompanied by wheezing, gasping, and sometimes coughing. U

ASTHO
Association of State and Territorial Health Officers. N

ASTM
American Society for Testing and Materials which is the world's largest source of voluntary consensus standards for materials, products, systems, and services. ASTM is a resource for sampling and testing methods, health and safety aspects of materials, safe performance guidelines, effects of physical and biological agents and chemicals. N

ASTSWMO
Association of State and Territorial Solid Waste Management Officials. N

asymptomatic
Showing no symptoms. N

at-the-source
At or before the commingling of delacquering scrubber liquor blowdown with other process or nonprocess wastewaters. A

ATA
Atmosphere absolute. O

atmosphere
The body of air surrounding the earth; the troposphere. N

atmosphere an
A standard unit of pressure representing the pressure exerted by a 29.92-inch column of mercury at sea level at 45' latitude and equal to 1000 grams per square centimeter. The whole mass of air surrounding the earth, composed largely of oxygen and nitrogen. N

atmospheric half-life
The time required for one-half of the quantity of an air pollutant to react and/or break down in the atmosphere. N

atmospheric pressure
The pressure of air at sea level, usually 14.7 p.s.i.a. (1 atmosphere), or 0 p.s.i.g. O

atmospheric residence time
The time required for removal of a substance from the atmosphere to the extent that l/e (approximately 37%) of the original material remains. N

atomic pile
A nuclear reactor. N

atomization
The process in which a stream of water or gas impinges upon a molten metal stream, breaking it into droplets which solidify as powder particles. A

atomize
To divide a liquid into extremely minute particles, either by impact with a jet of steam or compressed air, or by passage through some mechanical device. N

atrophy
Reduction in the size of a structure or organ resulting from lack of nourishment or functional activity, death and reabsorption of cells, diminished cellular proliferation, pressure, ischemia or hormone changes. N

ATSDR
Agency for Toxic Substances and Disease Registry (HHS). N

attainment area
For any air pollutant, an area which has been designated under Section 107 of the Clean Air Act as having ambient air quality levels better than any national primary or secondary ambient air quality standard for that pollutant. Standards have been set for sulfur oxides, particulate matter, nitrogen dioxide, carbon monoxide, ozone, lead, and hydrocarbons. For purposes of the Glossary, "attainment area" also refers to "unclassifiable area," which means, for any pollutants, an area designated under Section 107 as unclassifiable with respect to that pollutant due to insufficient information. N (2) An area considered to have air quality as good as or better than the national ambient air quality standards as defined in the Clean Air Act. An area may be an attainment area for one pollutant and a non-attainment area for others. N

attenuation
(1) A decrease in the concentration or quantity of a chemical or biological

material carried in a fluid, resulting from a physical, chemical, and/or biological reaction occurring in the period considered. (2) The process by which a compound is reduced in concentration over time, through adsorption, degradation, dilution, and/or transformation. N

attractant
All substances or mixtures of substances which, through their property of attracting certain animals, are intended to mitigate a population of, or destroy any vertebrate or invertebrate animals declared to be pests under 162.14. (i) Attractants include, but are not limited to: (A) Sensory stimulants (such as pheromones, synthetic attractants, and certain extracts from naturally-occurring organic materials) when used alone, or when in combination with toxicants that can kill certain vertebrate or invertebrate animals, that are intended to draw certain animals into traps or away from crops or sites; these sensory stimulants are considered to be active ingredients in pesticide products; and (B) Naturally-occurring foods and certain extracts from such foods, when in combination with toxicants that can kill certain vertebrate or invertebrate animals, that are intended to draw certain animals into traps or away from crops or sites; these foods and extracts are considered to be inert ingredients in pesticide products. (ii) Attractants do not include: (a) Substances or mixtures of substances intended to attract vertebrate or invertebrate animals for survey or detection purposes only, and (b) Naturally-occurring foods, when used alone or separately and not marketed in mixtures with toxicants, for the purpose of attracting vertebrate or invertebrates animals. O

attrition
Wearing or grinding down a substance by friction. A contributing factor in air pollution, as with dust. N

auction subaccount
An account in the Special Allowance Reserve, as specified in Section 416(b) of the Clean Air Act. The Auction Subaccount shall contain allowances to be sold at auction in the amount of 150,000 per year from 1995 through 1999, inclusive, and 200,000 per year for each year beginning in the calendar year 2000, subject to modifications noted in these regulations. A

audiogram
A chart, graph, or table resulting from an audiometric test showing an individual's hearing threshold levels as a function of frequency. O

audiologist
A professional, specializing in the study and rehabilitation of hearing, who is certified by the American Speech-Language-Hearing Association or licensed by a state board of examiners. O

audiometer
An instrument that measures hearing sensitivity. N

audit
A fiscal or accounting review, and sometimes a programmatic review, of a

grant period or a part thereof, or perhaps of several grants in one grantee institution. U

augmentation
A requirement for additional funds for a project previously awarded funds in the same funding/budget period. Project nature and scope are unchanged. (Requires a grant amendment). U

authorization
Basic substantive legislation enacted by Congress that sets up or continues the legal operation of a Federal program or agency. Such legislation is normally a prerequisite for subsequent appropriations, but does not usually provide budget authority. U

authorized account representative
A natural person who may transfer and otherwise dispose of allowances held in an account in the Allowance Tracking System, including, in the case of a unit account, the designated representative of the owners and operators of an affected unit. A

authorized employee
An employee whose duties require him to be in the regulated area and who has been specifically assigned by the employer. O

authorized person
(1) A person approved or assigned by the employer to perform a specific type of duty or duties or to be at a specific location or locations at the job site. O (2) Any person authorized by the employer and required by work duties to be present in regulated areas. O

auto-ignition temperature
The temperature to which a closed, or nearly closed container must be heated in order that the flammable liquid, when introduced into the container, will ignite spontaneously or burn. N

autogenous combustion
See autothermic combustion. U

automated method or analyzer
A method for measuring concentrations of an ambient air pollutant in which sample collection, analysis, and measurement are performed automatically. A

automatic
Self-acting, operating by its own mechanism when actuated by some impersonal influence, as, for example, a change in current strength, pressure, temperature, or mechanical configuration. O

automatic temperature compensator
A device that continuously senses the temperature of fluid flowing through a metering device and automatically adjusts the registration of the measured volume to the corrected equivalent volume at a base temperature. A

automobile
(1) A motor vehicle capable of carrying no more than 12 passengers. A (2) Any four-wheel vehicle propelled by a combustion engine using onboard fuel or by an electric motor

drawing current from rechargeable storage batteries or other portable energy storage devices (rechargeable using energy from a source off the vehicle such as residential electric service) which is manufactured primarily for use on public streets, roads, or highways (except any vehicle operated on a rail or rails) and which is rated at 8,500 pounds gross vehicle weight or less or is a type of vehicle which the Secretary determines is substantially used for the same purposes. A

autothermic combustion (or autogenous)
The burning of a wet organic material where the moisture content is at such a level that the heat of combustion of the organic material is sufficient to vaporize the water and maintain combustion. No auxiliary fuel is required except for start-up. U

autotrophic
An organism that produces food from inorganic substances. N

auxiliary emission control device
AECD. Any element of design which senses temperature, vehicle speed, engine RPM, transmission gear, manifold vacuum, or any other parameter for the purpose of activating, modulating, delaying, or deactivating the operation of any part of the emission control system. A

auxiliary power unit
Any engine installed in or on an aircraft exclusive of the propulsion engines. A

auxiliary-fuel firing equipment
Equipment used in an incinerator to supply additional heat by burning auxiliary fuel. Resulting higher temperatures (1) dry and ignite the waste material, (2) maintain their ignition, and (3) effect the complete combustion of combustible solids, vapors, and gases. U

available purchase power
Means the lesser of the following: (a) The sum of available system capacity in all neighboring companies. (b) The sum of the rated capacities of the power interconnection devices between the principal company and all neighboring companies, minus the sum of the electric power load on these interconnections. (c) The rated capacity of the power transmission lines between the power interconnection devices and the electric generating units (the unit in the principal company that has the malfunctioning flue gas desulfurization system and the unit(s) in the neighboring company supplying replacement electrical power) less the electric power load on these transmission lines. A

available system capacity
[For a utility system] the capacity determined by subtracting the system load and the system emergency reserves from the net system capacity. A

available to the public
Information in EPA's possession which EPA will furnish to any member of the public upon request and which EPA may make public, release or otherwise make available to any person

whether or not its disclosure has been requested. A

average concentration
As it relates to chlorine discharge is the average of analyses made over a single period of chlorine release which does not exceed two hours. A

average fuel economy
The unique fuel economy value as compiled under 40 CFR § 600.510 for a specific class of automobiles produced by a manufacturer that are subject to average fuel economy standards. A

average monthly discharge limitation
NPDES. The highest allowable average of "daily discharges" over a calendar month, calculated as the sum of all daily discharges measured during a calendar month divided by the number of daily discharges measured during that month. A

average process water usage flow rate
Where the rate of a contact cooling and heating water process [or a cleaning water process] in liters per day is equal to the volume of process water (liters) used per year by a process divided by the number of days per year the process operates. The "average process water usage flow rate" for a plant with more than one plastics molding and forming process that uses contact cooling and heating water [or cleaning water process] is the sum of the "average process water usage flow rates" for the contact cooling and heating processes [or the cleaning water process]. A

average sample
One that consists of proportionate parts from all sections of the container. A

average weekly discharge limitation
NPDES. The highest allowable average of "daily discharges" over a calendar week, calculated as the sum of all daily discharges measured during a calendar week divided by the number of daily discharges measured during that week. A

averaging time
The time period over which a function (e.g., average concentration of an air pollutant) is measured, yielding a time-weighted average. N

avg.
Abbreviation for average. A

award
The obligation of funds by the formal offer of a grant agreement to an applicant. U

awarding official
The official who obligates grant funds by signing the award documents; not to be confused with the "decision official." U

AWMA
Air and Waste Management Association. U

AWRA
American Water Resources Association. U

AWT
Advanced waste treatment. U

AWWA
American Water Works Association. N

AWWARF
American Water Works Association Research Foundation. N

axle clearance
The vertical distance from the level surface on which an automobile is standing to the lowest point on the axle differential of the automobile. A

axle ratio
(1) The number of times the input shaft to the differential (or equivalent) turns for each turn of the drive wheels. A (2) All ratios within ±3% of the axle ratio specified in the configuration in the test order. A

B

backend loader
A collection vehicle that loads refuse from the rear and compacts it. U

backend system
Informal term for any process that recovers valuable resources from organic solid waste. Examples are refuse-derived fuel recovery, fluid bed incineration, fiber reclamation, composting, and conversion to animal feed. U

backfill
The material used to refill a ditch or other excavation, or the process of doing so. N

background conditions
The biological, chemical, and physical conditions of a water body, upstream from the point or non-point source discharge under consideration. Background sampling location in an enforcement action will be upstream from the point of discharge, but not upstream from other inflows. If several discharges to any water body exist, and an enforcement action is being taken for possible violations to the standards, background sampling will be undertaken immediately upstream from each discharge. A

background level
With respect to air pollution, amounts of pollutants present in the ambient air due to natural sources. N

background patent
A foreign or domestic patent (regardless of its date of issue relative to the date of the EPA grant): (i) Which the grantee, but not the Government, has the right to license to others, and (ii) Infringement of which cannot be avoided upon the practice of a Subject Invention or Specified Work Object. A

background soil pH
The pH of the soil prior to the addition of substances that alter the hydrogen ion concentration. A

backhoe tamping
A processing step, often used in

direct-dump transfer systems, in which a conventional backhoe is used to compact waste contained in an open-top transfer trailer. U

BACM
Best availabe control measure. U

BACT
Best available control technology. A emission limitation based on the maximum degree of emission reduction which (considering energy, environmental, and economic impacts and other costs) is achievable through application of production processes and available methods, systems, and techniques. In no event does BACT permit emissions in excess of those allowed under any applicable Clean Air Act provisions. Use of the BACT concept is allowable on a case by case basis for major new or modified emissions sources in attainment and applies to each regulated pollutant. U

bacteria
(1) Single-celled microorganisms that possess cell walls. Some bacteria cause disease, and some are beneficial and promote the stabilization of solid waste. (2) Single-celled microorganisms lack chlorophyll. Some cause diseases, others aid in pollution control by breaking down organic matter in air and water. N (3) Can aid in the pollution control by consuming or breaking down organic matter in sewage, or by similarly acting on oil spills or other water pollutants. Bacteria in soil, water or air can also cause human, animal and plant health problems. N

BADCT
Best available demonstrated control technology. U

BADT
Best available demonstrated technology. U

baffle
A deflector that changes the direction of flow or velocity of water, sewage, or particulate matter. Also used to deaden sound. N

baffle chamber
In incinerator design, a chamber designed to promote the settling of fly ash and coarse particulate matter by changing the direction and/or reducing the velocity of the gases produced by the combustion of the refuse or sludge. N

bagasse
An agricultural waste material consisting of the dry pulp residue that remains after juice is extracted from sugar cane or sugar beets. The residue is used in the manufacture of pulp and paper. N

baghouse
An air pollution abatement device used to trap particulates by filtering gas streams through large fabric bags usually made of glass fibers. N

baghouse filter
Large fabric bag, usually made of glass fibers, used to eliminate intermediate and large (greater than 20 microns in diameter) particles. This device operates in a way similar to the bag of an electric vacuum

cleaner, passing the air and smaller particulate matter, while entrapping the larger particulates. N

bake oven
A device that uses heat to dry or cure coatings. A

balanced, indigenous population
An ecological community which: (1) Exhibits characteristics similar to those of nearby, healthy communities existing under comparable but unpolluted environmental conditions; or (2) May reasonably be expected to become reestablished in the polluted water body segment from adjacent waters if sources of pollution were removed. A

baler
A machine used to compress solid wastes, primary materials, or recoverable materials, with or without binding, to a density or from which will support handling and transportation as a material unit rather than requiring a disposable or reuseable container. This specifically excludes briquetters and stationary compaction equipment which is used to compact materials into disposable or reuseable containers. A

baling
Compacting solid waste into blocks to reduce volume. N

ballast
The flow of waters, from a ship, that is treated along with refinery wastewaters in the main treatment system. A

ballistic separator
A machine that sorts organic from inorganic matter for composting. N

band application
In pesticides, the spreading of chemicals over or next to each row of plants in a field. L

banking
A system for recording qualified air emission reductions for later use in bubble, offset, or netting transactions. (See: emissions trading). N

bar screen
In wastewater treatment, a device used to remove large solids. N

BARF
Best available retrofit facility. U

barometric condensing operations
Those operations or processes directly associated with or related to the concentration and crystallization of sugar solutions. A

barometric damper
A hinged or pivoted plate that automatically regulates the amount of air entering a duct, breeching, flue connection, or stack, thereby maintaining a constant draft in the incinerator. U

barrel
Forty-two United States gallons at sixty degrees Fahrenheit. A, D, O

barricade
A physical obstruction such as tapes, cones, or "A" frame type wood and/or metal structure intended to warn and limit access to a [hazardous work] area. O

barrier
(1) Any material or structure that

prevents or substantially delays movement of water or radionuclides toward the accessible environment. For example, a barrier may be a geologic, structure, a canister, a waste form with physical and chemical characteristics that significantly decrease the mobility of radionuclides, or a material placed over and around waste, provided that the material or structure substantially delays movement of water or radionuclides. A (2) A physical obstruction which is intended to prevent contact with energized lines or equipment, or to prevent unauthorized access to work area. O (3) A fence, wall or other structure or object placed between a single piece rim wheel and an employee during tire inflation, to contain the rim wheel components in the event of the sudden release of the contained air of the single piece rim wheel. O

barrier coating(s)
A layer of a material that acts to obstruct or prevent passage of something through a surface that is to be protected, e.g. grout, caulk, or various sealing compounds; sometimes used with polyurethane membranes to prevent corrosion or oxidation of metal surfaces, chemical impacts on various materials, or, for example, to prevent soil-gas-borne radon from moving through walls, cracks, or joints in a house. N

BART
Best available retrofit technology. U

basal application
In pesticides, the spreading of a chemical on plant stems or trunks just above the soil line. N

basal diet
The food or diet as it is prepared or received from the supplier, without the addition of any carrier, diluent, or test substance. A

base date
The date which is used as a reference for determination of compliance with regulations. A

base date period
The thirty day period immediately preceding the base date. A

base flood
A flood which has a one percent chance of occurrence in any given year (also known as a 100-year flood). This term is used in the National Flood Insurance Program (NFIP) to indicate the minimum level of flooding to be used by a community in its floodplain management regulations. A

base floodplain
The land area covered by a 100-year flood (one percent chance floodplain). Also see floodplain. A

base level
A unique combination of basic engine, inertia weight, and transmission class. A

base load
The load level at which a gas turbine is normally operated. A

base temperature
An arbitrary reference temperature for determining liquid densities or adjusting the measured volume of a liquid quantity. A

base vehicle
The lowest priced version of each body style that makes up a car line. A

based flood
A flood that has a 1 percent or greater chance of recurring in any year or a flood of a magnitude equalled or exceeded once in 100 years on the average over a significantly long period. A

baseline area
Any intrastate area (and every part thereof) designated as attainment or unclassifiable under section 107(d)(1)(D) or (E) of the CAA in which the major source or major modification establishing the baseline date would construct or would have an air quality impact equal to or greater than 1 ug/m³ (annual average) of the pollutant for which the baseline date is established. Area redesignations under section 107(d)(1)(D) or (E) of the CAA cannot intersect or be smaller than the area of impact of any major stationary source or major modification which: (a) Establishes a baseline date; or (b) Is subject to 40 CFR 52.21 and would be constructed in the same state as the state proposing the redesignation. A

baseline assessment survey
The planned sampling or measurement of parameters at set stations or in set areas in and near disposal sites for a period of time sufficient to provide synoptic data for determining water quality, benthic, or biological conditions as a result of ocean disposal operations. The minimum requirements for such surveys are given in [40 CFR] § 228.13. A

baseline concentration
That ambient concentration level which exists in the baseline area at the time of the applicable minor source baseline date. A baseline concentration is determined for each pollutant for which a baseline date is established and shall include: (a) the actual emissions representation of sources in existence on the applicable minor source baseline date, except as provided in 40 CFR § 52.21 paragraph (b)(13)(ii); (b) the allowable emissions of major stationary sources which commenced construction before the major source baseline date but were not in operation by the applicable minor source baseline date. (ii) the following will not be included in the baseline concentration and will affect the applicable maximum allowable increase(s): (a) The actual emissions representative of sources in existence on the applicable minor source baseline date. (b) actual emission increases and decreases at any stationary source occurring after the minor source baseline date. A

baseline configuration
The unretrofitted test configuration, tuned in accordance with the automobile manufacturer's specifications. [ed. Used in automobile emissions certification procedures]. A

baseline consumption allowances
The consumption allowances apportioned under [40 CFR] § 82.6. A

baseline date
(i) The earliest date after August 7, 1977, on which the first complete application under 40 CFR 52.21 is

submitted by a major stationary source or major modification subject to the requirements of 40 CFR 52.21. (ii) The baseline date is established for each pollutant for which increments or other equivalent measures have been established if: (a) the area in which the proposed source or modification would construct is designated as attainment or unclassifiable under section 107(d)(i) (D) or (E) of the CAA for the pollutant on the date of its complete application under 40 CFR 52.21; and (b) In the case of a major stationary source, the pollutant would be emitted in significant amounts, or, in the case of a major modification, there would be a significant net emissions increase of the pollutant. [ed. This definition established the date from which new sources will have to demonstrate they do not violate air quality increments designed to prevent significant deterioration of air quality]. A

baseline model year
With respect to any pollutant emitted from any vehicle or engine, or class or category thereof, the model year immediately preceding the model year in which Federal standards applicable to such vehicle or engine, or class or category thereof, first applied with respect to such pollutant. B

baseline production allowances
The production allowances apportioned under [40 CFR] § 82.5. A

basement
A story of a building or structure having one-half or more of its height below ground level and to which access for fire fighting purposes is unduly restricted. O

basic engine
A unique combination of manufacturer, engine displacement, number of cylinders, fuel system (as distinguished by number of carburetor barrels or use of fuel injection), catalyst usage, and other engine and emission control system characteristics specified by the Administrator of EPA. A

basic oxygen furnace
BOF. A furnace in which steel is produced from oxidation of a molten mixture of pig iron and steel scrap. Pure oxygen is introduced at supersonic speeds by a lance immersed in the mixture and left for 20 minutes. The process uses 35 percent or less of steel scrap. U

basic oxygen furnace steelmaking
The production of steel from molten iron, steel scrap, fluxes, and various combinations thereof, in refractory lined furnaces by adding oxygen. A

basic oxygen process furnace
BOPF. Any furnace producing steel by charging scrap steel, hot metal, and flux materials into a vessel and introducing a high volume of an oxygen-rich gas. A

basic vehicle frontal area
The area enclosed by the geometric projection of the basic vehicle along the longitudinal axis, which includes tires but excludes mirrors and air deflectors, onto a plane perpendicular

to the longitudinal axis of the vehicle. A

basin
Includes, but is not limited to, rivers and their tributaries, streams, coastal waters, sounds, estuaries, bays, lakes, and portions thereof, as well as the lands drained thereby. D

basis material
The coiled strip which is processed. A

BAT
Best available technology. A

batch
(1) Those alkaline cleaning operations which process steel products such as coiled wire, rods, and tubes in discrete batches or bundles. A (2) Those pickling operations which process steel products such as coiled wire, rods, and tubes in discrete batches or bundles. A (3) The collection of a substance or a product of the same category or configuration, as designated by the Administrator in a test request, from which a batch sample is to be randomly drawn and inspected to determine conformance with acceptability criteria. A (4) A quantity of a pesticide product or active ingredient used in producing a pesticide made in one operation or lot or if made in a continuous or semi-continuous process or cycle, the quantity produced during an interval of time to be specified by the producer. A

batch sample
The collection of substances or products of the same category, configuration or subgroup thereof which are drawn from a batch and from which test samples are drawn. A

batch-fed incinerator
An incinerator that is periodically charged with solid waste; one charge is allowed to burn down or burn out before another is added. U

BATEA
Best available technology economically achievable. N

battery
A modular electric power source where part or all of the fuel is contained within the unit and electric power is generated directly from a chemical reaction rather than indirectly through a heat cycle engine. In this regulation there is no differentiation between a single cell and a battery. A

battery configuration
The electrochemical type, voltage, capacity (in Watt-hours at the c/3 rate), and physical characteristics of the battery used as the tractive energy storage device. A

battery manufacturing operations
All of the specific processes used to produce a battery including the manufacture of anodes and cathodes and associated ancillary operations. These manufacturing operations are excluded from regulation under any other point source category. A

battery wall
A double or common wall between

two incinerator combustion chambers; both faces are exposed to heat. U

bauxite
Ore containing alumina monohydrate or alumina trihydrate which serves as the principal raw material for the production of alumina by the Bayer process or by the combination process. A

BCF
Bioconcentration factor. A

BCPCT
Best conventional pollution control technology. U

BCS
Buildings and community systems. U

BCT
(1) Best control technology. N (2) Best Conventional Pollutant Control Technology under section 304(b)(4) of the Clean Water Act. A

BDAT
Best demonstrated achievable (or available) technology. N

BDT
Best demonstrated technology. N

Be
Abbreviation for beryllium. A

bearer
A horizontal member of a scaffold upon which the platform rests and which may be supported by ledgers. O

beehive cokemaking
Those operations in which coal is heated with the admission of air in controlled amounts for the purpose of producing coke. There are no by-product recovery operations associated with beehive cokemaking operations. A

begin actual construction
Initiation of physical on-site construction activities on an emissions unit which are of a permanent nature. Such activities include, but are not limited to, installation of building supports and foundations, laying of underground pipework, and construction of permanent storage structures. With respect to a change in method of operating this term refers to those on-site activities other than preparatory activities which mark the initiation of the change. A

BEJ
Best engineering judgment. The specific requirements an owner or operator of a TSD must comply with are developed for each specific facility by permit writers, based on their best engineering judgment and the requirements of 40 CFR Part 264. Such requirements are then incorporated into the facility's operating permit. N

bell
An enclosed compartment, pressurized (closed bell) or unpressurized (open bell), which allows the diver to be transported to and from the underwater work area and which may be used as a temporary refuge during diving operations. O

belowground storage facility
A tank or other container located

other than as defined as "aboveground." A

belt pole
A device used in shifting belts on and off fixed pulleys on line or countershaft where there are no loose pulleys (sometimes called a "belt shipper" or "shipper pole.") O

belt shifter
A device for mechanically shifting belts from tight to loose pulleys or vice versa, or for shifting belts on cones of speed pulleys. O

belts
All power transmission belts, such as flat belts, round belts, V-belts, etc., unless otherwise specified. O

BEN
EPA's computer model for analyzing a violator's economic gain from not complying with the law. N

bench mark
A fixed, more or less permanent reference point or object of known elevation; the U.S. Geological Survey (USGS) installs brass caps in bridge abutments or otherwise permanently sets bench marks at convenient locations nationwide; the elevations on these marks are referenced to the National Geodetic Vertical Datum (NGVD), also commonly known as Mean Sea Level (MSL); locations of these bench marks on USGS topographic maps are shown as small triangles; since the marks are sometimes destroyed by construction or vandalism, the existence of any bench mark should be field verified before planning work which relies on a particular reference point; the USGS or local state surveyors office can provide information on the existence, exact location and exact elevation of bench marks. N

beneficial use
Produced water that is of good enough quality to be used for livestock watering or other agricultural uses and is being put to such use. A

beneficiation area
The area of land used to stockpile ore immediately before the beneficiation process, the area of land used for the beneficiation process, the area of land used to stockpile the tailings immediately after the beneficiation process, and the area of land from the stockpiled tailings to the treatment system (e.g., holding pond or settling pond, and the area of the treatment system). A

beneficiation process
The dressing or processing of gold bearing ores for the purpose of (i) Regulating the size of, or recovering, the ore or product, (ii) Removing unwanted constituents from the ore, and (iii) Improving the quality, purity, or assay grade of a desired product. A

benign
A condition of a neoplasm (tumor) in which the morphological and behavioral characteristics of the tumor differ minimally from the tissue from which it originates. A benign neoplasm (as distinct from malignant) may expand, but remains encapsulated,

and has limited potential to invade local structure and proliferate. N

benthic region
The bottom layer of a body of water. N

benzene
(Or priority pollutant No. 4). The value obtained by the standard method Number 602 specified in 44 FR 69464, 69570 (December 3, 1979). A

benzene storage tank
Any tank, reservoir, or container used to collect or store refined benzene. A

benzidine
The compound benzidine and its salts as identified by the chemical name 4,4'-diaminobiphenyl. A

benzidine manufacturer
A manufacturer who produces benzidine or who produces benzidine as an intermediate product in the manufacture of dyes commonly used for textile, leather and paper dyeing. A

benzidine-based dye applicator
An owner or operator who uses benzidine-based dyes in the dyeing of textiles, leather or paper. A

benzo(a)pyrene
(Or priority pollutant No. 73). The value obtained by the standard method Number 610 specified in 44 FR 69464, 69570 (December 3, 1979). A

beryllium
An airborne metal that can be hazardous to human health when inhaled. It is discharged by machine shops, ceramic and propellant plants, and foundries. N

beryllium alloy
Any metal to which beryllium has been added in order to increase its beryllium content and which contains more than 0.1 percent beryllium by weight. A

best available control measure
BACM. A term referring to the "best" measures (according to EPA guidance) for controlling small or dispersed sources of particulate matter, such as roadway dust, woodstoves, and open burning. N

best available control technology
BACT. An emissions limitation (including a visible emission standard) based on the maximum degree of reduction for each pollutant subject to regulation under the Clean Air Act which would be emitted from any proposed major stationary source or major modification which the EPA Administrator, on a case-by-case basis, taking into account energy, environmental, and economic impacts and other costs, determines is achievable for such source or modification through application of production processes or available methods, systems, and techniques, including fuel cleaning or treatment or innovative fuel combustion techniques for control of such pollutant. In no event shall application of best available control technology result in emissions of any pollutant which would exceed the emissions allowed by any applicable standard under 40 CFR parts

60 and 61. If the Administrator determines that technological or economic limitations on the application of measurement methodology to a particular emissions unit would make the imposition of an emission standard infeasible, a design, equipment, work practice, operational standard, or combination thereof, may be prescribed instead to satisfy the requirement for the application of best available control technology. Such standard shall, to the degree possible, set forth the emissions reduction achievable by implementation of such design, equipment, work practice or operation, and shall provide for compliance by means which achieve equivalent results. A

best available retrofit technology
BART. An emission limitation based on the degree of reduction achievable through the application of the best system of continuous emission reduction for each pollutant which is emitted by an existing stationary facility. The emission limitation must be established, on a case-by-case basis, taking into consideration the technology available, the costs of compliance, the energy and quality environmental impacts of compliance, any pollution control equipment in use or in existence at the source, the remaining useful life of the source, and the degree of improvement in visibility which may reasonably be anticipated to result from the use of such technology. A

best available technology
BAT. The best technology, treatment techniques, or other means which the Administrator finds, after examination for efficacy under field conditions and not solely under laboratory conditions, are available (taking cost into consideration). For the purposes of setting Maximum Contaminant Levels (MCLs) for synthetic organic chemicals, any BAT must be at least as effective as granular activated carbon. A

best available technology economically achievable
BATEA. Technology-based effluent limitations on direct dischargers are to meet by July 1, 1984, pursuant to 301 (b)(2)(A) of the FWPCA. The level of control is generally described as the "best of the best" technology in use and is to include controls on toxic pollutants. U

best conventional pollutant control technology
BCT. Technology-based effluent limitations for conventional pollutants that direct dischargers must meet by July 1, 1984, pursuant to 301 (b)(2)(E) of the FWPCA. The level of control is to be no less stringent than BPT. U

best management practice
(1) BMP. Schedules of activities, prohibitions of practices, maintenance procedures, and other management practices to prevent or reduce the pollution of waters of the United States from discharges of dredged or fill material. BMPs include methods, measures, practices, or design and performance standards which facilitate compliance with the section 404(b)(1) Guidelines (40 CFR Part 230), effluent limitations or prohibitions under section 307(a), and applicable water quality standards. A (2) Methods,

measures or practices selected by an agency to meet its nonpoint source control needs. BMPs include but are not limited to structural and nonstructural controls and operation and maintenance procedures. BMPs can be applied before, during and after pollution-producing activities to reduce or eliminate the introduction of pollutants into receiving waters. A

best practicable waste treatment technology
BPWTT. The cost-effective technology that can treat wastewater, combined sewer overflows and nonexcessive infiltration and inflow in publicly owned or individual wastewater treatment works, to meet the applicable provisions of: (i) 40 CFR part 133--secondary treatment of wastewater; (ii) 40 CFR part 125, subpart G--marine discharge waivers; (iii) 40 CFR 122.44-(d)--more stringent water quality standards and State standards; or (iv) 41 FR 6190 (February 11, 1976)--Alternative Waste Management Techniques for Best Practicable Waste Treatment (treatment and discharge, land application techniques and utilization practices and reuse). A

best practical control technology currently available
BPT. Technology-based effluent limitations direct dischargers were to meet by July 1, 1977, pursuant to §301(b)(1)(A) of the FWPCA. The level of control is generally described as the "average of the best" technology in use to control wastes from that industry. U

beta particle
An elementary particle emitted by radioactive decay that may cause skin burns. It is halted by a thin sheet of metal. N

beverage
Carbonated natural or mineral waters; soda water and similar carbonated soft drinks; and beer or other carbonated malt drinks in liquid form and intended for human consumption. A

beverage can
Any two-piece steel or aluminum container in which soft drinks or beer, including malt liquor, are packaged. The definition does not include containers in which fruit or vegetable juices are packaged. A

beverage container
(1) An air-tight container containing a beverage under pressure of carbonation. Cups and other open receptacles are specifically excluded from this definition. A (2) Any metal, glass, plastic, or wax-coated paper containers used to hold beverages. Such containers can become institutional, municipal, or residential solid waste. U

bhp
Abbreviation for brake horsepower. A

BHT
Butalyated hydroxytoluene. U

BIA
Bureau of Indian Affairs, United States Department of Interior. A

bicycle
A non-motorpowered, 2-wheeled vehicle. A

bicycle lane
A route for the exclusive use of bicycles, either constructed specifically for that purpose or converted from an existing lane. A

bicycle parking facility
Any storage facility for bicycles, which allows bicycles to be locked securely. A

BID
Background Information Document. N

biennial report
A report (EPA Form 8700-13A) submitted by generators of hazardous waste to the Regional Administrator due March 1 of each even-numbered year. The report includes information on the generator's activities during the previous calendar year. The owner or operator of a treatment, storage, and disposal facility must also prepare and submit a biennial report using EPA Form 8700-1313. N

BIF
Boilers, incinerators and furnaces. U

bike path
A route for the exclusive use of bicycles separated by grade or other physical barrier from motor traffic. A

bike route
A route in which bicycles share road space with motorized vehicles. A

bikeways
Bike paths, bike lanes and bike routes. A

bilge oil
Waste oil which accumulates, usually in small quantities, in the lower spaces in a ship, just inside the shell plating. Usually mixed with larger quantities of water. A

bioaccumulation
The uptake and, at least temporary, storage of a chemical by an exposed animal. The chemical can be retained in its original form and/or as modified by enzymatic and non-enzymatic reactions in the body. A

bioaccumulative
A characteristic of a chemical species when the rate of intake into a living organism is greater than the rate of excretion or metabolism. This results in an increase in tissue concentration relative to the exposure concentration. U

bioassay
Using living organisms to measure the effect of a substance, factor, or condition by comparing before-and-after data. Term is often used to mean cancer bioassays. N

bioavailability
(1) The rate and extent to which the administered compound is absorbed, i.e, reaches the systemic circulation. A (2) A measure of the degree to which a dose of a substance becomes physiologically available to the body tissues depending upon

absorption, distribution, metabolism and excretion rates. N

biochemical oxygen demand
BOD. (1) The dissolved oxygen required to decompose organic matter in water. It is a measure of pollution because heavy waste loads have a high demand for oxygen. N (2) A measure of the amount of oxygen consumed in the biological processes that break down organic matter in water. The greater the BOD, the greater the degree of pollution. N

bioconcentration
(1) The net accumulation of a substance directly from water into and onto aquatic organisms. A (2) Same as bioaccumulation; refers to the increase in concentration of a chemical in an organism. N

bioconcentration factor
The quotient of the concentration of a test substance in aquatic organisms at or over a discrete time period of exposure divided by the concentration in the test water at or during the same time period. A

bioconversion
A resource recovery method that uses the biological processes of living organisms to transform organic waste into usable material (e.g., humus, compost). U

biodegradable
Any substance that decomposes through the action of microorganisms. N

biodegradation
Decomposition of a substance into more elementary compounds by the action of microorganisms such as bacteria. U

BIOHAZARD
See biological hazard. U

biological additives
Microbiological cultures, enzymes, or nutrient additives that are deliberately introduced into an oil discharge for the specific purpose of encouraging biodegradation to mitigate the effects of the discharge. A

biological control
Using means other than chemicals to control pests, such as predatory organisms, sterilization, or inhibiting hormones. N

biological control agent
Any living organism applied to or introduced into the environment that is intended to function as a pesticide against another organism declared to be a pest by the [EPA] Administrator. A

biological half-life
The time required for the concentration of a chemical present in the body or in a particular body compartment to decrease by one-half through biological processes such as metabolism and excretion. N

biological hazard
Those infectious agents presenting a risk of death, injury or illness to employees. O

biological magnification
(1) The concentration of certain substances up a food chain. A very important mechanism in concentrating pesticides and heavy metals in organisms such as fish. N (2) Refers to the process whereby certain substances such as pesticides or heavy metals move up the food chain, work their way into a river of lake and are eaten by large birds, animals or humans. The substances become concentrated in tissues or internal orgrans as they move up the chain (See: bioaccumulative). N

biological markers/monitoring
Measuring chemicals or their metabolites in biological materials (e.g., blood, urine, breath) to estimate exposure, or to detect biochemical changes in the exposed subject before or during the onset of adverse health effects. Sometimes refers to a specific indicator for a particular disease/functional disturbance. U

biological monitoring
The determination of the effects on aquatic life, including accumulation of pollutants in tissue, in receiving waters due to the discharge of pollutants (A) by techniques and procedures, including sampling of organisms representative of appropriate levels of the food chain appropriate to the volume and the physical, chemical, and biological characteristics of the effluent, and (B) at appropriate frequencies and locations. D

biological oxidation
The process by which microorganisms decompose complex organic materials. The process is used in activated sludge wastewater treatment and in self-purification of bodies of water. Also called biochemical oxidation. U

biological treatment
A treatment technology that uses bacteria to consume waste. This treatment breaks down organic materials. N

biological waste
Waste derived from living organisms. U

biological wastewater treatment
A type of wastewater treatment in which bacterial or biochemical action is intensified to stabilize, oxidize, and nitrify the unstable organic matter present. Intermittent sand filters, contact beds, trickling filters, and activated sludge tanks are examples of the equipment used. U

biologically significant effect
A response in an organism or other biological system that is considered to have a substantial or noteworthy effect (positive or negative) on the well-being of the biological system. Used to distinguish statistically significant effects or changes, which may or may not be meaningful to the general state of health of the system. N

biologicals
Preparations made from living organisms and their products, including vaccines, cultures, etc., intended for use in diagnosing, immunizing or treating humans or

animals or in research pertaining thereto. A

biomass
(1) The amount of living matter in a given unit of the environment. (2) All of the living material in a given area, often refers to vegetation. Also called "biota." N

biomonitoring
(1) The use of living organisms to test the suitability of effluents for discharge into receiving waters and to test the quality of such waters downstream from the discharge. (2) Analysis of blood, urine, tissues, etc., to measure chemical exposure in humans. N

biopsy
Removal and examination of tissue from the living body. N

bioretention
See bioaccumulation. A

biosphere
The portion of earth and its atmosphere that can support life. N

biostabilizer
A machine that grinds and aerates organic waste materials to produce compost. U

biota
All living organisms that exist in an area. N

biotechnology
Techniques that use living organisms or parts of organisms to produce a variety of products (from medicines to industrial enzymes) to improve plants or animals or to develop microorganisms for specific uses such as removing toxics from bodies of water, or as pesticides. N

biotic community
A naturally occurring assemblage of plants and animals that live in the same environment and are mutually sustaining and interdependent. N

biotransformation
An enzymatic chemical alteration of a substance within the body that generally leads to a more excretable metabolite, sometimes producing a more toxic form of the substance. N

bird hazard
An increase in the likelihood of bird/aircraft collisions that may cause damage to the aircraft or injury to its occupants. A

bird hazards to aircraft
A facility or practice disposing of putrescible wastes that may attract birds and which occurs within 10,000 feet (3,048 meters) of any airport runway used by turbojet aircraft or within 5,000 feet (1,524 meters) of any airport runway used by only piston-type aircraft. A

bird poisons and repellents
All substances or mixtures of substances intended for preventing, destroying, repelling, or mitigating birds declared to be pests under 40 CFR 162.14. Bird poisons and repellents include, but are not limited to: (i) Toxicants intended to kill or

destroy certain birds; (ii) Toxicants intended to cause, by pharmacological action, repelling of birds away from certain sites; (iii) Sensory agents utilizing taste, sight, touch, or other means, intended to repel certain bird species or populations from certain sites, to reduce their predation of certain seed and crops, or to protect other organisms or objects from injury, soiling, or harassment; and (iv) Reproductive inhibitors intended to reduce or otherwise alter the reproductive capacity or potential of certain birds. A

bitterns
The saturated brine solution remaining after precipitation of sodium chloride in the solar evaporation process. A

bituminous coal
Solid fossil fuel classified as bituminous coal by A.S.T.M. Designation D-388-66. A

black liquor
The leftover liquid from wood chips treated by the sulfite process. (See: multiple-effect evaporater system). U

black lung
A disease of the lungs caused by habitual inhalation of coal dust. N

blackwater
Water that contains animal, human, or food wastes. N

blanket insulation
Relatively flat and flexible insulation in coherent sheet form, furnished in units of substantial area. Batt insulation is included in this term. A

blast furnace
Any furnace used to recover metal from slag. A

blast gate
A sliding metal damper in a duct, usually used to regulate the flow of forced air. U

bleached papers
Paper made of pulp that has been treated with bleaching agents. A

blend fertilizer
A mixture of dry, straight and mixed fertilizer materials. A

BLM
Bureau of Land Management. N

block group/enumeration district
BG/ED. The smallest geographic areas used by the Bureau of Census in conducting the population census. Block groups are designated for urban areas, while enumeration districts are designated for rural areas. BG/EDs data are frequently incorporated into exposure models to estimate population exposure to environmental pollutants. N

blood
Human blood, human blood components, and products made from human blood. O

blood products
Any product derived from human blood, including but not limited to

blood plasma, platelets, red or white blood corpuscles, and other derived licensed products, such as interferon, etc. A

bloodborne pathogens
Pathogenic microorganisms that are present in human blood and can cause disease in humans. These pathogens include, but are not limited to, hepatitis B virus (HBV) and human immunodeficiency virus (HIV). O

bloom
A proliferation of algae and/or higher aquatic plants in a body of water; often related to pollution, especially when pollutants accelerate growth. N

blow down
A general cleaning of a room or a part of a room by the use of compressed air. O

blow off
The use of compressed air for cleaning of short duration and usually for a specific machine or any portion of a machine. O

blowdown
The minimum discharge of recirculating water for the purpose of discharging materials contained in the process, the further buildup of which would cause concentrations or amounts exceeding limits established by best engineering practice. A

blower
A fan used to force air or gas under pressure. U

blowing still
The equipment in which air is blown through asphalt flux to change the softening point and penetration rate. A

blowing tap
Any tap in which an evolution of gas forces or projects jets of flame or metal sparks beyond the ladle, runner, or collection hood. A

blowout
A sudden violent escape of gas and oil from an oil well when high pressure gas is encountered and preventive measures have failed. A

BLS
Bureau of Labor Statistics. N

BMP
Best management practice. A

BMR
Baseline Monitoring Report (CWA). N

BOA
Basic ordering agreement. U

board insulation
Semi-rigid insulation preformed into rectangular units having a degree of suppleness, particularly related to their geometrical dimensions. A

boatswain's chair
A seat supported by slings attached to a suspended rope, designed to accommodate one workman in a sitting position. O

BOD
Biological oxygen demand. N

BOD5 input
The biochemical oxygen demand of the materials entered into process. It can be calculated by multiplying the fats, proteins and carbohydrates by factors of 0.890, 1.031 and 0.691 respectively. Organic acids (e.g., lactic acids) should be included as carbohydrates. Composition of input materials may be based on either direct analyses or generally accepted published values. A (2) The amount of dissolved oxygen consumed in five days by biological processes breaking down organic matter. N

BOD7
The biochemical oxygen demand as determined by incubation at 20° C for a period of 7 days using an acclimated seed. Agitation employing a magnetic stirrer set at 200 to 500 rpm may be used. A

body belt
A strap with means both for securing it about the waist and for attaching it to a lanyard, lifeline, or deceleration device. O

body burden
The total amount of a toxic material that a person has ingested or inhaled from all sources over time. N

body fluids
Liquid emanating or derived from humans and limited to blood; dialysate; amniotic, cerebrospinal, synovial, pleural, peritoneal and pericardial fluids; and semen and vaginal secretions. A

body harness
A design of straps which may be secured about the employee in a manner to distribute the fall arrest forces over at least the thighs, pelvis, waist, chest and shoulders with means for attaching it to other components of a personal fall arrest system. O

body style
A level of commonality in vehicle construction as defined by number of doors and roof treatment (e.g., sedan, convertible, fastback, hatchback) and number of seats (i.e., front seat, second or third seat) requiring seat belts pursuant to National Highway Traffic Safety Administration safety regulations. Station wagons and light trucks are identified as car lines. A

body type
A name denoting a group of vehicles that are either in the same car line or in different car lines provided the only reason the vehicles qualify to be considered in different car lines is that they are produced by separate divisions of a single manufacturer. A

BOF
Basic oxygen furnace. N

bog
Wet, spongy land usually poorly drained, highly acid and rich in plant residue; the result of lake eutrophication. N

boiler
Any enclosed combustion device that extracts useful energy in the form of steam. A

boiler operating day
A 24-hour period during which fossil fuel is combusted in a steam generating unit for the entire 24 hours. A

boiling point
The temperature at which the vapor pressure of a liquid is equal to the pressure of the atmosphere. A

boiling water reactor
BWR. A reactor in which water, used as both coolant and moderator, is allowed to boil in the core. The resulting steam can be used directly to drive a turbine. A

bond paper
A generic category of paper used in a variety of end use applications such as forms (see "form bond"), offset printing, copy paper, stationery, etc. In the paper industry, the term was originally very specific but is now very general. A

bond release
The time at which the appropriate regulatory authority returns a reclamation or performance bond based upon its determination that reclamation work (including, in the case of underground mines, mine sealing and abandonment procedures) has been satisfactorily completed. A

book paper
A generic category of papers produced in a variety of forms, weights, and finishes for use in books and other graphic arts applications, and related grades such as tablet, envelope, and converting papers. A

boom
A floating device used to contain oil on a body of water. N

booster cycle
The period during which additional hydraulic pressure is exerted to push the last charge of solid waste into a transfer trailer or a container attached to a stationary compactor. U

BOP
Basic oxygen process. N

BOPF
Basic oxygen process furnace. N

borosilicate recipe
Raw material formulation of the following approximate weight proportions: 72 percent silica; 7 percent nepheline syenite; 13 percent anhydrous borax; 8 percent boric acid; and 0.1 percent miscellaneous materials. A

borrowing authority
Statutory authority not necessarily provided through the appropriations process, that permits Federal agencies to incur obligations and to make payments from borrowed moneys. U

botanical pesticide
A pesticide whose active ingredient is a plant produced chemical such as nicotine or strychnine. N

bottle bill
Proposed or enacted legislation which requires a returnable deposit on beer or soda containers and provides for retail store or other redemption centers. Such legislation is designed

to discourage use of throw-away containers. N

bottom ash
The ash that drops out of the furnace gas stream in the furnace and in the economizer sections. Economizer ash is included when it is collected with bottom ash. A

bottom land hardwoods
Forested freshwater wetlands adjacent to rivers in the southeastern United States. They are especially valuable for wildlife breeding and nesting and habitat areas. N

bottom sample
A spot sample obtained from the material on the bottom surface of the tank, container, or line at its lowest point. A

bottom time
The total elapsed time measured in minutes from the time when the diver leaves the surface in descent to the time that the diver begins ascent. O

bounce
Unscheduled point contact opening(s) after initial closure and before scheduled reopening. A

boxboard
Paperboard used to manufacture boxes and cartons. U

BOYSNC
Beginning of year significant non-compliers. N

BP
Boiling point. N

BPJ
Best professional judgment. N

BPT
Best practicable control technology. N

BPTCA
The best practicable control technology currently available under section 304(b)(1) of the Clean Water Act. A

BPWTT
Best practicable waste treatment technology. The cost-effective technology that can treat wastewater, combined sewer overflows and nonexcessive infiltration and inflow in publicly owned or individual wastewater treatment works, to meet the applicable provisions of: (i) 40 CFR Part 133--secondary treatment of wastewater; (ii) 40 CFR Part 125, Subpart G--marine discharge waivers; (iii) 40 CFR 122.44(d)--more stringent water quality standards and State standards; or (iv) 41 FR 6190 (February 11, 1976) -- Alternative Waste Management Techniques for Best Practicable Waste Treatment (treatment and discharge, land application techniques and utilization practices, and reuse). A

brace
A tie that holds one scaffold member in a fixed position with respect to another member. O

brackish water
A mixture of fresh and salt water. N

brake
(1) The mechanism used on a mechanical power press to stop and/or hold the crankshaft, either directly or through a gear train, when the clutch is disengaged. O (2) A device used for retarding or stopping motion by friction or power means. O

branch circuit
The circuit conductors between the final overcurrent device protecting the circuit and the outlet(s). O

brass or bronze
Any metal alloy containing copper as its predominant constituent, and lesser amounts of zinc, tin, lead, or other metals. A

breakdown voltage
The voltage level at which the capacitor fails. A

breaker point
(1) A mechanical switch operated by the distributor cam to establish and interrupt the primary ignition coil current. A (2) The emissions-critical parameters for breaker points are: (A) Bounce; (B) Dwell Angle, and (C) Contact Resistance. A

breakover angle
The supplement of the largest angle, in the plan side view of an automobile, that can be formed by two lines tangent to the front and rear static loaded radii arcs and intersecting at a point on the underside of the automobile. A

breeching
A passage that conducts the products of combustion to a stack or chimney. U

breeching bypass
An arrangement in which breechings and dampers permit the intermittent use of two or more passages to direct or divert the flow of the products of combustion. U

breeder
A nuclear reactor that produces more fuel than it consumes. N

bricklayers' square scaffold
A scaffold composed of framed wood squares which support a platform, limited to light and medium duty. O

bridge wall
A partition between chambers over which the products of combustion pass. U

briquetter
A machine that compresses a material, such as metal turnings or coal dust, into small pellets. U

British thermal unit
BTU. The amount of heat required to raise the temperature of one pound of water one degree Fahrenheit at or near 39.2° F. The term is used in resource recovery to indicate the amount of heat energy available in a given unit of waste or recovered fuel. U

broadcast application
In pesticides, the spreading of chemicals over an entire area. N

broke
Paper that is discarded at any time during its manufacture. It is usually returned to a repulping unit for reprocessing. U

bronchial
Pertaining to the airways of the lung below the larynx that lead to the alveolar region of the lungs. Bronchial airways provide a passageway for air movement. N

bronchiectasis
Pathological dilation of a bronchus or of the bronchial tubes. N

bronchiole
Small branch of the bronchus. U

bronchiolitis
Inflammation of the smallest bronchial tubes. U

bronchitis
Inflammation of the mucous membrane of the bronchial tubes. It may aggravate an existing asthmatic condition. U

bronchoconstrictor
An agent that causes a reduction in the caliber (diameter) of a bronchial tube. U

bronchodilator
An agent which causes an increase in the caliber (diameter) of a bronchus or bronchial tube. U

bronchus
A major airway of the respiratory system. U

brood stock
The animals which are cultured to produce test organisms through reproduction. A

brown papers
Papers usually made from unbleached kraft pulp and used for bags, sacks, wrapping paper, and so forth. A

BSCO
Brake specific carbon monoxide. A

BSHC
Brake specific hydrocarbons. A

BSNO$_x$
Brake specific oxides of nitrogen. A

Btu
British thermal unit. A

BTX storage tank
Any tank, reservoir, or container used to collect or store benzene-toluene-xylene or other light-oil fractions. A

bubble policy
A concept which treats individual sources of pollution in an existing plant collectively rather than individually. As long as it meets an overall emissions reduction goal, a company can reduce emissions from different sources in the same plant by different amounts. N Emissions sources can propose alternate means to comply with a set of emissions limitations; under the bubble concept, sources can control more than required at one emission point where control costs are relatively low in return for a comparable relaxation of controls at

a second emission point where costs are higher. (See: emissions trading). N

bucket
An open container affixed to the movable arms of a wheeled or tracked vehicle to spread solid waste and cover material and to excavate soil. U

buckle
Any device for holding the body belt or body harness closed around the employee's body. O

buddy system
A system of organizing employees into work groups in such a manner that each employee of the work group is designated to be observed by at least one other employee in the work group. The purpose of the buddy system is to provide rapid assistance to employees in the event of an emergency. O

buddy-breathing device
An accessory to self-contained breathing apparatus which permits a second person to share the same air supply as that of the wearer of the apparatus. O

budget
The financial plan for expenditure of all Federal and non-Federal funds for a project, including other Federal assistance, developed by cost components in the grant application. U

budget amendment
A formal request submitted to the Congress by the President, after his formal budget transmittal but prior to completion of appropriate action by the Congress, that revises his previous budget request. U

budget authority
BA. Authority provided by law to enter into obligations that will result in immediate or future outlays. It may be classified by the period of availability (1-year, multiple-year, no-year), by the timing of congressional action (current or permanent), or by the manner of determining the amount available (definite or indefinite). The basic forms of budget authority are: Appropriations--budget authority provided through the congressional appropriation process that permits Federal agencies to incur obligations and to make payments. Borrowing authority--statutory authority not necessarily provided through the appropriations process, that permits Federal agencies to incur obligations and to make payments from borrowed moneys. Contract authority--statutory authority, not necessarily provided through the appropriations process, that permits Federal agencies to enter into contracts or incur other obligations in advance of an appropriation. U

budget period
The period specified in a grant agreement during which granted Federal funds are authorized to be expended, obligated, or firmly committed by the grantee for the purposes specified in the grant agreement. U

budget receipts
Money, net of refunds, collected from the public by the Federal

Government through the exercise of its governmental or sovereign powers, as well as gifts, contributions and premiums from voluntary participants in Federal social insurance programs closely associated with compulsory programs. Excluded are amounts received from strictly business-type transactions (such as sales, interest, or loan repayments) and payments between Governmental accounts. U

budget surplus or deficit
The difference between budget receipts and outlays. U

buffer
Any of certain combinations of chemicals used to stabilize the pH values or alkalinities of solutions. U

buffer strips
Strips of grass or other erosion-resisting vegetation between or below cultivated strips or fields. N

building
(1) A structure which stands alone or which is cut off from adjoining structures by fire walls with all openings therein protected by approved fire doors. A (2) Any frame structure with a roof. A

building insulation
A material, primarily designed to resist heat flow, which is installed between the conditioned volume of a building and adjacent unconditioned volumes or the outside. This term includes but is not limited to insulation products such as blanket, board, spray-in-place, and loose-fill that are used as ceiling, floor, foundation, and wall insulation. A

building manager
The person who manages one or several buildings under the authority of a Federal agency. For example, a building manager may be the GSA person who manages buildings for GSA. O

building, structure, facility, or installation
All of the pollutant-emitting activities which belong to the same industrial grouping, are located on one or more contiguous or adjacent properties, and are under the control of the same person (or persons under common control) except the activities of any vessel. Pollutant-emitting activities shall be considered as part of the same industrial grouping if they belong to the same "Major Group" (i.e., which have the same first two-digit code) as described in the *Standard Industrial Classification Manual*, 1972, as amended by the 1977 Supplement (U.S. Government Printing Office stock numbers 4101-0066 and 003-005-00176-0, respectively). A

building-related illness
A discrete, identifiable disease or illness. Can be traced to a specific pollutant or source within a building. (Contrast: sick building syndrome.) N

built-up roofing
A weather-proofing cover, applied over roof decks, consisting of either a liquid-applied system, a single-ply system, or a multiple-ply system. Liquid-applied systems generally

consist of silicone rubber, plastics, or similar material applied by spray or roller equipment. Single-ply systems generally consist of a single layer of synthetic rubber, plastic, or similar material, and a layer of adhesive. Multiple-ply systems generally consist of layers of felt and bitumen, and may be covered with a layer of mineral aggregate. O

bulk asbestos
Any quantity of asbestos fiber of any type or grade, or combination of types or grades, that is mined or milled with the purpose of obtaining asbestos. This term does not include asbestos that is produced or processed as a contaminant or an impurity. A

bulk container
A large container that can either be pulled or lifted mechanically onto a service vehicle or emptied mechanically into a service vehicle. A

bulk gasoline plant
A facility for the storage and dispensing of gasoline that employs tank trucks, trailers, railroad cars, or other mobile non-marine vessels for both incoming and outgoing gasoline transfer operations. A

bulk resin
A resin which is produced by a polymerization process in which no water is used. A

bulk terminal
Any facility which receives liquid product by pipelines, marine vessels, tank trucks, or railcars, and loads the product for further distribution into tank trucks, railcars, or marine vessels. A

bulky waste
Large items of solid waste such as household appliances, furniture, large auto parts, trees, branches, stumps, and other oversize wastes whose large size precludes or complicates their handling by normal solid wastes collection, processing, or disposal methods. A

bull clam
A tracked vehicle that has a hinged, curved bowl on top of the front of the blade. U

bulwark
The side of a ship above the upper deck. O

bundle
A structure composed of three or more fibers in a parallel arrangement with each fiber closer than one fiber diameter. A

bunker "c" oil
A general term used to indicate a heavy viscous fuel oil. A

bunker fuel
A general term for heavy oils used as fuel on ships and in industry; often refers to No. 5 or 6 fuel oil. A

bunkering
The process of fueling a ship. A

burial ground (graveyard)
A disposal site for unwanted radio-

active materials that uses earth or water for a shield. N

burn
The degree of heat treatment to which refractory bricks are subjected during their manufacture. U

burning agents
Those materials which, through physical or chemical means, improve the combustibility of the materials to which they are applied. A

burning area
The horizontal projection of a grate, a hearth, or both. U

burning hearth
A solid surface to support the solid fuel or solid waste in a furnace during drying, ignition, or combustion, without air openings in it; or, the surface upon which materials are placed for combustion. U

burning rate
The volume of solid waste incinerated or the amount of heat released during incineration. The rate is usually expressed in pounds of solid waste per square foot of burning area per hour or in British thermal units per sq. ft. of burning area per hour. U

burnishing
A surface finishing process in which minute surface irregularities are displaced rather than removed. A

bursting pressure
The pressure at which a pressure containment device would fail structurally. O

burying
Disposal of waste materials by depositing them in the earth. U

bus/carpool lane
A lane on a street or highway open only to buses (or buses and carpools), whether constructed especially for that purpose or converted from existing lanes. A

bushing
An insulating structure including a through conductor, or providing a passageway for such a conductor, with provisions for mounting on a barrier, conducting or otherwise, for the purpose of insulating the conductor from the barrier and conducting current from one side of the barrier to the other. O

business
Any person engaged in a business, trade, employment, calling or profession, whether or not all or any part of the net earnings derived from such engagement by such person inure (or may lawfully inure) to the benefit of any private shareholder or individual. A

business confidentiality claim
A claim or allegation that business information is entitled to confidential treatment for reasons of business confidentiality, or a request for a determination that such information is entitled to such treatment. A

business information
Any information which pertains to the interests of any business, which was developed or acquired by that

business, and (except where the context otherwise requires) which is possessed by EPA in recorded form. A

butterfly damper
A plate or blade installed in a duct, breeching, flue connection or stack that rotates on an axis to regulate the flow of gases. U

by-pass
The circumventing of a particular portion of a process or pollution control system. U

by-product
A material that is not one of the primary products of a production process and is not solely or separately produced by the production process. Examples are process residues such as slags or distillation column bottoms. The term does not include a co-product that is produced for the general public's use and is ordinarily used in the form it is produced by the process. A

by-product cokemaking
Those cokemaking operations in which coal is heated in the absence of air to produce coke. In this process, by-products may be recovered from the gases and liquids driven from the coal during cokemaking. A

byproduct
A chemical substance produced without a separate commercial intent during the manufacture, processing, use or disposal of another chemical substance(s) or mixture(s). A

byproduct utilization
The manufacture of products from bark and wood waste materials, but does not include the manufacture of insulation board, particleboard, or hardboard. A

C

C.
Celsius. U

CA
Corrective action. U

CAA
Clean Air Act. U

CAAA
Clean Air Act Amendments. U

CAB
Civil Aeronautics Board. U

cab
A housing which covers the rotating superstructure machinery and/or operator's station. On truck-crane trucks a separate cab covers the driver's station. O

cab over axle
The cab which contains the operator/passenger compartment is directly above the engine and front axle and the entire cab can be tilted forward to permit access to the engine compartment. A

cab over engine
See cab over axle. A

cabinet
An enclosure designed either for surface or flush mounting, and provided with a frame, mat, or trim in which a swinging door or doors are or may be hung. O

cable
(1) A conductor, or group of conductors, enclosed in a weatherproof sheath, that may be used to supply electrical power and/or control current for equipment or to provide voice communication circuits. O (2) A conductor with insulation, or a stranded conductor with or without insulation and other coverings (single-conductor cable) or a combination of conductors insulated from one another (multiple-conductor cable). O

cable-pullout unloading method
A procedure in which a landfill tractor empties a transfer trailer by pulling a cable network from the front to the rear of the vehicle. U

cadmium
A heavy metal element that accumulates in the environment. N

CAER
Community Awareness and Emergency Response Program. N

CAFE
Corporate average fuel economy. N

CAG
EPA's Carcinogen Assessment Group. N

cage
A guard that may be referred to as a cage or basket guard which is an enclosure that is fastened to the side rails of the fixed ladder or to the structure to encircle the climbing space of the ladder for the safety of the person who must climb the ladder. O

CAIR
Comprehensive Assessment Information Rule. U

caisson
A wood, steel, concrete or reinforced concrete, air- and water-tight chamber in which it is possible for men to work under air pressure greater than atmospheric pressure to excavate material below water level. O

cake
The solids discharged from a dewatering apparatus. U

cal.
Calorie. U

calcination
The process of heating a waste material to a high temperature without fusing in order to effect useful changes (e.g., oxidation, pulverization); commonly used in the treatment of hazardous waste, especially high-level radioactive waste. U

calcine
The solid materials produced by a roaster. A

calciner
A unit in which the moisture and organic matter of phosphate rock is reduced within a combustion chamber. A

calcining
The exposure of an inorganic chemical compound or mineral to a uniform high temperature to alter its chemical form and drive off a substance which was originally part of the compound. Most commonly used in processing high-level radioactive wastes. This process involves heating a solid waste material to high temperatures without melting to make useful changes, such as oxidation or pulverization. U

calcium carbide
Material containing 70 to 85 percent calcium carbide by weight. A

calcium sulfate storage pile runoff
The calcium sulfate transport water runoff from or through the calcium sulfate pile, and the precipitation which falls directly on the storage pile and which may be collected in a seepage ditch at the base of the outer

slopes of the storage pile, provided such seepage ditch is protected from the incursion of surface runoff from areas outside of the outer perimeter of the seepage ditch. A

calculated level
The level of production, exports or imports of controlled substances determined for each Group of controlled substances by: (1) Multiplying the amount (in kilograms) of production, exports or imports of each controlled substance's ozone depletion weight listed in appendix to this Part: and (2) Adding together the resulting products for the controlled substances within each group. A

calibrating gas
A gas of known concentration which is used to establish the response curve of an analyzer. A

calibration
The set of specifications, including tolerances, unique to a particular design, version or application of a component or component assembly capable of functionally describing its operation over its working range. A

calibration drift
CD. The difference in the CEMS output readings from the established reference value after a stated period of operation during which no unscheduled maintenance, repair, or adjustment takes place. A CD test is performed to demonstrate the stability of the CEMS calibration over time. A

calibration error
The difference between the pollutant concentration indicated by the measurement system and the known concentration of the test gas mixture. A

calibration of equipment
Measurement of dispersal or output of application equipment and adjustment of such equipment to control the rate of dispersal, and droplet or particle size of a pesticide dispersed by the equipment. A

California wastes
A category of wastes specified in Section 3004(d)(2) of HSWA [Hazardous and Solid Waste Amendments of RCRA]. N

CAMU
Corrective Action Management Unit. U

can
A container formed from sheet metal and consisting of a body and two ends or a body and a top. A

cancellation
Refers to Section 6 (b) of the Federal Insecticide, Fungicide and Rodenticide Act (FIFRA) which authorizes cancellation of a pesticide registration if unreasonable adverse effects to the environment and public health develop when a product is used according to widespread and commonly recognized practice, or if its labeling or other material required to be submitted does not comply with FIFRA provisions. N

cancer
An abnormal, potentially unlimited, disorderly new cell growth. U

candidate method
A method of sampling and analyzing the ambient air for an air pollutant for which an application for a reference method determination or an equivalent method determination is submitted in accordance with [applicable EPA] procedures. A

canmaking
The manufacturing process or processes used to manufacture a can from a basic metal. A

CAO
Corrective Action Order. N

CAP
Corrective Action Plan. U

cap
A layer of clay, or other highly impermeable material installed over the top of a closed landfill to prevent entry of rainwater and minimize production of leachate. N

capable of transportation of property on a street or highway
A vehicle that: (1) Is self propelled and is capable of transporting any material or fixed apparatus, or is capable of drawing a trailer or semi-trailer. (2) Is capable of maintaining a cruising speed of at least 25 mph over level, paved surface. (3) Is equipped or can readily be equipped with features customarily associated with practical street or highway use, such features including but not being limited to: A reverse gear and a differential, fifth wheel, cargo platform or cargo enclosures, and (4) Does not exhibit features which render its use on a street or highway impractical, or highly unlikely, such features including, but not being limited to, tracked road means, an inordinate size or features ordinarily associated with combat or tactical vehicles. A

capacitance
The property of a device which permits storage of electrically-separated charges when differences in electrical potential exist between the conductors and measured as the ratio of stored charge to the difference in electrical potential between conductors. A

capacitor
A device for accumulating and holding a charge of electricity, consisting of conducting surfaces separated by a dielectric. Types of capacitors are as follows: (1) "Small Capacitor" means a capacitor which contains less than 1.36 kg (3 lbs.) of dielectric fluid. The following assumptions may be used if the actual weight of the dielectric fluid is unknown. A capacitor whose total volume is less than 1,639 cubic centimeters (100 cubic inches) may be considered to contain less than 1.36 kg (3 lbs.) of dielectric fluid and a capacitor whose total volume is more than 3,278 cubic centimeters (200 cubic inches) must be considered to contain more than 1.36 kg (3 lbs.) of dielectric fluid. A capacitor whose volume is between 1,639 and 3,278

cubic centimeters may be considered to contain less than 1.36 kg (3 lbs.) of dielectric fluid if the total weight of the capacitor is less than 4.08 kg (9 lbs.). (2) "Large high voltage capacitor" means a capacitor which contains 1.36 kg (3 lbs.) or more of dielectric fluid and which operates at 2000 volts (a.c. or d.c.) or above. (3) "Large low voltage capacitor" means a capacitor which contains 1.36 kg (3 lbs.) or more of dielectric fluid and which operates below 2000 volts (a.c. or d.c.). A

capacity factor
The ratio of the average load on a machine or equipment for the period of time considered to the capacity rating of the machine or equipment. A

capillary
A vessel resembling a hair: fine, minute. Relating to a blood or lymphatic capillary vessel. U

capillary fringe
A zone immediately above the water table in which water is drawn upward from the water table by capillary action. N

capital expenditure
An expenditure for a physical or operational change to a stationary source which exceeds the product of the applicable "annual asset guideline repair allowance percentage" specified in the latest edition of Internal Revenue Service (IRS) Publication 534 and the stationary source's basis, as defined by section 1012 of the Internal Revenue Code. However, the total expenditure for a physical or operational change to a stationary source must not be reduced by any "excluded additions" as defined for stationary sources constructed after December 31, 1981, in IRS Publication 534, as would be done for tax purposes. In addition, "annual asset guideline repair allowance" may be used even though it is excluded for tax purposes in IRS Publication 534. A

capture
The containment or recovery of emissions from a process for direction into a duct which may be exhausted through a stack or sent to a control device. The overall abatement of emissions from a process with an add-on control device is a function both of the capture efficiency and of the control device. A

capture device
A hood, enclosed room floor sweep or other means of collecting solvent or other pollutants into a duct. The pollutant can then be directed to a pollution control device such as an afterburner or carbon adsorber. Sometimes the term is used loosely to include the control device. A

capture efficiency
The fraction of all organic vapors generated by a process that are directed to an abatement or recovery device. N

capture system
The equipment (including hoods, ducts, fans, dampers, etc.) used to capture or transport particulate matter generated by an affected electric submerged arc furnace to the control device. A

car coupling sound
A sound which is heard and identified by the observer as that of car coupling impact, and that causes a sound level meter indicator (FAST) to register an increase of at least ten decibels above the level observed immediately before hearing the sound. A

car line
A name denoting a group of vehicles within a make or car division which has a degree of commonality in construction (e.g., body, chassis). Car line does not consider any level of decor or opulence and is not generally distinguished by characteristics as roof line, number of doors, seats, or windows except for station wagons or light-duty trucks. Station wagons and light-duty trucks are considered to be different car lines than passenger cars. When applied to light trucks, the term "truck lines" will be used. A

car seal
A seal that is placed on the device used to change the position of a valve (e.g., from open to closed) such that the position of the valve cannot be changed without breaking the seal and requiring the replacement of the old seal, once broken, with a new seal. A

CARB
California Air Resources Board. U

carbon adsorber
An add-on control device which uses activated carbon to absorb volatile organic compounds from a gas stream. The VOCs are later recovered from the carbon. A

carbon dioxide
CO_2. A colorless, odorless nonpoisonous gas normally part of ambient air; fossil fuel combustion produces significant quantities of CO_2. N

carbon dioxide recorder
An instrument that continuously monitors the volume concentration (in percent) of carbon dioxide in a flue gas. U

carbon monoxide
CO. A colorless, odorless, very toxic gas produced by any process that involves the incomplete combustion of carbon-containing substances. One of the major air pollutants, it is primarily emitted through the exhaust of gasoline-powered vehicles. U

Carbon Monoxide National Ambient Air Quality Standard
CO NAAQS. The standards for carbon monoxide promulgated by the Administrator under section 109, 42 U.S.C. 7409, of the Clean Air Act and found in 40 CFR 50.8. A

carbon sorption
The process in which a substance (the sorbate) is brought into contact with a solid (the sorbent) and held there either by chemical or physical means. It is used in hazardous waste treatment and often employs activated carbon as the sorbent. U

carbon steel
Those steel products other than specialty steel products. A

carbon-nitrogen ratio
C/N. The ratio of the weight of carbon to the weight of nitrogen present in a compost or in materials being composted. U

carbonaceous matter
Pure carbon or carbon compounds present in the fuel or residue of a combustion process. U

carburetor accelerator pumps
The emission-critical parameter for accelerator pumps (plungers or diaphragms) is the average volume of fuel delivered per stroke by the pump within prescribed time limits. A

carcinogen
A chemical is considered to be a carcinogen if: (a) It has been evaluated by the International Agency for Research on Cancer (IARC), and found to be a carcinogen or potential carcinogen; or (b) It is listed as a carcinogen or potential carcinogen in the Annual Report on Carcinogens published by the National Toxicology Program (NTP) (latest edition); or, (c) it is regulated by OSHA as a carcinogen. O

carcinogenic
Cancer producing. N

carcinogenic process
A series of stages at the cellular level after which cancer will develop in an organism. Some believe there are at least 3 stages: initiation, promotion, and progression. While hypothesized as staged process, little is known about specific mechanisms of action. N

carcinoma
A malignant tumor or cancer; a new growth made up of epithelial cells tending to infiltrate other cells and give rise to metastases. N

carpenters' bracket scaffold
A scaffold consisting of wood or metal brackets supporting a platform. O

carpool
A vehicle containing three or more persons. A

carpool matching
Assembling lists of commuters whose daily travel plans indicate they might carpool with each other and making such lists available to such commuters to aid them in forming carpools. A

carriage
A wheeled vehicle used for the horizontal movement and support of other equipment. O

carrier
(1) A common carrier by railroad, or partly by railroad and partly by water, within the continental United States, subject to the Interstate Commerce Act, as amended, excluding street, suburban, and interurban electric railways unless operated as a part of a general railroad system of transportation. A (2) A solvent used to dissolve a test substance prior to delivery to the test chamber. A (3) Any material, including but not limited to feed, water, soil, nutrient media, with which the test substance is combined for administration to a test system. A (2) Any distributor who transports or

stores or causes the transportation or storage of gasoline or diesel fuel without taking title to or otherwise having any ownership of the gasoline or diesel fuel, and without altering either the quality or quantity of the gasoline or diesel fuel. A

carrier of contaminant
Dredged or fill material that contains contaminants. A

carrying capacity
(1) In recreation management, the amount of use a recreation area can sustain without deterioration of its quality. (2) In wildlife management, the maximum number of animals an area can support during a given period of the year. N

carrying case
The container used to store reusable hearing protectors. A

carryout collection
Collection of solid waste from a storage area proximate to the dwelling unit(s) or establishment. A

cartridge filter
A discrete filter unit containing both filter paper and activated carbon that traps and removes contaminants from petroleum solvent, together with the piping and ductwork used in the installation of this device. A

CAS
Chemical Abstract Service. N

CAS number
Chemical Abstracts Service Registry Number assigned to a chemical substance on the Inventory. A

CASAC
Clean Air Scientific Advisory Committee. N

case-control study
A retrospective epidemiologic study in which individuals with the disease under study (cases) are compared with individuals without the disease (controls) in order to contrast the extent of exposure in the diseased group with the extent of exposure in the controls. N

casing
A pipe or tubing of appropriate material, of varying diameter and weight, lowered into a borehole during or after drilling in order to support the sides of the hole and thus prevent the walls from caving, to prevent loss of drilling mud into porous ground, or to prevent water, gas, or other fluid from entering or leaving the hole. A

cask
A thick-walled container (usually lead) used to transport radioactive material. Also called a coffin. N

cast iron
An iron containing carbon in excess of the solubility in the austentite that exists in the alloy at the eutectic temperature. Cast iron also is defined here to include any iron-carbon alloys containing 1.2 percent or more carbon by weight. A

catalytic combustion system
A process in which a substance is introduced into an exhaust gas stream to burn or oxidize vaporized hydrocarbons or odorous contaminants; the substance itself remains intact. U

catalytic converter
An air pollution abatement device that removes organic contaminants by oxidizing them into carbon dioxide and water through chemical reaction. Can also be used to reduce nitrogen oxide emissions from motor vehicles. N

catalytic incinerator
A control device which oxidizes volatile organic compounds (VOCs) by using a catalyst to promote the combustion process. Catalytic incinerators require lower temperatures than conventional thermal incinerators, with resultant fuel and cost savings. N

catanadramous
Fish that swim downstream to spawn. N

catastrophic collapse
The sudden and utter failure of overlying strata caused by removal of underlying materials. A

catastrophic release
A major uncontrolled emission, fire, or explosion, involving one or more highly hazardous chemicals, that presents serious danger to employees in the work-place. O

categorical exclusion
A category of actions which do not individually or cumulatively have a significant effect on the human environment and which have been found to have no such effect in procedures adopted by a Federal agency in implementation of NEPA regulations (40 CFR §1507.3) and for which, therefore, neither an environmental impact statement is required. An agency may decide in its procedures or otherwise, to prepare environmental assessments for the reasons stated in 40 CFR § 1508.9 even though it is not required to do so. Any procedures under this section shall provide for extraordinary circumstances in which a normally excluded action may have a significant environmental effect. A

categorical pretreatment standard
A technology-based effluent limitation for an industrial facility which discharges into a municipal sewer system. Analogous in stringency to Best Available Technology (BAT) for direct dischargers. N

category I nonfriable asbestos-containing material (ACM)
Asbestos-containing packings, gaskets, resilient floor covering, and asphalt roofing products containing more than 1 percent asbestos as determined using the method specified in appendix A, subpart F, 40 CFR part 763, section 1, Polarized Light Microscopy. A

category II nonfriable ACM
Any material, excluding Category I nonfriable ACM, containing more than 1 percent asbestos as determined using the methods specified in appendix A, subpart F, 40 CFR part 763, section 1, Polarized Light Microscopy that, when

dry, cannot be crumbled, pulverized, or reduced to powder by hand pressure. A

category of chemical substances
A group of chemical substances the members of which are similar in molecular structure, in physical, chemical, or biological properties, in use, or in mode of entrance into the human body or into the environment, or the members of which are in some other way suitable for classification as such for purposes of the Toxic Substances Control Act, except that such term does not mean a group of chemical substances which are grouped together solely on the basis of their being new chemical substances. K

category of mixtures
A group of mixtures the members of which are similar in molecular structure, in physical, chemical, or biological properties, in use, or in the mode of entrance into the human body or into the environment, or the members of which are in some other way suitable for classification as such for the purposes of this [Toxic Substances Control] Act. K

Catfloc T
Polydiallyl dimethylamide. N

cathode ray tubes
Electronic devices in which electrons focus through a vacuum to generate a controlled image on a luminescent surface. This definition does not include receiving and transmitting tubes. A

cathodic protection
A technique to prevent corrosion of a metal surface by making that surface the cathode of an electrochemical cell. For example, a tank system can be cathodically protected through the application of either galvanic anodes or impressed current. A

cation exchange capacity
CEC. (1) The sum of exchangeable cations a soil can absorb expressed in milli-equivalents per 100 grams of soil as determined by sampling the soil to the depth of cultivation or solid waste placement, whichever is greater, and analyzing by the summation method for distinctly acid soils or the sodium acetate method for neutral, calcareous or saline soils ("Methods of Soil Analysis, Agronomy Monograph No. 9." C. A. Black, Ed., American Society of Agronomy, Madison, Wisconsin. pp. 891-901, 1965). A (2) The CEC is expressed in milliequivalents of negative charge per 100 grams (meq/100 g) or milliequivalents of negative charge per gram (meq/g) of soil. A

CATS
Corrective Action Tracking System. N

CAU
Carbon adsorption unit. N

caustic soda
Sodium hydroxide (NaOH), a strong alkaline substance used as the cleaning agent in some detergents. N

cave-in
The separation of a mass of soil or

rock material from the side of an excavation, or the loss of soil from under a trench shield or support system, and its sudden movement into the excavation, either by falling or sliding, in sufficient quantity so that it could entrap, bury, or otherwise injure and immobilize a person. O

C_{bi}
The concentration of VOC in each gas stream (i) for the time period entering the emission control device, in parts per million by volume. A

CBI
(1) Confidential business information. (2) Compliance Biomonitoring Inspection. D

CBOD5
The amount of dissolved oxygen consumed in 5 days from the carbonaceous portion of biological processes breaking down in an effluent. The test methodology is the same as for BOD5, except that nitrogen demand is suppressed. N

CCID
Confidential Chemicals Identification System. N

CCP
Composite Correction Plan (CWA). N

CC/RTS
Chemical Collection/Request Tracking System. N

CCTP
Clean Coal Technology Program. N

CD
Calibration drift. U

CDC
Centers for Disease Control (HHS). N

Cd S
Cadmium sulfide. U

CDM
Climatological dispersion model. N

CDNS
Climatological Data National Summary. N

CDS
Compliance Data System. N

CEA
(1) Council of Economic Advisors, White House staff office. (2) Cooperative Enforcement Agreement. N

CEAT
Contractor Evidence Audit Team. N

CEI
Compliance evaluation inspection. This is an overall review of the hazardous waste handler's performance. The inspection includes an onsite examination of records and other documents maintained by the handler and an evaluation of the handler's compliance with all applicable requirements. All applicable inspection checklists must be completed. N

ceiling insulation
A material, primarily designed to resist heat flow, which is installed between the conditioned area of a

building and an unconditioned attic as well as common ceiling floor assemblies between separately conditioned units in multi-unit structures. Where the conditioned area of a building extends to the roof, ceiling insulation includes such a material used between the underside and upperside of the roof. A

ceiling limit
A concentration limit in the work place that should not be exceeded, even for a short time, to protect workers against health effects. N

cell
Compacted solid wastes that are enclosed by natural soil or cover material in a land disposal site. A

cell height
The distance between the top and bottom of the compacted solid waste enclosed by natural soil or cover material in a sanitary landfill. U

cell thickness
The perpendicular distance between the cover materials placed over the last working faces of two successive cells in a sanitary landfill. U

cell-type incinerator
An incinerator whose grate areas are divided into cells, each of which has its own ash drop, underfire air control, and ash grate. U

cells
In solid waste disposal, holes where waste is dumped, compacted and covered with layers of dirt daily. N

cellular polyisocyanurate insulation
Insulation produced principally by the polymerization of polymeric polyisocyanates, usually in the presence of polyhydroxl compounds with the addition of catalysts, cell stabilizers, and blowing agents. A

cellular polystyrene insulation
An organic foam composed principally of polymerized styrene resin processed to form a homogenous rigid mass of cells. A

cellular polyurethane insulation
Insulation composed principally of the catalyzed reaction product of polyisocyanurates and polyhydroxl compounds, processed usually with a blowing agent to form a rigid foam having a predominantly closed cell structure. A

cellulose
Vegetable fiber such as paper, wood, and cane. A

cellulose fiberboard
Insulation composed principally of cellulose fibers usually derived from paper, paperboard stock, cane, or wood, with or without binders. A

cellulose fiber loose-fill
A basic material of recycled wood-based cellulosic fiber made from selected paper, paperboard stock, or ground wood stock, excluding contaminated materials which may reasonably be expected to be retained in the finished product, with suitable chemicals introduced to provide properties such as flame resistance, processing and handling characteris-

tics. The basic cellulosic material may be processed into a form suitable for installation by pneumatic or pouring methods. A

CEM
Continuous emission monitoring (CAA). N

cementing
The operation whereby a cement slurry is pumped into a drilled hole and/or forced behind the casing. A

CEMS
Continuous Emission Monitoring System. N

center pivot irrigation machine
A multi-motored irrigation machine which revolves around a central pivot and employs alignment switches or similar devices to control individual motors. O

central collection point
A location where a generator consolidates regulated medical waste brought together from original generation points prior to its transport off-site or its treatment on-site (e.g., incineration). A

central nervous system
The portion of the nervous system that includes the brain and spinal cord, and their connecting nerves. N

centrifugal collector
A mechanical system using centrifugal force to remove aerosols from a gas stream or to dewater sludge. N

CEPP
Chemical Emergency Preparedness Plan. U

CEQ
Council on Environmental Quality, a staff office of the Executive Office of the President. N

CEQA
California Environmental Quality Act. U

CERCLA
Comprehensive Environmental Response, Compensation and Liability Act of 1980. N (PL 96-510) ("Superfund"). U

CERCLIS
The abbreviation of the CERCLA Information System, EPA's comprehensive data base and management system that inventories and tracks releases addressed or needing to be addressed by the Superfund program. CERCLIS contains the official inventory of CERCLA sites and supports EPA's site planning and tracking functions. Sites that EPA decides do not warrant moving further in the site evaluation process are given a "No Further Response Action Planned" (NFRAP) designation in CERCLIS. This means that no additional federal steps under CERCLA will be taken at the site unless future information so warrants. Sites are not removed from the data base after completion of evaluations in order to document that these evaluations took place and to preclude the possibility that they be needlessly repeated. Inclusion of a specific site or area in the CERCLIS data base

does not represent a determination of any party's liability, nor does it represent a finding that any response action is necessary. Sites that are deleted from the NPL are not designated NFRAP sites. Deleted sites are listed in a separate category in the CERCLIS data base. A

CERI
Center for Environmental Research Information. N

CERMS
Continuous Emission Rate Monitoring System. U

certificate holder
The entity in whose name the certificate of conformity for a class of motor vehicles or motor vehicle engines has been issued. A

certificate of conformity
The document issued by the Administrator under section 206(a) of the Clean Air Act. A

certification
(1) In pesticide regulation, the recognition by a certifying agency that a person is competent and thus authorized to use or supervise the use of restricted use of pesticides; also, a certification by [EPA] that a pesticide chemical is useful for the purpose for which a tolerance or exemption is sought under FIFRA. A A statement of professional opinion based upon knowledge and belief. A (2) In the case of design certification/validation, that the manufacturer has reviewed and tested the design and manufacture, and in the case of installation certification /validation and annual recertification/revalidation, that the employer has reviewed and tested the installation, and concludes in both cases that the requirements of [29 CFR] § 1910.217(a) through (h) and Appendix A have been met. The certifications are made to the validation organization. O (3) A written statement regarding a specific fact or representation that contains the following language: Under civil and criminal penalties of law for the making or submission of false or fraudulent statements or representations (18 U.S.C. 1001 and 15 U.S.C. 2615), I certify that the information contained in or accompanying this document is true, accurate, and complete. As to the identified section(s) of this document for which I cannot personally verify truth and accuracy, I certify as the company official having supervisory responsibility for the persons who, acting under my direct instructions, made the verification that this information is true, accurate, and complete. A

certification vehicle
A vehicle which is selected by automobile manufacturers to be tested for compliance with new motor vehicle air pollutant emission limitations as a representative vehicle of that class of vehicle produced by that manufacturer. Test results from such vehicles determine whether EPA will issue a "certificate of conformity" necessary for the manufacturer to be able to market the vehicles. U

certification vehicle emission margin

A certified engine family means the difference between the EPA emission standards and the average FTP emission test results of that engine family's emission-data vehicles at the projected applicable useful life mileage point (i.e., useful life mileage for light-duty vehicles is 50,000 miles and for light-duty trucks is 120,000 miles for 1985 and later model years or 50,000 miles for 1984 and earlier model years). A

certified

Equipment is "certified" if it (a) has been tested and found by a nationally recognized testing laboratory to meet nationally recognized standards or to be safe for use in a specified manner, or (b) is of a kind whose production is periodically inspected by a nationally recognized testing laboratory, and (c) it bears a label, tag, or other record of certification. O

certified applicator

Any individual who is certified under section 4 of FIFRA as authorized to use or supervise the use of any pesticide which is classifed for restricted use. Any applicator who holds or applies registered pesticides, or use dilutions of registered pesticides consistent with section 2(e) of FIFRA, only to rovide a service of controlling pests without delivering any unapplied pesticide to any person so served is not deemed to be a seller or distributor of pesticides under this Act. A, C

certifying agency

The person or agency designated by the Governor of a State, by statute, or by other governmental act, to certify compliance with applicable water quality standards. If an interstate agency has sole authority to so certify for the area within its jurisdiction, such interstate agency shall be the certifying agency. Where a State agency and an interstate agency have concurrent authority to certify, the State agency shall be the certifying agency. Where water quality standards have been promulgated by the Administrator pursuant to section 10(c)(2) of the Federal Water Pollution Control Act, or where no State or interstate agency has authority to certify, the Administrator shall be the certifying agency. A

certifying official

For the purposes of part 73 [of 40 CFR], means: (1) for a corporation, a president, secretary, treasurer, or vice-president of the corporation in charge of a principal business function, or any other person who performs similar policy- or decision-making functions for the corporation; (2) for a partnership or sole proprietorship, a general partner or the proprietor, respectively; and (3) for a local government entity or State, Federal or other public agency, either a principal executive officer or ranking elected official. A

cesium

Cs. A silver-white, soft ductile element of the alkali metal group that is the most electropositive element known. Used especially in photoelectric cells. N

CFC-12
A chlorofluorocarbon with a trademark name of Freon, commonly used in refrigeration and automobile air conditioning. N

CFCs
Chlorofluorocarbons. A family of inert, nontoxic, and easily liquified chemicals used in refrigeration, air conditioning, packaging, insulation, or as solvents and aerosol propellants. Because CFCs are not destroyed in the lower atmosphere, they drift into the upper atmosphere where their chlorine components destroy ozone. N

cfh.
Cubic feet per hour. U

cfm.
Cubic feet per minute. A measure of the volume of a substance flowing through air within a fixed period of time. With regard to indoor air, refers to the amount of air, in cubic feet, that is exchanged with indoor air in a minute's time, or an air exchange rate. N (Also: cfm).

CFR
Code of Federal Regulations. A codification of the general and permanent rules published in the *Federal Register* by the departments and agencies of the Federal government. The Code is divided into 50 titles which represent broad areas subject to Federal regulation. It is issued quarterly and revised annually. N

cfs.
Cubic feet per second, a measure of the amount of water passing a given point. N

cfv.
Critical flow venture. U

CFV-CVS
Critical flow venture-constant volume sampler. U

chain grate stoker
A stoker with a moving chain as a grate surface. The grate consists of links mounted on rods to form a continuous surface that is generally driven by a shaft with sprockets. B

challenge agent
The air contaminant introduced into a test chamber so that its concentration inside and outside the respirator may be compared. A

chamber
An enclosed space inside an incinerator. A

change order
A written order issued by a recipient, or its designated agent, to its contractor authorizing an addition to, deletion from, or revision of, a contract, usually initiated at the contractor's request. A

changed use pattern
A significant change from a use pattern approved in connection with the registration of a pesticide product. Examples of significant changes include cude, but are not limited to, changes from nonfood to food use, outdoor to indoor use, ground to aerial

application, terrestrial to aquatic use, and nondomestic to domestic use. A

channelization
To straighten and deepen streams so water will move faster, a flood reduction or marsh drainage tactic that can interfere with waste assimilation capacity and disturb fish habitat. N

characteristic
Any one of the four categories used in defining hazardous waste: ignitability, corrosivity, reactivity, and toxicity. N

charge
(1) The amount of solid waste introduced into a furnace at one time. (2) The addition of iron and steel scrap or other materials into the top of an electric arc furnace. A

charge chrome
An alloy containing 52 to 70 percent by weight chromium, 5 to 8 percent by weight carbon, and 3 to 6 percent by weight silicon. A

charging chute
An overhead passage through which waste materials drop into an incinerator. U

charging equipment
The apparatus used to introduce refuse into an incinerator. U

charging gate
A horizontal, movable cover that closes the opening on a top-charging furnace. U

charging hopper
An enlarged opening at the top of a charging chute. U

check
A lengthwise separation of the wood, most of which occurs across the rings of annual growth. O

checker work
A pattern of multiple openings in a refractory structure through which the products of combustion pass to accelerate the turbulent mixing of gases. U

chemical
Any element, chemical compound or mixture of elements and/or compounds. O

chemical agents
Those elements, compounds, or mixtures that coagulate, disperse, dissolve, emulsify, foam, neutralize, precipitate, reduce, solubilize, oxidize, concentrate, congeal, entrap, fix, make the pollutant mass more rigid or viscous, or otherwise facilitate the mitigation of deleterious effects or removal of the pollutant from the water. A

chemical cartridge respirator
A respirator that uses various chemical substances to purify inhaled air of certain gases and vapors. This type respirator is effective for concentrations no more than ten times the TLV of the contaminant, if the contaminant has warning properties (odor or irritation) below the TLV. N

chemical coagulation
The destabilization and initial aggregation of colloidal and finely divided suspended matter by the addition of a floc-forming chemical. U

chemical composition
The name and percentage of weight of each compound in an additive and the name and percentage by weight of each element in an additive. A

chemical fixation
Any waste treatment process that involves reactions between the waste and certain chemicals, and results in solids that encapsulate, immobilize, or otherwise tie up hazardous components in the waste to minimize the leaching of such components and to render the waste nonhazardous and more suitable for disposal. U

Chemical Hazards Response Information System/Hazard Assessment Computer System
CHRIS/HACS, developed by the U.S. Coast Guard. HACS is a computerized model of the four CHRIS manuals that contain chemical-specific data. Federal on scene coordinators (OSCs) use HACS to find answers to specific questions during a chemical spill/response. State and local officials and industry representatives may ask an OSC to request a HACS run for contingency planning purposes. N

chemical hygiene officer
An employee who is designated by the employer, and who is qualified by training or experience, to provide technical guidance in the development and implementation of the provisions of the Chemical Hygiene Plan. This definition is not intended to place limitations on the position description or job classification that the designated individual shall hold within the employer's organizational structure. O

chemical hygiene plan
A written program developed and implemented by the employer which sets forth procedures, equipment, personal protective equipment and work practices that are capable of protecting employees from the health hazards presented by hazardous chemicals used in that particular workplace. O

chemical manufacturer
A person who imports, produces, or manufacturers a chemical substance. A person who extracts a component chemical substance from a previously existing chemical substance or a complex combination of substances is a manufacturer of that component chemical substance. A person who contracts with a manufacturer to manufacture or produce a chemical substance is also a manufacturer if (1) the manufacturer manufactures or produces the substance exclusively for that person, and (2) that person specifies the identify of the substance and controls the total amount produced and the basic technology for the plant process. A

chemical manufacturing plant(s)
(1) Any facility engaged in the production of chemicals by chemical, thermal, physical, or biological processes for use as a product, co-

product, by-product, or intermediate including but not limited to industrial organic chemicals, organic pesticide products, pharmaceutical preparations, paint and allied products, fertilizers, and agricultural chemicals. Examples of chemical manufacturing plants include facilities at which process units are operated to produce one or more of the following chemicals: benzene-sulfonic acid, benzene, chlorobenzene, cumene, cyclohexane, ethylene, ethyl-benzene, hydroquinone, linear alklyl-benzene, nitrobenzene, resorcinol, sulfolane, or styrene. A (2) Industrial plants which are classified by the Department of Commerce under Standard Industrial Classification (SIC) Code 28. A

chemical metal cleaning waste
Any wastewater resulting from the cleaning of any metal process equipment with chemical compounds, including, but not limited to, boiler tube cleaning. A

chemical mixture
Any combination of two or more substances regardless of source or of spatial or temporal proximity. N

chemical name
The scientific designation of a chemical substance in accordance with the nomenclature system developed by the International Union of Pure and Applied Chemistry or the Chemical Abstracts Service's rules of nomenclature, or a name which will clearly identify a chemical substance for the purpose of conducting a hazard evaluation. A O

chemical oxygen demand
COD. A measure of the oxygen required to oxidize all compounds in water, organic and inorganic. N

chemical plant
A large integrated plant or that portion of such a plant other than a refinery or distillery where flammable or combustible liquids are produced by chemical reactions or used in chemical reactions. O

chemical precipitation
(1) Precipitation induced by addition of chemicals. (2) The process of softening water by the addition of lime or lime and soda ash as the precipitants. [See: precipitation]. U

chemical protective clothing
Items of clothing that provide a protective barrier to prevent dermal contact with chemical substances of concern. Examples can include, but are not limited to: Full body protective clothing, boots, coveralls, gloves, jackets, and pants. A

chemical sensitivity
Health problems characterized by effects such as dizziness, eye and throat irritation, chest tightness, and nasal congestion that appear when certain individuals are exposed to certain chemicals. People may react to even trace amounts of chemicals to which they have become "sensitized." N

chemical structure
The molecular structure of a compound. A

chemical substance

Any organic or inorganic substance of a particular molecular identity, including--(i) any combination of such substances occurring in whole or in part as a result of a chemical reaction or occurring in nature, and (ii) any chemical element or uncombined radical. Such term does not include-- (i) any mixture, (ii) any pesticide (as defined in the Federal Insecticide, Fungicide, and Rodenticide Act) when manufactured, processed, or distributed in commerce for use as a pesticide, (iii) tobacco or any tobacco product, (iv) any source material, special nuclear material, or byproduct material (as such terms are defined in the Atomic Energy Act of 1954 and regulations issued under such Act), (v) any article the sale of which is subject to the tax imposed by section 4181 of the Internal Revenue Code of 1954 (determined without regard to any exemptions from such tax provided by section 4182 or 4221 or any other provision of such Code), any pistol, firearm, revolver, shells, or cartridges, and (vi) any food, food additive, drug, cosmetic, or device (as such terms are defined in section 201 of the Federal Food, Drug, and Cosmetic Act) when manufactured, processed, or distributed in commerce for use as a food, food additive, drug, cosmetic, or device. The term "food" as used in clause (vi) of this subparagraph includes poultry and poultry products (as defined in sections 4(e) and 4(f) of the Poultry Products Inspection Act), meat and meat food products (as defined in Section 1(j) of the Federal Meat Inspection Act), and eggs and egg products (as defined in section 4 of the Egg Products Inspection Act). K [Ed. This definition establishes the regulatory scope of TSCA].

Chemical Transportation Emergency Center

CHEMTREC. Operated by the Chemical Manufacturers Association this center provides information and/or assistance to emergency responders. CHEMTREC contacts the shipper or producer of the material for more detailed information, including on-scene assistance when feasible. Can be reached 24 hours a day by calling 800-424-9300. (See also: HIT). N

chemical treatment

Any one of a variety of technologies that use chemicals or a variety of chemical processes to treat waste. N

chemical waste

The waste generated by chemical, petrochemical, plastic, pharmaceutical, biochemical, or microbiological manufacturing processes. U

chemical waste landfill

A landfill at which protection against risk of injury to health or the environment from migration of PCBs to land, water, or the atmosphere is provided from PCBs and PCB Items deposited therein by locating, engineering, and operating the landfill as specified in [40 CFR] § 761.75. A

CHEMNET

A mutual aid network of chemical shippers and contractors. CHEMNET has more than fifty participating companies with emergency teams, twenty-three subscribers (who receive services in an incident from a participant and then reimburse response and cleanup costs), and several emergency response contractors. CHEMNET is activated when a member shipper cannot respond promptly to an incident involving that company's products(s) and requiring the presence of a chemical expert. If a member company cannot go to the scene of the incident, the shipper will authorize a CHEMNET-contracted emergency response company to go. Communications for the network are provided by CHEMTREC, with the shipper receiving notification and details about the incident from the CHEMTREC communicator. N

chemosterilant
A chemical that controls pests by preventing reproduction. N

CHEMTREC
Chemical Transportation Emergency Center. N

child-resistant packaging
Packaging that is designed and constructed to be significantly difficult for children under 5 years of age to open or obtain a toxic or harmful amount of the substance contained therein within a reasonable time, and that is not difficult for normal adults to use properly. A

chicken ladder
See crawling board. O

chilling effect
The lowering of the earth's temperature because of increased particles in the air blocking the sun's rays. (Compare greenhouse effect). N

CHIP
Chemical Hazard Information Profile. U

chipper
A size-reducing device with sharp blades attached to a rotating shaft (mandrel) that shaves or chips off pieces of objects such as tree branches or brush. U

CHLOREP
Chlorine Emergency Plan. U

chlorinated hydrocarbons
A class of persistent, broad-spectrum insecticides, notably DDT, that linger in the environment and accumulate in the food chain. Other examples are aldrin, dieldrin, heptachlor, chlordane, lindane, endrin, mirex, benzene, hexachloride, and toxaphene. N

chlorinated organic pesticides
A class of pesticides that include: Aldrin. BHC (benzene hexachloride). 1,1 - Bis(p-chlorophenyl) - 2, 2, 2- trichloroethanol. Chlorbenside (p-chlorobenzyl p-chlorophenyl sulfide). Chlordane. Chlorobenzilate (ethyl 4,4' - dichlorobenzilate). p-Chlorophenoxyacetic acid. p-Chlorophenyl-2, 4, 5 - trichlorphenyl sulfide. 2,4-D (2,4-dichlorophenoxyacetic acid). DDD (TDE). DDT. 1,1 - Dichloro - 2,2-bis (p-ethyphenyl) ethane. 2,6-Dichloro-4-nitroaniline. 2,4-Dichlorophenyl p-nitrophenyl ether. Dieldrin. Dodechachlorooctahydro-1,3,4 metheno - 2H-cyclobuta [cd]

pentalene. Endosulfan (6, 7, 8, 9, 10, 10- hexachloro- 1,5,5a,6,9,9a-hexahydro - 6,9-methano - 2,4,3-benzodioxathiepin - 3 - 0 oxide). Endosulfan sulfate (6,7,8,9,10,10-hexachloro- 1,5,5a, 6,9,9a- hexahydro-6,9 - methano - 2,4,3-benzodioxathiepin-3,3-dioxide). Heptachlor (1,4,5,6,7,8,8 - heptachlor -3a, 4, 7, 7a- tetrahydro - 4, 7-methanoindene). Heptachlor epoxide (1,4,5, 6,7,8,8-heptachloro -2,3 - epoxy - 2,3,3a,4,7,7a-hexahydro-4,7-methanoindene). Hexachlorophene (2,2' - methylenebis (3,4,6-trichlorophenol) and its monosodium salt. Isopropyl 4,4'-dichlorobenzilate. Lindane. Methoxychlor. Oven (p-chlorophenyl p-chlorobenzenesulfonate). Sesone (sodium 2,4-dichlorophenoxyethyl sulfate, SES). Sodium 2,4-dichlorophenoxyacetate. Sodium trichloroacetate. Sulphenone (p-chlorophenyl phenyl sulfone). Terpene polychlorinates (chlorinated mixture of camphene, pinene, and related terpenes 65-66 percent chlorine). 2,3,5,6-Tetrachloronitrobenzene. Tetradifon (2,4,5,4'-tetrachlorodiphenyl sulfone). Toxaphene (chlorinated camphene). Trichlorobenzoic acid. Trichlorobenzyl chloride. A

chlorinated solvent
An organic solvent containing chlorine atoms, e.g., methylene chloride and 1,1,1-trichloromethane which are used in aerosol spray containers and in traffic paint. N

chlorination
The application of chlorine to drinking water, sewage, or industrial waste to disinfect or to oxidize undesirable compounds. N

chlorinator
A device that adds chlorine to water in gas or liquid form. N

Chlorine Emergency Plan
CHLOREP, operated by the Chlorine Institute is a 24-hour mutual aid program. Response is activated by a CHEMTREC call to the designated CHLOREP contact, who notifies the appropriate team leader, based upon CHLOREP's geographical sector assignment for teams. The team leader in turn calls the emergency caller at the incident scene and determines what advice and assistance are needed. The team lead then decides whether or not to dispatch his team to the scene. N

chlorine-contact chamber
That part of a waste treatment plant where effluent is disinfected by chlorine before being discharged. N

chlorosis
Discoloration of normally green plant parts, that can be caused by disease, lack of nutrients, or various air pollutants. N

choke
A device to restrict air flow into a carburetor in order to enrich the air/fuel mixture delivered to the engine by the carburetor during cold-engine start and cold-engine operation. A

CHRIS/HACS
Chemical Hazards Response

Information System/Hazard Assessment Computer System. U

chrome pigments
Chrome yellow, chrome orange, molybdate chrome orange, anhydrous and hydrous chromium oxide, chrome green, and zinc yellow. A

chrome tan
The process of converting hides into leather using a form of chromium. A

chromium
Total chromium and is determined by the method specified in 40 CFR 136.3. A

chromosome abnormality
A group of conditions associated with abnormalities in the number or structure of chromosomes. These can be produced by insertion, deletion, or rearrangement of chromosomal segments. N

chromosome mutations
Chromosomal changes resulting from breakage and reunion of chromosomes. Chromosomal mutations are also produced through non-disjunction of chromosomes during cell division. A

chromosomes
Thread-like bodies occurring in animal and plant cell nuclei; they contain genes, the material that makes possible the transfer of characteristics from parent to offspring. U

chronic
Occurring over a long period of time, either continuously or intermittently; used to describe ongoing exposures and effects that develop only after a long exposure. Long-lasting or frequently recurring. N

chronic bronchitis
Inflammation of and anatomic changes in the bronchial tubes accompanied by persistent coughing and an excessive production of mucus. U

chronic exposure
Long-term, low level exposure to a toxic chemical. U

chronic health effect
An adverse effect on a human or animal body with symptoms that develop slowly over a long period of time or that recur frequently. N (Compare: acute health effect).

chronic obstructive pulmonary disease
A disease of the lung, involving increased resistance to air flow in the bronchial airways and loss of tissue elasticity, that leads to decreased ability of the lungs to perform ventilation. The pathological changes that lead to COPD can be caused by chronic bronchitis, pulmonary emphysema, chronic asthma, and chronic bronchiolitis. N

chronic respiratory disease
A persistent or long-lasting intermittent disease of the respiratory tract. U

chronic toxicity
(1) The property of a substance or mixture of substances to cause adverse effects in an organism upon repeated or continuous exposure over a period

of at least 1/2 the lifetime of that organism. A (2) The lowest concentration of a constituent causing observable effects (i.e., considering lethality, growth, reduced reproduction, etc.) over a relatively long period of time, usually a 28-day test period for small fish test species. A

chronic toxicity test
A method used to determine the concentration of a substance in water that produces an adverse effect on a test organism over an extended period of time. In this test guideline, mortality and reproduction (and optionally, growth) are the criteria of toxicity. A

chute-fed incinerator
An incinerator that is charged through a chute that extends two or more floors above it. U

CIAQ
Council on Indoor Air Quality. U

CIIT
Chemical Industry Institute of Toxicology. U

cilia
Hair-like cells that line the airways and by their sweeping motion propel the dirt and germ-filled mucus out of the respiratory tract. U

ciliated epithelial cell
A cell with cilia that lines the tracheobronchial region of the lung. The beating of the cilia moves mucus and substances (such as inhaled particles trapped on/in the mucus) upwards and out of the lung, thereby contributing significantly to lung clearance. N

circuit
A conductor or system of conductors through which an electric current is intended to flow. O

circuit breaker
(i) (600 volts nominal, or less). A device designed to open and close a circuit by nonautomatic means and to open the circuit automatically on a predetermined overcurrent without injury to itself when properly applied within its rating. (ii) (Over 600 volts nominal). A switching device capable of making, carrying, and breaking currents under normal circuit conditions, and also making, carrying for a specified time, and breaking currents under specified abnormal circuit conditions, such as those of short circuit. O

cirrhosis
A liver disease characterized by increased fibrous tissue, accompanied by other abnormal physiological changes. Clinical signs of cirrhosis include the loss of functional liver cells and increased resistance to blood flow through the liver. N

city
A political subdivision of a State within a defined area over which a municipal corporation has been established to provide local government functions and facilities. A

city fuel economy
The fuel economy determined by

operating a vehicle (or vehicles) over the driving schedule in the Federal Emission Test Procedure. A

civil action
A law suit filed in court against a person who has either failed to comply with statutory or regulatory requirements or an administrative order or has contributed to a release of hazardous wastes or constituents. There are four types of civil action: compliance; corrective; monitoring and analysis; and imminent hazard. N

civil judgment
The disposition of a civil action by any court of competent jurisdiction, whether entered by verdict, decision, settlement, stipulation, or otherwise creating a civil liability for the wrongful acts complained of; or a final determination of liability under the Program Fraud Civil Remedies Act of 1988 (31 U.S.C. 3801-12). A

cl.
Chemiluminescence. U

claim
(1) An assertion made by a manufacturer regarding the effectiveness of his product. A (2) A demand or written assertion by a contractor seeking, as a matter of right, changes in contract duration, costs, or other provisions, which originally have been rejected by the recipient. A

claims-made policy
An insurance policy that provides coverage of an occurrence if a claim is filed during the term of a policy. A

clamshell bucket
A vessel used to hoist and convey materials; it has two jaws that clamp together when it is lifted by specially attached cables. U

clarification
Clearing action that occurs during waste water treatment when solids settle out, often aided by centrifugal action and chemically induced coagulation. N

clarifier
A settling tank where solids are mechanically removed from waste water. N

class
A group of vehicles which are identical in all material aspects with respect to the parameters listed in 40 CFR § 205.155. A

class I, II and III
Geographical classification system for attainment areas under the Clean Air Act. Class I areas -- primarily national parks and wilderness areas-- allow virtually no emissions and therefore no economic development. Class II areas allow limited development and Class III areas the most development. N

class I sludge management facility
Any POTW identified under 40 CFR 403.8(a) as being required to have an approved pretreatment program (including such POTWs located in a State that has elected to assume local program responsibilities pursuant to 40 CFR 403.10(e)) and any other treatment works treating domestic

sewage classified as a Class I sludge management facility by the Regional Administrator in conjunction with the State Program Director because of the potential for its sludge use or disposal practices to adversely affect public health or the environment. A

class P1
All aircraft piston engines, except radial engines. A

class T1
Aircraft turbofan or turbojet engines except engines of Class T5 of rated power less than 8,000 pounds thrust. A

class T2
All turbofan or turbojet aircraft engines except engines of Class T3, T4, and T5 of rated power of 8,000 pounds thrust or greater. A

class T3
All aircraft gas turbine engines of the JT3D model family. A

class T4
All aircraft gas turbine engines of the JT8D model family. A

class T5
All aircraft gas turbine engines employed for propulsion of aircraft designed to operate at supersonic flight speeds. A

class T8
All aircraft gas turbine engines of the JT8D model family. A

class TF
All turbofan or turbojet aircraft engines except engines of Class T3, T8, and TSS. A

class TP
All aircraft turboprop engines. A

class TSS
All aircraft gas turbine engines employed for propulsion of aircraft designed to operate at supersonic flight speeds. A

classification
The separation and rearrangement of waste materials according to composition (organic or inorganic), size, weight, color, shape, and the like, using specialized equipment. U

classification of railroads
The division of railroad industry operating companies by the Interstate Commerce Commission into three categories. As of 1978, Class I railroads must have annual revenues of $50 million or greater, Class II railroads must have annual revenues of between $10 and $50 million, and Class III railroads must have less than $10 million in annual revenues. A

classified information
Official information which has been assigned a security classification category in the interest of the national defense or foreign relations of the United States. A

classified material
Any document, apparatus, model, film, recording, or any other physical object from which classified information can be derived by study,

analysis, observation, or use of the material involved. A

classified waste
Waste material that has been given security classification in accordance with 50 U.S.C. 401 and Executive Order 11652. A

clastogenic
Able to break chromosomes and thereby produce chromosome abnormalities, a form of genotoxicity. This results in the gain, loss, or rearrangement of pieces of chromosomes. N

Claus sulfur recovery plant
A process unit which recovers sulfur from hydrogen sulfide by a vapor-phase catalytic reaction of sulfur dioxide and hydrogen sulfide. A

clay mineral analysis
The estimation or determination of the kinds of clay-size minerals and the amount present in a sediment or soil. A

clean air
Air of such purity that it will not cause harm or discomfort to an individual if it is inhaled for extended periods of time. O

Clean Air Act
CAA. 42 U.S.C § 7401 *et seq.* U

clean air standards
Any enforceable rule, regulations, guidelines, standards, limitation, orders, controls, prohibitions, or other requirements which are contained in, issued under, or otherwise adopted pursuant to the Air Act or Executive Order 11738, an applicable implementation plan as adopted pursuant to section 110 of the Clean Air Act, an approved implementation procedure or plan under section 111(c) or section 111(d), (of the Clean Air Act), or an approved implementation procedure under section 112(d) of the Clean Air Act. A

clean area
A controlled environment which is maintained and monitored to assure a low probability of asbestos contamination to materials in that space. Clean areas used in this method have HEPA filtered air under positive pressure and are capable of sustained operation with an open laboratory blank which on subsequent analysis has an average of less than 18 structures/mm^2 in an area of 0.057 mm^2 (nominally 10 200-mesh grid openings) and a maximum of 53 structures/mm^2 for any single preparation for that same area. A

clean change room
A room where employees put on clean clothing and/or protective equipment in an environment free of the hazardous material. The clean change room shall be contiguous to and have an entry from a shower room, when the shower room facilities are otherwise required. O

clean coal technology
Any technology not in widespread use as of the date of enactment of the Clean Air Act amendments which will achieve significant reductions in

pollutants associated with the burning of coal. N

clean fuels
Blends and/or substitutes for gasoline fuels. These include compressed natural gas, methanol, ethanol, and others. N

clean room
An uncontaminated room having facilities for the storage of employees' street clothing and uncontaminated materials and equipment. A

Clean Water Act
CWA. Clean Water Act (formerly referred to the Federal Water Pollution Control Act) Pub. L. 92-500, as amended by Pub. L. 95-217 and Pub. L. 95-576, 33 U.S.C. 1251 et seq. D

clean water standards
Any enforceable limitation, control, condition, prohibition, standard, or other requirement which is promulgated pursuant to the Clean Water Act or contained in a permit issued to a discharger by EPA, or by a State under an approved program, as authorized by section 402 of the Clean Water Act, or by a local government to ensure compliance with pretreatment regulations as required by section 307 of the Clean Water Act. A

cleaning
A chemical solution bath and a rinse or series of rinses designed to produce a desired surface finish on the workpiece. This term includes air pollution control scrubbers which are sometimes used to control fumes from chemical solution baths. Conversion coating and anodizing when performed as an integral part of the aluminum forming operations are considered cleaning or etching operations. When conversion coating or anodizing are covered here they are not subject to regulation under the provisions of 40 CFR Part 433, Metal Finishing. A

cleanup
Actions taken to deal with a release or threat of release of a hazardous substance that could affect humans and/or the environment. The term "cleanup" is sometimes used interchangeably with the terms remedial action, removal action, response action, or corrective action. N

cleanup operation
An operation where hazardous substances are removed, contained, incinerated, neutralized, stabilized, cleared-up, or in any other manner processed or handled with the ultimate goal of making the site safer for people or the environment. O

clear cut
A forest management technique that involves harvesting all the trees in one area at one time. Under certain soil and slope conditions it can contribute sediment to water pollution. N

clearance
The disappearance of a compound from a specific organ or body compartment or the whole body. In pulmonary toxicology, clearance refers specifically to removal of an inhaled substance that deposits on the lung surface. N

clearance sample
A spot sample taken 4 inches (100 mm) below the level of the tank outlet. A

cleats
Ladder crosspieces of rectangular cross-section placed on edge on which a person may step in ascending or descending. O

clinical laboratory
A workplace where diagnostic or other screening procedures are performed on blood or other potentially infectious materials. O

clinkers
Hard, sintered, or fused pieces of residue formed in a fire by the agglomeration of ash, metals, glass, and ceramics. U

CLIPS
Chemical List Index and Processing System. N

cloning
In biotechnology, obtaining a group of genetically identical cells from a single cell. This term has assumed a more general meaning that includes making copies of a gene. N

closed container
A container so sealed by means of a lid or other device that neither liquid nor vapor will escape from it at ordinary temperatures. O

closed course competition event
An organized competition event covering an enclosed, repeated or confined route intended for easy viewing of the entire route by all spectators. Such events include short tract, dirt track, drag race, speedway, hillclimb, ice race, and the Bonneville Speed Trials. A

closed portion
That portion of a facility which an owner or operator has closed in accordance with the approved facility closure plan and all applicable closure requirements. A

closed system
An operation where containment prevents the release of the hazardous material into regulated areas, non-regulated areas, or the external environment. O

closed-loop recycling
Reclaiming or reusing wastewater for non-potable purposes in an enclosed process. N

closed-vent system
A system that is not open to atmosphere and that is composed of piping, connections, and, if necessary, flow-inducing devices that transport gas or vapor from a piece or pieces of equipment to a control device. A

closeout
The final EPA or recipient actions taken to assure satisfactory completion of project work and to fulfill administrative requirements, including financial settlement, submission of acceptable required final reports, and resolution of any outstanding issues under the Cooperative Agreement and/or Superfund State Contract. A

closing volume
CV. The lung volume at which the flow from the lower parts of the lungs becomes severely reduced or stops during expiration, presumably because of airway closure. U

closure
The act of securing a "Hazardous Waste Management Facility" pursuant to the requirements of 40 CFR Part 264 (RCRA). A

closure plan
The plan for closure prepared in accordance with the requirements of § 264.112 [of 40 CFR parts 260-299]. A

CLSA
Closed-loop stripping analyses. N

clusters
A new approach to environmental regulation. Clustering is the coordination across programs of regulations that affect particular industries and pollutants such as lead, groundwater and indoor air. N

clutch
(1) A friction, electromagnetic, hydraulic, pneumatic, or positive mechanical device for engagement or disengagement of power. O (2) The coupling mechanism used on a mechanical power press to couple the flywheel to the crankshaft, either directly or through a gear train. O

CMA
Chemical Manufacturers Association. N

CMB
Chemical mass balance. N

CME
Comprehensive [groundwater] monitoring evaluation. This is an overall review of a facility's compliance with all applicable RCRA requirements. It includes everything covered in CEI [compliance evalation inspections] for groundwater monitoring facilities, and a more detailed investigation of the engineering features and effectiveness of the groundwater monitoring system and the facility's hydrogeological conditions. In many situations, CMEs will include sampling and analysis of groundwater. N

CMEL
Comprehensive (groundwater) Monitoring Evaluation Log. N

CNS
Central nervous system. N

CN,T
Cyanide, total. A

CO
Carbon monoxide. U

CO NAAQS
Carbon Monoxide National Ambient Air Quality Standard. U

co-product
A chemical substance produced for a commercial purpose during the manufacture, processing, use, or disposal of another chemical substance(s) or mixture(s). A

CO_2
Carbon dioxide. U

coagulation
(1) A clumping of particles in waste water to settle out impurities, often induced by chemicals such as lime or alum. N   (2) In reference to primary drinking water regulations and related regulations applicable to public water systems, a process using coagulant chemicals and mixing by which colloidal and suspended materials are destabilized and agglomerated into flocs. A

coal
All solid fossil fuels classified as anthracite, bituminous, subbituminous, or lignite by the American Society for Testing and Materials. Designation D388-77. A

coal gasification
Any number of processes for converting coal to gas by adding hydrogen in the presence of steam at high temperature and pressure. U

coal liquefaction
Any number of processes for converting coal to partially liquid form by heating it without oxygen but with other additives. U

coal mine
An active mining area, including all land and property placed upon, under or above the surface of such land, used in or resulting from the work of extracting coal from its natural deposits by any means or method, including secondary recovery of coal from refuse or other storage piles derived from the mining, cleaning, or preparation of coal. A

coal pile runoff
The rainfall runoff from or through any coal storage pile. A

coal preparation plant
A facility where coal is subjected to cleaning, concentrating, or other processing or preparation in order to separate coal from its impurities and then is loaded for transit to a consuming facility. A

coal preparation plant associated areas
The coal preparation plant yards, immediate access roads, coal refuse piles and coal storage piles and facilities. A

coal preparation plant water circuit
All pipes, channels, basins, tanks, and all other structures and equipment that convey, contain, treat, or process any water that is used in coal preparation processes within a coal preparation plant. A

coal processing and conveying equipment
Any machinery used to reduce the size of coal or to separate coal from refuse, and the equipment used to convey coal to or remove coal and refuse from the machinery. This includes, but is not limited to, breakers, crushers, screens, and conveyor belts. A

coal refuse
(1) Waste-products of coal mining, cleaning, and coal preparation operations (e.g., culm, gob, etc.)

containing coal, matrix material, clay, and other organic and inorganic material. A (2) Any byproduct of coal mining or coal cleaning operations with an ash content greater than 50 percent, by weight, and a heating value less than 13,900 kJ/kg (6,000 Btu/lb) on a dry basis. A

coal refuse disposal pile
Any coal refuse deposited on the earth and intended as permanent disposal or long-term storage (greater than 180 days) of such material, but does not include coal refuse deposited within the active mining area or coal refuse never removed from the active mining area. A

coal storage system
Any facility used to store coal except for open storage piles. A

coal treatment facility
All structures which contain, convey, and as necessary, chemically or physically treat coal mine drainage, coal preparation plant process wastewater, or drainage, from coal preparation plant associated areas, which remove pollutants regulated by this part from such waters. This includes all pipes, channels, ponds, basins, tanks and all other equipment serving such structures. A

coaming
The raised frame, as around a hatchway in the deck, to keep out water. O

coarse papers
Papers used for industrial purposes, as distinguished from those used for cultural or sanitary purposes. A

coastal
(1) Any body of water landward of the territorial seas as defined in 40 CFR 125.1(gg), or (2) any wetlands adjacent to such waters. A

coastal waters
(1) Generally, those U.S. waters navigable by deep draft vessels, the contiguous zone, the high seas and other waters subject to tidal influence. A (2) For the purposes of classifying the size of discharges. The waters of the coastal zone except for the Great Lakes and specified ports and harbors on inland rivers. A (3) For the purpose of the National Contingency Plan. All United States waters subject to the tide, United States waters of the Great Lakes, specified ports and harbors on inland rivers, waters of the contiguous zone, other waters of the high seas subject to the NCP, and the land surface or land substrata, ground waters, and ambient air proximal to those waters. The term coastal zone delineates an area of federal responsibility for response action. Precise boundaries are determined by EPA/USCG agreements and identified in federal regional contingency plans. A (4) Lands and waters adjacent to the coast that exert an influence on the uses of the sea and its ecology, or, inversely, whose uses and ecology are affected by the sea. N

coating
Any organic material that is applied to the surface of metal coil. A

coating application station
That portion of a large surface coating operation where a prime coat or a top coat is applied to products (e.g., dip tank, spray booth, or flow coating unit). That portion of the metal coil surface coating operation where the coating is applied to the surface of the metal coil. Included as part of the coating application station is the flashoff area between the coating application station and the curing oven. A

coating blow
The process in which air is blown through hot asphalt flux to produce coating asphalt. The coating blow starts when the air is turned on and stops when the air is turned off. A

coating operations
All of the operations associated with preparation and application of the vitreous coating. Usually this includes ballmilling, slip transport, application of slip to the workpieces, cleaning and recovery of faulty parts, and firing (fusing) of the enamel coat. A

COCO
Contractor-owned/contractor-operated. N

COD
Chemical oxygen demand. U

codisposal
The technique in which sludge is combined with other combustible materials (e.g., refuse-derived fuels) to form a furnace feed with a higher heat value than pure sludge. U

COE
Corps of Engineers. U

coefficient of haze
COH. A measurement of visibility interference in the atmosphere. N

coffin
A thick-walled container (usually lead) used for transporting radioactive materials. N

COH
Coefficient of haze. N

cohort study
A study of a group of persons sharing a common experience (e.g., exposure to a substance) within a defined time period; this experiment is used to determine if an increased risk of a health effect (disease) is associated with that exposure. N

coil
(1) A device used to provide high voltage in an inductive ignition system. A (2) A strip of basis material rolled into a roll for handling. A

coil coating
The process of converting basis material strip into coated stock. Usually cleaning, conversion coating, and painting are performed on the basis material. This regulation covers processes which perform any two or more of the three operations. A

coke
Bituminous coal from which the volatile components have been driven

off by heat, leaving fixed carbon and ash fused together. U

coke by-product recovery plant
Any facility designed and operated for the separation and recovery of coal tar derivatives (by-products) evolved from coal during the coking process of a coke oven battery. A

coke oven
An oven in which coal is changed to coke by destructive distillation. Coke is an essential component in pig iron and steel production. U

coker feed (or fuel)
A special fuel oil used in a coker furnace, one of the operating elements of a refinery. A

cold drying hearth
A surface upon which unheated waste materials are placed to dry or to burn. Hot combustion gases are then passed over the materials. U

cold worked pipe and tube
Those cold forming operations that process unheated pipe and tube products using either water or oil solutions for cooling and lubrication. A

coliform index
A rating of the purity of water based on a count of fecal bacteria. N

coliform organism
Microorganisms found in the intestinal tract of humans and animals. Their presence in water indicates fecal pollution and potentially dangerous bacterial contamination by disease-causing microorganisms. N

collection
The act of removing solid waste (or materials which have been separated for the purpose of recycling) from a central storage point. A

collection center
An area or facility designated to accept particular waste materials (e.g., cans, glass bottles, newspapers) from the public; or a central receiving point for refuse collected by a municipal agency or private firm. U

collection frequency
The number of times collection is provided in a given period of time. A

collector hauler
A person engaged in the collection of refuse and/or in its transport between storage and processing facilities. U

collector ring
An assembly of slip rings for transferring electrical energy from a stationary to a rotating member. O

collector sewer
The common lateral sewers, within a publicly owned treatment system, which are primarily installed to receive wastewaters directly from facilities which convey wastewater from individual systems, or from private property, and which include service "Y" connections designed for connection with those facilities including: (i) Crossover sewers connecting more than one property on one side of a major street, road, or highway to a lateral sewer on the other side when more cost effective

than parallel sewers; and (ii) Except as provided in paragraph (b)(10)(iii) of [40 CFR § 32.2005], pumping units and pressurized lines service individual structures or groups of structures when such units are cost effective and are owned and maintained by the grantee. (iii) This definition excludes other facilities which convey wastewater from individual structures, from private property to the public lateral sewer, or its equivalent and also excludes facilities associated with alternatives to conventional treatment works in small communities. A

colloidal dispersion
A mixture resembling a true solution but containing one or more substances that are finely divided but large enough to prevent passage through a semipermeable membrane. It consists of particles which are larger than molecules, which settle out very slowly with time, which scatter a beam of light, and which are too small for resolution with an ordinary light microscope. A

colloidal matter
Finely divided solids which will not settle but may be removed by coagulation or biochemical action or membrane filtration. U

color
(1) That color as measured by the testing method presented in the National Council for Air and Stream Improvement, (Inc.) "Technical Bulletin 253," December 1971. Color units are to be assumed equal to mg/l. (2) That color as measured by the modified tristimulus method as developed by the American Dye Manufacturers Institute and described in the Proceedings of the 28th Industrial Waste Conference, Purdue University, and in Appendix A in the "Development Document for Effluent Limitations Guidelines and New Source Performance Standards for the Textile Mills Point Source Category." A

color sorting of glass
A technique for sorting glass recovered from solid waste by color. Two methods have been developed: (1) optical sorting, which compares the reflected light from each piece of glass with that of a standard and successively uses different light source filters and standards for color selectivity; and (2) magnetic sorting, which differentiates clear glass from colored by using high-intensity magnetic forces to attract the iron compounds found only in colored glass. U

column dryer
Any equipment used to reduce the moisture content of grain in which the grain flows from the top to the bottom in one or more continuous packed columns between two perforated metal sheets. A

combination
Those cold rolling operations which include recirculation of rolling solutions at one or more mill stands, and once-through use of rolling solutions at the remaining stand or stands. A

combination acid pickling
Those operations in which steel products are immersed in solutions of more than one acid to chemically remove scale and oxides, and those rinsing steps associated with such immersions. A

combined cycle gas turbine
A stationary turbine combustion system where heat from the turbine exhaust gases is recovered by a steam generating unit. A

combined cycle system
A system in which a separate source, such as a gas turbine, internal combustion engine, kiln, etc., provides exhaust gas to a heat recovery steam generating unit. A

combined fuel economy
The fuel economy value determined for a vehicle (or vehicles) by harmonically averaging the city and highway fuel economy values, weighted 0.55 and 0.45 respectively, for gasoline-fueled and diesel vehicles. Four electric vehicles, the term means the equivalent petroleum-based fuel economy value as determined by the calculation procedure promulgated by the Secretary of Energy. A

combined metals
The total of gold, platinum and palladium. A

combined sewers
A sewer system that carries both sewage and stormwater runoff. Normally, its entire flow goes to a waste treatment plant, but during a heavy storm, the storm water volume may be so great as to cause overflows. When this happens untreated mixtures of storm water and sewage may flow into receiving waters. Stormwater runoff may also carry toxic chemicals from industrial areas or streets into the sewer system. N

combustible
Various materials in the waste stream which are burnable, such as paper, plastic, lawn clippings, leaves and other organic materials. N

combustible liquid
Any liquid having a flashpoint at or above 140 degrees F. O

combustible waste
Waste materials that are burnable (e.g., paper, plastics, food, plant trimmings, wood). U

combustibles
Materials that can be ignited at a specific temperature in the presence of air to release heat energy. A

combustion
(1) The production of heat and light energy through a chemical process-- usually oxidation. One of the three basic contributing processes of air pollution, the others being attrition and vaporization. (2) Any chemical process that involves oxidation sufficient to produce light or heat. A

combustion air
The air used for burning a fuel. U

combustion gases
The mixture of gases and vapors produced by burning. U

commence construction
As applied to construction of a major stationary source or major modification means that the owner or operator has all necessary preconstruction approvals or permits and either has: (i) begun, or caused to begin, a continuous program of actual on-site construction of the source, to be completed within a reasonable time or (ii) entered into binding agreements or contractual obligations, which cannot be cancelled or modified without substantial loss to the owner or operator, to undertake a program of actual construction of the source to be completed within a reasonable time. A

commenced
With respect to the definition of "new source" in section 111(a)(2) of the Clean Air Act, that an owner or operator has undertaken a continuous program of construction or modification or that an owner or operator has entered into a contractual obligation to undertake and complete, within a reasonable time, a continuous program of construction or modification. A

commenced commercial operation
To have begun to generate electricity for sale, including test generation. A

comment period
Time provided for the public to review and comment on proposed governmental action or rulemaking after it is published in the *Federal Register*. N

commerce
(1) Trade, traffic, commerce, or transportation, or communication among the several States, or between a State and any place outside thereof, or within the District of Columbia, or a possession of the United States (other than the Trust Territory of the Pacific Islands), or between points in the same State but through a point outside thereof. A, H (2) Trade, traffic or transportation (A) between any place in any State and any place outside thereof; and (B) commerce wholly within the District of Columbia. G, K

commercial aircraft engine
Any aircraft engine used or intended for use by an "air carrier," (including those engaged in "intrastate air transportation") or a "commercial operator" (including those engaged in "intrastate air transportation") as these terms are defined in the Federal Aviation Act and the Federal Aviation Regulations. A

commercial applicator
An applicator (whether or not he is private applicator with respect to some uses) who uses or supervises the use of any pesticide which is classified for restricted use for any purpose or on any property other than as provided by paragraph (2) [of FIFRA]. C

commercial asbestos
Any variety of asbestos which is produced by extracting asbestos from asbestos ore. A

commercial establishment
Stores, offices, restaurants, warehouses and other non-manufacturing activities. A

commercial item
(1) Any machine, manufacture, or composition of matter which, at the time of a request for a license has been sold, offered for sale or otherwise made available commercially to the public in the regular course of business, at terms reasonable in the circumstances, and (2) Any process which, at the time of a request for a license, is in commercial use, or is offered for commercial use, so the results of the process or the products produced thereby are or will be accessible to the public at terms reasonable in the circumstances. A

commercial item descriptions
A series of simplified item descriptions under the Federal specifications-and-standards program used in the acquisition of commercial off-the-shelf and commercial type products. A

commercial parking facility
Any lot, garage, building or structure, or combination or portion thereof, on or in which motor vehicles are temporarily parked for a fee, excluding (i) a parking facility, the use of which is limited exclusively to residents (and guests of residents) of a residential building or group of buildings under common control, and (ii) parking on public streets. A

commercial parking space
Any parking space in which the parking of a single motor vehicle is permitted for a fee. It includes on-street parking governed by parking meters, and excludes employee and residential parking spaces. A

commercial property
Any property that is normally accessible to the public and that is used for any of the purposes described in the following standard land use codes (reference *Standard Land Use Coding Manual*. U.S. DOT/FHWA, reprinted March 1977): 53-59, Retail Trade; 61-64, Finance, Insurance, Real Estate, Personal, Business and Repair Services; 652-659, Legal and other professional services; 671, 672, and 673 Governmental Services; 692 and 699, Welfare, Charitable and Other Miscellaneous Services; 712 and 719, Nature exhibitions and other Cultural Activities; 721, 723, and 729, Entertainment, Public and other Public Assembly; and 74-79, Recreational, Resort, Park and other Cultural Activities. A

commercial solid waste
All types of solid wastes generated by stores, offices, restaurants, warehouses, and other non-manufacturing activities, excluding residential and industrial wastes. A

commercial storer of PCB waste
The owner or operator of each facility which is subject to the PCB storage facility standards of [40 CFR] § 761.65, and who engages in storage activities involving PCB waste generated by others, or PCB waste that was removed while servicing the equipment owned by others and

brokered for disposal. The receipt of a fee or any other form of compensation for storage services is not necessary to qualify as a commercial storer of PCB waste. It is sufficient under this definition that the facility stores PCB waste generated by others or the facility removed the PCB waste while servicing equipment owned by others. A generator who stores only the generator's own waste is subject to the storage requirements of [40 CFR] § 761.65, but is not required to seek approval as a commercial storer. If a facility's storage of PCB waste at no time exceeds 500 liquid gallons of PCBs, the owner or operator is not required to seek approval as a commercial storer of PCB waste. A

commercial use
The use of a chemical substance or any mixture containing the chemical substance in a commercial enterprise providing saleable goods or a service to consumers (e.g., a commercial dry cleaning establishment or painting contractor). A

commercial use request
Refers to a request from or on behalf of one who seeks information for a use or purpose that furthers the commercial, trade or profit interests of the requestor or the person on whose behalf the request is made. In determining whether a requestor properly belongs in this category, EPA must determine the use to which a requestor will put the documents requested. Moreover, where EPA has reasonable cause to doubt the use to which a requestor will put the records

sought, or where that use is not clear from the request itself, EPA may seek additional clarification before assigning the request to a specific category. A

commercial vessels
Those vessels used in the business of transporting property for compensation or hire, or in transporting property in the business of the owner, lessee, or operator of the vessel. D

commercial waste
Material which originates in wholesale, retail or service establishments such as office buildings, stores, markets, theaters, hotels and warehouses. N

comminuter
A machine that shreds or pulverizes solids to make waste treatment easier. N

comminution
Mechanical shredding or pulverizing of waste, used in solid waste management and waste water treatment. N

commission finishing
The finishing of textile materials, 50 percent or more of which are owned by others, in mills that are 51 percent or more independent (i.e., only a minority ownership by company(ies) with greige or integrated operations); the mills must process 20 percent or more of their commissioned production through batch, noncontinuous processing operations with 50 percent or more of their commissioned orders

processed in 5000 yard or smaller lots. A

commission scouring
The scouring of wool, 50 percent or more of which is owned by others, in mills that are 51 percent or more independent (i.e., only a minority ownership by company(ies) with greige or integrated operations); the mills must process 20 percent or more of their commissioned production through batch, noncontinuous processing operations. A

commitment of funds
Formal action by a program office (technically an "allowance holder") to set aside a specific portion of its allowance for a designated project. A document control register is maintained to record the commitments (Compare: obligation of funds). U

committee
A group of qualified scientists designated by the National Academy of Sciences according to agreement under the FIFRA Act to submit an independent report to the Administrative Law Judge on questions of scientific fact referred from a hearing under subpart B of 40 CFR parts 150-189. A

common carrier by motor vehicle
Any person who holds himself out to the general public to engage in the transportation by motor vehicle in interstate or foreign commerce of passengers or property or any class or classes thereof for compensation, whether over regular or irregular routes. A

common exposure route
A likely way (oral, dermal, respiratory) by which a pesticide may reach and/or enter an organism. A

common name
Any designation or identification such as code name, code number, trade name, brand name, or generic chemical name used to identify a chemical substance other than by its chemical name. A

Community Awareness and Emergency Response Program
CAER. Program developed by the Chemical Manufacturers Association, which provides guidance for chemical plant managers to assist them in taking the initiative in cooperating with local communities to develop integrated (community/industry) hazardous materials response plans. N

Community Relations Plan
CRP. A management and planning tool outlining the specific community relations activities to be undertaken during the course of a response. It is designed to provide for two-way communication between the affected community and the agencies responsible for conducting a response action, and to assure public input into the decision-making process related to the affected communities. A

community water system
A public water system which serves at least 15 service connections used by year-round residents or regularly serves at least 25 year-round residents. N, A

compact cars
Interior volume index greater than or equal to 100 cubic feet but less than 110 cubic feet. A

compaction
The process of reducing the bulk of solid waste by rolling and tamping or compressing and crushing. U

compaction pit transfer system
A transfer system in which solid waste is compacted in a storage pit by a crawler tractor before being pushed into an open-top transfer trailer. U

compactor
(1) Any power-driven, mechanical device that reduces the volume of solid waste by compression and crushing. (2) A truck-mounted solid waste compactor, which comprises an engine powered truck cab and chassis or trailer, equipped with a compactor body and associated machinery for receiving, compacting, transporting and unloading solid waste. A

compactor collection vehicle
A vehicle with an enclosed body containing mechanical devices that convey solid waste into the main compartment of the body and compress it into a smaller volume of greater density. A

compartmentalized vehicle
A collection vehicle which has two or more compartments for placement of solid wastes or recyclable materials. The compartments may be within the main truck body or on the outside of that body as in the form of metal racks. A

compatibility
That property of a pesticide which permits its use with other chemicals without undesirable results being caused by the combination. A

compatible
The ability of two or more substances to maintain their respective physical and chemical properties upon contact with one another for the design life of the tank system under conditions likely to be encountered in the UST. A

compatible industrial wastewater
Wastewater that is produced by an industrial user, has a pollutant strength and other characteristics similar to those of domestic wastewater, and can be efficiently and effectively transported and treated with domestic wastewater. This definition includes wastewater from sanitary conveniences at an industrial user's facility. A

competent
Properly qualified to perform functions associated with pesticide application, the degree of capability required being directly related to the nature of the activity and the associated responsibility. A

competent person
One who is capable of identifying existing and predictable hazards in the surroundings or working conditions which are unsanitary, hazardous, or dangerous to employees, and who has authorization to take prompt corrective measures to eliminate them. O

competition motorcycle
Any motorcycle designed and marketed solely for use in closed course competition events. A

complainant
(1) Any person authorized to issue a complaint on behalf of the EPA to persons alleged to be in violation of an Act. The complainant shall not be the Judicial Officer, Regional Judicial Officer, or any other person who will participate or advise in the decision. A (2) The EPA acting through any person authorized by the Administrator to issue a complaint to alleged violators of the Act. The complainant shall not be the judicial officer or the Administrator. A

complete
In reference to an application for a permit, that the application contains all the information necessary for processing the application. Designating an application complete for purposes of permit processing does not preclude the reviewing authority from requesting or accepting any additional information. A

complete carcinogen
Chemicals that are capable of inducing tumors in animals or humans without supplemental exposure to other agents. Complete refers to the three stages of carcinogenesis, initiation, promotion, and progression which need to be present in order to induce a cancer. N

complete destruction
Alteration by physical or chemical processes to inorganic forms. A

complete waste treatment system
A complete waste treatment system consists of all the connected treatment works necessary to meet the requirements of Title III of the [Clean Water] Act and involved in: (a) The transport of wastewaters from individual homes or buildings to a plant or facility wherein treatment of the wastewater is accomplished; (b) the treatment of the wastewaters to remove pollutants; and (c) the ultimate disposal, including recycling or reuse, of the treated wastewaters and residues resulting from the treatment process. One complete waste treatment system would, normally, include one treatment plant or facility, but in instances where two or more treatment plants are interconnected, all of the interconnected treatment works will be considered as one waste treatment system. A

completed project
A funded grant for which work has been completed and an acceptable final report received. The term has nothing to do with whether or not closeout has been effectuated. U

compliance
Compliance with clean air or water standards. Also, compliance with a schedule or plan ordered or approved by a court of competent jurisdiction, the Environmental Protection Agency, or an air or water pollution control agency, in accordance with the requirements of the Air or Water Act and regulations issued pursuant thereto. A

compliance date
The date upon which a source is required to meet applicable pollution control requirements. U

compliance date period
The thirty day period immediately preceding the compliance date. U

compliance level
(1) An emission level determined during a Production Compliance Audit pursuant to subpart L of 40 CFR part 86-99. A (2) The deteriorated pollutant emissions level at the 60th percentile point for a population of heavy-duty engines or heavy-duty vehicles subject to Production Compliance Audit testing pursuant to the requirements of this subpart. A compliance level for a population can only be determined for a pollutant for which an upper limit has been established. A

compliance monitoring
Measuring and analyzing pollutant sources, review of reports and information obtained from dischargers, and all other activities conducted by the State to verify compliance with effluent limits and compliance schedules. A

compliance order/action
An order or action issued under Section 3008(a) of RCRA, requires any person who is not complying with a requirement of RCRA to take steps to come into compliance. N

compliance safety and health officer
CSHO. A person authorized by the Occupational Safety and Health Administration, U.S. Department of Labor, to conduct inspections. O

compliance schedule
(1) legally enforceable schedule specifying a date or dates by which a source or category of sources must comply with specific emission or effluent standards contained in a State implementation plan or NPDES permit or with any increments of progress to achieve such compliance. A (2) The date or dates by which a source or category of sources is required to comply with the standards of 40 CFR parts 86-99, and with any steps toward such compliance which are set forth in a waiver of compliance under § 61.11. A

compliance use date
The first calendar year for which an allowance may be used for purposes of meeting a unit's sulfur dioxide emissions limitation requirements. A

composite sample
A sample composed of no less than eight grab samples taken over the compositing period. A

compost
A mixture of garbage and degradable trash with soil in which certain bacteria in the soil break down the garbage and trash into organic fertilizer. N

composting
The natural biological decomposition of organic material in the presence of air to form a humus-like material.

Controlled methods of composting include mechanical mixing and aerating, ventilating the materials by dropping them through a vertical series of aerated chambers, or placing the compost in piles out in the open air and mixing it or turning ir periodically. N

compound leachate collection
This system consists of a gravity flow drainfield installed under the waste disposal facility liner and above a secondary installed liner. This design is recommended for use when semi-liquid or leachable solid wastes are placed in a lined pit excavated into relatively permeable soil. A

compressor configuration
The basic classification unit of a manufacturer's product line and is comprised of compressor lines, models or series which are identical in all material respects with regard to the parameters listed in [40 CFR] § 204.55-3. A

computer paper
A type of paper used in manifold business forms produced in rolls and/or fan folded. It is used with computers and word processors to print out data, information, letters, advertising, etc. It is commonly called computer printout. A

computer-aided carpool matching
A carpool matching system in which the work of assembling lists of commuters with similar daily travel patterns is done by computer. A

conc.
Concentration. U

concealed
Rendered inaccessible by the structure or finish of the building. Wires in concealed raceways are considered concealed, even though they may become accessible by withdrawing them. O

concentration
An exposure level. Exposure is expressed as weight or volume of test substance per volume of air (mg/l), or as parts per million (ppm). A

concentration measurement system
The total equipment required for the continuous determination of SO_2 gas concentration in a given source effluent. A

concentration of a solution
The amount of solute in a given amount of solvent and can be expressed as a weight/weight or weight/volume relationship. The conversion from a weight relationship to one of volume incorporates density as a factor. For dilute aqueous solutions, the density of the solvent is approximately equal to the density of the solutions; thus, concentrations in mg/dm^3 are approximately equal to 10^{-3} $g/10^3$ g or parts per million (ppm); ones in ug/dm^3 are approximately equal to 10^{-6} $g/10^3$ g or parts per billion (ppb). In addition, concentration can be expressed in terms of molarity, normality, molality, and mole fraction. For example, to convert from weight/volume to

molarity one incorporates molecular mass as a factor. A

concentration vs. time study
Results in a graph which plots the measured concentration of a given compound in a solution as a function of elapsed time. Usually, it provides a more reliable determination of equilibrium water solubility of hydrophobic compounds than can be obtained by single measurements of separate samples. A

concretion
A localized concentration of chemical compounds (e.g., calcium carbonate and iron oxide) in the form of a grain or nodule of varying size, shape, hardness, and color, concretions of significance in hydric soils are usually iron oxides and manganese oxides occurring at or near the soil surface, which have developed under conditions of fluctuating water tables. N

concurrent
Acting in conjunction, and used to describe a situation wherein two or more controls exist in an operated condition at the same time. O

condensate
Hydrocarbon liquid separated from natural gas which condenses due to changes in the temperature and/or pressure and remains liquid at standard conditions. A

condensate stripper system
A column, and associated condensers, used to strip, with air or steam, TRS compounds from condensate streams from various processes within a kraft pulp mill. A

condenser stack gases
The gaseous effluent evolved from the stack of processes utilizing heat to extract mercury metal from mercury ore. A

conditional registration
Under special circumstances, the Federal Insecticide, Fungicide, and Rodenticide Act (FIFRA) permits registration of pesticide products that is "conditional" upon the submission of additional data. These special circumstances include a finding by the EPA Administrator that a new product or use of an existing pesticide will not significantly increase the risk of unreasonable adverse effects. A product containing a new (previously unregistered) active ingredient may be conditionally registered only if the Administrator finds that such conditional registration is in the public interest, that a reasonable time for conducting the additional studies has not elapsed, and the use of the pesticide for the period of conditional registration will not present an unreasonable risk. N

conditioned
Heated and/or mechanically cooled. A

conditioning
(1) Exposure of construction materials, test chambers, and testing apparatus to dilution water or to the test solution prior to the start of the test in order to minimize the sorption of test substance onto the test

facilities or the leaching of substances from test facilities into the dilution water or the test solution. A (2) Pretreatment of a sludge to facilitate removal of water in a thickening or dewatering process. Methods are as follows: Chemical (inorganic and organic), Elutriation, Heat treatment. U

conduction
The transfer of heat by physical contact between substances. U

conduction velocity
The speed at which the compound nerve action potential traverses a nerve. A

conductor
(1) A material, usually in the form of a wire, cable, or bus bar suitable for carrying an electric current. O (2) (a) Bare. A conductor having no covering or electrical insulation whatsoever. (b) Covered. A conductor encased within material of composition or thickness that is not recognized as electrical insulation. (c) Insulated. A conductor encased within material of composition and thickness that is recognized as electrical insulation. O

confidence limit
The confidence interval is a range of values that has a specified probability (e.g., 95 percent) of containing a given parameter or characteristic. The confidence limit refers to the upper value of the range (e.g. upper confidence limit). N

confidential business information
Trade secrets or confidential commercial or financial information under FIFRA section 10(b) or 5 U.S.C. 552(b)(3) or (4). A

configuration
(1) The mechanical arrangement, calibration, and condition of a test automobile, with particular respect to carburetion, ignition timing, and emission control systems. A (2) The basic classification unit of a manufacturer's product line and is comprised of all vehicle designs, models or series which are identical in material aspects with respect to the parameters listed in [40 CFR] § 205.55-3. A

confined aquifer
An aquifer bounded above and below by impermeable beds or by beds of distinctly lower permeability than that of the aquifer itself; an aquifer containing confined ground water. A

confined space
Any area which has limited openings for entry and exit that would make escape difficult in an emergency, has a lack of ventilation, contains known and potential hazards, and is not intended nor designated for continuous human occupancy. N

confining bed
A body of impermeable or distinctly less permeable material stratigraphically adjacent to one or more aquifers. A

confining zone
A geological formation, group of formations, or part of a formation that is capable of limiting fluid movement above an injection zone. A

confluent growth
In reference to primary drinking water regulations and related regulations applicable to public water systems, a continuous bacterial growth covering the entire filtration area of a membrane filter, or a portion thereof, in which bacterial colonies are not discrete. A

conical burner
A hollow, cone-shaped combustion chamber with an exhaust vent at its point and a door at its base through which waste materials are charged; air is delivered to the burning solid waste inside the cone. Also called teepee burner. U

consent agreement
Any written document, signed by the parties, containing stipulations or conclusions of fact or law and a proposed penalty or proposed revocation or suspension acceptable to both complainant and respondent. A

consent decree
A legal document, approved by a judge, that formalizes an agreement reached between litigants. In Superfund cases it sets the terms by which potentially responsible parties (PRPs) will conduct all or part of a cleanup action at a Superfund site; cease or correct actions or processes that are polluting the environment; or otherwise comply with regulations where the PRP's failure to comply caused EPA to initiate regulatory enforcement actions. The consent decree describes the actions PRP's will take and may be subject to a public comment period. N

conservation
Avoiding waste of, and renewing when possible, human and natural resources. The protection, improvement, and use of natural resources according to principles that will assure their highest economic or social benefits. N

consistent POTW removal
Reduction in the amount of a pollutant or alteration of the nature of a pollutant in the influent to a POTW to a less toxic or harmless state in the effluent which is achieved by that POTW in 95 percent of the samples taken when measured according to specified procedures. The reduction or alteration can be obtained by physical, chemical or biological means and may be the result of specifically designed POTW capabilities or it may be incidental to the operation of the treatment system. Removal as used in this subpart shall not mean dilution of a pollutant in the POTW or its sewer system. The inability of monitoring equipment to detect pollutants in the influent to the POTW shall not by itself, constitute removal, except where the pollutant is shown by the POTW to be degradable during the time it is in the POTW or its sewer system. A

consolidated grants
A grant funded under more than one grant authority by EPA or a grant awarded in conjunction with one or more Federal agencies (e.g., Joint Funded Assistance). Application for and award and administration of a consolidated grant must conform to this subchapter, except as the

Director, Grants Administration Division, may otherwise direct with respect to substatutory requirements. Those conditions and procedures will conform to this Subchapter to the greatest extent practicable. A

consolidated premanufacture notice
Any PMN submitted to EPA that covers more than one chemical substance (each being assigned a separate PMN number by EPA) as a result of a prenotice agreement with EPA (See 48 FR 21734). A

consortium
An association of manufacturers and/or processors who have made an agreement to jointly sponsor testing. A

constant controls
Systems which limit the quantity, rate, or concentration, excluding the use of dilution, and emissions of air pollutants on a continuous basis. A

construction
(1) Under the Water Pollution Act, any one or more of the following: preliminary planning to determine the feasibility of treatment works, engineering, architectural, legal, fiscal, or economic investigations or studies, surveys, designs, plans, working drawings, specifications, procedures, or other necessary actions, erection, building, acquisition, alteration, remodeling, improvement, or extension of treatment works, or the inspection or supervision of any of the foregoing items. D (2) Under the Clean Air Act, any physical change or change in the method of operation (including fabrication, erection, installation, demolition, or modification of an emissions unit) which would result in a change in actual emissions. [ed. The definition is used for determining whether a new source review under the CAA is required]. A (3) Under RCRA, (A) the erection or building of new structures and acquisition of lands or interests therein, or the acquisition, replacement, expansion, remodeling, alteration, modernization, or extension of existing structures, and (B) the acquisition and installation of initial equipment of, or required in connection with, new or newly acquired structures or the expanded, remodeled, altered, modernized or extended part of existing structures (including trucks and other motor vehicles, and tractors, cranes, and other machinery) necessary for the proper utilization and operation of the facility after completion of the project; and includes preliminary planning to determine the economic and engineering feasibility and the public health and safety aspects of the project, the engineering, architectural, legal, fiscal, and economic investigations and studies, and any surveys, designs, plans, working drawings, specifications, and other action necessary for the carrying out of the project, and (C) the inspection and supervision of the process of carrying out the project to completion. A, I (4) Under Superfund, erection, building, alternation, remodeling, improvement, or extension of buildings, structures or other property; construction also includes remedial actions in response to a release, or a threat of a release, of a hazardous

substance into the environment as determined by CERCLA. A, L

construction and demolition waste
The waste building materials, packaging, and rubble resulting from construction, remodeling, repair, and demolition operations on pavements, houses, commercial buildings and other structures. A

construction material
Any article, material, or supply brought to the construction site for incorporation in the building or work. A

construction runoff
The point source rainfall runoff from any construction activity and any earth surface disturbed by such activity from the inception of the construction until construction is complete and any disturbed earth is returned to a vegetative or other cover commensurate with the intended land use. A

construction work
The construction, rehabilitation, alteration, conversion, extension, demolition or repair of buildings, highways, or other changes or improvements to real property, including facilities providing utility services. The term also includes the supervision, inspection, and other on-site functions incidental to the actual construction. A

consumer
(1) A private individual who uses a chemical substance or any product containing the chemical substance in or around a permanent or temporary household or residence, during recreation, or for any personal use or enjoyment. A (2) Any person who purchases a beverage in a beverage container for final use or consumption. A

Consumer Price Index
CPI. The United States government's primary indicator of the monetary inflation rate as published monthly by the U. S. Department of Labor, Bureau of Labor Statistics, Consumer Price Indices Branch, in the CPI Detailed Report and in the Monthly Labor Review. For purposes of part 73, the administrator will use the "Consumer Price Index for all urban consumers for the U.S. City Average, for all Items on the Official Reference Base" (CPI-U), or if such index is no longer published, such other index as the Administrator in his discretion determines meets the requirements of the Clean Air Act Amendments of 1990. (1) CPI (1990) means the most recently adjusted CPI for all urban consumers as of August 31, 1989. The CPI for 1990 is 124.6 (with 1982-84 = 100). (2) CPI (year) means the most recently adjusted CPI for all urban consumers as of August 31 of the previous year. A

consumer product
A chemical substance that is directly, or as part of a mixture, sold or made available to consumers for their use in or around a permanent or temporary household or residence, in or around a school, or in recreation. A

consumer waste
Materials used and discarded by the buyer, or consumer, as opposed to waste created and discarded in-plant during the manufacturing process. U

consumption allowances
The privileges granted by this Part to produce and import calculated levels of controlled substances; however, consumption allowances may be used to produce controlled substances only in conjunction with production allowances. A person's consumption allowances are the total of the allowances he obtains under § 82.7 (1991 allowances for Group I, Group II and Group III controlled substances), [40 CFR] § 82.8 (1991 allowances for Group IV and § 82.10 (additional consumption allowances), as may be modified under § 82.12 (transfer of allowances). A

contact cooling water
(1) Any wastewater which contacts the metal workpiece or the raw materials used in forming metals for the purpose of removing heat from the metal. A (2) Water used to reduce temperature which comes into contact with a raw material, intermediate product, waste product other than heat, or finished product. N

contact pesticide
A chemical that kills pests when it touches them, rather than by being eaten (stomach poison). Also, soil that contains the minute skeletons of certain algae that scratches and dehydrates waxy-coated insects. N

contact resistance
The opposition to the flow of current between the mounting bracket and the insulated terminal. A

container
(1) Any portable device in which a material is stored, transported, treated, disposed of, or otherwise handled. A (2) Any bag, barrel, bottle, box, can, cylinder, drum, reaction vessel, storage tank, or the like that contains a hazardous chemical. For purposes of this section, pipes or piping systems, and engines, fuel tanks, or other operating systems in a vehicle, are not considered to be containers. O (3) Any portable waste management unit in which a material is stored, transported, treated, or otherwise handled. Examples of containers are drums, barrels, tank trucks, barges, dumpsters, tank cars, dump trucks, and ships. A

container glass
Glass made of soda-lime recipe, clear or colored, which is pressed and/or blown into bottles, jars, ampoules, and other products listed in Standard Industrial Classification 3221 (SIC 3221). A

container train
Small trailers, hitched in series, that are pulled by a motor vehicle and used to collect and transport solid waste. U

containerized refuse
Solid waste that has been deposited into a receptacle for storage or transport. U

containment
Any method or technology that prevents migration of hazardous waste into the environment. N

contaminant
(1) Any material which by reason of its action upon, within, or to a person is likely to cause physical harm. O (2) A chemical or biological substance in a form that can be incorporated into, onto or be ingested by and that harms aquatic organisms, consumers of aquatic organisms, or users of the aquatic environment, and includes but is not limited to the substances on the 307(a)(1) list of toxic pollutants promulgated on January 31, 1978 (43 FR 4109). A

contaminate
To introduce a substance that would cause: (i) the concentration of that substance in the ground water to exceed the maximum contaminant level or (ii) an increase in the concentration of that substance in the ground water where the existing concentration of that substance exceeds the maximum contaminant level. A

contaminated
The presence or the reasonably anticipated presence of blood or other potentially infectious materials on an item or surface. O

contaminated non-process wastewater
Any water including precipitation runoff which, during manufacturing or processing, comes into incidental contact with any raw material, intermediate product, finished product, by-product or waste product by means of: (1) Precipitation runoff; (2) accidental spills; (3) accidental leaks caused by the failure of process equipment and which are repaired or the discharge of pollutants therefrom contained or terminated within the shortest reasonable time which shall not exceed 24 hours after discovery or when discovery should reasonably have been made, whichever is earliest; and (4) discharges from safety showers and related personal safety equipment, and from equipment washings for the purpose of safe entry, inspection and maintenance; provided that all reasonable measures have been taken to prevent, reduce, eliminate and control to the maximum extent feasible such contact and provided further that all reasonable measures have been taken that will mitigate the effects of such contact once it has occurred. A

contaminated runoff
Runoff which comes into contact with any raw material, intermediate product, finished product, by-product or waste product located on petroleum refinery property. A

contaminated sharps
Any contaminated object that can penetrate the skin including, but not limited to, needles, scalpels, broken glass, broken capillary tubes, and exposed ends of dental wires. O

contiguous zone
The zone of the high seas, established by the United States under Article 24 of the Convention on the Territorial Sea and Contiguous Zone, which is contiguous to the territorial sea and which extends nine miles

seaward form the outer limit of the territorial sea. A, D

contingency plan
A document setting out an organized, planned, and coordinated course of action to be followed in case of a fire, explosion, or release of hazardous waste or hazardous waste constituents which could threaten human health or the environment. A

continuing planning process
The continuing planning process, including any revision thereto, required by sections 208 and 303(e) of the [Clean Water] Act for State agencies and section 208(b) of the [Clean Water] Act for designated areawide agencies. A

continuing resolution
Legislation enacted by Congress to provide budget authority for specific ongoing activities when a regular appropriation for such activities has not been enacted by the beginning of the fiscal year. U

continuous casting
The production of sheet, rod, or other long shapes by solidifying the metal while it is being poured through an open-ended mold. A

continuous discharge (NPDES)
A "discharge" which occurs without interruption throughout the operating hours of the facility, except for infrequent shutdowns for maintenance, process changes, or other similar activities. A

continuous disposal
A method of tailings management and disposal in which tailings are dewatered by mechanical methods immediately after generation. The dried tailings are then placed in trenches or other disposal areas and immediately covered to limit emissions consistent with applicable Federal standards. A

continuous emission rate monitoring system
(1) CERMS. A monitoring system for continuously measuring the emissions of a pollutant from an affected facility. A (2) A continuous monitor is one in which the sample to be analyzed passes the measurement section of the analyzer without interruption, and which evaluates the detector response to the sample at least once each 15 seconds and computes and records the results at least every 60 seconds. A CERMS consists of all the equipment used to acquire data and includes the sample extraction and transport hardware, the analyzer(s), and the data recording/processing hardware and software. A (3) The total equipment required for the determination and recording of the pollutant mass emission rate (in terms of mass per unit of time). A

continuous feed incinerator
An incinerator into which solid waste is charged almost continuously to maintain a steady rate of burning. U

continuous monitoring
The taking and recording of

measurements at regular and frequent intervals during operation of a facility. A

continuous monitoring system
The total equipment, required under the emission monitoring sections in applicable subparts, used to sample and condition (if applicable), to analyze, and to provide a permanent record of emissions or process parameters. A

continuous operations
The introduction by an industrial user of regulated wastewaters to a POTW throughout the operating hours of the facility, except for infrequent shut-downs for maintenance, process changes, or other similar activities. A

continuous recorder
A data-recording device recording an instantaneous data value at least once every 15 minutes. A

continuous sample
One obtained from a pipeline in such manner as to give a representative average of a moving stream. A

contour plowing
Farming methods that break ground following the shape of the land in a way that discourages erosion. N

contract
(1) An award of funds or other assistance by means of a written contractual agreement under Federal Procurement Regulations. (2) Any contract or other agreement made with an Executive Branch agency for the procurement of goods, materials, or services (including construction), and includes any subcontract made thereunder. A

contract authority
Statutory authority, not necessarily provided through the appropriations process, that permits Federal agencies to enter into contracts or incur other obligations in advance of an appropriation. U

contract carrier by motor vehicle
Any person who engages in transportation by motor vehicle of passengers or property in interstate or foreign commerce for compensation under continuing contracts with one person or a limited number of persons either (1) for the furnishing of transportation services through the assignment of motor vehicles for a continuing period of time to the exclusive use of each person served or (2) for the furnishing of transportation services designed to meet the distinct need of each individual customer. A

contract collection
Refuse collection performed in accordance with a written agreement in which the rights and duties of the contractual parties are set forth. U

contract specifications
The set of specifications prepared for an individual construction project which contains design, performance, and material requirements for that project. A

contractor
Any person with whom an Executive Branch agency has entered into, extended or renewed a contract, and

includes subcontractors or any person holding a subcontract. A

contrails
Long, narrow clouds caused when high-flying jet aircraft disturb the atmosphere. N

control
(1) An exposure of test organisms to dilution water only or dilution water containing the test solvent or carrier (no toxic agent is intentionally or inadvertently added). A (2) Any remedial action intended to stabilize, inhibit future misuse of, or reduce emissions or effluents from residual radioactive materials. A (3) (Including the terms "controlling," "controlled by," and "under common control with") means the power to direct or cause the direction of the management and policies of a person or organization, whether by the ownership of stock, voting rights, by contract, or otherwise. [ed. Relevant to determining what entities may be liable for polluting activities]. A (4) A mechanism used to regulate or guide the operation of the equipment. O

control authority
The POTW if it has an approved pretreatment program; in the absence of such a program, the NPDES state if it has an approved pretreatment program or EPA if the State does not have an approved program. A

control device
(1) The air pollution control equipment used to collect particulate matter emissions. A (2) An enclosed combustion device, vapor recovery system, or flare. A

control efficiency
The ratio of the amount of a pollutant removed from effluent gases by a control device to the total amount of pollutant without control. U

control group
A group of subjects observed in the absence of the exposure agent for comparison with exposed groups. N

control strategy
A combination of measures designated to achieve the aggregate reduction of emissions necessary for attainment and maintenance of a national standard, including, but not limited to, measures such as: (1) Emission limitations. (2) Federal or State emission charges or taxes or other economic incentives or disincentives. (3) Closing or relocation of residential, commercial, or industrial facilities. (4) Changes in schedules or methods of operation of commercial or industrial facilities or transportation systems, including, but not limited to, short-term changes made in accordance with standby plans. (5) Periodic inspection and testing of motor vehicle emission control systems, at such time as the Administrator determines that such programs are feasible and practicable. (6) Emission control measures applicable to in-use motor vehicles, including, but not limited to, measures such as mandatory maintenance, installation of emission control devices, and conversion to gaseous fuels. (7) Measures to reduce motor

vehicle traffic, including, but not limited to, measures such as commuter taxes, gasoline rationing; parking restrictions, or staggered working hours. (8) Expansion or promotion of the use of mass transportation facilities through measures such as increases in the frequency, convenience, and passenger-carrying capacity of mass transportation systems or providing for special bus lanes on major streets and highways. (9) Any land use or transportation control measures not specifically delineated herein. (10) Any variation of, or alternative to, any measure delineated herein. (11) Control or prohibition of a fuel or fuel additive used in motor vehicles, if such control or prohibition is necessary to achieve a national primary or secondary air quality standard and is approved by the Administrator under section 211(c)(4)(C) of the Clean Air Act. [ed. A necessary part of an approvable State implementation plan under § 110 of the Clean Air Act]. A

control substance
Any chemical substance or mixture, or any other material other than a test substance, feed, or water, that is administered to the test system in the course of a study for the purpose of establishing a basis for comparison with the test substance for known chemical or biological measurements. A

control system
Equipment and/or procedures intended to reduce the amount of a pollutant, or pollutants, in effluent gases. U

control techniques guidelines
Technology assessments prepared by EPA to provide guidance on the best controls available for use by categories of existing sources; used to establish RACT. U

controlled area
(1) A surface location, to be identified by passive institutional controls, that encompasses no more than 100 square kilometers and extends horizontally no more than five kilometers in any direction from the outer boundary of the original location of the radioactive wastes in a disposal system; and (2) the subsurface underlying such a surface location. A

controlled substance
Any substance, whether existing alone or in a mixture, but excluding any such substance or mixture that is in a manufactured product other than a container used for the transportation or storage of the substance or mixture. Any amount of a listed substance which is not part of a use system containing the substance is a controlled substance. If a listed substance or mixture must first be transferred from a bulk container to another container, vessel, or piece of equipment in order to realize its intended use, the listed substance or mixture is a controlled substance. Controlled substances are divided into five groups, Group I, Group II, Group III, Group IV, and Group V. A

controlled surface mine drainage
Any surface mine drainage that is pumped or siphoned from the active mining area. A

controlled vehicles
Light-duty vehicles sold nationally (except in California) in the 1968 model-year and later and light-duty vehicles sold in California in the 1966 model-year and later. A

controlled-air incinerator
An incinerator with two or more combustion areas in which the amounts and distribution of air are controlled. Partial combustion takes place in the first zone, and gases are burned in a subsequent zone or zones. U

controller
A device or group of devices that serves to govern, in some predetermined manner, the electric power delivered to the apparatus to which it is connected. O

conveniently available
Service facility and spare parts for small-volume manufacturers means that the vehicle manufacturer has a qualified service facility at or near the authorized point of sale or delivery of its vehicles and maintains an inventory of all emission-related spare parts or has made arrangements for the part manufacturers to supply the parts by expedited shipment (e.g., utilizing overnight express delivery service, UPS, etc.). A

conventional filtration treatment
In reference to primary drinking water regulations and related regulations applicable to public water systems, a series of processes including coagulation, flocculation, sedimentation, and filtration resulting in substantial particulate removal. A

conventional mine
An open pit or underground excavation for the production of minerals. A

conventional pollutants
Statutorily listed pollutants which are understood well by scientists. These may be in the form of organic waste, sediment, acid, bacteria and viruses, nutrients, oil and grease, or heat. N

conventional sewage treatment system
A collection and treatment system consisting of minimum size (six or eight inch) gravity collector sewers normally with manholes, force mains, pumping and lift stations, and interceptors leading to a central treatment plant. A

conventional system
A collection and treatment system consisting of minimum size (6 or 8 inch) gravity collector sewers, normally with manholes, force mains, pumping and lift stations, and interceptors leading to a central treatment plant. A

conventional technology
(1) Wastewater treatment processes and techniques involving the treatment of wastewater at a centralized treatment plant by means of biological or physical/chemical unit processes followed by direct point source discharge to surface waters. A (2) Wet flue gas desulfurization (FGD) technology, dry FGD technology, atmospheric fluidized bed combustion technology, and oil hydrodesulfurization technology. A

conversion
A resource recovery method that uses biological, chemical, or mechanical processes to transform solid waste materials into usable forms. See bioconversion, recycling, reprocessing, and transformation. U

conversion efficiency
The measure of the catalytic converter's ability to oxidize HC/CO to CO_2/H_2O under fully warmed-up conditions. A

conveying system
A device for transporting materials from one piece of equipment or location to another location within a plant. Conveying systems include but are not limited to the following: feeders, belt conveyors, bucket elevators and pneumatic systems. A

conviction
A judgment of conviction of a criminal offense by any court of competent jurisdiction, whether entered upon a verdict or a plea, including a plea of nolo contendere. A

coolant
A liquid or gas used to reduce the heat generated by power production in nuclear reactors, electric generators, various industrial and mechanical processes, and automobile engines. N

cooling air
Ambient air that is added to hot combustion gases to cool them. Also called tempering air. U

cooling lake
Any manmade water impoundment which impedes the flow of a navigable stream and which is used to remove waste heat from heated condenser water prior to recirculating the water to the main condenser. A

cooling pond
Any manmade water impoundment which does not impede the flow of a navigable stream and which is used to remove waste heat from heated condenser water prior to returning the recirculated cooling water to the main condenser. A

cooling sprays
Water sprays directed into flue gases to cool them and, in most cases, to remove some fly ash. U

cooling tower
A device that aids in heat removal from water used as a coolant in electric power generating plants. N

cooling water intake structure
The total structure used to direct water into the components of the cooling systems wherein the cooling function is designed to take place, provided that the intended use of the major portion of the water so directed is to absorb waste heat rejected from the process or processes employed or from auxiliary operations on the premises, including air conditioning. A

cooperating agency
Any Federal agency other than a lead agency which has jurisdiction by law or special expertise with respect to any environmental impact involved in a proposal (or a reasonable alternative) for legislation or other

major Federal action significantly affecting the quality of the human environment. The selection and responsibilities of a cooperating agency are described in 40 CFR §1501.6. A State or local agency of similar qualifications or, when the effects are on a reservation, an Indian Tribe, may by agreement with the lead agency become a cooperating agency. A

cooperative agreement
A legal instrument EPA uses to transfer money, property, services, or anything of value to a recipient to accomplish a public purpose in which substantial EPA involvement is anticipated during the performance of the project. A

cooperator
Any person who grants permission to a permittee or a permittee's designated participant to use an experimental-use pesticide at an application site owned or controlled by the cooperator. N

copper
Total copper and is determined by the method specified in 40 CFR 136.3. A

copy of study
The written presentation of the purpose and methodology of a study and its results. A

core
The uranium-containing heart of a nuclear reactor, where energy is released. N

Corps
U.S. Army Corps of Engineers. A

corrective order/action
An order EPA issues that requires corrective action under RCRA Section 3008(h) at a facility when there has been a release of hazardous waste or constituents into the environment. Corrective action may be required beyond the facility boundary and can be required regardless of when the waste was placed at the facility. N

corrosion
The gradual wearing away of a substance by chemical action. U

corrosion expert
A person who, by reason of his knowledge of the physical sciences and the principles of engineering and mathematics, acquired by a professional education and related practicable experience, is qualified to engage in the practice of corrosion control on buried or submerged metal piping systems and metal tanks. Such a person must be certified as being qualified by the National Association of Corrosion Engineers (NACE) or be a registered professional engineer who has certification or licensing that includes education and experience in corrosion control on buried or submerged metal piping systems and metal tanks. A

corrosion inhibitor
In reference to primary drinking water regulations and related regulations applicable to public water systems, a substance capable of reducing the corrosivity of water toward metal plumbing materials, especially lead and copper, by forming

a protective film on the interior surface of those materials. A

corrosive
(1) A chemical agent that reacts with the surface of a material causing it to deteriorate or wear away. N (2) A chemical that causes visible destruction of, or irreversible alterations in, living tissue by chemical action at the site of contact. For example, a chemical is considered to be corrosive if, when tested on the intact skin of albino rabbits by the method described by the U.S. Department of Transportation in appendix A to 49 CFR part 173, it destroys or changes irreversibly the structure of the tissue at the site of contact following an exposure period of four hours. O

corrosivity
A characteristic of hazardous waste which identifies waste that must be segregated because of its ability to extract and solubilize toxic contaminants (especially heavy metals) from other waste; identifies waste that requires the use of corrosion-resistant containers for disposal. U

corrugated box
A container for goods which is composed of an inner fluting of material (corrugating medium) and one or two outer liners of material (linerboard). A

cosmic radiation
Radiation of many sorts but mostly atomic nuclei (protons) with very high energies, originating outside the earth's atmosphere. Cosmic radiation is part of the natural background radiation. Some cosmic rays are more energetic than any manmade forms of radiation. U

cost of production
For a car line, this is the aggregate of the products of: (1) The average U.S. dealer wholesale price for such car line as computed from each official dealer price list effective during the course of a model year, and (2) The number of passenger automobiles within the car line produced during the part of the model year that the price list was in effect. A

cost per ton per minute
A unit that is often used in cost comparisons between transfer (in which there is an intermediate step between refuse collection and processing or disposal in a sanitary landfill) and direct-haul (in which collected refuse is transported directly to processing plants or sanitary landfills) operations. U

cost recovery
A legal process by which potentially responsible parties who contributed to contamination at a Superfund site can be required to reimburse the Trust Fund for money spent during any cleanup actions by the federal government. N

cost sharing
The portion of allowable project costs that a recipient contributes toward completing its project (i.e., non-Federal share, matching share). A

cost-effective alternative
An alternative control or corrective method identified after analysis as being the best available in terms of reliability, permanence, and economic considerations. Although costs are one important consideration, when regulatory and compliance methods are being considered, such analysis does not require EPA to choose the least expensive alternative. For example, when selecting a method for cleaning up a site on the Superfund National Priorities List, the Agency balances costs with the long-term effectiveness of the various methods proposed. N

cost-effectiveness analysis
An analysis performed to determine which waste treatment management system or component part thereof will result in the minimum total resources costs over time to meet the Federal, State, or local requirements. A

cost-sharing
(1) Participation by a grantee in the costs of conducting the project. For EPA grants, cost-sharing is mandatory at a minimum of five percent of allowable actual project costs, unless otherwise required by statute. (2) The portion of allowable project costs that a recipient contributes toward completing its project (i.e., non-Federal share, matching share). A

cost/benefit analysis
A quantitative evaluation of the costs which would be incurred versus the overall benefits to society of a proposed action such as the establishment of an acceptable dose of a toxic chemical. N

cotton fiber content papers
Paper that contains a minimum of 25 percent and up to 100 percent cellulose fibers derived from lint cotton, cotton linters, and cotton or linen cloth cuttings. It is also known as rag content paper or rag paper. It is used for stationery, currency, ledgers, wedding invitations, maps, and other specialty papers. A

Council
The Council on Environmental Quality established under title II of the National Environmental Policy Act of 1969 (42 U.S.C. 4321 through 4347). A

counterbalance
The mechanism that is used to balance or support the weight of the connecting rods, slide, and slide attachments. O

counterweight
A weight used to supplement the weight of the machine in providing stability for lifting working loads. O

coupler
A device for locking together the component parts of a tubular metal scaffold. O

cover
A device or system which is placed on or over a waste placed in a waste management unit so that the entire waste surface area is enclosed and sealed to minimize air emissions. A cover may have openings necessary for operation, inspection, and maintenance of the waste management unit such as access hatches, sampling ports, and

gauge wells provided that each opening is closed and sealed when not in use. Examples of covers include a fixed roof installed on a tank, a lid installed on a container, and an air-supported enclosure installed over a waste management unit. A

cover material
Soil used to cover compacted solid waste in a sanitary landfill. N

cover paper
See cover stock. A

cover stock
A heavyweight paper commonly used for covers, books, brochures, pamphlets, and the like. A

covered
A conductor encased within material of composition or thickness that is not recognized as electrical insulation. O

covered federal action
Any of the following federal actions: (1) The awarding of any federal contract; (2) The making of any federal grant; (3) The making of any federal loan; (4) The entering into of any cooperative agreement; and (5) The extension, continuation, renewal, amendment, or modification of any federal contract, grant, loan, or cooperative agreement. Covered federal action does not include receiving from an agency a commitment providing for the United States to insure or guarantee a loan. Loan guarantees and loan insurance are addressed independently. A

covered states
Those States that are participating in the demonstration medical waste tracking program and includes: Connecticut, New Jersey, New York, Rhode Island, and Puerto Rico. Any other State is a Non-Covered State. A

CPI
Consumer Price Index. A

CPM
Continuous particle monitor. U

CPSA
Consumer Product Safety Act. U

CPSC
Consumer Product Safety Commission. N

crankcase emissions
Airborne substances emitted to the atmosphere from any portion of the engine crankcase ventilation or lubrication systems. A

crawler-dozer
One of the most commonly used machines on sanitary landfills because of its capacity to perform a variety of operations: site preparation, spreading, compacting, covering, construction and maintenance of access roads and because of its excellent flotation and tractive abilities. A

crawling board
A plank with cleats spaced and secured at equal intervals, for use by a worker on roofs, not designed to carry any material. O

criminal action
A prosecuting action taken by the U.S. government or a state towards any person(s) who has knowingly and willfully not complied with the law. Such an action can result in the imposition of fines or imprisonment. N

criteria
(1) Descriptive factors taken into account by EPA in setting standards for various pollutants. These factors are used to determine limits on allowable concentration levels, and to limit the number of violations per year. When issued by EPA, the criteria provide guidance to the states on how to establish their standards. N (2) As used in the Clean Air Act, information on adverse effects of air pollutants on human health or the environment at various concentrations. The information is collected pursuant to section 108 of the Clean Air Act and used to set national ambient air quality standards. U

criteria pollutants
The 1970 amendments to the Clean Air Act required EPA to set National Ambient Air Quality Standards for certain pollutants known to be hazardous to human health. EPA has identified and set standards to protect human health and welfare for six pollutants: ozone, carbon monoxide, total suspended particulates, sulfur dioxide, lead, and nitrogen oxide. The term, "criteria pollutants" derives from the requirement that EPA must describe the characteristics and potential health and welfare effects of these pollutants. It is on the basis of these criteria that standards are set or revised. N

criterion sound level
A sound level of 90 decibels. O

critical emission-related components
Those components which are designed primarily for emission control, or whose failure may result in a significant increase in emissions accompanied by no significant impairment (or perhaps even an improvement) in performance, driveability, and/or fuel economy as determined by the Administrator. A

critical emission-related maintenance
That maintenance to be performed on critical emission-related components. A

critical endpoint
A chemical may elicit more than one toxic effect (endpoint), even in one test animal, in tests of the same or different duration (acute, subchronic, and chronic exposure studies). The doses that cause these effects may differ. The critical endpoint used in the dose-response assessment is the one that occurs at the lowest dose. In the event that data from multiple species are available, it is often the most sensitive species that determines the critical endpoint. This term is applied in the derivation of risk reference doses. N

critical organ
The most exposed human organ or tissue exclusive of the integumentary system (skin) and the cornea. A

critical pollutant
The pollutant or pollutant combination (TSP x SO_2) with the highest subindex during the reporting period. [ed. for the PSD areas]. A

cross braces
The horizontal members of a shoring system installed perpendicular to the sides of the excavation, the ends of which bear against either uprights or wales. O

cross grain
Cross grain (slope of grain) is a deviation of the fiber direction from a line parallel to the sides of the piece. O

cross recovery furnace
A furnace used to recover chemicals consisting primarily of sodium and sulfur compounds by burning black liquor which on a quarterly basis contains more than 7 weight percent of the total pulp solids from the neutral sulfite semichemical process and has a green liquor sulfidity of more than 28 percent. A

cross-sectional study
An epidemiologic study assessing the prevalence of a disease in a population. These studies are most useful for conditions or diseases that are not expected to have a long latent period and do not cause death or withdrawal from the study population. Potential bias in case ascertainment and exposure duration must be addressed when considering cross-sectional studies. N

CRP
Community Relations Plan. U

crude oil
Petroleum as it is extracted from the earth. There may be several thousands of different substances in crude oil, some of which evaporate quickly while others persist indefinitely. The physical characteristics of crude oils may vary widely. Crude oils are often identified in trade jargon by their regions of origin. This identification may not relate to the apparent physical characteristics of the oil. Commercial gasoline, kerosene, heating oils, diesel oils, lubricating oils, waxes, and asphalts are all obtained by refining crude oil. A

crude petroleum
Hydrocarbon mixtures that have a flash point below 150 degrees F. and which have not been processed in a refinery. O

crusher
A machine used to crush any metallic mineral and includes feeders or conveyors located immediately below the crushing surfaces. Crushers include, but are not limited to, the following types: jaw, gyratory, cone, and hammermill. A

Cs
Cesium. U

CSI
Compliance Sampling Inspection. U

CSMA
Chemical Specialties Manufacturers Association. U

ct.
Closed throttle. U

CTG
Control Techniques Guideline. U

cu.
Cubic. U

cu.ft.
Cubic feet. U

cu.in.
Cubic inch(es). U

cubic feet per minute
CFM. A measure of the volume of a substance flowing through air within a fixed period of time. With regard to indoor air, refers to the amount of air, in cubic feet, that is exchanged with indoor air in minute's time, or an air exchange rate. N

cullet
Clean, color-sorted, crushed-glass that is used in glassmaking to expedite the melting of silica sand. U

cullet water
That water which is exclusively and directly applied to molten glass in order to solidify the glass. A

cultivating
Physical methods of soil treatment employed within established farming, ranching and silviculture lands upon planted farm, ranch, or forest crops to aid and improve their growth, quality or yield. A

cultural eutrophication
Increasing rate at which water bodies "die" by pollution from human activities. N

cumulative impact
The impact on the environment which results from the incremental impact of the action when added to the other past, present, and reasonably foreseeable future actions regardless of what agency (Federal or non-Federal) or person undertakes such other actions. Cumulative impacts can result from individually minor but collectively significant actions taking place over a period of time. A

cumulative toxicity
The adverse effects of repeated doses occurring as a result of prolonged action on, or increased concentration of, the administered test substance or its metabolites in susceptible tissue. A

cumulative working level months
CWLM. The sum of lifetime exposure to radon working levels expressed in total working level months. N

curb collection
Collection of solid waste placed adjacent to a street. A

curb mass
The actual or manufacturer's estimated mass of the vehicle with fluids at nominal capacity and with all equipment specified by the Administrator. A

curb-idle
(1) For manual transmission code light-duty trucks, the engine speed

with the transmission in neutral or with the clutch disengaged and with the air conditioning system, if present, turned off. For automatic transmission code light-duty trucks, curb-idle means the engine speed with the automatic transmission in the Park position (or the Neutral position if there is no Park position), and with the air conditioning system, if present, turned off. (2) For manual transmission code heavy-duty engines, the manufacturer's recommended engine speed with the transmission in neutral or with the clutch disengaged. For automatic transmission code heavy-duty engines, curb-idle means the manufacturer's recommended engine speed with the automatic transmission in gear and the output shaft stalled. A

curie

(1) A measure of radioactivity. N (2) The amount of radioactive material which produces 37 billion nuclear transformations per second. One picocurie (pCi) = 10^{-12} Ci. A

curing oven

A device that uses heat or radiation to dry or cure the coating(s) applied to metal parts or products. A

current assets

Cash or other assets or resources commonly identified as those which are reasonably expected to be realized in cash or sold or consumed during the normal operating cycle of the business. A

current liabilities

Obligations whose liquidation are reasonably expected to require the use of existing resources properly classifiable as current assets or the creation of other current liabilities. A

curtail

To cease operations to the extent technically feasible to reduce emissions. A

curtain wall

A refractory construction or baffle that deflects combustion gases downward. U

custody transfer

The transfer of produced petroleum and/or condensate, after processing and/or treating in the producing operations, from storage tanks or automatic transfer facilities to pipelines or any other forms of transportation. A

custom blend

A mixture of pesticide and another compound (usually herbicides with fertilizers), which is prepared to the order of the end user and not held in inventory. N

custom blender

Any establishment which provides the service of mixing pesticides to a customer's specifications, usually a pesticide(s)-fertilizer(s), pesticide-pesticide, or a pesticide-animal feed mixture, when: (1) the blend is prepared to the order of the customer and is not held in inventory by the blender; (2) the blend is to be used on the customer's property (including leased or rented property); (3) the pesticide(s) used in the blend bears end-use labeling directions which do not prohibit use of the product in such a blend; (4) the blend is prepared from registered pesticides; (b) the blend is delivered to the end-user along with a copy of the end-use labeling of each pesticide used in the blend and a statement specifying the composition of mixture; and (6) no other pesticide production activity is performed at the establishment. A

custom-molded device
A hearing protective device that is made to conform to a specific ear canal. This is usually accomplished by using a moldable compound to obtain an impression of the ear and ear canal. The compound is subsequently permanently hardened to retain this shape. A

customer
Any person to whom a manufacturer, importer, or processor directly distributes any quantity of a chemical substance, mixture containing the substance or mixture, or article containing the substance or mixture, whether or not a sale is involved. A

customs territory of the United States
The 50 States, Puerto Rico, and the District of Columbia. A

cut
The portion of a land surface from which earth or rock is excavated; the distance between an original ground surface and an excavated surface. U

cutback asphalts
Asphalts diluted with solvents to reduce viscosity for low temperature applications. A

cutie-pie
An instrument used to measure radiation levels. N

cutout or by-pass
Devices which vary the exhaust system gas flow so as to discharge the exhaust gas and acoustic energy to the atmosphere without passing through the entire length of the exhaust system, including all exhaust system sound attenuation components. A

cutting
To penetrate with a sharp-edged instrument and includes sawing, but does not include shearing, slicing, or punching. A

cvs.
Constant volume sampler. U

CWA
Clean Water Act (formerly referred to the Federal Water Pollution Control Act) Pub. L. 92-500, as amended by Pub. L. 95-217 and Pub. L. 95-576, 33 U.S.C. 1251 *et seq.* U

CWA and regulations
The Clean Water Act (CWA) and applicable regulations promulgated thereunder. In the case of an approved State program, it includes State program requirements. A

CWLM
Cumulative working level months. The sum of lifetime exposure to radon working levels expressed in total working level months. N

cwt.
Hundred weight. U

CWTC
Chemical Waste Transportation Council. N

cyanosis
Bluish discoloration, especially of the skin and mucous membranes and fingernail beds caused by deficient oxygenation of the blood. N

cyclone collector
(1) An incinerator collector in which an inlet gas stream is made to move vortically; its centrifugal force tends to drive suspended particles to the cyclone wall, where they fall to the bottom and are collected. (2) A device that uses centrifugal force to pull large particles from polluted air. N

cyclone separator
A separator that uses a swirling air flow to sort mixed materials according to the size, weight, and density of the pieces. U

cyclonic flow
A spiraling movement of exhaust gases within a duct or stack. A

cylinder
A pressure vessel for the storage of gases. O

cytochrome P-448 and P-450
Enzymes which are important in the detoxification by biotransformation of many chemical substances. Cytochrome P-448 and P-450 enzymes, integral in the metabolic activation and detoxification of many compounds, are found primarily in the liver and, to a lesser extent, in the lung and other tissues. N

cytology
The scientific study of cells. N

cytotoxicity
Producing a specific toxic action upon cells. N

D

daily cover
Cover material that is spread and compacted on the top and side slopes of compacted solid waste at least at the end of each compacting day in order to control vectors, fire, moisture, and erosion and to assure an aesthetic appearance. A

daily discharge
NPDES. The "discharge of a pollutant" measured during a calendar day or any 24-hour period that reasonably reports the calendar day for purposes of sampling. For pollutants with limitations expressed in units of mass, the "daily discharge" is calculated as the total mass of the pollutant discharged over the day. For pollutants with limitations expressed in other units of measurement, the "daily discharge" is calculated as the average measurement of the pollutant over the day. A

dairy waste
The waste generated by dairy plants in their processing of milk to produce cream, butter, cheese, ice cream, and other dairy products; it consists primarily of organic materials and suspended solids. U

damper
A manually or automatically controlled valve or plate in a breeching, duct, or stack that is used to regulate a draft or the rate of flow of air or other gases. U

Dano biostabilizer system
An aerobic, thermophilic composting process in which optimum conditions of moisture, air, and temperature are maintained in a single, slowly revolving cylinder that retains the compostable solid waste for 1 to 5 days; the material is later windrowed. U

DASHO
Designated Agency Safety and Health Official. The executive official of a Federal Department or Agency who is responsible for safety and occupational health matters within a Federal agency, and is so designated or appointed by the head of the agency. N

147

data call-in
A part of the Office of Pesticide Programs (OPP) process of developing key required test data, especially on the long-term, chronic effects of existing pesticides, in advance of scheduled Registration Standard reviews. Data Call-In is an adjunct of the Registration Standards program intended to expedite reregistration and involves the "calling-in" of data from manufacturers. N

data fleet
A fleet of automobiles tested at "zero device-miles" in "baseline configuration," the "retrofitted configuration," and in some cases the "adjusted configuration," in order to determine the changes in fuel economy and exhaust emissions due to the "retrofitted configuration," and where applicable the changes due to the "adjusted configuration," as compared to the fuel economy and exhaust emissions of the "baseline configuration." A

data gap
The absence of any valid study or studies in the Agency's files that would satisfy a specific data requirement for a particular pesticide product. A

data recorder
That portion of the system that records a permanent record of the measurement values. The data recorder may include automatic data reduction capabilities. A

data submitters list
The current Agency list, entitled "Pesticide Data Submitters by Chemical," of persons who have submitted data to the Agency. A

daughter
A nuclide formed by the radioactive decay of another nuclide, which in this context is called the parent. U

day-night sound level (L_{dn})
The 24-hour time of day weighted equivalent sound level, in decibels, for any continuous 24-hour period, obtained after addition of ten decibels to sound levels produced in the hours from 10 p.m. to 7 a.m. A

days
Calendar days. A

dB(A)
The standard abbreviation for A-weighted sound levels in decibels. A

DBMS
Data Base Management System. N

dcf.
Dry cubic feet. U

dcm.
Dry cubic meter. U

DDT
The first chlorinated hydrocarbon insecticide (chemical name: 1,1,1-trichlorous-2, 2-bis (p-chloriphenyl)-ethane). It has a half-life of 15 years and can collect in fatty tissues of certain animals. EPA banned registration and interstate sale of DDT for virtually all but emergency uses in the U.S. in 1972 because of its persistence in the environment and accumulation in the food chain. N

DDT formulator
A person who produces, prepares or processes a formulated product comprising a mixture of DDT and inert materials or other diluents into a product intended for application in any use registered under the Federal Insecticide, Fungicide and Rodenticide Act, as amended (7 U.S.C. 135, et seq.). A

DDT manufacturer
A manufacturer, excluding any source which is exclusively a DDT formulator, who produces, prepares or processes technical DDT, or who uses DDT as a material in the production, preparation or processing of another synthetic organic substance. A

dead (deenergized)
Free from any electrical connection to a source of potential difference and from electrical charges: not having a potential difference from that of earth. Note: The term is used only with reference to current-carrying parts which are sometimes alive (energized). O

dead front
Without live parts exposed to a person on the operating side of the equipment. O

deadweight tonnage
The actual weight in tons of cargo, stores, etc., required to bring a vessel down to her load line, from the light condition. Cargo deadweight is, as its name implies, the actual weight in tons of the cargo when loaded, as distinct from stores, ballast, etc. A

dealer
(1) A person who resides or is located in the United States, any territory of the United States or the District of Columbia and who is engaged in the sale or distribution of new automobiles to the ultimate purchaser. [ed. Used for provisions of CAA that prevent tampering with pollution control equipment in automobiles]. A (2) Any person who is engaged in the sale or the distribution of new motor vehicles or new motor vehicle engines to the ultimate purchaser. B

dealership
Any site owned or operated by a restricted use pesticide retail dealer where any restricted use pesticide is made available for use, or where the dealer offers to make available for use any such pesticide. A

death
(1) The lack of opercular movement by a test fish. A (2) The lack of reaction of a test organism to gentle prodding. A

debarment
An action taken by the Director, Grants Administration Division, U.S. EPA under 40 CFR Part 32 to deny an individual, organization or unit of government the opportunity to participate in EPA grant agreements or to receive subagreements. A

debris
Woody material such as bark, twigs, branches, heartwood or sapwood that will not pass through a 2.54 cm (1.0 in) diameter round opening and is

present in the discharge from a wet storage facility. A

decay
Disintegration of wood substance due to action of wood-destroying fungi. It is also known as dote and rot. O

decel.
Deceleration. U

dechlorination
Removal of chlorine from a substance by chemically replacing it with hydrogen or hydroxide ions in order to detoxify the substances involved. N

decibel
dB. The unit measurement of sound level calculated by taking ten times the common logarithm of the ratio of the magnitude of the particular sound pressure to the standard reference sound pressure of 20 micropascals and its derivatives. A

declared value
For imported components, the value at which components are declared by the importer to the U.S. Customs Service at the date of entry into the customs territory of the United States, or, with respect to imports into Canada, the declared value of such components as if they were declared as imports into the United States at the date of entry into Canada. A

decommissioning
The process of removing a facility or area from operation and decontaminating and/or disposing of it or placing it in a condition of standby with appropriate controls and safeguards. U

decompression chamber
A pressure vessel for human occupancy such as a surface decompression chamber, closed bell, or deep diving system used to decompress divers and to treat decompression sickness. O

decompression sickness
A condition with a variety of symptoms which may result from gas or bubbles in the tissues of divers after pressure reduction. O

decompression table
A profile or set of profiles of depth-time relationships for ascent rates and breathing mixtures to be followed after a specific depth-time exposure or exposures. O

decontamination
(1) The use of physical or chemical means to remove, inactivate, or destroy bloodborne pathogens on a surface or item to the point where they are no longer capable of transmitting infectious particles and the surface or item is rendered safe for handling, use, or disposal. O (2) The removal of hazardous substances from employees and their equipment to the extent necessary to preclude the occurrence of foreseeable adverse health affects. O (3) The inactivation of the hazardous material or its safe disposal. O

decontamination area
An enclosed area adjacent and connected to the regulated area and consisting of an equipment room, shower area, and clean room, which is used for the decontamination of

workers, materials, and equipment contaminated with asbestos. A

deep-well disposal
The deposition of raw or treated, filtered hazardous waste by pumping it into deep wells, where it is contained in the pores of permeable subsurface rock and separate, stores, etc. U

deep-well injection
The subsurface implacement of fluids through a bored, drilled or driven well, or through a dug well whose depth is greater than the largest surface dimension. N

defeat device
An AECD [air emission control device] that reduces the effectiveness of the emission control system under conditions which may reasonably be expected to be encountered in normal urban vehicle operation and use, unless (1) such conditions are substantially included in the Federal emission test procedure, or (2) the need for the AECD is justified in terms of protecting the vehicle against damage or accident, or (3) the AECD does not go beyond the requirements of engine starting. A

defect
Any characteristic or condition which tends to weaken or reduce the strength of the tool, object, or structure of which it is a part. O

defoliant
All substances or mixtures of substances intended for causing the leaves or foliage to drop from plants. Defoliants include, but are not limited to, harvest-aid agents intended for defoliating plants (such as cotton) to facilitate harvesting. C

degassing
The removal of dissolved hydrogen from the molten aluminum prior to casting. Chemicals are added and gases are bubbled through the molten aluminum. Sometimes a wet scrubber is used to remove excess chlorine gas. A

degradation
(1) The process by which a chemical is reduced to a less complex form. N (2) Stated as the biochemical oxygen demand (BOD) within 28 days as a percentage of either the theoretical oxygen demand (TOD) or the chemical oxygen demand (COD). A

degradation products
Those chemicals resulting from partial decomposition or chemical breakdown of pesticides. A

degreasing
(1) The removal of oils and greases from the surface of the metal workpiece. This process can be accomplished with detergents as in alkaline cleaning or by the use of solvents. A (2) The operation of using an organic solvent as a surface cleaning agent. A

deinking
A process in which most of the ink, filler, and other extraneous material is removed from printed paper waste or broke. The result is a pulp that can be used in the manufacture of new paper. U

delayed compliance order
An order issued by a state or by the administrator to a stationary source which postpones the date by which the source is required to comply with any requirement contained in the applicable state implementation plan. O

delegated state
A state (or other governmental entity) which has applied for, and received authority to administer, within its territory, its state regulatory program as the federal program required under a particular federal statute. As used in connection with NPDES, UIC, and PWS programs, the term does not connote any transfer of federal authority to a state. N

delist
Use of the petition process to have a facility's toxic designation rescinded. N

demolition
The wrecking or taking out of any load-supporting structural member of a facility together with any related handling operations. A

demonstration
The initial exhibition of a new technology process or practice or a significantly new comination or use of technologies, processes or practices, subsequent to the development stage, for the purpose of proving technological feasibility and cost effectiveness. I

demulsibility
The resistance of an oil to emulsification, or the ability of an oil to separate from any water with which it is mixed. The better the demulsibility rating, the more quickly the oil separates from water. A

denitrification
The anaerobic biological reduction of nitrate nitrogen to nitrogen gas. N

densified refuse-derived fuel
d-RDF. A refuse-derived fuel that has been compressed to improve certain handling or burning characteristics. B

density
The mass of a unit volume of a material. It is a function of temperature, hence the temperature at which it is measured should be specified. For a solid, it is the density of the impermeable portion rather than the bulk density. For solids and liquids, suitable units of measurement are g/cm^3. The density of a solution is the mass of a unit volume of the solution and suitable units of measurement are g/cm^3. A

denuder
A horizontal or vertical container which is part of a mercury chlor-alkali cell and in which water and alkali metal amalgam are converted to alkali metal hydroxide, mercury, and hydrogen gas in a shortcircuited, electrolytic reaction. A

deoxyribonucleic acid
DNA. The molecule in which the genetic information for most living cells is encoded. Viruses, too, can contain RNA. N

departure angle
The smallest angle, in a plan side

view of an automobile, formed by the level surface on which the automobile is standing and a line tangent to the rear tire static loaded radius arc and touching the underside of the automobile rearward of the rear tire. A

depletion curve
In hydraulics, a graphical representation of water depletion from storage-stream channels, surface soil, and ground water. A depletion curve can be drawn for base flow, direct runoff, or total flow. N

deposit
The sum paid to the dealer by the consumer when beverages are purchased in returnable beverage containers, and which is refunded when the beverage container is returned. A

deposition
Specific to air toxics, the adsorption on the respiratory tract surface of inhaled, gaseous, or particulate pollutants. Also, adsorption of a gaseous or particulate air pollutant at the surface of the ground, vegetation, or water. N

depressurization
A condition that occurs when the air pressure inside a structure is lower than the air pressure outside. Depressurization can occur when household appliances that consume or exhaust house air, such as fireplaces or furnaces, are not supplied with enough makeup air. Radon-containing soil gas may be drawn into a house more rapidly under depressurized conditions. N

depuration
The elimination of a test substance from a test organism. A

depuration phase
The portion of a bioconcentration test after the uptake phase during which the organisms are in flowing water to which no test substance is added. A

dermal corrosion
The production of irreversible tissue damage in the skin following the application of the test substance. A

dermal exposure
Contact between a chemical and the skin. N

dermal irritation
The production of reversible inflammatory changes in the skin following the application of a test substance. A

dermal toxicity
The ability of a pesticide or toxic chemical to poison people or animals by contact with the skin. N

dermatitis
Inflammation of the skin. N

DES
Diethylstilbestrol. A synthetic estrogen used as a growth stimulant in food animals. Residues in meat are thought to be carcinogenic. N

desalinization
Removing salt from ocean or brackish water. N

desiccant
(1) Chemical agents that absorb moisture; some desiccants are capable of drying out plants or insects, causing death. N (2) All substances or mixtures of substances intended for artificially accelerating the drying of plant tissue. Desiccants include, but are not limited to, harvest-aid agents whose use is intended to cause sufficient foliage injury so as to result in accelerated drying and death (maturation) of certain crop plants, such as cotton and soybeans. O

design capacity
The weight of solid waste of a specified gross calorific value that a thermal processing facility is designed to process in 24 hours of continuous operation; usually expressed in tons per day. A

design value
EPA-computed statistic that characterizes air quality and determines the nature of pollution controls. In nonattainment areas, the design value is the fourth highest daily reading at the "worst case" monitor--the monitor with the highest pollutant readings during any one of three consecutive years. N

designated area
An area which may be used for work with "select carcinogens," reproductive toxins or substances which have a high degree of acute toxicity. A designated area may be the entire laboratory, an area of a laboratory or a device such as a laboratory hood. N

designated areawide planning agency
That agency designated in accordance with section 208(a)(2),(3), or (4) of the [Clean Water] Act. A

designated areawide planning area
All areas designated pursuant to section 208 (a) (2), (3), or (4) of the [Clean Water] Act and [40 CFR] §130.13. A

designated employee
A qualified person delegated to perform specific duties under the conditions existing. O

designated facility
A hazardous waste treatment, storage, or disposal facility which (1) has received a permit (or interim status), (2) has received a permit (or interim status) from a State, or (3) is regulated under § 261.6(c)(2) or subpart F of part 266 of 40 CFR parts 260-299, and (4) that has been designated on the manifest by the generator pursuant to § 260.20. A

designated high-altitude location
Certain counties which have substantially all of their area located above 1,219 meters (4,000 feet). A

designated liability area
The geographic area within which emissions from a source may significantly affect the ambient air quality. A

designated pollutant
(1) An air pollutant which is neither a criteria nor hazardous pollutant, as described in the Clean Air Act, but for which new sources performance standards exist. The Clean Air Act requires states to control these

pollutants, which include acid mist, total reduced sulfur (TRS), and fluorides. N (2) Any air pollutant, emissions of which are subject to a standard of performance for new stationary sources but for which air quality criteria have not been issued, and which is not included on a list published under section 108(a) or section 112(b)(1)(A) of the [Clean Air] Act. A

designated representative
Any individual or organization to whom an employee gives written authorization to exercise a right of access. For the purposes of access to employee exposure records and analyses using exposure or medical records, a recognized or certified collective bargaining agent shall be treated automatically as a designated representative without regard to written employee authorization. O

designated uses
Those water uses identified in state water quality standards which must be achieved and maintained as required under the Clean Water Act. Uses can include cold water fisheries, public water supply, agriculture, etc. N

designated volatility nonattainment area
Any area designated as being in nonattainment with the National Ambient Air Quality Standard for ozone pursuant to rulemaking under section 107(d)(4)(A)(ii) of the Clean Air Act. A

Designated Agency Safety and Health Official
DASHO. The executive official of a Federal Department or Agency who is responsible for safety and occupational health matters within a Federal agency, and is so designated or appointed by the head of the agency. N

designer bugs
Popular term for microbes developed through biotechnology that can degrade specific toxic chemicals at their source in toxic waste dumps or in ground water. N

desizing facilities
Those facilities that desize more than 50 percent of their total production. These facilities may also perform other processing such as fiber preparation, scouring, mercerizing, functional finishing, bleaching, dyeing and printing. A

desorption efficiency
Of a particular compound applied to a sorbent and subsequently extracted with a solvent is the weight of the compound which can be recovered from the sorbent divided by the weight of the compound originally sorbed. A

destination facility
The disposal facility, the incineration facility, or the facility that both treats and destroys regulated medical waste, to which a consignment of such is intended to be shipped, specified in Box 8 of the Medical Waste Tracking Form. A

destroyed regulated medical waste
Regulated medical waste that is no longer generally recognizable as

medical waste because the waste has been ruined, torn apart, or mutilated (it does not mean compaction) through: (1) processes such as thermal treatment or melting, during which treatment and destruction could occur; or (2) processes such as shredding, grinding, tearing, or breaking, during which only destruction would take place. A

destruction facility
A facility that destroys regulated medical waste by ruining or mutilating it, or tearing it apart. A

destruction removal efficiency
DRE. A specific mathematical formula used to determine how efficiently an incinerator works. By law, incinerators must destroy and remove 99.99 - 99.9999% of each POHC [principal organic hazardous constituent]. N

destructive distillation
The airless heating of organic matter that results in the evolution of volatile substances and produces a solid char consisting of fixed carbon and ash. U

desulfurization
Removal of sulfur from fossil fuels to reduce pollution. N

detection level
The minimum concentration of a substance which analytical techniques can detect with some degree of accuracy in various environmental samples such as ground water. A detection level varies between substances, environmental conditions, samples, and laboratory equipment and technique. N

detergent
Synthetic washing agent that helps to remove dirt and oil. Some contain compounds which kill useful bacteria and encourage algae growth when they are in wastewater that reaches receiving waters. N

detoxification
Reduction of a chemical's toxic properties by means of biotransformation processes, to form a more readily excreted, or a less toxic chemical than the parent compound. N

developer
A person, government unit, or company that proposes to build a hazardous waste treatment, storage, or disposal facility. N

developmental toxicity
Adverse effects on the developing organism that may result from exposure prior to conception (either parent), during prenatal development, or postnatally to the time of sexual maturation. Adverse developmental effects may be detected at any point in the life span of the organism. Major manifestations of developmental toxicity include: death of the developing organism; induction of structural abnormalities (teratogenicity); altered growth; and functional deficiency. N

deviation
A formal exception to a Section or Sections of EPA grant regulations or the *EPA Grants Administration Manual*

based on written justification, and provided for by a grant amendment. U

device
(1) Any instrument or contrivance (other than a firearm) which is intended for trapping, destroying, repelling, or mitigating any pest or any other form of plant or animal life (other than man and other than bacteria, virus, or other microorganism on or in living man or other living animals); but not including equipment used for the application of pesticides when sold separately therefrom. A, C (2) A unit of an electrical system which is intended to carry but not utilize electric energy. O (3) Any device or class of device as defined by the FIFRA Act and determined by the Administrator to be subject to the provisions of the FIFRA Act. A

device integrity
The durability of a device and effect of its malfunction on vehicle safety or other parts of the vehicle system. A

dewater
(1) To remove the water from recently produced tailings by mechanical or evaporative methods such that the water content of the tailings does not exceed 30 percent by weight. A (2) The removal of water by such processes as filtration, centrifugation, pressing, and coagulation to prepare sewage sludge for disposal by burning or landfill. The term also applies to the removal of water from pulp or other materials. U

DHEW
Former U.S. Department of Health, Education and Welfare, now Department of Health and Human Services. A

diagnostic-feasibility study
A two part study to determine a lake's current condition and to develop possible methods for lake restoration and protection. (a) The diagnostic portion of the study includes gathering information and data to determine the limnological, morphological, demographic, socio-economic, and other pertinent characteristics of the lake and its watershed. This information will provide recipients an understanding of the quality of the lake, specifying the location and loading characteristics of significant sources polluting the lake. (b) The feasibility portion of the study includes: (1) Analyzing the diagnostic information to define methods and procedures for controlling the sources of pollution; (2) Determining the most energy and cost efficient procedures to improve the quality of the lake for maximum public benefit; (3) Developing a technical plan and milestone schedule for implementing pollution control measures and in-lake restoration procedures; and (4) If necessary, conducting pilot scale evaluations. A

dialysis
A process by which various substances in solution with widely differing molecular weights may be separated by solute diffusion through semipermeable membranes. It is a suitable means of separation for hazardous wastes that form aqueous solutions. U

diaphragm displacement
The distance through which the center of the diaphragm moves when activated. In the case of a non-modulated stem, diaphragm displacement corresponds to stem displacement. A

diathermy
The generation of heat in tissues for medical or surgical purposes by electric currents. U

diatomaceous earth
Diatomite. A chalk-like material (fossilized diatoms) used to filter out solid waste in waste-water treatment plants; also used as an active ingredient in some powdered pesticides. N

diazinon
An insecticide. In 1986, EPA banned its use on open areas such as sod farms and golf courses because it posed a danger to migratory birds who gathered on them in large numbers. The ban did not apply to its use in agriculture, or on lawns of homes and commercial establishments. N

dicofol
A pesticide used on citrus fruits. N

die
The tooling used in a press for cutting or forming material. An upper and a lower die make a complete set. O

dielectric material
A material that does not conduct direct electrical current. Dielectric coatings are used to electrically isolate UST systems from the surrounding soils. Dielectric bushings are used to electrically isolate portions of the UST system (e.g., tank from piping). A

dielectric strength
The ability of the spark plug's ceramic insulator material to resist electrical breakdown. A

diesel engine
A type of internal combustion engine that uses a fuel injector and produces combustion temperatures by compression. U

diesel fuel
Any fuel sold in any State and suitable for use in diesel motor vehicles and diesel motor vehicle engines, and which is commonly or commercially known or sold as diesel fuel. A

dietary LC$_{50}$
A statistically derived estimate of the concentration of a test substance in the diet that would cause 50 percent mortality to the test population under specified conditions. A

differentiation
The process by which single cells grow into particular forms of specialized tissue, e.g., root, stem, leaf. N

diffused air
A type of aeration that forces oxygen into sewage by pumping air through perforated pipes inside a holding tank and bubbling it through the sewage. N

diffusion
The movement of suspended or dissolved particles from a more concentrated to a less concentrated region as a result of the random movement of individual particles; the process tends to distribute them uniformly throughout the available volume. N

digester
In wastewater treatment, a closed tank; in solid waste conversion, a unit in which bacterial action is induced and accelerated in order to break down organic matter and establish the proper carbon to nitrogen ratio. N

digestion
The biochemical decomposition of organic matter. Digestion of sewage sludge occurs in tanks where it breaks down into gas, liquid, and mineral matter. N

dike
(1) An embankment or ridge of either natural or man-made materials used to prevent the movement of liquids, sludges, solids, or other materials. A (2) A low wall that can act as a barrier to prevent a spill from spreading. N

diluent
The material added to a pesticide by the user or manufacturer to reduce the concentration of active ingredient in the mixture. A

dilution ratio
The relationship between the volume of water in a stream and the volume of incoming waste. It can affect the ability of the stream to assimilate waste. N

dilution ventilation
Air flow designed to dilute contaminants to acceptable levels. N

dilution water
The water used to produce the flow-through conditions of the test to which the test substance is added and to which the test species is exposed. A

dilution zone
See mixing zone. U

dinocap
A fungicide used primarily by apple growers to control summer diseases. EPA, in 1986, proposed restrictions on its use when laboratory tests found it caused birth defects in rabbits. N

dinoseb
A herbicide that is also used as a fungicide and insecticide. It was banned by EPA in 1986 because it posed the risk of birth defects and sterility. N

dioxin
Any of a family of compounds known chemically as dibenzo-p-dioxins. Concern about them arises from their potential toxicity and as contaminants in commercial products. Tests on laboratory animals indicate that it is one of the more toxic man-made chemicals known. N

diploid
The chromosome state in which each homologous chromosome is present in

pairs. Normal human somatic (non-reproductive) cells are diploid (i.e., they have 46 chromosomes), whereas reproductive cells, with 23 chromosomes are haploid. N

direct application
Those cold rolling operations which include once-through use of rolling solutions at all mill stands. A

direct chill casting
The pouring of molten aluminum into a water-cooled mold. Contact cooling water is sprayed onto the aluminum as it is dropped into the mold, and the aluminum ingot falls into a water bath at the end of the casting process. A

direct costs
Those costs which can be identified specifically with the grant project or which can be directly assigned to it with a high degree of accuracy. U

direct discharge
The discharge of a pollutant. A

direct discharger
(1) A source that places pollutants directly into navigable waters. Sources that dispose of pollutants into a sewer system and non-point sources, that add pollutants to uncontrolled runoff, are not direct dischargers. (2) A municipal or industrial facility which introduces pollution through a defined conveyance or system; a point source. N

direct drive
The type of driving arrangement wherein no clutch is used; coupling and decoupling of the driving torque is accomplished by energization and deenergization of a motor. Even though not employing a clutch, direct drives match the operational characteristics of "part revolution clutches" because the driving power may be disengaged during the stroke of the press. O

direct feed incinerator
An incinerator that accepts solid waste directly into its combustion chamber. U

direct filtration
A series of processes including coagulation and filtration but excluding sedimentation resulting in substantial particulate remove. A

direct financial interest
Ownership or part ownership by an employee of land, stocks, bonds, debentures, warrants, a partnership, shares, or other holdings and also means any other arrangement where the employee may benefit from his or her holding in or salary from coal mining operations. Direct financial interests include employment, pensions, creditor, real property and other financial relationships. A

direct photolysis
The direct absorption of light by a chemical followed by a reaction which transforms the parent chemical into one or more products. A

direct sale subaccount
An account in the special allowance reserve, as defined in section 416(b) of the Clean Air Act. The direct sale subaccount will contain Phase II allowances to be sold in the amount of

25,000 per year, beginning in calendar year 1993 and of 50,000 per year beginning in calendar year 2000. A

direct training
All technical and managerial training conducted directly by EPA for personnel of state and local governmental agencies, other Federal agencies, private industries, universities, and other non-EPA agencies and organizations. A

director
The chief administrative officer of a State or Interstate water pollution control agency with an NPDES permit program approved pursuant to section 402(b) of the Clean Water Act and an approved State pretreatment program. A

director of an approved state
The chief administrative officer of a state agency responsible for implementing the state municipal solid waste permit program or other system of prior approval that is deemed to be adequate by EPA under regulations published pursuant to sections 2002 and 4005 of RCRA. A

disaggregation
The result of breaking down a sum total of population or economic activity for a State or other jurisdiction (i.e., designated 208 area or SMSA) into portions, each representing a smaller area or jurisdiction. A

disallowed costs
Those charges to a grant which EPA or its representative determine to be unallowable. U

discharge
(1) Water-borne pollutants released to a receiving stream directly or indirectly or to a sewerage system. A (2) [For purposes of Section 311 of the CWA], includes, but is not limited to, any spilling, leaking, pumping, pouring, emitting, emptying or dumping, but excludes (A) discharges in compliance with a permit under section 402 of this [Federal Water Pollution Control] Act, (B) discharges resulting from circumstances identified and reviewed and made a part of the public record with respect to a permit issued or modified under section 402 of this Act, and subject to a condition in such permit, and (C) continuous or anticipated intermittent discharges from a point source, identified in a permit or permit application under section 402 of this Act, which are caused by events occurring within the scope of relevant operating or treatment systems. D (3)(A) [In connection with activities under the Outer Continental Shelf Lands Act or the Deepwater Port Act of 1974, or which may affect natural resources belonging to, appertaining to, or under the exclusive management authority of the United States including resources under the Fishery Conservation and Management Act of 1976]. A discharge into any waters beyond the contiguous zone from any vessel or onshore or offshore facility, which vessel or facility is subject to or is engaged in activities under the Outer Continental Shelf Lands Act or the Deepwater Port Act of 1974, and (B) any discharge into any waters beyond the contiguous zone which contain, cover, or support any natural resource

belonging to, appertaining to, or under the exclusive management authority of the United States (including resources under the Fishery Conservation and Management Act of 1976). A (4) When used without qualification includes a discharge of a pollutant, and a discharge of pollutants. D

discharge allowance
The amount of pollutant (mg per kg of production unit) that a plant will be permitted to discharge. A

Discharge Monitoring Report
DMR. The EPA uniform national form, including any subsequent additions, revisions, or modifications, for the reporting of self-monitoring results by NPDES permitees. DMRs must be used by "approved States" as well as by EPA. EPA will supply DMRs to any approved State upon request. The EPA national forms may be modified to substitute the state agency name, address, logo, and other similar information, as appropriate, in place of EPA's. A

discharge of a pollutant
(1)(a) Any addition of any "pollutant" or combination of pollutants to "waters of the United States" from any "point source," or (b) any addition of any pollutant or combination of pollutants to the waters of the "contiguous zone" or the ocean from any point source other than a vessel or other floating craft which is being used as a means of transportation. (2) This definition includes additions of pollutants into waters of the United States from: surface runoff which is collected or channelled by man; discharges through pipes, sewers, or other conveyances owned by a State, municipality, or other person which do not lead to a treatment works; and discharges through pipes, sewers, or other conveyances leading into privately owned treatment works. This term does not include an addition of pollutants by any "indirect discharger." A

discharge of dredged material
Any addition from any "point source" of "dredge material" into "waters of the United States." The term includes the addition of dredged material into waters of the United States and the runoff or overflow from a contained land or water dredged material disposal area. Discharges of pollutants into waters of the United States resulting from the subsequent onshore processing of dredged material are not included within this term and are subject to the NPDES program even though the extraction and deposit of such material may also require a permit from the Corps of Engineers or the State section 404 program [of the FWPCA]. A

discharge of fill material
The addition from any "point source" of "fill material" into "waters of the United States." The term includes the following activities in waters of the United States: Placement of fill that is necessary for the construction of any structure; the building of any structure or impoundment requiring rock, sand, dirt, or other materials for its construction; site-develoment fills for recreational, industrial, commercial,

residential, and other uses; causeways or road fills; dams and dikes; artificial islands; property protection and/or reclamation devices such as riprap, groins, seawalls, breakwaters, and revetments; beach nourishment; levees; fill for structures such as sewage treatment facilities, intake and outfall pipes associated with power plants and subaqueous utility lines, and artificial reefs. A

discharge of pollutant or pollutants
Each means (1) any addition of any pollutant to navigable waters other than the territorial sea, from any point source, (2) any addition of any pollutant to the waters of the territorial sea, the contiguous zone or the ocean from any point source other than a vessel or other floating craft. A, D

discharge of pollutants associated with an aquaculture project
The addition or discharge of specific pollutants in a controlled manner from a point source to an aquaculture project to enhance the growth or propagation of the species under culture. A

discharge point
The point within the disposal site at which the dredged or fill material is released. A

disconnecting (or isolating) switch
(Over 600 volts, nominal). A mechanical switching device used for isolating a circuit or equipment from a source of power. O

disconnecting means
A device, or group of devices, or other means by which the conductors of a circuit can be disconnected from their source of supply. O

disinfectant
(1) Any oxidant, including but not limited to chlorine, chlorine dioxide, chloramines, and ozone added to water in any part of the treatment or distribution process, that is intended to kill or inactivate pathogenic microorganisms. A (2) A chemical or physical process that kills pathogenic organisms in water. Chlorine is often used to disinfect sewage treatment effluent, water supplies, wells, and swimming pools. N

disinfection
In reference to primary drinking water regulations and related regulations applicable to public water systems, a process which inactivates pathogenic organisms in water by chemical oxidants or equivalent agents. A

dispenser
The permanent (intended to be refilled) or disposable (discarded when empty) container designed to hold more than one complete set of hearing protector(s) for the express purpose of display to promote sale or display to promote use or both. A

dispersant
(1) A chemical agent used to break up concentrations of organic material such as spilled oil. M (2) An agent that emulsifies, disperses, or solubilizes oil into the water column

or promotes the surface spreading of oil slicks to facilitate dispersal of the oil into the water column. A

dispersants
Those chemical agents that emulsify, disperse, or solubilize oil into the water column or promote the surface spreading of oil slicks to facilitate dispersal of the oil into the water column. A

dispersion model
A mathematical model or computer simulation used to predict the movement of airborne pollution. Models take into account a variety of mixing mechanisms which dilute effluents and transport them away from the point of emission. N

dispersion technique
(1) The use of dilution to attain ambient air quality levels including any intermittent or supplemental control of air pollutants varying with atmospheric conditions. B Increase in stack height is an example of a dispersion technique. (2) Any technique which attempts to affect the concentration of a pollutant in the ambient air by using that portion of a stack which exceeds good engineering practice stack height, varying the rate of emission of a pollutant according to atmospheric conditions or ambient concentrations of that pollutant, or by addition of a fan or reheater to obtain a less stringent emission limitation. The preceding sentence does not include: (a) The reheating of a gas stream, following use of a pollution control system, for the purpose of returning the gas to the temperature at which it was originally discharged from the facility generating the gas stream; (b) the use of smoke management in agricultural or silvicultural programs; or (c) combining the exhaust gases from several stacks into one stack. A

disposable device
A hearing protective device that is intended to be discarded after one period of use. A

disposal
(1) The planned release or placement of waste in a manner that precludes recovery. (2) The discharge, deposit, injection, dumping, spilling, leaking, or placing of any solid waste or hazardous waste into or on any land or water so that such solid waste or hazardous waste or any constituent thereof may enter the environment or be emitted into the air or discharged into any waters, including ground waters. I (3) Final placement or destruction of toxic, radioactive, or other wastes; surplus or banned pesticides or other chemicals; polluted soils; and drums containing hazardous materials from removal actions or accidental releases. Disposal may be accomplished through use of approved secure landfills, surface impoundments, land farming, deep well injection, ocean dumping, or incineration. N (4) Permanent isolation of spent nuclear fuel or radioactive waste from the accessible environment with no intent of recovery, whether or not such isolation permits the recovery of such fuel or waste. For example, disposal of waste in a mined geologic repository occurs when all of the shafts to the repository are backfilled

and sealed. A (5) The collection, storage, treatment, utilization, processing, or final disposal of solid waste. A (6) Intentionally or accidentally to discard, throw away, or otherwise complete or terminate the useful life of PCBs and PCB Items. Disposal includes spills, leaks, and other uncontrolled discharges of PCBs as well as actions related to containing, transporting, destroying, degrading, decontaminating, or confining PCBs and PCB Items. A (7) The safe removal of the hazardous material from the work environment. O

disposal facility
A facility or part of a facility at which "hazardous waste" is intentionally placed into or on the land or water, and at which hazardous waste will remain after closure. A

disposal site
An interim or finally approved and precise geographical area within which ocean dumping of wastes is permitted under conditions specified in permits issued under sections 102 and 103 of the Act. Such sites are identified by boundaries established by (1) coordinates of latitude and longitude for each corner, or by (2) coordinates of latitude and longitude for the center point and a radius in nautical miles from that point. Boundary coordinates shall be identified as precisely as is warranted by the accuracy with which the site can be located with existing navigational aids or by the implantation of transponders, buoys or other means of marking the site. A (2) The region within the smallest perimeter of residual radioactive material (excluding cover materials) following completion of control activities. A

disposal site designation study
The collection, analysis and interpretation of all available pertinent data and information on a proposed disposal site prior to use, including but not limited to, that from baseline surveys, special purpose surveys of other Federal agencies, public data archives, and social and economic studies and records of areas which would be affected by use of the proposed site. A

disposal site evaluation study
The collection, analysis, and interpretation of all pertinent information available concerning an existing disposal site, including but not limited to, data and information from trend assessment surveys, monitoring surveys, special purpose surveys of other Federal agencies, public data archives, and social and economic studies and records of affected areas. A

disposal system
Any combination of engineered and natural barriers that isolate spent nuclear fuel or radioactive waste after disposal. A

disposal well
A well used for the disposal of waste into a subsurface stratum. A

disposer of PCB waste
As the term is used in subpart J and K of 40 CFR Parts 700-789, means any person who owns or operates a facility approved by EPA for the disposal of

PCB waste which is regulated for disposal under the requirements of subpart D of this part. A

disposition
The movement and fate of chemicals in the body, including absorption, distribution, biotransformation, and excretion. N

dissolved chromium, dissolved nickel or dissolved iron
That portion of chromium, nickel or iron, respectively, determined utilizing the approved method for total chromium, total nickel or total iron, respectively, following preliminary treatment as described in paragraph 4.1.1, page 86, of the *Methods for Chemical Analysis of Water and Wastes*, 1971, EPA, Analytical Quality Control Laboratory, Cincinnati, Ohio. A

dissolved oxygen
DO. (1) A measure of the amount of oxygen available for biochemical activity in a given amount of water. Adequate levels of DO are needed to support aquatic life. Low dissolved oxygen concentrations can result from inadequate waste treatment. N (2) The oxygen freely available in water. Dissolved oxygen is vital to fish and other aquatic life and for the prevention of odors. Traditionally, the level of dissolved oxygen has been accepted as the single most important indicator of a water body's ability to support desirable aquatic life. Secondary and advanced waste treatment are generally designed to protect DO in waste-receiving waters. N

dissolved solids
(1) The total of disintegrated organic and inorganic material contained in water. Excesses can make water unfit to drink or use in industrial processes. N (2) Disintegrated organic and inorganic material contained in water. N

distillate oil
Fuel oils that contain 0.05 weight percent nitrogen or less and comply with the specifications for fuel oil numbers 1 and 2, as defined by the American Society of Testing and Materials in ASTM D396-78, Standard Specifications for Fuel Oils (incorporated by reference--see [40 CFR] § 60.17). A

distillation
The act of purifying liquids through boiling, so that the steam condenses to a pure liquid and the pollutants remain in a concentrated residue. N

distillery
A plant or that portion of a plant where flammable or combustible liquids produced by fermentation are concentrated, and where the concentrated products may also be mixed, stored, or packaged. O

distribute in commerce
(1) Sell in, offer for sale in, or introduce or deliver for introduction into, commerce. A (2) When used to describe an action taken with respect to a chemical substance or mixture or article containing a substance or mixture, to sell, or the sale of, the substance, mixture, or article in commerce; to introduce or deliver for

introduction into commerce, or the introduction or delivery for introduction into commerce of, the substance, mixture, or article; or to hold, or the holding of, the substance, mixture, or article after its introduction into commerce. K (3) To sell in commerce, to introduce or deliver for introduction into commerce, or to hold after introduction into commerce. A

distribution
Transport of a substance through the body by physical means (e.g., active transport or diffusion). Distribution is dependent on the chemical properties of the toxicant or its metabolites and, to some extent, the route of exposure as well as physiologic variables. N

distributor
(1) Any person who transports or stores or causes the transportation of storage of gasoline at any point between any gasoline refinery and any retail outlet or wholesale-purchaser-consumer's facilities. A (2) A device for directing the secondary current from the induction coil to the spark plugs at the proper intervals and in the proper firing orders. A (3) A business, other than a chemical manufacturer or importer, which supplies hazardous chemicals to other distributors or to employers. O

distributor firing angle
The angular relationship of breaker point opening from one opening to the next in the firing sequence. A

district engineer
The district engineer for the U.S. Army Corps of Engineers District in which dredged or fill material is proposed to be discharged or such other individual as may be designated by the Secretary of the Army to issue or deny permits under section 404 of the [Clean Water] Act. A

diuresis
Increased production of urine. N

diurnal breathing loss
Fuel evaporative emissions as a result of the daily range in temperature to which the fuel system is exposed. A

diver
An employee working in water using underwater apparatus which supplies compressed breathing gas at the ambient pressure. O

diving mode
A type of diving requiring specific equipment, procedures and techniques (SCUBA, surface-supplied air, or mixed gas). O

dL
Deciliter. N

DL
Detection limit. U

DMA
Designated Management Agency. A

DMR
Discharge Monitoring Reports (EPA). U

DNA
Deoxyribonucleic acid. The molecule in which the genetic information for

most living cells is encoded. Viruses, too, can contain RNA. N

DO
Dissolved oxygen. U

DOC
Department of Commerce. U

DOD
Department of Defense. U

DOE
Department of Energy. U

DOI
Department of the Interior. U

DOJ
Department of Justice. U

DOL
Department of Labor. U

domestic
Within the geographical boundaries of the 50 United States, including the District of Columbia, the Commonwealth of Puerto Rico, the Virgin Islands, Guam, American Samoa, the Northern Mariana Islands, and any other territory or possession of the United States. A

domestic application
Application of a pesticide directly to humans or pets, or application of a pesticide in, on or around all structures, vehicles or areas associated with the household or home life, patient care areas of health related institutions, or areas where children spend time including but not limited to: (1) Gardens, non-commercial greenhouses, yards, patios, houses, pleasure marine craft, mobile homes, campers and recreational vehicles, non-commercial campsites, home swimming pools and kennels; (2) Articles, objects, devices or surfaces handled or contacted by humans or pets in all structures, vehicles or areas listed above; (3) Patient care areas of nursing homes, mental institutions, hospitals, and convalescent homes; (4) Educational, lounging and recreational areas of preschools, nurseries and day camps. A

domestic construction material
An unmanufactured construction material which has been mined or produced in the United States, or manufactured construction material which has been manufactured in the United States if the cost of its components which are mined, produced, or manufactured in the United States exceeds 50 percent of the cost of all its components. A

domestic wastewater
Wastewater of the type commonly introduced into a treatment works by residential users. A

DOS
Department of State. U

dose
(1) The quantity of a chemical to which an organism is exposed. N (2) A general term denoting the quality of radiation or energy absorbed. For special purposes it must be appropriately qualified. If unqualified, it refers to absorbed dose. (3) In radiology, the quantity of energy or

radiation absorbed. N (4) The amount of test substance administered. Dose is expressed as weight of test substance (g, mg) per unit weight of test animal (e.g., mg/kg) or as weight of test substance per unit weight of food or drinking water. A

dose equivalent
The product of the absorbed dose from ionizing radiation and such factors as account for differences in biological effectiveness due to the type of radiation and its distribution in the body as specified by the International Commission on Radiological Units and Measurements (ICRU). The unit of the dose equivalent is the rem. A

dose rate
Absorbed dose delivered per unit time. U

dose-response
The relationship between the dose and the proportion of a population sample showing a defined effect. A

dose-response relationship
A relationship between: (1) the dose, often actually based on "administered dose" (i.e., exposure) rather than absorbed dose, and (2) the extent of toxic injury produced by that chemical. Response can be expressed either as the severity of injury or proportion of exposed subjects affected. A dose-response assessment is one of the four steps in a risk assessment. N

dosimeter
An instrument that measures exposure to radiation. N

dosimetry
In general, the measurement or modeling of the amount, rate, and distribution of a drug or toxicant especially as it pertains to producing a particular biological effect. N

DOT
Department of Transportation. U

DOT container
A container constructed in accordance with the applicable requirements of 49 CFR chapter 1. A

DOT specifications
Regulations of the Department of Transportation published in 49 CFR. O

downpass
A chamber or gas passage placed between two combustion chambers to carry the products of combustion downward. U

draft
The difference between the pressure in an incinerator, or any component part, and that in the atmosphere; it causes air or the products of combustion to flow from the incinerator to the atmosphere. U

draft controller
An automatic device that maintains a uniform furnace draft by regulating a damper. U

Draft Environmental Impact Statement
DEIS. The document prepared by EPA, or under EPA guidance, which attempts to identify and analyze the environmental impacts of a proposed EPA action and feasible alternatives,

and is circulated for public comment prior to preparation of the final environmental impact statement (final EIS). A

draft permit
A document prepared under 40 CFR §124.6 indicating the Director's tentative decision to issue or deny, modify, revoke and reissue, terminate, or reissue a "permit." A notice of intent to terminate a permit, and a notice of intent to deny a permit, as discussed in 40 CFR §124.5 are types of "draft permits." A denial of a request for modification, revocation and reissuance, or termination, as discussed in 40 CFR §124.5, is not a "draft permit." A "proposed permit" is not a "draft permit." A

drag conveyor
A conveyor that uses vertical steel plates fastened between two continuous chains to drag material across a smooth surface. U

drag plate
A plate beneath a traveling or chain grate stoker used to support the returning grates. U

dragline
A revolving shovel that carries a bucket attached only by cables and digs by pulling the bucket toward itself. U

drain sample
A tap sample obtained from the draw-off or discharge valve. Occasionally, a drain sample may be the same as a bottom sample, as in the case of a tank car. A

drainage water
Incidental surface waters from diverse sources such as rainfall, snow melt or permafrost melt. A

drawing
The process of pulling metal through a die or succession of dies to reduce the metal's diameter or alter its shape. There are two aluminum forming subcategories based on the drawing process. In the drawing with neat oils subcategory, the drawing process uses a pure or neat oil as a lubricant. In the drawing with emulsions or soaps subcategory, the drawing process uses an emulsion or soap solution as a lubricant. A

dredge
Self-contained combination of an elevating excavator (e.g., bucket line dredge), the beneficiation or gold-concentrating plant, and a tailings disposal plant, all mounted on a floating barge. A

dredged material
(1) Any material excavated or dredged from the navigable waters of the United States. (2) [ed. Dredged material often contains high levels of toxic and other pollutants that have precipitated into bottom sediments. Disposal of dredged material can cause serious environmental problems. Disposal in navigable waters requires a permit under Section 404 of CWA]. (3) Material that is excavated or dredged from "waters of the United States." A

dredging
Removal of mud from the bottom of

water bodies using a scooping machine. This disturbs the ecosystem and causes silting that can kill aquatic life. Dredging of contaminated mud can expose aquatic life to heavy metals and other toxics. Dredging activities may be subject to regulation under Section 404 of the Clean Water Act. N

drift
Movement of a pesticide during or immediately after application or use through air to a site other than the intended site of application or use. A

drilling and production facility
All drilling and servicing equipment, wells, flow lines, separators, equipment, gathering lines, and auxiliary non-transportation-related equipment used in the production of petroleum but does not include natural gasoline plants. A

drilling mud
A heavy suspension used in drilling an "injection well," introduced down the drill pipe and through the drill bit. A

drinking water supply
Any raw or finished water source that is or may be used by a public water system (as defined in the Safe Drinking Water Act) or as drinking water by one or more individuals. L

drivetrain configuration
A unique combination of engine code, transmission configuration and axle ratio. A

drop-off center
A central point for collecting recyclable or compostable materials. The materials are taken by individuals to the collection site or center and deposited into designated containers. U

dross reverberatory furnace
Any furnace used for the removal or refining of impurities from lead bullion. A

drum mill
A long, inclined steel drum that rotates and grinds solid wastes in its rough interior; finer ground material falls through holes near the end of the drum and coarser material drops out of the end. The drum mill is used in some composting operations. U

dry cleaning operation
That process by which an organic solvent is used in the commercial cleaning of garments and other fabric materials. A

dry limestone process
An air pollution control method that uses limestone to absorb the sulfur oxides in furnaces and stack gases. N

dryer
A unit in which the moisture content of a substance is reduced by contact with a heated gas stream. A

drying hearth
A solid surface in an incinerator upon which wet waste materials, liquids, or waste matter that may turn to liquid before burning are placed to dry or to burn with the help of hot combustion gases. U

dscf.
Dry cubic feet at standard conditions. U

dscm.
Dry cubic meter at standard conditions. U

duct burner
A device that combusts fuel and that is placed in the exhaust duct from another source, such as a stationary gas turbine, internal combustion engine, kiln, etc., to allow the firing of additional fuel to heat the exhaust gases before the exhaust gases enter a heat recovery steam generating unit. A

ductile iron
A cast iron that has been treated while molten with a master alloy containing an element such as magnesium or cerium to induce the formation of free graphite as nodules or spherules, which imparts a measurable degree of ductility to the cast metal. A

dump
A site used to dispose of solid wastes without environmental controls. N

dump plate
A hinged plate in an incinerator that supports residue and from which residue may be discharged by rotating the plate. U

dumping
[As used in regulation of ocean disposal] a disposition of material: Provided, That it does not mean a disposition of any effluent from any outfall structure to the extent that such disposition is regulated under the provisions of the Federal Water Pollution Control Act, as amended, under the provisions of [33 USC § 407], or under the provisions of the Atomic Energy Act of 1954, as amended, nor does it mean a routine discharge of effluent incidental to the propulsion of, or operation of motor-driven equpment on, vessels: Provided further, That it does not mean the construction of any fixed structure or artificial island nor the intentional placement of any device in ocean waters or on or in the submerged land beneath such waters, for a purpose other than disposal, when such construction or such placement is otherwise regulated by Federal or State law or occurs pursuant to an authorized Federal or State program: And provided further, That it does not include the deposit of oyster shells, or other materials when such deposit is made for the purpose of developing, maintaining, or harvesting fisheries resources and is otherwise regulated by Federal or State law or occurs pursuant to an authorized Federal or State program. A, E

duplicator paper
Writing papers used for masters or copy sheets in the aniline ink or hectograph process of reproduction (commonly called spirit machines). A

durability fleet
A fleet of automobiles operated for mileage accumulation used to assess deterioration effects associated with the retrofit device. A

dust
Fine grain particles light enough to be suspended in air. N

dust collector
A device or combination of devices for separating dust from the air handled by an exhaust ventilation system. O

dust loading
The amount of dust in a gas; usually expressed in grains per cubic foot or pounds per thousand pounds of gas. U

dust-handling equipment
Any equipment used to handle particulate matter collected by the air pollution control device (and located at or near such device) serving any electric submerged arc furnace subject to this subpart. A

dustfall jar
An open container used to collect large particles from the air for measurement and analysis. N

dwell angle
The number of degrees of distributor mechanical rotation during which the breaker points are capable of conducting current. A

dye penetrant testing
A nondestructive method for finding discontinuities that are open to the surface of the metal. A dye is applied to the surface of metal and the excess is rinsed off. Dye that penetrates surface discontinuities will not be rinsed away, thus marking these discontinuities. A

dynamometer-idle
For automatic transmission code heavy-duty engines, the manufacturer's recommended engine speed without a transmission that simulates recommended engine speed with a transmission and with the transmission in neutral. A

dystrophic lakes
Shallow bodies of water that contain much humus and/or organic matter, that contain many plants but few fish, and are highly acidic. N

E

E
The VOC emission reduction efficiency (as a fraction) of the emission control device during performance testing. A

EO
Executive Order. A Presidential directive to executive agencies that is promulgated under Constitutional or statutory authority. For certain E.O.'s, independent agencies may voluntarily comply. E.O.'s are published in the Federal Register and in Title 3 of the Code of Federal Regulations. U

EA
Environmental assessment. F

EAP
Environmental Action Plan. N

ear insert device
A hearing protective device that is designed to be inserted into the ear canal, and to be held in place principally by virtue of its fit inside the ear canal. A

ear muff device
A hearing protective device that consists of two acoustic enclosures which fit over the ears and which are held in place by a spring-like headband to which the enclosures are attached. A

early life stage toxicity test
A test to determine the minimum concentration of a substance which produces a statistically significant observable effect on hatching, survival, development and/or growth of a fish species continuously exposed during the period of their early development. A

EC_{50}
That experimentally derived concentration of test substance in dilution water that is calculated to affect 50 percent of a test population during continuous exposure over a specified period of time. In this guideline, the effect measured is immobilization. A

ecological impact
The effect that a man-made or natural activity has on living organisms and their non-living (abiotic) environment. N

ecology
(1) The relationship of living things to one another and their environment, or the study of such relationships. (2) The study of the interrelationships between living organisms and their environment, both physical and biological. N

economic poisons
Chemicals used to control pests and to defoliate cash crops such as cotton. N

ecosphere
(1) The layer of earth and troposphere inhabited by or suitable for the existence of living organisms. (2) The "bio-bubble" that contains life on earth, in surface waters, and in the air. (Compare: biosphere). N

ecosystem
The interacting system of a biological community and its nonliving surroundings. N

ecotoxicological studies
Measurement of effects of environmental toxicants on indigenous populations of organisms. N

ECRA
Environmental Cleanup and Responsibility Act, effective December 31, 1983 in New Jersey. U

ECSL
Enforcement Compliance Schedule Letters. U

ECX
The experimentally derived chemical concentration that is calculated to effect X percent of the test criterion. A

EDA
Economic Development Administration. U

EDB
Ethylene dibromide. A chemical used as an agricultural fumigant and in certain industrial processes. Extremely toxic and found to be a carcinogen in laboratory animals. EDB has been banned for most agricultural uses in the United States. N

EDD
Enforcement Decision Document. U

eddy current separator
A separator that uses an alternating current to temporarily magnetize a piece of metal making it possible to deflect it and separate it out. This is used to sort out aluminum and other nonmagnetic metals. Also called aluminum magnet and electrodynamic separator. U

edema
An accumulation of an excessive amount of fluid in cells, tissues, or serous cavity. Lung edema is the accumulation of fluid in the lung. N

EDF
Environmental Defense Fund. U

education
Planned and organized activity by a consultant to impart information to employers and employees to enable them to establish and maintain employment and a place of employment which is safe and healthful. O (2) The process of imparting knowledge or skill through systematic instruction. It does not require formal classroom instruction. O

EEC
European Economic Community, headquartered in Brussels. U

EEI
Edison Electric Institute. N

EENET
Emergency Education Network (FEMA). N

EER
Excess Emission Report. N

effective date
(1) The date of promulgation in the *Federal Register* of an applicable standard or other regulation. A (2) The sum of the products of the dose equivalents to individual organs and tissues and appropriate weighing factors representing the risk relative to that for an equal dose to the whole body. A

effective dose equivalent
The sum of the products of absorbed dose and appropriate factors to account for differences in biological effectiveness due to the quality of radiation and its distribution in the body of reference man. The unit of the effective dose equivalent is the rem. The method for calculating effective dose equivalent and the definition of reference man are outlined in the International Commission on Radiological Protection's Publication No. 26. A

effectively grounded
Intentionally connected to earth through a ground connection or connections of sufficiently low impedance and having sufficient current-carrying capacity to prevent buildup of voltages which may result in undue hazard to connected equipment or to persons. O

effects
(a) Direct effects, which are caused by the action and occur at the same time and place. (b) Indirect effects, which are caused by the action and are later in time or farther removed in distance, but are still reasonably foreseeable. Indirect effects may include growth inducing effects and other effects related to induced changes in the pattern of land use, population density or growth rate, and related effects on air and water and other natural systems, including ecosystems. Effects and impacts as used in these regulations are synonymous. Effects includes ecological (such as the effects on natural resources and on the components, structures, and functioning of affected ecosystems), aesthetic, historic, cultural, economic, social, or health, whether direct, indirect, or cumulative. Effects may also include those resulting from actions which may have both beneficial and detrimental effects,

even if on balance the agency believes that the effect will be beneficial. [ed. Used for determining the application of NEPA]. A

effects on welfare
All language referring to effects on welfare includes, but is not limited to, effects on soils, water, crops, vegetation, man-made materials, animals, wildlife, weather, visibility, and climate, damage to and deterioration of property, and hazards to transportation, as well as effects on economic values and on personal comfort and well being. B

efficacy
The capacity of a pesticide product when used according to label directions to control, kill, or induce the desired action in the target pest. A

efficiency
The ability of the air cleaner of the unit under test to remove contaminant. A

efficiency rating
The degree to which a desired effect takes place. The efficiency rating of a piece of control equipment is based on the proportion of pollution it can remove. U

effluent
(1) Wastewater--treated or untreated--that flows out of a treatment plant, sewer, or industrial outfall. Generally refers to wastes discharged into surface waters. N (2) Dredged material or fill material, including return flow from confined sites. A

effluent limitation
(1) Any restriction imposed by the Director on quantities, discharge rates, and concentrations of pollutants which are discharged from point sources into waters of the United States, the waters of the contiguous zone, or the ocean. A (2) Any effluent limitation which is established as a condition of a permit issued or proposed to be issued by a state or by the Environmental Protection Agency pursuant to section 402 of the Federal Water Pollution Control Act; any toxic or pretreatment effluent standard established under section 307 of the Federal Water Pollution Control Act; any standard of performance established under section 306 of the Federal Water Pollution Control Act; and any effluent limitation established under section 302, section 316, or section 318 of the Federal Water Pollution Control Act. A

effluent limitation guideline
A regulation published by the Administrator under Section 304(b) of the Clean Water Act to adopt or revise effluent limitations. N

effluent standard
Any effluent standard or limitation, which may include a prohibition of any discharge, established or proposed to be established for any toxic pollutant under section 307(a) of the Federal Water Pollution Control Act. A

eggshell thickness
The thickness of the shell and the membrane of the egg at several points around the girth after the egg has been opened, washed out, and the

shell and membrane dried for at least 48 hours at room temperature. Values are expressed as the average thickness of the several measured points in millimeters. A

EGR
Exhaust gas recirculation. N

EHS
Extremely hazardous substances. U

EI
Emissions Inventory. N

EIA
(1) Environmental impact assessment. (2) Economic impact assessment. N

EIL
Environmental impairment liability. N

EIR
(1) Environmental Impact Report. (2) Endangerment Information Report. N

EIS/AS
Emissions Inventory System/Area Source. N

EIS/PS
Emissions Inventory System/Point Source. N

EKMA
Empirical kinetic modeling approach. N

EL
Exposure level. U

electric arc furnace steelmaking
The production of steel principally from steel scrap and fluxes in refractory lined furnaces by passing an electric current through the scrap or steel bath. A

electric sign
A fixed, stationary, or portable self-contained, electrically illuminated utilization equipment with words or symbols designed to convey information or attract attention. O

electric submerged arc furnace
Any furnace wherein electrical energy is converted to heat energy by transmission of current between electrodes partially submerged in the furnace charge. A

electric supply lines
Those conductors used to transmit electric energy and their necessary supporting or containing structures. Signal lines of more than 400 volts to ground are always supply lines within the meaning of the rules, and those of less than 400 volts to ground may be considered as supply lines, if so run and operated throughout. O

electric traction motor
An electrically powered motor which provides tractive energy to the wheels of a vehicle. A

electric utility combined cycle gas turbine
Any combined cycle gas turbine used for electric generation that is constructed for the purpose of supplying more than one-third of its potential electric output capacity and more than 25 MW electrical output to any utility power distribution system for sale. Any steam distribution system that is

constructed for the purpose of providing steam to a steam electric generator that would produce electrical power for sale is also considered in determining the electrical energy output capacity of the affected facility. A

electric utility company
The largest interconnected organization, business or governmental entity that generates electric power for sale (e.g., a holding company with operating subsidiary companies). A

electric utility stationary gas turbine
Any stationary gas turbine constructed for the purpose of supplying more than one-third of its potential electric output capacity to any utility power distribution system for sale. A

electric utility steam generating unit
Any steam electric generating unit that is constructed for the purpose of supplying more than one-third of its potential electric output capacity and more than 25 MW electrical output to any utility power distribution system for sale. Any steam supplied to a steam distribution system for the purpose of providing steam to a steam-electric generator that would produce electrical energy for sale is also considered in determining the electrical energy output capacity of the affected facility. A

electrical charging system
A device to convert 60 Hz alternating electric current, as commonly available in residential electric service in the United States, to a proper form for recharging the energy storage device. A

electrically-heated choke
A device which contains a means for applying heat to the thermostatic coil by electrical current. A

electrocoating
The electrodeposition of a metallic or nonmetallic coating onto the surface of a workpiece. A

electrodialysis
A process that uses electrical current applied to permeable membranes to remove minerals from water. Often used to desalinize salty or brackish water. N

electroless plating
The deposition of conductive material from an autocatalytic plating solution without application of electrical current. A

electromagnetic radiation
Restricted to that portion of the spectrum commonly defined as the radio frequency region, which includes the microwave frequency region. O

electron volt
(eV). A unit of energy equivalent to the energy gained by an electron in passing through a potential difference of one volt. Larger multiples of the electron volt are frequently used: KeV for thousand or kilo electron volts: MeV for million or mega electron volts (1 eV = 1.6 x 10^{-12} erg). U

electronic crystals
Crystals or crystalline material which because of their unique structural and electronic properties are

used in electronic devices. Examples of these crystals are crystals comprised of quartz, ceramic, silicon, gallium arsenide, and idium arsenide. A

elementary neutralization unit
(1) Is used for neutralizing wastes which are hazardous wastes only because they exhibit the corrosivity characteristic defined in 40 CFR § 261.22 of this chapter, or are listed in Subpart D of Part 261 of Title 40 only for this reason; and (2) Meets the definition of tank, container, transport vehicle, or vessel in 40 CFR § 260.10. U

ELF
Extremely low frequency. U

eligible costs
The construction costs for wastewater treatment works upon which EPA grants are based. N

elimination
A reaction of an organic chemical (RX) in water in which the X group is lost. These reactions generally follow the same type of rate laws that hydrolysis reactions follow. A

elutriation
A process for separating lighter particles from heavier particles by washing solid waste with a slowly moving upward stream of fluid that carries the lighter particles with it. It is used in sludge conditioning to reduce the need for conditioning chemicals and to improve sedimentation and filtration by removing excess alkalinity and dissolved solids. U

embryo
(1) The young sporophytic plant before the start of germination. A (2) In mammals, the stage in the developing organism at which organs and organ systems are developing. For humans, this involves the stage of development between the second through eighth weeks (inclusive) post conception. N

embryo cup
A small glass jar or similar container with a screened bottom in which the embryos of some species (i.e., minnow) are placed during the incubation period and which is normally oscillated to ensure a flow of water through the cup. A

embryotoxicity
Any toxic effect on the conceptus as a result of prenatal exposure during the embryonic stages of development. These effects may include malformations and variations, altered growth, in utero death, and altered postnatal function. N

emergency
Any occurrence such as, but not limited to, equipment failure, rupture of containers, or failure of control equipment which may result in a release of--which is (insert appropriate quantitative or qualitative level of release which constitutes an emergency). O

emergency (chemical)
A situation created by an accidental release or spill of hazardous chemicals which poses a threat to the safety of

workers, residents, the environment, or property. N

emergency action plan
A plan for a workplace, or parts thereof, describing what procedures the employer and employees must take to ensure employee safety from fire or other emergencies. O

emergency condition
(1) An urgent, non-routine situation that requires the use of a pesticide(s) and shall be deemed to exist when: (A) no effective pesticides are available under the FIFRA Act that have labeled uses registered for control of the pest under the conditions of the emergency; and (B) no economically or environmentally feasible alternative practices which provide adequate control are available; and (C) the situation: (i) involves the introduction or dissemination of a pest new to or not theretofore known to be widely prevalent or distributed within or throughout the United States and its territories; or (ii) will present significant risks to human health; or (iii) will present significant risks to threatened or endangered species, beneficial organisms, or the environment; or (iv) will cause significant economic loss due to: (a) an outbreak or an expected outbreak of a pest; or (b) a change in plant growth or development caused by unusual environmental conditions where such change can be rectified by the use of a pesticide(s). A (2) That period of time when: (a) The electrical output of an affected facility with a malfunctioning flue gas desulfurization system cannot be reduced or electrical output must be increased because: (1) All available system capacity in the principal company interconnected with the affected facility is being operated, and (2) All available purchase power interconnected with the affected facility is being obtained, or (b) The electric generation demand is being shifted as quickly as possible from an affected facility with a malfunctioning flue gas desulfurization system to one or more electrical generating units held in reserve by the principal company or by a neighboring company, or (c) An affected facility with a malfunctioning flue gas desulfurization system becomes the only available unit to maintain a part or all of the principal company's system emergency reserves and the unit is operated in spinning reserve at the lowest practical electric generation load consistent with not causing significant physical damage to the unit. If the unit is operated at a higher load to meet load demand, an emergency condition would not exist unless the conditions under (a) of this definition apply. A

emergency episode
(See: air pollution episode). N

emergency escape route
The route that employees are directed to follow in the event they are required to evacuate the workplace or seek a designated refuge area. O

emergency fuel
A fuel fired by a gas turbine only during circumstances, such as natural gas supply curtailment or breakdown of delivery system, that makes it

impossible to fire natural gas in the gas turbine. A

emergency gas turbine
Any stationary gas turbine which operates as a mechanical or electrical power source only when the primary power source for a facility has been rendered inoperable by an emergency situation. A

emergency level
For air quality contingency plans, the emergency level indicates that air quality is continuing to degrade toward a level of significant harm to the health of persons and that the most stringent control actions are necessary. An emergency will be declared when any one of the following levels is reached at any monitoring site: (1) SO_2--2,100 ug/m^3 (0.08 ppm), 24-hour average. (2) Particulate--875 ug/m^3, 24-hour average. (3) SO_2 and particulate combined--product of SO_2 ug/m^3, 24-hour average and particulate ug/m^3, 24-hour average equal to 393 x 10^3. (4) CO--46 mg/m^3 (40 ppm), 8-hour average. (5) Ozone (O_3)--1,000 ug/m^3 (0.05 ppm), 1-hour average. (6) NO_2--3,000 ug/m^3 (1.6 ppm), 1-hour average; 750 ug/m^3 (0.04 ppm), 24-hour average and meteorological conditions are such that pollutant concentrations can be expected to remain at the above levels for twelve (12) or more hours or increase, or in the case of ozone, the situation is likely to reoccur within the next 24 hours unless control actions are taken. A

Emergency Management Institute
EMI is a component of FEMA's National Emergency Training Center located in Emmitsburg, Maryland. It conducts resident and nonresident training activities for Federal, State, and local government officials, managers in the private economic sector, and members of professional and volunteer organizations on subjects that range from civil nuclear preparedness systems to domestic emergencies caused by natural and technological hazards. N

emergency permits
For any of the materials listed in [40 CFR] § 227.6, except as trace contaminants, after consultation with the Department of State with respect to the need to consult with parties to the Convention on the Prevention of Marine Pollution by Dumping of Wastes and Other Matter that are likely affected by the dumping, emergency permits may be issued to dump such materials where there is demonstrated to exist an emergency requiring the dumping of such materials, which poses an unacceptable risk relating to human health and admits of no other feasible solution. As used herein, "emergency" refers to situations requiring action with a marked degree of urgency, but is not limited in its application to circumstances requiring immediate action. Emergency permits may be issued for other materials, except those prohibited by § 227.5, without consultation with the Department of State when the Administrator determines that there exists an emergency requiring the dumping of such materials which poses an unacceptable risk to human health and admits of no other feasible solution. A

Emergency Planning and Community Right-to-Know Act of 1986
Title III of Superfund Amendments and Reauthorization Act of 1986 (SARA). N

emergency project
A project involving the removal, enclosure, or encapsulation of friable asbestos-containing material that was not planned but results from a sudden unexpected event. A

emergency renovation operation
A renovation operation that was not planned but results from a sudden, unexpected event that, if not immediately attended to, presents a safety or public health hazard, is necessary to protect equipment from damage, or is necessary to avoid imposing an unreasonable financial burden. This term includes operations necessitated by nonroutine failures of equipment. A

emergency response
A response effort by employees from outside the immediate release area or by other designated responders (i.e., mutual-aid groups, local fire departments, etc.) to an occurrence which results, or is likely to result, in an uncontrolled release of a hazardous substance. Responses to incidental releases of hazardous substances where the substance can be absorbed, neutralized, or otherwise controlled at the time of release by employees in the immediate release area, or by maintenance personnel are not considered to be emergency responses within the scope of this standard. Responses to releases of hazardous substances where there is no potential safety or health hazard (i.e., fire, explosion, or chemical exposure) are not considered to be emergency responses. O

emergency situation (PCB)
For continuing use of a PCB Transformer exists when: (1) Neither a non-PCB transformer nor a PCB-Contaminated transformer is currently in storage for reuse or readily available (i.e., available within 24 hours) for installation. (2) Immediate replacement is necessary to continue service to power users. A

EMF
Electro magnetic field. U

EMI
Emergency Management Institute. U

eminent domain
Government taking--or forced acquisition--of private land for public use, with compensation paid to the landowner. N

emission
(1) Gas-borne pollutants released to the atmosphere. A (2) Pollution discharged into the atmosphere from smokestacks, other vents, and surface areas of commercial or industrial facilities; from residential chimneys; and from motor vehicle, locomotive, or aircraft exhausts. N

emission control diagnostics
Computerized devices placed on vehicles to detect malfunction of emissions controls and notify the owner of the need for repair. N

emission critical parameters
Those critical parameters and tolerances which, if equivalent from one part to another, will not cause the vehicle to exceed applicable emission standards with such parts installed. A

emission factor
The relationship between the amount of pollution produced and the amount of raw material processed. For example, an emission factor for a blast furnace making iron would be the number of pounds of particulates per ton of raw materials. N

emission inventory
A listing, by source, of the amount of air pollutants discharged into the atmosphere of a community. It is used to establish emission standards. N

emission limitation
A requirement established by a State, local government, or the Administrator which limits the quantity, rate, or concentration of emissions of air pollutants on a continuous basis, including any requirements which limit the level of opacity, prescribe equipment, set fuel specifications, or prescribe operation or maintenance procedures for a source to assure continuous emission reduction. A

emission measurement system
All of the equipment necessary to transport and measure the level of emissions. This includes the sample system and the instrumentation system. A

emission outlet pathlength
The depth of effluent at the location emissions are released to the atmosphere. A

emission rate
The amount of pollutant emitted per unit of time. U

emission related parts
Those parts installed for the specific purpose of controlling emissions or those components, systems, or elements of design which must function properly to assure continued vehicle emission compliance. A

emission short test
Any test prescribed under 40 CFR § 85.2201 et seq., and meeting all of the requirements thereunder. A

emission standard
(1) The maximum amount of a pollutant that is permitted to be discharged from a single polluting source; e.g., the number of pounds of fly ash per cubic foot of air that may be emitted from a coal-fired boiler. (2) The maximum amount of air polluting discharge legally allowed from a single source, mobile or stationary. N (3) A legally enforceable regulation setting forth an allowable rate of emissions into the atmosphere, or prescribing equipment specifications for control of air pollution emissions. A (4) See: emission limitation.

emission-related defect
A defect in design, materials, or workmanship in a device, system, or assembly described in the approved Application for Certification (required by 40 CFR § 86.077-22, and like

provisions of Part 85 and Part 86 of Title 40 of the *Code of Federal Regulations*) which affects any parameter or specification enumerated in Appendix VIII. A

emission-related maintenance
That maintenance which does substantially affect emissions or which is likely to affect the deterioration of the vehicle or engine with respect to emissions, even if the maintenance is performed at some time other than that which is recommended. A

emission-related standards
Those critical parameters and tolerances which, if equivalent from one part to another, will not cause the vehicle to exceed applicable emission standards with such parts installed. A

emissions trading
EPA policy that allows a plant complex with several facilities to decrease pollution from some facilities while increasing it from others, so long as total results are equal to or better than previous limits. Facilities where this is done are treated as if they exist in a bubble in which total emissions are averaged out. Complexes that reduce emissions substantially may "bank" their "credits" or sell them to other industries. N

emissions unit
Any part of a stationary source which emits or would have the potential to emit any pollutant subject to regulation under the Clean Air Act. A

employee
(1) A current employee, a former employee, or an employee being assigned or transferred to work where there will be exposure to toxic substances or harmful physical agents. In the case of a deceased or legally incapacitated employee, the employee's legal representative may directly exercise all the employee's rights under this section. O (2) Every laborer or mechanic under the [OSHA] Act regardless of the contractual relationship which may be alleged to exist between the laborer and mechanic and the contractor or subcontractor who engaged him. "Laborer and mechanic" are not defined in the OSHA Act, but the identical terms are used in the Davis-Bacon Act (40 U.S.C. § 276a), which provides for minimum wage protection on Federal and federally assisted construction contracts. The use of the same term in a statute which often applies concurrently with section 107 of the Act has considerable precedential value in ascertaining the meaning of "laborer and mechanic" as used in the Act. "Laborer" generally means one who performs manual labor or who labors at an occupation requiring physical strength; "mechanic" generally means a worker skilled with tools. See 18 Comp. Gen. 341. O

employee exposure
That exposure to airborne asbestos that would occur if the employee were not using respiratory protective equipment. O

employee exposure record
A record containing any of the

following kinds of information: (i) environmental (workplace) monitoring or measuring of a toxic substance or harmful physical agent, including personal, area, grab, wipe, or other form of sampling, as well as related collection and analytical methodologies, calculations, and other background data relevant to interpretation of the results obtained; (ii) biological monitoring results which directly assess the absorption of a toxic substance or harmful physical agent by body systems (e.g., the level of a chemical in the blood, urine, breath, hair, fingernails, etc.) but not including results which assess the biological effect of a substance or agent or which assess an employee's use of alcohol or drugs; (iii) material safety data sheets indicating that the material may pose a hazard to human health; or (iv) in the absence of the above, a chemical inventory or any other record which reveals where and when used and the identity (e.g., chemical, common, or trade name) of a toxic substance or harmful physical agent. O

employee medical record
A record concerning the health status of an employee which is made or maintained by a physician, nurse, or other health care personnel or technician including:
(A) Medical and employment questionnaires or histories (including job description and occupational exposures),
(B) The results of medical examinations (pre-employment, pre-assignment, periodic, or episodic) and laboratory tests (including chest and other X-ray examinations taken for the purposes of establishing a baseline or detecting occupational illness, and all biological monitoring not defined as an "employee exposure record"),
(C) Medical opinions, diagnoses, progress notes, and recommendations,
(D) First aid records,
(E) Descriptions of treatments and prescriptions, and
(F) Employee medical complaints.
(i) "Employee medical record" does not include medical information in the form of:
(A) Physical specimens (e.g., blood or urine samples) which are routinely discarded as a part of normal medical practice; or
(B) Records concerning health insurance claims if maintained separately from the employer's medical program and its records, and not accessible to the employer by employee name or other direct personal identifier (e.g., social security number, payroll number, etc.); or
(C) Records created solely in preparation for litigation which are privileged from discovery under the applicable rules of procedure or evidence; or
(D) Records concerning voluntary employee assistance programs (alcohol, drug abuse, or personal counseling programs) if maintained separately from the employer's medical program and its records. O

employer
(1) A person engaged in a business affecting commerce who has employees, but does not include the United States or any State or political subdivision of a State. H (2) The

public department, agency, or entity which hires an employee. The term includes, but is not limited to, any State, County, City, or other local governmental entity which operates or administers schools, a department of health or human services, a library, a police department, a fire department, or similar public service agencies or offices. A (3) Any manufacturer, importer, processor, or user of chemical substances or mixtures. A

employment facility
Any single location of a business nature with 250 or more employees working, at minimum, the same six core hours. A

EMS
Enforcement Management System under NPDES program. D

EMTS
Exposure Monitoring Test Site. N

emulsified asphalts
Asphalts dispersed in water with an emulsifying agent. A

emulsion
A mechanical mixture of two liquids which do not naturally mix as oil and water. Water-in-oil emulsions have the water as the internal phase and oil as the external. Oil-in-water emulsions have water as the external phase and the internal phase is oil. A

encapsulate
To seal a pesticide, and its container if appropriate, in an impervious container made of plastic, glass, or other suitable material which will not be chemically degraded by the contents. This container then should be sealed within a durable container made from steel, plastic, concrete, or other suitable material of sufficient thickness and strength to resist physical damage during and subsequent to burial or storage. A

encapsulation
The treatment of ACBM with a material that surrounds or embeds asbestos fibers in an adhesive matrix to prevent the release of fibers, as the encapsulant creates a membrane over the surface (bridging encapsulant) or penetrates the material and binds its components together (penetrating encapsulant). A

enclosed
Surrounded by a case, cage, or fence, which will protect the contained equipment and prevent accidental contact of a person with live parts. O

enclosed process
A manufacturing or processing operation that is designed and operated so that there is no intentional release into the environment of any substance present in the operation. An operation with fugitive, inadvertent, or emergency pressure relief releases remains an enclosed process so long as measures are taken to prevent worker exposure to and environmental contamination from the releases. A

enclosure
(1) The case or housing of apparatus, or the fence or walls

surrounding an installation to prevent personnel from accidentally contacting energized parts, or to protect the equipment from physical damage. O (2) An airtight, impermeable, permanent barrier around ACBM to prevent the release of asbestos fibers into the air. A

end box
A container(s) located on one or both ends of a mercury chlor-alkali electrolyzer which serves as a connection between the electrolyzer and denuder for rich and stripped amalgam. A

end box ventilation system
A ventilation system which collects mercury emissions from the end-boxes, the mercury pump sumps, and their water collection systems. A

end use product
A pesticide product whose labeling (1) includes directions for use of the product (as distributed or sold, or after combination by the user with other substances) for controlling pests or defoliating, desiccating, or regulating the growth of plants, and (2) Does not state that the product may be used to manufacture or formulate other pesticide products. A

endangered species
Animals, birds, fish, plants, or other living organisms threatened with extinction by man-made or natural changes in their environment. Requirements for declaring a species endangered are contained in the Endangered Species Act. N

endangerment assessment
(1) A site-specific risk assessment of the actual or potential danger to human health or welfare and the environment from the release of hazardous substances or waste. The endangerment assessment document is prepared in support of enforcement actions under CERCLA or RCRA. N (2) A study conducted to determine the nature and extent of contamination at a site on the National Priorities List and the risks posed to public health of the environment. EPA or the state conduct the study when a legal action is to be taken to direct potentially responsible parties to clean up a site or pay for the cleanup. An endangerment assessment supplements a remedial investigation. N

endemic
Present in a community or among a group of people; said of a disease prevailing continually in a region. N

endothelial
Pertaining to the layer of flat cells lining the inner surface of blood and lymphatic blood vessels, and the surface lining of serosa and synovial membranes. N

endpoint
A biological effect used as an index of the effect of a chemical on an organism. N

energized
Connected to an energy source or containing residual or stored energy. O

energy
The capacity to do work. It may take a number of forms, among them mechanical, chemical, and radiant, and can be transformed from one form to another, but cannot be created or destroyed. U

energy average level
A quantity calculated by taking ten times the common logarithm of the arithmetic average of the antilogs of one-tenth of each of the levels being averaged. The levels may be of any consistent type, e.g. maximum sound levels, sound exposure levels, and day-night sound levels. A

energy recovery
A form of resource recovery in which the organic fraction of waste is converted to some form of usable energy, such as burning processed or raw refuse to produce steam. U

energy storage device
A rechargeble means of storing tractive energy on board a vehicle such as storage batteries or a flywheel. A

energy summation of levels
A quantity calculated by taking ten times the common logarithm of the sum of the antilogs of one-tenth of each of the levels being summed. The levels may be of any consistent type, e.g., day-night sound level or equivalent sound level. A

enforceable requirements of the Act
Those conditions or limitations of section 402 or 404 [FWPCA] permits which, if violated, could result in the issuance of a compliance order or initiation of a civil or criminal action under section 309 of the Act. If a permit has not been issued, the term shall include any requirement which, in the Regional Administrator's judgment, would be included in the permit when issued. Where no permit applies, the term shall include any requirement which the Regional Administrator determines is necessary to meet applicable criteria for best practicable waste treatment technology (BPWTT). A

enforcement
EPA, state, or local legal actions to obtain compliance with environmental laws, rules, regulations, or agreements and/or obtain penalties or criminal sanctions for violations. Enforcement procedures may vary, depending on the specific requirements of different environmental laws and related implementing regulatory requirements. Under CERCLA, for example, EPA will seek to require potentially responsible parties to clean up a Superfund site, or pay for the cleanup, whereas under the Clean Air Act the agency may invoke sanctions against cities failing to meet ambient air quality standards that could prevent certain types of construction or federal funding. In other situations, if investigations by EPA and state agencies uncover willful violations, criminal trials and penalties are sought. N

Enforcement Decision Document
EDD. A document that provides an explanation to the public of EPA's selection of the cleanup alternative at enforcement sites on the National

Priorities List. Similar to a Record of Decision. N

Enforcement Division Director
One of the Directors of the Enforcement Divisions within the Regional offices of the Environmental Protection Agency or the designated representative of the Enforcement Division Director. A

engine code
A unique combination, within an engine-system combination (as defined in 40 CFR Part 86), of displacement, carburetor (or fuel injection) calibration, distributor calibration, choke calibration, auxiliary emission control devices and other engine and emission control system components specified by the Administrator of EPA. A

engine configuration
A subclassification of an engine-system combination on the basis of engine code, inertia weight class, transmission type and gear ratios, final drive ratio, and other parameters which may be designated by the Administrator of EPA. A

engine displacement
Volumetric engine capacity as defined in 40 CFR § 205.153. A

engine family
The basic classification unit of a vehicle's product line for a single model year used for the purpose of emission-data vehicle or engine selection and as determined in accordance with 40 CFR 86.078-24. A

engine family group
A combination of engine families for the purpose of determining a minimum deterioration factor under the Alternative Durability Program. A

engine lubricating oils
Petroleum-based oils used for reducing friction in engine parts. A

engine malfunction
Not operating according to specifications (e.g., those specifications listed in the application for [motor vehicle] certification). A

engine model
All commercial aircraft turbine engines which are of the same general series, displacement, and design characteristics and are usually approved under the same type certificate. A

engine sidescreen
A rugged screen that fits on the engine housing of a vehicle used at a sanitary landfill to prevent paper and other objects from accumulating and damaging the engine. U

engine-displacement-system combination
An engine family-displacement-emission control system combination. A

engine-system combination
An engine family-exhaust emission control system combination. A

engineered storage
This disposal method is considered a last alternative for those wastes for which no adequate disposal methods

exist (particularly radioactive wastes). A facility would temporarily store harmful substances until a permanent disposal site is developed. Engineered storage facilities must provide safe keeping for solidified hazardous wates for long periods of time and the wastes must be retrievable at any point in time. This method is being proposed as an option for long term storage of high-level radioactive wastes. U

engineering controls
Controls (e.g., sharps disposal containers, self-sheathing needles) that isolate or remove the bloodborne pathogens hazard from the workplace. O

enhanced inspection & maintenance (enhanced I&M)
An improved automobile inspection and maintenance program that includes, as a minimum, increases in coverage of vehicle types and model years, tighter stringency of inspections and improved management practices to ensure more effectiveness. This may also include annual, computerized, or centralized inspections; under-the-hood inspections to detect tampering with pollution control equipment; and increased repair waiver cost. The purpose of Enhanced I&M is to reduce automobile emissions by assuring that cars are running properly. N

enrichment
The addition of nutrients (e.g., nitrogen, phosphorous, carbon compounds) from sewage effluent or agricultural runoff to surface water. This process greatly increases the growth potential for algae and aquatic plants. N

envelopes
Brown, manila, padded, or other mailing envelopes not included with "stationery." O

environment
(1) The natural and physical environment and excludes social, economic and other environments. A (2) Water, air, land, and all plants and man and other animals living therein, and the interrelationships which exist among these. C (3) (a) The navigable waters, the waters of the contiguous zone, and the ocean waters of which the natural resources are under the exclusive management authority of the United States under the Fishery Conservation and Management Act of 1976, and (b) any other surface water, ground water, drinking water supply, land surface or subsurface strata, or ambient air within the United States or under the jurisdiction of the United States. L (4) The sum of all external conditions affecting the life, development and survival of an organism. N

Environmental Appeals Board
The Board within the EPA described in [40 CFR] § 1.25. The Administrator delegates authority to the Environmental Appeals Board to issue final decisions in appeals filed under this part. An appeal directed to the Administrator, rather than to the Environmental Appeals Board, will not be considered. This delegation of authority to the Environmental Appeals Board does not preclude the

Environmental Appeals Board from referring an appeal or motion filed under this part to the Administrator for decision when the Environmental Appeals Board, in its discretion, deems it appropriate to do so. When an appeal or motion is referred to the Administrator, all parties shall be so notified and the rules in this part referring to the Environmental Appeals Board shall be interpreted as referring to the Administrator. A

environmental assessment
(1) A written environmental analysis which is prepared pursuant to the National Environmental Policy Act to determine whether a federal action would significantly affect the environment and thus require preparation of a more detailed environmental impact statement. N (2) A concise public document for which a Federal agency is responsible that serves to: (a) Briefly provide sufficient evidence and analysis for determining whether to prepare an environmental impact statement or a finding of no significant impact. (b) Aid an agency's compliance with the Act when no environmental impact statement is necessary. (c) Facilitate preparation of a statement when one is necessary. (3) Shall include brief discussions of the need for the proposal, of alternatives as required by § 102(2)(E) of NEPA, of the environmental impacts of the proposed action and alternatives, and a listing of agencies and persons consulted. A

environmental audit
(1) An independent assessment of the current status of a company's compliance with applicable environmental requirements. (2) An independent evaluation of a company's environmental compliance policies, practices, and controls. N

environmental education and training
Educational activities and training activities involving elementary, secondary, and postsecondary students, as such terms are defined in the State in which they reside, and environmental education personnel, but does not include technical training activities directed toward environmental management professionals or activities primarily directed toward the support of noneducational research and development. A

environmental fate
The destiny of a chemical or biological pollutant after release into the environment. Environmental fate involves temporal and spatial considerations of transport, transfer, storage, and transformation. N

environmental impact appraisal
An environmental review supporting a negative declaration [i.e., the action is not a major Federal action significantly affecting the environment]. It describes a proposed EPA action, its expected environmental impact, and the basis for the conclusion that no significant impact is anticipated [and no NEPA Statement is required]. A

Environmental Impact Assessment
EIA. The report, prepared by the applicant for an NPDES permit to

discharge as a new source, which identifies and analyzes the environmental impacts of the applicant's proposed source and feasible alternatives. U

Environmental Impact Statement
EIS. A document required of federal agencies by the National Environmental Policy Act for major projects or legislative proposals significantly affecting the environment. A tool for decision making, it describes the positive and negative effects of the undertaking and lists alternative actions. N

environmental information document
Any written analysis prepared by an applicant, grantee or contractor describing the environmental impacts of a proposed action. This document will be of sufficient scope to enable the responsible official to prepare an environmental assessment as described in the remaining subparts of this regulation. A

environmental noise
The intensity, duration, and the character of sounds from all sources. A

Environmental Protection Agency
EPA. An independent agency of the Federal government formed in 1970 and responsible for pollution abatement and control programs, including programs in air and water pollution control, water supply and radiation protection, solid and toxic waste management, pesticides control, and noise abatement. U

Environmental Response Team
EPA experts located in Edison, NJ, and Cincinnati, OH, who can provide around-the-clock technical assistance to EPA regional offices and states during all types of emergencies involving hazardous waste sites and spills of hazardous substances. N

Environmental Review
The process whereby an evaluation is undertaken by EPA to determine whether a proposed Agency action may have a significant impact on the environment and therefore require the preparation of the EIS. A

environmental transformation product
Any chemical substance resulting from the action of environmental processes on a parent compound that changes the molecular identity of the parent compound. A

environmentally related measurements
Any data collection activity or investigation involving the assessment of chemical, physical, or biological factors in the environment which affect human health or the quality of life. The following are examples of environmentally related measurements: (a) a determination of pollutant concentrations from sources or in the ambient environment, including studies of pollutant transport and fate; (b) a determination of the effects of pollutants on human health and on the environment; (c) a determination of the risk/benefit of pollutants in the environment; (d) a determination of the quality of environmental data used in economic studies; and (e) a determination of the environmental

impact of cultural and natural processes. A

environmentally sensitive areas
Areas having beneficial qualities or termed "natural assets" by the Environmental Protection Agency, which include wetlands, floodplains, permafrost areas, critical habitats of endangered species, and recharge zones of sole-source aquifers. U

environmentally transformed
A chemical substance is "environmentally transformed" when its chemical structure changes as a result of the action of environmental processes on it. A

enzyme
Any of numerous substances produced by living cells that affect or bring about chemical changes in the body without being changed themselves. U

EOP
End of pipe. U

EP
(1) Extraction Procedure. U (2) End point. U

EP tox
Extraction procedure toxicity. U

EPA
The U.S. Environmental Protection Agency, established in 1970 by Presidential Executive Order, bringing together parts of various government agencies involved with the control of pollution. N

EPA assistance
Any grant or cooperative agreement, loan, contract (other than a procurement contract or a contract of insurance or guaranty), or any other arrangement by which EPA provides or otherwise makes available assistance in the form of: (1) Funds; (2) Services of personnel; or (3) Real or personal property or any interest in or use of such property, including: (i) Transfers or leases of such property for less than fair market value or for reduced consideration; and (ii) Proceeds from a subsequent transfer or lease of such property if EPA's share of its fair market value is not returned to EPA. A

EPA Enforcement Officer
Any officer or employee of the Environmental Protection Agency so designated in writing by the Administrator (or by his designee). A

EPA hazardous waste number
The number assigned by EPA to each hazardous waste listed in part 261, subpart D, [of 40 CFR parts 260-299] and to each characteristic identified in part 261, subpart C. A

EPA identification number
(1) The number assigned by EPA to each generator, transporter, and treatment, storage, or disposal facility. A (2) PCB. The 12-digit number assigned to a facility by EPA upon notification of PCB waste activity under [40 CFR] § 761.205. A

EPA Legal Office
The EPA General Counsel and any EPA office over which the General

Counsel exercises supervisory authority, including the various Offices of Regional Counsel. A

EPA office
Any organizational element of EPA, at any level or location. The terms "EPA office" and "EPA legal office" are used in subpart [B of 40 CFR parts 1-51] for the sake of brevity and ease of reference. A

EPA record
Any document, writing, photograph, sound or magnetic recording, drawing, or other similar thing by which information has been preserved, from which the information can be retrieved and copied, and which is, was, or is alleged to be possessed by EPA and used to support an EPA decision or action. The term includes informal writings (such as handwritten notes, drafts, and the like), and also includes information preserved in a form which must be translated or deciphered by machine in order to be intelligible to humans. The term includes documents and the like which were created or acquired by EPA, its predecessors, its officers, and employees by use of Government funds or in the course of transacting official business. However, the term does not include materials which are legally owned by an EPA officer or employee in his or her purely personal capacity. Nor does the term include materials published by non-Federal organizations which are readily available to the public, such as books, journals, and periodicals available through reference libraries, even if such materials are in EPA's possession. U

EPA region
The states and territories found in any one of the following ten regions:
Region I-Maine, Vermont, New Hampshire, Massachusetts, Connecticut, and Rhode Island.
Region II - New York, New Jersey, Commonwealth of Puerto Rico, and the U.S. Virgin Islands.
Region III - Pennsylvania, Delaware, Maryland, West Virginia, Virginia, and the District of Columbia.
Region IV - Kentucky, Tennessee, North Carolina, Mississippi, Alabama, Georgia, South Carolina, and Florida.
Region V - Minnesota, Wisconsin, Illinois, Michigan, Indiana, and Ohio.
Region VI - New Mexico, Oklahoma, Arkansas, Louisiana, and Texas.
Region VII - Nebraska, Kansas, Missouri, and Iowa.
Region VIII - Montana, Wyoming, North Dakota, South Dakota, Utah, and Colorado.
Region IX - California, Nevada, Arizona, Hawaii, Guam, American Samoa, Commonwealth of the Northern Mariana Islands.
Region X - Washington, Oregon, Idaho, and Alaska. N

EPA share
That portion of allowable project costs provided by EPA under EPA grant programs. A

EPA-approved emission test
Any test prescribed under 40 CFR § 85.2201 *et seq.*, and meeting all of the requirements thereunder. A

ephippium
A resting egg which develops under

the carapace in response to stress conditions in daphnids. A

epidemic
Widespread outbreak of a disease, or a large number of cases of a disease in a single community or relatively small area. N

epidemiology
The study of diseases as they affect population, including the distribution of disease, or other health-related states and events in human populations, the factors (e.g. age, sex, occupation, economic status) that influence this distribution, and the application of this study to control health problems. N

episode (pollution)
An air pollution incident in a given area caused by a concentration of atmospheric pollution reacting with meteorological conditions that may result in a significant increase in illnesses or deaths. Although most commonly used in relation to air pollution, the term may also be used in connection with other kinds of environmental events such as a massive water pollution situation. N

epithelial
Pertaining to the cell layer that covers all internal and external surfaces of the body, including the gastrointestinal, respiratory, and urinary tracts. N

EPR
Engine pressure ratio. U

EPTC
Extraction Procedure Toxicity Characteristic Test. N

eq.
Equivalent. U

equilibrium
(1) The state in which opposing forces are exactly counteracted or balanced. Types of equilibrium include acid-base, colloid, dynamic, homeostatic, and chemical. Used in risk assessment of toxic air pollutants to generally describe the chemical equilibrium between a pollutant in the inhaled air and the level in the body. N (2) In relation to radiation, the state at which the radioactivity of consecutive elements within a radioactive series is neither increasing nor decreasing. N

equipment room
A contaminated room located within the decontamination area that is supplied with impermeable bags or containers for the disposal of contaminated protective clothing and equipment. A

equivalence data
Chemical data or biological test data intended to show that two substances or mixtures are equivalent. A

equivalent
(1) That a chemical substance or mixture is able to represent or substitute for another in a test or series of tests, and that the data from one substance can be used to make scientific and regulatory decisions concerning the other substance. A

(2) Alternative designs, materials, or methods that the employer can demonstrate will provide an equal or greater degree of safety for employees than the method or item specified in the standard. O

equivalent method
Any method of sampling and analyzing for an air pollutant which has been demonstrated to the Administrator's satisfaction to have a consistent and quantitatively known relationship to the reference method, under specified conditions. A

equivalent petroleum-based fuel economy value
A number which represents the average number of miles traveled by an electric vehicle per gallon of gasoline. A

equivalent sound level
The level, in decibels, of the mean-square A-weighted sound pressure during a stated time period, with reference to the square of the standard reference sound pressure of 20 micropascals. It is the level of the sound exposure divided by the time period and is abbreviated as L_{eq}. A

equivalent test weight
The weight, within an inertia weight class, which is used in the dynamometer testing of a vehicle and which is based on its loaded vehicle weight or adjusted loaded vehicle weight. A

ERA
(1) Economic Regulatory Administration of the U.S. Department of Energy. (2) Expedited response action. N

erase stack
An expanding connection on the outlet of a fan or in an airflow passage to convert kinetic energy into static pressure. U

erosion
The wearing away of land surface by wind or water. Erosion occurs naturally from weather or runoff but can be intensified by land-clearing practices related to farming, residential or industrial development, road building, or timber-cutting. N

ERP
Enforcement response policy, at EPA, aimed at high priority violators under RCRA. U

ERT
Environmental Response Team. U

ESP
Electrostatic precipitator. U

established federal standard
Any operative occupational safety and health standard established by any agency of the United States and presently in effect, or contained in any Act of Congress in force on the date of enactment of [OSHA]. H

establishment
(1) Each site where a pesticide, as defined by FIFRA, or a device is produced, regardless of whether such site is independently owned or operated and regardless of whether such site is domestic and producing

any pesticide or device for export only or whether the site is foreign and producing any pesticide or device for import into the United States. A (2) Any place where a pesticide or device or active ingredient used in producing a pesticide is produced, or held, for distribution or sale. C (3) A single physical location where business is conducted or where services or industrial operations are performed. (For example: A factory, mill, store, hotel, restaurant, movie theater, farm, ranch, bank, sales office, warehouse, or central administrative office). Where distinctly separate activities are performed at a single physical location (such as contract construction activities operated from the same physical location as a lumber yard), each activity shall be treated as a separate establishment. (4) For firms engaged in activities such as agriculture, construction, transportation, communications, and electric, gas and sanitary services, which may be physically dispersed, records may be maintained at a place to which employees report each day. (5) Records for personnel who do not primarily report or work at a single establishment, and who are generally not supervised in their daily work, such as traveling salesmen, technicians, engineers, etc., shall be maintained at the location from which they are paid or the base from which personnel operate to carry out their activities. O

estuarine zones
An environmental system consisting of an estuary and those transitional areas which are consistently influenced or affected by water from an estuary such as, but not limited to, salt marshes, coastal and intertidal areas, bays, harbors, lagoons, inshore waters, and channels, and the term "estuary" means all or part of the mouth of a river or stream or other body of water having unimpaired natural connection with open sea and within which the sea water is measurably diluted. U

estuary
Region of interaction between rivers and nearshore ocean waters, where tidal action and river flow create a mixing of fresh and salt water. These areas may include bays, mouths of rivers, salt marshes, and lagoons. These brackish water ecosystems shelter and feed marine life, birds, and wildlife. (See: wetlands). N

etching
See cleaning. A

ethanol blending plant
Any refinery at which gasoline is produced solely through the addition of ethanol to gasoline, and at which the quality or quantity of gasoline is not altered in any other manner. A

ethylene dibromide
EDB. A chemical used as an agricultural fumigant and in certain industrial processes. Extremely toxic and found to be a carcinogen in laboratory animals. EDB has been banned for most agricultural uses in the United States. N

etiology
All of the factors that contribute to the cause of a disease or an abnormal condition; a branch of medical science

concerned with the causes and origins of disease. N

ETS
Environmental tobacco smoke. U

eutrophic lakes
(1) Shallow, murky bodies of water that have excessive concentrations of plant nutrients causing excessive algal production. (See: dystrophic lakes). N (2) A lake that exhibits any of the following characteristics: (a) Excessive biomass accumulations of primary producers; (b) rapid organic and/or inorganic sedimentation and shallowing; or (c) seasonal and/or diurnal dissolved oxygen deficiencies that may cause obnoxious odors, fish kills, or a shift in the composition of aquatic fauna to less desirable forms. A

eutrophication
The slow aging process during which a lake, estuary, or bay evolves into a bog or marsh and eventually disappears. During the later stages of eutrophication the water body is choked by abundant plant life as the result of increased amounts of nutritive compounds such as nitrogen and phosphorus. Human activities that add nutrients to a water body can accelerate the process. N

evap.
Evaporative. U

evaporation
The physical transformation of a liquid to a gas at any temperature below its boiling point. U

evaporation ponds
Areas where sewage sludge or other wastes are dumped and allowed to dry out. N

evaporation rate
The rate at which a material will vaporize (evaporate) when compared to the known rate of vaporization of a standard material. The evaporation rate can be useful in evaluating the health and fire hazards of a material. The designated standard material is usually normal butyl acetate (NBUAC or n-BuAc), with a vaporization rate designated as 1.0. Vaporization rates of other solvents or materials are then classified as: FAST evaporating if greater than 3.0. Examples: Methyl Ethyl Ketone = 3.8, Acetone = 5.6, Hexane = 8.3.; MEDIUM evaporating if 0.8 to 3.0 Examples: 190 proof (95%) Ethyl Alcohol = 1.4, VM&P Naphtha = 1.4, MIBK = 1.6.; SLOW evaporating if less than 0.8. Examples: Xylene = 0.6, Isobutyl Alcohol = 0.6, Normal Butyl Alcohol = 0.4, Water = 0.3, Mineral Spirits = 0.1. N

evaporative emission code
A unique combination in an evaporative emission family on a vehicle--evaporative emission control system combination, of purge system calibrations, fuel tank and carburetor bowl vent calibrations and other fuel system and evaporative emission control system components and calibrations specified by the Administrator of EPA. A

evaporative emissions
Hydrocarbons emitted into the

atmosphere from a motor vehicle, other than exhaust and crankcase emissions. A

evaporative vehicle configuration
A unique combination of basic engine, engine code, body type, and evaporative emission code. A

evapotranspiration
The loss of water from the soil both by evaporation and by transpiration from the plants growing in the soil. N

excavation
Any man-made cut, cavity, trench, or depression in an earth surface, formed by earth removal. O

excavation zone
The volume containing the tank system and backfill material bounded by the ground surface, walls, and floor of the pit and trenches into which the UST system is placed at the time of installation. A

exceedance
Violation of environmental protection standards by exceeding allowable limits or concentration levels. N

exception report
A report that generators who transport waste off-site must submit to the Regional Administrator [EPA] if they do not receive a copy of the manifest signed and dated by the owner or operator of the designated facility to which their waste was shipped within 45 days from the date on which the initial transporter accepted the waste. N

exposure information report
An assessment of the potential public exposure to hazardous substances. This report(s) accompanies a facility permit application, and review of this report(s) becomes part of the Administrative Record. N

excess ammonia-liquor storage tank
Any tank, reservoir, or container used to collect or store a flushing liquor solution prior to ammonia or phenol recovery. A

excess combustion air
The quantity of air in excess of theoretical air, and usually expressed as a percentage of the theoretical air. U

excess emissions
An [air pollutant] emission rate which exceeds any applicable emission limitation. The averaging time and test procedures for determining such excess emissions shall be as specified as part of the applicable emission limitation. A

excess emissions and monitoring systems performance report
A report that must be submitted periodically by a source in order to provide data on its compliance with stated emission limits and operating parameters, and on the performance of its monitoring systems. A

excess risk
An increased risk of disease above the normal background rate. N

excessive concentrations
For the purpose of determining good

engineering practice stack height in a fluid model or field study, a maximum concentration due to downwash wakes, or eddy effects produced by structures or terrain features which is at least 40 percent in excess of the maximum concentration experienced in the absence of such downwash, wakes or eddy effects. A

excessive infiltration/inflow
The quantities of infiltration/inflow which can be economically eliminated from a sewerage system by rehabilitation, as determined in a cost-effectiveness analysis that compares the costs for correcting the infiltration/inflow conditions to the total costs for transportation and treatment of the infiltration/inflow, subject to the provisions in [40 CFR] § 35.927. A

excluded manufacturing process (PCB)
A manufacturing process in which quantities of PCBs, as determined in accordance with the definition of inadvertently generated PCBs, calculated as defined, and from which releases to products, air, and water meet the requirements of paragraphs (1) through (5) of this definition, or the importation of products containing PCBs as unintentional impurities, which products meet the requirements of paragraphs (1) and (2) of this definition. (1) The concentration of inadvertently generated PCBs in products leaving any manufacturing site or imported into the United States must have an average of less than 25 ppm, with a 50 ppm maximum. (2) The concentration of inadvertently generated PCBs in components of detergent bars leaving the manufacturing site or imported into the United States must be less than 5 ppm. (3) The release of inadvertently generated PCBs at the point at which emissions are vented to ambient air must be less than 10 ppm. (4) The amount of inadvertently generated PCBs added to water discharged from a manufacturing site must be less than 100 micrograms per resolvable gas chromatographic peak per liter of water discharged. (5) Disposal of any other process wastes above concentrations of 50 ppm PCB must be in accordance with subpart D of this part. A

excluded PCB products
PCB materials which appear at concentrations less than 50 ppm, including but not limited to: (1) Non-Aroclo inadvertently generated PCBs as a byproduct or impurity resulting from a chemical manufacturing process. (2) Products contaminated with Aroclor or other PCB materials from historic PCB uses (investment casting waxes are one example). (3) Recycled fluids and/or equipment contaminated during use involving the products described in paragraphs (1) and (2) of this definition (heat transfer and hydraulic fluids and equipment and other electrical equipment components and fluids are examples). (4) used oils, provided that in the cases of paragraphs (1) through (4) of this definition: (i) The products or source of the products containing less than 50 ppm concentration PCBs were legally manufactured, processed, distributed in commerce, or used before October 1, 1984. (ii) The

products or source of the products containing less than 50 ppm concentrations PCBs were legally manufactured, processed, distributed in commerce, or used, i.e., pursuant to authority granted by EPA regulation, by exemption petition, by settlement agreement, or pursuant to other Agency-approved programs; (iii) The resulting PCB concentration (i.e., below 50 ppm) is not a result of dilution, or leaks and spills of PCBs in concentrations over 50 ppm. A

exclusionary
Any form of zoning ordinance that tends to exclude specific classes of persons or businesses from a particular district or area. N

exclusive bus lane
A lane on a street or highway for the exclusive use of buses, whether constructed especially for that purpose or converted from an existing lane. A

exclusive use study
A study that meets each of the following requirements: (1) The study pertains to a new active ingredient (new chemical) or new combination of active ingredients (new combination) first registered after September 30, 1978; (2) The study was submitted in support of, or as a condition of approval of, the application resulting in the first registration of a product containing such new chemical or new combination (first registration), or an application to amend such registration to add a new use; and (3) The study was not submitted to satisfy a data requirement imposed under FIFRA section 3(c)(2)(B); Provided that, a study is an exclusive study only during the 10-year period following the date of the first registration. A

excretion
Elimination or discharge of excess and waste chemicals from the body. Chemicals may be excreted through feces, urine, exhaled breath, etc. N

exempt solvent
Specific organic compounds that are not subject to requirements of regulation because they have been deemed by EPA to be of negligible photochemical reactivity. N

exempted aquifer
Underground bodies of water defined in the Underground Injection Control program as aquifers that are sources of drinking water (although they are not being used as such) and that are exempted from regulations barring underground injection activities. N

exemption
An exemption from a testing requirement of a test rule promulgated under section 4 of the [TSCA] Act and part 799. A

exemption application
Any application submitted to EPA under section 5(h)(2) of the [TSCA] Act. A

exemption category
A category of chemical substances for which a person(s) has applied for or been granted an exemption under section 5(h)(4) of the Toxic Substances Control Act. A

ENVIRONMENTAL REGULATORY GLOSSARY

exemption certification
A certified statement delineating those actions specifically exempted from NEPA compliance by existing legislation. A

exemption notice
Any notice submitted to EPA under [40 CFR] § 723.175. A

exhaust emissions
Substances emitted to the atmosphere from any opening downstream from the exhaust port of a motor vehicle engine. A

exhaust gas
Any offgas (the constituents of which may consist of any fluids, either as a liquid and/or gas) discharged directly or ultimately to the atmosphere that was initially contained in or was in direct contact with the equipment for which gas limits are prescribed in 40 CFR §§ 61.62(a) and (b); 61.63(a); 61.64(a)(1),(b),(c), and (d); 61.65 (b)(1)(ii), (b)(2), (b)(3), (b)(5), (b)(6)(ii), (b)(7), and (b)(9)(ii); and 61.65(d). A leak as defined in paragraph (w) of this section is not an exhaust gas. Equipment which contains exhaust gas is subject to § 61.65(b)(8), whether or not that equipment contains 10 percent by volume vinyl chloride. A

exhaust gas recirculation-air bleed
EGR. A system or device (such as modification of the engine's carburetor or positive crankcase ventilation system) that results in engine operation at an increased air-fuel ratio so as to achieve reductions in exhaust emissions of hydrocarbons and carbon monoxide. A

exhaust header pipe
Any tube of constant diameter which conducts exhaust gas from an engine exhaust port to other exhaust system components which provide noise attenuation. Tubes with cross connections or internal baffling are not considered to be "exhaust header pipes." O

exhaust system
The system comprised of a combination of components which provides for enclosed flow of exhaust gas from engine exhaust port to the atmosphere. A

exhauster
A fan located between the inlet gas flange and outlet gas flange of the coke oven gas line that provides motive power for coke oven gases. A

existing facility
(1) With reference to a stationary source, any apparatus of the type for which a new source performance standard is promulgated and the construction or modification of which was commenced before the date of proposal of that standard; or any apparatus which could be altered in such a way as to be of that type. A
(2) A facility which was in operation or for which construction began on or before November 19, 1980. N

existing hazardous waste management (HWM) facility (existing facility)
A facility which was in operation or for which construction commenced on

or before November 19, 1980. A facility has commenced construction if: (1) The owner or operator has obtained the Federal, State and local approvals or permits necessary to begin physical construction; and either (2)(i) A continuous on-site, physical construction program has begun; or (ii) The owner or operator has entered into contractual obligations--which cannot be cancelled or modified without substantial loss--for physical construction of the facility to be completed within a reasonable time. A

existing impoundment
Any uranium mill tailings impoundment which is licensed to accept additional tailings and is in existence as of December 15, 1989. A

existing indirect dischargers
Only those two iron blast furnace operations with discharges to publicly owned treatment works prior to May 27, 1982. A

existing injection well
An injection well other than a new injection well. N

existing MSWLF unit
Any municipal solid waste landfill unit that is receiving solid waste. Waste placement in existing units must be consistent with past operating practices or modified practices to ensure good management. A

existing source
Any stationary source which is not a new source. A

existing tank system or existing component
A tank system or component that is used for the storage or treatment of hazardous waste and that is in operation, or for which installation has commenced on or prior to July 14, 1986. Installation will be considered to have commenced if the owner or operator has obtained all Federal, State, and local approvals or permits necessary to begin physical construction of the site or installation of the tank system and if either (1) a continuous on-site physical construction or installation program has begun, or (2) the owner or operator has entered into contractual obligations-- which cannot be canceled or modified without substantial loss--for physical construction of the site or installation of the tank system to be completed within a reasonable time. A

existing vessel
Includes every description of watercraft or other artificial contrivance used, or capable of being used, as a means of transportation on the navigable waters, the construction of which is initiated before promulgation of standards and regulations under [§ 312 of FWPCA]. D

expedited hearing
A hearing commenced as the result of the issuance of a notice of intention to suspend or the suspension of a registration of a pesticide by an emergency order, and is limited to a consideration as to whether a pesticide presents an imminent hazard which justifies such suspension. A

expendable personal property
Expendable personal property refers to all tangible personal property (including consumable materials) other than nonexpendable personal property. A

experimental animals
Individual animals or groups of animals, regardless of species, intended for use and used solely for research purposes and does not include animals intended to be used for any food purposes. A

experimental start date
The first date the test substance is applied to the test system. A

experimental technology
Means a technology which has not been proven feasible under the conditions in which it is being tested. A

experimental termination date
The last date on which data are collected directly from the study. A

experimental use permit review
Review of an application for a permit pursuant to section 5 of FIFRA to apply a limited quantity of a pesticide in order to accumulate information necessary to register the pesticide. The application may be for a new chemical or for a new use of an old chemical. The fee applies to such experimental uses of a single unregistered active ingredient (no limit on the number of other active ingredients, in a tank mix, already registered for the crops involved) and no more than three crops. This fee does not apply to experimental use permits required for small-scale field testing of microbial pest control agents (40 CFR 172.3). A

expiratory (maximum) flow rate
The maximum rate at which air can be expelled from the lungs. U

explosion-proof apparatus
Apparatus enclosed in a case that is capable of withstanding an explosion of a specified gas or vapor which may occur within it and of preventing the ignition of a specified gas or vapor surrounding the enclosure by sparks, flashes, or explosion of the gas or vapor within, and which operates at such an external temperature that it will not ignite a surrounding flammable atmosphere. O

explosive
A chemical that causes a sudden, almost instantaneous release of pressure, gas, and heat when subjected to sudden shock, pressure, or high temperature. N, O

explosive gases
The concentration of explosive gases generated by the facility or practice shall not exceed: (1) twenty-five percent (25%) of the lower explosive limit for the gases in facility structures (excluding gas control or recovery system components); and (2) the lower explosive limit for the gases at the property boundary. A

export
The transport of virgin, used or recycled controlled substances from inside the United States or its

territories to persons outside the United States or its territories, excluding United States military bases and ships for on-board use. A

export exemption
(1) An exemption from the prohibitions of Section 10(a)(3) and (4) of FIFRA; this type of exemption is granted by statute under Section 10(b)(2) of FIFRA for the purpose of exporting regulated products. A (2) An exemption granted by statute under section 203(b)(3) of the Clean Air Act for the purpose of exporting new motor vehicles or new motor vehicle engines. A

exporter
The person who, as the principal party in interest in the export transaction, has the power and responsibility for determining and controlling the sending of the chemical substance or mixture to a destination out of the customs territory of the United States. A

exposed
(As applied to live parts). Capable of being inadvertently touched or approached nearer than a safe distance by a person. It is applied to parts not suitably guarded, isolated, or insulated. (See "Accessible and Concealed"). O (3) (1) (As applied to wiring methods). On or attached to the surface or behind panels designed to allow access. [See "Accessible. (As applied to wiring methods)."] O (4) (For the purposes of 40 CFR § 1926.408(d), Communications systems). Where the circuit is in such a position that in case of failure of supports or insulation, contact with another circuit may result. O

exposure
(1) Contact with a chemical or physical agent. N (2) The amount of radiation or pollutant present in an environment which represents a potential health threat to the living organisms in that environment. N (3) That an employee is subjected to a toxic substance or harmful physical agent in the course of employment through any route of entry (inhalation, ingestion, skin contact or absorption, etc.), and includes past exposure and potential (e.g., accidental or possible) exposure, but does not include situations where the employer can demonstrate that the toxic substance or harmful physical agent is not used, handled, stored, generated, or present in the workplace in any manner different from typical non-occupational situations. O

exposure assessment
The determination or estimation (qualitative or quantitative) of the magnitude, frequency, duration, route, and extent (number of people) of exposure to a chemical. N

exposure incident
A specific eye, mouth, other mucous membrane, non-intact skin, or parenteral contact with blood or other potentially infectious materials that results from the performance of an employee's duties. O

exposure pathways
The environmental routes through

which living organisms can be exposed to hazardous waste. N

external environment
Any environment external to regulated and nonregulated areas. O

external floating roof
A pontoon-type or double-deck type cover with certain rim sealing mechanisms that rests on the liquid surface in a waste management unit with no fixed roof. A

external radiation
Radiation from a source outside the body. U

extinguisher classification
The letter classification given an extinguisher to designate the class or classes of fire on which an extinguisher will be effective. O

extinguisher rating
The numerical rating given to an extinguisher which indicates the extinguishing potential of the unit based on standardized tests developed by Underwriters' Laboratories, Inc. O

extinguishing media
The fire fighting substance to be used to control a material in the event of a fire. It is usually named by its generic name, such as fog, foam, water, etc. N

extraction plant
A facility chemically processing beryllium ore to beryllium metal, alloy, or oxide, or performing any of the intermediate steps in these processes. A

extraction site
The place from which the dredged or fill material proposed for discharge is to be removed. A

extraction test procedure
A series of laboratory operations and analyses designed to determine whether, under severe conditions, a solid waste, stabilized waste or landfilled material can yield a hazardous leachate. U

extrapolation
Estimation of unknown values by extending or projecting from known values. N

extrathoracic
Situated or occurring outside the thorax (the part of the respiratory tract above the trachea). N

extremely hazardous substances
Any of 406 chemicals identified by EPA on the basis of toxicity, and listed under SARA Title III. The list is subject to revision. N

extrusion
The application of pressure to a billet of metal, forcing the metal to flow through a die orifice. A

extrusion die cleaning
The process by which the steel dies used in extrusion of aluminum are cleaned. The term includes a dip into a concentrated caustic bath to dissolve the aluminum followed by a water rinse. It also includes the use of a wet scrubber with the die cleaning operation. A

eye corrosion
The production of irreversible tissue damage in the eye following application of a test substance to the anterior surface of the eye. A

eye irritation
The production of reversible changes in the eye following the application of a test substance to the anterior surface of the eye. A

F

F
Fahrenheit. U

FAA
Federal Aviation Administration. U

fabric filter
A cloth device that catches dust and particles from industrial emissions. N

fabricating
Any processing (e.g., cutting, sawing, drilling) of a manufactured product that contains commercial asbestos, with the exception of processing at temporary sites (field fabricating) for the construction or restoration of facilities. In the case of friction products, fabricating includes bonding, debonding, grinding, sawing, drilling, or other similar operations performed as part of fabricating. A

faces or sides
The vertical or inclined earth surfaces formed as a result of excavation work. O

facilities plan
A preliminary plan prepared as the basis for construction of publicly owned waste treatment works under Title II of FWPCA, as amended. A

facility
(1) An identifiable piece of process equipment. A source is composed of one or more [air] pollutant-emitting facilities. A (2) (a) Any building, structure, installation, equipment, pipe or pipeline (including any pipe into a sewer or publicly owned treatment works), well, pit, pond, lagoon, impoundment, ditch, landfill, storage container, motor vehicle, rolling stock, or aircraft, or (b) any site or area where a hazardous substance has been deposited, stored, disposed of, or placed, or otherwise come to be located; but does not include any consumer product in consumer use or any vessel. L (3) Any HWM facility, UIC underground injection well, NPDES point source, PSD stationary source, or any other facility or activity (including land or appurtenances thereto) that is subject to

209

regulation under the RCRA, UIC, NPDES, or PSD programs. N (4) Any resource recovery system or component thereof, any system, program or facility for resource conservation, and any facility for collection, source separation, storage, transportation, transfer, processing, treatment or disposal of solid waste, including hazardous waste, whether such facility is associated with facilities generating such wastes or not. A (5) All thermal processing equipment, buildings, and grounds at a specific site. A (6) Any process equipment (e.g., reactor, distillation column) to convert raw materials or feedstock chemicals into controlled substances. A

facility component
Any part of a facility including equipment. A

facility structures
Any buildings and sheds or utility or drainage lines on the facility. A

facultative bacteria
Those bacteria able to live and grow under more than one set of conditions, with or without oxygen. U

facultative species
Species that can occur both in wetlands and uplands; there are three subcategories of facultative species: (1) Facultative Wetland Plants (FACW) that usually occur in wetlands (estimated probability 67-99%), but occasionally are found in nonwetlands, (2) Facultative Plants (FAC) that are equally likely to occur in wetlands or nonwetlands (estimated probability 34-66%), and (3) Facultative Upland Plants (FACU) that usually occur in nonwetlands (estimated probability 67-99%); occasionally are found in wetlands (estimated probability 1-33%). N

fail-safe
A provision designed to automatically stop or safely control any motion in which a malfunction occurs. O

failing compressor
The measured noise emissions of the compressor, when measured in accordance with the applicable procedure, exceeds the applicable standard. A

failing exhaust system
When installed on any federally regulated motorcycle for which it is designed and marketed, the motorcycle and exhaust system exceed the applicable standards. A

failing vehicle
The measured emissions of the vehicle, when measured in accordance with the applicable procedure, exceeds the applicable standard. A

failure
The breakage, displacement, or permanent deformation of a structural member or connection so as to reduce its structural integrity and its supportive capabilities. O

fair market value
The price at which property would change hands between a willing buyer and a willing seller, neither being under any compulsion to buy or to sell and both having reasonable knowledge or relevant facts. O

family NO_x emission limit
The NO_x emission level to which an engine family is certified in the light-duty truck NO_x averaging program, expressed to one-tenth of a gram per mile accuracy. A

family particulate emission limit
The diesel particulate emission level to which an engine family is certified in the particulate averaging program, expressed to an accuracy of one hundredth gram-per-mile. A

farm field equipment
Tractors or implements, including self-propelled implements, or any combination thereof used in agricultural operations. O

farm tank
A tank located on a tract of land devoted to the production of crops or raising animals, including fish, and associated residences and improvements. A farm tank must be located on the farm property. "Farm" includes fish hatcheries, rangeland and nurseries with growing operations. A

farm worker
Any person or persons engaged in agricultural hand labor in the field. A

fast meter response
The "fast" response of the sound level meter shall be used. The fast dynamic response shall comply with the meter dynamic characteristics in paragraph 5.3 of the American National Standard Specification for Sound Level Meters. ANSI S1.4-1971. This publication is available from the American National Standards Institute, Inc., 1430 Broadway, New York, New York 10018. A

fast turnaround operation of a spray drying tower
An operation involving more than 6 changes of formulation in a 30 consecutive day period that are of such degree and type (e.g., high phosphate to no phosphate) as to require cleaning of the tower to maintain minimal product quality. A

fast turnaround operation of automated fill lines
An operation involving more than 8 changes of formulation in a 30 consecutive day period that are of such degree and type as to require thorough purging and washing of the fill line to maintain minimal product quality. A

fault
A surface or zone of rock fracture along which there has been displacement. A

fault-tree analysis
A means of analyzing hazards. Hazardous events are first identified by other techniques such as HAZOP. Then all combinations of individual failures that can lead to that hazardous event are shown in the logical format of the fault tree. By estimating the individual failure probabilities, and then using the appropriate arithmetical expressions, the top-event frequency can be calculated. N

FCC
Federal Communications Commission. U

FCs
(1) Fluorocarbons. A gas used as a propellant in aerosols, thought to be modifying the ozone layer in the stratosphere thereby allowing more harmful solar radiation to reach the Earth's surface. N (2) Any of a number of organic compounds analogous to hydrocarbons in which one or more hydrogen atoms are replaced by flourine. Once used in the United States as a propellant in aerosols, they are now primarily used in coolants and some industrial processes. FCs containing chlorine are called chlorofluorocarbons (CFCs). They are believed to be modifying the ozone layer in the stratosphere, thereby allowing more harmful solar radiation to reach the Earth's surface. N

FD&CA
Food, Drug and Cosmetic Act as amended (21 U.S.C. § *et seq.*) U

FDA
Food and Drug Administration. N

FDAA
Federal Disaster Assistance Administration. N

FDCA
The Food, Drug & Cosmetic Act as amended (21 U.S.C. 321 *et seq.*) U

FDF
Fundamentally different factors. N

FE
Fugitive emissions. N

feasibility study
FS. (1) A process undertaken by the lead agency (or responsible party if the responsible party will be developing a cleanup proposal) for developing, evaluating, and selecting remedial actions which emphasizes data analysis. The feasibility study is generally performed concurrently and in an interdependent fashion with the remedial investigation. In certain situations, the lead agency may require potentially responsible parties to conclude initial phases of the remedial investigation prior to initiation of the feasibility study. The feasibility study process uses data gathered during the remedial investigation. These data are used to define the objectives of the response action and to broadly develop remedial action alternatives. Next, an initial screening of these alternatives is required to reduce the number of alternatives to a workable number. Finally, the feasibility study involves a detailed analysis of a limited number of alternatives which remain after the initial screening stage. The factors that are considered in screening and analyzing the alternatives are public health, economics, engineering practicality, environmental impacts, and institution issues. A (2) Analysis of the practicability of a proposal; e.g., a description and analysis of the potential cleanup alternatives for a site or alternatives for a site on the National Priorities List. The feasibility study usually recommends selection of a cost-effective alternative. It usually starts as soon as the

remedial investigation is underway; together, they are commonly referred to as the "RI/FS." The term can apply to a variety of proposed corrective or regulatory actions. (3) In research, a small-scale investigation of a problem to ascertain whether or not a proposed research approach is likely to provide useful data. N

fecal coliform bacteria
Those organisms associated with the intestines of warm-blooded animals that are commonly used to indicate the presence of fecal material and the potential presence of organisms capable of causing human disease. A

federal agency
(1) Any department, agency, or other instrumentality of the federal government, and any independent agency or establishment of the federal government including any government corporation and the Government Printing Office. A, I, J (2) All agencies of the Federal Government. It does not mean the Congress, the Judiciary, or the President, including the performance of staff functions for the President in his Executive Office. It also includes, for purposes of these regulations, States and units of general local government and Indian tribes assuming NEPA responsibilities under section 104(h) of the Housing and Community Development Act of 1974. A

federal assistance
The entire Federal contribution to a project, including, but not limited to, the EPA grant amount. U

federal contract
An acquisition contract awarded by an agency, including those subject to the Federal Acquisition Regulation (FAR), and any other acquisition contract for real or personal property or services not subject to the FAR. A

federal delayed compliance order
A delayed compliance order issued by the administrator under section 113(d) (1), (3), (4) or (5) of the OSHA Act. O

federal emission test procedure
The dynamometer driving schedule, dynamometer procedure, and sampling and analytical procedures described in [40 CFR] Part 86 for the respective model year, which are used to derive city fuel economy data. A

Federal Environmental Impact Statement
FEIS. The document prepared by a Federal agency or department or under Federal guidance which identifies and analyzes in detail the environmental impacts of a proposed Federal action and incorporates comments made on the draft EIS. A

federal facility
(1) Any building, installation, structure, land, or public work owned by or leased to the federal government. Ships at sea, aircraft in the air, land forces on maneuvers, and other mobile facilities are not considered federal facilities for the purpose of these guidelines. United States government installations located on foreign soil or on land outside the jurisdiction of the United States

government are not considered federal facilities for the purpose of these guidelines. A (2) Any facility owned or operated by any department, commission, agency, office, bureau or other unit of the government of the United States of America except for facilities owned or operated by the Department of Energy. A

federal financial assistance
Any financial benefits provided directly as aid to a project by a department, agency, or instrumentality of the Federal government in any form including contracts, grants, and loan guarantees. Actions or programs carried out by the Federal government itself such as dredging performed by the Army Corps of Engineers do not involve Federal financial assistance. Actions performed for the Federal government by contractors, such as construction of roads on Federal lands by a contractor under the supervision of the Bureau of Land Management, should be distinguished from contracts entered into specifically for the purpose of providing financial assistance, and will not be considered programs or actions receiving Federal financial assistance. Federal financial assistance is limited to benefits earmarked for a specific program or action and directly awarded to the program or action. Indirect assistance, e.g., in the form of a loan to a developer by a lending institution which in turn receives Federal assistance not specifically related to the project in question is not Federal financial assistance. U

federal government
Includes the legislative, executive, and judicial branches of the Government of the United States, and the government of the District of Columbia. A

federal grant
An award of financial assistance in the form of money, or property in lieu of money, by the federal government or a direct appropriation made by law to any person. The term does not include technical assistance which provides services instead of money, or other assistance in the form of revenue sharing, loans, loan guarantees, loan insurance, interest subsidies, insurance, or direct United States cash assistance to an individual. A

Federal Implementation Plan
FIP. A plan developed by EPA pursuant to § 110(c) of the Clean Air Act and imposed on a State that fails to produce its own plan to comply with the Act by a certain date. N

federal land manager
With respect to any lands in the United States, the Secretary of the department with authority over such lands. A

federal loan
A loan made by an agency. The term does not include loan guarantee or loan insurance. A

Federal Register
A daily federal government publication that announces all proposed and final federal regulations. It also contains notices of public meetings

and other events the agency may schedule. Most major libraries carry the *Federal Register*.

Federal Register document
A document intended for publication in the *Federal Register* and bearing in its heading an identification code including the letters FRL.

federally assisted construction contract
Any agreement or modification thereof between any applicant and any person for construction work which is paid for in whole or in part with funds obtained from the Agency or borrowed on the credit of the Agency pursuant to any Federal program involving a grant, contract, loan, insurance, or guarantee, or undertaken pursuant to any Federal program involving such grant, contract, loan, insurance, or guarantee, or any application or modification thereof approved by the Agency for a grant, contract, loan, insurance, or guarantee under which the applicant itself participates in the construction work.

federally enforceable
[For purposes of the Clean Air Act] all limitations and conditions which are enforceable by the Administrator, including requirements developed pursuant to 40 CFR Parts 60 and 61, requirements within any applicable State Implementation Plan, and any permit requirements established pursuant to 40 CFR 52.21 or under regulations approved pursuant to this section, 40 CFR 51.18, or 51.24.

federally permitted release
(A) Discharges in compliance with a permit under section 402 of the Federal Water Pollution Control Act, (B) discharges resulting from circumstances identified and reviewed and made part of the public record with respect to a permit issued or modified under section 402 of the Federal Water Pollution Control Act and subject to a condition of such permit, (C) continuous or anticipated intermittent discharges from a point source, identified in a permit or permit application under section 402 of the Federal Water Pollution Control Act, which are caused by events occurring within the scope of relevant operating or treatment systems, (D) discharges in compliance with a legally enforceable permit under section 404 of the Federal Water Pollution Control Act, (E) releases in compliance with a legally enforceable final permit issued pursuant to section 3005 (a) through (d) of the Solid Waste Disposal Act from a hazardous waste treatment, storage, or disposal facility when such permit specifically identifies the hazardous substances and makes such substances subject to a standard of practice, control procedure or bioassay limitation or condition, or other control on the hazardous substances in such releases, (F) any release in compliance with a legally enforceable permit issued under section 102 of section 103 of the Marine Protection, Research, and Sanctuaries Act of 1972, (G) any injection of fluids authorized under Federal underground injection control programs or State programs submitted for Federal approval (and not disapproved by the Administrator of the Environmental Protection Agency) pursuant to part C of the

Safe Drinking Water Act, (H) any emission into the air subject to a permit or control regulation under section 111, section 112, title I part C, title I part D, or State implementation plans submitted in accordance with section 110 of the Clean Air Act (and not disapproved by the Administrator of the Environmental Protection Agency), including any schedule or waiver granted, promulgated, or approved under these sections, (I) any injection of fluids or other material authorized under applicable State law (i) for the purpose of stimulating or treating wells for the production of crude oil, natural gas, or water, (ii) for the purpose of secondary, tertiary, or other enhanced recovery of crude oil or natural gas, or (iii) which are brought to the surface in conjunction with the production of crude oil or natural gas and which are reinjected, (J) the introduction of any pollutant into a publicly owned treatment works when such pollutant is specified in and in compliance with applicable pretreatment standards of section 307(b) or (c) of the Clean Water Act and enforceable requirements in a pretreatment program submitted by a State or municipality for Federal approval under section 402 of such Act, and (K) any release of source, special nuclear, or byproduct material, as those terms are defined in the Atomic Energy Act of 1954, in compliance with a legally enforceable license, permit, regulation, or order issued pursuant to the Atomic Energy Act of 1954. [ed. Used to create exclusions from the reporting requirements of Superfund]. L

federally registered
Currently registered under sec. 3 of the FIFRA Act, after having been initially registered under the Federal Insecticide, Fungicide, and Rodenticide Act of 1947 (Pub.L. 86-139; 73 Stat. 286; June 25, 1947) by the Secretary of Agriculture or under FIFRA by the [EPA] Administrator. A

feed gas
The chemical composition of the exhaust gas measured at the converter inlet. A

feeder
All circuit conductors between the service equipment, or the generator switchboard of an isolated plant, and the final branch-circuit overcurrent device. O

feedlot
A concentrated, confined animal or poultry growing operation for meat, milk or egg production, or stabling, in pens or houses wherein the animals or poultry are fed at the place of confinement and crop or forage growth or production is not sustained in the area of confinement. A

feedlot waste
High concentrations of animal excrement that result from raising large numbers of animals on a relatively small, confined area of land. The soil cannot handle the excessive amounts of excrement, as it does under open-range conditions, so run-off from feedlots contributes excessive quantities of nitrogen, phosphorus, and potassium to nearby waterways. U

feedstock
(1) The raw materials supplied to manufacturing or processing plants for use in the production of goods or for treatment, respectively. Waste from one industry may be the feedstock for another industry. (2) The crude oil and natural gas liquids fed to the topping units. A

FEMA
Federal Emergency Management Agency. A

fen
(1) Low-lying land partly covered with water. N (2) A type of wetland that accumulates peat deposits. Fens are less acidic than bogs, deriving most of their water from groundwater rich in calcium and magnesium. (See: wetlands.) N

fence line concentration
Modeled or measured concentrations of air pollutants found at the boundaries of a property on which a pollution source is located. Usually assumed to be the nearest location at which an exposure of the general population could occur. N

FEPCA
Federal Environmental Pesticide Control Act. U

FERC
Federal Energy Regulatory Commission. U

fermentation
Chemical reactions accompanied by living microbes that are supplied with nutrients and other critical conditions such as heat, pressure, and light that are specific to the reaction at hand. N

ferrofluid systems
A means of separating nonmagnetic materials or immersing them in a ferrofluid held within a magnetic field. The "apparent density" for the ferrofluid thus created causes separation of any two substances differing in density by 5 to 10 percent or more according to a float/sink technique. U

ferromanganese silicon
That alloy containing 63 to 66 percent by weight manganese, 28 to 32 percent by weight silicon, and a maximum of 0.08 percent by weight carbon. A

ferrosilicon
That alloy as defined by ASTM Designation A100-69 (Reapproved 1974) (incorporated by reference-see § 60.17) grades A, B, C, D, and E, which contains 50 or more percent by weight silicon. A

ferrous
Describes those metals that are predominantly composed of iron and are most commonly magnetic. U

fertility
The ability to achieve conception and to produce offspring. For litter-bearing species, the number of offspring per litter is also used as a measure of fertility. Reduced fertility is sometimes referred to as subfertility. N

fertilizer
Materials such as nitrogen and

phosphorous that provide nutrients for plants. Commercially sold fertilizers may contain other chemicals or may be in the form of processed sewage sludge. N

fetus
The post-embryonic stage of the developing young. In humans, from the end of the second month of pregnancy up to birth. N

FFDCA
The Federal Food, Drug and Cosmetic Act, as amended (21 U.S.C. 321 et seq). A

FGD
Flue gas desulfurization. N

FHA
Federal Housing Administration. U

FHLBB
Federal Home Loan Bank Board. U

FHSA
Federal Hazardous Substances Act. This act allows the Consumer Product Safety Commission to ban or regulate hazardous materials produced for use by consumers. Under the act, the commission has labeling authority over consumer products that are toxic, corrosive, flammable, irritant or radioactive. N

FHWA
Federal Highway Administration. U

fiber
A particulate form of asbestos, 5 micrometers or longer, with a length-to-diameter ratio of at least 3 to 1. O

fiber boxes
Boxes made from container board, either solid fiber or corrugated paperboard (general term); or boxes made from solid paperboard of the same material throughout (specific term). A

fiber release episode
Any uncontrolled or unintentional disturbance of ACBM resulting in visible emission. A

fiberboard boxes
See fiber boxes. A

fiberglass insulation
Insulation which is composed principally of glass fibers, with or without binders. A

fibrosis
Formation of scar tissue in the lung or other tissues, usually as a result of inflammation occurring over a long period of time. N

FID
Flame ionization detector. N

field capacity of solid waste
The amount of water retained in solid waste after it has been saturated and has drained freely. Also called moisture-holding capacity. U

field testing
Practical and generally small-scale testing of innovative or alternative technologies directed to verifying performance and/or refining design parameters not sufficiently tested to resolve technical uncertainties which prevent the funding of a promising

improvement in innovative or alternative treatment technology. A

FIFRA
Federal Insecticide, Fungicide and Rodenticide Act. C

fill material
Any "pollutant" which replaces portions of the "waters of the United States" with dry land or which changes the bottom elevation of a water body for any purpose. A

filling
(1) Depositing dirt and mud, often raised by dredging, into marshy areas to create stable land generally for development. It can destroy the marsh ecology. N (2) Depositing dirt and mud or other materials into aquatic areas to create more dry land, usually for agricultural or commercial development purposes. Such activities often damage the ecology of the area. N

film badge
A piece of masked photographic film worn by nuclear workers to monitor their exposure to radiation. Nuclear radiation darkens the film. N

film wet mixture
A water or organic solvent-based suspension, solution, dispersion, or emulsion used in the manufacture of an instant photographic or peel-apart film article. A

filter
A porous device through which a gas or liquid is passed to remove suspended particles or dust. U

filter collector
A mechanical filtration system for removing particulate matter from a gas stream, for measurement, analysis, or control; also called bag collector. Filters are designed in a variety of sizes and materials for specific purposes. U

filtration
(1) The physical removal of the solid constituents from aqueous waste streams by means of a filter medium. Most aqueous waste streams that contain solids are treated by this process. U (2) In reference to primary drinking water regulations and related regulations applicable to public water systems, a process for removing particulate matter from water by passage through porous media. A

final authorization
Approval by EPA of a State program which has met the requirements of section 3006(b) of RCRA and the applicable requirements of part 271, subpart A. A

final closure
(1) The measures which must be taken by a facility to render the landfill portion environmentally innocuous when it determines that it will no longer accept waste for treatment, storage, or disposal on the entire facility. (2) The closure of all hazardous waste management units at the facility in accordance with all applicable closure requirements so that hazardous waste management activities under 40 CFR Parts 264 and 265 are no longer conducted at the facility

unless subject to the provisions in § 262.34. A

final cover
Cover material at a landfill that serves the same functions as daily cover but, in addition, may be permanently exposed on the surface. A

final environmental impact statement
FEIS. The document prepared by a Federal agency or department or under Federal guidance which identifies and analyzes in detail the environmental impacts of a proposed Federal action and incorporates comments made on the draft EIS. A

final order
(a) An order issued by the Administrator after an appeal of an initial decision, accelerated decision, decision to dismiss, or default order, disposing of a matter in controversy between the parties, or (b) an initial decision which becomes a final order. A

final printed labeling
(1) The printed label and the labeling which will appear on or will accompany the pesticide product. A (2) The label or labeling of the product when distributed or sold. Final printed labeling does not include the package of the product, unless the labeling is an integral part of the package. A

final product
A new chemical substance (as "new chemical substance" is defined in [40 CFR] § 720.3) that is manufactured by a person for distribution in commerce, or for use by the person other than as an intermediate. A

final status
A TSD facility that has interim status acquires final status when final administrative disposition has been made of its permit application. U

finding of no significant impact
A document by a Federal agency briefly presenting the reasons why an action, not otherwise excluded (40 CFR § 1508.4), will not have a significant effect on the human environment and for which an environmental impact statement therefore will not be prepared. It shall include the environmental assessment or a summary of it and shall note any other environmental documents related to it (40 CFR § 1501.7(a)(5)). If the assessment is included, the finding need not repeat any of the discussion in the assessment but may incorporate it by reference. A

FINDS
Facility Index System (OIRM). N

fines
Fine particulates; aerosols. U

finish coat operation
The coating application station, curing oven, and quench station used to apply and dry or cure the final coating(s) on the surface of the metal coil. Where only a single coating is applied to the metal coil, that coating is considered a finish coat. A

FIP
Federal Implementation Plan. U

FIPS
Federal Information Procedures System. N

fire brigade
An organized group of employees that are knowledgeable, trained, and skilled in the safe evacuation of employees during emergency situations and in assisting in fire fighting operations. O

fire, class A
A fire involving ordinary combustible materials such as paper, wood, cloth, and some rubber and plastic materials. O

fire, class B
A fire involving flammable or combustible liquids, flammable gases, greases and similar materials, and some rubber and plastic materials. O

fire, class C
A fire involving energized electrical equipment where safety to the employee requires the use of electrically nonconductive extinguishing media. O

fire, class D
A fire involving combustible metals such as magnesium, titanium, zirconium, sodium, lithium and potassium. O

fire point
The lowest temperature at which an oil vaporizes rapidly enough to burn for at least 5 seconds after ignition, under standard conditions. A

fire resistance
So resistant to fire that, for a specified time and under conditions of a standard heat intensity, it will not fail structurally and will not permit the side away from the fire to become hotter than a specified temperature. For purposes of this part, fire resistance shall be determined by the Standard Methods of Fire Tests of Building Construction and Materials, NFPA 251-1969. O

fire-fighting turbine
Any stationary gas turbine that is used solely to pump water for extinguishing fires. A

firebrick
Refractory brick made from fireclay. U

fireclay
A sedimentary clay containing only small amounts of fluxing impurities. It is high in hydrous aluminum silicates and is, therefore, capable of withstanding high temperatures. U

fires
A facility or practice shall not pose a hazard to the safety of persons or property from fires. This may be accomplished through compliance with [40 CFR] § 257.3-7 and through the periodic application of cover material or other techniques as appropriate. A

first aid
Any one-time treatment, and any followup visit for the purpose of observation, of minor scratches, cuts, burns, splinters, and so forth, which do not ordinarily require medical care. Such one-time treatment, and followup visit for the purpose of observation, is

considered first aid even though provided by a physician or registered professional personnel. O

first attempt at repair
Rapid action taken for the purpose of stopping or reducing leakage of organic material to atmosphere using best practices. A

first food use
Refers to the use of a pesticide on a food or in a manner which otherwise would be expected to result in residues in a food, if no permanent tolerance, exemption from the requirement of a tolerance, or food additive regulation for residues of the pesticide on any food has been established for the pesticide under section 408 (d) or (e) or 409 of the Federal Food, Drug, and Cosmetic Act. A

first pass effect
Reduction in a substance's systemic availability resulting from metabolism or excretion by the first major organ of contact with such capability after the absorption process. This phenomenon of removing chemicals after absorption before entering the general systemic circulation can occur in the lung or liver. N

first-order half-life
t1/2. The time required for the concentration of the chemical to be reduced to one-half its initial value. A

first-order reaction
A reaction in which the rate of disappearance of a chemical is directly proportional to the concentration of the chemical and is not a function of the concentration of any other chemical present in the reaction mixture. A

fiscal year
A budget term. The federal fiscal year runs from October to September 30 as opposed to the calendar year which runs from January 1 to December 31. U

fish poisons and repellents
All substances or mixtures of substances intended for destroying, repelling, or mitigating fish declared to be pests under 40 CFR § 162.14. Fish poisons and repellents include, but are not limited to: (i) Toxicants intended to kill fish in lakes, ponds, or streams; (ii) Repellents intended to repel species dangerous to man or injurious to aquatic organisms which man wishes to protect; and (iii) Sex influence agents intended to control sexual development of fish, such as to cause young to develop into all-female populations. A

fission
The splitting of atomic nuclei into smaller nuclei, accompanied by the release of great quantities of energy. U

FIT
Field Investigation Team. N

fitting
An accessory such as a locknut, bushing, or other part of a wiring system that is intended primarily to perform a mechanical rather than an electrical function. O

fixed capital cost
The capital needed to provide all the depreciable components. A

fixed carbon
The ash-free carbonaceous material that remains after volatile matter is driven off during the proximate analysis of a dry solid waste sample. U

fixed grate
A grate without moving parts; also called a stationary grate. A stationary grate through which no air passes is called a dead plate. U

fixed roof
A cover that is mounted on a waste management unit in a stationary manner and that does not move with fluctuations in liquid level. A

fixed station monitoring
The repeated, long-term sampling or measurement of parameters at representative points for the purpose of determining air or water quality trends and characteristics. A

FL
Full load. U

flame resistance
The property of materials, or combinations of component materials, to retard ignition and restrict the spread of flame. O

flammable
A chemical that includes one of the following categories: (a) Aerosol, flammable. An aerosol that, when tested by the method described in 16 CFR 1500.45, yields a flame projection exceeding 18 inches at full valve opening, or a flashback (a flame extending back to the valve) at any degree of valve opening; (b) Gas, flammable. (1) A gas that, at ambient temperature and pressure, forms a flammable mixture with air at a concentration of 13 percent by volume or less; or (2) A gas that, at ambient temperature and pressure, forms a range of flammable mixtures with air wider than 12 percent by volume, regardless of the lower limit; (c) Liquid, flammable. Any liquid having a flashpoint below 100° F (37.8° C), except any mixture having components with flashpoints of 100° F (37.8° C) or higher, the total of which make up 99 percent or more of the total volume of mixture. (d) Solid, flammable. A solid, other than a blasting agent or explosive as defined in CFR 1910.109-(a), that is liable to cause fire through friction, absorption of moisture, spontaneous chemical change, or retained heat from manufacturing or processing, or which can be ignited readily and when ignited burns so vigorously and persistently as to create a serious hazard. A solid is a flammable solid if, when tested by the method described in 16 CFR 1500.44, it ignites and burns with a self-sustained flame at a rate greater than one tenth of an inch per second along its major axis. N

flammable liquid
(1) Any liquid having a flashpoint below 100 degrees F. (37.8 degrees C.) O (2) Any liquid having a flash point below 140 degrees F. and having a vapor pressure not exceeding 40

pounds per square inch (absolute) at 100 degrees F. O

flash drying
The process of drying a wet organic material by passing it through a high temperature zone at such a rate that the water is rapidly evaporated but the organic material, protected by the boiling point of water, is not overheated. U

flash point
(1) The minimum temperature at which a liquid gives off a vapor in sufficient concentration to ignite when tested by the following methods: (a) Tagliabue Closed Tester (see American National Standard Method of Test for Flash Point by Tag Closed Tester, Z11.24 1979 [ASTM D56-79]). (b) Pensky-Martens Closed Tester (see American National Standard Method of Test for Flash Point by Pensky-Martens Closed Tester, Z11.7-1979 [ASTM D93-79]). (c) Setaflash Closed Tester (see American National Standard Method of Test for Flash Point by Setaflash Closed Tester [ASTM D 3278-78]). N (2) The minimum temperature at which a liquid or solid gives off sufficient vapor to form an ignitable vapor-air mixture near the surface of the liquid or solid. U

flash-off area
The structure on automobile and light-duty truck assembly lines between the coating application system (dip tank or spray booth) and the bake oven. A

flashover
The discharge of ignition voltage at any point other than at the spark plug gap. A

flat glass
Glass made of soda-lime recipe and produced into continuous flat sheets and other products listed in SIC 3211. A

fleet vehicle
Any of 5 or more light duty vehicles operated by the same person(s), business, or governmental entity and used principally in connection with the same or related occupations or uses. This definition shall also include any taxicab (or other light duty vehicle-for-hire) owned by any individual or business. A

flight conveyor
A drag conveyor that uses rollers interspersed in its pull chains to reduce friction. U

floc
A clump of solids formed in sewage by biological or chemical action. N

flocculation
Separation of suspended solids during waste water treatment by chemical creation of clumps of flocs. N

flood or flooding
A general and temporary condition of partial or complete inundation of normally dry land areas from the overflow of inland and/or tidal waters, and/or the unusual and rapid accumulation or runoff of surface waters from any source, or flooding from any other source. A

floodplain
The lowland and relatively flat areas adjoining inland and coastal waters and other floodprone areas such as offshore islands, including at a minimum, that area subject to a one percent or greater chance of flooding in any given year. The base floodplain shall be used to designate the 100-year floodplain (one percent chance floodplain). The critical action floodplain is defined as the 500-year flood plain (0.2 percent chance floodplain). A

floor hole
An opening measuring less than 12 inches but more than 1 inch in its least dimension, in any floor, platform, pavement, or yard, through which materials but not persons may fall; such as a belt hole, pipe opening, or slot opening. O

floor insulation
A material, primarily designed to resist heat flow, which is installed between the first level conditioned area of a building and an unconditioned basement, a crawl space, or the outside beneath it. Where the first level conditioned area of a building is on a ground level concrete slab, floor insulation includes such a material installed around the perimeter of or on the slab. In the case of mobile homes, floor insulation also means skirting to enclose the space between the building and the ground. A

floor opening
An opening measuring 12 inches or more in its least dimension, in any floor, platform, pavement, or yard through which persons may fall; such as a hatchway, stair or ladder opening, pit, or large manhole. Floor openings occupied by elevators, dumbwaiters, conveyors, machinery, or containers are excluded. O

floor sweep
A vapor collection designed to capture vapors which are heavier than air and which collect along the floor. N

flotation
The rising of suspended matter to the surface of the liquid in a tank as scum by aeration, the evolution of gas, chemicals, electrolysis, heat, or bacterial decomposition and the subsequent removal of the scum by skimming. U

flow coating
A method of applying coatings in which the part is carried through a chamber containing numerous nozzles which direct unatomized streams of coatings from many different angles onto the surface of the part. A

flow proportional composite sample
A sample composed of grab samples collected continuously or discretely in proportion to the total flow at time of collection or to the total flow since collection of the previous grab sample. The grab volume or frequency of grab collection may be varied in proportion to flow. A

flow rate
The volume per time unit given to the flow of gases or other fluid substance which emerges from an

orifice, pump, turbine or passes along a conduit or channel. A

flow-through
A continuous or an intermittent passage of test solution or dilution water through a test chamber or a holding or acclimation tank, with no recycling. A

flow-through process tank
A tank that forms an integral part of a production process through which there is a steady, variable, recurring, or intermittent flow of materials during the operation of the process. Flow-through process tanks do not include tanks used for the storage of materials prior to their introduction into the production process or for the storage of finished products or by-products from the production process. A

flow-through test
A toxicity test in which water is renewed continuously in the test chambers, the test chemical being transported with the water used to renew the test medium. A

flowmeter
(1) A gauge that shows the speed of waste water moving through a treatment plant. N (2) Also used to measure the speed of liquids moving through various industrial processes. N

FLPMA
Federal Land Policy and Management Act. N

flue
Any passage designed to carry combustion gases and entrained particulates. U

flue dust
Solid particles (smaller than 100 microns) carried in the products of combustion. U

flue gas
The air and pollutants emitted to the atmosphere after a production process or combustion takes place; also called stack gas. U

flue gas desulfurization
Any pollution control process which treats stationary source combustion flue gas to remove sulfur oxides. A

flue gas scrubber
A type of equipment that removes fly ash or other objectionable materials from flue gas by using sprays, wet baffles, or other means that require water as the primary separation mechanism. Also called flue gas washer, gas scrubber, and gas washer. B

flue-fed incinerator
An incinerator that is charged through a shaft that functions as a chute for charging waste and has a flue to carry the products of combustion. U

fluid
Any material or substance which flows or moves whether in a semisolid, liquid, sludge, gas, or any other form or state. A

fluidized bed combustion technology
Combustion of fuel in a bed or

series of beds (including but not limited to bubbling bed units and circulating bed units) of limestone aggregate (or other sorbent materials) in which these materials are forced upward by the flow of combustion air and the gaseous products of combustion. A

fluidized bed technique
A combustion process in which heat is transferred from finely divided particles, such as sand, to combustible materials in a fluid bed incinerator. In one such incinerator, combustion is confined within a bed of waste and sand that is fluidized by an upward-controlled flow of air with enough velocity to float some of the solids. Volatile gases are collected above the bed. U

fluidized bed combustion
The burning of pulverized coal kept in motion by a current of air so that the mass appears to be boiling. U

flume
A natural or man-made channel that diverts water. N

fluorescent light ballast
A device which electrically controls fluorescent light fixtures and includes a capacitor containing 0.1 kg or less of dielectric. A

fluorides
Gaseous, solid, or dissolved compounds containing fluorine that result from industrial processes. N

fluorocarbons
(1) FCs. A gas used as a propellant in aerosols, thought to be modifying the ozone layer in the stratosphere thereby allowing more harmful solar radiation to reach the Earth's surface. N (2) Any of a number of organic compounds analogous to hydrocarbons in which one or more hydrogen atoms are replaced by flourine. Once used in the United States as a propellant in aerosols, they are now primarily used in coolants and some industrial processes. FCs containing chlorine are called chlorofluorocarbons (CFCs). They are believed to be modifying the ozone layer in the stratosphere, thereby allowing more harmful solar radiation to reach the Earth's surface. N

fluorosis
An abnormal condition caused by excessive intake of fluorine, characterized chiefly by mottling of the teeth. N

flush
(1) To open a cold-water tap to clear out all the water which may have been sitting for a long time in the pipes. In new homes, to flush a system means to send large volumes of water gushing through the unused pipes to remove loose particles of solder and flux. (2) To force large amounts of water through liquid to clean out piping or tubing, storage or process tanks. N

flux density (neutron)
A term used to express the number of neutrons entering a sphere of unit cross-sectional area in unit time. For neutrons of given energy, the product of neutron density and speed. U

fluxing
The use of a substance to promote fusion of metals or minerals by removing impurities. U

fly ash
(1) The component of coal which results from the combustion of coal, and is the finely divided mineral residue which is typically collected from boiler stack gases by electrostatic precipitator or mechanical collection devices. (2) The ash that is carried out of the furnace by the gas stream and collected by mechanical precipitators, electrostatic precipitators, and/or fabric filters. Economizer ash is included when it is collected with fly ash. A (3) Suspended particles, charred paper, dust, soot, and other partially oxidized matter carried in the products of combustion. A

fly ash collector
The equipment used to remove fly ash from incinerator combustion gases. U

FMC
Federal Maritime Commission. U

FMD
EPA's Financial Management Division. U

FMSHRC
Federal Mine Safety and Health Review Commission. U

foam
A stable aggregation of small bubbles which flow freely over a burning liquid surface and form a coherent blanket which seals combustible vapors and thereby extinguishes the fire. O

foam-in-place insulation
Foam is rigid cellular foam produced by catalyzed chemical reactions that hardens at the site of the work. The term includes spray-applied and injected applications such as spray-in-place foam and pour-in-place. A

fog
Suspended liquid particles formed by condensation of vapor. N

fogging
Applying a pesticide by rapidly heating the liquid chemical so that it forms very fine droplets that resemble smoke. It is used to destroy mosquitoes and blackflies. N

FOIA
Freedom of Information Act N

folding boxboard
A paperboard suitable for the manufacture of folding cartons. A

fomite
An inanimate object that can harbor or transmit pathogenic organisms. U

FONSI
Finding of No Significant Impact (NEPA). N

food
Any article used for food or drink for man or animals. A

food additive
Any substance the intended use of which results or may reasonably be expected to result, directly or indirectly, in its becoming a component of or otherwise affecting the

characteristics of any food (including any such substance intended for use in producing, manufacturing, packing, processing, preparing, treating, packaging, transporting, or holding food), except that such term does not include: (1) A pesticide chemical in or on a raw agricultural commodity. (2) A pesticide chemical to the extent that it is intended for use or is used in the production, storage, or transportation of any raw agricultural commodity. (3) A color additive. (4) Any substance used in accordance with a sanction or approval granted prior to September 6, 1958, pursuant to the FFDCA, the Poultry Products Inspection Act, or the Federal Meat Inspection Act. (5) A new animal drug. (6) A substance that is generally recognized, among experts qualified by scientific training and experience to evaluate its safety, as having been adequately shown through scientific procedures (or, in the case of a substance used in food prior to January 1, 1958, through either scientific procedures or experience based on common use in food) to be safe under the conditions of its intended use. A

food additive regulation
A regulation issued pursuant to FFDCA section 409 that states the conditions under which a food additive may be safely used. A food additive regulation under this part ordinarily establishes a tolerance for pesticide residues in or on a particular processed food or a group of such foods. It may also specify: (1) The particular food or classes of food in or on which a food additive may be used. (2) The maximum quantity of the food additive which may be used in or on such food. (3) The manner in which the food additive may be added to or used in or on such food. (4) Directions or other labeling or packaging requirements for the food additive. A

food chain
A sequence of organisms, each of which uses the next lower member of the sequence as a food source. N

food-chain crops
Tobacco, crops grown for human consumption, and crops grown for feed for animals whose products are consumed by humans. A

food-processing waste
The waste resulting from operations that alter the form or composition of agricultural products for marketing purposes. U

food waste
The organic residues generated by the handling, storage, sale, preparation, cooking, and serving of foods, commonly called garbage. A

forced draft
The positive pressure created by the action of a fan or blower, which supplies the primary or secondary combustion air in an incinerator. U

forced expiratory volume
FEV. The maximum volume of air that can be forcibly expired when starting from maximal-inspiration. Can also be expressed for a specific time interval, e.g., FEV (one second). U

forced vital capacity
FVC. The greatest amount of air that can be forcefully exhaled following maximum inhalation. N

foreseeable emergency
Any potential occurrence such as, but not limited to, equipment failure, rupture of containers, or failure of control equipment which could result in an uncontrolled release of a hazardous chemical into the workplace. N

forest
A concentration of trees and related vegetation in non-urban areas sparsely inhabited by and infrequently used by humans; characterized by natural terrain and drainage patterns. A

forging
Deforming metal, usually hot, with compressive force into desired shapes, with or without dies. Where dies are used, the metal is forced to take the shape of the die. A

form board
A lightweight commodity paper designed primarily for business forms including computer printout and carbonless paper forms. (See manifold business forms). A

formaldehyde
CH_2O. (1) A pungent, irritating gas formed by the oxidation of hydrocarbons. (2) A colorless, pungent, irritating gas, CH_2O, used chiefly as a disinfectant and preservative and in synthesizing other compounds and resins. N

formation
UIC. A body of consolidated or unconsolidated rock characterized by a degree of lithologic homogeneity which is prevailingly, but not necessarily, tabular and is mappable on the earth's surface or traceable in the subsurface. A

formation fluid
Fluid present in a formation under natural conditions as opposed to introduced fluids, such as drilling mud. A

forming
A set of manufacturing operations in which metals and alloys are made into semifinished products by hot or cold working. A

formulation
(1) The process of mixing, blending, or dilution of one or more active ingredients with one or more other active or inert ingredients, without an intended chemical reaction, to obtain a manufacturing use product or an end use product, or (2) The repackaging of any registered product. A (3) The substance or mixture of substances which is comprised of all active and inert ingredients in a pesticide. N

forward mutation
A gene mutation from the wild (parent) type to the mutant condition. A

fossil fuel
Natural gas, petroleum, coal, and any form of solid, liquid, or gaseous fuel derived from such materials for the purpose of creating useful heat. A

fossil-fuel fired steam generating unit
A furnace or boiler used in the process of burning fossil fuel for the purpose of producing steam by heat transfer. A

fouling
The impedance to the flow of gas or heat that results when material accumulates in gas passages or on heat-absorbing surfaces in an incinerator or other combustion chamber. U

foundation insulation
A material, primarily designed to resist heat flow, which is installed in foundation walls between conditioned volumes and unconditioned volumes and the outside or surrounding earth, at the perimeters of concrete slab-on-grade foundations, and at common foundation wall assemblies between conditioned basement volumes. A

four-wheel drive general utility vehicle
A four-wheel drive, general purpose automobile capable of off-highway operation that has a wheelbase not more than 110 inches and that has a body shape similar to a 1977 Jeep CJ-5 or CJ-7, or the 1977 Toyota Land Cruiser, as defined by the Secretary of Transportation at 49 CFR 533.4. A

FRA
Federal Railroad Administration. U

fraction
Refinery term for a product of fractional distillation having a restricted boiling range. A

franchise collection
Refuse collection by a private firm that is given exclusive rights to collect, for a fee paid by customers, in a specific territory or from specific types of customers. U

frank effect level
FEL. Related to biological response to chemical exposures (compare with NOAEL and LOEL); the exposure level that produces an unmistakable adverse health effect (such as inflammation, severe convulsions, or death). N

free available chlorine
The value obtained using the amperometric titration method for free available chlorine described in *Standard Methods for the Examination of Water and Wastewater*, page 112 (13th edition). A

free fall
The act of falling before the personal fall arrest system begins to apply force to arrest the fall. O

free liquids
Liquids which readily separate from the solid portion of a waste under ambient temperature and pressure. A

free moisture
Liquid that will drain freely by gravity from solid materials. A

free product
A regulated substance that is present as a non-aqueous phase liquid (e.g., liquid not dissolved in water). A

free stall barn
Specialized facilities wherein

producing cows are permitted free movement between resting and feeding areas. A

freeboard
The vertical distance between the top of a tank or surface impoundment dike, and the surface of the waste contained therein. A

frequency
Number of cycles, revolutions, or vibrations completed in a unit of time [See: Hertz]. U

fresh water
(1) Water that generally contains less than 1,000 milligrams-per-liter of dissolved solids. N (2) Underground source of drinking water. A

freshwater lake
Any inland pond, reservoir, impoundment, or other similar body of water that has recreational value, that exhibits no oceanic and tidal influences, and that has a total dissolved solids concentration of less than 1 percent. A

friable
Material, which when dry, may be crumbled, pulverized, or reduced to powder by hand pressure, and includes previously nonfriable material after such previously nonfriable material becomes damaged to the extent that when dry it may be crumbled, pulverized, or reduced to powder by hand pressure. A

friable asbestos material
Any material containing more than 1 percent asbestos as determined using the method specified in appendix A, subpart F, 40 CFR part 763 section 1, Polarized Light Microscopy, that, when dry, can be crumbled, pulverized, or reduced to powder by hand pressure. A

friable material
Any material applied onto ceilings, walls, structural members, piping, ductwork, or any other part of the building structure which, when dry, may be crumbled, pulverized, or reduced to powder by hand pressure. A

front panel
That portion of the label of a pesticide product that is ordinarily visible to the purchaser under the usual conditions of display for sale. A

frontend loader
A collection vehicle with mechanical arms in the front that engage a refuse container, lift it up over the cab, empty it into the vehicle's body, where it is compressed, and return it to the ground. U

frontend recovery system
Nontechnical term for any process that separates and recovers valuable resources from inorganic solid waste. Examples are air classification, flotation, grinding, magnetic separation, screening, and shredding. U

froth flotation
A process for separating small solid particles according to type by immersing them in a tank of water with a chemical surface-active agent and introducing air bubbles at the bottom of the tank. The agent causes one type of material to have a

greater affinity for air than water and to rise to the surface with the bubbles for collection. The process is used to recover tiny particles of glass by separating them from rock and stone. U

FRS
Federal Reserve System. U

FS
Feasibility Study. N

FSR
Financial Status Report (EPA). U

fsw
Feet of seawater (or equivalent static pressure head). O

FTC
Federal Trade Commission. U

fuel
(1) Any material which is capable of releasing energy or power by combustion or other chemical or physical reaction. A (2) (a) Gasoline and diesel fuel for gasoline- or diesel-powered automobiles or (b) electrical energy for electrically powered automobiles. A

fuel bed
The layer of solid fuel or solid waste on a furnace grate or hearth. U

fuel-burning equipment
Any furnace, boiler, apparatus, stack, and all appurtenances thereto, used in the process of burning fuel for the primary purpose of producing heat or power by indirect heat transfer. A

fuel cell
A device for converting chemical energy into electrical energy. U

fuel cycle
The complete series of steps involved in supplying fuel for nuclear power reactors. It includes mining, refining, the original fabrication of fuel elements, their use in a reactor, chemical processing to recover the fissionable material remaining in the spent fuel, reenrichment of the fuel material, refabrication into new fuel elements, and management of radioactive waste. U

fuel economy
(1) The average number of miles traveled by an automobile or group of automobiles, per gallon of gasoline or diesel fuel as computed in 40 CFR § 600.207 or (2) the equivalent petroleum based fuel economy for an electrically powered automobile as determined by the Secretary of Energy. A

fuel economy data vehicle
A vehicle used for the purpose of determining fuel economy which is not a certification vehicle. A

fuel economy standard
The Corporate Average Fuel Economy Standard (CAFE) which went into effect in 1978. It was meant to enhance the national fuel conservation effort by slowing fuel consumption through a miles-per-gallon requirement for motor vehicles. N

fuel evaporative emissions
Vaporized fuel emitted into the

atmosphere from the fuel system of a motor vehicle. A

fuel gas
Any gas which is generated at a petroleum refinery and which is combusted. Fuel gas also includes natural gas when the natural gas is combined and combusted in any proportion with a gas generated at a refinery. Fuel gas does not include gases generated by catalytic cracking unit, catalyst regenerators and fluid coking burners. A

fuel gas combustion device
Any equipment, such as process heaters, boilers and flares used to combust fuel gas, except facilities in which gases are combusted to produce sulfur or sulfuric acid. A

fuel manufacturer
Any person who, for sale or introduction into commerce, produces or manufactures a fuel or causes or directs the alteration of the chemical composition of, or the mixture of chemical compounds in, a bulk fuel by adding to it an additive. A

fuel oil grade
Numerical ratings ranging from 1 to 6. The lower the grade number, the thinner the oil is and the more easily it evaporates. A high number indicates a relatively thick, heavy oil. No. 1 and No. 2 fuel oils are usually used in domestic heaters, and the others are used by industry and ships. No. 5 and 6 oils are solids which must be liquified by heating. Kerosene, coal oil, and range oil are all No. 1 oil. No. 3 fuel oil is no longer used as a standard term. A

fuel pretreatment
A process that removes a portion of the sulfur in a fuel before combustion of the fuel in a steam generating unit. A

fuel supply agreement
A legally binding document between a firm associated with a new independent power production facility (IPPF) or a new IPPF and a fuel supplier that establishes the terms and conditions under which the fuel supplier commits to provide fuel to be delivered to a specific new IPPF. A

fuel system
The combination of fuel tank, fuel pump, fuel lines, and carburetor, or fuel injection components, and includes all fuel system vents and fuel evaporative emission control systems. A

fuel venting emissions
All raw fuel, exclusive of hydrocarbons in the exhaust emissions, discharged from aircraft gas turbine engines during all normal ground and flight operations. A

fugitive dust
Particulate matter composed of soil which is uncontaminated by pollutants resulting from industrial activity. Fugitive dust may include emissions from haul roads, wind erosion of exposed soil surfaces and soil storage piles, and other activities in which soil is either removed, stored, transported, or redistributed; also,

solid, airborne particulate matter emitted from any source other than through a stack. A

fugitive emission
Particulate matter that is not collected by a capture system and is released to the atmosphere at the point of generation. A

fugitive emissions
(1) Those emissions which could not reasonably pass through a stack, chimney, vent, or other functionally equivalent opening. (2) Any air pollutants emitted to the atmosphere other than from a stack. A

fugitive source
Any source of emissions not controlled by an air pollution control device. A

full capacity
Operation of the steam generating unit at 90 percent or more of the maximum steady-state design heat input capacity. A

full scale
The maximum measuring limit for a given range. A

fume
Solid particles under 1 micron in diameter, formed as vapors condense or as chemical reactions take place. U

fume scrubber
A wet air pollution control device used to remove and clean the fumes originating in the pickling [and hot coating] operation. A

fume suppression system
The equipment comprising any system used to inhibit the generation of emissions from steelmaking facilities with an inert gas, flame, or steam blanket applied to the surface of molten iron or steel. A

fumigant
A pesticide that is vaporized to kill pests; often used in buildings or greenhouses. N

functional developmental toxicity
The study of the causes, mechanisms, and manifestations of alterations or delays in functional competence of the organism or organ system following exposure to an agent during critical periods of development pre- and/or postnatally. This is a subset of development toxicity. N

functional equivalent
EPA's decision-making process and its relationship to the environmental review conducted under the National Environmental Policy Act (NEPA). A review is considered functionally equivalent when it addresses the substantive components of a NEPA review. N

functional residual capacity
FRC. The volume of gas remaining in the lungs at the end of a normal expiration. U

functional space
A room, group of rooms, or homogeneous area (including crawl spaces or the space between a dropped ceiling and the floor or roof deck above), such as classroom(s), a cafeteria,

gymnasium, hallways(s), designated by a person accredited to prepare management plans, design abatement projects, or conduct response actions. A

fund or trust fund
The Hazardous Substance Response Fund established by section 221 [of CERCLA] or, in the case of a hazardous waste disposal facility for which liability has been transferred under section 107(k) of the Act, the Postclosure Liability Fund established by section 232 of the Act. L

fungi
(1) (Singular, Fungus) Molds, mildews, yeasts, mushrooms, and puffballs, a group of organisms that lack chlorophyll (i.e., are not photosynthetic and which are usually nonmobile, filamentous, and multicellular). Some grow in the ground, others attach themselves to decaying trees and other plants, getting their nutrition from decomposing organic matter. Some cause disease, others stabilize sewage and break down solid wastes in composting. N Non-chlorophyll-bearing thallophyte (that is, any non-chlorophyll-bearing plant of a lower order than mosses and liverworts), as for example, rust, smut, mildew, mold, yeast, and bacteria, except those on or in living man or other animals and those on or in processed food, beverages, or pharmaceuticals. C

fungicides
All substances or mixtures of substances intended for preventing or inhibiting the growth of, or destroying any fungi. A

furnace
(1) A combustion chamber; an enclosed structure in which heat is produced. (2) A solid fuel burning appliance that is designed to be located outside of ordinary living areas and that warms spaces other than the space where the appliance is located, by the distribution of air heated in the appliance through ducts. The appliance must be tested and listed as a furnace under accepted American or Canadian safety testing codes unless exempted from this provision by the Administrator. A manufacturer may request an exemption in writing from the Administrator by stating why the testing and listing requirement is not practicable and by demonstrating that his appliance is otherwise a furnace. A (3) The chambers of the combustion train where drying, ignition, and combustion of waste material and evolved gases occur. A

furnace arch
A nearly horizontal structure that extends into a furnace and serves to deflect gases. U

furnace charge
Any material introduced into the electric submerged arc furnace, and may consist of, but is not limited to, ores, slag, carbonaceous material, and limestone. A

furnace cycle
The time period from completion of a furnace product tap to the completion of the next consecutive product tap. A

furnace power input
The resistive electrical power consumption of an electric submerged arc furnace as measured in kilowatts. A

furnace pull
That amount of glass drawn from the glass furnace or furnaces. A

furnace volume
The total internal volume of combustion chambers. U

FURS
Federal Underground Injection Control Reporting System. N

FWPCA
Federal Water Pollution Control Act, as amended (33 U.S.C. 1251 et seq.). A

FWS
U.S. Fish and Wildlife Service. A

G

GAAP
Generally accepted accounting principles. N

GAC
Granulated activated carbon. U

gal.
Gallon (U.S.). U

galvanizing
Coating steel products with zinc by the hot dip process including the immersion of the steel product in a molten bath of zinc metal, and the related operations preceding and subsequent to the immersion phase. A

game fish
Species like trout, salmon, bass, etc. caught for sport. They show more sensitivity to environmental changes than "rough" fish. N

gamma multi-hit model
A dose-response model that can be derived under the assumption that the response is induced if the target site has undergone some number of independent biological events (hits). N

gamma radiation
Gamma rays are true rays of energy in contrast to alpha and beta radiation. The properties are similar to x-rays and other electromagnetic waves. They are the most penetrating waves of radiant nuclear energy but can be blocked by dense materials such as lead. N

gap spacing
The distance between the center electrode and the ground electrode where the high voltage ignition arc is discharged. A

garbage
Waste materials that are likely to decompose or putrefy. [See food waste]. U

gas barrier
Any device or material used to divert the flow of gases produced in a sanitary landfill or by other land disposal techniques. U

238

gas stream
The air, clean or polluted, that is present during a production process or combustion and is eventually vented to the atmosphere. U

gas turbine model
A group of gas turbines having the same nominal air flow, combuster inlet pressure, combuster inlet temperature, firing temperature, turbine inlet temperature and turbine inlet pressure. A

gas well
Any well which produces natural gas in a ratio to the petroleum liquids produced greater than 15,000 cubic feet of gas per 1 barrel (42 gallons) of petroleum liquids. A

gas-tight
Operated with no detectable emissions. A

gasification
Conversion of a solid material, such as coal, into a gas for use as fuel. N

gasoline
Any petroleum distillate having a Reid vapor pressure of 4 pounds or greater which is produced for use as a motor fuel and is commonly called gasoline. A

gasoline blending stock or component
Any liquid compound which is blended with other liquid compounds or with lead additives to produce gasoline. A

gasoline importer
A person who imports gasoline or gasoline blending stocks or components from a foreign country into the United States (including the Commonwealth of Puerto Rico, the Virgin Islands, Guam, American Samoa, and the Northern Mariana Islands). A

gasoline service station
Any site where gasoline is dispensed to motor vehicle fuel tanks form stationary storage tanks. A

gasoline terminal
A facility for the storage and dispensing of gasoline where incoming gasoline loads are received by pipeline, marine tanker or barge, and where outgoing gasoline loads are transferred by tank truck, trailers, railroad cars, or other non-marine mobile vessels. A

gasoline volatility
The property of gasoline whereby it evaporates into a vapor. Gasoline volatility is measured in pounds per square inch (psi), with a higher number reflecting more gasoline evaporation. Gasoline vapor is a volatile organic compound (VOC). N

gastrointestinal
Pertaining to the intestines and stomach. N

gauge pressure (p.s.i.g.)
Pressure measured by a gauge and indicating the pressure exceeding atmospheric. O

gavage
Experimental exposure regimen in which a substance is administered to an animal into the stomach via a tube. N

GCWR
Gross combination weight rating. U

GD
(EPA) Guidance Document. U

gear oils
Petroleum-based oils used for lubricating machinery gears. A

Geiger counter
An electrical device that detects the presence of radioactivity. N

gene
A length of DNA that directs the synthesis of a protein. N

gene library
A collection of DNA fragments from cells or organisms. So far, no simple way for sorting the contents of gene libraries has been devised. However, DNA pieces can be moved into bacterial cells where sorting according to gene function becomes feasible. N

general permit
(1) An NPDES "permit" issued under [40 CFR] § 122.28 authorizing a category of discharges under the CWA within a geographical area. A (2) A permit applicable to a class or category of dischargers. N

generation
The act or process of generating solid waste. A

generation rate
The quantity of solid waste that originates from a defined activity; or a defined number of solid waste producers per unit of time. U

generator
(1) Any person, by site location, whose act, or process produces "hazardous waste" identified or listed in 40 CFR part 261. A (2) A facility whose act or process produces hazardous waste. (3) A device that changes mechanical energy into electrical energy. N (4) A facility or mobile source that emits pollutants into the air releases hazardous wastes into water or soil. N

generator column
Used to produce or generate saturated solutions of a solute in a solvent. The column is packed with a solid support coated with the solute, i.e., the organic compound whose solubility is to be determined. When water (the solvent) is pumped through the column, saturated solutions of the solute are generated. A

genetic engineering
A process of inserting new genetic information into existing cells in order to modify any organism for the purpose of changing one of its characteristics. N

genetically significant dose
GSD. The gonadal dose which, if received by every member of the population, would be expected to produce the same total genetic effect on the population as the sum of the individual doses that are actually received. It is not a forecast of predictable adverse effects on any individual person or his/her unborn children. U

genotoxic
A broad term that usually refers to a chemical which has the ability to damage DNA or the chromosomes. This can be determined directly by measuring mutations or chromosome abnormalities or indirectly by measuring DNA repair, sister-chromated exchange, etc. Mutagenicity is a subset of genotoxicity. N

GEP
Good engineering practice. N

germ cell
A cell capable of developing into a gamete (ovum (egg) or sperm). N

germicide
Any compound that kills disease-carrying microorganisms. These must be registered as pesticides with EPA. N

germination
The resumption of active growth by an embryo. The primary root should attain a length of 5 mm for the seed to be counted as having germinated. A

GI
Government Institutes, publishers of this *Glossary* and other information. U

glass fiberreinforced polyisocyanurate/ polyurethane foam
Cellular polyisocyanurate or cellular polyurethane insulation made with glass fibers within the foam core. A

glass melting furnace
A unit comprising a refractory vessel in which raw materials are charged, melted at high temperature, refined, and conditioned to produce molten glass. The unit includes foundations, superstructure and retaining walls, raw material charger systems, heat exchangers, melter cooling system, exhaust system, refractory brick work, fuel supply and electrical boosting equipment, integral control systems and instrumentation, and appendages for conditioning and distributing molten glass to forming apparatuses. The forming apparatuses, including the float bath used in flat glass manufacturing, are not considered part of the glass melting furnace. A

GLC
Ground level concentration. U

global commons
That area (land, air, water) outside the jurisdiction of any nation. A

glomerulus
Part of the nephron, the basic structure of the kidney. N

glove bag
A sealed compartment with attached inner gloves used for the handling of asbestos-containing materials. Properly installed and used, glove bags provide a small work area enclosure typically used for small-scale asbestos stripping operations. Information on glove-bag installation, equipment and supplies, and work practices is contained in the Occupational Safety and Health Administration's (OSHA's) final rule on occupational exposure to asbestos (appendix G to 29 CFR 1926.58). A

GLP
Good laboratory practice. U

gm
  gram. N

GOB
  Grants Operations Balance of EPA's Grants Administration Division. U

GOCO
  Government-owned/contractor-operated. N

GOGO
  Government-owned/government-operated. N

good engineering practice stack height
  GEP. The greater of: (1) 65 meters; 2(i) For stacks in existence on January 12, 1979 and for which the owner or operator had obtained all applicable preconstruction permits or approvals required under this Parts 51 and 52 of Title 40, H_g = 2.5 H; (ii) for all other stacks,
  H_g = H + 1.5 L, where
  H_g = good engineering practice stack height, measured from the ground-level elevation at the base of the stack.
  H = height of nearby structure(s) measured from the ground-level elevation at the base of the stack.
  L = lesser dimension (height or projected width) of nearby structure(s);
  (3) The height demonstrated by a fluid model or a field study approved by the reviewing agency, which ensures that the emissions from a stack do not result in excessive concentrations of any air pollutant as a result of atmospheric downwash, wakes, or eddy effects created by the source itself, structures, or terrain obstacles. A

governing instruments
  Those legal documents which establish the existence of an organization and define its powers and parameters of operation. They include such documents as the Articles of Incorporation or Association, Constitution, Charter and By-Laws. A

government contract
  Any agreement or modification thereof between any contracting agency and any person for the furnishing of supplies or services or for the use of real or personal property, including lease arrangements. The term "services," as used in this definition includes, but is not limited to, the following services: utility, construction, transportation, research, insurance, and fund depository. The term "government contract" does not include (1) agreements in which the parties stand in the relationship of employer and employee, and (2) federally assisted construction contracts. A

government-sponsored enterprises
  Enterprises with completely private ownership, such as Federal land banks and Federal home loans banks, established and chartered by the Federal Government to perform specialized functions. These enterprises are not included in the budget totals, but financial information on their operations is published in a separate part of the appendix to the President's budget. U

gr.
  Grain. U

grab sample
A single sample which is collected at a time and place most representative of total discharge. A

grade
The slope of a surface such as a roadway. Also, the elevation of a real or planned surface or structure. O

grading and contouring
A process for minimizing water infiltration of a sanitary landfill by reshaping the site to fill depressions and to create runoff patterns with shorter slopes that discharge to lined troughs. U

grain
(1) A unit of weight equal to 65 milligrams or 2/1,000 of an ounce. N (2) Corn wheat, sorghum, rice, rye, oats, barley, and soybeans. A

grain elevator
Any plant or installation at which grain is unloaded, handled, dried, cleaned, stored, or loaded. A

grain loading
The rate at which particles are emitted from a pollution source--measurement is made by the numbers of grains per cubic foot of gas emitted. N

grain terminal elevator
Any grain elevator which has a permanent storage capacity of more than 88,100 m^3 (ca. 2.5 million U.S. bushels), except those located at animal food manufacturers, pet food manufacturers, cereal manufacturers, breweries, and livestock feedlots. A

grant
Any grant or cooperative agreement awarded by an Executive Branch agency including all subagreements awarded thereunder. This includes grants-in-aid, except where such assistance is solely in the form of general revenue sharing funds, distributed under the State and Local Fiscal Assistance Act of 1972, 31 U.S.C. 1221 *et seq.* A

grant agreement
The written agreement and admendments thereto between an agency or department and a grantee in which the terms and conditions governing the grant are stated and agreed to by both parties pursuant to grant regulations. U

grant award official
The EPA official authorized to execute a grant agreement on behalf of the Government. A

grantee
(1) The party which has accepted a grant award and includes entities controlled by the grantee. The term "controlled" means the direct or indirect ownership of more than 50 percent of outstanding stock entitled to vote for the election of directors, or a directing influence over such stock; provided, however, that foreign entities not wholly owned by the grantee shall not be considered as "controlled." A (2) Any individual, agency, or entity which has been awarded wastewater treatment construction grant assistance. A

granular activated carbon treatment
GAC. A filtering system often used in small water systems and individual homes to remove organics. GAC can be highly effective in removing elevated levels of radon from water. N

grapple
A clamshell-type bucket with three or more jaws that is used in excavating. Also called star or orange peel bucket. U

grate
A piece of furnace equipment used to support solid waste or solid fuel during the drying, igniting, and burning processes. Openings in its surface permit air to flow through the fuel and permit ash and unburned residue to be removed after combustion. U

grate siftings
The materials that fall from the solid waste fuel bed through the grate openings. A

gravity separation
(1) The treatment of mineral particles which exploits differences between their specific gravities. The separation is usually performed by means of sluices, jigs, classifiers, spirals, hydrocyclones, or shaking tables. A (2) The separation of mixed material immersed in a liquid according to the differential specific gravities of its components. It is used in solid waste recovery to separate nonferrous metals from other heavy materials. U

grease skimmer
A device for removing floating grease or scum from the surface of wastewater in a tank. U

green belts
Certain areas restricted from being used for building and houses; they often serve as separating buffers between pollution sources and concentrations of population. U

greenhouse effect
The warming of our atmosphere caused by build-up of carbon dioxide, which allows light from the Sun's rays to heat the Earth but prevents loss of the heat. N

grid casting facility
The facility which includes all lead melting pots and machines used for casting the grid used in battery manufacturing. A

grinder
A unit which is used to pulverize dry phosphate rock to the final product size used in the manufacture of phosphate fertilizer and does not include crushing devices used in mining. A

grinder pump
A mechanical device which shreds solids and raises the fluid to higher elevation through pressure sewers. N

grinding
(1) To reduce to powder or small fragments and includes mechanical chipping or drilling. A (2) The process of removing stock from a workpiece by the use of a tool consisting of abrasive grains held by a rigid or semi-rigid grinder. Grinding

includes surface finishing, sanding, and slicing. A

gross calorific value
Heat liberated when waste is burned completely and the products of combustion are cooled to the initial temperature of the waste. Usually expressed in British thermal units per pound. A

gross combination weight rating
GCWR. The value specified by the manufacturer as the loaded weight of a combination vehicle. A

gross production of fiberboard products
The air dry weight of hardboard or insulation board following formation of the mat and prior to trimming and finishing operations. A

gross tonnage
One hundred cubic feet of permanently enclosed space is equal to one gross ton--nothing whatever to do with weight. This is usually the registered tonnage although it may vary somewhat according to the classifying authority or nationality. A

gross vehicle weight
GVW. The manufacturer's gross weight rating for the individual vehicle. A

gross vehicle weight rating
GVWR. The value specified by the manufacturer as the maximum design loaded weight of a single vehicle. A

ground
A conducting connection, whether intentional or accidental, between an electrical circuit or equipment and the earth, or to some conducting body that serves in place of the earth. O

ground cover
Plants grown to keep soil from eroding. N

ground water
(1) The supply of fresh water under the earth's surface that forms a natural reservoir. N (2) Water below the land surface in the zone of saturation. A (3) Water in a saturated zone or stratum beneath the surface of land or water. A, L

ground water flow
The direction of groundwater movement and of any contaminants it contains; governed primarily by the hydraulic gradient. N

ground water quality
The ambient chemical, physical and biological quality of ground water; generally defined by State and local standards to determine suitability as a drinking-water source. Uncontaminated ground water's suitability as a drinking-water source is generally based on its total dissolved solids (TDS) content. N

ground water recharge
The addition of water to the ground water system by natural or artificial processes. N

groundwater contamination
The pollution of springs and wells from their sources underground. It can result from indiscriminate land

disposal of potentially hazardous waste materials that are then dissolved or suspended in free liquids, usually water, and leach downward through the unsaturated profile to the zone of saturation or from improperly constructed or operated wells. Movement of the toxic materials in the saturated zone is horizontal, and the rate of flow is determined by the gradient of the aquifer and its permeability. Correction of the problem is seldom limited to one site. U

groundwater infiltration
Water which enters the treatment facility as a result of the interception of natural springs, aquifers, or run-off which percolates into the ground and seeps into the treatment facility's tailings pond or wastewater holding facility and that cannot be diverted by ditching or grouting the tailings pond or wastewater holding facility. A

groundwater monitoring
The periodic sampling and analysis of changes in concentrations of chemical constituents in groundwater. U

growth
A relative measure of the viability of an algal population based on the number and/or weight of algal cells per volume of nutrient medium or test solution in a specified period of time. A

growth rate
An increase in biomass or cell numbers of algae per unit time. A

GSA
General Services Administration. U

GSD
Genetically significant dose. U

guarantor
Any person, other than the owner or operator, who provides evidence of financial responsibility of an owner or operator under CERCLA (Superfund). L

guard or shield
A barrier designed to protect against employee contact with a hazard created by a moving machinery part. O

guarded
Protected by personnel, covered, fenced, or enclosed by means of suitable casings, barrier rails, screens, mats, platforms, or other suitable devices in accordance with standard barricading techniques designed to prevent dangerous approach or contact by persons or objects. O

guardrail
A barrier secured to uprights and erected along the exposed sides and ends of platforms to prevent falls of persons. O

guidance
Documents issued mainly to elaborate and provide direction on the implementation of regulations. N

guide coat operation
The guide coat spray booth, flash-off area and bake oven(s) which are used to apply and dry or cure a surface coating between the prime coat and topcoat operation on the components of automobile and light-duty truck bodies. U

guide specification
A general specification--often referred to as a design standard or design guideline--which is a model standard and is suggested or required for use in the design of all of the construction projects of an agency. A

guillotine damper
An adjustable plate, used to regulate the flow of gases, installed vertically in a breeching. U

GVW
Gross vehicle weight. U

GVWR
Gross vehicle weight rating. U

GWPS
Ground Water Protection Standards. U

H

h.
Hour(s). U

H₂O
Water. U

H₂S
Hydrogen sulfide. U

H2SO4
Sulfuric acid. U

habitat
The sum of environmental conditions in a specific place that is occupied by an organism, population, or community. N

hair pulp
The removal of hair by chemical dissolution. A

hair save
The physical or mechanical removal of hair which has not been chemically dissolved, and either selling the hair as a by-product or disposing of it as a solid waste. A

half-life
(1) The time taken by certain materials to lose half their strength. For example the half life of DDT is 15 years; of radium 1,580 years. M (2) The time required for a pollutant to lose half its affect on the environment. For example, the half-life of DDT in the environment is 15 years, of radium, 1,580 years. The time required for half of the atoms of a radioactive element to undergo decay. The time required for the elimination of one half a total dose from the body. N

half-life of a chemical
The time required for the concentration of the chemical substance being tested to be reduced to one-half its initial value. A

halocarbon
The chemical compounds $CFCl_3$ and CF_2Cl_2 and such other halogenated compounds as the Administrator [of EPA] determines may reasonably be anticipated to contribute to reductions

in the concentration of ozone in the stratosphere. B

halogen
Any of a group of 5 chemically-related nonmetallic elements that includes bromine, fluorine, chlorine, iodine, and astatine. N

halon
Bromine-containing compounds with long atmospheric lifetimes whose breakdown in the stratosphere cause depletion of ozone. Halons are used in fire-fighting. N

hammer provision
Statutory requirements that go into effect automatically if EPA fails to issue regulations by certain dates specified in the statute. N

hammermill
A high- speed machine with hammers and cutters to crush, grind, chip, or shred solid wastes. N

hand glass melting furnace
A glass melting furnace where the molten glass is removed from the furnace by a glassworker using a blowpipe or a pontil. A

handicapped person
Any person who (1) has a physical or mental impairment which substantially limits one or more major life activities, (2) has a record of such an impairment, or (3) is regarded as having such an impairment. For purposes of employment, the term "handicapped person" does not include any person who is an alcoholic or drug abuser whose current use of alcohol or drugs prevents such individual from performing the duties of the job in question or whose employment, by reason of such current drug or alcohol abuse, would constitute a direct threat to property or the safety of others. A

handrail
A bar or pipe supported on brackets from a wall or partition, as on a stairway or ramp, to furnish persons with a handhold in case of tripping. O

hang-up
The process of hydrocarbon molecules being absorbed, adsorbed, condensed, or by any other method removed from the sample flow prior to reaching the instrument detector. It also refers to any subsequent desorption of the molecules into the sample flow when they are assumed to be absent. A

HAP
Hazardous air pollutant. B

hard water
Alkaline water containing dissolved mineral salts, that interfere with some industrial processes and prevent soap from lathering. N

hardness
(1) A characteristic of water, imparted by salts of calcium, magnesium, and iron such as bicarbonates, carbonates, sulfates, chlorides, and nitrates, that cause curding of soap, deposition of scale in boilers, damage in some industrial processes, and sometimes objectionable taste. It may be determined by a standard laboratory procedure or

computed from the amounts of calcium and magnesium as well as iron, aluminum, manganese, barium, strontium, and zinc, and is expressed as equivalent calcium carbonate. (2) The total concentration of the calcium and magnesium ions in water expressed as calcium carbonate (mg CaCO₃/liter). A

hardpan
(1) A hardened, compacted, or cemented soil layer. (2) A very dense soil layer caused by compaction or cementation of soil particles by organic matter, silica, sesquioxides, or calcium carbonate, for example. N

harvesting
Physical measures employed directly upon farm, forest, or ranch crops within established agricultural and silvicultural lands to bring about their removal from farm, forest, or ranch land, but does not include the construction of farm, forest, or ranch roads. A

hatch
Eggs or young birds that are the same age and that are derived from the same adult breeding population, where the adults are of the same strain and stock. A

hatchability
Embryos that mature, pip the shell, and liberate themselves from the eggs on day 23 or 24 of incubation. Values are expressed as percentage of viable embryos (fertile eggs). A

hatchback
A passenger automobile where the conventional luggage compartment, i.e., trunk, is replaced by a cargo area which is open to the passenger compartment and accessed vertically by a rear door which encompasses the rear window. A

haul time
The elapsed or cumulative time spent transporting solid waste between two specific locations. U

hazard
A probability that a given pesticide [or other pollutant] will have an adverse effect on man or the environment in a given situation, the relative likelihood of danger or ill effect being dependent on a number of interrelated factors present at any given time. A

hazard and operability study
HAZOP. A systematic technique for identifying hazards or operability problems throughout an entire facility. One examines each segment of a process and lists all possible deviations for normal operating conditions and how they might occur. The consequences on the process are assessed, and the means available to detect and correct the deviations are examined. N

hazard correction
The elimination or control of a workplace hazard in accord with the requirements of applicable federal or state statutes, regulations or standards. O

hazard identification
The process of determining whether exposure to a substance is causally related to the incidence and/or

severity of an adverse health effect (e.g., cancer, birth defects, etc.). Hazard identification involves gathering and evaluating data on the types of health injury or disease that may be produced by a chemical and on the conditions of exposure under which injury or disease is produced. It may also involve characterization of the behavior of a chemical within the body and the interactions it undergoes within organs, cells, or even parts of cells. Hazard identification is the first step in the risk assessment process. N

hazard information transmission program
HIT. This program provides a digital transmission of the CHEMTREC emergency chemical report to first responders at the scene of a hazardous materials incident. The report advises the responder on the hazards of the materials, the level of protective clothing required, mitigating action to take in the event of a spill, leak or fire, and first aid for victims. HIT is a free public service provided by the Chemical Manufacturing Association. Reports are sent in emergency situations only to organizations that have pre-registered with HIT. Brochures and registration forms may be obtained by writing: Manager, CHEMTREC/ CHEMNET, 2501 M Street, N.W., Washington, DC 20037. N

hazard ranking system
HRS. The principle screening tool used by EPA to evaluate risks to public health and the environment associated with abandoned or uncontrolled hazardous waste sites. The HRS calculates a score based on the potential of hazardous substances spreading from the site through the air, surface water, or ground water and on other factors such as nearby population. This score is the primary factor in deciding if the site should be on the National Priorities List and, if so, what ranking it should have compared to other sites on the list. N

hazard warning
Any words, pictures, symbols, or combination thereof appearing on a label or other appropriate form of warning which convey the hazard(s) of the chemical(s) in the container(s). O

hazardous air pollutant
(1) An air pollutant to which no ambient air quality standard is applicable and which in the judgment of the Administrator [of EPA] causes, or contributes to, air pollution which may reasonably be anticipated to result in an increase in mortality or an increase in serious irreversible, or incapacitating reversible, illness. B (2) An air pollutant which is not covered by ambient air quality standards but which, as defined in the Clean Air Act, may reasonably be expected to cause or contribute to irreversible illness or death. Such pollutants include asbestos, beryllium, mercury, benzene, coke oven emissions, radionuclides, and vinyl chloride. N

hazardous chemical
Any chemical which is a physical hazard or a health hazard. O

hazardous constituents
Constituents that have been detected in groundwater in the uppermost

aquifer underlying a regulated unit and that are reasonably expected to be in or derived from waste contained in a regulated unit. N

hazardous material
A material which has one or more of the following characteristics: (1) Has a flash point below 140° F, closed cup, or is subject to spontaneous heating; (2) Has a threshold limit value below 500 ppm for gases and vapors, below 500 mg/m^3 for fumes, and below 25 mppcf (million particles per cubic foot) for dusts; (3) Has a single dose oral LD$_{50}$ below 50 mg/kg; (4) Is subject to polymerization with the release of large amounts of energy; (5) Is a strong oxidizing or reducing agent; (6) Causes first degree burns to skin [from a] short time exposure, or is systemically toxic by skin contact; or (7) In the course of normal operations, may produce dusts, gases, fumes, vapors, mists, or smokes which have one or more of the above characteristics. N

hazardous materials response (HAZMAT) team
An organized group of employees, designated by the employer, who are expected to perform work to handle and control actual or potential leaks or spills of hazardous substances requiring possible close approach to the substance. The team members perform responses to releases or potential releases of hazardous substances for the purpose of control or stabilization of the incident. A HAZMAT team is not a fire brigade nor is a typical fire brigade a HAZMAT team. A HAZMAT team, however, may be a separate component of a fire brigade or fire department. O

hazardous substance
(1) Any material that poses a threat to human health and/or the environment. Typical hazardous substances are toxic, corrosive, ignitable, explosive, or chemically reactive. Any substance designated by EPA to be reported if a designated quantity of the substance is spilled in the waters of the United States or if otherwise emitted to the environment. (2) (A) Any substance designated pursuant to section 311(b)(2)(A) of the Federal Water Pollution Control Act, (B) Any element, compound, mixture, solution, or substance designated pursuant to section 102 of the Act, (C) Any hazardous waste having the characteristics identified under or listed pursuant to section 3001 of the Solid Waste Disposal Act (but not including any waste the regulation of which under the Solid Waste Disposal Act has been suspended by Act of Congress), (D) Any toxic pollutant listed under section 307(a) of the Federal Water Pollution Control Act, (E) Any hazardous air pollutant listed under section 112 of the Clean Air Act, and (F) Any imminently hazardous chemical substance or mixture with respect to which the Administrator has taken action pursuant to section 7 of the Toxic Substances Control Act. The term does not include petroleum, including crude oil or any fraction thereof which is not otherwise specifically listed or designated as a hazardous substance under subparagraphs (A) through (F) of this paragraph, and the term does not

include natural gas, natural gas liquids, liquefied natural gas, or synthetic gas usable for fuel (or mixtures of natural gas and such synthetic gas). [ed. Establishes the substances covered by Superfund]. L (2) Any substance designated or listed under paragraphs (A) through (D) of this definition, exposure to which results or may result in adverse affects on the health or safety of employees: (A) Any substance defined under [29 CFR] section 101(14) of CERCLA; (B) Any biological agent and other disease-causing agent which after release into the environment and upon exposure, ingestion, inhalation, or assimilation into any person, either directly from the environment or indirectly by ingestion through food chains, will or may reasonably be anticipated to cause death, disease, behavioral abnormalities, cancer, genetic mutation, physiological malfunctions (including malfunctions in reproduction) or physical deformations in such persons or their offspring; (C) Any substance listed by the U.S. Department of Transportation as hazardous materials under 49 CFR 172.01 and appendices; and (D) hazardous waste as herein defined. O

hazardous substance UST system

An underground storage tank system that contains a hazardous substance defined in section 101(14) of the Comprehensive Environmental Response, Compensation and Liability Act of 1980 (but not including any substance regulated as a hazardous waste under subtitle C) or any mixture of such substances and petroleum, and which is not a petroleum UST system. A

hazardous waste

(1) A solid waste, or combination of solid wastes, which because of its quantity, concentration, or physical, chemical or infectious characteristics may (A) cause, or significantly contribute to an increase in mortality or an increase in serious irreversible, or incapacitating reversible, illness; or (B) pose a substantial present or potential hazard to human health or the environment when improperly treated, stored, transported, or disposed of, or otherwise managed. I
(2) Any waste or combination of wastes which pose a substantial present or potential hazard to human health or living organisms because such wastes are nondegradable or persistent in nature or because they can be biologically magnified, or because they can be lethal, or because they may otherwise cause or tend to cause detrimental cumulative effects; also, a waste or combination of wastes of a solid, liquid, contained gaseous, or semisolid form which may cause, or contribute to, an increase in mortality or an increase in serious irreversible, or incapacitating reversible illness, taking into account the toxicity of such waste, its persistence and degradability in nature, its potential for accumulation or concentration in tissue, and other factors that may otherwise cause or contribute to adverse acute or chronic effects on the health of persons or other organisms. A [ed. Hazardous wastes will be those wastes listed by EPA or meeting characteristics specified by EPA in their criteria pursuant to the Resource Conservation Recovery Act (RCRA).]

hazardous waste constituent
A constituent that caused the Administrator to list the hazardous waste in part 261, subpart D, [of 40 CFR parts 260-261], or a constituent listed in table 1 of § 261.24 [of this same CFR]. A

Hazardous Waste Data Management System (HWDMS)
A database maintained by the EPA in which brief summary conclusions from inspection reports are tracked. N

hazardous waste discharge
The accidental or intentional spilling, leaking, pumping, pouring, emitting, emptying or dumping of hazardous waste into or on any land or water. A

hazardous waste generation
The act or process of producing hazardous waste. I

hazardous waste management
The systematic control of the collection, source separation, storage, transportation, processing, treatment, recovery, and disposal of hazardous wastes. I

hazardous waste management facility
HWM facility. All contiguous land, and structures, other appurtenances, and improvements on the land used for treating, storing, or disposing of hazardous waste. A facility may consist of several treatment, storage, or disposal operational units (for example, one or more landfills, surface impoundments, or combination of them). A

hazardous waste management unit
A contiguous area of land on or in which hazardous waste is placed, or the largest area in which there is significant likelihood of mixing hazardous waste constituents in the same area. Examples of hazardous waste management units include a surface impoundment, a waste pile, a land treatment area, a landfill cell, an incinerator, a tank and its associated piping and underlying containment system and a container storage area. A container alone does not constitute a unit; the unit includes containers and the land or pad upon which they are placed. A

hazardous waste management unit shutdown
A work practice or operational procedure that stops operation of a hazardous waste management unit or part of a hazardous waste management unit. An unscheduled work practice or operational procedure that stops operation of a hazardous waste management unit or part of a hazardous waste management unit for less than 24 hours is not a hazardous waste management unit shutdown. The use of spare equipment and technically feasible bypassing of equipment without stopping operation are not hazardous waste management unit shutdowns. A

hazardous waste site post-closure plan
The plan for post-closure care prepared in accordance with the requirements of 40 CFR § 265.117 through § 265.120. A

hazards analysis
The procedures involved in (1) identifying potential sources of release of hazardous materials from fixed facilities or transportation accidents; (2) determining the vulnerability of a geographical area to a release of hazardous materials; and (3) comparing hazards to determine which present greater or lesser risks to a community. N

hazards identification
Providing information on which facilities have extremely hazardous substances, what those chemicals are, and how much there is at each facility. The process also provides information on how the chemicals are stored and whether they are used at high temperature. N

HAZMAT
Hazardous material. N

HAZOP
Hazard and Operability Study. U

HBV
Hepatitis B virus. O

HC
Hydrocarbons. U

HCFA
Health Care Financing Administration. U

HCFCs
Chlorofluorocarbons that have been chemically altered by the addition of hydrogen, and which are significantly less damaging to stratospheric ozone than other CFCs. N

HCl
Hydrochloric acid. U

HCRS
Heritage Conservation and Recreation Service. U

HEA
Health effects assessment. N

headband
The component of hearing protective device which applies force to, and holds in place on the head, the component which is intended to acoustically seal the ear canal. A

health and safety data
(1) (a) Any study of any effect of a chemical substance or mixture on health, on the environment, or on both, including underlying data and epidemiological studies; studies of occupational exposure to a chemical substance or mixture; and toxicological, clinical, and ecological studies of a chemical substance or mixture; (b) Any test performed under the TSCA Act; and (c) Any data reported to, or otherwise obtained by, EPA from a study described in paragraph (a)(3)(i)(A) of [40 CFR § 2.306] or a test described in paragraph (a)(#)(i)(B) of [40 CFR § 2.306]. A

health and safety plan
A plan that specifies the procedures that are sufficient to protect on-site personnel and surrounding communities from the physical, chemical, and/or biological hazards of the site. The health and safety plan outlines: (i) Site hazards; (ii) Work areas and site control procedures; (iii) Air

surveillance procedures; (iv) Levels of protection; (v) Decontamination and site emergency plans; (vi) Arrangements for weather-related problems; and (vii) Responsibilities for implementing the health and safety plan. A

health and safety study
Any study of any effect of a chemical substance or mixture on health or the environment or on both, including underlying data and epidemiological studies, studies of occupational exposure to a chemical substance or mixture, toxicological, clinical, and ecological, or other studies of a chemical substance or mixture, and any test performed under the TSCA Act. Chemical identity is always part of a health and safety study. A

health assessment
An evaluation of available data on existing or potential risks to human health posed by a Superfund site. The Agency for Toxic Substances and Disease Registry of the U.S. Department of Health and Human Services is required to perform a health assessment at every site on the National Priorities List. N

health care facilities
Buildings or portions of buildings and mobile homes that contain, but are not limited to, hospitals, nursing homes, extended care facilities, clinics, and medical and dental offices, whether fixed or mobile. O

health hazard
A chemical, mixture of chemicals or a pathogen for which there is statistically significant evidence based on at least one study conducted in accordance with established scientific principles that acute or chronic health effects may occur in exposed employees. The term "health hazard" includes chemicals which are carcinogens, toxic or highly toxic agents, reproductive toxins, irritants, corrosives, sensitizers, heptaotoxins, nephrotoxins, neurotoxins, agents which act on the hematopoietic system, and agents which damage the lungs, skin, eyes, or mucous membranes. It also includes stress due to temperature extremes. Further definition of the terms used above can be found in appendix A to 29 CFR 1910.1200. O

health professional
A physician, occupational health nurse, industrial hygienist, toxicologist, or epidemiologist, providing medical or other occupational health services. O

hearing
(1) A hearing on the record open to the public and conducted under rules of practice. A (2) A public hearing which is conducted pursuant to the provisions of chapter 5, subchapter II of title 5 of the United States Code and the regulations of 40 CFR part 150-189. A

hearing clerk
The Hearing Clerk, A-110, United States Environmental Protection Agency, 401 M St. S.W., Washington, D.C. 20460. A

hearing officer
The individual or board of individuals designated to conduct hearings. A

hearing protective device
Any device or material, capable of being worn on the head or in the ear canal, that is sold wholly or in part on the basis of its ability to reduce the level of sound entering the ear. This includes devices of which hearing protection may not be the primary function, but which are nonetheless sold partially as providing hearing protection to the user. This term is used interchangeably with the terms "hearing protector" and "device." A

hearth
The bottom of a furnace, on which waste materials or fuels are exposed to the flame. U

heat balance
An accounting of the distribution of the heat input and output of an incinerator or boiler, usually on an hourly basis. U

heat exchanger
A device that transfers heat from one fluid to another without allowing them to mix. U

heat input
The total gross calorific value (where gross calorific value is measured by ASTM Method D2015-66, D240-64, or D1826-64) of all fuels burned. O

heat island effect
The haze dome created in cities by pollutants combining with the heat trapped in the spaces between tall buildings. This haze prevents natural cooling of air, and in the absence of strong winds can hold high concentrations of pollutants in one place. N

heat rating
That measurement of engine indicated mean effective pressure (IMEP) value obtained on the engine at a point when the supercharge pressure is 25.4mm (one inch) Hg below the preignition point of the spark plug, as rated according to SAE J549A Recommended Practice. A

heat release rate
The amount of heat liberated during complete combustion in unit time. It is usually expressed in British thermal units per hour per cubic foot of the internal volume of the furnace in which combustion takes place. U

heat treatment
The application of heat of specified temperature and duration to change the physical properties of the metal. A

heating oil
Petroleum that is No. 1, No. 2, No. 4-light, No. 4-heavy, No. 5-light, No. 5-heavy, and No. 6 technical grades of fuel oil; other residual fuel oils (including Navy Special Fuel Oil and Bunker C); and other fuels when used as substitutes for one of these fuel oils. Heating oil is typically used in the operation of heating equipment, boilers, or furnaces. A

heavy duty scaffold
A scaffold designed and constructed to carry a working load not to exceed 75 pounds per square foot. O

heavy duty vehicle
(1) A truck, bus, or other vehicle manufactured primarily for use on the public streets, roads, and highways (not including any vehicle operated exclusively on a rail or rails) which has a gross vehicle weight (as determined under regulations promulgated by the Administrator) in excess of six thousand pounds. Such term includes any such vehicle which has special features enabling off-street or off-highway operation and use. B (2) Any motor vehicle rated at more than 8,500 pounds GVWR or that has a vehicle curb weight of more than 6,000 pounds or that has a basic vehicle frontal area in excess of 45 square feet. A

heavy light-duty truck
Any light-duty truck rated greater than 6000 lbs GVWR. A

heavy media separation
The separation of mixed material immersed in a colloidal suspension according to its differential densities, or the float /sink technique. The colloidal medium is a water suspension of a finely ground, dense mineral, usually magnetite, ferrosilicon, or galena. U

heavy metals
(1) Metallic elements like mercury, chromium, cadmium, arsenic, and lead, with high molecular weights. They can damage living things at low concentrations and tend to accumulate in the food chain. N (2) All uranium, plutonium, or thorium placed into a nuclear reactor. A

heavy-duty engine
Any engine which the engine manufacturer could reasonably expect to be used for motive power in a heavy-duty vehicle. A

heavy-passenger cars
For the 1984 model year only, a passenger car or passenger car derivative capable of seating 12 passengers or less, rated at 6,000 pounds GVW or more and having an equivalent test weight of 5,000 pounds or more. A

HEI
Health Effects Institute. N

helmet
A head protective device consisting of a rigid shell, energy absorption system, and chin strap intended to be worn to provide protection for the head or portions thereof, against impact, flying or falling objects, electric shock, penetration, heat and flame. O

hemangiosarcoma
A malignant neoplasm characterized by rapidly proliferating, extensively infiltrating, anaplastic cells derived from blood vessels and lining blood-filled spaces. N

herbicide
All substances or mixtures of substances, except defoliants intended for use in preventing or inhibiting the growth of or killing or destroying plants and plant parts which are declared to be pests under 40 CFR § 162.14. Herbicides include, but are not limited to: (i) Direct contact

herbicides intended to kill or destroy weeds, unwanted brush and trees, or unwanted plant parts, or to mitigate their adverse effects on desirable plants; (ii) Soil treatment herbicides intended to kill or destroy weeds, unwanted brush and trees, or unwanted plant parts, or to prevent the establishment of any or all plants; (iii) Pre-emerges herbicides intended to prevent or inhibit the germination or growth of weed seeds or seedlings; (iv) Root control herbicides intended to prevent the growth of, or kill roots in certain sites such as sewer lines and drainage tiles; (v) Aquatic herbicides intended to prevent, inhibit, or control the growth of, or kill aquatic weeds; (vi) Algaecides, except, slimicides intended to prevent or inhibit the multiplication of, or destroy algae in ponds, swimming pools, aquaria or similar confined sites; (vii) Debarking agents intended to kill trees by treatment of bark on trunks; and (viii) Biological weed-control agents such as specific pathogenic organisms or entities prepared and utilized by man. O

herbivore
An animal that feeds on plants. N

heritable translocations
Reciprocal translocations transmitted from parent to the succeeding progeny. A

hertz
Unit of frequency equal to one cycle per second, generally applied to nonionizing radiation. U

heterotrophic organisms
(1) Humans and animals that can't make food from inorganic chemicals. M (2) Consumers such as humans and animals, and decomposers--chiefly bacteria and fungi--that are dependent on organic matter for food. N

HEW
U.S. Department of Health, Education and Welfare, now HHS or Health and Human Services. U

hexavalent chromium
Chromium VI. The value obtained by the method specified in 40 CFR 136.3. A

HFID
Heated flame ionization detector. U

Hg
Mercury. U

HHS
U.S. Department of Health and Human Services. U

HI
Hazard Index. U

hi-volume sampler
A device used to measure and analyze suspended particulate pollution. N

hide
Any animal pelt or skin as received by a tannery as raw material to be processed. A

high air
Air pressure used to supply power to pneumatic tools and devices. O

high altitude
Any elevation over 1,219 meters (4,000 feet). A

high concentration PCBs
PCBs that contain 500 ppm or greater PCBs, or those materials which EPA requires to be assumed to contain 500 ppm or greater PCBs in the absence of testing. A

high density polyethylene
A material used to make plastic bottles that produces toxic fumes when burned. N

high dose
Shall not exceed the lower explosive limit (LEL) and ideally should induce minimal toxicity. A

high radiation area
Any area, accessible to personnel, in which there exists radiation at such levels that a major portion of the body could receive in any one hour a dose in excess of 100 millirem. O

high terrain area
With respect to any facility, any area having an elevation of 900 feet or more above the base of the stack of such facility, and the term "low terrain area" means any area other than a high terrain area. B

high velocity air filter
HVAF. An air pollution control filtration device for the removal of sticky, oily, or liquid aerosol particulate matter from exhaust gas streams. A

high-altitude conditions
A test altitude of 1,620 meters (5,315 ft.) plus or minus 100 meters (328 ft.), or equivalent observed barometric test conditions of 83.3 $\pm$ 1 kilopascals. A

high-altitude efficiency modification
The provision of increased air flow, restricted fuel flow, or other modification [in automobile engines] having the effect of compensating for the adverse effects on combustion efficiency of decreased air density at high altitudes. A

high-altitude reference point
An elevation of 1,620 meters (5,315 feet) plus or minus 100 meters (328 feet), or equivalent observed barometric test conditions of 83.3 kPa (24.2 inches Hg), plus or minus 1 kPa (0.30 inches Hg). A

high-contact industrial surface
A surface in an industrial setting which is repeatedly touched, often for relatively long periods of time. Manned machinery and control panels are examples of high-contact industrial surfaces. High-contact industrial surfaces are generally of impervious solid material. Examples of low-contact industrial surfaces include ceilings, walls, floors, roofs, roadways and sidewalks in the industrial area, utility poles, unmanned machinery, concrete pads beneath electrical equipment, curbing, exterior structural building components, indoor vaults, and pipes. A

high-contact residential/commercial surface
A surface in a residential/commercial

area which is repeatedly touched, often for relatively long periods of time. Doors, wall areas below 6 feet in height, uncovered flooring, windowsills, fencing, bannisters, stairs, automobiles, and children's play areas such as outdoor patios and sidewalks are examples of high-contact residential/commercial surfaces. Examples of low-contact residential/commercial surfaces include interior ceilings, interior wall areas above 6 feet in height, roofs, asphalt roadways, concrete roadways, wooden utility poles, unmanned machinery, concrete pads beneath electrical equipment, curbing, exterior structural building components (e.g., aluminum/ vinyl siding, cinder block, asphalt tiles), and pipes. A

high-grade paper
Letterhead, dry copy papers, miscellaneous business forms, stationery, typing paper, tablet sheets, and computer printout paper and cards, commonly sold as "white ledger," "computer printout" and "tab card" grade by the wastepaper industry. A

high-hazard contents
High-hazard contents shall be classified as those which are liable to burn with extreme rapidity or from which poisonous fumes or explosions are to be feared in the event of fire. O

high-level liquid waste
The aqueous waste resulting from the operation of the first-cycle extraction system, equivalent concentrated wastes from a process not using solvent extraction, in a facility for processing irradiated reactor fuels. U

high-level radioactive waste
The aqueous waste resulting from the operation of the first cycle solvent extraction system, or equivalent and the concentrated waste from subsequent extraction cycles, or equivalent, in a facility for reprocessing irradiated reactor fuels, or irradiated fuel from nuclear power reactors. E

highly toxic
A chemical falling within any of the following categories: (a) A chemical that has a median lethal dose (LD_{50}) of 50 milligrams or less per kilogram of body weight when administered orally to albino rats weighing between 200 and 300 grams each. (b) A chemical that has a median lethal dose (LD_{50}) of 20_0 milligrams or less per kilogram of body weight when administered by continuous contact for 24 hours (or less if death occurs within 24 hours), with the bare skin of albino rabbits weighing between two and three kilograms each. (c) A chemical that has a median lethal concentration (LC_{50}) in air of 200 parts per million by volume or less of gas or vapor, or 2 milligrams per liter or less of mist, fume, or dust, when administered by continuous inhalation for one hour (or less if death occurs within one hour) to albino rats weighing between 200 and 300 grams each. N, O

highway
The streets, roads, and public ways in any State. A

highway fuel economy
The fuel economy determined by

operating a vehicle (or vehicles) over the driving schedule in the Federal Highway Fuel Economy Test Procedure. A

histology
The study of the structure of cells and tissues; usually involves microscopic examination of tissue slices. N

HIT
Hazard information transmission program. U

HIV
Human immunodeficiency virus. O

HMTA
Hazardous Materials Transportation Act. This act provides authority for regulating the transportation of hazardous material by road, air and rail. The Department of Transportation's (DOT) Materials Transportation Bureau (MTB) identified particular quantities and forms of materials as hazardous and specifies packaging, labeling and shipping requirements for the materials that pose a risk to health, safety or property. N

HOCs
Halogenated organic compounds. U

hoistway
Any shaftway, hatchway, well hole, or other vertical opening or space in which an elevator or dumb-waiter is designed to operate. O

holding pond
A pond or reservoir usually made of earth built to store waste stream or polluted runoff. N

homeostasis
Maintenance of a constant internal environment in an organism. N

homogeneous area
An area of surfacing material, thermal system insulation material, or miscellaneous material that is uniform in color and texture. A

homogeneous waste
Solid waste composed of similar materials, e.g., newsprint, stationery, and cardboard. U

hood
For the purposes of 40 CFR § 42.741, a partial enclosure or canopy for capturing and exhausting, by means of a draft, the organic vapors or other fumes rising from a coating process or other source. A

hood capture efficiency
The emission from a process which are captured by hood and directed into the control device, expressed as a percent of all emissions. N

hormone
A chemical substance, formed in one organ or part of the body and carried in the blood to another organ or part where it alters the functional activity, and sometimes the structure, of one or more organs by its specific chemical activity. N

host
(1) Any plant or animal on or in which another lives for nourishment,

development, or protection. A (2) In genetics, the organisms, typically a bacterium, into which a gene from another organism is transplanted. In medicine, an animal infected by or parasitized by another organism. N

host defense(s)/systems
A complex system that defends the body against biological or chemical agents. Often referred to with respect to the lungs where the system clears the lungs of microbes and particulate pollutants. Also refers to chemical defenses such as antioxidant substances that defend against oxidants such as ozone or nitrogen dioxide. N

hot
Slang for radioactive material. N

hot drying hearth
A surface upon which waste materials are placed to dry or to burn. Hot combustion gases first pass over the materials and then under the hearth. U

hot soak loss
Fuel evaporative emissions during the 1-hour hot soak period which begins immediately after an automobile engine is turned off. A

housed lot
Totally roofed buildings which may be open or completely enclosed on the sides wherein animals or poultry are housed over solid concrete or dirt floors, slotted (partially open) floors over pits or manure collection areas in pens, stalls or cages, with or without bedding materials and mechanical ventilation. A

household waste
Any solid waste (including garbage, trash, and sanitary waste in septic tanks) derived from households (including single and multiple residences, hotels and motels, bunkhouses, ranger stations, crew quarters, campgrounds, picnic grounds, and day-use recreation areas). A

hp.
Horsepower. U

hp.- hr.
Horsepower-hour. U

HRS
Hazard ranking system. N

HSL
Hazardous substance list. N

HSWA
The Hazardous and Solid Waste Amendments of 1984. Public Law 98-616 that amended RCRA. N

HUD
U.S. Department of Housing and Urban Development. U

human environment
The natural and physical environment and the relationship of people with that environment. This means that economic or social effects are not intended by themselves to require preparation of an environmental impact statement. When an environmental impact statement is prepared and economic or social and natural or physical environmental effects are interrelated, then the environmental impact statement will

discuss all of these effects on the human environment. N

human equivalent dose
The human dose of an agent expected to induce the same type and severity of toxic effect that an animal dose has induced. N

human exposure model
HEM. A mathematical model used in exposure assessments for toxic air pollutants to quantify the number of people exposed to pollutants emitted by stationary sources and the pollutant concentrations they are exposed to. Input data include plant characteristics such as location, emission, parameters, etc. as well as Bureau of Census data used in the estimation of persons exposed and appropriate meteorological data. N

human subject
A living individual about whom an investigator (whether professional or student) conducting research obtains (1) Data through intervention nor interaction with the individual, or (2) identifiable private information. "Intervention" includes both physical procedures by which data are gathered (for example, venipuncture) and manipulations subject or the subject's environment that are performed for research purposes. "Interaction" includes communication or interpersonal contact between investigator and subject. "Private information" includes information about behavior that occurs in a context in which an individual can reasonably expect that no observation or recording is taking place, and information which has been provided for specific purposes by an individual and which the individual can reasonably expect will not be made public (for example, a medical record). Private information must be individually identifiable (i.e., the identity of the subject is or may readily be ascertained by the investigator or associated with the information) in order for obtaining the information to constitute research involving human subjects. A

humus
The dark brown or black residue found in soil resulting from the decomposition of organic matter. Residues in well-digested sludges and activated sludge are similar to humus in appearance and behavior. U

HVAF
High velocity air filter. U

HW
Hazardous wastes. U

HWDMS
Hazardous Waste Data Management System (OSWER). N I

hybrid
A cell or organism resulting from a cross between two unlike plant or animal cells or organisms. N

hybridoma
A hybrid cell that produces monoclonal antibodies in large quantities. N

hydraulic barkers
Wood processing equipment that has the function of removing bark from

wood, using water under a pressure of 68atm (1000 psi) or greater. A

hydraulic fluids
Petroleum-based hydraulic fluids. A

hydraulic gradient
The direction of groundwater flow. N

hydraulic tipper
A device that unloads a transfer trailer by raising its front end to a 70 degree angle. U

hydrocarbon
Any of a vast family of compounds containing carbon and hydrogen in various combinations: found especially in fossil fuels. Some of the hydrocarbon compounds are major air pollutants: they may be carcinogenic or active participants in photochemical process. U

hydrochloric acid pickling
Those operations in which steel products are immersed in hydrochloric acid solutions to chemically remove oxides and scale, and those rinsing operations associated with such immersions. A

hydrogen peroxide
H_2O_2. A fast-reaching liquid used as a bleaching agent; can be formed from gases during the photochemical process; gives off oxygen easily. U

hydrogen sulfide
H_2S. The gas emitted during organic decomposition that smells like rotten eggs. It is also a byproduct of oil refining and burning and can cause illness in heavy concentrations. N

hydrogeology
The geology of ground water, with particular emphasis on the chemistry and movement of water. N

hydrology
The science dealing with the properties, distribution, and circulation of water. N

hydrolysis
(1) A chemical process of decomposition in which the elements of water react with another substance to yield one or more entirely new substances. An example is the breakdown of cellulose into carbohydrates and ultimately to glucose. (2) The reaction of an organic chemical with water, such that one or more bonds are broken and the reaction products of the transformation incorporate the elements of water (H_2O). This type of transformation often results in the next exchange of a group X, on an organic chemical RX, for the OH group from water. This can be written as:
RX + HOH---\ ROH + HX. A

hydrotesting
The testing of piping or tubing by filling with water and pressurizing to test for integrity. A

hyperbaric conditions
Pressure conditions in excess of surface pressure. O

hypersensitivity
Exaggerated response by the immune system to an allergen. Sometimes used incorrectly in a non-immune sense to

indicate increased susceptibility to the effects of a pollutant. N

hypertrophy
Enlargement of an organ due to increase in cell size with no change in the cell number. For example, liver hypertrophy occurs in mice exposed to chlorinated hydrocarbons or to phenobarbital. N

hyperventilation
Overventilation; increased rate of air exchange relative to metabolic carbon dioxide production so that alveolar carbon dioxide pressure tends to fall below normal. N

hypo
Prefix, pertaining to a less than normal value. U

I

I.D.
Inside diameter. U

IAGs
Interagency agreements. U

IAQ
Indoor air quality. U

IARC
International Agency for Research on Cancer. N

IBP
Initial boiling point. U

ICC
Interstate Commerce Commission. U

ice fog
An atmospheric suspension of highly reflective ice crystals. A

ICI
Independent commercial importer. U

ICRP
International Commission on Radiological Protection. K

identity
(1) Any chemical or common name used to identify a chemical substance or a mixture containing that substance. A (2) Any chemical or common name which is indicated on the material safety data sheet (MSDS) for the chemical. The identity used shall permit cross-references to be made among the required list of hazardous chemicals, the label and the MSDS. O

idle
That condition where all engines capable of providing motive power to the locomotive are set at the lowest operating throttle position; and where all auxiliary non-motive power engines are not operating. A

idle adjustments
A series of adjustments which include idle revolutions per minute, idle air/fuel ratio, and basic timing. A

idle emission test
A sampling procedure for exhaust emissions which requires operation of

267

the engine in the idle mode only. At a minimum, the idle test must consist of the following procedures carried out on a fully warmed-up engine: A verification that the idle revolutions per minute is within manufacturer's specified limits and a measurement of the exhaust carbon monoxide and/or hydrocarbon concentrations during the period of time from 15 to 25 seconds after the engine either was used to move the car or was run at 2,000 to 2,500 r/min with no load for 2 or 3 seconds. A

IDLH
Immediately dangerous to life and health. U

ignitability
An Environmental Protection Agency characteristic of hazardous waste which identifies waste that presents a fire hazard because it is ignitable under routine waste disposal and storage conditions. U

ignition arch
A refractory furnace arch or surface located over a fuel bed to radiate heat and to accelerate ignition. U

ignition temperature
The lowest temperature of a fuel at which combustion becomes self-sustaining. U

immediate container
That container which is directly in contact with the pesticide or device. A

immediate use
A chemical substance is for the "immediate use" of a person if it is under the control of, and used only by, the person who transferred it from a labeled container and will only be used by that person within the work shift in which it is transferred from the labeled container. A

immediately dangerous to life and health
(1) IDLH. The maximum level to which a healthy individual can be exposed to a chemical for 30 minutes and escape without suffering irreversible health effects or impairing symptoms. Used as a "level of concern." N (2) An atmospheric concentration of any toxic, corrosive or asphyxiant substance that poses an immediate threat to life or would cause irreversible or delayed adverse health effects or would interfere with an individual's ability to escape from a dangerous atmosphere. O

imminent danger
Any conditions or practices in a place of employment which are such that a danger exists which could reasonably be expected to cause death or serious physical harm immediately or before the imminence of such danger can be eliminated. O

imminent hazard
A situation which exists when the continued use of a pesticide during the time required for cancellation proceedings would be likely to result in unreasonable adverse effects on the environment or will involve unreasonable hazard to the survival of a species declared endangered by the Secretary of the Interior under Pub. L. 91-135. A, C

imminent hazard order
Used by the responsible agency under authority of RCRA Section 7003 to force any person contributing to an imminent and substantial endangerment to human health or the environment caused by the handling of non-hazardous or hazardous solid waste to take steps to clean up the problem. N

immobilization
The lack of movement by the test organisms except for minor activity of the appendages. A

immune system
All internal structures and processes providing defense against disease causing organisms (viruses, bacteria, fungi, parasites). Includes nonspecific defense mechanisms, such as interferon production, epithelialmembranes and phagocytic cells, as well as specific immune responses of cells producing antibodies in response to antigens entering the body. N

immunodeficiency
A condition resulting from ineffective functioning of the immunological system. Immunodeficiency may be primary (due to a defect in the immune mechanism per se) or secondary (dependent upon another disease process or toxicant exposure). N

immunosuppression
Decrease of immunologic response, usually resulting from exposure to chemical, pharmacologic, physical, or immunologic agents. N

impact mill
A machine that grinds material by throwing it against heavy metal projections rigidly attached to a rapidly rotating shaft. U

impedance
The rate at which a substance absorbs and transmits sound. N

impermeable liner
A layer of natural and/or manufactured material of sufficient composition, density, and thickness to have a maximum permeability for water of 10^{-7} centimeters per second at the maximum anticipated hydrostatic pressure. U

impervious
Chemical protective clothing is "impervious" to a chemical substance if the substance causes no chemical or mechanical degradation, permeation, or penetration of the chemical protective clothing under the conditions of, and the duration of, exposure. A

implementation
Putting a plan into practice by carrying out planned activities, including compliance and enforcement activities, or ensuring such activities are carried out. A

implementation plan
The plan, or revision thereof, which has been approved or promulgated by EPA under section 110 of the Clean Air Act and which is designed to attain and maintain a national primary or secondary ambient air quality standard in a State or portion thereof. A

import for commercial purposes
To import with the purpose of obtaining an immediate or eventual commercial advantage for the importer, and includes the importation of any amount of a chemical substance or mixture. If a chemical substance or mixture containing impurities is imported for commercial purposes, then those impurities also are imported for commercial purposes. A

import in bulk form
To import a chemical substance (other than as part of a mixture or article) in any quantity, in cans, bottles, drums, barrels, packages, tanks, bags, or other containers, if the chemical substance is intended to be removed from the container and the substance has an end use or commercial purpose separate from the container. A

importer
(1) Any person who imports any chemical substance or any chemical substance as part of a mixture or article into the customs territory of the United States, and includes: (A) The person primarily liable for the payment of any duties on the merchandise, or (B) an authorized agent acting on his behalf (as defined in 19 CFR 1.11). (2) Importer also includes, as appropriate: (A) The consignee; (B) The importer of record; (C) The actual owner if an actual owner's declaration and superseding bond has been filed in accordance with 19 CFR 141.20; (D) The transferee, if the right to draw merchandise in a bonded warehouse has been transferred in accordance with Subpart C of 19 CFR part 144. For the purpose of this definition, the customs territory of the United States consists of the 50 states, Puerto Rico, and the District of Columbia. A (2) The first business with employees within the Customs Territory of the United States which receives hazardous chemicals produced in other countries for the purpose of supplying them to distributors or employers within the United States. O

impoundment
A body of water confined by a dam, dike, floodgate, or other barrier. N

improved discharge
The volume, composition and location of an applicant's discharge following: (1) construction of planned outfall improvements, including, without limitation, outfall relocation, outfall repair, or diffuser modification; or (2) construction of planned treatment system improvements to treatment levels or discharge characteristics; or (3) implementation of a planned program to improve operation and maintenance of an existing treatment system or to eliminate or control the introduction of pollutants into the applicant's treatment works. A

impulsive noise
An acoustic event characterized by very short rise time and duration. A

impurity
(1) A chemical substance which is unintentionally present with another chemical substance or mixture. A (2) Any substance (or group of structurally similar substances if specified by the Agency) in a pesticide

product other than an active ingredient or an inert ingredient, including unreacted starting materials, side reaction products, contaminants, and degradation products. A

impurity associated with an active ingredient
(1) Any impurity present in the technical grade of active ingredient; and (2) Any impurity which forms in the pesticide product through reactions between the active ingredient and any other component of the product or packaging of the product. A

in existence
The owner or operator has obtained all necessary preconstruction approvals or permits required by Federal, State, or local air pollution emissions and air quality laws or regulations and either has (1) begun, or caused to begin, a continuous program of physical on-site construction of the facility or (2) entered into binding agreements or contractual obligations, which cannot be cancelled or modified without substantial loss to the owner or operator, to undertake a program of construction of the facility to be completed in a reasonable time. A

in operation
(1) Engaging in activity related to the primary design function of the source. A (2) A facility which is treating, storing, or disposing of hazardous waste. N

in or near commercial buildings
Within the interior of, on the roof of, attached to the exterior wall of, in the parking area serving, or within 30 meters of a non-industrial non-substation building. Commercial buildings are typically accessible to both members of the general public and employees, and include: (1) Public assembly properties, (2) educational properties, (3) institutional properties, (4) residential properties, (5) stores, (6) office buildings, and (7) transportation centers (e.g., airport terminal buildings, subway stations, bus stations, or train stations). A

in personem
An action in personem is instituted against an individual, usually through the personal service of process, and may result in the imposition of a liability directly upon the person of a defendant. A

in poor condition
The binding of the material is losing its integrity as indicated by peeling, cracking, or crumbling of the material. A

in the hands of the manufacturer
Vehicles that are still in the possession of the manufacturer and have not had their bills of lading transferred to another person for the purpose of transporting. A

in vinyl chloride service
A piece of equipment either contains or contacts a liquid that is at least 10 percent vinyl chloride by weight or a gas that is at least 10 percent by volume vinyl chloride as determined according to the provisions of § 61.67(h). The provisions of 40 CFR § 61.67(h) also specify how to determine

that a piece of equipment is not in vinyl chloride service. A

in vitro studies
Studies of chemical effects conducted in tissues, cells or subcellular extracts from an organism (i.e., not in the living organism). N

in vivo studies
(1) Studies of chemical effects conducted in intact living organisms. N (2) In the living body of a plant or animal. In vivo tests are those laboratory experiments carried out on whole animals or human volunteers. N

in VOC service
The piece of equipment that contains or contacts a process fluid that is at least 10 percent VOC by weight (see 40 CFR 60.2 for the definition of volatile organic compound or VOC and 40 CFR 60.485(d) to determine whether a piece of equipment is not in VOC service). A

in volatile hazardous air pollutant (VHAP) service
A piece of equipment that either contains or contacts a fluid (liquid or gas) that is at least 10 percent by weight a volatile hazardous air pollutant (VHAP) as determined according to the provisions of 40 CFR § 61.245(d). A

in-kind contribution
The value of a non-cash contribution provided by (a) the grantee, (b) other public agencies and institutions, (c) private organizations and individuals, or (d) EPA. An in-kind contribution may consist of charges for real property and equipment and value of goods and services directly benefiting and specifically identifiable to the grant program. A

in-process control technology
The conservation of chemicals and water throughout the production operations to reduce the amount of wastewater to be discharged. A

in-situ
Systems that perform an analysis without removing a sample from the stack. Point in-situ analyzers place the sensing or detecting element directly in the flue gas stream. Cross-stack in-situ analyzers measure the parameter of interest by placing a source beam on one side of the stack and the detector (in single-pass instruments) or a retroreflector (in double-pass instruments) on the other side, and measuring the parameter of interest (e.g., CO) by the attenuation of the beam by the gas in its path. A

in-situ uranium leach methods
The processes involving the purposeful introduction of suitable leaching solutions into a uranium ore body to dissolve the valuable minerals in place and the purposeful leaching of uranium ore in a static or semistatic condition either by gravity through an open pile, or by flooding a confined ore pile. It does not include the natural dissolution of uranium by ground waters, the incidental leaching of uranium by mine drainage, nor the rehabilitation of aquifers and the monitoring of these aquifers. A

inability to provide records
The incapacity of any person to

maintain, furnish or permit access to any records required by an environmental statute where such incapacity arises out of causes beyond the control and without the fault or negligence of such person. Such causes may include, but are not restricted to acts of God or the public enemy, fires, floods, epidemics, quarantine restrictions, strikes, and unusually severe weather, but in every case, the failure must be beyond the control and without the fault or negligence of said person. A

inactive stack
A stack to which no further routine additions of phosphogypsum will be made and which is no longer used for water management associated with the production of phosphogypsum. If a stack has not been used for either purpose for two years, it is presumed to be inactive. A

inactive waste disposal site
Any disposal site or portion of it where additional asbestos-containing waste material will not be deposited and where the surface is not disturbed by vehicular traffic. A

incidence
The number of new cases of a disease within a specified time period. It is frequently presented as the number of new cases per 1,000, 10,000 or 100,000. The incidence rate is a direct estimate of the probability or risk of developing a disease during a specified time period. N

incidence rates
The number of injuries and illnesses, or lost workdays, per 100 fulltime workers. Rates are calculated as

$$\frac{N \times 200{,}000}{EH}$$

N = number of injuries and illnesses, or number of lost workdays.
EH = total hours worked by all employees during a month, a quarter, or fiscal year
200,000 = base for 100 fulltime equivalent workers (working 40 hours per week, 50 weeks per year. O

incineration
(1) The controlled process which combustible solid, liquid, or gaseous wastes are burned and changed into noncombustible gases. A (2) Burning of certain types of solid, liquid or gaseous materials. (3) A treatment of technology involving destruction of waste by controlled burning at high temperatures, e.g., burning sludge to remove the water and reduce the remaining residues to a safe, nonburnable ash which can be disposed of safely on land, in some waters or in underground locations. N

incineration at sea
Disposal of waste by burning at sea on specially-designed incinerator ships. N

incinerator
(1) Any furnace used in the process of burning waste for the primary purpose of reducing the volume of the waste by removing combustible matter. (2) An enclosed device using controlled flame combustion, the primary purpose of which is to thermally break down hazardous waste. Examples of

incinerators are rotary kiln, fluidized bed, and liquid injection incinerators. A

incinerator collector
Any device used to remove suspended particles from the gaseous emissions produced in an incinerator during combustion. U

incinerator stoker
A mechanically operable moving grate arrangement for supporting, burning, or transporting solid waste in a furnace and discharging the residue. C

incipient L$_{C50}$
That test substance concentration, calculated from experimentally-derived mortality data, that is lethal to 50 percent of a test population when exposure to the test substance is continued until the mean increase in mortality does not exceed 10 percent in any concentration over a 24-hour period. A

inclined plate conveyor
A separating device that operates by feeding material onto an inclined steel plate belt conveyor so that heavy and resilient materials, such as glass, bounce down the conveyor and light and inelastic materials are carried upward by the motion of the belt. U

incompatible waste
A hazardous waste which is unsuitable for: (1) Placement in a particular device or facility because it may cause corrosion or decay of containment materials (e.g., container inner liners or tank walls); or (2) Commingling with another waste or material under uncontrolled conditions because the commingling might produce heat or pressure, fire or explosion, violent reaction, toxic dusts, mists, fumes, or gases, or flammable fumes or gases. A

incomplete gasoline-fueled heavy-duty vehicle
Any gasoline-fueled heavy-duty vehicle which does not have the primary load-carrying device, or passenger compartment, or engine compartment or fuel system attached. A

incomplete truck
Any truck which does not have the primary load carrying device or container attached. A

incorporated into the soil
The injection of solid waste beneath the surface of the soil or the mixing of solid waste with the surface soil. A

increments of progress
Steps to achieve compliance which must be taken by an owner or operator of a designated facility, including: (1) Submittal of a final control plan for the designated facility to the appropriate air pollution control agency; (2) Awarding of contracts for emission control systems or for process modifications, or issuance of orders for the purchase of component parts to accomplish emission control or process modification; (3) Initiation of on-site construction or installation of emission control equipment or process change; (4) Completion of on-site construction or installation of emission control

equipment or process change; and (5) Final compliance; increments of progress are individually enforceable. A

independent commercial importer
ICI. An importer who is not an original equipment manufacturer (OEM) or does not have a contractual agreement with an OEM to act as its authorized representative for the distribution of motor vehicles or motor vehicle engines in the U.S. market. A

independent laboratory
A test facility operated independently of any product manufacturer capable of performing evaluation tests. Additionally, the laboratory shall have no financial interests in the outcome of these tests other than a fee charged for each test performed. A

independently audited
An audit performed by an independent certified public accountant in accordance with generally accepted auditing standards. A

index or **index mark**
A mark on a choke thermostat housing, located in a fixed relationship to the thermostatic coil tang position to aid in assembly and service adjustment of the choke. A

Indian governing body
The governing body of any tribe, band, or group of Indians subject to the jurisdiction of the United States and recognized by the United States as possessing power of self-government. A [ed. Indian tribes generally have authority to impose their own pollution control requirements]. U

Indian lands
"Indian country" as defined in 18 U.S.C. 1151. That section defines Indian country as: (a) All land within the limits of any Indian reservation under the jurisdiction of the United States government, notwithstanding the issuance of any patent, and, including rights-of-way running through the reservation; (b) All dependent Indian communities within the borders of the United States whether within the original or subsequently acquired territory thereof, and whether within or without the limits of a State. A

Indian reservation
Any federally-recognized reservation established by treaty, agreement, Executive order, or act of Congress. A

Indian tribe
Any Indian Tribe, band, pueblo or community, including Native villages and Native groups as defined in the Alaska Native Claims Settlement Act, which is recognized by the Federal Government as eligible for services from the Bureau of Indian Affairs. A

indicator
(1) An event, entity, or condition that typically characterizes a prescribed environment or situation; indicators determine or aid in determining whether or not certain stated circumstances exist or criteria are satisfied. (2) In biology, an organism, species, or community that shows the presence of certain environmental conditions. N

indicator parameters
Waste constituents, (reaction

products or parameters such as specific conductance, total organic carbon, or total organic halogen), that provide a reliable indication of the presence of hazardous constituents in groundwater. N

indictment
Indictment for a criminal offense. An information or other filing by competent authority charging a criminal offense shall be given the same effect as an indictment. A

indirect ammonia recovery system
Those systems which recover ammonium hydroxide as a by-product from coke oven gases and waste ammonia liquors. A

indirect costs
Those costs incurred for a common or joint purpose but benefiting more than one cost objective, and not readily identifiable to the costs objectives specifically benefited. U

indirect discharge
(1) The discharge or the introduction of nondomestic pollutants from any source regulated by the pretreatment requirements of section 307 (b) or (c) of the FWPCA, into a POTW. A (2) Introduction of pollutants from a non-domestic source into a publicly owned waste treatment system. Indirect dischargers can be commercial or industrial facilities whose wastes go into the local sewers. N

indirect discharger
A nondomestic discharger introducing "pollutants" to a "publicly owned treatment works." A

indirect financial interest
The same financial relationships as for direct ownership, but where the employee reaps the benefits of such interests, including interests held by his or her spouse, minor child and other relatives, including in-laws, residing in the employee's home. The employee will not be deemed to have an indirect financial interest if there is no relationship between the employee's functions or duties and the coal mining operation in which the spouse, minor children or other resident relative holds a financial interest. A

indirect source
A facility, building, structure, installation, real property, road, or highway which attracts, or may attract, mobile sources of pollution. Such term includes parking lots, parking garages, and other facilities subject to any measure for management of parking supply (within the meaning of section 110(c)(2)(D)(ii)) [of the CAA], including regulation of existing off-street parking but such term does not include new or existing on-street parking. Direct emissions sources or facilities at, within, or associated with, any indirect source shall not be deemed indirect sources. B

indirect source review program
The facility-by-facility review of indirect sources of air pollution including such measures as are necessary to assure, or assist in assuring, that a new or modified indirect source will not attract mobile sources of air pollution, the emissions

from which would cause or contribute to air pollution concentrations--(i) exceeding any national primary ambient air quality standard for a mobile source-related air pollutant after the primary standard attainment date, or (ii) preventing maintenance of any such standard after such date. B

individual generation site
The contiguous site at or on which one or more hazardous wastes are generated. An individual generation site, such as a large manufacturing plant, may have one or more sources of hazardous waste but is considered a single or individual generation site if the site or property is contiguous. A

individual risk
The increased risk for a person exposed to a specific concentration of a toxicant. N

individual sewage treatment systems
Privately owned alternative wastewater treatment works (including dual waterless/graywater systems) serving one or more principal residences or small commercial establishments which are neither connected into nor a part of any conventional treatment works. Normally, these are on-site systems with localized treatment and disposal of wastewater with minimal or no conveyance of untreated wastewater. Limited conveyance of treated or partially treated effluents to further treatment or disposal sites can be a function of individual systems where cost-effective. A

individual systems
Privately owned alternative wastewater treatment works (including dual waterless/gray water systems) serving one or more principal residences or small commercial establishments. Normally these are on-site systems with localized treatment and disposal of wastewater, but may be systems utilizing small diameter gravity, pressure or vacuum sewers conveying treated or partially treated wastewater. These systems can also include small diameter gravity sewers carrying raw wastewater to cluster systems. A

indoor air
The breathing air inside a habitable structure or conveyance. N

indoor air pollution
Chemical, physical, or biological contaminants in indoor air. N

indoor climate
Temperature, humidity, lighting, and noise levels in a habitable structure or conveyance. Indoor climate can affect indoor air pollution. N

indoor/outdoor ratio
The ratio of the indoor concentration of an air pollutant to the outdoor concentration of that pollutant. N

induced draft
The negative pressure created by the action of a fan, blower, or ejector located between an incinerator and a stack. U

induced-draft fan
A fan that exhausts hot gases from heat-absorbing equipment, dust collectors, or scrubbers. U

industrial building
A building directly used in manufacturing or technically productive enterprises. Industrial buildings are not generally or typically accessible to other than workers. Industrial buildings include buildings used directly in the production of power, the manufacture of products, the mining of raw materials, and the storage of textiles, petroleum products, wood and paper products, chemicals, plastics, and metals. A

industrial cost recovery
(a) The grantee's recovery from the industrial users of a treatment works of the grant amount allocable to the treatment of waste from such users under section 204(b) of the Clean Water Act. (b) The grantee's recovery from the commercial users of an individual system of the grant amount allocable to the treatment of waste from such users under section 201(h) of the Clean Water Act. A

industrial cost recovery period
That period during which the grant amount allocable to the treatment of wastes from industrial users is recovered from the industrial users of such works. A

industrial furnace
Any of the following enclosed devices that are integral components of manufacturing processes and that use controlled flame devices to accomplish recovery of materials or energy: (1) Cement kilns; (2) Lime kilns; (3) Aggregate kilns; (4) Phosphate kilns; (5) Coke ovens; (6) Blast furnaces; (7) Smelting, melting and refining furnaces (including pyrometallurgical devices such as cupolas, reverberator furnaces, sintering machine, roasters, and foundry furnaces); (8) Titanium dioxide chloride process oxidation reactors; (9) Methane reforming furnaces; (10) Pulping liquor recovery furnaces; (11) Combustion devices used in the recovery of sulfur values from spent sulfuric acid; (12) Such other devices as the Administrator may, after notice and comment, add to this list on the basis of one or more of the following factors: (i) The design and use of the device primarily to accomplish recovery of material products; (ii) The use of the device to burn or reduce raw materials to make a material product; (iii) The use of the device to burn or reduce secondary materials as effective substitutes for raw materials, in processes using raw materials as principal feedstocks; (iv) The use of the device to burn or reduce secondary materials as ingredients in an industrial process to make a material product; (v) The use of the device in common industrial practice to produce a material product; and (vi) Other factors, as appropriate. A

industrial incinerator
An incinerator designed to burn a particular industrial waste. U

industrial solid waste
Solid waste generated by manufacturing or industrial processes that is not a hazardous waste

regulated under subtitle C of RCRA. Such waste may include, but is not limited to, waste resulting from the following manufacturing processes: electric power generation; fertilizer/agricultural chemicals; food and related products/by-products; inorganic chemicals; iron and steel manufacturing; leather and leather products; nonferrous metals manufacturing/foundries; organic chemicals; plastics and resins manufacturing; pulp and paper industry; rubber and miscellaneous plastic products; stone, glass, clay, and concrete products; textile manufacturing; transportation equipment; and water treatment. This term does not include mining waste or oil and gas waste. A

industrial source
Any source of nondomestic pollutants regulated under section 307 (b) or (c) of the Clean Water Act which discharges into a POTW. A

industrial source complex (ISC) model
A Gaussian dispersion model used to predict the movement of a plume of air pollution and concentrations the general population may be exposed to near a facility. There are two versions of the ISC model, short-term and long-term. This is a standard model used by the U.S. EPA and incorporates detailed source and emissions characteristics and appropriate meteorological data. N

industrial user
(a) Any nongovernmental, nonresidential user of a publicly owned treatment works which discharges more than the equivalent of 25,000 gallons per day (gpd) of sanitary wastes and which is identified in the Standard Industrial Classification Manual, 1972, Office of Management and Budget, as amended and supplemented under one of the following divisions:
Division A. Agriculture, Forestry, and Fishing.
Division B. Mining.
Division D. Manufacturing.
Division E. Transportation, Communications, Electric, Gas, and Sanitary Services.
Division I. Services.
(1) In determining the amount of a user's discharge for purposes of industrial cost recovery, the grantee may exclude domestic wastes or discharges for sanitary conveniences.
(2) After applying the sanitary waste exclusion (if the grantee chooses to do so), dischargers in the above divisions that have a volume exceeding 25,000 gpd or the weight of biochemical oxygen demand (BOD) or suspended solids (SS) equivalent to that weight found in 25,000 gpd of sanitary waste are considered industrial users. Sanitary wastes, for purposes of this calculation of equivalency, are the wastes discharged from residential users. The grantee, with the Regional Administrator's approval, shall define the strength of the residential discharges in terms of parameters including, as a minimum, BOD and SS per volume of flow.
(b) Any nongovernmental user of a publicly owned treatment works which discharges wastewater to the treatment works which contains toxic pollutants or poisonous solids, liquids, or gases in sufficient quantity either singly or by interaction with other wastes, to

contaminate the sludge of any municipal systems, or to injure or to interfere with any sewage treatment process, or which constitutes a hazard to humans or animals, creates a public nuisance, or creates any hazard in or has an adverse effect on the waters receiving any discharge from the treatment works.

(c) All commercial users of an individual system constructed with grant assistance under section 201(h) of the Clean Water Act and this subpart. (See [40 CFR] § 35.918(a)(3)). A

industrial waste
Any solid, semisolid, or liquid waste generated by a manufacturing or processing plant the ocean dumping of which may unreasonably degrade or endanger human health, welfare, or amenities, or the marine environment, ecological systems, and economic potentialities. E

industrial waste exchange
An information clearinghouse for industrial waste that provides information on the specific wastes available and puts companies interested in using wastes as feedstock in touch with the waste generators. The waste exchange thus fosters resource recovery and conservation. U

industrial waste treatment systems needs
(1) The anticipated industrial point source wasteload reductions required to attain and maintain applicable water quality standards and effluent limitations for at least a 20-year planning period (in 5-year increments).
(2) Any alternative considerations for industrial sources connected to municipal systems should be reflected in the alternative considerations for such municipal waste treatment system. A

industrial wipers
Paper towels especially made for industrial cleaning and wiping. A

ineligible
Excluded from participation in Federal nonprocurement programs pursuant to a determination of ineligibility under statutory, executive order, or regulatory authority, other than Executive Order 12549 and its agency implementing regulations; for example, excluded pursuant to the Davis-Bacon Act and its implementing regulations, the equal employment opportunity acts and executive orders, or the environmental protection acts and executive orders. A person is ineligible where the determination of ineligibility affects such person's eligibility to participate in more than one covered transaction. A

inert ingredients
All ingredients [in a pesticide] which are not active ingredients including, but not limited to, the following types of ingredients (except when they are pesticidal efficacy of their own): Solvents such as water; baits such as sugar, starches, and meat scraps; dust carriers such as talc and clay; fillers; wetting and spreading agents; propellents in aerosol dispensers; emulsifiers. A, C

inertia weight class
The class, which is a group of test

weights, into which a vehicle is grouped based on its loaded vehicle weight in accordance with the provisions of 40 CFR Part 86. A

inertial grate stoker
A stoker with a fixed bed of plates that is carried on rollers and activated by an electrically driven mechanism; it draws the bed slowly back against a spring and then releases it so that the entire bed moves forward until stopped abruptly by another spring. The inertia of the solid waste carries it a small distance forward along the stoker surface, and then the cycle is repeated. D

inertial separator
A device that uses centrifugal force to separate waste particles. N

infectious agent
Any organism (such as a virus or a bacteria) that is capable of being communicated by invasion and multiplication in body tissues and capable of causing disease or adverse health impacts in humans. A

infectious waste
(1) Equipment, instruments, utensils, and fomites of a disposable nature from the rooms of patients who are suspected to have or have been diagnosed as having a communicable disease and must, therefore, be isolated as required by public health agencies; (2) laboratory wastes, such as pathological specimens (e.g., all tissues, specimens of blood elements, excreta, and secretions obtained from patients or laboratory animals) and disposable fomites (any substance that may harbor or transmit pathogenic organisms) attendant thereto; (3) surgical operating room pathologic specimens and disposable fomites attendant thereto, and similar disposable materials from outpatient areas and emergency rooms. A

infectiousness
A characteristic of hazardous waste under consideration by the Environmental Protection Agency that would identify waste that contains contagious pathogenic organisms. U

infertile
Lacking fertility, inability to conceive offspring. Infertility may be temporary or permanent; permanent infertility is termed sterility. N

infiltration
(1) Water other than wastewater that enters a sewer system (including sewer service connections and foundation drains) from the ground through such means as defective pipes, pipe joints, connections, or manholes. Infiltration does not include, and is distinguished from inflow. A (2) The penetration of water through the ground surface into sub-surface soil or the penetration of water from the soil into sewer or other pipes through defective joints, connections, or manhole walls. (3) A land application technique where large volumes of waste water are applied to land, allowed to penetrate the surface and percolate through the underlying soil. (See: percolation). N

infiltration air
Air that leaks into the chambers or ducts of an incinerator. U

infiltration water
That water which permeates through the earth into the plant site. A

infiltration/inflow
The total quantity of water from both infiltration and inflow without distinguishing the source. A

inflammation
A protective tissue response to injury that serves to destroy, dilute, or wall off both the injurious agent and the injured tissue. It is characterized by symptoms such as pain, heat, redness, swelling and loss of function. Under some circumstances, it can be a toxic response due to local accumulations of cells and mediators. N

inflow
Water other than wastewater that enters a sewerage system (including sewer service connections) from sources such as roof leaders, cellar drains, yard drains, area drains, foundation drains, drains from springs and swampy areas, manhole covers, cross connections between storm sewers and sanitary sewers, catch basins, cooling towers, storm waters, surface runoff, street wash waters, or drainage. Inflow does not include, and is distinguished from, infiltration. A

influencing
Making, with the intent to influence, any communications to or appearance before an officer or employee or any agency, a Member of Congress, an officer or employee of Congress, or an employee of a Member of Congress in connection with any covered Federal action. A

information file
In the Superfund program, a file that contains accurate, up-to-date documents on a Superfund site. The file is usually located in a public building such as a school, library, or city hall that is convenient for local residents. N

ingredient statement
A statement which contains--(1) the name and percentage of each active ingredient, and total percentage of all inert ingredients, in the pesticide; and (2) if the pesticide contains arsenic in any form, a statement of the percentages of total and water soluble arsenic, calculated as elementary arsenic. C

inground tank
A device meeting the definition of "tank" whereby a portion of the tank wall is situated to any degree within the ground, thereby preventing visual inspection of that external surface area of the tank that is in the ground. A

inhalation LC_{50}
A concentration of a substance, expressed as milligrams per liter of air or parts per million parts of air, that is lethal to 50 percent of the test population of animals under specified test conditions. A

inherently low-polluting propulsion system
A propulsion system that does not require control devices for exhaust emissions that are external to the energy releasing activities of the propulsion system. A

inhibition
Any decrease in the growth rate of the test algae compared to the control algae. A

initial decision
(1) In some EPA proceedings, the decision of the Administrative Law Judge supported by findings of fact and conclusions regarding all material issues of law, fact, or discretion, as well as reasons therefor. Such decision shall become the final decision and order of the Administrator without further proceedings unless an appeal therefrom is taken or the Administrator orders review thereof as provided in EPA regulations. A (2) The decision issued by the Presiding Officer based upon the record of the proceedings out of which it arises. A

initial failure rate
The percentage of vehicles rejected because of excessive emissions of a single pollutant during the first inspection cycle of an inspection/maintenance program. (If inspection is conducted for more than one pollutant, the total failure rate may be higher than the failure rates for each single pollutant). A

initiation of construction
The issuance to a construction contractor of a notice to proceed, or, if no such notice is required, the execution of a construction contract. A

initiator
An agent capable of starting but not necessarily completing the process of producing an abnormal, uncontrolled growth of tissue usually by altering a cell's genetic material. Initiated cells may or may not be transformed into tumors. N

injection interval
That part of the injection zone in which the well is screened, or in which the waste is otherwise directly emplaced. A

injection well
A well into which fluids are injected for purposes such as waste disposal, improving the recovery of crude oil, or solution mining. N

injection zone
UIC. A geological formation group of formations or part of a formation receiving fluids through a well. A

inland oil barge
A non-self-propelled vessel carrying oil in bulk as cargo and certificated to operate only in the inland waters of the United States, while operating in such waters. D

inland waters of the United States
(1) Those waters of the United States lying inside the baseline from which the territorial sea is measured and those waters outside such baseline which are a part of the Gulf Intracoastal Waterway. D (2) For the

purposes of classifying the size of discharges, "inland waters" means those waters of the U.S. in the inland zone, waters of the Great Lakes, and specified ports and harbors on inland rivers. A

inland zone

The environment inland of the coastal zone excluding the Great Lakes and specified ports and harbors of inland rivers. The term inland zone delineates the area of Federal responsibility for response action. Precise boundaries are determined by EPA/USCG agreement and identified in Federal regional contingency plans. A

innage

Space occupied in a product container. A

inner liner

A continuous layer of material placed inside a tank or container which protects the construction materials of the tank or container from the contained waste or reagents used to treat the waste. A

innovative control technology

Any system of air pollution control that has not been adequately demonstrated in practice, but would have a substantial likelihood of achieving greater continuous emissions reduction than any control system in current practice or of achieving at least comparable reductions at lower cost in terms of energy, economics, or nonair quality environmental impacts. A

innovative technology

A production process, a pollution control technique, or a combination of the two which satisfies one of the criteria in [40 CFR] § 125.23 and which has not been commercially demonstrated in the industry of which the requesting discharger is a part. A

innovative wastewater processes and techniques

Innovative waste water treatment processes and techniques are developed methods which have not been fully proven under the circumstances of their contemplated use and which represent a significant advancement over the state of the art in terms of meeting the national goals of cost reduction, increased energy conservation or recovery, greater recycling and conservation of water resources (including preventing the mixing of pollutants with water), reclamation or reuse of effluents and resources (including increased productivity of arid lands), improved efficiency and/or reliability, the beneficial use of sludges or effluent constituents, better management of toxic materials or increased environmental benefits. Innovative waste water treatment processes and techniques are generally limited to new and improved applications of those alternative processes and techniques including both treatment at centralized facilities and individual and other onsite treatment. Treatment processes based on the conventional concept of treatment (by means of biological or physical/chemical unit processes) and discharge to surface waters shall not be considered

innovative waste water treatment processes and techniques except where it is demonstrated that these processes and techniques, as a minimum, meet cost-reduction or energy-reduction criterion. Treatment and discharge systems include primary treatment, suspended-growth or fixed-growth biological systems for secondary or advance waste water treatment, physical/chemical treatment, disinfection, and sludge processing. The term "innovative" does not include collector sewers, interceptors, storm or sanitary sewers or the separation of them, or major sewer rehabilitation, except insofar as they meet the criteria in paragraph 6 of these guidelines and are alternatives to conventional treatment works for small communities under 40 CFR § 35.915-1(e) or part of individual systems under 40 CFR § 35.918. A

inoculum
(1) Bacteria placed in compost to start biological action. (2) A medium containing organisms which is introduced into cultures or living organisms. N

inorganic chemicals
Chemical substances of mineral origin, not of basically carbon structure. N

inorganic matter
Chemical substances of mineral origin, not containing carbon-to-carbon bonding. Generally structured through ionic bonding. U

inorganic pesticides
Noncarbon-containing substances used as pesticides. A

inorganic refuse
Solid waste composed of matter other than plant, animal, and certain carbon compounds (e.g., metals and glass). B

inorganic solid debris
Nonfriable inorganic solids contaminated with D004-D011 hazardous wastes that are incapable of passing through a 9.5 mm standard sieve; and that require cutting, or crushing and grinding in mechanical sizing equipment prior to stabilization; and, are limited to the following inorganic or metal materials: (1) Metal slags (either dross or scoria); (2) Glassified slag; (3) Glass; (4) Concrete (excluding cementitious or pozzolanic stabilized hazardous wastes); (5) Masonry and refractory bricks; (6) Metal cans, containers, drums, or tanks; (7) Metal nuts, bolts, pipes, pumps, valves, appliances, or industrial equipment; (8) Scrap metal as defined in 40 CFR 261.1(c)(6). A

inprocess wastewater
Any water which, during manufacturing or processing, comes into direct contact with the plant's product or results from the production or use of any raw material, intermediate product, finished product, by-product, or waste product but which has not been discharged to a wastewater treatment process or discharged untreated as wastewater. A

insect
Any of the numerous small invertebrate animals generally having the body more or less obviously

segmented, for the most part belonging to the class insecta, comprising six-legged, usually winged forms, as for example, beetles, bugs, bees, flies, and to other allied classes of arthropods whose members are wingless and usually have more than six legs, as for example, spiders, mites, ticks, centipedes, and wood lice. C

insecticide

(1) A pesticide compound specifically used to kill or control the growth of insects. N All substances or mixtures of substances intended for preventing or inhibiting the establishment, reproduction, development, or growth of, destroying or repelling any member of the Class Insecta or other allied Classes in the Phylum Arthropoda declared to be pests under 40 CFR § 162.14. Insecticides include, but are not limited to: (i) Plant protection insecticides intended for use directly or indirectly against insects or allied organisms that attack or infest plants or plant parts, to prevent or mitigate their injury, debilitation, or destruction; (ii) Animal protection insecticides intended for use directly or indirectly against insects or allied organisms that attack or infest plants or plant parts, to prevent or mitigate their injury, debilitation, or destruction; (ii) Animal protection insecticides intended for use directly or indirectly against insects or allied organisms that attack or infest man, other mammals, birds, or certain other animals, to prevent or mitigate their injury, irritation, harassment, or debilitation; (iii) Premise and indoor insecticides intended for use directly or indirectly against insects or allied organisms to prevent or mitigate their decimation or contamination of man's stored food and animal feeds, injury to raw or manufactured goods, or weakening or destruction of buildings and building materials; and (iv) Biological insect control agents such as specific pathogenic organisms or entities prepared and utilized by man. A

inside information

Information obtained by a Federal employee as a result of Government employment which has not been made available to the general public or would not be made available on request. A

inspection

Any inspection of an employer's factory, plant, establishment, construction site, or other area, workplace or environment where work is performed by an employee of an employer, and includes any inspection conducted pursuant to a complaint, any reinspection, followup inspection, accident investigation or other inspection. O

inspection and maintenance

I/M. (1) Activities to assure proper emissions-related operation of mobile sources of air pollutants, particularly automobile emissions controls. (2) Also applies to wastewater treatment plants and other anti-pollution facilities and processes. N

inspection and maintenance program
also **inspection/maintenance**

A program to reduce emissions from in-use vehicles through identifying vehicles that need emission control related maintenance and requiring that such maintenance be performed. A

inspection criteria
The rejection and acceptance numbers associated with a particular sampling plan. A

installation
(1) An identifiable piece of process equipment. A (2) Any building or structure or any group of buildings or structures at a single demolition or renovation site that are under the control of the same owner or operator (or owner or operator under common control). A

instant photographic film article
A self-developing photographic film article designed so that all the chemical substances contained in the article, including the chemical substances required to process the film, remain sealed during distribution and use. A

institution of higher education
An educational institution described in the first sentence of section 1201 of the Higher Education Act of 1965 (other than an institution of any agency of the United States) which is accredited by a nationally recognized accrediting agency or association approved by the Administrator for this purpose. For purposes of this subsection, the Administrator shall publish a list of nationally recognized accrediting agencies or associations which he determined to be reliable authority as to the quality of training offered. D

institutional solid waste
Solid wastes generated by educational, health care, correctional, and other institutional facilities. A

institutional use
Any application of a pesticide in or around any property or facility that functions to provide a service to the general public or to public or private organizations, including but not limited to: (1) Hospitals and nursing homes; (2) Schools other than preschools and day care facilities; (3) Museums and libraries; (4) Sports facilities; (5) Office buildings. A

instream use
Water use taking place within a stream channel, e.g., hydro-electric power generation, navigation, water-quality improvement, fish propagation, recreation. N

instrumental detection limit
The concentration equivalent to a signal, due to the analyte, which is equal to three times the standard deviation of a series of ten replicate measurements of a reagent blank signal at the same wavelength. A

instrumentation system
The system which consists of the analytical instruments necessary to measure the level of emissions plus any required support equipment. A

insulated wall
A furnace wall on which refractory material is installed over insulation. U

insulating brick
Firebrick with a low thermal

conductivity and a bulk density of less than 70 pounds per cubic feet, which is suitable for insulating industrial furnaces. Also called insulating block. U

insurer
A company authorized to do business as an insurance carrier under the laws of a state or the District of Columbia. O

intake
Amount of material inhaled, ingested, or absorbed dermally during a specified period of time. N

integral vista
A view perceived from within the mandatory Class I Federal area of a specific landmark or panorama located outside the boundary of the mandatory Class I Federal area. A

integrated exposure assessment
A summation over time, in all media, of the magnitude of exposure to a toxic chemical. N

integrated facility
A facility that performs electroplating as only one of several operations necessary for manufacture of a product at a single physical location and has significant quantities of process wastewater from non-electroplating manufacturing operations. In addition, to qualify as an "integrated facility" one or more plant electroplating process wastewater lines must be combined prior to or at the point of treatment (or proposed treatment) with one or more plant sewers carrying process wastewater from non-electroplating manufacturing operations. A

integrated pest management
IPM. A mixture of pesticide and non-pesticide methods to control pests. N

integrated solid waste management
The practice of disposing of solid waste that utilizes several complementary components, such as source reduction, recycling, composting, incineration (waste to energy), and landfilling. U

integrated system
A process for producing a pesticide product that: (1) Contains any active ingredient derived from a source that is not an EPA-registered product; or (2) Contains any active ingredient that was produced or acquired in a manner that does not permit its inspection by the Agency under FIFRA sec. 9(a) prior to its use in the process. A

intensive survey
The frequent sampling or measurement of parameters at representative points for a relatively short period of time to determine water quality conditions, causes, effects, or cause and effect relationships of such conditions. A

interceptor sewer
A sewer which is designed for one or more of the following purposes: (i) To intercept wastewater from a final point in a collector sewer and convey such wastes directly to a treatment facility or another interceptor. (ii) To

replace an existing wastewater treatment facility and transport the wastes to an adjoining collector sewer or interceptor sewer for conveyance to a treatment plant. (iii) To transport wastewater from one or more municipal collector sewers to another municipality or to a regional plant for treatment. (iv) To intercept an existing major discharge of raw or inadequately treated wastewater for transport directly to another interceptor or to a treatment plant. A

interconnected
Two or more electric generating units are electrically tied together by a network of power transmission lines, and other power transmission equipment. A

interference
(1) An inhibition or disruption of the POTW, its treatment processes or operations, or its sludge processes, use or disposal which is a cause of or significantly contributes to either a violation of any requirement of the POTW's NPDES permit (including an increase in the magnitude or duration of a violation) or to the prevention of sewage sludge use or disposal by the POTW in accordance with the following statutory provisions and regulations or permits issued thereunder (or more stringent state or local regulations): Section 405 of the Clean Water Act, the Solid Waste Disposal Act (including title II more commonly referred to as the Resource Conservation and Recovery Act (RCRA) and including state regulations contained in any state sludge management plan prepared pursuantto Subtitle D of the Solid Waste Disposal Act), the Clean Air Act, and the Toxic Substances Control Act. An Industrial User significantly contributes to such a permit violation or prevention of sludge use or disposal in accordance with above-cited authorities whenever such User: (1) Discharges a daily pollutant loading in excess of that allowed by contract with the POTW or by federal, state or local law; (2) Discharges wastewater which substantially differs in nature or constituents from the User's average discharge; or (3) Knows or has reason to know that its discharge, alone or in conjunction with discharges from other sources, would result in a POTW permit violation or prevent sewage sludge use or disposal in accordance with the above-cited authorities as they apply to the POTW's selected method of sludge management. (2) The discharge of sulfides in quantities which can result in human health hazards and/or risks to human life, and an inhibition or disruption of POTW as defined in 40 CFR 403.3(i). A

interference equivalent
(1) The portion of indicated input concentration due to the presence of an interferant. (2) Positive or negative response caused by a substance other than the one being measured. A

interflow
That portion of precipitation that infiltrates the soil and moves laterally underground until intercepted by a stream channel or until it resurfaces downslope from ion its point of infiltration. U

intergovernmental agreement

Any written agreement between units of government under which one public agency performs duties for or in concert with another public agency using EPA assistance. This includes substate and interagency agreements. A

interim (permit) status

Period during which treatment, storage and disposal facilities coming under RCRA in 1980 are temporarily permitted to operate while awaiting denial or issuance of a permanent permit. Permits issued under these circumstances are usually called "Part A" or "Part B" permits. U

interim authorization

Approval by EPA of a State hazardous waste program which has met the requirements of section 3006(c) of RCRA and applicable requirements of 40 CFR Part 271, Subpart B. A

interim permits

Prior to April 23, 1978, interim permits may be issued in accordance with subpart A of part 227 to dump materials which are not in compliance with the environmental impact criteria of subpart B of part 227, or which would cause substantial adverse effects as determined in accordance with the criteria of subpart D or E of part 227 or for which an ocean disposal site has not been designated on other than an interim basis pursuant to part 228 of this subchapter H; provided, however, no permit may be issued for the ocean dumping of any materials listed in [40 CFR] § 227.5, or for any of the materials listed in § 227.6, except as trace contaminants; provided further that the compliance date of April 23, 1978, does not apply to the dumping of wastes by existing dumpers when the regional administrator determines that the permittee has exercised his best efforts to comply with all requirements of a special permit by April 23, 1978, and has an implementation schedule adequate to allow phasing out of ocean dumping or compliance with all requirements necessary to receive a special permit by December 31, 1981, at the latest. No interim permit will be granted for the dumping of waste from a facility which has not previously dumped wastes in the ocean from a new facility, or for the dumping of an increased amount of waste from the expansion or modification of an existing facility, after the effective date of these regulations (except when the facility is operated by a municipality now dumping such wastes). No interim permit will be issued for the dumping of any material in the ocean for which an interim permit had previously been issued unless the applicant demonstrates that he has exercised his best efforts to comply with all provisions of the previously issued permits. Interim permits shall specify an expiration date no later than one year from the date of issue. A

interlock

A device designed to ensure that operations or motions occur in proper sequence. O

intermediate

(1) Any chemical substance (a)

which is intentionally removed from the equipment in which it is manufactured, and (b) which either is consumed in whole or in part in chemical reaction(s) used for the intentional manufacture of other chemical substance(s) or mixture(s), or is intentionally present for the purpose of altering the rate of such chemical reaction(s). Note: The "equipment in which it was manufactured" includes the reaction vessel in which the chemical substance was manufactured and other equipment which is strictly ancillary to the reaction vessel, and any other equipment through which the chemical substance may flow during a continuous flow process, but does not include tanks or other vessels in which the chemical substance is stored after its manufacture. A (2) Any chemical substance which is consumed in whole or in part in a chemical reaction(s) used for the intentional manufacture of other chemical substances or mixtures, or that is intentionally present for the purpose of altering the rates of such chemical reactions. A

intermediate cover

Cover material for landfills that serves the same functions as daily cover, but must resist erosion for a longer period of time, because it is applied on areas where additional disposal cells are not to be constructed for extended periods of time. A

intermediate handler

A facility that either treats regulated medical waste or destroys regulated medical waste but does not do both.

The term, as used [here], does not include transporters. A

intermediate premanufacture notice

Any PMN submitted to EPA for a chemical substance which is an intermediate as in the production of a final product, provided that the PMN for the intermediate is submitted to EPA at the same time as, and together with, the PMN for the final product and that the PMN for the intermediate identifies the final product and describes the chemical reactions leading from the intermediate to the final product. If PMNs are submitted to EPA at the same time for several intermediates used in the production of a final product, each of these is an intermediate PMN if they all identify the final product and every other associated intermediate PMN and are submitted to EPA at the same time as, and together with, the PMN for the final product. A

intermediate processing center

Usually refers to a facility that processes residentially collected mixed recyclables into new products for market; also known as a materials recovery facility (MRF). U

intermediate speed

Peak torque speed if peak torque speed occurs between 60 and 75 percent of rated speed. If the peak torque speed is less than 60 percent of rated speed, intermediate speed means 60 percent of rated speed. If the peak torque speed is greater than 75 percent of rated speed, intermediate speed means 75 percent of rated speed. A

intermediate-level liquid waste

Fluid materials, disposed as a result of Hanford [Washington nuclear engineering facility] operations, which contain from 5×10^{-5} microcuries per milliliter to 100 microcuries per milliliter of mixed fission products, including less than 2 microcuries per milliliter of cesium-137, strontium-90, or long-lived alpha emitters. U

intermunicipal agency

(a) Under the Clean Air Act, an agency of two or more municipalities located in the same State or in different States and having substantial powers or duties pertaining to the prevention and control of air pollution. (b) Under the Resource Conservation and Recovery Act, an agency established by two or more municipalities with responsibility for planning or administration of solid waste. I (c) In all other cases, an agency of two or more municipalities having substantial powers or duties pertaining to the control of pollution. A

internal combustion engine

An engine in which both the heat energy and the ensuing mechanical energy are produced inside the engine proper. U

internal compaction transfer system

A transfer method in which the reciprocating action of a hydraulically powered bulkhead contained within an enclosed trailer packs solid waste against the rear doors. U

internal radiation

Radiation from a source within the body as a result of deposition of radionuclides in body tissues by ingestion, inhalation, or implantation. U

internal subunit

A subunit that is covalently linked to at least two other subunits. Internal subunits of polymer molecules are chemically derived from monomer molecules that have formed covalent links between two or more other molecules. A

international shipment

The transportation of hazardous waste into or out of the jurisdiction of the United States. A

interspecies

Between different species. N

interspecies scaling factors

Numerical values used in the determination of the equivalent doses between species, (e.g. frequently a known animal dose is scaled to estimate an equivalent human dose). The U.S.EPA's cancer risk assessment guidelines (50 FR 33992) note that commonly used dosage scales include milligram per kilogram body weight per day, parts per million in soil or water or air, milligram per square meter body surface area per day, and milligram per kilogram body weight per lifetime. The guidelines for carcinogen assessment generally recommend using the surface area approach unless there is evidence to the contrary. The dose as mg/kg of body weight/day is generally used to scale between species for non-cancer effects of chemicals after dermal, oral, or perenteral exposure. N

interstate agency
(a) Under the Clean Air Act, an agency established by two or more States, or by two or more municipalities located in different States, having substantial powers or duties pertaining to the prevention and control of air pollution. (b) Under the Federal Water Pollution Control Act, an agency of two or more States established by or pursuant to an agreement or compact approved by the Congress or any other agency of two or more States, having substantial powers or duties pertaining to the control of pollution of waters. (c) Under the Resource Conservation and Recovery Act, an agency of two or more municipalities in different States or an agency established by two or more States, with authority to provide for the disposal of solid wastes and serving two or more municipalities located in different States. (d) In all other cases, an agency of two or more States having substantial powers or duties pertaining to the control of pollution. A, D, I

interstate air quality control region
A geographic area, designated under section 107 of the Clean Air Act, that includes areas in two or more States. A

interstate carrier water supply
A source of water for drinking and sanitary use on planes, buses, trains, and ships operating in more than one state. These sources are federally regulated. N

interstate commerce
The commerce between any place in a State and any place in another State, or between places in the same State through another State, whether such commerce moves wholly by rail or partly by rail and partly by motor vehicle, express, or water. A

interstate waters
(1) Waters that flow across or form a part of State or international boundaries, e.g., the Great Lakes, the Mississippi River, or coastal waters. N

interstitial monitoring
The continuous surveillance of the space between the walls of an underground storage tank. N

intervener
A person who files a motion to be made a party under [40 CFR] § 209.15 or § 209.16, and whose motion is approved. A

intramuscular
Within the muscle; refers to injection. N

intraperitoneal
Within the membrane surrounding the organs of the abdominal cavity; refers to injection. N

intraspecies
Within a particular species. N

intravascular
Within the blood vessels; refers to

injection, usually into the veins (intravenous or i.v.). N

intrinsically safe equipment
Equipment and associated wiring in which any spark or thermal effect, produced either normally or in specified fault conditions, is incapable, under certain prescribed test conditions, of causing ignition of a mixture of flammable or combustible material in air in its most easily ignitible concentration. O

intrusion coefficient
A number expressing the level of protection provided by a gas tight totally-encapsulating chemical protective suit. The intrusion coefficient is calculated by dividing the test room challenge agent concentration by the concentration of challenge agent found inside the suit. The accuracy of the intrusion coefficient is dependent on the challenge agent monitoring methods. The larger the intrusion coefficient the greater the protection provided by the TECP suit. O

inventory
The list of chemical substances manufactured or processed in the United States that EPA compiled and keeps current under section 8(b) of the Toxic Substances Control Act. A

inversion
An atmospheric condition caused by a layer of warm air preventing the rise of cool air trapped beneath it. This holds down pollutants that might otherwise be dispersed, and can cause an air pollution episode. N

invertebrate animal poisons and repellents
Invertebrate animal poisons and repellents include, but are not limited to: (A) Antifouling agents intended for use on boat and ship bottoms, pier and dock pilings, and similar submerged structures to prevent attachment or damage and destruction by marine invertebrates; (B) Mollusk control agents intended to repel or destroy snails or slugs; and (C) Protozoa control agents intended to destroy disease-inducing and/or parasitic protozoa in aquatic situations. A

invitation for bids
The solicitation for prospective suppliers by a purchaser requesting their competitive price quotations. A

ion change
By interchanging ions between a liquid and solid phase, this process allows the undesirable materials to be collected. The mechanisms of ion exchange is chemical, using resins that react either positively or negatively. This method can be used to remove trace metals and cyanides from industrial sources, as well as fluorides and nitrates from drinking water supplies. The contaminants can then be recovered for recycling or disposed of safely. U

ion exchange
The reversible interchange of ions of like charge between an insoluble solid and the surrounding liquid phase in which there is no permanent change in the structure of the solid. The process is used in hazardous waste

treatment to remove objectionable levels of metals and cyanides from certain waste streams and excessive levels of fluorides, nitrates, and manganese from drinking water. U

ionization
The process by which a neutral atom or molecule acquires a positive or negative charge. U

ionization chamber
A device that detects and measures the intensity of ionizing radiation. N

ionizing radiation
Radiation that can remove electrons from atoms, i.e., alpha, beta, and gamma radiation. N

IPM
Integrated pest management. N

IPPF
Independent power production facility. A

IR
(1) Intermediate range. N (2) Infrared. N

IRB
Institutional Review Board. A

IRB approval
The determination of the IRB [institutional review board] that the research has been reviewed and may be conducted at an institution within the constraints set forth by the IRB and by other institutional and federal requirements. A

IRLG
Interagency Regulatory Liaison Group. U

IRPTC
International Register of Potentially Toxic Chemicals. N

irradiated food
Food that has been subject to brief radioactivity, usually by gamma rays, to kill insects, bacteria, and mold, and preserve it without refrigeration or freezing. N

irradiation
Exposure to radiation of wavelengths shorter than those of visible light (gamma, x-ray, or ultraviolet), for medical purposes, the destruction of bacteria in milk or other foodstuffs, or for inducing polymerization of monomers or vulcanization of rubber. N

irreparable harm
Significant undesirable effect occurring after the date of permit issuance which will not be reversed after cessation or modification of the discharge. A

irrigation
Technique for applying water or wastewater to land areas to supply the water and nutrient needs of plants. N

irrigation return flow
Surface water, other than navigable waters, containing pollutants which result from the controlled application of water by any person to land used primarily for crops, forage growth, or nursery operations; the ditches and

other structure that collects such surface water. This term includes water used for cranberry harvesting, rice crops, and other such controlled application of water to land for purposes of farm management. A

irritant
A chemical, which is not corrosive, but which caused a reversible inflammatory effect on living tissue by chemical action at the site of contact. A chemical is a skin irritant if, when tested on the intact skin of albino rabbits by the methods of 16 CFR 1500.41 for four hours exposure or by other appropriate techniques, it results in an empirical score of five or more. A chemical is an eye irritant if so determined under the procedure listed in 16 CFR 1500.42 or other appropriate techniques. O

irritating
An irritating material, as defined by DOT, is a liquid or solid substance which, upon contact with fire or when exposed to air, gives off dangerous or intensely irritating fumes (not including poisonous materials). (See: Poison, Class A and Poison, Class B). N

ischemia
Local lack of oxygen due to mechanical obstruction (mainly arterial narrowing) of the blood supply. U

ISO standard day conditions
288 degrees Kelvin, 60 percent relative humidity and 101.3 kilopascals pressure. A

isokinetic sampling
Sampling in which the linear velocity of the gas entering the sampling nozzle is equal to that of the undisturbed gas stream at the sample point. A

isolated
Not readily accessible to persons unless special means for access are used. O

isolated power system
A system comprising an isolating transformer or its equivalent, a line isolation monitor, and its ungrounded circuit conductors. O

isolated source
A source of air pollutant emissions located a substantial distance from any other source of such air pollutants and that will assume legal responsibility for all violations of the applicable national standards in its designated liability area. A

isolated system
A fully enclosed structure other than the vessel of containment of the hazardous material, which is impervious to the passage of the hazardous material and which would prevent the entry of the hazardous material into regulated areas, nonregulated areas, or the external environment, should leakage or spillage from the vessel of containment occur. O

isolation waste
Discarded materials originating from the diagnosis, core, or treatment of patients placed in quarantine because of known or suspected infectious diseases. (See: infectious waste). U

isotope

A variation of an element that has the same atomic number but a different weight because of its neutrons. Isotopes of an element may have different radioactive behavior. N

ITC

(1) Interagency Testing Committee. N (2) International Trade Commission. U

IU

Industrial user. U

J

J.
Joule. (See: Joule). U

Jacob's ladder
A marine ladder of rope or chain with wooden or metal rungs. O

jigging
A process for separating presized solid materials of different densities by using the periodic pulsations of a liquid (usually water) through a bed of the mixed material to float the lighter solids. U

job shop
A facility which owns not more than 50% (annual area basis) of the materials undergoing metal finishing. A

joint sponsor
A person who sponsors testing pursuant to section 4(b)(3)(A) of the [TSCA] Act. A

joint submitters
Two or more persons who submit a [TSCA] section 5 notice together. A

jointly-funded projects
A project for which assistance is sought, on a combined or coordinated basis, involving two or more Federal programs or funding authorities. A

Joule
J. A unit of energy or work which is equivalent to one watt per second or 0.737 foot-pounds. U

judicial officer
(1) The person designated by the Administrator under 40 CFR §22.04 (b) to serve as the Judicial Officer. (2) An attorney who is a permanent or temporary employee of the United States Environmental Protection Agency and serves as counsel on matters appealed to the Administrator of EPA. A

junk
Unprocessed, discarded materials that are usually suitable for reuse or recycling (e.g., rags, paper, toys, metal, furniture). U

K

K.
Kelvin. U

K-factor
The chemical conductivity of a material, expressed as British thermal units per square foot per hour per degree Fahrenheit per foot of thickness. See: thermal conductivity. U

K_d
See adsorption ratio. A

kg.
Kilogram(s). U

kickout
The accidental release or failure of a cross brace. O

kinetic energy
Energy possessed by a mass because of its motion; e.g., the falling water of a dam has the energy to put turbines into motion. U

kinetic rate coefficient
A number that describes the rate at which a water constituent such as a biochemical oxygen demand or dissolvedoxygen increases or decreases. N

kkg.
1000 kilogram(s). U

km.
Kilometer(s). U

knife hog
See chipper. U

knot
A branch or limb, imbedded the tree and cut through in the process of lumber manufacture, classified according to size, quality, and occurrence. The size of the knot is determined as the average diameter on the surface of the piece. O

known human effects
A commonly recognized human health effect of a particular substance or mixture as described either in: (i) Scientific articles or publications

299

abstracted in standard reference sources. (ii) The firm's product labeling or material safety data sheets (MSDS). A

known to or reasonably ascertainable
All information in a person's possession or control, plus all information that a reasonable person similarly situated might be expected to know, or could obtain without unreasonable burden or cost. A

knows or has reason to know
That a person, with respect to a claim or statement--(a) Has actual knowledge that the claim or statement is false, fictitious, or fraudulent; (b) Acts in deliberate ignorance of the truth or falsity of the claim or statement; or (c) Acts in reckless disregard of the truth or falsity of the claim or statement. A

kpa.
Kilopascals. U

kraft paper
A comparatively coarse paper noted for its strength and used primarily as a wrapper or packaging material. It is made from wood pulp produced by the sulfate pulping process. U

kraft pulp mill
Any stationary source which produces pulp from wood by cooking (digesting) wood chips in a water solution of sodium hydroxide and sodium sulfide (white liquor) at high temperature and pressure. Regeneration of the cooking chemicals through a recovery process is also considered part of the kraft pulp mill. A

kwh.
Kilowatt hour; the provision of one kilowatt of electrical energy for one hour. U

L

l.
   Liter. U

label
(1) The written, printed, or graphic matter on, or attached to, the pesticide or device or any of its containers or wrappers. C (2) Use of a pesticide in a manner not consistent with the label is a prohibited misuse of the product subject to enforcement under FIFRA. (3) A sticker that contains fuel economy information and is affixed to new automobiles in accordance with EPA vehicle certification regulations. A (4) Any written, printed, or graphic sign or symbol displayed on or affixed to containers of hazardous chemicals pursuant to OSHA requirements. A label should contain identity of the hazardous material; appropriate hazard warnings; and name and address of the chemical manufacturer, importer, or other responsible party. N

labeled
Equipment is "labeled" if there is attached to it a label, symbol, or other identifying mark of a nationally recognized testing laboratory which, (a) makes periodic inspections of the production of such equipment, and (b) whose labeling indicates compliance with nationally recognized standards or tests to determine safe use in a specified manner. O

labeling
All labels and all other written, printed, or graphic matter--(A) accompanying the pesticide or device at any time; or (B) to which reference is made on the label or in literature accompanying the pesticide or device, except to current official publications of the Environmental Protection Agency, the United States Departments of Agriculture and Interior, the Department of Health, Education and Welfare [now the Department of Health and Human Services], State experiment stations, State agricultural colleges, and other similar Federal or State institutions or agencies authorized by law to conduct research in the field of pesticides. C

laboratory
Any research, analytical, or clinical facility that performs health care related analysis or service. This includes medical, pathological, pharmaceutical, and other research, commercial, or industrial laboratories. A

laboratory waste
Discarded materials generated by research and analytical activities in the laboratory. U

LADD
Lifetime average daily dose. N

ladder
An appliance usually consisting of two side rails joined at regular intervals by crosspieces called steps, rungs, or cleats, on which a person may step in ascending or descending. O

ladder safety device
Any device, other than a cage or well, designed to eliminate or reduce the possibility of accidental falls and which may incorporate such features as life belts, friction brakes, and sliding attachments. A

LAER
Lowest achievable emission rate. A

lag time
The time interval from a step change in input concentration at the instrument inlet to the first corresponding change in the instrument output. A

lagoon
(1) A shallow pond where sunlight, bacterial action, and oxygen work to purify waste water, also used for storage of wastewaters or spent nuclear fuel rods. N (2) Shallow body of water, often separated from the sea by coral reefs or sandbars. N

land
Any surface or subsurface land that is not part of a disposal site and is not covered by an occupiable building. A

land application unit
An area where wastes are applied onto or incorporated into the soil surface (excluding manure spreading operations) for agricultural purposes or for treatment and disposal. A

land disposal
Placement in or on the land and includes, but is not limited to, placement in a landfill, surface impoundment, waste pile, injection well, land treatment facility, salt dome formation, salt bed formation, underground mine or cave, concrete vault or bunker intended for disposal purposes and placement in or on the land by means of open detonation. The term "land disposal" does not encompass ocean disposal. U

land treatment facility
A facility or part of a facility at which hazardous waste is applied onto or incorporated into the soil surface; such facilities are disposal facilities if the waste will remain after closure. A

landfarming
The application of waste to land

and/or incorporation into the surface soil, including the use of such waste as a fertilizer or soil conditioner. Also called landspreading. U

landfill
(1) Sanitary landfills are land disposal sites for non-hazardous solid wastes at which the waste is spread in layers, compacted to the smaller practical volume, and cover material applied at the end of each operating day. (2) Secure chemical landfills are disposal sites for hazardous waste. They are selected and designed to minimize the chance of release of hazardous substances into the environment. N (3) A disposal facility or part of a facility where hazardous waste is placed in or on land and which is not a pile, a land treatment facility, a surface impoundment, an underground injection well, a salt dome formation, a salt bed formation, an underground mine, or a cave. A (4) An area of land or an excavation in which wastes are placed for permanent disposal, and that is not a land application unit, surface impoundment, injection well, or waste pile. A

landfill cell
A discrete volume of a hazardous waste landfill which uses a liner to provide isolation of wastes from adjacent cells or wastes. Examples of landfill cells are trenches and pits. A

landfill gas
The gas produced in sanitary landfills during anaerobic digestion of the organic contents, which goes on constantly. It has a volume composition of 40 to 60 percent methane, a gas valued as a fuel and raw material in chemical syntheses and which could be recovered from municipal solid waste disposal sites. U

landyard
A rope, suitable for supporting one person. One end is fastened to a safety belt or harness and the other end is secured to a substantial object or a safety line. O

Lantz process
A destructive distillation technique in which the combustible components of solid waste are converted into combustible gases, charcoal, and a variety of distillates. U

large appliance product
Any organic surface-coated metal range, oven, microwave oven, refrigerator, freezer, washer, dryer, dishwasher, water heater, or trash compactor manufactured for household, commercial, or recreational use. A

latency
Time from the first exposure to a chemical until the appearance of a toxic effect. N

lateral expansion
A horizontal expansion of the waste boundaries of an existing MSWLF unit. A

lateral sewer
A sewer which connects the collector sewer to the interceptor sewer. A

lavage
A washing of a hollow organ, such

as the stomach, using a tube and fluids, used in animal feeding studies. N

lb-ft.
Pound feet. U

LC$_{50}$
Lethal concentration. (1) The concentration of material which is lethal to one-half of the test population of aquatic animals upon continuous exposure for 96 hours or less. A (2) Median level concentration, a standard measure of toxicity. It tells how much of a substance is needed to kill half of a group of experimental organisms at a specific time of observation. (See LD$_{50}$). N

LC$_{Lo}$
Lethal concentration low. The lowest concentration of a substance in air, other than LC$_{50}$, that has been reported to have caused death in humans or animals. The reported concentrations may be entered for periods of exposure that are less than 24 hours (acute) or greater than 24 hours (subacute and chronic). N

LD$_0$
The highest concentration of a toxic substance at which none of the test organisms die. N

LD$_{50}$
Lethal dose. (1) The dose of a chemical taken by mouth or absorbed by the skin which is expected to cause death in 50 percent of the test animals so treated. M (2) The dose of a toxicant that will kill 50 percent of the test organisms within a designated period of time. The lower the LD$_{50}$, the more toxic the compound. N

LD$_{Lo}$
Lethal dose low. See: Lethal dose low. N

LDR
Land disposal restrictions. U

leach
To undergo the process by which materials in the soil are moved into a lower layer of soil or are dissolved and carried through soil by water. A

leachate
(1) Liquid that has passed through or emerged from solid waste and contains soluble, suspended or miscible materials removed from such wastes. A (2) Any liquid, including any suspended components in the liquid, that has percolated through or drained from hazardous waste. A

leachate collection system
A system that gathers leachate and pumps it to the surface for treatment. N

leaching
The process by which nutrient chemicals or contaminants are dissolved and carried away by water, or are moved into a lower layer of soil. N

lead
A heavy metal that may be hazardous to health if breathed or swallowed. M [ed. National ambient

air quality standards have been promulgated for lead].

lead additive
Any substance containing lead or lead compounds. A

lead agency
(1) The federal agency, state agency, political subdivision, or Indian Tribe that has primary responsibility for planning and implementing a response action under CERCLA. A (2) The agency or agencies preparing or having taken primary responsibility for preparing the environmental impact statement. A

lead recipe
Raw material formulation of the following approximate weight proportions: 56 percent silica; 8 percent potassium carbonate; and 36 percent red lead. A

lead reclamation facility
The facility that remelts lead scrap and casts it into lead ingots for use in the battery manufacturing process. A

leaded gasoline
(1) Gasoline which is produced with the use of any lead additive or which contains more than 0.05 gram of lead per gallon or more than 0.005 gram of phosphorus per gallon. A (2) Gasoline to which lead has been added to raise the octane level. N

leak
(1) (a) The migration of liquid wastes outside of containment structures. N (b) Any of several events that indicate interruption of confinement of vinyl chloride within process equipment. Leaks include events regulated under subpart V of 40 CFR parts 61-80 such as: (1) An instrument reading of 10,000 ppm or greater measured according to Method 21 (see appendix A of 40 CFR part 60); (2) A sensor detection of failure of a seal system, failure of a barrier fluid system, or both; (3) Detectable emissions as indicated by an instrument reading of greater than 500 ppm above background for equipment designated for no detectable emissions measured according to Test Method 21 (see appendix A of 40 CFR part 60); and (4) In the case of pump seals regulated under § 61.242-2, indications of liquid dripping constituting a leak under § 61.242-2. Leaks also include events regulated under § 61.65(b)(8)(i) for detection of ambient concentrations in excess of background concentrations. A relief valve discharge is not a leak. A (2) Any instance in which a PCB Article, PCB Container, or PCB Equipment has any PCBs on any portion of its external surface. A

leak-detection system
A system capable of detecting the failure of either the primary or secondary containment structure or the presence of a release of hazardous waste or accumulated liquid in the secondary containment structure. Such a system must employ operational controls (e.g., daily visual inspections for releases into the secondary containment system of aboveground tanks) or consist of an interstitial monitoring device designed to detect continuously and automatically the

failure of the primary or secondary containment structure or the presence of a release of hazardous waste into the secondary containment structure. A

leak-tight
Solids or liquids cannot escape or spill out. It also means dust-tight. A

ledge plate
A plate that is adjacent to or overlaps the edge of a stoker. U

ledger paper
A type of paper generally used in a broad variety of recordkeeping type applications such as in accounting machines. A

ledgers (stringers)
A horizontal scaffold member which extends from post to post and which supports the putlogs or bearers forming a tie between the posts. O

legal defense costs
Any expenses that an insurer incurs in defending against claims of third parties brought under the terms and conditions of an insurance policy. A

legal proceedings
Any criminal proceeding or any civil judicial proceeding to which the Federal Government or a State or local government or quasi-governmental authority is a party. The term includes appeals from such proceedings. A

legislation
[For the purpose of determining whether an EIS is required under NEPA], a bill or legislative proposal to Congress developed by or with the significant cooperation and support of a Federal agency, but does not include requests for appropriations. The test for significant cooperation is whether the proposal is in fact predominantly that of the agency rather than another source. Drafting does not by itself constitute significant cooperation. Proposals for legislation includes requests for ratification of treaties. Only the agency which has primary responsibility for the subject matter involved will prepare a legislative environmental impact statement. A

LEL
Lower explosive limit. Refers to the lowest concentration of gas or vapor (percent by volume in air) that will burn or explode if an ignition source is present at ambient temperatures. The LEL is constant up to 250° F. Decrease it by 0.7 at temperatures above 250° F because explosibility increases with higher temperature. N

LEPC
Local Emergency Planning Committee. A committee appointed by the state emergency response commission, as required by SARA Title III to formulate a comprehensive emergency plan for its jurisdiction. N

LERC
Local Emergency Response Committee. P

lesion
A pathologic or traumatic

discontinuity of tissue or loss of function. N

lethal
Deadly; fatal. N

lethal concentration low
LC_{Lo}. The lowest concentration of a substance in air, other than LC_{50}, that has been reported to have caused death in humans or animals. The reported concentrations may be entered for periods of exposure that are less than 24 hours (acute) or greater than 24 hours (subacute and chronic). N

lethal dose
See LD_{50}. U

lethal dose low
LD_{Lo}. The lowest dose (other than LD_{50}) of a substance introduced by any route, other than inhalation, over any period of time in one or more divided portions and reported to have caused death in humans or animals. N

leukemia
A progressive, malignant disease of the blood-forming tissues, marked by an excessive number of white blood cells and their precursors. N

level of concern
LOC. The concentration in air of an extremely hazardous substance above which there may be serious immediate health effects to anyone exposed to it for short periods of time. N

LFL
Lower flammable limit. U

liabilities
Probable future sacrifices of economic benefits arising from present obligations to transfer assets or provide services to other entities in the future as a result of past transactions or events. A

liability
The state of being legally responsible for property damage or bodily injury caused during operation, closure or post-closure phases of a hazardous waste management facility. N

license or permit
An authorization granted by an agency of the Federal Government or a State or Local government to conduct any activity which may result in any discharge into the navigable waters of the United States, emissions of air pollutants into the atmosphere, or other polluting activity. The license or permit will establish the conditions under which the polluting activity can take place, including specific limitations on amounts of pollutants that may be released. Violations of permit conditions are usually enforceable by the Federal, State or Local government. U

licensed material
Source material, special nuclear material, or byproduct material received, possessed, used, or transferred under a general or special license issued by the U.S. Energy Research and Development Administration or a State. U

licensed site
The area contained within the boundary of a location under the control of persons generating or storing uranium byproduct materials under a license issued by the Commission. This includes such areas licensed by Agreement States, i.e., those States which have entered into an effective agreement under section 274(b) of the Atomic Energy at of 1954, as amended. A

licensing or permitting agency
Any agency of the Federal Government to which application is made for a license or permit. A

life cycle
The stages an organism passes through during its existence. N

lifeline
A component consisting of a flexible line for connection to an anchorage at one end to hang vertically (vertical lifeline), or for connection to anchorages at both ends to stretch horizontally (horizontal lifeline), and which serves as a means for connecting other components of a personal fall arrest system to the anchorage. O

lifetime
Covering the lifespan of an organism (generally considered 70 years for humans). N

lift
In a sanitary landfill, a compacted layer of solid waste and the top layer of cover material. N

lifting station
(See: pumping station). N

light-duty truck
Any motor vehicle rated at 8500 pounds GVWR or less which has a vehicle curb weight of 6000 pounds or less and which has a basic vehicle frontal area of 45 square feet or less, which is: (1) Designed primarily for purposes of transportation of property or is a derivation of such a vehicle, or (2) Designed primarily for transportation of persons and has a capacity of more than 12 persons, or (3) Available with special features enabling off-street or off-highway operation and use. A

light-duty truck 1
Any light light-duty truck up through 3750 lbs loaded vehicle weight. A

light-duty truck 2
Any light light-duty truck greater than 3750 lbs loaded vehicle weight. A

light-duty truck 3
Any heavy light-duty truck up through 5750 lbs adjusted loaded vehicle weight. A

light-duty truck 4
Any heavy light-duty truck greater than 5750 lbs adjusted loaded vehicle weight. A

light-duty vehicle
(1) A gasoline-powered motor vehicle rated at 6,000 lb. gross vehicle weight (GVW) or less. A (2) A passenger car

or passenger car derivative capable of seating 12 passengers or less. A

light-off time
LOT. The time required for a catalytic converter (at ambient temperature 68-86 degrees F) to warm-up sufficiently to convert 50 percent of the incoming HC and CO to CO_2 and H_2O. A

light-oil condenser
Any unit in the light-oil recovery operation that functions to condense benzene-containing vapors. A

light-oil decanter
Any vessel, tank, or other type of device in the light-oil recovery operation that functions to separate light oil from water downstream of the light-oil condenser. A light-oil decanter also may be known as a light-oil separator. A

light-oil storage tank
Any tank, reservoir, or container used to collect or store crude or refined light-oil. A

light-oil sump
Any tank, pit, enclosure, or slop tank in light-oil recovery operations that functions as a wastewater separation device for hydrocarbon liquids on the surface of the water. A

lighting outlet
An outlet intended for the direct connection of a lampholder, a lighting fixture, or a pendant cord terminating in a lampholder. O

lignite
Coal that is classified as lignite A or B according to the American Society of Testing and Materials' (ASTM) Standard Specification for Classification of Coals by Rank D388-77. U

lime (or limestone) scrubbing process
(1) Any of a number of methods using lime and a scrubber to remove sulfur dioxide from flue gases. (2) Process in which sulfur gases moving towards a smokestack are passed through a limestone and water solution to remove sulfur before it reaches the atmosphere. N

limited evidence
According to the U.S. EPA carcinogen risk assessment guidelines, limited evidence is a collection of facts and accepted scientific inferences that suggests the agent may be causing an effect but the suggestion is not strong enough to be an established fact. N

limited water-soluble substances
Chemicals which are soluble in water at less than 1,000 mg/l. A

limiting factor
A condition whose absence, or excessive concentration, exerts some restraining influence upon a population through incompatibility with species requirements or tolerance. M

limiting permissible concentration of the liquid phase of a material
(1) That concentration of a constituent which, after allowance for

initial mixing, does not exceed applicable marine water quality criteria; or, when there are not applicable marine water quality criteria. (2) That concentration of waste or dredged material in the receiving water which, after allowance for initial mixing, will not exceed a toxicity threshold defined as 0.01 of a concentration shown to be acutely toxic to appropriate sensitive marine organisms in a bioassay carried out in accordance with approved EPA procedures. (3) When there is reasonable scientific evidence on a specific waste material to justify the use of an application factor other than 0.01, such alternative application factor shall be used in calculating the LPC. A

limiting permissible concentration of the suspended particulate and solid phases of a material
That concentration which will not cause unreasonable acute or chronic toxicity or other sublethal adverse effects based on bioassay results using appropriate sensitive marine organisms in the case of the suspended particulate phase, or appropriate sensitive benthic marine organisms in the case of the solid phase; and which will not cause accumulation of toxic materials in the human food chain. These bioassays are to be conducted in accordance with procedures approved by EPA, or, in the case of dredged material, approved by EPA and the Corps of Engineers. A

limnology
The study of the physical chemical, meteorological, and biological aspects of fresh water. N

linear accelerators
A device for accelerating charged particles. It employs alternate electrodes and gaps arranged in a straight line, so proportioned that when potentials are varied in the proper amplitude and frequency, particles passing through the waveguide receive successive increments of energy. U

linearity
The maximum deviation between an actual instrument reading and the reading predicted by a straight line drawn between upper and lower calibration points. A

liner
(1) The material used on the inside of a furnace wall to insure a chamber impervious to escaping gases; the material used on the inside of a sanitary landfill to insure the basin is impervious to fluids, thereby preventing leaching of wastes to the environment. (2) A continuous layer of natural or man-made materials, beneath or on the sides of a surface impoundment, landfill, or landfill cell, which restricts the downward or lateral escape of hazardous waste, hazardous waste constituents, or leachate. A

lining
A material permanently attached to the inside of the outer shell of a

garment for the purpose of thermal protection and padding. O

lipid solubility
The maximum concentration of a chemical that will dissolve in fatty substances; lipid soluble substances are insoluble in water. If a substance is lipid soluble it will very selectively disperse through the environment via living tissue. N

liquefaction
Changing a solid into a liquid form. N

liquefied petroleum gases
LPG and LP Gas mean and include any material which is composed predominantly of any of the following hydrocarbons, or mixtures of them, such as propane, propylene, butane (normal butane or iso-butane), and butylenes. O

liquid trap
Sumps, well cellars, and other traps used in association with oil and gas production, gathering, and extraction operations (including gas production plants), for the purpose of collecting oil, water, and other liquids. These liquid traps may temporarily collect liquids for subsequent disposition or reinjection into a production or pipeline stream, or may collect and separate liquids from a gas stream. A

liquid-mounted seal
A foam or liquid-filled primary seal mounted in contact with the liquid between the tank wall and the floating roof continuously around the circumference of the tank. A

liquified petroleum gases or LP-gas
LPG. Any material which is composed predominantly of any of the following hydrocarbons, or mixtures of them; propane, propylene, butanes (normal butane or isobutane) and butylenes. O

listed
Equipment is "listed" if it is of a kind mentioned in a list which, (a) is published by a nationally recognized laboratory which makes periodic inspection of the production of such equipment, and (b) states such equipment meets nationally recognized standards or has been tested and found safe for use in a specified manner. O

listed waste
Wastes listed as hazardous under RCRA but which have not been subjected to the Toxic Characteristics Listing Process because the dangers they present are considered self-evident. N

lithology
The description of rocks on the basis of their physical and chemical characteristics. A

lithosphere
The solid part of the earth below the surface, including any ground water contained within it. A

litter tax
Charges levied against items appearing in litter (e.g., cigarette

butts, candy wrappers, convenience food packaging) to finance their collection and disposal. U

live load
The total static weight of workers, tools, parts, and supplies that the equipment is designed to support. O

LLRW
Low-level radioactive waste. Wastes less hazardous than most of those generated by a nuclear reactor. Usually generated by hospitals, research laboratories, and certain industries. The Department of Energy, Nuclear Regulatory Commission, and EPA share the responsibilities for managing them. (See: high-level radioactive wastes). N

load cell
A device external to the locomotive, of high electrical resistance, used in locomotive testing to simulate engine loading while the locomotive is stationary. (Electrical energy produced by the diesel generator is dissipated in the load cell resistors instead of the traction motors). A

load on top
A procedure for ballasting and cleaning unloaded tankers without discharging oil. Half of the tanks are first filled with seawater while the others are cleaned by hosing. Then oil from the cleaned tanks, along with oil which has separated out in the full tanks, is pumped into a single slop tank. The clean water in the full tanks is then discharged while the freshly-cleaned tanks are filled with seawater. Ballast is thus constantly maintained. A

load-bearing resistance of a refractory
The degree to which a refractory resists deformation when subjected to a specified compressive load at a specified temperature and time. U

loaded emissions test
A sampling procedure for exhaust emissions which requires exercising the engine under stress (i.e., loading) by use of a chassis dynamometer to simulate actual driving conditions. As a minimum requirement, the loaded emission test must include running the vehicle and measuring exhaust emissions at two speeds and loads other than idle. A

loaded vehicle mass
Curb mass plus 80 kg (176 lb.), average driver mass. A

loaded vehicle weight
The vehicle curb weight plus 300 pounds. A

loading
(1) The introduction of waste into a waste management unit but not necessarily to complete capacity (also referred to as filling). A (2) The ratio of daphnid biomass (grams, wet weight) to the volume (liters) of test solution in a test chamber at a point in time, or passing through the test chamber during a specific interval. A (3) The ratio of fish biomass (grams, wet weight) to the volume (liters) of test solution passing through the test

chamber during a 24-hr. period. A (4) The ratio of the biomass of gammarids (grams, wet weight) to the volume (liters) of test solution in either a test chamber or passing through it in a 24-hour period. A

loading cycle
The time period from the beginning of filling a tank truck, railcar, or marine vessel until flow to the control device ceases, as measured by the flow indicator. A

loading rack
The loading arms, pumps, meters, shutoff valves, relief valves, and other piping and valves necessary to fill tank trucks, railcars, or marine vessels. A

LOAEL
Lowest observed adverse effect level. N

loam
A soft, easily crumbled soil composed of a mixture of sand, silt, and clay. U

LOC
Level of concern. The concentration in air of an extremely hazardous substance above which there may be serious immediate health effects to anyone exposed to it for short periods of time. N

local agency
Any local government agency, other than the State agency, which is charged with the responsibility for carrying out a portion of a pollution control plan. A

local education agency
(1) Any local educational agency as defined in section 198 of the Elementary and Secondary Education Act of 1965 (20 U.S.C. 3381). (2) The owner of any nonpublic, nonprofit elementary, or secondary school building. (3) The governing authority of any school operated under the defense dependents' education system provided for under the Defense Dependents' Education Act of 1978 (20 U.S.C. 921, *et seq.*). A

local effect
A biological response occurring at the site of first contact between the toxic substance and the organism. N

local emergency planning committee
LEPC. A committee appointed by the state emergency response commission, as required by SARA Title III to formulate a comprehensive emergency plan for its jurisdiction. N

local government
A county, municipality, city, town, township, local public authority (including any public and Indian housing agency under the United States Housing Act of 1937), school district, special district, intrastate district, council of governments (whether or not incorporated as a nonprofit corporation under state law), any other regional or interstate government entity, or any agency or instrumentality of a local government. A

local share
The amount of the total grant eligible and allowable project costs

which a public body is obligated to pay under the grant. A

location
(a) Damp location. Partially protected locations under canopies, marquees, roofed open porches, and like locations, and interior locations subject to moderate degrees of moisture, such as some basements. (b) Dry location. A location not normally subject to dampness or wetness. A location classified as dry may be temporarily subject to dampness or wetness, as in the case of a building under construction. (c) Wet location. Installations underground or in concrete slabs or masonry in direct contact with the earth, and locations subject to saturation with water or other liquids, such as locations exposed to weather and unprotected. O

lockout
The placement of a lockout device on an energy isolating device, in accordance with an established procedure, ensuring that the energy isolating device and the equipment being controlled cannot be operated until the lockout device is removed. O

lockout device
A device that utilizes a positive means such as a lock, either key or combination type, to hold an energy isolating device in a safe position and prevent the energizing of a machine or equipment. Included are blank flanges and bolted slip blinds. O

locomotive
A self-propelled vehicle designed for and used on railroad tracks in the transport or rail cars, including self-propelled rail passenger vehicles. A

locomotive load cell test stand
The load cell and associated structure, equipment, trackage and locomotive being tested. A

LOE
Level of effort. N

LOEL
Lowest observed effect level. N

logit model
A dose-response model that can be derived under the assumption that the individual tolerance level is a random variable following the logit distribution. N

long term stabilization
The addition of material on a uranium mill tailings pile for purpose of ensuring compliance with the requirements of 40 CFR 192.02(a) or 192.32(b)(i). These actions shall be considered complete when the Nuclear Regulatory Commission determines that the requirements of 40 CFR 192.02(a) or 192.32(b)(i) have been met. A

long-term contract
When used in relation to solid waste supply, a contract of sufficient duration to assure the viability of a resource recovery facility (to the extent that such viability depends upon solid waste supply). I

loose-fill insulation
Insulation in granular, nodular,

fibrous, powdery, or similar form, designed to be installed by pouring, blowing or hand placement. A

lost workdays
The number of days (consecutive or not) after, but not including, the day of injury or illness during which the employee would have worked but could not do so; that is, could not perform all or any part of his normal assignment during all or any part of the workday or shift, because of the occupational injury or illness. O

LOT
Light-off time. U

low air
Air supplied to pressurize working chambers and locks. O

low altitude
Any elevation less than or equal to 1,219 meters (4000 feet). A [ed. Used to determine high altitude areas where changes in vehicle emission control systems are allowed to improve engine performance].

low altitude conditions
A test altitude less than 549 meters (1,800 feet). A

low dose
Should correspond to 1/10 of the high dose. A

low hazard contents
Those of such low combustibility that no self-propagating fire therein can occur and that consequently the only probable danger requiring the use of emergency exits will be from panic, fumes, or smoke, or fire from some external source. O

low NOx burners
One of several combustion technologies used to reduce emissions of NOx. N

low terrain
Any area other than high terrain. A

low-concentration PCBs
PCBs that are tested and found to contain less than 500 ppm PCBs, or those PCB-containing materials which EPA requires to be assumed to be at concentrations below 500 ppm (i.e., untested mineral oil dielectric fluid). A

low-emission vehicle
Any motor vehicle which--(A) emits any air pollutant in amounts significantly below new motor vehicle standards applicable under section 202 [of the CAA] at the time of procurement to that type of vehicle; and (B) with respect to all other air pollutants meets the new motor vehicle standards applicable under section 202 at the time of procurement to that type of vehicle. U

low-level liquid waste
Fluid materials that are contaminated by less than 5×10^{-5} microcuries per milliliter of mixed fission products. U

low-level radioactive waste
LLRW. Wastes less hazardous than most of those generated by a nuclear reactor. Usually generated by hospitals, research laboratories, and

certain industries. The Department of Energy, Nuclear Regulatory Commission, and EPA share the responsibilities for managing them. (See: high-level radioactive wastes.) N

low-mileage emissions target
For a particular pollutant, the value in grams per mile resulting from the division of the emission standard by the applicable engine family deterioration factor derived from the certification process for the applicable model year. A

low-noise emission product
Any product which emits noise in amounts significantly below the levels specified in noise emission standards under regulations applicable under section 6 [of the Noise Control Act] at the time of procurement to that type of product. G

low-noise emission product determination
The Administrator's determination whether or not a product, for which a properly filed application has been received, meets the low-noise-emission product criterion. A

low-pitched roof
A roof having a slope less than or equal to four in twelve. O

low-pressure tank
A storage tank which has been designed to operate at pressures above 0.5 p.s.i.g. but not more than 15 p.s.i.g. O

low-volume waste sources
Taken collectively as if from one source, wastewater from all sources except those for which specific limitations are otherwise established. Low volume waste sources would include but are not limited to wastewaters from wet scrubber air pollution control systems, ion exchange water treatment systems, water treatment evaporator blowdown, laboratory and sampling streams, boiler blowdown, floor drains, cooling tower basin cleaning wastes and recirculating house service water systems. Sanitary wastes and air conditioning wastes are not included. A

lower explosive limit
LEL. (1) The lowest percent by volume of a mixture of explosive gases which will propagate a flame in air at 25° C and atmospheric pressure. A (2) Refers to the lowest concentration of gas or concentration of gas or vapor (percent by volume in air) that will burn or explode if an ignition source is present at ambient temperatures. The LEL is constant up to 250° F. Decrease it by 0.7 at temperatures above 250° F because explosibility increases with higher temperature. N

lower flammable limit
LFL. For a vapor or gas, the lowest concentration (lowest percentage of the substance in air) that will produce a flash of fire when an ignition source (heat, arc, or flame) is present. At concentrations lower than the LFL, the mixture is too "lean" to burn. N

lower respiratory tract
That part of the respiratory tract below the larynx. N

lower sample
A spot sample obtained at the level of the fixed tank outlet or the swing line outlet. A

lowest achievable emission rate
The rate of emissions which reflects for any source, the more stringent rate of emissions based on the following: (A) the most stringent emission limitation which is contained in the implementation plan of any State for such class or category of source, unless the owner or operator of the proposed source demonstrates that such limitations are not achievable, or (B) the most stringent emissions limitation which is achieved in practice by such class or category of source, whichever is more stringent. This limitation, when applied to a modification, means the lowest achievable emissions rate for the new or modified emissions units within the stationary source. In no event shall the application of this term permit a proposed new or modified source to emit any pollutant in excess of the amount allowable under applicable new source standards of performance. A, B [ed. This is the minimum level of air pollutant emissions control required to be achieved by a new or modified stationary source that seeks to locate in an area not achieving ambient air quality standards].

lowest dose of a substance
TD_{LO}. The lowest dose of a substance introduced by any route other than inhalation over any given period of time and reported to produce any toxic effect in humans or to produce tumorigenic or reproductive effects in animals or humans. N

lowest observed adverse effect level
LOAEL. The lowest dose or exposure level of a chemical in a study at which there is a statistically or biologically significant increase in the frequency or severity of an adverse effect in the exposed population as compared with an appropriate, unexposed control group. N

lowest observed effect level
LOEL. In a study, the lowest dose or exposure level at which a statistically or biologically significant effect is observed in the exposed population compared with an appropriate unexposed control group. N

LPG
See liquified petroleum gases. U

lpm.
Liter per minute. U

LTO
Landing take off. U

LTU
Land Treatment Unit. N

lubricating oil
The fraction of crude oil which is sold for purposes of reducing friction in any industrial or mechanical device. Such term includes re-refined oil. A, I

luminescent materials
Materials that emit light upon excitation by such energy sources as photons, electrons, applied voltage, chemical reactions or mechanical energy and which are specifically used as coatings in fluorescent lamps and cathode ray tubes. Luminescent materials include, but are not limited to, calcium halophosphate, yttrium oxide, zinc sulfide, and zinc-cadmium sulfide. A

LUST
Leaking underground storage tank. U

lysimeter
A device used to measure the quantity or rate of water movement through or from a block of soil or other material, such as solid waste, or used to collect percolated water for quality analysis. U

M

m.
Meter(s). U

M10
Those offshore facilities continuously manned by ten (10) or more persons. A

m³
Cubic meter. U

M9IM
Those offshore facilities continuously manned by nine (9) or fewer persons or only intermittently manned by any number of persons. A

MABs
Monoclonal antibodies. U

machine shop
A facility performing cutting, grinding, turning, honing, milling, deburring, lapping, electrochemical machining, etching, or other similar operations. A

macrophage
A specialized cell of the immune system capable of engulfing and digesting foreign particles. N

MACT
Maximum achievable control technology. N

MADCAP
Model of advection, diffusion, and chemistry for air pollution. N

made
When used in connection with any invention, the conception or first actual reduction to practice of such invention. A

MAER
Maximum allowable emission rate. N

magazine
Any building or structure, other than an explosives manufacturing building, used for the storage of explosives. A

magnetic separation
The process by which a permanent magnet or electromagnet is used to

319

attract materials away from mixed waste. U

major disaster
Any hurricane, tornado, storm, flood, high water, wind-driven water, tidal wave, earthquake, drought, fire, or other catastrophe in any part of the United States which, in the determination of the President, is or threatens to become of sufficient severity and magnitude to warrant disaster assistance by the Federal Government to supplement the efforts and available resources of States and local governments and relief organizations in alleviating the damage, loss, hardship, or suffering caused thereby. A

major discharge
A discharge of more than 10,000 gallons of oil to the inland waters or more than 100,000 gallons of oil to the coastal waters. A

major emitting facility
Any of the following stationary sources of air pollutants which emit, or have the potential to emit, one hundred tons per year or more of any air pollutant from the following types of stationary sources: fossil-fuel fired steam electric plants of more than two hundred and fifty million British thermal units per hour heat input, coal cleaning plants (thermal dryers), kraft pulp mills, Portland Cement plants, primary zinc smelters, iron and steel mill plants, primary aluminum ore reduction plants, primary copper smelters, municipal incinerators capable of charging more than two hundred and fifty tons of refuse per day, hydrofluoric, sulfuric, and nitric acid plants, petroleum refineries, lime plants, phosphate rock processing plants, coke oven batteries, sulfur recovery plants, carbon black plants (furnace process) primary lead smelters, fuel conversion plants, sintering plants, secondary metal production facilities, chemical process plants, fossil-fuel boilers of more than two hundred and fifty million British thermal units per hour heat input, petroleum storage and transfer facilities with a capacity exceeding three hundred thousand barrels, taconite ore processing facilities, glass fiber processing plants, charcoal production facilities. Such term also includes any other source with the potential to emit two hundred and fifty tons per year or more of any air pollutant. This term shall not include new or modified facilities which are nonprofit health or education institutions which have been exempted by the State. [See: major stationary source]. B

major employment facility
Any single employer location having 250 or more employees. A

major facility
Any NPDES facility or activity classified as such by the Regional Administrator, or, in the case of approved State programs, the Regional Administrator in conjunction with the State Director. A

major federal action
Actions with effects that may be major and which are potentially subject to federal control and

responsibility. Major reinforces but does not have a meaning independent of significantly (40 CFR § 1508.27). Actions include the circumstance where the responsible officials fail to act and that failure to act is reviewable by courts or administrative tribunals under the Administrative Procedure Act or other applicable law as agency action. (a) Actions include new and continuing activities, including projects and programs entirely or partly financed, assisted, conducted, regulated, or approved by federal agencies; new or revised agency rules, regulations, plans, policies, or procedures; and legislative proposals (40 CFR §§ 1506.8, 1508.17). Actions do not include funding assistance solely in the form of general revenue sharing funds, distributed under the State and Local Fiscal Assistance Act of 1972, 31 U.S.C. 1221 *et seq.*, with no federal agency control over the subsequent use of such funds. Actions do not include bringing judicial or administrative civil or criminal enforcement actions. (b) Federal actions tend to fall within one of the following categories: (1) Adoption of official policy, such as rules, regulations, and interpretations adopted pursuant to the Administrative Procedure Act, 5 U.S.C. 551 *et seq.*; treaties and international conventions or agreements; formal documents establishing an agency's policies which will result in or substantially alter agency programs. (2) Adoption of formal plans, such as official documents prepared or approved by federal agencies which guide or prescribe alternative uses of federal resources, upon which future agency actions will be based. (3) Adoption of programs, such as a group of concerted actions to implement a specific policy or plan; systematic and connected agency decisions allocating agency resources to implement a specific statutory program or executive directive. (4) Approval of specific projects, such as construction or management activities located in a defined geographic area. Projects include actions approved by permit or other regulatory decision as well as federal and federally assisted activities. A

major live activities
Functions such as caring for one's self, performing manual tasks, walking, seeing, hearing, speaking, breathing, learning, and working. A

major modification
Used to define modifications with respect to Prevention of Significant Deterioration and New Source Review under the Clean Air Act and refers to modifications to major stationary sources of emissions and provides significant pollutant increase levels below which a modification is not considered major. N (i) Any physical change in or change in the method of operation of a major stationary source that would result in a significant net emissions increase of any pollutant subject to regulation under the [Clean Air] Act. (ii) Any net emissions increase that is considered significant for volatile organic compounds shall be considered significant for ozone. (iii) A physical change or change in the method of operation shall not include: (a) routine maintenance, repair, and replacement; (b) use of an alternative

fuel or raw material by reason of an order under sections 2(a) and (b) of the Energy Supply and Environmental Coordination Act of 1974 (or any superseding legislation) or by reason of a natural gas curtailment plan pursuant to the Federal Power Act; (c) use of an alternative fuel by reason of an order or rule under section 125 of the Act; (d) use of an alternative fuel at a steam generating unit to the extent that the fuel is generated from municipal solid waste; (e) use of an alternative fuel or raw material by a stationary source which (1) the source was capable of accommodating before December 21, 1976, unless such change would be prohibited under any federally enforceable permit condition which was established after December 21, 1976, pursuant to 40 CFR 52.21 or under regulations approved pursuant to 40 CFR 51.18 or 40 CFR 51.24; or (2) the source is approved to use under any permit issued under this ruling; (f) an increase in the hours of operation or in the production rate, unless such change is prohibited under any federally enforceable permit condition which was established after December 21, 1976 pursuant to 40 CFR 52.21 or under regulations approved pursuant to 40 CFR 51.18 or 40 CFR 51.24; (g) any change in ownership at a stationary source. A

major release
A release of any quantity of hazardous substance(s), pollutant(s), or contaminant(s) that poses a substantial threat to public health or welfare or the environment or results in significant public concern. A

major source baseline date
(a) In the case of particulate matter and sulfur dioxide, January 6, 1975, and (b) In the case of nitrogen dioxide, February 8, 1988. A

major stationary source
Used to determine to applicability of Prevention of Significant Deterioration and new source regulations. In a non-attainment area, any stationary pollutant source that has a potential to emit more than 100 tons per year is considered a major stationary source. In PSD areas the cutoff level may be either 100 or 250 tons, depending upon the type of source. N (i)(a) Any stationary source of air pollutants which emits, or has the potential to emit, 100 tons per year or more of any pollutant subject to regulation under the Act; or (b) Any physical change that would occur at a stationary source not qualifying under paragraph (f)(5)(i)(a) of this section [§ 52.24], as a major stationary source, if the change would constitute a major stationary source by itself. (ii) A major stationary source that is major for volatile for organic compounds shall be considered major for ozone. [See: major emitting facility]. A

make available for use
To distribute, sell, ship, deliver for shipment, or receive and (having so received) deliver, to any person. However, the term excludes transactions solely between persons who are pesticide producers, registrants, wholesalers, or retail sellers, acting only in those capacities. A

makes
Wherever it appears, shall include the terms presents, submits, and causes to be made, presented, or submitted. As the context requires, "making" or "made" shall likewise include the corresponding forms of such terms. A

malformation
A permanent structural change in a developing organism that may adversely affect survival, development, or function. N

malfunction
(1) Any sudden and unavoidable failure of air pollution control equipment or process equipment or of a process to operate in a normal or usual manner so that emissions of asbestos are increased. Failures of equipment shall not be considered malfunctions if they are caused in any way by poor maintenance, careless operation, or any other preventable upset conditions, equipment breakdown, or process failure. A (2) Not operating according to specifications (e.g., those specifications listed in the application for certification). A

malignant
A condition of a neoplasm (tumor) in which it has escaped normal growth regulation and has demonstrated the ability to invade local or distant structures, thereby disrupting the normal architecture or functional relationships of the tissue system. N

malleable iron
A cast iron made by a prolonged anneal of white cast iron in which decarburization or graphitization, or both, take place to eliminate some or all of the cementite. Graphite is present in the form of temper carbon. A

mammal poisons and repellents
All substances, or mixtures of substances, except rodenticides, intended for preventing, destroying, repelling, or mitigating mammals declared to be pests under 40 CFR §162.14. Mammal poisons and repellents include, but are not limited to: (i) Taste, odor, and irritant repellents intended to repel mammals or their adverse, undesired, or destructive activities such as attacking, foraging, chewing, gnawing, urinating, or defecating in or on specific sites or on or near specific objects, person, plants, or animals; (ii) Predacides intended to kill certain mammals that prey upon other vertebrate animals which man deems necessary to protect; (iii) Toxicants, baits, and poisons intended to kill certain mammals causing injury or destruction to crops, stored foods, or other organisms and objects which man deems necessary to protect; and (iv) Reproductive inhibitors intended to reduce or otherwise alter the reproductive capacity or potential of certain mammals. A

man lock
A chamber through which men pass from one air pressure environment to another. O

man-made beta particle and photon emitters
All radionuclides emitting beta

particles and/or photons listed in Maximum Permissible Body Burdens and Maximum Permissible Concentration of Radionuclides in Air or Water for Occupational Exposure, NBS Handbook 69, except the daughter products of thorium-232, uranium-235 and uranium-238. A

man-rem
The product of the average individual dose in a population times the number of individuals in the population. Syn: person-rem. U

management
Any activity, operation, or process (except for transportation) conducted to prepare spent nuclear fuel or radioactive waste for storage or disposal, or the activities associated with placing such fuel or waste in a disposal system. A

management agencies
(1) The identification of those agencies recommended for designation by the Governor pursuant to Section 208 of the FWPCA to carry out each of the provisions of the water quality management plan. The identification shall include those agencies necessary to construct, operate and maintain all treatment works identified in the plan and those agencies necessary to implement the regulatory programs. (2) Depending upon an agency's assigned responsibilities under the plan, the agency must have adequate authority and capability: (i) To carry out its assigned portions of an approved State water quality management plan(s) (including the plans developed for areawide planning areas designated pursuant to Section 208(a) (2), (3), or (4) of the Act) developed under this part; (ii) To effectively manage waste treatment works and related point and nonpoint source facilities and practices serving such area in conformance with the approved plan; (iii) Directly or by contract, to design and construct new works, and to operate and maintain new and existing works as required by any approved water quality management plan developed under this part; (iv) To accept and utilize grants or other funds from any source for waste treatment management or nonpoint source control purposes; (v) To raise revenues, including the assessment of user charges; (vi) To incur short and long term indebtedness; (vii) To assure, in implementation of an approved water quality management plan, that each participating community pays its proportionate share of related costs; (viii) To refuse to receive any wastes from a municipality or subdivision thereof, which does not comply with any provision of an approved water quality management plan applicable to such areas; and (ix) To accept for treatment industrial wastes. A

management authority
The EPA organizational entity assigned responsibility for implementing the management functions identified in [40 CFR] § 228.3. A

management of migration
Actions that are taken to minimize and mitigate the migration of hazardous substances or pollutants or contaminants and the effects of such

migration. Management of migration actions may be appropriate where the hazardous substances or pollutants or contaminants are no longer at or near the area where they were originally located or situations where a source cannot be adequately identified or characterized. Measures may include, but are not limited to, provision of alternative water supplies, management of a plume of contamination, or treatment of a drinking water aquifer. A

management or hazardous waste management
The systematic control of collection, source separation, storage, transportation, processing, treatment, recovery, and disposal of hazardous waste. A

management system
The total equipment required for the determination of the gas volumetric flow rate in a duct or stack. The system consists of three major subsystems: (A) Analyzer--that portion of the measurement system which senses the stack gas flow rate or velocity pressure and generates a signal output that is a function of the flow rate or velocity of the gases. (B) Data presentation--that portion of the measurement system that provides a display of the output signal in terms of volumetric flow rate units, or other units which are convertible to volumetric flow rate units. (C) Sampling interface--that portion of the measurement system that performs one or more of the following operations: delineation, acquisition, transportation, and conditioning of a signal from the stack gas and protection of the analyzer from any hostile aspects of the source environment. A

mandatory recycling
Programs under statute that require consumers to separate their trash to make all recyclable materials available for recycling. U

manhole
A subsurface enclosure which personnel may enter and which is used for the purpose of installing, operating, and maintaining equipment and/or cable. O

manifest
(1) The form used for identifying the quantity, composition, and the origin, routing, and destination of hazardous waste during its transportation from the point of generation to the point of disposal, treatment, or storage. I (2) The shipping document EPA form 8700-22 and, if necessary, EPA form 8700-22A, originated and signed by the generator in accordance with the instructions included in the appendix to part 262 [title 40 CFR]. A

manifest document number
The U.S. EPA twelve digit identification number assigned to the generator plus a unique five digit document number assigned to the [Hazardous Waste] Manifest by the generator for recording and reporting purposes. A

manifest system
The clerical procedure to be followed by an owner / operator of a

facility that receives hazardous waste accompanied by a manifest or delivery document. U

manifold business forms
A type of product manufactured by business forms manufacturers that is commonly produced as marginally punched continuous forms in small rolls or fan folded sets with or without carbon paper interleaving. It has a wide variety of uses such as invoices, purchase orders, office memoranda, shipping orders, and computer printout. A

manmade air pollution
Air pollution which results directly or indirectly from human activities. B

manmade wetland
Any wetland area that has been purposely or accidentally created by some activity of man; also called artificial wetlands. N

manned control center (PCB)
An electrical power distribution control room where the operating conditions of a PCB Transformer are continuously monitored during the normal hours of operation (of the facility), and, where the duty engineers, electricians, or other trained personnel have the capability to deenergize a PCB Transformer completely within 1 minute of the receipt of a signal indicating abnormal operating conditions such as an overtemperature condition or overpressure condition in a PCB Transformer. A

manometer
An instrument for measuring pressure.
It usually consists of a U-shaped tube containing a liquid, the surface of which in one end of the tube moves proportionally with changes in pressure on the liquid in the other end. Also, a tube type of differential pressure gauge. U

manual method
A method for measuring concentrations of an ambient air pollutant in which sample collection, analysis, or measurement, or some combination thereof, is performed manually. A

manual separation
The separation of mixed waste by hand (e.g., the practice of keeping newspapers separate from garbage in the home). U

manufacture
To produce or manufacture in the United States or import into the customs territory of the United States. A

manufacture for commercial purposes
(1) To produce, with the purpose of obtaining an immediate or eventual commercial advantage for the manufacturer, and includes among other things such "manufacture" of any amount of a chemical substance or mixture: (i) For commercial distribution, including for test marketing. (ii) For use by the manufacturer, including use for product research and development, or as an intermediate. (2) Manufacture for commercial purposes also applies to substances that are produced coincidentally during the manufacture,

processing, use, or disposal of another substance or mixture, including byproducts and impurities. Such byproducts and impurities may, or may not, in themselves have commercial value. They are nonetheless produced for the purpose of obtaining a commercial advantage since they are part of the manufacture of a chemical product for a commercial purpose. A

manufacture of electronic crystals
The growing of crystals and/or the production of crystal wafers for use in the manufacture of electronic devices. A

manufacture of semi-conductors
Those processes, beginning with the use of crystal wafers, which lead to or are associated with the manufacture of semiconductor devices. A

manufacture or import for commercial purposes
(1) For distribution in commerce, including for test marketing purposes, or (2) For use by the manufacturer, including for use as an intermediate. A

manufacture solely for export
To manufacture for a commercial purpose solely for export from the United States under the following restrictions on domestic activity: (1) Processing is limited solely to sites under the control of the manufacturer. (2) Distribution in commerce is limited to purposes of export. (3) The manufacturer may not use the substance except in small quantities solely for research and development. A

manufacturer
(1) Any person engaged in the manufacturing or assembling of new products, or the importing of new products for resale, or who acts for, and is controlled by, any such person in connection with the distribution of such products, including any establishment engaged in the mechanical or chemical transformation of materials or substances into new products including but not limited to the blending of materials such as pesticidal products, resins, or liquors. A , B, G (2) A person who imports, produces or manufactures a chemical substance. A person who extracts a component chemical substance from a previously existing chemical substance or a complex combination of substances is a manufacturer of that component chemical substance. A person who contracts with a manufacturer to manufacture or produce a chemical substance is also a manufacturer if (1) the manufacturer manufactures or produces the substance exclusively for that person, and (2) that person specifies the identity of the substance and controls the total amount produced and the basic technology for the plant process. A

manufacturer parts
Parts produced or sold by the manufacturer of the motor vehicle or motor vehicle engine. A

manufacturers formulation
A list of substances or component parts as described by the maker of a coating, pesticide or other product containing chemicals or other substances. N

manufacturing activities
All those activities at one site which are necessary to produce a substance identified in Subpart D of 40 CFR Parts 700-789 and make it ready for sale or use as the listed substance, including purifying or importing the substance. A

manufacturing process
(1) All of a series of unit operations operating at a site, resulting in the production of a product. A (2) A method whereby a process emission source or series of process emission sources is used to convert raw materials, feed stocks, subassemblies, or other components into a product, either for sale or for use as a component in a subsequent manufacturing process. A

manufacturing stream
All reasonably anticipated transfer, flow, or disposal of a chemical substance, regardless of physical state or concentration, through all intended operations of manufacture, including the cleaning of equipment. A

manufacturing use product
(1) Any pesticide product other than an end use product. A product may consist of the technical grade of active ingredient only, or may contain inert ingredients, such as stabilizers or solvents. A (2) Any pesticide product other than a product to be labeled with directions for end use. This term includes any product intended for use as a pesticide after re-formulation or re-packaging. A

Mar Ad
Maritime Administration in the U.S. Department of Commerce. U

margin of exposure
MOE. The ratio of the no-observed-adverse-effect level (NOAEL) to the estimated human exposure. The MOE was formerly referred to as the margin of safety (MOS). N

margin of safety
When setting primary standards-- by law, based entirely on health considerations -- EPA first determines the concentration of a pollutant that is safe for most people. It then sets the standard at a **lower** concentration level. The difference in the two levels -- the margin of safety-- protects people who may be especially vulnerable to air pollution. See primary standards. N

marine bays and estuaries
Semi-enclosed coastal waters which have a free connection to the territorial sea. A

marine environment
That territorial seas, the contiguous zone and the oceans. A

marine sanitation device
Any equipment installed on board a vessel to receive, retain, treat, or discharge sewage and any process to treat such sewage. N, A, D

marine vessel
Any tank ship or tank barge which transports liquid product such as benzene. A

mark
The descriptive name, instructions, cautions, or other information applied

to chemical substances, mixtures, articles, containers, equipment, or other objects or activities described in these regulations. A

market/marketers
The processing or distributing in commerce, or the person who processes or distributes in commerce, used oil fuels to burners or other marketers, and may include the generator of the fuel if it markets the fuel directly to the burner. A

marking
The act of physically indicating the classification assignment on classified material. A

MARPOL
The International Convention for the Prevention of Pollution from Ships, 1973, as modified by the Protocol of 1978 relating thereto, Annex I, which regulates pollution from oil and which entered into force on October 2, 1983. A

marsh
(1) Wet, soft, low-lying land that provides a habitat for many plants and animals. It can be destroyed by dredging and filling. (2) A type of wetland that does not accumulate appreciable peat deposits and is dominated by herbaceous vegetation. Marshes may be either fresh or saltwater and tidal or non-tidal. N

masking
Blocking out a sight, sound, or smell with another. N

mass balance
A quantitative accounting of the distributions of chemical in plant components, support medium, and test solutions. It also means a quantitative determination of uptake as the difference between the quantity of gas entering an exposure chamber, the quantity leaving the chamber, and the quantity adsorbed to the chamber walls. A

mass median aerodynamic diameter
MMAD. Median of the distribution of mass with respect to the aerodynamic diameter of a particle. N

master inventory file
EPA's comprehensive list of chemical substances which constitute the Chemical Substances Inventory compiled under section 8(b) of the [TSCA] Act. A

MATC
Maximum Acceptable Toxicant Concentration. The maximum concentration at which a chemical can be present and not be toxic to the test organism. A

matching share
That portion of the project costs that is not derived from Federal assistance. See: cost-sharing. U

material
Matter of any kind or description, including, but not limited to, dredged material, solid waste, incinerator residue, garbage, sewage, sewage sludge, munitions, radiological, chemical, and biological warfare agents, radioactive materials,

chemicals, biological and laboratory waste, wreck or discarded equipment, rock, sand, excavation debris, and industrial, municipal, agricultural, and other waste; but such term does not mean sewage from vessels within the meaning of [33 USC] §1322. Oil within the meaning of [33 USC] §1321 of this title shall be included only to the extent that such oil is taken on board a vessel or aircraft for the purpose of dumping. E

material balance
An accounting of the weights of materials entering or leaving a processing unit, such as an incinerator, usually on an hourly basis. U

material exchange
An industrial waste exchange that also buys and sells the waste. U

material safety data sheet
MSDS. A compilation of information required under the OSHA Communication Standard on the identity of hazardous chemicals, health, and physical hazards, exposure limits, and precautions. Section 311 of SARA requires facilities to submit MSDSs under certain circumstances. N

material specification
A specification that stipulates the use of certain materials to meet the necessary performance requirements. A

material storage runoff
The rainfall runoff from or through any coal, ash or other material storage pile. A

materials lock
A chamber through which materials and equipment pass from one air pressure environment into another. O

materials market
The combined commercial interests that buy recyclable materials and process them for reuse. The demand for goods made of recycled materials determines the economic feasibility of recycling. U

materials recovery
Extraction of materials from the waste stream for reuse or recycling. Examples include source separation, front-end recovery, in-plant recycling, post combustion recovery, leaf composting, etc. U

maximum achievable control technology
MACT. Emissions limitations based on the best demonstrated control technology or practices in similar sources to be applied to major sources emitting one or more of the listed toxic pollutants. N

maximum contaminant level
(1) The maximum permissible level of a contaminant in water which is delivered to the free flowing outlet of the ultimate user of a public water system, except in the case of turbidity where the maximum permissible level is measured at the point of entry to the distribution system. Contaminants added to the water under circumstances controlled by the user, except those resulting from corrosion of piping and plumbing caused by water quality, are excluded from this definition. A (2) The maximum

permissible level of a contaminant in water which is delivered to any user of a public water system. J MCLs are enforceable standards. N

maximum contaminant level goal
MCLG. The maximum level of a contaminant in drinking water at which no known or anticipated adverse effect on the health of persons would occur, and which allows an adequate margin of safety. Maximum contaminant level goals are nonenforceable health goals. A

maximum daily discharge limitation
The highest allowable "daily discharge." A

maximum for any one day
Based on the daily average mass of material processed during the peak thirty consecutive day production period. A

maximum individual risk
MIR. The increased risk for a person exposed to the highest measured or predicted concentration of a toxicant. N

maximum likelihood estimate
MLE. A statistical best estimate of the value of a parameter from a given data set. N

maximum permissible dose equivalent
MPDE. The greatest dose equivalent that a person or specified part of the body shall be allowed to receive in a given period of time. U

maximum rated capacity
When the portable air compressor, operating at the design full speed with the compressor on load, delivers its rated cfm output and pressure, as defined by the manufacturer. U

maximum rated horsepower
The maximum brake horsepower output of an engine as stated by the manufacturer in his sales and service literature and his application for certification under 40 CFR § 86.082-21. A

maximum rated RPM
The engine speed measured in revolutions per minute (RPM) at which peak net brake power (SAE J-245) is developed for motorcycles of a given configuration. A

maximum rated torque
The maximum torque produced by an engine as stated by the manufacturer in his sales and service literature and his application for certification under 40 CFR § 86.082-21. A

maximum sound level
The greatest A-weighted sound level in decibels measured at fast meter response during the designated time interval or during the event. It is abbreviated as L_{max}. A

maximum tolerated dose
MTD. The highest dose of a toxicant that causes toxic effects without causing death during a chronic exposure and that does not decrease the body weight by more than 10%. N

maximum total trihalomethane (THM) potential
MTP. The maximum concentration of total trihalomethanes produced in a

given water containing a disinfectant residual after 7 days at a temperature of 25 degrees C or above. A

may
If a discretionary right, privilege, or power is conferred, the word "may" is used. If a right, privilege, or power is abridged or if an obligation to abstain from acting is imposed, the word "may" is used with a restrictive "no," "not," or "only." (E.g., no employer may . . .; an employer may not . . .; only qualified persons may. . . .) O

mbbl.
1,000 barrels (one barrel = 42 gallons). U

MCAs
MABs, monoclonal antibodies. U

MCL
Maximum contaminant level. U

MCLG
Maximum contaminant level goal. A

MDL
Method detection limit. U

mean retention time
The time obtained by dividing a reservoir's mean annual minimum total storage by the non-zero 30-day, ten-year low-flow from the reservoir. A

means of egress
A continuous and unobstructed way of exit travel from any point in a building or structure to a public way and consists of three separate and distinct parts: The way of exit access, the exit, and the way of exit discharge. A means of egress comprises the vertical and horizontal ways of travel and shall include intervening room spaces, doorways, hallways, corridors, passageways, balconies, ramps, stairs, enclosures, lobbies, escalators, horizontal exits, courts, and yards. O

means of emission limitation
A system of continuous emission reduction (including the use of specific technology or fuels with specified pollution characteristics). B

measurement period
A continuous period of time during which noise of railroad yard operations is assessed, the beginning and finishing times of which may be selected after completion of the measurements. A

mechanical aeration
Use of mechanical energy to inject air into water to cause a waste stream to absorb oxygen. N

mechanical and thermal integrity
The ability of a converter to continue to operate at its previously determined efficiency and light-off time and be free from exhaust leaks when subject to thermal and mechanical stresses representative of the intended application. A

mechanical collector
A device that traps particulate matter by the use of mechanical energy, rather than chemically or electrically. U

mechanical composting
A method in which the compost is

continuously and mechanically mixed and aerated. U

mechanical energy
Energy in a form which can do work directly. U

mechanical equipment
All motor or human propelled wheeled equipment except for wheelbarrows and mopcarts. O

mechanical removal methods
Include the use of pumps, skimmers, booms, earthmoving equipment, and other mechanical devices. A

mechanical separation
The separation of mixed material by mechanical means (e.g., air classifier, spiral classifier). See separator. U

mechanical torque rate
A term applied to a thermostatic coil, defined as the torque accumulation per angular degree of deflection of a thermostatic coil. A

mechanical turbulence
Random irregularities of fluid motion in air caused by buildings or mechanical, non-thermal processes. N

media
Specific environments -- air, water, soil -- which are the subject of regulatory concern and activities. N

medical consultation
A consultation which takes place between an employee and a licensed physician for the purpose of determining what medical examinations or procedures, if any, are appropriate in cases where a significant exposure to a hazardous chemical may have taken place. O

medical lock
A special chamber in which employees are treated for decompression illness. It may also be used in preemployment physical examinations to determine the adaptability of the prospective employee to changes in pressure. O

medical pathology
A disorder or disease. O

medical treatment
Treatment administered by a physician or by registered professional personnel under the standing orders of a physician. Medical treatment does not include first aid treatment even though provided by a physician or registered professional personnel. O

medical waste
Any solid waste which is generated in the diagnosis, treatment (e.g., provision of medical services), or immunization of human beings or animals, in research pertaining thereto, or in the production or testing of biologicals. The term does not include any hazardous waste identified or listed under [40 CFR] Part 261 or any household waste as defined in [40 CFR] § 261.4(b)(I). Note to this definition: Mixtures of hazardous waste and medical waste are subject to this part except as provided in [40 CFR] § 259.31. A

medium discharge
A discharge of 1,000 to 10,000 gallons of oil to the inland waters or a discharge of 10,000 to 100,000 gallons of oil to the coastal waters. A

medium release
All releases not meeting the criteria for classification as a minor or major release. A

mega-
A prefix meaning 1 million. J

meiosis
Cell and nuclear division in which the number of chromosomes is reduced from diploid (2n) to haploid (n). This process is characteristic of germ cells (spermatocyte or oocyte) division in which two successive divisions of the nucleus produce four cells that contain half the number of chromosomes present in the somatic cells. Each of the four daughter cells obtain, at random, any one of the two copies of each chromosome from parent cell. These cells may mature to sperm or egg cells. N

meltdown and refining period
(1) That phase of the steel production cycle when charge material is melted and undesirable elements are removed from the metal. A (2) The time period commencing at the termination of the initial charging period and ending at the initiation of the tapping period, excluding any intermediate charging periods. A

membrane barrier
A thin layer of material impervious to the flow of gas or water. U

meq.
Milliequivalent. U

merchant
Those by-product cokemaking operations which provide more than fifty percent of the coke produced to operations, industries, or processes other than iron making blast furnaces assocated with steel production. A

metabolism
(1) The study of the sum of the processes by which a particular substance is handled in the body and includes absorption, tissue distribution, biotransformation, and excretion. A (2) The biochemical reactions by which energy is made available for the use of an organism. Metabolism includes all chemical transformations occurring in an organism from the time a nutrient substance enters, until it has been utilized and the waste products eliminated. In toxicology, metabolism of a toxicant consists of a series of chemical transformations that take place within an organism. A wide range of enzymes act on toxicants, that may increase water solubility, and facilitate elimination from the organism. In some cases, however, metabolites may be more toxic than their parent compound. N

metabolite
Any substance produced in or by living organisms by biological processes and derived from a pesticide. A

metal cleaning waste
Any wastewater resulting from cleaning [with or without chemical

cleaning compounds] any metal process equipment including, but not limited to, boiler tube cleaning, boiler fireside cleaning, and air preheater cleaning. A

metal coil surface coating operation
The application system used to apply an organic coating to the surface of any continuous metal strip with thickness of 0.15 millimeter (mm) (0.006 in.) or more that is packaged in a roll or coil. A

metal preparation
Any and all of the metal processing steps preparatory to applying the enamel slip. Usually this includes cleaning, pickling and applying a nickel flash or chemical coating. A

metallic shoe seal
Includes but is not limited to a metal sheet held vertically against the tank wall by springs or weighted levers and is connected by braces to the floating roof. A flexible coated fabric (envelope) spans the annular space between the metal sheet and the floating roof. A

metallo-organic active ingredients
Carbon containing active ingredients containing one or more metallic atoms in the structure. A

metallo-organic pesticides
A class of organic pesticides containing one or more metal or metalloid atoms in the structure. A

metalworking fluid
A liquid of any viscosity or color containing intentionally added water and used in metal machining operations for the purpose of cooling, lubricating, or rust inhibition. A

metaplasia
The abnormal transformation of an adult, fully differentiated tissue of one kind into a differentiated tissue of another kind. N

metastasis
The transmission of a disease from one part of the body to another. N

methane
(1) A colorless, nonpoisonous, flammable gas created by anaerobic decomposition of organic compounds. N (2) A colorless, nonpoisonous, flammable gas emitted by marshes and dumps undergoing anaerobic decomposition. N [ed. The principal component of natural gas].

methods of operation
The installation, emplacement, or introduction of materials, including those involved in construction, to achieve a process or procedure to control: Surface water pollution from non-point sources, i.e. agricultural, forest practices, mining, construction; ground or surface water pollution from well, subsurface, or surface disposal operations; activities resulting in salt water intrusion; or changes in the movement, flow, or circulation of navigable or ground waters. A

metric ton
Or tonne, is equal to 2,200 pounds. U

metropolitan planning organization
MPO. The organization designated under 23 U.S.C. 134 and 23 CFR part 450.106. A

MF
Modifying factor. N

MFBI
Major fuel burning installation. N

Mg.
Megagram = 10^6 grams. U

mg.
Abbreviation for milligram(s). U

mg/m³
Milligrams per cubic meter of air. N

mgal.
1,000 gallons. U

microbes
(1) Tiny plants and animals, some that cause disease are found in sewage. N (2) Microscopic organisms such as algae, animals, viruses, bacteria, fungus, and protozoa, some of which cause diseases. (See: microorganism). N

microbial inoculation
The process in which microorganisms are introduced into organic waste materials to initiate decomposition. It is a practical approach to site restoration if the depth of contamination is fairly shallow, the extent of contamination is relatively small, and the waste materials are organic compounds. U

microbial pesticide
A microorganism that is used to control a pest. They are of low toxicity to man. N

microorganism
Living organisms so small that individually they can usually only be seen through a microscope. N

MICROMORT
A one-in-a-million chance of death from an environmental hazard. N

microenvironment
The immediate local environment of an organism. N

micron
Unit of measurement equal to 1/1,000,000 of a meter. J

micron efficiency curve
A curve showing how well a collector traps micron-size dust particles. U

microscale
The concentrations in air volumes associated with area dimensions ranging from several meters up to about 100 meters. A

midden
A refuse pile in which bones, broken tools, and pottery have been accumulating, layer by layer, in long inhabited places since human beings lived in caves. It is the earliest historical evidence of waste materials. U

middle scale
The concentration typical of areas up to several city blocks in size with

dimensions ranging from about 100 meters to 0.5 kilometer. A

midnight dumper
An idiomatic term referring to a person who disposes of hazardous or noxious wastes in a stealthy, illegal manner. U

midrange
The value of oxygen or carbon dioxide concentration that is representative of the normal conditions in the stack gas of the affected facility at typical operating rates. A

military engine
Any engine manufactured solely for the Department of Defense to meet military specifications. A

mill
A preparation facility within which the metal ore is cleaned, concentrated or otherwise processed prior to shipping to the consumer, refiner, smelter or manufacturer. A mill includes all ancillary operations and structures necessary for the cleaning, concentrating or other processing of the metal ore such as ore and gangue storage areas, and loading facilities. A

mill broke
Any paper waste generated in a paper mill prior to completion of the papermaking process. It is usually returned directly to the pulping process. Mill broke is excluded from the definition of "recovered materials." O

milled refuse
Solid waste that has been mechanically reduced in size. C

millfeed
The ore and other material introduced into the milling process. U

milli-
A prefix meaning 1/1,000; abbreviated by the letter m, such as milligram (mg). J

milligram
10^{-3} gram. U

milliliter
10^{-3} liter. U

millirem (mrem)
10^{-3} rem. U

mimeo paper
A grade of writing paper used for making copies on stencil duplicating machines. A

mine
An active mining area, including all land and property placed, under or above the surface of such land, used in or resulting from the work of extracting metal ore or minerals from their natural deposits by any means or method, including secondary recovery of metal ore from refuse or other storage piles, wastes, or rock dumps and mill tailings derived from the mining, cleaning, or concentration of metal ores. A

mine dewatering
Any water that is impounded or that collects in the mine and is pumped,

drained or otherwise removed from the mine through the efforts of the mine operator. This term shall also include wet pit overflows caused solely by direct rainfall and ground water seepage. However, if a mine is also used for treatment of process generated waste water, discharges of commingled water from the mine shall be deemed discharges of process generated waste water. A

mine drainage
Any drainage, and any water pumped or siphoned, from an active mining area or a post-mining area. A

miner of asbestos
A person who produces asbestos by mining or extracting asbestos containing ore so that it may be further milled to produce bulk asbestos for distribution in commerce, and includes persons who conduct milling operations to produce bulk asbestos by processing asbestos-containing ore. Milling involves the separation of the fibers from the ore, grading and sorting the fibers, or fiberizing crude asbestos ore. To mine or to mill is to "manufacture" for commercial purposes under TSCA. A

mineral fiber insulation
Insulation (rock wool or fiberglass) which is composed principally of fibers manufactured from rock, slag or glass, with or without binders. A

mineral handling and storage facility
The areas in asphalt roofing plants in which minerals are unloaded from a carrier, the conveyor transfer points between the carrier and the storage silos, and the storage silos. A

minimal risk
That the probability and magnitude of harm or discomfort anticipated in the research are not greater in and of themselves than those ordinarily encountered in daily life or during the performance of routine physical or psychological examinations or tests. A

minimum detectable sensitivity
The smallest amount of input concentration that can be detected as the concentration approaches zero. A

minimum maintained velocity
The velocity of air movement which must be maintained in order to meet minimum specified requirements for health and safety. O

mining overburden returned to the mine site
Any material overlying an economic mineral deposit which is removed to gain access to that deposit and is then used for reclamation of a surface mine. A

mining wastes
Residues which result from the extraction of raw materials from the earth. A

minor discharge
(1) A discharge to the inland waters of less than 1,000 gallons of oil or a discharge to the coastal waters of less than 10,000 gallons of oil. A (2) Any discharge which (a) has a total volume of less than 50,000 gallons on every day of the year, (b) does not

affect the waters of any other State, and (c) is not identified by the Director, the Regional Administrator, or by the Administrator [of EPA] in regulations issued pursuant to section 307(a) of the [Federal Water Pollution Control] Act as a discharge which is not a minor discharge. If there is more than one discharge from a facility and the sum of the volumes of all discharges from the facility exceeds 50,000 gallons on any day of the year, then no discharge from the facility is a "minor discharge" as defined herein. A

minor release
A release of a quantity of hazardous substance(s), pollutant(s), or contaminant(s) that poses minimal threat to public health or welfare or the environment. A

minor source baseline date
The earliest date after the trigger date on which a major stationary source or a major modification subject to 40 CFR 52.21 or to regulations approved pursuant to 40 CFR 51.166 submits a complete application under the relevant regulations. A

minority business enterprise
A business which is (1) certified as socially and economically disadvantaged by the Small Business Administration, (2) certified as a minority business enterprise by a state or federal agency, or (3) an independent business concern which is at least 51 percent owned and controlled by minority group member(s). A minority group member is an individual who is a citizen of the United States and one of the following: (i) Black American; (ii) Hispanic American (with origins from Puerto Rico, Mexico, Cuba, South or Central America); (iii) Native American (American Indian, Eskimo, Aleut, native Hawaiian), or (iv) Asian-Pacific American (with origins from Japan, China, the Philippines, Vietnam, Korea, Samoa, Guam, the U.S. Trust Territories of the Pacific, Northern Marianas, Laos, Cambodia, Taiwan or the Indian subcontinent). A

minute volume
The minute volume of breathing; a product of tidal volume times the respiratory frequency in one minute. U

MIR
Maximum individual risk. N

misbranded
A pesticide is misbranded under FIFRA if--(A) its labeling bears any statement, design, or graphic representation relative thereto or to its ingredients which is false or misleading in any particular; (B) it is contained in a package or other container or wrapping which does not conform to the standards established by the Administrator pursuant to section 25(c)(3); (C) it is an imitation of, or is offered for sale under the name of, another pesticide; (D) its label does not bear the registration number assigned under section 7 to each establishment in which it was produced; (E) any word, statement, or other information required by or under authority of FIFRA to appear on the label or labeling is not prominently placed thereon with such conspicuousness (as compared with other words, statements, designs, or

graphic matter in the labeling) and in such terms as to render it likely to be read and understood by the ordinary individual under customary conditions of purchase and use; (F) the labeling accompanying it does not contain directions for use which are necessary for effecting the purpose for which the product is intended and if complied with, together with any requirements imposed under section 3(d) of FIFRA, are adequate to protect health and the environment; (G) the label does not contain a warning or caution statement which may be necessary and if complied with, together with any requirements imposed under section 3(d) of this Act, is adequate to protect health and the environment; or (H) in the case of a pesticide not registered in accordance with section 3 of FIFRA and intended for export, the label does not contain, in words prominently placed thereon with such conspicuousness (as compared with other words, statements, designs, or graphic matter in the labeling) as to render it likely to be noted by the ordinary individual under customary conditions of purchase and use, the following: "Not Registered for Use in the United States of America." (2) A pesticide is misbranded if--(A) the label does not bear an ingredient statement on that part of the immediate container (and on the outside container or wrapper of the retail package, if there be one, through which the ingredient statement on the immediate container cannot be clearly read) which is presented or displayed under customary conditions of purchase, except that a pesticide is not misbranded under this subparagraph if: (i) the size or form of the immediate container, or the outside container or wrapper of the retail package, makes it impracticable to place the ingredient statement on the part which is presented or displayed under customary conditions of purchase: and (ii) the ingredient statement appears prominently on another part of the immediate container, or outside container or wrapper, permitted by the Administrator; (B) the labeling does not contain a statement of the use classification under which the product is registered; (C) there is not affixed to its container, and to the outside container or wrapper of the retail package, if there be one, through which the required information on the immediate container cannot be clearly read, a label bearing (i) the name and address of the producer, registrant, or person for whom produced; (ii) the name, brand, or trademark under which the pesticide is sold; (iii) the net weight or measure of the content: Provided, That the Administrator may permit reasonable variations; and (iv) when required by regulation of the Administrator to effectuate the purposes of this Act, the registration number assigned to the pesticide under this Act, and the use classification; and (D) the pesticide contains any substance or substances in quantities highly toxic to man, unless the label shall bear, in addition to any other matter required by this Act (i) the skull and crossbones; (ii) the word "poison" prominently in red on a background of distinctly contrasting color; and (iii) a statement of a practical treatment (first aid or otherwise) in case of poisoning by the pesticide. A, C

miscellaneous material
Interior building material on structural components, structural members or fixtures, such as floor and ceiling tiles, and does not include surfacing material or thermal system insulation. A

mist
Liquid particles measuring 500 to 40 microns, that are found by condensation of vapor. By comparison, fog particles are smaller than 40 microns. N

mitigation
(1) Avoiding the impact altogether by not taking a certain action or parts of an action. (2) Minimizing impacts by limiting the degree or magnitude of the action and its implementation. (3) Rectifying the impact by repairing, rehabilitating, or restoring the affected environment. (4) Reducing or eliminating the impact over time by preservation and maintenance operations during the life of the action. (5) Compensating for the impact by replacing or providing substitute resources or environments. A

mitosis
Cellular and nuclear division that involves duplication of the chromosomes of a parent cell, and formation of two daughter cells. This type of cell division occurs in most somatic cells. N

mixed fertilizer
A mixture of wet and/or dry straight fertilizer materials, mixed fertilizer materials, fillers and additives prepared through chemical reaction to a given formulation. A

mixed liquor
Activated sludge and water containing organic matter being treated in an aeration tank. N

mixed-waste processing
A system that involves the centralized treatment of collected, mixed, municipal waste to sort out reusable or recyclable materials and/or to convert mixed fractions into new forms of marketable materials or fuels. U

mixing chamber
A chamber usually placed between the primary and secondary combustion chambers and in which the products of combustion are thoroughly mixed by turbulence that is created by increased velocities of gases, checker work, or turns in the direction of the gas flow. U

mixing depth
The expanse in which air rises from the earth and mixes with the air above it until it meets air equal or warmer in temperature. U

mixing zone
(1) The zone extending from the sea's surface to seabed and extending laterally to a distance of 100 meters in all directions from the discharge point(s) or to the boundary of the zone of initial dilution as calculated by a plume model, whichever is greater, unless the director determines that the more restrictive mixing zone or another definition of the mixing zone is more appropriate for a specific discharge. A (2) A limited volume of water serving as a zone of initial

dilution in the immediate vicinity of a discharge point where receiving water quality may not meet quality standards or other requirements otherwise applicable to the receiving water. The mixing zone should be considered as a place where wastes and water mix and not as a place where effluents are treated. A

mixture
Any combination of two or more chemical substances if the combination does not occur in nature and is not, in whole or part, the result of a chemical reaction; except that such term does include (1) any combination which occurs, in whole or in part, as a result of a chemical reaction if the combination could have been manufactured for commercial purposes without a chemical reaction at the time the chemical substances comprising the combination were combined, and if all the chemical substances comprising the combination are not new chemical substances, and (2) hydrates of a chemical substance or hydrated ions formed by association of a chemical substance with water, so long as the nonhydrated form is itself not a new chemical substance. [40 CFR §720.3]. A [40 CFR §712.3 varies the definition from this point and continues: "and if all of the chemical substances comprising the combination are included in the EPA, TSCA Chemical Substance Inventory after the effective date of the premanufacture notification requirement under 40 CFR § 720, and (2) hydrates of a chemical substance or hydrated ions formed by association of a chemical substance with water. The term mixture includes alloys, inorganic glasses, ceramics, frits, and cements, including Portland Cement."] A

ml.
Milliliter(s). U

MLE
Maximum likelihood estimate. N

mm.
Abbreviation for millimeter(s). U

MMAD
Mass median aerodynamic diameter. N

MOA
Memorandum of agreement. D

mobile compactor
A vehicle with an enclosed body containing mechanical devices that convey solid waste into the main compartment of the body and compress it. U

mobile source
A moving producer of air pollution, mainly forms of transportation -- cars, motorcycles, planes. N

mobile X-ray
X-ray equipment mounted on a permanent base with wheels and/or casters for moving while completely assembled. O

model
(1) A specific combination of carline, body style, and drivetrain configuration. A (2) A computer program designed to simulate actual conditions, e.g. air movement, used to

predict environmental effects of proposed new sources of pollution. U

model plant
A description of a typical but theoretical plant used for developing economic, environmental impact and energy impact analyses as support for regulations or regulatory guidelines. It is an imaginary plant, with features of existing or future plants used to estimate the cost of incorporating air pollution control technology as the first step in exploring the economic impact of a potential NSPS. N

model specific code
The designation used for labeling purposes in 40 CFR §§ 205.158 and 205.169 for identifying the motorcycle manufacturer, class, and "advertised engine displacement," respectively. A

model type
A unique combination of car line, basic engine, and transmission class. A

model year
The manufacturer's annual production period (as determined by the Administrator) which includes January 1 of such calendar year; Provided, That if the manufacturer has no annual production period, the term "model year" shall mean the calendar year in which a vehicle is modified. A certificate holder shall be deemed to have produced a vehicle or engine when the certificate holder has modified the nonconforming vehicle or engine. A

modeling
(1) An investigative technique using a mathematical or physical representation of a system or theory that accounts for all or some of its known properties. Models are often used to test the effect of changes of system components on the overall performance of the system. N (2) Use of mathematical equations to simulate and predict real events and processes. N

modification
Any physical change in, or change in the method of operation of, a stationary source which increases the amount of any air pollutant emitted by such source or which results in the emission of any air pollutant not previously emitted, except that: (1) Routine maintenance, repair, and replacement shall not be considered physical changes, and (2) The following shall not be considered a change in the method of operation: (i) An increase in the production rate, if such increase does not exceed the operating design capacity of the stationary source; (ii) An increase in hours of operation. A

modified discharge
The volume, composition and location of the discharge proposed by the applicant for which a modification under section 301(h) of the Clean Water Act is requested. A modified discharge may be a current discharge, improved discharge, or altered discharge. A

modified source
Any physical change in, or change in the method of operation of, a stationary source which increases the emission rate of any pollutant for

which a national standard has been promulgated under [40 CFR] Part 50 of this chapter or which results in the emission of any such pollutant not previously emitted, except that: (1) Routine maintenance, repair, and replacement shall not be considered a physical change, and (2) The following shall not be considered a change in the method of operation: (i) An increase in the production rate, if such increase does not exceed the operating design capacity of the source; (ii) An increase in the hours of operation; (iii) Use of an alternative fuel or raw material, if prior to the effective date of a paragraph in this Part which imposes conditions on or limits modifications, the source is designed to accommodate such alternative use. A

modifying factor
MF. A factor that is greater than zero and less than or equal to 10; used in the operational derivation of a reference dose. Its magnitude depends upon an assessment of the scientific uncertainties of the toxicological data base not explicitly treated with standard uncertainty factors (e.g., number of animals tested). The default value for the MF is 1. N

modular combustion unit
One of a series of incinerator units designed to operate independently and can handle small quantities of solid waste. U

modulated stem
A stem attached to the vacuum break diaphragm in such a manner as to allow stem displacement independent of diaphragm displacement. A

modulated stem displacement
The distance through which the modulated stem may move when actuated independent of diaphragm displacement. A

MOE
Margin of exposure. N

moisture content of solid waste
The weight loss (expressed as a percentage) when a sample of solid waste is dried to a constant weight at a temperature of 100° C to 105° C. U

moisture penetration
The depth to which irrigation water or precipitation penetrates soil before the rate of downward movement becomes negligible. U

mol.
Mole, or weight in grams of a compound equal to its mol. wt. U

mol. wt.
Molecular weight. U

molecule
The smallest part of a substance that can exist separately and still retain its chemical properties and characteristic composition; the smallest combination of atoms that will form a given chemical compound. U

monitor
To measure and record. A

monitor pathlength
The depth of effluent at the installed location of the continuous monitoring system. A

monitoring
Periodic or continuous surveillance or testing to determine the level of compliance with statutory requirements and / or pollutant levels in various media or in humans, animals, and other living things. N

monitoring activity
Includes but is not limited to, the following: the collection of samples, including preservation and transport, and the collection of information concerning the quality or condition of ambient waters, including ground waters, or aquatic biota; the collection of samples, including preservation and transport, and the collection of information concerning the physical, chemical, or biological character of waste discharges to ambient waters, including ground waters; the operation and maintenance of field and laboratory support facilities including approved quality assurance practices; the processing, analysis, interpretation, and reporting of resulting data and information; and the management of such activities in terms of staffing, funding, scheduling, and coordination with other agents, including other State, interstate, Federal, local, and private entities or agencies. A

monitoring and analysis order
Used to evaluate the nature and extent of a substantial hazard to human health or the environment that exists at a TSD. It can be issued to either the current owner or to a past owner or operator if the facility is not currently in operation, or if the present owner could not be expected to have knowledge of the release potential. N

monitoring device
The total equipment, required under the monitoring of operations sections in applicable subparts, used to measure and record (if applicable) process parameters. A

monitoring system
Any system, required under the monitoring sections in applicable subparts, used to sample and condition (if applicable), to analyze, and to provide a record of emissions or process parameters. A

monitoring well
(1) A well used to obtain water samples for water quality analysis or to measure groundwater levels. (2) A well drilled at a hazardous waste management facility or Superfund site to collect ground-water samples for the purpose of physical, chemical, or biological analysis to determine the amounts, types, and distribution of contaminants in the ground water beneath the site. N

monoclonal antibodies
MABs and MCAs. Molecules of living organisms that selectively find and attach to other molecules to which their structure conforms exactly. This could also apply to equivalent activity by chemical molecules. N

monthly average
The arithmetic average of eight individual data points from effluent sampling and analysis during any calendar month. A

Montreal Protocol
An international environmental agreement to control chemicals that deplete the ozone layer. The protocol, which was renegotiated in June 1990, calls for a phase-out of CFCs, halons, and carbon tetrachloride by the year 2000, a phase-out of chloroform by 2005, and provides financial assistance to help developing countries make the transition from ozone-depleting substances. N

morbidity
The number of sick individuals or cases of disease in a population. N

morphology
Study of the form or structure of cells, tissues, organs, or organisms. N

morphometry
Quantitative measure of morphology. U

mortality
The number of individual deaths in a population. N

MOS
Margin of safety. N

motor activity
Any movement of the experimental animal. A

motor carrier
A common carrier by motor vehicle, a contract carrier by motor vehicle, or a private carrier of property by motor vehicle as those terms are defined by paragraphs (14), (15), and (17) of § 203(a) of the Interstate Commerce Act {49 U.S.C. 303(a)}. A

motor controller
An electronic or electromechanical device to convert energy stored in an energy storage device into a form suitable to power the traction motor. A

motor fuel
Petroleum or a petroleum-based substance that is motor gasoline, aviation gasoline, No. 1 or No. 2 diesel fuel, or any grade of, gasohol, and is typically used in the operation of a motor engine. A

motor vehicle
(1) Any vehicle, machine, tractor, trailer, or semitrailer propelled or drawn by mechanical power and used upon the highways in the transportation of passengers or property, or any combination thereof, but does not include any vehicle, locomotive, or car operated exclusively on a rail or rails. A (2) Any self-propelled vehicle designed for transporting persons or property on a street or highway. B

motor vehicle manufacturer
As used in sections 202, 203, 206, 207, and 208 [of the Clean Air Act], any person engaged in the manufacturing or assembling of new motor vehicles or new motor vehicle engines, or importing such vehicles or engines for resale, or who acts for and is under the control of any such person in connection with the distribution of new motor vehicles or new motor vehicle engines, but shall not include any dealer with respect to new motor vehicles or new motor

vehicle engines received by him in commerce. B

motorcycle
Any motor vehicle, other than a tractor, that: (i) has two or three wheels; (ii) has a curb mass less than or equal to 680 kg (1499 lb); and (iii) is capable, with an 80 kg (176 lb) driver, of achieving a maximum speed of at least 24 km/h (15 mph) over a level paved surface. A

motorcycle noise level
The A-weighted noise level of a motorcycle as measured by the acceleration test procedure. N

MOU
Memorandum Of Understanding. N

movable grate
A grate with moving parts. A movable grate designed to feed solid fuel or solid waste to a furnace is called a stoker. U

move laterally (in soils)
To undergo transfer through soil generally in a horizontal plane from the original site of application or use by physical, chemical, or biological means. A

movement
Hazardous waste transported to a facility in an individual vehicle. A

mpc.
1,000 pieces. U

MPD
Minimum premarket data. U

MPO
Metropolitan Planning Organization. A

MPRSA
Marine Protection Research & Sanctuaries Act of 1972. N

MPTDS
MPTER model with deposition and settling of pollutants. N

MPTER
Multiple point source model with terrain. N

MSA
(1) Metropolitan Statistical Area as defined by the Department of Commerce. A (2) Management system audits. U

MSBu.
1,000 standard bushels. U

MSDS
Material Safety Data Sheet, the written listing of data for the chemical substance as required under [40 CFR] § 721.72(c). A

MSHA
Mine Safety & Health Administration. U

MSS systems
(Motion-stopping-safety systems). Fall protection using the following equipment singly or in combination: standard railings (guardrails) as described in [40 CFR] § 1926.500(f); scaffolds or platforms with guardrails as described in § 1926.451; safety nets

as described in § 1926.105; and safety belt systems as described in § 1926.104. O

MSW
Municipal solid waste. U

MTD
Maximum tolerated dose. N

MTP
Maximum total trihalomethane (THM) potential. A

MTU
Mobile treatment unit(s). U

muck soils
Earth made from decaying plant materials. N

mucociliary clearance
Removal of materials from the respiratory tract via ciliary action. U

mucociliary transport
The process by which mucus is transported, by ciliary action, from the lungs. U

mucus
The sticky fluid covering the airways of the respiratory system. U

mulch
A layer of material (wood chips, straw, leaves) placed around plants to hold moisture, prevent weed growth, and enrich soil. N

multicyclone collector
A dust collector consisting of several cyclone collectors that operate in parallel; the volume and velocity of incinerator combustion gas can be regulated by dampers to maintain efficiency over a given load range. U

multipurpose dry chemical
A dry chemical which is approved for use on Class A, Class B and Class C fires. O

multistage model
A mathematical function used to extrapolate the probability of incidence of disease from a bioassay in animals using high doses, to that expected to be observed at the low doses that are likely to be found in chronic human exposure. This model is commonly used in quantitative carcinogenic risk assessments where the chemical agent is assumed to be a complete carcinogen and the risk is assumed to be proportional to the dose in the low region. N

multiple-chamber incinerator
An incinerator that consists of two or more chambers, arranged as in-line or retort types, interconnected by gas passage ports or ducts. U

multiple-effect evaporator system
The multiple-effect evaporators and associated condenser(s) and hotwell(s) used to concentrate the spent cooking liquid that is separated from the pulp (black liquor). A

multiple use
Harmonious use of land for more than one purpose; i.e., grazing of livestock, wildlife production, recreation, watershed and timber production. Not necessarily the

combination of uses that will yield the highest economic return or greatest unit output. N

mungo
Reclaimed wool of poor quality, which is combined with other fibers to make low-quality cloth. U

municipal air pollution control agency
A city, county, or other local government agency responsible for enforcing ordinances or laws relating to the prevention and control of air pollution. A

municipal collection
Refuse collection by public employees and equipment under the supervision and direction of a municipal department or office. U

municipal incinerator
A privately or publicly owned incinerator primarily designed and used to burn residential and commercial solid waste within a community. U

municipal sanitary landfill
The disposal site for residential and commercial solid waste generated, collected, and processed within a community. U

municipal separate storm sewer
A conveyance or system of conveyances including roads with drainage systems, municipal streets, catch basins, curbs, gutters, ditches, manmade channels, or storm drains: (i) Owned or operated by a State, city, town, borough, county, parish, district, association, or other public body (created by or pursuant to State law) having jurisdiction over disposal of sewage, industrial wastes, storm water, or other wastes, including special districts under State law such as a sewer district, flood control district or drainage district, or similar entity, or an Indian tribe or an authorized Indian tribal organization, or a designated and approved management agency under section 208 of the Clean Water Act that discharges to water of the United States; (ii) Designed or used for collecting or conveying storm water; (iii) Which is not a combined sewer; and (iv) Which is not part of a Publicly Owned Treatment Works (POTW) as defined at 40 CFR 122.2. A

municipal solid waste landfill unit
MSWLF. A discrete area of land or an excavation that receives household waste, and that is not a land application unit, surface impoundment, injection well, or waste pile, as those terms are defined in this section. A MSWLF unit also may receive other types of RCRA Subtitle D wastes, such as commercial solid waste, nonhazardous sludge, and industrial solid waste. Such a landfill may be publicly or privately owned. An MSWLF unit may be a new MSWLF unit, an existing MSWLF unit or a lateral expansion. A

municipal solid wastes
Garbage, refuse, sludges, wastes, and other discarded materials resulting from residential and non-industrial operations and activities, such as household activities, office functions, and commercial housekeeping wastes. A

municipal waste combustor
MWC. Any device that combusts, solid, liquid, or gasified MSW including, but not limited to, field-erected incinerators (with or without heat recovery), modular incinerators (starved air or excess air), boilers (i.e., steam generating units), furnaces (whether suspension-fired, grate-fired, mass-fired, or fluidized bed-fired) and gasification/combustion units. This does not include combustion units, engines, or other devices that combust landfill gases collected by landfill gas collection systems. A

municipal-type solid waste
MSW. Household, commercial/retail, and/or institutional waste. Household waste includes material discarded by single and multiple residential dwellings, hotels, motels, and other similar permanent or temporary housing establishments or facilities. Commercial/retail waste includes material discarded by stores, offices, restaurants, warehouses, nonmanufacturing activities at industrial facilities, and other similar establishments or facilities. Institutional waste includes material discarded by schools, hospitals, nonmanufacturing activities at prisons and government facilities and other similar establishments or facilities. Household, commercial/retail, and institutional waste do not include sewage, wood pallets, construction and demolition wastes, industrial process or manufacturing wastes, or motor vehicles (including motor vehicle parts or vehicle fluff). Municipal-type solid waste does include motor vehicle maintenance materials, limited to vehicle batteries, used motor oil, and tires. Municipal type solid waste does not include wastes that are solely segregated medical wastes. However, any mixture of segregated medical wastes and other wastes which contains more than 30 percent waste medical waste discards, is considered to be municipal-type solid waste. A

municipality
(A) A city, town, borough, county, parish, district, association, or other public body created by or pursuant to State law, with responsibility for the planning or administration of solid waste management, or an Indian tribe or authorized Indian tribal organization or Alaska Native village or organization, and (B) includes any rural community or unincorporated town or village or any other public entity for which an application for assistance is made by a State or political subdivision thereof. I And having jurisdiction over disposal of sewage, industrial wastes, or other waste, or a designated and approved management agency under section 208 of the FWPCA. (a) This definition includes a special district created under State law such as a water district, sewer district, sanitary district, utility district, drainage district, or similar entity or an integrated waste management facility, as defined in section 201(e) of the FWPCA, which has as one of its principal responsibilities the treatment, transport, or disposal of domestic wastewater in a particular geographic area. (b) This definition excludes the following: (1) Any revenue producing

entity which has as its principal responsibility an activity other than providing wastewater treatment services to the general public, such as an airport, turnpike, port facility, or other municipal utility. (2) Any special district (such as school district or a park district) which has the responsibility to provide wastewater treatment services in support of its principal activity at specific facilities, unless the special district has the responsibility under State law to provide waste water treatment services to the community surrounding the special district's facility and no other municipality, with concurrent jurisdiction to serve the community, serves or intends to serve the special district's facility or the surrounding community. A, B, J

mutagen
Any substance that causes changes in the genetic structure in subsequent generations. N

mutagenesis
The induction of heritable changes in the genetic material of either somatic or germinal cells. O

mutagenic
The property of a substance or mixture of substances to induce changes in the genetic complement of either somatic or germinal tissue in subsequent generations. A

mv.
Millivolt(s). U

MVAPCA
Motor Vehicle Air Pollution Control Act. U

MVIACSA
Motor Vehicle Information and Cost Saving Act. U

MVICSA
Motor Vehicle Information and Cost Savings Act. U

MWC
Municipal waste combustor or MWC unit. A

Mwh.
Megawatt hour(s). U

MWTA
Medical Waste Tracking Act of 1988. I

MYDP
Multi-year development plans. N

N

NAAQS
National ambient air quality standard. U

NACA
National Agricultural Chemicals Association. N

NAMS
National air monitoring station(s). Collectively the NAMS are a subset of the SLAMS ambient air quality monitoring network. A

nano-
A prefix that divides a basic unit by one billion (10^9). U

NAPAP
National Acid Precipitation Assessment Program. B

naphthalene
(Or priority pollutant No. 55). The value obtained by the standard method Number 610 specified in 44 FR 69464, 69571 (December 3, 1979). A

naphthalene processing
Any operations required to recover naphthalene including the separation, refining, and drying of crude or refined naphthalene. A

NAR
National Asbestos Registry. U

NARA
National Air Resources Act. U

narcosis
A disorder characterized by drowsiness or unconsciousness, caused by the action of a toxicant on the central nervous system. N

NAS
National Academy of Sciences. U

NASA
National Aeronautics & Space Administration. U

NATICH
National Air Toxics Information Clearinghouse. U

national ambient air quality standard
A federally promulgated maximum level of an air pollutant that can exist in the ambient air without producing adverse effect to humans (primary standard) or the public welfare (secondary standard). U

national and global scales
Measurement scales representing concentrations characterizing the nation and the globe as a whole. A

National Commission on Air Quality
A national commission created by the Clean Air Act Amendments of 1977 which studied the implementation of the CAA and made recommendations to the Congress regarding necessary changes to the CAA. U

national consensus standard
Any standard or modification thereof which (1) has been adopted and promulgated by a nationally recognized standards-producing organization under procedures whereby it can be determined by the Secretary of Labor or by the Assistant Secretary of Labor that persons interested and affected by the scope or provisions of the standard have reached substantial agreement on its adoption, (2) was formulated in a manner which afforded an opportunity for diverse views to be considered, and (3) has been designated as such a standard by the Secretary or the Assistant Secretary, after consultation with other appropriate Federal agencies. O

national contingency plan
The national contingency plan published under section 311(c) of the Federal Water Pollution Control Act or revised pursuant to section 105 of CERCLA. L

national data bank
A facility or system established or to be established by the Administrator [of EPA] for the purposes of assembling, organizing, and analyzing data pertaining to water quality and the discharge of pollutants. A

National Emissions Standards for Hazardous Air Pollutants
NESHAPS. Emissions standards set by EPA for an air pollutant not covered by NAAQS that may cause an increase in deaths or in serious irreversible, or incapacitating illness. N

National Fire Protection Association
NFPA. An international membership organization which promotes/improves fire protection and prevention and establishes safeguards against loss of life and property by fire. Best known on the industrial scene for the National Fire Codes -- 16 volumes of codes, standards, recommended practices and manuals developed (and periodically updated) by NFPA technical committees. Among these is NFPA 704, the code for showing hazards of materials as they might be encountered under fire or related emergency conditions, using the familiar diamond-shaped label or placard with appropriate numbers or symbols. N

National Institute for Occupational Safety and Health
NIOSH, U.S. Public Health Service, U.S. Department of Health and Human Services (DHHS), among other activities, tests and certifies respiratory protective devices and air sampling detector tubes, recommends occupational exposure limits for various substances, and assists OSHA and MSHA in occupational safety and health investigations and research. N

National Oil and Hazardous Substances Contingency Plan
NOHSCP/NCP. The federal regulation that guides determination of the sites to be corrected under the Superfund program and the program to prevent or control spills into surface waters or other portions of the environment. N

National Pollutant Discharge Elimination System
NPDS. The national program for issuing, modifying, revoking and reissuing, terminating, monitoring and enforcing permits, and imposing and enforcing pretreatment requirements, under sections 307, 402, 318, and 405 of the Clean Water Act. The term includes an approved program. A

national pretreatment standard or pretreatment standard
Any regulation containing pollutant discharge limits promulgated by the EPA in accordance with section 307 (b) and (c) of the FWPCA, which applies to Industrial Users. This term includes prohibitive discharge limits established pursuant to [40 CFR] § 403.5. A

National Primary Drinking Water Regulations
NPDWR. D

National Priorities List
(1) NPL. EPA's list of the most serious uncontrolled or abandoned hazardous waste sites identified for possible long-term remedial action under Superfund. A site must be on the NPL to receive money from the Trust Fund for remedial action. The list is based primarily on the score a site receives from the Hazard Ranking System. EPA is required to update the NPL at least once a year. N (2) The list, compiled by EPA pursuant to CERCLA section 105, of uncontrolled hazardous substances releases in the United States that are priorities for long-term remedial evaluation and response. A

National Program Assistance Agreements
Assistance Agreements approved by the EPA Assistant Administrator for Water for work undertaken to accomplish broad NEP goals and objectives. A

National Response Center
NRC. (1) The federal operations center that receives notifications of all releases of oil and hazardous substances into the environment. The Center, open 24 hours a day, is operated by the U.S. Coast Guard, which evaluates all reports and notifies the appropriate agency. (2) A notification center which must be called when significant oil or chemical spills or other environment-related

accidents occur. The toll-free telephone number is 1-800-424-8802. N

National Response Team
NRT. Representatives of 13 federal agencies that, as a team, coordinate federal responses to nationally significant incidents of pollution and provide advice and technical assistance to the responding agency(ies) before and during a response action. N

national security exemption
An exemption which may be granted under section 203(b)(1) of the CAA for the purpose of national security. A

national standard
Either a primary or secondary standard. A

National Toxicology Program
NTP. Federal activity overseen by PHHS with resources from NIH, FDA, and the Center for Disease Control. Its goals are to develop tests useful for public health regulations of toxic chemicals, to develop toxicological profiles of materials, to foster testing of materials, and to communicate the results for use by others. N

nationally recognized testing laboratory
NRTL. An organization which is recognized by OSHA and which tests for safety, and lists or labels or accepts, equipment or materials and which meets all of the following criteria:
(1) For each specified item of equipment or material to be listed, labeled or accepted, the NRTL has the capability (including proper testing equipment and facilities, trained staff, written testing procedures, and calibration and quality control programs) to perform: (i) testing and examining of equipment and materials for workplace safety purposes to determine conformance with appropriate test standards; or (ii) experimental testing and examining of equipment and materials for workplace safety purposes to determine conformance with appropriate test standards or performance in a specified manner. (2) The NRTL shall provide, to the extent needed for the particular equipment or materials listed, labeled, or accepted, the following controls or services: (i) implements control procedures for identifying the listed and labeled equipment or materials; (ii) inspects the run of production of such items at factories for product evaluation purposes to assure conformance with the test standards; and (iii) conducts field inspections to monitor and to assure the proper use of its identifying mark or labels on products; (3) The NRTL is completely independent of employers subject to the tested equipment requirements, and of any manufacturers or vendors of equipment or materials being tested for these purposes; and,
(4) The NRTL maintains effective procedures for: (i) producing creditable findings or reports that are objective and without bias; and (ii) handling complaints and disputes under a fair and reasonable system. O

natural barrier
A natural object that effectively precludes or deters access. Natural barriers include physical obstacles such

as cliffs, lakes or other large bodies of water, deep and wide ravines, and mountains. Remoteness by itself is not a natural barrier. A

natural conditions
Naturally occurring phenomena that reduce visibility as measured in terms of visual range, contrast, or coloration. A

natural draft
The negative pressure created by the height of a stack or chimney and the difference in temperature between flue gases and the atmosphere. U

natural draft opening
Any opening in a room, building, or total enclosure that remains open during operation of the facility and that is not connected to a duct in which a fan is installed. The rate and direction of the natural draft across such an opening is a consequence of the difference in pressures on either side of the wall containing the opening. A

natural gas
(1) Naturally occurring mixture of hydrocarbon and nonhydrocarbon gases found in geologic formations beneath the earth's surface, of which the principal constituent is methane; or (2) liquid petroleum gas, as defined by the American Society for Testing and Materials in ASTM D1835-82, "Standard Specification for Liquid Petroleum Gases" (IBR-see 40 CFR § 60.17). A

natural resources
Land, fish, wildlife, biota, air, water, ground water, drinking water supplies, and other such resources belonging to, managed by, held in trust by, appertaining to, or otherwise controlled by the United States (including the resources of the exclusive economic zone defined by the Magnuson Fishery Conservation and Management Act of 1976), any state or local government, any foreign government, any Indian tribe, or, if such resources are subject to a trust restriction or alienation, any member of an Indian tribe. A

natural selection
The process of survival of the fittest, by which organisms that adapt to their environment survive and those that do not disappear. N

navigable waters
As defined by 40 CFR 110.1, means the waters of the United States, including the territorial seas. The term includes:
(a) All waters that are currently used, were used in the past, or may be susceptible to use in interstate or foreign commerce, including all waters that are subject to the ebb and flow of the tide;
(b) Interstate waters, including interstate wetlands;
(c) All other waters such as intrastate lakes, rivers, streams (including intermittent streams), mudflats, sandflats, and wetlands, the use, degradation, or destruction of which would affect or could affect interstate or foreign commerce including any such waters:
(1) That are or could be used by interstate or foreign travelers for recreational or other purposes; (2)

From which fish or shellfish are or could be taken and sold in interstate or foreign commerce; (3) That are used or could be used for industrial purposes by industries in interstate commerce; (d) All impoundments of waters otherwise defined as navigable waters under this section; (e) Tributaries of waters identified in paragraphs (a) through (d) of this definition, including adjacent wetlands; and (f) Wetlands adjacent to waters identified in paragraphs (a) through (e) of this definition: Provided, that waste treatment systems (other than cooling ponds meeting the criteria of this paragraph) are not waters of the United States. A

NBAR
Nonbinding preliminary allocation of responsibility. N

NCA
(1) Noise Control Act. U (2) National Coal Association. U

NCAQ
National Commission on Air Quality. N

NCC
National Climatic Center. N

NCHS
National Center for Health Statistics (NIH). N

NCI
National Cancer Institute, United States Department of Health and Human Services, or designee. O

NCM
Notice of Commencement of Manufacture (TSCA). U

NCO
Negotiated Consent Order. N

NCP
(1) National Contingency Plan (CERCLA). N (2) Noncompliance Penalties (CAA). N (3) A nonconformance penalty as described in section 206(g) of the Clean Air Act. A

NCTR
National Center for Toxicological Research. U

ND
Not detectable. N

NDA
New drug application. U

NDIR
Nondispersive infrared. U

neat oil
Pure oil with no or few impurities added. A

neat soap
The solution of completely saponified and purified soap containing about 20-30 percent water which is ready for final formulation into a finished product. A

necessary and adequate
Refers to additions, alterations, or methods of operation in the absence of which a small business concern could not comply with one or more

applicable standards. This can be determined with reference to design specifications provided by manufacturers, suppliers, or consulting engineers; including, without limitations, additions, alterations, or methods of operation the design specifications of which will provide a measure of treatment or abatement of pollution in excess of that required by the applicable standard. A

necessary preconstruction approvals or permits
(1) Those permits or approvals required under federal air quality control laws and regulations and those air quality control laws and regulations which are part of the applicable State Implementation Plan. [ed. Affects date a source is considered to have commenced construction in NSD areas]. A (2) Those permits or approvals required by the permitting authority as a precondition to undertaking any [regulated] activity. A, B

necrosis
Death of cells that can discolor areas on a plant or kill the entire plant. N

NEDS
National Emissions Data System. N

negative declaration
A written announcement, prepared after the environmental review, which states that EPA has decided not to prepare an EIS and summarizes the environmental impact appraisal. A

negligible residue
Any amount of a pesticide chemical remaining in or on a raw agricultural commodity or group of raw agricultural commodities that would result in a daily intake regarded as toxicologically insignificant on the basis of scientific judgment of adequate safety data. Ordinarily this will add to the diet an amount which will be less than 1/2,000th of the amount that has been demonstrated to have no effect from feeding studies on the most sensitive animal species tested. Such toxicity studies shall usually include at least 90-day feeding studies in two species of mammals. A

NEIC
National Enforcement Investigations Center based in Denver, Colorado (EPA). U

neighborhood scale
Concentrations within some extended area of the city that has relatively uniform land use with dimensions in the 0.5 to 4.0 kilometers range. A

neighboring company
Any one of those electric utility companies with one or more electric power interconnections to the principal company and which have geographically adjoining service areas. A

nematicides
All substances or mixtures of substances intended for preventing or inhibiting the multiplication or establishment of, preventing or mitigating the adverse effects of, repelling, or destroying any members of the Class Nematoda of the Phylum Nemathelminthes declared to be pests under 40 CFR § 162.14. (i)

Nematicides include but are not limited to, plant parasitic nematode control agents intended for use in or on plants, plant parts, soil, or certain infested agricultural commodities or articles. (ii) Nematicides do not include those substances or mixtures of substances subject to the provisions of the Federal Food, Drug and Cosmetic Act, as amended (21 U.S.C. 301 et seq.), such as substances or mixtures of substances intended for use in preventing reproduction of, inactivating, or destroying nematodes in living man or other animals. A

nematode
Invertebrate animals of the phylum nemathelminthes and class nematoda; unsegmented round worms with elongated, fusiform, or saclike bodies covered with cuticle and inhabiting soil, water, plants, or plant parts; may also be called nemas or eelworms. C

neonatal
Newly born; in humans, up to 6 weeks of age. N

neoplasm
A new or abnormal tissue growth that is uncontrollable and progressive. A

NEPA
National Environmental Policy Act. U

NEPA-associated documents
Any one or combination of: notices of intent, negative declarations, exemption certifications, environmental impact appraisals, news releases, EIS's, and environmental assessments. Associated with a Federal agency or department's compliance with NEPA. A

NESHAPS
National Emissions Standards for Hazardous Air Pollutants. N

net emissions increase
(i) The amount by which the sum of the following exceeds zero: (a) any increase in actual emissions from a particular physical change or change in the method of operation at a stationary source; and (b) any other increases and decreases in actual emissions at the source that are contemporaneous with the particular change and are otherwise creditable. (ii) An increase or decrease in actual emissions is contemporaneous with the increase from the particular change only if it occurs between: (a) the date five years before construction on the particular change commences and (b) the date that the increase from the particular change occurs. (iii) An increase or decrease in actual emissions is creditable only if the Administrator has not relied on it in issuing a permit for the source under this Ruling which permit is in effect when the increase in actual emissions from the particular change occurs. (iv) An increase or decrease in actual emissions of sulfur dioxide or particulate matter which occurs before the applicable baseline date is creditable only if it is required to be considered in calculating the amount of maximum allowable increases remaining available. (v) An increase in actual emissions is creditable only to the extent that the new level of actual emissions exceeds the old level.

(vi) A decrease in actual emissions is creditable only to the extent that: (a) the old level of actual emissions or the old level of allowable emissions, whichever is lower, exceeds the new level of actual emissions; (b) it is federally enforceable at and after the time that actual construction on the particular change begins; and (c) it has approximately the same qualitative significance for public health and welfare as that attributed to the increase from the particular change. (vii) An increase that results from a physical change at a source occurs when the emissions unit on which construction occurred becomes operational and begins to emit a particular pollutant. Any replacement unit that requires shakedown becomes operational only after a reasonable shakedown period, not to exceed 180 days. A

net evaporation
The evaporation rate exceeds the precipitation rate during a one year period. A

net precipitation
The precipitation rate exceeds the evaporation rate during a one year period. A

net system capacity
The sum of the net electric generating capability (not necessarily equal to rated capacity) of all electric generating equipment owned by an electric utility company (including steam generating units, internal combustion engines, gas turbines, nuclear units, hydroelectric units, and all other electric generating equipment) plus firm contractual purchases that are interconnected to the affected facility that has the malfunctioning flue gas desulfurization system. The electric generating capability of equipment under multiple ownership is prorated based on ownership unless the proportional entitlement to electric output is otherwise established by contractual arrangement. A

net working capital
Current assets minus current liabilities. A

net worth
Total assets minus total liabilities and is equivalent to owner's equity. A

netting
A concept under the Clean Air Act by which a company can modify an existing plant without a new source review. The company must make compensatory reductions elsewhere in the plant that bring the net emissions increase below a threshold amount. N

neurotoxic effect
See neurotoxicity. A

neurotoxicity
The adverse effect on the structure or function of the central and/or peripheral nervous system related to exposure to a chemical substance or agent. N

neutralize
To eliminate potential hazards by inactivating strong acids, caustics, and oxidizers. For example, acids can be neutralized by adding an appropriate

amount of caustic substance to the spill. N

new biochemical and microbial registration review
Review of an application for registration of a biochemical or microbial pesticide product containing a biochemical or microbial active ingredient not contained in any other pesticide product that is registered under FIFRA at the time the application is made. A

new chemical
An active ingredient not contained in any currently registered pesticide. A

new chemical registration review
Review of an application for registration of a pesticide product containing a chemical active ingredient which is not contained as an active ingredient in any other pesticide product that is registered under FIFRA at the time the application is made. A

new chemical substance
Any chemical substance which is not included in the chemical substance list compiled and published under section 8(b). K [ed. This determines which newly produced chemicals must undergo notification and review by EPA before production pursuant to the Toxic Substances Control Act]. A

new discharger
Any building, structure, facility, or installation: (a) From which there is or may be a discharge of pollutants, (b) That did not commence the discharge of pollutants at a particular site prior to August 13, 1979; (c) Which is not a new source, and (d) Which has never received a finally effective NPDES permit for discharges at that site. A

new HWM facility
A Hazardous Waste Management facility which began operation or for which construction commenced after November 19, 1980. A

new independent power production facility
For the purposes of this part a unit(s) that: (1) Commences commercial operation on or after November 15, 1990; (2) Is nonrecourse project-financed, as defined in 10 CFR part 715; (3) Sells 80% of electricity generated at wholesale; and (4) Does not sell electricity to any affiliate or, if it does, demonstrates it cannot obtain the required allowances from such an affiliate. A

new injection well
A well which begins injection after a UIC program for the State in which the well is located is approved. N

new motor vehicle engine
An engine in a new motor vehicle or a motor vehicle engine, the equitable or legal title to which has never been transferred to the ultimate purchaser. B

new MSWLF unit
Any municipal solid waste landfill unit that has not received waste prior to the effective date of this part (October 9, 1993). A

new product
(1) A product, the equitable or legal

title of which has never been transferred to an ultimate purchaser, or (2) A product which is imported or offered for importation into the United States and which is manufactured after the effective date of a regulation under section 6 or section 8 [of the Noise Control Act] which would have been applicable to such product had it been manufactured in the United States. G (3) A pesticide product which is not a federally registered product. A

new source
(1) Any building, structure, facility, or installation from which there is or may be a discharge of pollutants, the construction of which commenced (a) After promulgation of standards of performance under section 306 of the Clean Water Act which are applicable to such source, or (b) After proposal of standards of performance in accordance with section 306 of the Clean Water Act which are applicable to such source, but only if the standards are promulgated in accordance with section 306 within 120 days of their proposal. A (2) Any stationary source, the construction or modification of which is commenced after the publication in the Federal Register of proposed national emission standards for hazardous air pollutants which will be applicable to such source. A

new source and environmental questionnaire
NS/EQ. An initial document submitted by an applicant for a new source NPDES permit. This document will furnish information on the status of the proposed source that will allow determination of whether the facility is a new or existing source. In addition, the NS/EQ will also furnish information on the potential environmental impacts of the proposed source. It is the Agency's intention that in the case of sources which will probably have insignificant environmental impacts, the NS/EQ will normally provide sufficient information to fulfill the requirements for an environmental impact assessment. A

new source coal mine
(1) A coal mine (excluding coal preparation plants and coal preparation plant associated areas): (i) The construction of which is commenced after May 29, 1981 (the date of publication of the proposal of these regulations); or (ii) Which is determined by the EPA Regional Administrator to constitute a "major alteration." In making this determination, the Regional Administrator shall take into account the occurrence of one or more of the following events, in connection with the mine for which the NPDES permit is being considered, after the date of proposal of applicable new source performance standards: (A) A mine operation initiates extraction of a coal seam not previously extracted by that mine; (B) A mine operation discharges into a drainage area not previously affected by wastewater discharges from the mine; (C) A mine operation causes extensive new surface disruption; (D) A mine operation initiates construction of a new shaft, stope, or drift; (E) A mine operation acquires additional land or mineral rights; (F) A mine operation makes significant capital investment in

additional equipment or additional facilities; and (G) Such other factors as the Regional Administrator deems relevant. (2) No provision in this part shall be deemed to affect the classification as a new source, pursuant to EPA's promulgation of January 13, 1981 (46 FR 3136), of a coal mine on which construction began prior to May 29, 1981. A

new source performance standards
NSPS. Uniform national EPA air emission and water effluent standards which limit the amount of pollution allowed from new sources or from existing sources that have been modified. N

new tank system
A tank system that will be used to contain an accumulation of regulated substances and for which installation has commenced after December 22, 1988. A

new use
When used with respect to a product containing a particular active ingredient, means: (1) Any proposed use pattern that would require the establishment of, the increase in, or the exemption from the requirement of, a tolerance or food additive regulation under section 408 or 409 of the Federal Food, Drug and Cosmetic Act; (2) Any aquatic, terrestrial, outdoor, or forestry use pattern, if no product containing the active ingredient is currently registered for that use pattern; or (3) Any additional use pattern that would result in a significant increase in the level of exposure, or a change in the route of exposure, to the active ingredient of man or other organisms. A

new use pattern registration review
Review of an application for registration, or for amendment of a registration entailing a major change to the use pattern of an active ingredient contained in a product registered under FIFRA or pending Agency decision on a prior application at the time of application. Examples of major changes include but are not limited to, changes from non-food to food use, outdoor to indoor use, ground to aerial application, terrestrial to aquatic use, and non-residential to residential use. A

new uses of asbestos
Commercial uses of asbestos not identified in [40 CFR] § 763.165 the manufacture, importation or processing of which would be initiated for the first time after August 25, 1989. The following products are also not new uses of asbestos. Acetylene cylinders, arc chutes, asbestos diaphragms, battery separators, high grade electrical paper, missile liner, packing, reinforced plastic, sealant tape, specialty industrial gaskets, and textiles. A

new vessel
Includes every description of watercraft or other artificial contrivance used, or capable of being used, as a means of transportation on the navigable waters, the construction of which is initiated after promulgation of standards and regulation under § 312 of FWPCA. D

new water
Water from any discrete source such as a river, creek, lake or well which is deliberately allowed or brought into the plant site. A

newly certified aircraft gas turbine engine
An aircraft gas turbine engine which is originally type certified on or after the effective date of the applicable emission standard. A

newsprint
Paper of the type generally used in the publication of newspapers or special publications like the Congressional Record. It is made primarily from mechanical wood pulps combined with some chemical wood pulp. A

NFPA
National Fire Protection Association. An international membership organization which promotes/improves fire protection and prevention and establishes safeguards against loss of life and property by fire. Best known on the industrial scene for the National Fire Codes -- 16 volumes of codes, standards, recommended practices and manuals developed (and periodically updated) by NFPA technical committees. Among these is NFPA 704, the code for showing hazards of materials as they might be encountered under fire or related emergency conditions, using the familiar diamond-shaped label or placard with appropriate numbers or symbols. N

ng.
Abbreviation for nanogram. U

NHLBI
National Heart, Lung, and Blood Institute. U

NHTSA
National Highway Traffic Safety Administration. U

NIAID
National Institute of Allergy and Infectious Diseases. U

NIAMDD
National Institute of Arthritis, Metabolism and Digestive Diseases. U

NICHHD
National Institute of Child Health and Human Development. U

nickel
Total nickel and is determined by the method specified in 40 CFR 136.3. A

NIDA
National Institute of Drug Abuse. U

NIEHS
National Institute of Environmental Health Sciences, United States Department of Health and Human Services, or designee. O

NIM
National impact model. N

NIMBY
Not in my backyard. N

NIOSH
National Institute for Occupational Safety and Health, U.S. Public Health Service, U.S. Department of Health

and Human Services (DHHS), among other activities, tests and certifies respiratory protective devices and air sampling detector tubes, recommends occupational exposure limits for various substances, and assists OSHA and MSHA in occupational safety and health investigations and research. N

NIPDWR
National interim primary drinking water regulations. U

nitric acid plant
Any facility producing nitric acid 30 to 70 percent in strength by either the pressure or atmospheric pressure process. A

nitric oxide
NO. A gas formed by combustion under high temperature and high pressure in an internal combustion engine. It changes into nitrogen dioxide in the ambient air and contributes to photochemical smog. N

nitrification
The process whereby ammonia in wastewater is oxidized to nitrite and then to nitrate by bacterial or chemical reactions. N

nitrilotriacetic acid
NTA. A compound being used to replace phosphates in detergents. N

nitrite
(1) An intermediate in the process of nitrification. (2) Nitrous oxide salts used in food preservation. N

nitrogen dioxide
The result of nitric oxide combining with oxygen in the atmosphere; a major component of photochemical smog. N

nitrogenous wastes
Animal or plant residues that contain large amounts of nitrogen. N

nm.
Nanometer, 10^{-9} gram. U

NMFS
National Marine Fisheries Service. A

NO
(1) Abbreviation for nitric oxide. U
(2) NO_x is used by nitric oxides. U

no detectable emissions
Less than 500 parts per million by volume (ppmv) above background levels, as measured by a detection instrument reading in accordance with the procedures specified in [40 CFR] § 61.355(h). A

no discernible adverse effect
No adverse effect observable within the limitations and sensitivity specified in the Registration Guidelines promulgated pursuant to the Federal Insecticide, Fungicide and Rodenticide Act. A

no discharge of free oil
A discharge does not cause a film or sheen upon or a discoloration on the surface of the water or adjoining shorelines or cause a sludge or emulsion to be deposited beneath the surface of the water or upon adjoining shorelines. A

NO flowmeter
A calibrated flowmeter capable of measuring and monitoring NO flowrates with an accuracy of $\pm$ 2% of the measured flowrate. (Rotameters have been reported to operate unreliably when measuring low NO flows and are not recommended). U

no observed adverse effect level
NOAEL. The highest experimental dose at which there is no statistically or biologically significant increases in frequency or severity of adverse health effects, as seen in the exposed population compared with an appropriate, unexposed population. Effects may be produced at this level, but they are not considered to be adverse. N

no observed effect concentration
NOEC. The highest tested concentration in an acceptable early life stage test: (i) which did not cause the occurrence of any specified adverse effect (statistically different from the control at the 95 percent level); and (ii) below which no tested concentration caused such an occurrence. A

no observed effect level
NOEL. The highest experimental dose at which there is no statistically or biologically significant increases in frequency or severity of toxic effects seen in the exposed compared with an appropriate, unexposed population. N

no reasonable alternatives
(1) No land-based disposal sites, discharge point(s) within internal waters, or approved ocean dumping sites within a reasonable distance of the site of the proposed discharge the use of which would not cause unwarranted economic impacts on the discharger, or, notwithstanding the availability of such sites. U

no-adverse-effect level
See no-effect level. A

no-effect level
The maximum does used in a test which produces no observed adverse effects. A no-observed-effect level is expressed in terms of the weight of a substance given daily per unit weight of test animal (mg/kg). When administered to animals in food or drinking water, the no-observed-effect level is expressed as mg/kg of food of mg/ml of water. A

no-toxic-effect-level
See no-effect level. A

NO₂
Abbreviation for nitrogen dioxide. U

NOAA
National Oceanic and Atmospheric Administration (DOC). N

NOAEL
No observed adverse effect level; the highest dose in an experiment which did not produce an observable adverse effect. N [See: LOAEL].

NOEC
No observed effect concentration. A

NOEL
No observed effects level. N

NOHSCP
National Oil and Hazardous Substances Contingency Plan. N

NOI
Notice Of Intent. N

noise
Spontaneous deviations from a mean output not caused by input concentration changes. A

noise control system
Includes any vehicle part, component or system the primary purpose of which is to control or cause the reduction of noise emitted from a vehicle. A

noise dose
The ratio, expressed as a percentage, of (1) the time integral, over a stated time or event, of the 0.6 power of the measured SLOW exponential time-averaged, squared A-weighted sound pressure and (2) the product of the criterion duration (8 hours) and the 0.6 power of the squared sound pressure corresponding to the criterion sound level (90 dB). O

noise dosimeter
An instrument that integrates a function of sound pressure over a period of time in such a manner that it directly indicates a noise dose. O

noise emission test
A test conducted pursuant to the measurement methodology specified. A

noise reduction rating
NRR. A single number noise reduction factor in decibels, determined by an empirically derived technique which takes into account performance variation of protectors in noise reducing effectiveness due to differing noise spectra, fit variability and the mean attenuation of test stimuli at the one-third octave band test frequencies. A

nominal concentration
The amount of an ingredient which is expected to be present in a typical sample of a pesticide product at the time the product is produced, expressed as a percentage by weight. A

nominal fuel tank capacity
The volume of the fuel tank(s), specified by the manufacturer to the nearest tenth of a U.S. gallon, which may be filled with fuel from the fuel tank filler inlet. A

NOMS
National Organics Monitoring Survey. N

NON
Notice Of Noncompliance. K

non-commercial scientific institution
An institution that is not operated on a commercial basis as that term is referenced in paragraph (e) of [40 CFR] § 2.100 and which is operated solely for the purposes of conducting scientific research the results of which are not intended to promote any particular product or industry. A

non-community water system
A public water system that is not a community water system. A

non-compliance penalty
A penalty required by section 120 of the CAA that is calculated to take away the financial advantage a source derives from not complying with air pollution requirements. U

non-continuous discharger
A mill which is prohibited by the NPDES authority from discharging pollutants during specific periods of time for reasons other than treatment plant upset control, such periods being at least 24 hours in duration. A mill shall not be deemed a non-continuous discharger unless its permit, in addition to setting forth the prohibition described above, requires compliance with the effluent limitations established by this subpart for non-continuous dischargers and also requires compliance with maximum day and average of 30 consecutive days effluent limitations. Such maximum day and average of 30 consecutive days effluent limitations for non-continuous dischargers shall be established by the NPDES authority in the form of concentrations which reflect wastewater treatment levels that are representative of the application of the best practicable control technology currently available, the best conventional pollutant control technology, or new source performance standards in lieu of the maximum day and average of 30 consecutive days effluent limitations for conventional pollutants set forth in this subpart. A

non-emission related maintenance
That maintenance which does not substantially affect emissions and which does not have a lasting effect on the deterioration of the vehicle or engine with respect to emissions once the maintenance is performed at any particular date. A

non-enclosed process
Any equipment system (such as an open-top reactor, storage tank, or mixing vessel) in which a chemical substance is manufactured, processed, or otherwise used where significant direct contact of the bulk chemical substance and the workplace air may occur. A

non-industrial use
Use other than at a facility where chemical substances or mixtures are manufactured, imported, or processed. A

non-ionizing electromagnetic radiation
(1) Radiation that does not change the structure of atoms but does heat tissue and may cause harmful biological effects. (2) Microwaves, radio waves, and low-frequency elecetromagnetic fields from high-voltage transmission lines. N

non-transient non-community water system
NTNCWS. A public water system that is not a community water system and that regularly serves at least 25 of the same persons over 6 months per year. A

non-transportation-related onshore and offshore facilities
(A) Fixed onshore and offshore oil well drilling facilities including all equipment and appurtenances related thereto used in drilling operations for

exploratory or development wells, but excluding any terminal facility, unit or process integrally associated with the handling or transferring of oil in bulk to or from a vessel. (B) Mobile onshore and offshore oil well drilling platforms, barges, trucks, or other mobile facilities including all equipment and appurtenances related thereto when such mobile facilities are fixed in position for the purpose of drilling operations for exploratory or development wells, but excluding any terminal facility, unit or process integrally associated with the handling or transferring of oil in bulk to or from a vessel. (C) Fixed onshore and offshore oil production structures, platforms, derricks, and rigs including all equipment and appurtenances related thereto, as well as completed wells and the wellhead separators, oil separators, and storage facilities used in the production of oil, but excluding any terminal facility, unit or process integrally associated with the handling or transferring of oil in bulk to or from a vessel. (D) Mobile onshore and offshore oil production facilities including all equipment and appurtenances related thereto as well as completed wells and wellhead equipment, piping from wellheads to oil separators, oil separators, and storage facilities used in the production of oil when such mobile facilities are fixed in position for the purpose of oil production operations, but excluding any terminal facility, unit or process integrally associated with the handling or transferring of oil in bulk to or from a vessel. (E) Oil refining facilities including all equipment and appurtenances related thereto as well as in-plant processing units, storage units, piping, drainage systems and waste treatment units used in the refining of oil, but excluding any terminal facility, unit or process integrally associated with the handling or transferring of oil in bulk to or from a vessel. (F) Oil storage facilities including all equipment and appurtenances related thereto as well as fixed bulk plant storage, terminal oil storage facilities, consumer storage, pumps and drainage systems used in the storage of oil, but excluding inline or breakout storage tanks needed for the continuous operation of a pipeline system and any terminal facility, unit or process integrally associated with the handling or transferring of oil in bulk to or from a vessel. (G) Industrial, commercial, agricultural or public facilities which use and store oil, but excluding any terminal facility, unit or process integrally associated with the handling or transferring of oil in bulk to or from a vessel. (H) Waste treatment facilities including in-plant pipelines, effluent discharge lines, and storage tanks, but excluding waste treatment facilities located on vessels and terminal storage tanks and appurtenances for the reception of oily ballast water or tank washings from vessels and associated systems used for off-loading vessels. (I) Loading racks, transfer hoses, loading arms and other equipment which are appurtenant to a nontransportation-related facility or terminal facility and which are used to transfer oil in bulk to or from highway vehicles or railroad cars. (J) Highway vehicles and railroad cars which are used for the transport of oil exclusively within the confines of a nontransportation-related facility and which are not intended to transport oil in interstate or intrastate commerce. (K) Pipeline systems which are used for the transport of oil exclusively within the confines of a nontransportation-related facility or terminal facility and which are not intended to transport oil in interstate or intrastate commerce, but excluding pipeline systems used to transfer oil in bulk to or from a vessel. A

nonattainment area
For any air pollutant, an area which is shown by monitored data or which is calculated by air quality modeling (or other methods determined by the Administrator to be reliable) to exceed any national ambient air quality standard for such pollutant. B

nonconforming vehicle or engine
A motor vehicle or motor vehicle engine which is not covered by a certificate of conformity prior to final or conditional importation and which has not been finally admitted into the United States under the provisions of [40 CFR] § 85.1505, § 85.1509 or the applicable provisions of [40 CFR] § 85.1512 covering EPA approved manufacturer and U.S. Government Agency catalyst and O₂ sensor control programs. A

nonconsumer article
Any article subject to TSCA which is not a "consumer product" within the meaning of the Consumer Product Safety Act (CPSA), 15 U.S.C. 2052. A

noncontact cooling water
(1) Water used for cooling which does not come into direct contact with any raw material, intermediate product, waste product or finished product. A (2) Water which is used in a cooling system designed so as to maintain constant separation of the cooling medium from all contact with process chemicals but which may on the occasion of corrosion, cooling system leakage or similar cooling system failures contain small amounts of process chemicals: Provided, that all reasonable measures have been taken to prevent, reduce, eliminate and control to the maximum extent feasible such contamination: And provided further, That all reasonable measures have been taken that will mitigate the effects of such contamination once it has occurred. A

noncontinental area
The State of Hawaii, the Virgin Islands, Guam, American Samoa, the Commonwealth of Puerto Rico, or the Northern Mariana Islands. A

nondegradation clause
A legal provision stipulating that the present air quality of an area must not be lowered. The provision is meant to protect those areas whose air quality is already better than federal standards demand. A [ed. nondegradation is also a policy applied to water quality of navigable waters].

nonexcessive infiltration
The quantity of flow which is less than 120 gallons per capita per day (domestic base flow and infiltration)

or the quantity of infiltration which cannot be economically and effectively eliminated from a sewer system as determined in a cost-effectiveness analysis. (See [40 CFR] §35.2005(b)(16) and 35.2120). A

nonexcessive inflow
The maximum total flow rate during storm events which does not result in chronic operational problems related to hydraulic overloading of the treatment works or which does not result in a total flow of more than 275 gallons per capita per day (domestic base flow plus infiltration plus inflow). Chronic operational problems may include surcharging, backups, bypasses, and overflows. [See 40 CFR] § 35.2005(b)(16) and 35.2120). A

nonexpendable personal property
Tangible personal property having a useful life of more than 1 year and an acquisition cost of $300 or more per unit. A grantee may use its own definition of nonexpendable personal property provided that such definition would at least include all nonexpendable personal property as defined herein. A

nonferrous
Metals that contain no iron. Nonferrous waste usually includes aluminum, copper, brass, and bronze materials. U

nonferrous metal
Any pure metal other than iron or any metal alloy for which a metal other than iron is its major constituent in percent by weight. A

nonfriable asbestos-containing material
Any material containing more than 1 percent asbestos as determined using the method specified in appendix A, subpart F, 40 CFR part 763, section 1, Polarized Light Microscopy, that, when dry, cannot be crumbled, pulverized, or reduced to powder by hand pressure. A

nonimpervious solid surfaces
Solid surfaces which are porous and are more likely to absorb spilled PCBs prior to completion of the cleanup requirements prescribed in this policy. Nonimpervious solid surfaces include, but are not limited to, wood, concrete, asphalt, and plasterboard. A

nonindustrial source
Any source of pollutants which is not an industrial source. A

nonisolated intermediate
Any intermediate that is not intentionally removed from the equipment in which it is manufactured, including the reaction vessel in which it is manufactured, equipment which is ancillary to the reaction vessel, and any equipment through which the chemical substance passes during a continuous flow process, but not including tanks or other vessels in which the substance is stored after its manufacture. A

nonoperational storage tank
ny underground storage tank in which regulated substances will not be deposited or from which regulated substances will not be dispensed after the date of the enactment of the

Hazardous and Solid Waste Amendments of 1984. I

nonperishable raw agricultural commodity
Any raw agricultural commodity not subject to rapid decay or deterioration that would render it unfit for consumption. Examples are cocoa beans, coffee beans, field-dried beans, field-dried peas, grains, and nuts. Not included are eggs, milk, meat, poultry, fresh fruits, vegetables such as onions, parsnips, potatoes, and carrots. A

nonpoint source
Causes of water pollution that are not associated with point sources, such as agricultural fertilizer runoff, sediment from construction. Examples include (i) Agriculturally related nonpoint sources of pollution including runoff from manure disposal areas, and from land used for livestock and crop production; (ii) Silviculturally related nonpoint sources of pollution; (iii) Mine-related sources of pollution including new, current and abandoned surface and underground mine runoff; (iv) Construction activity related sources of pollution; (v) Sources of pollution from disposal on land, in wells or in subsurface excavations that affect ground and surface water quality; (vi) Salt water intrusion into rivers, lakes, estuaries and groundwater resulting from reduction of fresh water flow from any cause, including irrigation, obstruction, groundwater extraction, and diversion; and (vii) Sources of pollution related to hydrologic modifications, including those caused by changes in the movement, flow, or circulation of any navigable waters or groundwaters due to construction and operation of dams, levees, channels, or flow diversion facilities. A

nonpoint source assessment
An assessment of water quality problems caused by nonpoint sources of pollutants. (1) The assessment shall include a description of the type of problem, an identification of the waters affected (by segment or other appropriate planning area), an evaluation of the seriousness of the effects on those waters, and an identification of nonpoint sources contributing to the problem. (2) Any nonpoint sources of pollutants originating outside a segment which materially affect water quality within the segment shall be considered. (3) The results of this assessment should be reflected in the States' report required under Section 305(b) of the Federal Water Pollution Control Act. A

nonpoint source control needs
(1) For each category of nonpoint sources of pollutants to be considered in any specified area as established in the State/EPA agreement, an identification and evaluation of all measures necessary to produce the desired level of control through application of best management practices (recognizing the application of best management practices may vary from area to area depending upon the extent of water quality problems). (2) The evaluation shall include an assessment of nonpoint source control measures applied thus far, the period of time required to achieve the desired control, the proposed regulatory

programs to achieve the controls, the management agencies needed to achieve the controls, and the costs by agency and activity, presented by 5-year increments, to achieve the desired controls, and a description of the proposed actions necessary to achieve such controls. A

nonprocurement list
The portion of the *List of Parties Excluded from Federal Procurement or Nonprocurement Programs* complied, maintained and distributed by the General Services Administration (GSA) containing the names and other information about persons who have been debarred, suspended, or voluntarily excluded under Executive Order 12549 and these regulations, and those who have been determined to be ineligible. A

nonprofit organization
Any corporation, trust, foundation, or institution (a) which is entitled to exemption under section 501(c)(3) of the Internal Revenue Code, or (b) which is not organized for profit and no part of the net earnings of which inure to the benefit of any private shareholder or individual. U

nonrestricted access areas
Any area other than restricted access, outdoor electrical substations, and other restricted access locations. In addition to residential/commercial areas, these areas include unrestricted access rural areas (areas of low density development and population where access is uncontrolled by either man-made barriers or naturally occurring barriers, such as rough terrain, mountains, or cliffs). A

nonscheduled renovation operation
A renovation operation necessitated by the routine failure of equipment, which is expected to occur within a given period based on past operating experience, but for which an exact date cannot be predicted. A

nonsudden accident
An unforeseen and unexpected occurrence which takes place over time and involves continuous or repeated exposure. A

nonsudden accidental occurrence
An occurrence which takes place over time and involves continuous or repeated exposure. A

nonthreshold toxicant
An agent considered to produce a toxic effect from any dose; any level of exposure is deemed to involve some risk. Usually used only in regard to carcinogenesis. N

nontidal
Not influenced by tides. N

nonvapor tight
Any tank truck, railcar, or marine vessel that does not pass the required vapor-tightness test. A

nonwetland
Any area that has sufficiently dry conditions that hydrophytic vegetation, hydric soils, and/or wetland hydrology are lacking; it includes upland as well as former wetlands that are effectively drained. N

normal ambient value
That concentration of a chemical species reasonably anticipated to be present in the water column, sediments, or biota in the absence of disposal activities at the disposal site in question. A

normal liquid detergent operations
All such operations except those defined as fast turnaround operation of automated fill lines. A

normal operation of a spray tower
Operation utilizing formulations that present limited air quality problems from stack gases and associated need for extensive wet scrubbing; without more than 6 turnarounds in a 30 consecutive day period, thus permitting essentially complete recycle of waste water. A

normal standing position
Standing erect and straight with arms down along the sides and looking straight ahead. A

NORS
National organics reconnaissance survey. N

nose
That portion of a tread projecting beyond the face of the riser immediately below. O

notice
A written communication served in person or sent by certified mail, return receipt requested, or its equivalent, to the last known address of a party, its identified counsel, its agent for service of process, or any partner, officer, director, owner, or joint venturer of the party. Notice, if undeliverable, shall be considered to have been received by the addressee five days after being properly sent to the last address known by the agency. A

notice
A written communication served in person or sent by certified mail, return receipt requested, or its equivalent, to the last known address of a party, its identified counsel, its agent for service of process, or any partner, officer, director, owner, or joint venturer of the party. Notice, if undeliverable, shall be considered to have been received by the addressee five days after being properly sent to the last address known by the agency. A

notice of intent
The written announcement to Federal, State and local agencies, and to interested persons, that a draft environmental impact statement will be prepared. The notice shall briefly describe the EPA action, its location, and the issues involved. The purpose of a notice of intent is to involve other government agencies and interested persons as early as possible in the planning and evaluation of actions which may have significant environmental impacts. This notice should encourage public input in the preparation of a draft EIS and assure that environmental values will be identified and weighed from the outset, rather than accommodated by adjustments at the end of the decision-making process. A

NOV
Notice Of Violation. N

NO$_x$
Abbreviation for nitrogen oxides or oxides of nitrogen. U

nozzle sample
One obtained from a diesel pump nozzle which dispenses diesel fuel from a storage tank at a retail outlet or a wholesale purchaser-consumer facility. A

NPDES
National Pollutant Discharge Elimination System. U

NPDES application
The uniform national forms (including the NPDES application short forms, NPDES application standard forms, and any subsequent additions, revisions or modifications duly promulgated by the Administrator [of EPA] pursuant to the [Federal Water Pollution Control] Act) for application for an NPDES permit. A

NPDES permit
Any permit or equivalent document or requirements issued by the Administrator, or, where appropriate, by the Director [of a state agency], after enactment of the Federal Water Pollution Control Amendments of 1972, to regulate the discharge of pollutants pursuant to section 402 of the Act. A

NPDES reporting form
The uniform national forms (including subsequent additions, revisions, or modifications duly promulgated by the Administrator [of EPA] pursuant to the [Federal Water Pollution Control] Act) for reporting data and information pursuant to monitoring and other conditions of NPDES permits. A

NPDES state
A State or Interstate water pollution control agency with an NPDES permit program approved pursuant to section 402(b) of the [Federal Water Pollution Control] Act. A

NPDS
National Pollutant Discharge System. The national program for issuing, modifying, revoking and reissuing, terminating, monitoring and enforcing permits, and imposing and enforcing pretreatment requirements, under sections 307, 402, 318, and 405 of the Clean Water Act. The term includes an approved program. A

NPDWR
National Primary Drinking Water Regulations. D

NPL
National Priorities List. A

NPRM
Notice of Proposed Rulemaking. The document issued by an agency, and published in the Federal Register, that solicits public comment on a proposed regulatory action. Under the Administrative Procedure Act, it must include, at a minimum: (a) a statement of the time, place and nature of the public rulemaking proceedings; (b) reference to the legal authority under which the rule is proposed; and (c) either the terms or substance of the regulation under

development, or a description of the subject and issues involved. U

NPS
Non-point source. U

NRC
(1) Nuclear Regulatory Commission. U
(2) National Response Center. U

NRC-licensed facility
Any facility licensed by the Nuclear Regulatory Commission or any Agreement State to receive title to, receive, possess, use, transfer, or deliver any source, by-product, or special nuclear material. A

NRDC
Natural Resources Defense Council. U

NRT
National Response Team consisting of representatives of 14 government agencies (DOD, DOI, DOT/RSPA, DOT/USCG, EPA, DOC, FEMA, DOS, USDA, DOJ, HHS, DOL, Nuclear Regulatory Commission, and DOE), is the principal organization for implementing the NCP. When the NRT is not activated for a response action, it serves as a standing committee to develop and maintain preparedness, to evaluate methods of responding to discharges or releases, to recommend needed changes in the response organization, and to recommend revisions to the NCP. The NRT may consider and make recommendations to appropriate agencies on the training, equipping, and protection of response teams; and necessary research, development, demonstration, and evaluation to improve response capabilities. U

NRTL
See nationally recognized testing laboratory. U

NSF
National Science Foundation. U

NSO
[Primary] Nonferrous Smelter Order under section 119 of the Clean Air Act. U

NSR
New source (pre-construction) review. U

NSPS
New Source Performance Standards under section 306 of the Clean Water Act (or section 111 of the Clean Air Act). A

NSWMA
National Solid Waste Management Association. U

NTA
(1) Negotiated testing agreement. U
(2) Nitrilotriacetic acid. A compound being used to replace phosphates in detergents. N

NTIS
National Technical Information Service. Under the Department of Commerce is the central point in the United States for the public sale of government funded research and development reports and other analyses prepared by federal agencies, their contractors, or grantees. U

NTNCWS
Non-Transient Non-Community Water System. A public water system that is not a community water system and that regularly serves at least 25 of the same persons over 6 months per year. A

NTP
National Toxicology Program. U

NTU
Nephelometric turbidity unit. N

nuclear energy
The force released by nuclear decay; radioactivity. U

nuclear fuel cycle
The operations defined to be associated with the production of electrical power for public use by any fuel cycle through utilization of nuclear energy. A

nuclear power plant
A device that converts atomic energy into usable power; heat produced by a reactor makes steam to drive electricity-generating turbines. N

nuclear winter
Prediction by some scientists that smoke and debris rising from massive fires resulting from a nuclear war could enter the atmosphere and block out sunlight for weeks or months. The scientists making this prediction project a cooling of the earth's surface, and changes in climate which could, for example, negatively effect world agricultural and weather patterns. N

nuclide
A species of atom characterized by the constitution of its nucleus. The nuclear constitution is specified by the number of protons (Z), number of neutrons (N) and energy content; or alternatively, by the atomic number (Z), mass number A = (N + Z), and atomic mass. To be regarded as a distinct nuclide, the atom must be capable of existing for a measurable time. Thus, nuclear isomers are separate nuclides, whereas promptly decaying excited nuclear states and unstable intermediates in nuclear reactions are not so considered. U

number of employees
Unless otherwise specified, the maximum number of employees present at any one time on a regular shift. O

nutrient(s)
(1) Any substance assimilated by living things that promotes growth. The term is generally applied to nitrogen and phosphorus in wastewater, but is also applied to other essential and trace elements. N
(2) Elements or compounds essential to growth and development of living things; carbon, oxygen, nitrogen, potassium and phosphorus. N

NVACP
Neighborhoods, voluntary associations and consumer protection. U

NWPA
The Nuclear Waste Policy Act of 1982 (Pub. L. 97-425). A

NWQSS
National Water Quality Surveillance System (EPA). U

O

O.D.
Outside diameter. U

O₂
Oxygen. U

O₃
Ozone. U

OALJ
Office of Administrative Law Judges. U

OAR
Office of Air and Radiation at EPA. U

OAQPS
Office of Air Quality Planning & Standards (EPA). U

objective evidence
The objective evidence of an emission related repair means all diagnostic information and data, the actual parts replaced during repair, and any other information directly used to support a warranty claim, or to support denial of such a claim. A

obligation of funds
Formal assignment by the EPA, through a Financial Management Officer, of a specified portion of appropriated funds to support a given project. For EPA, R&D grants funds are obligated when a GAD official signs the grant agreement or amendment. U

obligations
Amounts of orders placed, contracts awarded, services rendered, or other commitments made by Federal agencies during a given period, that will require outlays during the same or some future period. U

observation period
The portion of the test that begins after the test birds have been dosed and extends at least 14 days. A

observed effect concentration
OEC. The lowest tested concentration in an acceptable early life stage test: (i) Which caused the occurrence of any specified adverse effect (statistically different from the

379

control at the 95 percent level); and (ii) above which all tested concentrations caused such an occurrence. A

obstruction detector
A control that will stop the suspended or supported unit in the direction of travel if an obstruction is encountered, and will allow the unit to move only in a direction away from the obstruction. O

occupational exposure
Reasonably anticipated skin, eye, mucous membrane, or parenteral contact with blood or other potentially infectious materials that may result from the performance of an employee's duties. O

occupational safety and health standard
A standard which requires conditions, or the adoption or use of one or more practices, means, methods, operations, or processes, reasonably necessary or appropriate to provide safe or healthful employment and places of employment. H

occurrence
An accident, including continuous or repeated exposure to conditions, which results in bodily injury or property damage which the owner or operator neither expected nor intended to occur. A

OCE
(1) Office of Civil Enforcement. U (2) Office of Criminal Enforcement. N

ocean
Those waters of the open seas lying seaward of the baseline from which the territorial sea is measured, as provided for in the Convention on the Territorial Sea and the Contiguous Zone (15 UST 1606; TIAS 5639); this definition includes the waters of the territorial sea, the contiguous zone and the oceans as defined in section 502 of the FWPCA. A

ocean dumping
(1) The disposal of materials of any kind at sea, subject to regulation pursuant to the Marine Protection, Research and Sanctuaries Act. A (2) A disposition of material: Provided, That it does not mean a disposition of any effluent from any outfall structure to the extent that such disposition is regulated under the provisions of the Federal Water Pollution Control Act, as amended (33 USC 1251-1376) under the provisions of section 13 of the Rivers and Harbors Act of 1899, as amended (33 USC 407), or under the provisions of the Atomic Energy Act of 1954, as amended (42 USC 2011, et seq.), nor does it mean a routine discharge of effluent incidental to the propulsion of, or operation of motor-driven equipment on, vessels. Provided further, That it does not mean the construction of any fixed structure or artificial island nor the intentional placement of any device in ocean waters or on or in the submerged land beneath such waters, for a purpose other than disposal, when such construction or such placement is otherwise regulated by federal or state law or occurs pursuant to an authorized federal or state program. And provided further, That it does not include the deposit of

oyster shells or other materials when such deposit is made for the purpose of developing, maintaining, or harvesting fisheries resources and is otherwise regulated by federal or state law or occurs pursuant to an authorized federal or state law or occurs pursuant to an authorized federal or state program. A, E (3) The disposal of pesticides in or on the oceans and seas as defined in Pub. L. 92-532. A

ocean waters
(1) Those waters of the open seas lying seaward of the base line from which the territorial sea is measured, as provided for in the Convention on the Territorial Sea and the Contiguous Zone (15 UST 1606; TIAS 5639). E (2) Those coastal waters landward of the baseline of the territorial seas, and the deep waters of the territorial seas, or the waters of the contiguous zone. A Also see ocean.

OCS
Outer continental shelf. N

OCSLA
Outer Continental Shelf Lands Act. N

octave band attenuation
The amount of sound reduction determined according to the measurement procedure of 40 CFR § 211.206 for one-third octave bands of noise. A

OCZM
Office of Coastal Zone Management. U

OD
Optical density. Refers to the light refractive characteristics of a lens. O

odor threshold
The lowest concentration of an airborne odor that a human being can detect. U

OE
Office of Enforcement at EPA. U

OEC
Observed effect concentration. A

OECD
Organization for Economic Cooperation and Development, headquartered in Paris, France. U

OEM
Original equipment manufacturer. U

off-budget federal entities
Organizational entities, federally owned in whole or in part, whose transactions belong in the budget under current budget accounting concepts but which have been excluded from the budget totals under provisions of law. While these transactions are not included in the budget totals, information on these entities is presented in various places in the budget documents. U

off-kilogram (off-pound)
The mass of aluminum or aluminum, copper, or copper alloy removed from a forming or ancillary operation at the end of a process cycle for transfer to a different machine or process. A

off-road motorcycle
Any motorcycle that is not a street motorcycle or competition motorcycle. A

off-road vehicles
Forms of motorized transportation that do not require prepared surfaces and which can be used to reach remote areas. M

off-site facility
A hazardous waste treatment, storage or disposal area that is located at a place away from the generating site. N

offal
The viscera and trimmings of a slaughtered animal removed from the carcass. U

office papers
Note pads, loose-leaf fillers, tablets, and other papers commonly used in offices, but not defined elsewhere. A

office waste
Discarded materials that consist primarily of paper waste, including envelopes, ledgers, and brochures. U

offset printing paper
An uncoated or coated paper designed for offset lithography. A

offsets
A condition of new source review in nonattainment areas under the Clean Air Act, whereby a company must obtain a reduction in emissions from some other source that equals or exceeds any increase in emissions from a new or modified plant. N

offshore facility
Any facility of any kind located in, on, or under, any of the navigable waters of the United States, and any facility of any kind which is subject to the jurisdiction of the United States and is located in, on, or under any other waters, other than a vessel or a public vessel. D

offshore platform gas turbines
Any stationary gas turbine located on a platform in an ocean. A

OGC
Office of General Counsel. U

OIA
Office of International Activities at EPA. U

OIG
Office of the Inspector General. N

oil
(1) Oil of any kind or in any form, including, but not limited to, petroleum, fuel oil, sludge, oil refuse, and oil mixed with wastes other than dredged spoil. D (2) Crude oil or petroleum or a liquid fuel derived from crude oil or petroleum, including distillate and residual oil. A

oil "fingerprinting"
A method that identifies oil spills so they can be traced back to their sources. N

oil and grease
(1) Those components of a waste water amenable to measurement by the method described in *Methods for Chemical Analysis of Water and*

Wastes, 1971, Environmental Protection Agency, Analytical Quality Control Laboratory, page 217. A (2) The value obtained by the method specified in 40 CFR 136.3. A

oil feedstock
The crude oil and natural gas liquids fed to the topping units. A

oil pollution fund
The fund established by section 311(k) of the Clean Water Act. A

oil spill
Accidental discharge into bodies of water, can be controlled by chemical dispersion, combustion, mechanical containment, and absorption. N

old chemical registration review
Review of an application for registration of a new product containing active ingredients and uses which are substantially similar or identical to those currently registered or for which an application is pending Agency decision. A

oligotrophic lakes
Deep clear lakes with low nutrient supplies. They contain little organic matter and have a high dissolved oxygen level. N

OMB
Office of Management and Budget, a White House staff office that controls the Federal budget. U

OMS
Office of Mobile Sources at EPA. U

on ground tank
A device meeting the definition of "tank" in 40 CFR § 260.10 and that is situated in such a way that the bottom of the tank is on the same level as the adjacent surrounding surface so that the external tank bottom cannot be visually inspected. A

on site
Within the boundaries of a contiguous property unit. A (See: on-site).

on-premise sales
Sales transactions in which beverages are purchased by a consumer for immediate consumption within the area under control of the dealer. A

on-scene coordinator
OSC. The Federal official predesignated by EPA or USCG to coordinate and direct Federal responses and removals under the NCP; or the DOD official designated to coordinate and direct the removal actions from releases of hazardous substances, pollutants, or contaminants from DOD vessels and facilities. When the NRC receives notification of a pollution incident, the NRC Duty Officer notifies the appropriate OSC, depending on the location of an incident. Based on this initial report and any other information that can be obtained, the OSC makes a preliminary assessment of the need for a Federal response. If an onscene response is required, the OSC will go the scene and monitor the response of the responsible party of State or local government. If the responsible party is unknown or not

taking appropriate action, and the response is beyond the capability of State and local governments, the OSC may initiate Federal actions, using funding from the FWPCA Pollution Fund for oil discharges and the CERCLA Trust Fund (Superfund) for hazardous substance releases. N

on-site
The same or geographically contiguous property which may be divided by public or private right-of-way, provided the entrance and exit between the properties is at a crossroads intersection, and access is by crossing as opposed to going along, the right-of-way. Non-contiguous properties owned by the same person but connected by a right-of-way which he controls and to which the public does not have access, is also considered on-site property. A

on-site disposal
Any methods or processes to eliminate or reduce the volume or weight of solid waste on the property of the generator. U

on-site facility
A hazardous waste treatment, storage or disposal area that is located on the generating site. N

on-site incinerator
An incinerator that burns solid waste on the property used by the generator thereof. U

onboard controls
Devices placed on vehicles to capture gasoline vapor during refueling and then route the vapors to the engine when the vehicle is started so that they can be efficiently burned. N

once through cooling water
(1) Those waters discharged that are used for the purpose of heat removal and that do not come into direct contact with any raw material, intermediate or finished product. A (2) Water passed through the main cooling condensers in one or two passes for the purpose of removing waste heat. A

oncogenic
The property of a substance or a mixture of substances to produce or induce benign or malignant tumor formations in living animals. A

oncology
Study of cancer. N

one-hour period
Any 60-minute period commencing on the hour. A

one-hundred-year flood plain
Areas adjacent to streams where the probability of flooding in any given year is one in a hundred. N

one-year, 24-hour precipitation event
The maximum 24-hour precipitation event with a probable recurrence interval of once in one year as defined by the National Weather Service and Technical Paper No. 40, "Rainfall Frequency Atlas of the U.S.," May 1961, or equivalent regional or rainfall probability information developed therefrom. A

onshore

(1) All land areas landward of the territorial seas as defined in 40 CFR 125.1(gg). A (2) All facilities except those that are located in the territorial seas or on the outer continental shelf. A

onshore facility

Any facility (including, but not limited to, motor vehicles and rolling stock) of any kind located in, on, or under, any land or nonnavigable waters within the United States; and (b), as defined by section 311(a)(10) of the CWA, any facility (including, but not limited to, motor vehicles and rolling stock) of any kind located in, on, or under any land within the United States other than submerged land. A, L, N

onshore oil storage facility

Any facility (excluding motor vehicles and rolling stock) of any kind located in, on, or under, any land within the United States, other than submerged land. A

onsite consultation

The provision of consultative assistance on an employer's occupational safety and health program and on specific workplace hazards through a visit to an employer's worksite. It includes a written report to the employer on the findings and recommendations resulting from the visit. It may include training and education needed to address hazards, or potential hazards, at the worksite. O

opacity

(1) Degree of obscuration of light. For example, a window has zero opacity; a wall is 100 percent opaque. The Ringelmann Chart of evaluating smoke density is based on opacity. (2) The fraction of a beam of light, expressed in percent, which fails to penetrate a plume of smoke. A (3) The degree to which emissions reduce the transmission of light and obscure the view of an object in the background. A (4) The fraction of a beam of light, expressed in percent, which fails to penetrate a plume of smoke. A

opacity rating

The apparent obscuration of an observer's vision that equals the apparent obscuration of smoke of a given rating on the Ringelmann Chart. U

open burning

(1) The uncontrolled burning of waste materials in the open, in outdoor ininerators, or in an open dump either intentionally or accidentally. (2) The combustion of any material without the following characteristics: (a) Control of combustion air to maintain adequate temperature for efficient combustion, (b) Containment of the combustion-reaction in an enclosed device to provide sufficient residence time and mixing for complete combustion, and (c) Control of emission of the gaseous combustion products. A (3) The combustion of a pesticide or pesticide container in any fashion other than incineration. A

open combustion

Those basic oxygen furnace

steelmaking wet air cleaning systems which are designed to allow excess air to enter the air pollution control system for the purpose of combusting the carbon monoxide in furnace gases. A

open cut mine
Any form of recovery of ore from the earth except by a dredge. A

open dump
(1) Any facility or site where solid waste is disposed of which is not a sanitary landfill which meets the criteria promulgated under section 4004 of RCRA and which is not a facility for disposal of hazardous waste. A, I [ed. All open dumps will eventually be prohibited by RCRA]. (2) A land disposal site at which solid wastes are disposed of in a manner that does not protect the environment, are susceptible to open burning, and are exposed to the elements, vectors, and scavengers. A

open hearth furnace
(1) A long, wide, shallow reverberatory furnace used to produce steel from cast or pig iron. Now being replaced by the basic oxygen furnace. U (2) A steel-making furnace in which the oxidation of a molten mixture of pig iron and steel scrap by chemicals and combustible gas takes place in a large, long, shallow pool (the hearth) that is enclosed by a brickwork ceiling. Heat is introduced by combustion products flowing between the molten mixture and the ceiling. The process uses large quantities of scrap. U

open hearth furnace steelmaking
The production of steel from molten iron, steel scrap, fluxes, and various combinations thereof, in refractory lined fuel-fired furnaces equipped with regenerative chambers to recover heat from the flue and combustion gases. A

open land
Any surface or subsurface land which is not a disposal site and is not covered by a building. A

open site
An area that is essentially free of large sound-reflecting objects, such as barriers, walls, board fences, signboards, parked vehicles, bridges, or buildings. A

open space
A relatively undeveloped green or wooded area provided usually within an urban development to minimize feelings of congested living. M

open-ended valve
Any valve, except pressure relief valves, having one side of the valve seat in contact with process fluid and one side open to atmosphere, either directly or through open piping. A

open-pit incinerator
A burning apparatus that has an open top and a system of closely spaced nozzles that place a stream of high-velocity air over the burning zone. U

operable treatment works
An operable treatment works is a treatment works that: (a) Upon completion of construction will treat

wastewater, transport wastewater to or from treatment, or transport and dispose of wastewater in a manner which will significantly improve an objectionable water quality related situation or health hazard in existence prior to construction of the treatment works, and (b) Is a component part of a complete waste treatment system which, upon completion of construction for the complete waste treatment system (or completion of construction of other treatment works in the system in accordance with a schedule approved by the Regional Administrator [of EPA]) will comply with all applicable statutory and regulatory requirements. A

operable unit
(1) A discrete action, as described in the Cooperative Agreement or SSC, that comprises an incremental step toward comprehensively addressing site problems. The cleanup of a site can be divided into a number of operable units, depending on the complexity of the problems associated with the site. Operable units may address geographical portions of a site, specific site problems, or initial phases of an action, or may consist of any set of actions performed over time or any actions that are concurrent but located in different parts of a site. A (2) Term for each of a number of separate activities undertaken as part of a Superfund site cleanup. A typical operable unit would be removing drums and tanks from the surface of a site. N

operating control
A mechanism regulating or guiding the operation of equipment that ensures a specific operating mode. O

operating device
A device actuated manually to activate a control. O

operating humidity range
The range of ambient relative humidity over which the instrument will meet all performance specifications. A

operating temperature range
The range of ambient temperatures over which the instrument will meet all performance specifications. A

operation
Any step in the electroless plating process in which a metal is electrodeposited on a basis material and which is followed by a rinse; this includes the related operations of alkaline cleaning, acid pickle, and stripping, when each operation is followed by a rinse. A

operation and maintenance
(1) Activities conducted at a site after a Superfund site action is completed to ensure that the action is effective and operating properly. (2) Actions taken after construction to assure that facilities constructed to treat waste water will be properly operated, maintained, and managed to achieve efficiency levels and prescribed effluent limitations in an optimum manner. N

operation period
(1) A minimum period of time over which a measurement system is expected to operate within certain performance specifications without unscheduled maintenance, repair, or

adjustment. A (2) The period of time over which the instrument can be expected to operate unattended within specifications. A

operational
A uranium mill tailings pile that is licensed to accept additional tailings, and those tailings can be added without violating subpart W or any other Federal, state or local rule or law. A pile cannot be considered operational if it is filled to capacity or the mill it accepts tailings from has been dismantled or otherwise decommissioned. A

operational test period
A minimum period of time over which the continuous monitoring system is expected to operate within certain performance specifications without unscheduled maintenance, repair, or adjustment. A

operations and maintenance program (asbestos)
A program of work practices to maintain friable ACBM in good condition, ensure clean up of asbestos fibers previously released, and prevent further release by minimizing and controlling friable ACBM disturbance or damage. A

operator
The person responsible for the overall operation of a facility. M

OPPTS
Office of Prevention, Pesticides, and Toxic Substances at EPA. U

option
Any available equipment or feature not standard equipment on a model. A

oral toxicity
Adverse effects resulting from taking a substance into the body by mouth. Ordinarily used to denote effects in experimental animals. N

ORD
Office of Research and Development at EPA. U

ordinance
A statute enacted by the legislative body of a local, generally a municipal, government. U

ore
Gold placer deposit consisting of metallic gold-bearing gravels, which may be: residual, from weathering of rocks in-situ; river gravels in active streams; river gravels in abandoned and often buried channels; alluvial fans; sea-beaches; and sea-beaches now elevated and inland. Ore is the raw "bank run" material measured in place, before being moved by mechanical or hydraulic means to a beneficiation process. A

organic
Referring to or derived from living organisms. In chemistry, any compound containing carbon. N

organic active ingredients
Carbon-containing active ingredients used in pesticides, excluding metallo-organic active ingredients. A

organic chemicals/compounds
Animal or plant-produced substances containing mainly carbon, hydrogen, and oxygen. N

organic chlorine
The chlorine associated with all chlorine-containing compounds that elute just before lindane to just after mirex during gas chromatographic analysis using a halogen detector. A

organic coating
Any coating used in a surface coating operation, including dilution solvents, from which VOC emissions or volatile organic compound emissions occur during the application or the curing process. A

organic content
The ratio of carbon compounds, whether from living organisms or not, to the total chemical composition of a substance. U

organic materials
Chemical compounds of carbon excluding carbon monoxide, carbon dioxide, carbonic acid, metallic carbides, metallic carbonates, and ammonium carbonate. A

organic matter
The organic fraction of the sediment or soil; it includes plant and animal residues at various stages of decomposition, cells and tissues of soil organisms, and substances synthesized by the microbial population. A

organic peroxide
An organic compound that contains the bivalent-O-O-structure and which may be considered to be a structural derivative of hydrogen peroxide where one or both of the hydrogen atoms has been replaced by an organic radical. O

organic pesticides
Carbon-containing substances used as pesticides, excluding metallo-organic compounds. A

organic refuse
Solid waste composed of carbon compounds and generally, but not exclusively, by-products of plant and animal life processes (e.g., paper, wood, excreta, yard trimmings). U

organic solvents
Organic materials, including diluents and thinners, which are liquids at standard conditions and which are used as dissolvers, viscosity reducers, or cleaning agents. A

organism
Any living thing. N

organochlorine pesticides
Those pesticides which contain carbon and chlorine such as aldrin, DDD, DDE, DDT, dieldrin, endrin, and heptachlor. A

organophosphates
Pesticide chemicals that contain phosphorus, used to control insects. They are short-lived but some can be toxic when first applied. N

organotins
Chemical compounds used in antifoulant paints to protect the hulls of

boats and ships, buoys, and dock pilings from marine organisms such as barnacles. N

orientation sensitivity
The angular tolerance to which the sensor can be misaligned from its correct orientation to measure the flow rate vector before a specified error occurs in the indicated flow rate compared to the reference flow rate. A

original equipment manufacturer
OEM. The entity which originally manufactured the motor vehicle or motor vehicle engine prior to conditional importation. A

original equipment market part
Any part installed in or on a motor vehicle in the manufacturer's production line. A

original equipment part
A part present in or on a vehicle at the time the vehicle is sold to the ultimate purchaser, except for components installed by a dealer which are not manufactured by the vehicle manufacturer or are not installed at the direction of the vehicle manufacturer. A

original generation point
The location where regulated medical waste is generated. Waste may be taken from original generation points to a central collection point prior to off-site transport or on-site treatment. A

original production (OP) year
The calendar year in which the motor vehicle or motor vehicle engine was originally produced by the OEM. A

original production (OP) years old
The age of a vehicle as determined by subtracting the original production year of the vehicle from the calendar year of importation. A

ORM
Other regulated material. DOT hazard classification of a particular hazardous material to label it in transport. ORM-A; a class of materials with an anesthetic, irritating, noxious, toxic, or other property whose leakage can cause extreme discomfort to transportation personnel. ORM-B: a class of materials (including solids wet with water) that can cause damage to a vehicle if they leak during transport. ORM-E: materials that are not in any other hazard classification but are subject to DOT regulations. A

ORP
Oxidation-reduction potential. U

Orsat
An apparatus used to analyze flue gases volumetrically by dissolving the constituent gases selectively in various solvents. U

Osborne separator
A separator that uses a pulsed, rising column of air to separate small particles of glass, metal, or other dense items from compost. U

OSC
See on-scene coordinator. A

oscillating-grate stoker
A stoker whose entire grate surface oscillates to move the solid waste and residue over the grate surface. U

OSHA
The Federal Occupational Safety and Health Administration or the state agency responsible under a plan approved under section 18 of the [OSH] Act for the enforcement of occupational safety and health standards in that state. O (2) Occupational Safety and Health Act. U

OSHA Area Director
The Director for the Occupational Safety and Health Administration Area Office having jurisdiction over the geographic area in which the employer's establishment is located. O

OSHRC
Occupational Safety and Health Review Commission. U

OSM
Office of Surface Mining, Department of Interior. U

osmosis
The tendency of a fluid to pass through a permeable membrane such as the wall of a living cell into a less concentrated solution so as to equalize the concentrations on both sides of the membrane. N

OSTP
Office of Science and Technology Policy (White House). N

OSW
Office of Solid Waste at EPA. U

OSWER
Office of Solid Waste and Emergency Response. N

OTA
Office of Technology Assessment (U.S. Congress). N

other coatings
Coating steel products with metals other than zinc or terne metal by the hot dip process including the immersion of the steel product in a molten bath of metal, and the related operations preceding the subsequent to the immersion phase. A

other lead-emitting operation
Any lead-acid battery manufacturing plant operation from which lead emissions are collected and ducted to the atmosphere and which is not part of a grid casting, lead oxide manufacturing, lead reclamation, paste mixing, or three-process operation facility. U

other significant evidence
Factually significant information that relates to the uses of the pesticide and their adverse risk to man or to the environment but does not include evidence based only on misuse of the pesticide unless such misuse is widespread and a commonly recognized practice. A

otolaryngologist
A physician specializing in diagnosis and treatment of disorders of the ear, nose and throat. O

outage
Space left in a product container to

allow for expansion during temperature changes it may undergo during shipment and use. Measurement of space not occupied. A

outdoor application or use
Any pesticide application or use that occurs outside enclosed manmade structures or the consequences of which extend beyond enclosed manmade structures, including, but not limited to, pulp and paper mill water treatments and industrial cooling water treatments. A

outdoor electrical substations
Outdoor, fenced-off, and restricted access areas used in the transmission and/or distribution of electrical power. Outdoor electrical substations restrict public access by being fenced or walled off as defined under [40 CFR] § 761.30(1)(1)(ii). For purposes of this TSCA policy, outdoor electrical substations are defined as being located at least 0.1 km from a residential/commercial area. Outdoor fenced-off and restricted access areas used in the transmission and/or distribution of electrical power which are located less than 0.1 km from a residential/commercial area are considered to be residential/commercial areas. A

outfall
(1) A point source as defined by 40 CFR 122.2 at the point where a municipal separate storm sewer discharges to waters of the United States and does not include open conveyances connecting two municipal separate storm sewers, or pipes, tunnels or other conveyances which connect segments of the same stream or other waters of the United States and are used to convey waters of the United States. A (2) The place where an effluent is discharged into receiving waters. N

outrigger
A device, used singly or in pairs, for suspending a working platform from work, storage, and rigging locations on the building being serviced. Unlike davits, an outrigger reacts its operating moment load as at least two opposing vertical components acting into two or more distinct roof points and/or attachments. O

outside air
The air outside buildings and structures, including, but not limited to, the air under a bridge or in an open air ferry dock. A

over-the-head position
The mode of use of a device with a headband, in which the headband is worn such that it passes over the user's head. This is in contrast to the behind-the-head and under-the-chin positions. A

overburden
Any material of any nature, consolidated or unconsolidated, that overlies a mineral deposit, excluding topsoil or similar naturally-occurring surface materials that are not disturbed by mining operations. A

overfill release
A release that occurs when a tank is filled beyond its capacity, resulting

in a discharge of the regulated substance to the environment. A

overfire air
(1) Air forced into the top of an incinerator or boiler to fan the flames. N (2) Air under control as to quantity and direction, introduced above and beyond a fuel bed by induced or forced draft. A

overfire air fan
A fan used to provide air above a fuel bed. U

overland flow
A land application technique that cleanses waste water by allowing it to flow over a sloped surface. As the water flows over the surface, the contaminants are removed and the water is collected at the bottom of the slope for reuse. N

overload
Operation of equipment in excess of normal, full load rating, or of a conductor in excess of rated ampacity which, when it persists for a sufficient length of time, would cause damage or dangerous overheating. A fault, such as a short circuit or ground fault, is not an overload. O

oversaturated solution
A solution that contains a greater concentration of a solute than is possible at equilibrium under fixed conditions of temperature and pressure. A

oversized regulated medical waste
Medical waste that is too large to be placed in a plastic bag or standard container. A

oversubscription payment deadline
Thirty calendar days prior to the allowance transfer deadline. A

overturn
The period of mixing (turnover), by top to bottom circulation, of previously stratified water masses. This phenomenon may occur in spring and/or fall; the result is a uniformity of physical and chemical properties of the water at all depths. N

OW
Office of Water at EPA. U

owned or controlled
Leased, operated, controlled, supervised, or in ten percent or greater part, owned. A

owned or controlled by the parent company
The parent owns or controls 50 percent or more of the other company's voting stock or other equity rights, or has the power to control the management and policies of the other company. A

owner
The original purchaser or any subsequent purchaser of a vehicle. A

owner
(1) Any of the following persons: (a) Any holder of any portion of the legal or equitable title in an affected unit; or (b) Any holder of a leasehold interest in an affected unit; or (c) Any purchaser of power from an

affected unit under a life-of-the-unit, firm power contractual arrangement as that term is used in section 408(i) of the Clean Air Act. However, unless expressly provided for in a leasehold agreement, owner shall not include a passive lessor, or a person who has an equitable interest through such lessor, whose rental payments are not based, either directly or indirectly, upon the revenues or income from the affected unit. A (2) In the case of an UST system in use on November 8, 1984, or brought into use after that date, any person who owns an UST system used for storage, use, or dispensing of regulated substances; and in the case of any UST system in use before November 8, 1984, but no longer in use on that date, any person who owned such UST immediately before the discontinuation of its use. A

owner or operator

(1) (A)(i) In the case of a vessel, any person owning, operating, or chartering by demise, such vessel, and (ii) in the case of an onshore facility, or an offshore facility, any person owning or operating such facility, and (iii) in the case of any abandoned facility, the person who owned, operated, or otherwise controlled activities at such facility immediately prior to such abandonment. Such term does not include a person, who, without participating in the management of a vessel or facility, holds indicia of ownership primarily to protect his security interest in the vessel or facility. O (B) In the case of a hazardous substance which has been accepted for transportation by a common or contract carrier and except as provided in section 107(a) (3) or (4) of CERCLA, (i) the term "owner or operator" shall mean such common carrier or other bona fide for hire carrier acting as an independent contractor during such transportation, (ii) the shipper of such hazardous substance shall not be considered to have caused or contributed to any release during such transportation which resulted solely from circumstances or conditions beyond his control; (C) In the case of a hazardous substance which has been delivered by a common or contract carrier to a disposal or treatment facility and except as provided in section 107(a) (3) or (4) (i) the term "owner or operator" shall not include such common or contract carrier and (ii) such common or contract carrier shall not be considered to have caused or contributed to any release at such disposal or treatment facility resulting from circumstances or conditions beyond its control. A, L (2) Any person who owns, leases, operates or supervises a facility, building, structure or installation which emits or has the potential to emit any air pollutant regulated by EPA under the Clean Air Act. A

owner or operator of a demolition or renovation activity

Any person who owns, leases, operates, controls, or supervises the facility being demolished or renovated or any person who owns, leases, operates, controls, or supervises the demolition or renovation operation, or both. A

owner's manual
The instruction booklet normally provided to the purchaser of a vehicle. A

OX
Abbreviation for photochemical oxidants (ozone). U

oxidant
A substance containing oxygen that reacts chemically in air to produce a new substance; primary source of photochemical smog. N

oxidation
Oxygen combining with other elements. N

oxidation control system
(1) An emission control system which reduces emissions from sulfur recovery plants by converting these emissions to sulfur dioxide. A (2) The addition of oxygen which breaks down organic waste or chemicals such as cyanides, phenols, and organic sulfur compounds in sewage by bacterial and chemical means. (3) Oxygen combining with other elements. (4) The process in chemistry whereby electrons are removed from a molecule. N

oxidation pond
(1) A holding area where organic wastes are broken down by aerobic bacteria. (2) A man-made lake or body of water in which waste is consumed by bacteria. It is used most frequently with other waste treatment processes. An oxidation pond is basically the same as a sewage lagoon. N

oxidation-reduction process
A complex of biochemical reactions in soil that influences the valence state of elements and their ions found in the soil; long periods of soil saturation during the growing season tend to elicit anaerobic conditions that shift the overall process to a reducing condition. N

oxide
A compound of two elements, one of which is oxygen. U

oxides of nitrogen
The sum of the nitric oxide and nitrogen dioxide contained in a gas sample as if the nitric oxide were in the form of nitrogen dioxide. A

oxidizer
(1) An oxidizer or oxidizing material is a substance that yields oxygen readily to stimulate the combustion (oxidation) of organic matter. A (2) A chemical other than a blasting agent or explosive as defined in [29 CFR] § 1910.109(a), that initiates or promotes combustion in other materials, thereby causing fire either of itself or through the release of oxygen or other gases. O

oxidizing catalyst
A device installed in the exhaust system of the vehicle that utilizes a catalyst and, if necessary, an air pump to reduce emissions of hydrocarbons and carbon monoxide by 50 percent from that vehicle. A

oxygen deficiency
That concentration of oxygen by volume below which atmosphere

supplying respiratory protection must be provided. It exists in atmospheres where the percentage of oxygen by volume is less than 19.5 percent oxygen. O

oxygenated fuels
Gasoline which has been blended with alcohols or ethers that contain oxygen in order to reduce carbon monoxide and other emissions. N

oxygenated solvent
An organic solvent containing oxygen as part of the molecular structure. Alcohols and ketones are oxygenated compounds often used as paint solvents. N

oxyhemoglobin
Hemoglobin in combination with oxygen. It is the predominant form of hemoglobin present in arterial blood. U

ozonator
A device that adds ozone to water. N

ozone
O3. (1) A pungent, colorless, toxic gas that contributes to photochemical smog. [ed. The natural ambient air quality standard for photochemical oxidants was changed to an ozone standard]. (2) Found in two layers of the atmosphere, the stratosphere and the troposphere. In the stratosphere (the atmospheric layer beginning 7 to 10 miles above the earth's surface) ozone is a form of oxygen found naturally which provides a protective layer shielding the earth from ultraviolet radiation's harmful health effects on humans and the environment. In the troposphere (the layer extending up 7 to 10 miles from the earth's surface), ozone is a chemical oxidant and major component of photochemical smog. Ozone can seriously affect the human respiratory systems and is one of the most prevalent and widespread of all the criteria pollutants for which the Clean Air Act required EPA to set standards. Ozone in the troposphere is produced through complex chemical reactions of nitrogen oxides, which are among the primary pollutants emitted by combustion sources, hydrocarbons, released into the atmosphere through the combustion, handling and processing of petroleum products; and sunlight. N

ozone depletion
Destruction of the stratospheric ozone layer which shields the earth from ultraviolet radiation harmful to biological life. This destruction of ozone is caused by the breakdown of certain chlorine and/or bromine-containing compounds (chlorofluorocarbons or halons) which break down when they reach the stratosphere and catalytically destroy ozone molecules. N

P

PA
Preliminary assessment. U

PA/SI
Preliminary assessment/site inspection. U

PAC
Powdered activated carbon. N

package or **packaging**
(1) The immediate container or wrapping in which any pesticide is contained for consumption, use or storage. "Package" does not include: (a) Any shipping container or wrapping used solely for the transportation of any pesticide in bulk or in quantity to manufacturers, packers or processors, or to wholesale or retail distributors thereof; or (b) Any shipping container or other wrapping used by retailers to ship or deliver any pesticide to consumers unless it is the only such container or wrapping. A (2) The container in which a hearing protective device is presented for purchase or use. The package in some cases may be the same as the carrying case. A

packed tower
A pollution control device that forces dirty air through a tower packed with crushed rock or wood chips while liquid is sprayed over the packing material. The pollutants in the air stream either dissolve or chemically react with the liquid. N

packer
A device lowered into a well which can be expanded to produce a watertight seal. A

PAH
Polycyclic aromatic hydrocarbons. Components in organic materials that may pose a risk of cancer. A

PAIR
Preliminary Assessment Information Rule. U

pandemic
Widespread throughout an area, nation or the world. N

paper
(1) Generally, the term for all kinds

of matted or felted sheets of fiber laid down on a fine screen from a water suspension. Specifically, as one of the two subdivisions of the general term, paper refers to materials that are lighter in basis weight, thinner, and more flexible than paperboard, the other subdivision. It is used primarily for printing, writing, and wrapping. (2) One of two broad subdivisions of paper products, the other being paperboard. Paper is generally lighter in basis weight, thinner, and more flexible than paperboard. Sheets 0.012 inch or less in thickness are generally classified as paper. Its primary uses are for printing, writing, wrapping, and sanitary purposes. However, in this guideline, the term paper is also used as a generic term that includes both paper and paperboard. It includes the following types of papers: bleached paper, bond paper, book paper, brown paper, coarse paper, computer paper, cotton fiber content paper, cover stock or cover paper, duplicator paper, form bond, ledger paper, manifold business forms, mimeo paper, newsprint, office papers, offset printing paper, printing paper, stationery, tabulating paper, unbleached papers, writing paper, and xerographic/copy paper. A

paper napkins
Special tissues, white or colored, plain or printed, usually folded, and made in a variety of sizes for use during meals or with beverages. A

paper product
Any item manufactured from paper or paperboard. The term "paper product" is used in this guideline to distinguish such items as boxes, doilies, and paper towels from printing and writing papers. It includes the following types of products: corrugated boxes, doilies, envelopes, facial tissue, fiberboard boxes, folding boxboard, industrial wipers, paper napkins, paper towels, tabulating cards, and toilet tissue. A

paper towels
Paper toweling in folded sheets, or in raw form, for use in drying or cleaning, or where quick absorption is required. A

paperboard
One of the two broad categories of paper products. It is distinguished from paper, the other category, by a heavier basis weight and greater thickness and rigidity. The category includes container board, boxboard, building board, and automobile board, and it can be manufactured from virgin pulp or a combination of recycled fibers. U

paperstock
Paper waste that is recovered and reused. It is the principal ingredient in the manufacture of certain types of paperboard. U

PAPR
Powered air purifying respirator. N

parameter
A quantitative or characteristic element which describes physical, chemical, or biological conditions of water. A

parent corporation
A corporation which directly owns

at least 50 percent of the voting stock of the corporation which is the facility owner or operator; the latter corporation is deemed a "subsidiary" of the parent corporation. A

parenteral
Piercing mucous membranes or the skin barrier through such events as needlesticks, human bites, cuts, and abrasions. O

park and ride lot
A parking facility for the parking of private automobiles and bicycles of mass transit users. A

parking surcharge regulation
A regulation imposing or requiring the imposition of any tax, surcharge, fee, or other charge on parking spaces, or any other area used for the temporary storage of motor vehicles. B

PARS
Precision and accuracy reporting system. N

Parshall flume
A calibrated device developed by Parshall for measuring the flow of liquid in an open conduit. It consists essentially of a contracting length, a throat, and an expanding length. At the throat is a sill over which the flow passes at critical depth. The upper and lower heads are each measured at a definite distance from the sill. The lower head need not be measured unless the sill is submerged more than about 67 percent. U

part A
The first part of the two part application that must be submitted by a TSD facility to receive a permit. It contains general facility information such as location, waste types, quantities, process types, and capacities. There is a standard form for the PART A. N

part B
The second part of the permit application that includes detailed and highly technical information concerning the TSD in question. There is no standard form for the PART B, instead the facility must submit information, based on the regulatory requirements, on exactly how the operator or owner will comply with RCRA. N

partial closure
The closure of a hazardous waste management unit in accordance with the applicable closure requirements of parts 264 and 265 of [40 CFR] at a facility that contains other active hazardous waste management units. A

particleboard
Board products that are composed of distinct particles of wood or other lignocellulosic materials not reduced to fibers which are bonded together with an organic or inorganic binder. A

particulate asbestos material
Finely divided particles of asbestos material. A

particulate loading
(1) The introduction of particulates into ambient air. (2) The mass of particulates per unit volume of air or water. N

particulate matter
(1) Any finely divided solid or liquid material, other than uncombined water, as measured by the reference methods specified under each applicable subpart, or an equivalent or alternative method. A (2) Any airborne finely divided solid or liquid material with an aerodynamic diameter smaller than 100 micrometers. A

particulates
Fine liquid or solid particles such as dust, smoke, mist, fumes, or smog, found in the air or emissions. N

parts per million
ppm. A volume unit of measurement; the number of parts of a given pollutant in a million parts of air. U

party
(1) Any person, group, organization, or Federal agency or department that participates in a hearing. A (2) Any nation that is a party to the Montreal Protocol. A

Pascal (Pa)
The standard international unit of vapor pressure and is defined as newtons per square meter (N/m^2). A newton is the force necessary to give acceleration of one meter per second squared to one kilogram of mass. A

pass through
(1) A discharge which exits the POTW into waters of the United States in quantities or concentrations which, alone or in conjunction with a discharge or discharges from other sources, is a cause of a violation of any requirement of the POTW's NPDES permit (including an increase in the magnitude or duration of a violation). O (2) The discharge of pollutants through the POTW into navigable waters in quantities or concentrations which are a cause of or significantly contribute to a violation of any requirement of the POTW's NPDES permit (including an increase in the magnitude or duration of a violation). An industrial user significantly contributes to such permit violation where it: (1) Discharges a daily pollutant loading in excess of that allowed by contract with the POTW or by federal, state, or local law; (2) Discharges wastewater which substantially differs in nature and constituents from the user's average discharge; (3) Knows or has reason to know that its discharge, alone or in conjunction with discharges from other sources, would result in a permit violation; or (4) Knows or has reason to know that the POTW is, for any reason, violating its final effluent limitations in its permit and that such industrial user's discharge either alone or in conjunction with discharges from other sources, increases the magnitude or duration of the POTW's violations. A

passenger automobile
Any automobile which the Secretary determines is manufactured primarily for use in the transportation of no more than 10 individuals. A

passive institutional control
(1) Permanent markers placed at a disposal site, (2) public records and archives, (3) government ownership and regulations regarding land or

resource use, and (4) other methods of preserving knowledge about the location, design, and contents of a disposal system. A

paste mixing facility
The facility including lead oxide storage, conveying, weighing, metering, and charging operations; paste blending, handling, and cooling operations; and plate pasting, takeoff, cooling, and drying operations. A

pasture crops
Crops such as legumes, grasses, grain stubble and stover which are consumed by animals while grazing. A

pathogen
Microorganisms that can cause disease in other organisms or in humans, animals and plants. They may be bacteria, viruses, or parasites and are found in sewage, in runoff from animal farms or rural areas populated with domestic and/or wild animals, and in water used for swimming. Fish and shellfish contaminated by pathogens, or the contaminated water itself, can cause serious illnesses. N

pathogenic
Capable of causing disease. N

pathogenic bacteria
Bacteria which may cause disease in the host organisms by their parasitic growth. U

pathogenic waste
Discarded materials that contain organisms capable of causing disease. See infectious waste and isolation waste. U

pathology
The study of disease. N

PbB
Blood Lead. N

PBBs
Polybrominated biphenyls. Chemical substances the compositions of which, without regard to impurities, consist of brominated biphenyl molecules having the molecular formula $C_{12}H_xBr_y$ where $x+y = 10$ and y ranges from 1 to 10. A

PCA
Production compliance audit as described in § 86.1106-87 of this 40 CFR parts 86-99. A

PCB and PCBs
Any chemical substance that is limited to the biphenyl molecule that has been chlorinated to varying degrees or any combination of substances which contains such substance. Refer to [40 CFR] § 761.1(b) for applicable concentrations of PCBs. PCB and PCBs as contained in PCB items are defined in [40 CFR] § 761.3. Inadvertently generated non-Aroclor PCBs are defined as the total PCBs calculated following division of the quantity of monochlorinated biphenyls by 50 and dichlorinated biphenyls by 5. A

PCB article
Any manufactured article, other than a PCB container that contains PCBs and whose surface(s) has been in direct contact with PCBs. "PCB article" includes capacitors, transformers, electric motors, pumps,

pipes and any other manufactured item (1) which is formed to a specific shape or design during manufacture, (2) which has end use function(s) dependent in whole or in part upon its shape or design during end use, and (3) which has either no change of chemical composition during its end use or only those changes of composition which have no commercial purpose separate from that of the PCB article. A

PCB closed manufacturing process

A manufacturing process in which PCBs are generated but from which less than 10 micrograms per cubic meter from any resolvable gas chromatographic peak are contained in any release to air; less than 100 micrograms per liter from any resolvable gas chromatographic peak are contained in any release to water; and less than 2 micrograms per gram from any resolvable gas chromatographic peak are contained in any product, or any process waste. A

PCB container

Any package, can, bottle, bag, barrel, drum, tank, or other device that contains PCBs or PCB articles and whose surface(s) has been in direct contact with PCBs. A

PCB contaminated electrical equipment

Any electrical equipment, including but not limited to transformers (including those used in railway locomotives and self-propelled cars), capacitors, circuit breakers, reclosers, voltage regulators, switches (including sectionalizers and motor starters), electromagnets, and cable, that contain 50 ppm or greater PCB, but less than 500 ppm PCB. Oil-filled electrical equipment other than circuit breakers, reclosers, and cable whose PCB concentration is unknown must be assumed to be PCB-Contaminated Electrical Equipment. (See: [40 CFR] § 761.30(a) and (h) for provisions permitting reclassification of electrical equipment containing 500 ppm or greater PCBs to PCB-Contaminated Electrical Equipment. A

PCB controlled waste manufacturing process

A manufacturing process in which PCBs are generated but from which less 10 micrograms per cubic meter from any resolvable gas chromatographic peak are contained in any release to air; less than 100 micrograms per liter from any resolvable gas chromatographic peak are contained in any release to water; less than 2 micrograms per gram from any resolvable gas chromatographic peak are contained in any product, and the remainder of PCBs generated are incinerated in a qualified incinerator, landfilled in a landfill approved under the provisions of [40 CFR] § 761.75, or stored for such incineration or landfilling in accordance with the requirements of § 761.65(b)(1). A

PCB equipment

Any manufactured item, other than a PCB container or a PCB article container, which contains a PCB article or other PCB equipment, and includes microwave ovens, electronic equipment, and fluorescent light ballasts and fixtures. A

PCB item
Any PCB article, PCB article container, PCB container, or PCB equipment, that deliberately or unintentionally contains or has a part of it any PCB or PCBs at a concentration of 50 ppm or greater. A

PCB mixture
Any mixture which contains 0.05 percent (on a dry weight basis) or greater of a PCB chemical substance, and any mixture which contains less than 0.05 percent PCB chemical substance because of any dilution of a mixture containing more than 0.05 percent PCB chemical substance. This definition includes, but is not limited to, dielectric fluid and contaminated solvents, oils, waste oils, other chemicals, rags, soil, paints, debris, sludge, slurries, dredge spoils, and materials contaminated as a result of spills. A

PCB qualified incinerator
Means one of the following: (1) An incinerator approved under the provisions of [40 CFR] § 761.70. Any concentration of PCBs can be destroyed in an incinerator approved under 21 §761.70. (2) A high efficiency boiler approved under the provisions of § 761.60(a)(3). Only PCBs in concentrations below 500 ppm can be destroyed in a high-efficiency boiler approved under §761.60(a)(3). (3) An incinerator approved under section 3005(c) of the Resource Conservation and Recovery Act (42 U.S.C. 6925(c)) (RCRA). Only PCBs in concentrations below 50 ppm can be destroyed in a RCRA-approved incinerator. The manufacturer seeking to qualify a process as a controlled waste process by disposing of wastes in a RCRA-approved incinerator must make a determination that the incinerator is capable of destroying less readily burned compounds than the PCB homologs to be destroyed. The manufacturer may use the same guidance used by EPA in making such determination when issuing an approval under section 3005(c) of RCRA. The manufacturer is also responsible for obtaining a reasonable assurance that the incinerator, when burning PCB wastes, will be operated under conditions which have been shown to enable the incinerator to destroy the less readily burned compounds. A

PCB transformer
Any transformer that contains 500 ppm PCB or greater. A

PCB waste(s)
Those PCBs and PCB Items that are subject to the disposal requirements of subpart D of [40 CFR parts 700-789]. A

PCE
(1) Pollution control equipment. N

pCi
Picocurie. A

PCS
Permit Compliance System, a national data base under NPDES. U

PCV valve
A device to control the flow of blow-by gasses and fresh air from the crankcase to the fuel induction system of the engine. A

PDP-CVS
Positive displacement pump-constant volume sampler. U

peak air flow
The maximum engine intake mass air flow rate measure during the 195 second to 202 second time interval of the Federal Test Procedure. A

peak load
One hundred percent of the manufacturer's design capacity of the gas turbine at ISO standard day conditions. A

peak optical response
The wavelength of maximum sensitivity of the instrument. A

peak torque speed
The speed at which an engine develops maximum torque. A

peat
Partially decomposed organic material. U

PEL
Permissible exposure limit. N

percent load
The fraction of the maximum available torque at a specified engine speed. A

percent removal
A percentage expression of the removal efficiency across a treatment plant for a given pollutant parameter, as determined from the 30-day average values of the raw wastewater influent pollutant concentrations to the facility and the 30-day average values of the effluent pollutant concentrations for a given time period. A

percent volatile
Percent volatile by volume is the percentage of a liquid or solid (by volume) that will evaporate at an ambient temperature of 70° F (unless some other temperature is specified). Examples: butane, gasoline, and paint thinner (mineral spirits) are 100 percent volatile; their individual evaporation rates vary, but, in time each will evaporate completely. N

percentage of completion method
A system under which payments are made for construction work according to the percentage of completion of the work, rather than to the grantee's cost incurred. A

perceptible leaks
Any petroleum solvent vapor or liquid leaks that are conspicuous from visual observation or that bubble after application of a soap solution, such as pools or droplets of liquid, open containers or solvent, or solvent laden waste standing open to the atmosphere. A

percolation
The movement of water downward and radially through the sub-surface soil layers, usually continuing downward to the ground water. N

performance assessment
An analysis that: (1) identifies the processes and events that might affect the disposal system; (2) examines the effects of these processes and events on the performance of the disposal

system; and (3) estimates the cumulative releases of radionuclides, considering the associated uncertainties, caused by all significant processes and events. These estimates shall be incorporated into an overall probability distribution of cumulative release to the extent practicable. A

performance averaging period
Thirty calendar days, one calendar month, or four consecutive weeks as specified. A

performance evaluation sample
A reference sample provided to a laboratory for the purpose of demonstrating that the laboratory can successfully analyze the sample within limits of performance specified by the Agency. The true value of the concentration of the reference material is unknown to the laboratory at the time of the analysis. A

performance specification
A specification that states the desired operation or function of a product but does not specify the materials from which the product must be constructed. A

performance standard
The EPA-set limit of emissions from an individual source within a specific source category. A source category is designated when the Environmental Protection Agency determines that sources within the category contributes significantly to air [or water] pollution. A national standard of performance applies to new sources and is based on control achievable with the best available technology. U

performance test method
PTM. The sampling and analysis procedure used to obtain reference measurements for comparison to CEMS measurements. The applicable test methods are Method 10, 10A, or 10B (for the determination of CO) and Method 3 or 3A (for the determination of O_2). These methods are found in 40 CFR part 60, appendix A. A

periodic application of cover material
The application and compaction of soil or other suitable material over disposed solid waste at the end of each operating day or at such frequencies and in such a manner as to reduce the risk of fire and to impede disease vectors' access to the waste. A

perlite composite board
Insulation board composed of expanded perlite and fibers formed into rigid, flat, rectangular units with a suitable sizing material incorporated in the product. It may have on one or both surfaces a facing or coating to prevent excessive hot bitumen strike-in during roofing installation. A

permanent storage capacity
Grain storage capacity which is inside a building, bin, or silo. A

permanent total enclosure
PTE. A permanently installed enclosure that completely surrounds a source of emissions such that all VOC emissions are captured and contained for discharge through a control device. A

permanently installed decorative fountains and reflection pools
Those that are constructed in the ground, on the ground, or in a building in such a manner that the pool cannot be readily disassembled for storage and are served by electrical circuits of any nature. These units are primarily constructed for their aesthetic value and not intended for swimming or wading. O

permanently installed swimming pools, wading and therapeutic pools
Those that are constructed in the ground, on the ground, or in a building in such a manner that the pool cannot be readily disassembled for storage whether or not served by electrical circuits of any nature. O

permeability
(1) The quality of the soil that enables water to move downward through the profile, measured as the number of inches per hour that water moves downward through the saturated soil. N (2) The capacity of a porous medium to conduct or transmit fluids. U

permissible dose
The dose of a chemical or radiation that may be received by an individual without the expectation of significantly harmful result. N

permissible exposure limit
The exposure, inhalation or dermal permissible exposure limit specified in 29 CFR part 1910, subparts G and Z. O

permit
(1) An authorization, license, or equivalent control document issued by EPA or an approved state agency to implement the requirements of an environmental regulation; e.g., a permit to operate a wastewater treatment plant or to operate a facility that may generate harmful emission. N (2) An entitlement to commence and continue operation of a facility as long as both procedural and performance standards are met. The term "permit" includes any functional equivalent such as a registration or license. A (3) An authorization, license, or equivalent control document issued by EPA or an approved State to implement the requirements of [40 CFR § 270] and parts 271 and 124. Permit includes permit by rule (§ 270.60), and emergency permit (§ 270.61). Permit does not include RCRA interim status (subpart G of this part), or any permit which has not yet been the subject of final agency action, such as a draft permit or a proposed permit. A (4) The written certification by the employer authorizing employees to perform identified work operations subject to specified precautions. O

permit area
The area of land specified or referred to in an NPDES permit in which active mining and related activities may occur that result in the discharge regulated under the terms of the permit. Usually this is specifically delineated in an NPDES permit or permit application, but in other cases may be ascertainable from an Alaska Tri-agency permit application or similar document specifying the mine location, mining plan and similar data. A

permit-by-rule
A provision of regulations stating that a facility or activity is deemed to have a permit if it meets the requirements of the provision. A

permits for incineration at sea
Permits for incineration of wastes at sea will be issued only as research permits or as interim permits until specific criteria to regulate this type of disposal are promulgated, except in those cases where studies on the waste, the incineration method and vessel, and the site have been conducted and the site has been designated for incineration at sea in accordance with the procedures of [40 CFR] § 228.4(b). In all other respects the requirements of parts 220 through 228 apply. A

permitting authority
The District Engineer of the U.S. Army Corps of Engineers or such other individual as may be designated by the Secretary of the Army to issue or deny permits under section 404 of the Clean Water Act; or the State Director of a permit program approved by EPA under section 404(g) and section 404(h) or his delegated representative. A (Ed. There are other permit programs. This definition is only applicable to the 404 permit program).

persistence
Refers to the length of time a compound, once introduced into the environment, stays there. A compound may persist for less than a second or indefinitely. N

persistent pesticides
Pesticides that do not break down chemically and remain in the environment after a growing season. N

person
(1) Under most environmental statutes, the term includes an individual, corporation, firm, company, joint venture, partnership, sole proprietorship, association, or any other business entity, any State or political subdivision thereof, any municipality, any interstate body and any department, agency, or instrumentality of the United States and any officer, agent, or employee thereof. A, B, D, G, H, I, J, O. Also any organized group of persons whether incorporated or not. A, C [Ed. "Person" is defined numerous times. The above is an edited definition from these]. (2) An individual, partnership, corporation, association, scientific or academic establishment, or organizational unit thereof, and any other legal entity. A (3) An applicant, registrant, manufacturer, pesticide user, environmental group, labor union, or other individual or group of individuals interested in pesticide regulation. A

person-rem
The product of the average individual dose in a population times the number of individuals in the population. [Syn: man-rem]. U

personal property
(1) Any property that is not real property and that is movable or not attached to the land. Personal property can be a single or multi-component or multi-material product.

A (2) Except as otherwise defined by State law, tangible property of any kind except real property. A (2) Property other than real property. It may be tangible (having physical existence), such as equipment and supplies, or intangible (having no physical existence), such as patents, inventions, and copyrights. A

personal protective equipment
(1) Specialized clothing or equipment worn by an employee for protection against a hazard. General work clothes (e.g., uniforms, pants, shirts or blouses) not intended to function as protection against a hazard are not considered to be personal protective equipment. O (2) Any chemical protective clothing or device placed on the body to prevent contact with, and exposure to, an identified chemical substance or substances in the work area. Examples include, but are not limited to, chemical protective clothing, aprons, hoods, chemical goggles, face splash shields, or equivalent eye protection, and various types of respirators. Barrier creams are not included in this definition. A

personnel monitoring equipment
Devices designed to be worn or carried by an individual for the purpose of measuring the dose received (e.g., film badges, pocket chambers, pocket dosimeters, film rings, etc.). O

pest
(1) Any insect, rodent, nematode, fungus, weed, or (2) any other form of terrestrial or aquatic plant or animal life or virus, bacteria, or other microorganism (except viruses, bacteria, or other micro-organisms on or in living man or other living animals) which the Administrator declares to be a pest under section 25(c)(1) [of FIFRA]. C

pest problem
(1) A pest infestation and its consequences, or (2) any condition for which the use of plant regulators, defoliants, or desiccants would be appropriate. A

pesticidal product report
Information showing the types and amounts of pesticidal products which were: (1) produced in the past calendar year; (2) produced in the current calendar year; and, (3) sold or distributed in the past calendar year. For active ingredients, the pesticidal product report must include information on the types and amounts of an active ingredient for which there is actual or constructive knowledge of its use or intended use as a pesticide. This pesticidal product report also pertains to those products produced for export only which must also be reported. A positive or a negative annual report is required in order to maintain registration for the establishment. A

pesticide
Any substance or mixture of substances intended for preventing, destroying, repelling, or mitigating any pest, or intended for use as a plant regulator, defoliant, or desiccant, other than any article that: (1) Is a new animal drug under FFDCA sec. 201(w), or (2) Is an animal drug that has been determined by regulation of

the Secretary of Health and Human Services not to be a new animal drug, or (3) Is an animal feed under FFDCA sec. 201(x) that bears or contains any substances described by paragraph (s) (1) or (2) of this section. O, A, C

pesticide chemical
Any substance which alone, or in chemical combination with or in formulation with one or more other substances, is a "pesticide" within the meaning of FIFRA and which is used in the production, storage, or transportation of any raw agricultural commodity or processed food. The term includes any substance that is an active ingredient, intentionally-added inert ingredient, or impurity of such a "pesticide." A

pesticide formulation
The substance or mixture of substances comprised of all active and inert (if any) ingredients of a pesticide product. A

pesticide incinerator
Any installation capable of the controlled combustion of pesticides, at a temperature of 1000° C (1832° F) for two seconds dwell time in the combustion zone, or lower temperatures and related dwell times that will assure complete conversion of the specific pesticide to inorganic gases and solid ash residues. A

pesticide product
A pesticide in the particular form (including composition, packaging, and labeling) in which the pesticide is, or is intended to be, distributed or sold. The term includes any physical

apparatus used to deliver or apply the pesticide if distributed or sold with the pesticide. A

pesticide residue
A residue of a pesticide chemical or of any metabolite or degradation product of a pesticide chemical. A

pesticide tolerance
The amount of pesticide residue allowed by law to remain in or on a harvested crop. By using various safety factors, EPA sets these levels well below the point where the chemicals might be harmful to consumers. N

pesticide use
A use of a pesticide (described in terms of the application site and other applicable identifying factors) that is included in the labeling of a pesticide product which is registered, or for which an application for registration is pending, and the terms and conditions (or proposed terms and conditions) of registration for the use. A

pesticide-related wastes
All pesticide-containing wastes or by-products which are produced in the manufacturing or processing of a pesticide and which are to be discarded, but which, pursuant to acceptable pesticide manufacturing or processing operations, are not ordinarily a part of or contained within an industrial waste stream discharged into a sewer or the waters of a state. A

pesticides report
Information showing the types and

amounts of pesticides or devices which are being produced in the current calendar year, have been produced in the past calendar year, and which have been sold or distributed in the past calendar year. A

PET
Polyethylene Terephthalate. A plastic resin used to make packaging, particularly soft drink bottles. U

petitioner
Any person adversely affected by a notice of the [EPA] Administrator who requests a public hearing. A

petrochemical operations
The production of second generation petrochemicals (i.e., alcohols, ketones, cumene, styrene, etc.) or first generation petrochemicals and isomerization products (i.e., BTX, olefins, cyclohexane, etc.) when 15 percent or more of refinery production is first generation petrochemicals and isomerization products. A

petroleum
The crude oil removed from the earth and the oils derived from tar sands, shale, and coal. A

petroleum dry cleaner
A dry cleaning facility that uses petroleum solvent in a combination of washers, dryers, filters, stills, and settling tanks. A

petroleum liquids
Petroleum, condensate, and any finished or intermediate products manufactured in a petroleum refinery but does not mean Number 2 through Number 6 fuel oils as specified in ASTM D396-78, gas turbine fuel oils Numbers 2-GT through 4-GT as specified in ASTM D-2880-78, or diesel fuel oils Numbers 2-D and 4-D as specified in ASTM D-975-78. A

petroleum marketing facilities
All facilities at which petroleum is produced or refined and all facilities from which petroleum is sold or transferred to other petroleum marketers or to the public. A

petroleum refinery
(1) Any facility engaged in producing gasoline, kerosene, distillate fuel oils, residual fuel oils, lubricants, or other products through distillation of petroleum or through redistillation, cracking, extracting or reforming of unfinished petroleum derivatives. A (2) Industrial plants as classified by the Department of Commerce under Standard Industrial Classification (SIC) Code 29. A

pH
(1) The logarithm of the reciprocal of hydrogen ion concentration. A (2) A symbol for the degree of acidity or alkalinity. U

pharmaceutical
Any compound or mixture, other than food, used in the prevention, diagnosis, alleviation, treatment, or cure of disease in man and animal. A

pharmacokinetics
(1) The dynamic behavior of chemicals inside biological systems; it includes the processes of uptake, distribution, metabolism, and excretion.

N (2) The study of the rates of absorption, tissue distribution, biotransformation, and excretion. A

phased disposal
A method of tailings management and disposal which uses lined impoundments which are filled and then immediately dried and covered to meet all applicable Federal standards. A

phenolic insulation
Insulation made with phenolic plastics which are plastics based on resins made by the condensation of phenols, such as phenol or cresol, with aldehydes. A

phenols
Organic compounds that are by-products of petroleum refining, tanning, textile, dye, and resin manufacture. Low concentrations can cause taste and odor problems in water, higher concentrations can kill aquatic life. N

phenols 4AAP
Phenolic compounds. The value obtained by the method specified in 40 CFR 136.3. A

phosphate rock plant
Any plant which produces or prepares phosphate rock product by any or all of the following processes: mining, beneficiation, crushing, screening, cleaning, drying, calcining, and grinding. A

phosphate rock feed
All material entering the process unit including, moisture and extraneous material as well as the following ore minerals: fluorapatite, hydroxyapatite, chlorapatite, and carbonateapatite. A

phosphates
Chemical compounds containing phosphorus. N

phosphorus
An essential food element that can contribute to the eutrophication of water bodies. N

photo-degradable
Refers to plastics which will decompose if left exposed to light. U

photochemical oxidants
Air pollutants formed by the action of sunlight on oxides of nitrogen and hydrocarbons. N

photochemical process
The chemical changes brought about by the radiant energy of the sun acting upon various polluting substances. The products are known as photochemical smog. N

photochemical smog
Air pollution caused by not one pollutant but by chemical reactions of various pollutants emitted from different sources. N

photoperiod
The light and dark periods in a 24 hour day. This is usually expressed in a form such as 17 hours light/7 hours dark or 17L/7D. A

photosynthesis
The manufacture by plants of carbohydrates and oxygen from carbon dioxide and water in the presence of chlorophyll, using sunlight as an energy source. N

physical and chemical treatment system

(1) Processes generally used in large-scale waste-water treatment facilities. Physical processes may involve air-stripping or filtration. Chemical treatment includes coagulation, chlorination, or ozone addition. The term can also refer to treatment processes, treatment of toxic materials in surface waters and ground waters, oil spills, and some methods of dealing with hazardous materials on or in the ground. N (2) Those full scale coke plant wastewater treatment systems incorporating full scale granular activated carbon adsorption units which were in operation prior to January 7, 1981, the date of proposal of the regulation. A

physical and thermal integrity

The ability of the material to resist physical and thermal breakdown. A

physical construction

[In the RCRA program] Excavation, movement of earth, erection of forms or structures, or similar activity to prepare a HWM facility to accept hazardous waste. N

physical hazard

A chemical for which there is scientifically valid evidence that it is a combustible liquid, a compressed gas, explosive, flammable, an organic peroxide, an oxidizer, pyrophoric, unstable (reactive) or water-reactive. O

physical or mental impairment

(i) Any physiological disorder or condition, cosmetic disfigurement, or anatomical loss affecting one or more of the following body systems: neurological; musculoskeletal; special sense organs; respiratory, including speech organs; cardiovascular; reproductive; digestive; genito-urinary; hemic and lymphatic; skin; and endocrine; and (ii) any mental or psychological disorder, such as mental retardation, organic brain syndrome, emotional or mental illness, and specific learning disabilities. The term "physical or mental impairment" includes, but is not limited to, such diseases and conditions as orthopedic, visual, speech, and hearing impairments, cerebral palsy, epilepsy, muscular dystrophy, multiple sclerosis, cancer, heart disease, diabetes, mental retardation, emotional illness, and drug addiction and alcoholism. A

phytoplankton

That portion of the plankton community comprised of tiny plants, e.g., algae, diatoms. N

phytotoxic

Something that harms plants. N

PIAT

Public Information Assist Team. U

PIC

Products of incomplete combustion. N

picking belt or table

A table or belt on which solid waste is manually sorted and certain items are removed. It is normally used in composting and salvage operations. U

pickling bath
Any chemical bath (other than alkaline cleaning) through which a workpiece is processed. A

pickling fume scrubber
The process of using an air pollution control device to remove particulates and fumes from air above a pickling bath by entraining the pollutants in water. A

pickling liquor
A corrosive liquid (usually an acid) used to remove scale and oxides from metals. N

pickling rinse
A rinse, other than alkaline cleaning rinse, through which a workpiece is processed. A rinse consisting of a series of rinse tanks is considered as a single rinse. A

pickup truck
A light truck which has a passenger compartment and an open cargo bed. A

picocurie
pCi. Measurement of radioactivity. A picocurie is one million millionth, or a trillionth, of a curie, and represents about 2.2 radioactive particle disintegration per minute. A

PIG
(1) Program implementation guideline. [See: regulatory interpretative memoranda for description]. U (2) Container, usually lead, used to ship or store radioactive materials. N

piggyback collection
Crew collection of refuse and paper, simultaneously, at the curb. Bundled newspapers are placed on a rack installed beneath the compactor body, and refuse is placed in the body. U

PIGS
Pesticides in Groundwater Strategy. N

pile
(1) A nuclear reactor. N (2) Any non-containerized accumulation of solid, nonflowing hazardous waste that is used for treatment or storage. A

pilot program
A program that is initiated on a limited basis for the purpose of facilitating a future full scale regional program. A

PIN
Procurement Information Notice. N

pitch
Pitch is the included angle between the horizontal and the ladder, measured on the opposite side of the ladder from the climbing side. O

pitch and bark pockets
A pitch pocket is an opening extending parallel to the annual growth rings containing, or that has contained, pitch, either solid or liquid. A bark pocket is an opening between annual growth rings that contains bark. O

PL
Public Law. U

plankton
Tiny plants and animals that live in water. N

planned [asbestos] renovation operations
A renovation operation, or a number of such operations, in which the amount of friable asbestos material that will be removed or stripped within a given period of time can be predicted. Individual nonscheduled operations are included if a number of such operations can be predicted to occur during a given period of time based on operating experience. A

planning
Identifying problems, defining objectives, collecting information, analyzing alternatives and determining necessary activities and courses of action. A

plans
Reports and drawings, including a narrative operating description, prepared to describe the facility and its proposed operation. A

plant
All of the pollutant-emitting activities which belong to the same industrial grouping, are located on one or more contiguous or adjacent properties, and are under the control of the same person (or persons under common control), except the activities of any marine vessel. Pollutant-emitting activities shall be considered as part of the same industrial grouping if they belong to the same "Major Group" (i.e., which have the same two-digit code) as described in the "Standard Industrial Classification Manual, 1987" (incorporated by reference as specified in 40 CFR 52.742). A

plant blending records
Those records which document the weight fraction of organic solvents and solids used in the formulation or preparation of inks at the vinyl or urethane printing plant where they are used. A

plant community
The plant populations existing in a shared habitat or environment. N

plant regulator
(1) Any substance or mixture of substances intended, through physiological action, for accelerating or retarding the rate of growth or rate of maturation, or for otherwise altering the behavior of plants or the produce thereof, but shall not include substances to the extent that they are intended as plant nutrients, trace elements, nutritional chemicals, plant inoculants, and soil amendments. Also, the term 'plant regulator' shall not be required to include any of such of those nutrient mixtures or soil amendments as are commonly known as vitamin-hormone horticultural products, intended for improvement, maintenance, survival, health, and propagation of plants, and as are not for pest destruction and are nontoxic, nonpoisonous in the undiluted packaged concentration. C (2) Include but are not limited to, substances or mixtures of substances intended to cause fruit thinning, fruit setting, stem elongation, stimulation or retardation, abscission inhibition,

branch structure modification, sucker control, flower induction or inhibition, increased flowering, altered sex expression, extended flowering periods, fruit ripening stimulation, physiological disease inhibition, rooting of cuttings, or dormancy induction or release. A

plant site (mining)
The area occupied by the mine, necessary haulage ways from the mine to the beneficiation process, the beneficiation area, the area occupied by the wastewater treatment facilities and the storage areas for waste materials and solids removed from the wastewaters during treatment. A

plasmid
A circular piece of DNA that exists apart from the chromosome and replicates independently of it. Bacterial plasmids carry information that renders the bacteria resistant to antibiotics. Plasmids are often used in genetic engineering to carry desired genes into organisms. N

plastic body
An automobile or light-duty truck body constructed of synthetic organic material. A

plastic body component
Any component of an automobile or light-duty truck exterior surface constructed of synthetic organic material. A

plastic rigid foam
Cellular polyurethane insulation, cellular polyisocyanurate insulation, glass fiber reinforced polyisocyanurate/polyurethane foam insulation, cellular polystyrene insulation, phenolic foam insulation, spray-in-place foam and foam-in-place insulation. A

plastics
Non-metallic compounds that result from a chemical reaction, and are molded or formed into rigid or pliable structural material. N

platform
(1) A working space for persons, elevated above the surrounding floor or ground, such as a balcony or platform for the operation of machinery and equipment. O (2) An extended step or landing breaking a continuous run of stairs. O

platform ladder
A self-supporting ladder of fixed size with a platform provided at the working level. The size is determined by the distance along the front rail from the platform to the base of the ladder. O

plowing
All forms of primary tillage, including moldboard, chisel, or wide-blade, plowing, discing, harrowing, and similar physical means utilized on farm, forest or ranch land for the breaking up, cutting, turning over, or stirring of soil to prepare it for the planting of crops. The term does not include the redistribution of soil, rock, sand, or other surficial materials in a manner which changes any area of the waters of the United States to dry land. For example, the redistribution of surface materials by blading,

grading, or other means to fill in wetland areas is not plowing. Rock crushing activities which result in the loss of natural drainage characteristics, the reduction of water storage and recharge capabilities, or the overburden of natural water filtration capacities do not constitute plowing. Plowing will never involve a discharge of dredged or fill material. A

plugging
The act or process of stopping the flow of water, oil, or gas into or out of a formation through a borehole or well penetrating that formation. A

plugging record
A systematic listing of permanent or temporary abandonment of water, oil, gas, test, exploration and waste injection wells, and may contain a well log, description of amounts and types of plugging material used, the method employed for plugging, a description of formations which are sealed and a graphic log of the well showing formation location, formation thickness, and location of plugging structures. A

plume
(1) A visible or measurable discharge of a contaminant from a given point of origin. Can be visible or thermal in water, or visible in the air as, for example, a plume of smoke. (2) The area of measurable and potentially harmful radiation leaking from a damaged reactor. 3) The distance from a toxic release considered dangerous for those exposed to the leaking fumes. N

plume impaction
Concentrations measured or predicted to occur when the plume interacts with elevated terrain. A

plutonium
A radioactive metallic element similar chemically to uranium. N

PM
Particulate matter. U

PM_{10}
Particulate matter with an aerodynamic diameter less than or equal to a nominal 10 micrometers as measured by a reference method based on appendix J of part 50 [40 CFR] and designated in accordance with part 53 or by an equivalent method designated in accordance with part 53. A

PM_{10} emissions
Finely divided solid or liquid material, with an aerodynamic diameter less than or equal to a nominal 10 micrometers emitted to the ambient air as measured by an applicable reference method, or an equivalent or alternative method, specified in [40 CFR] or by a test method specified in an approved State implementation plan. A

PM_{15}
Particulate matter (nominally 15m and less). N

PMN
(1) Premanufacture notification. Section 5(a) of TSCA requires that a manufacturer must notify EPA 90 days before producing a new chemical; see premanufacture notice. U

ENVIRONMENTAL REGULATORY GLOSSARY 417

pneumatic ash handling
A system of pipes and cyclone separators that conveys fly ash or floor dust to a bin via an air stream. U

pneumatic coal-cleaning equipment
Any facility which classifies bituminous coal by size or separates bituminous coal from refuse by application of air stream(s). A

pneumatic collection of solid waste
A mechanical system that uses a high-velocity air stream to convey solid waste dropped from standard gravity chutes through transport pipes to a collection point. U

pneumoconiosis
A condition of the lung in which there is permanent deposition of particulate matter and the tissue reaction to its presence. It may range from relatively harmless forms of iron oxide deposition to destructive forms of silicosis. N

POE
Point of exposure. N

POHC
Principal organic hazardous constituents. U

point of access
All areas used by employees for work-related passage from one area or level to another. Such open areas include doorways, passageways, stairway openings, studded walls, and various other permanent or temporary openings used for such travel. O

point of operation
That point at which cutting, shaping, or forming is accomplished upon the stock and shall include such other points as may offer a hazard to the operator in inserting or manipulating the stock in the operation of the machine. O

point of waste generation
The location where samples of a waste stream are collected for the purpose of determining the waste flow rate, water content, or benzene concentration in accordance with procedures specified in § 61.355 of [40 CFR]. For a chemical manufacturing plant or petroleum refinery, the point of waste generation is a location after the waste stream exits the process unit component, product tank, or waste management unit generating the waste, and before the waste is exposed to the atmosphere or mixed with other wastes. For a coke-by-product recovery plant subject to and complying with the control requirements of §§ 61.132, 61.133, or 61.134 of [40 CFR], the point of waste generation is a location after the waste stream exits the process unit component or waste management unit controlled by that subpart, and before the waste is exposed to the atmosphere. For other facilities subject to [40 CFR], the point of waste generation is a location after the waste enters the facility, and before the waste is exposed to the atmosphere or placed in a facility waste management unit. A

point source
(1) Any discernible, confined, and

discrete conveyance, including but not limited to, any pipe, ditch, channel, tunnel, conduit, well, discrete fissure, container, rolling stock, concentrated animal feeding operation, landfill leachate collection system, vessel or other floating craft from which pollutants are or may be discharged. This term does not include return flows from irrigated agriculture or agricultural storm water runoff. A (2) For particulate matter, sulfur oxides, carbon monoxide, hydrocarbons, and nitrogen dioxide--(a) Any stationary source the actual emissions of which are in excess of 90.7 metric tons (100 tons) per year of the pollutant in a region containing an area whose 1970 "urban place" population, as defined by the U.S. Bureau of the Census, was equal to or greater than 1 million; (b) Any stationary source the actual emissions of which are in excess of 22.7 metric tons (25 tons) per year of the pollutant in a region containing an area whose 1970 "urban place" population, as defined by the U.S. Bureau of the Census was less than 1 million; or (c) Without regard to amount of emissions, stationary sources such as those listed in Appendix C to this part. (3) For lead, any stationary source the actual emissions of which are in excess of 4.54 metric tons (5 tons) per year of lead or lead compounds measured as elemental lead. A

point source load allocations
(1) For each water quality segment, the individual load allocation for point sources of pollutants, including thermal load allocations. (Note: In those segments where water quality standards are established at levels less stringent than necessary to achieve the 1983 water quality goals specified in Section 101(a)(2) of the [Federal Water Pollution Control] Act, the Regional Administrator may request the State to provide appropriate information, such as wasteload allocation information which may be relevant in making water quality related effluent limitation determinations pursuant to Section 302 of the [Federal Water Pollution Control] Act). A [ed. Load allocations determine how much pollution each source in a stream segment can contribute without water quality standards being violated].

point-of-entry treatment device
A treatment device applied to the drinking water entering a house or building for the purpose of reducing contaminants in the drinking water distributed throughout the house or building. A

poison, class A
A DOT term for extremely dangerous poisons -- poisonous gases or liquids that, in very small amounts, either as gas or as vapor of the liquid, mixed with air, are dangerous to life. Examples: phosgene, cyanogen, hydrocyanic acid, nitrogen peroxide. N

poison, class B
A DOT term for liquid, solid, paste or semisolid substances--other than Class A poisons or irritating materials --that are known (or presumed on the basis of animal tests) to be so toxic

to humans that they are a hazard to health during transportation. N

polarization
In electromagnetic waves, refers to the direction of the electric field vector. U

pollen
(1) A fine dust produced by plants. (2) The fertilizing element of flowering plants. (3) A natural or background air pollutant. N

pollutant
Dredged spoil, solid waste, incinerator residue, filter backwash, sewage, garbage, sewage sludge, munitions, chemical wastes, biological materials, radioactive materials (except those regulated under the Atomic Energy Act of 1954, as amended (42 U.S.C. 2011 et seq.)), heat, wrecked or discarded equipment, rock, sand, cellar dirt and industrial, municipal, and agricultural waste discharged into water. It also does not mean sewage from vessels, or water, gas, or other material which is injected into a well to facilitate production of oil and gas, or water derived in association with oil and gas production and disposed of in a well, if the well used either to facilitate production or for disposal purposes is approved by authority of the State in which the well is located, and if the State determines that the injection or disposal will not result in the degradation of ground or surface water resources. A

pollutant (NPDES and 404 of FWPCA)
(1) Generally, any substance introduced into the environment that adversely affects the usefulness of a resource. N (2) Dredged spoil, solid waste, incinerator residue, sewage, garbage, sewage sludge, munitions, chemical wastes, biological materials, radioactive materials, heat, wrecked or discarded equipment, rock, sand, cellar dirt and industrial, municipal, and agricultural waste discharged into water. It does not mean: (a) "sewage from vessels" within the meaning of section 312 of this [Clean Water] Act; or (b) water, gas, or other material which is injected into a well to facilitate production of oil or gas, or water derived in association with oil and gas production and disposed of in a well, if the well used either to facilitate production or for disposal purposes is approved by authority of the state in which the well is located, and if the state determines that such injection or disposal will not result in the degradation of ground or surface water resources. D Radioactive materials covered by the Atomic Energy Act are those encompassed in its definition of source, byproduct, or special nuclear produced isotopes. See *Train v. Colorado Public Interest Research Group, Inc.*, 426 U.S. 1 (1976). A

pollutant or contaminant (CERCLA)
Any element, substance, compound, or mixture, including disease causing agents, which after release into the environment and upon exposure, ingestion, inhalation, or assimilation into any organism, either directly from the environment or indirectly by ingesting through food chains, will or may reasonably be anticipated to cause death, disease, behavioral

abnormalities, cancer, genetic mutation, physiological malfunctions (including malfunctions in reproduction), or physical deformation in such organisms or their offspring. The term does not include petroleum, including crude oil and any fraction thereof which is not otherwise specifically listed or designated as a hazardous substance under section 101(14) (A) through (F) of CERCLA, nor does it include natural gas, liquified natural gas, or synthetic gas of pipeline quality (or mixtures of natural gas and synthetic gas). The term pollutant or contaminant means any pollutant or contaminant which may present an imminent and substantial danger to public health or welfare. (as defined by section 104(a)(2) of CERCLA). A

pollutant standard index
PSI. Measure of adverse health effects of air pollution levels in major cities. N

pollution
(1) The presence of matter or energy whose nature, location or quantity produces undesired environmental effects; for purposes of the Federal Water Pollution Control Act, pollution is the man-made or man induced alteration of the chemical, physical, biological and radiological integrity of water. L, D (2) The man-made or man induced alteration of the chemical, physical, biological and radiological integrity of water. A

polyaromatic hydrocarbons
A highly reactive group of organiccompounds, at least some of which are carcinogens. U

polychlorinated biphenyls
(1) PCBs. A mixture of compounds composed of the biphenyl molecule which has been chlorinated to varying degrees. A (2) Solid waste containing concentrations of PCBs equal to or greater than 10 mg/kg (dry weight) is incorporated into the soil when applied to land used for producing animal feed, including pasture crops for animals raised for milk. Incorporation of the solid waste into the soil is not required if it is assured that the PCB content is less than 0.2 mg/kg (actual weight) in animal feed or less than 1.5 mg/kg (fat basis) in milk. A

polyectrolytes
Synthetic chemicals that help solids to clump during sewage treatment. N

polyethylene
A family of resins obtained by polymerizing ethylene gas. They are grouped into two major categories, HDPE and PET. U

polymer
Any of the natural or synthetic compounds of usually high molecular weight that consist of many repeated links, each link being a relatively light and simple molecule. A

polyvinyl chloride
A plastic that releases hydrochloric acid when burned. L

POM
Polycyclic organic matter. N

pond water surface area
When used for the purpose of

calculating the volume of waste water shall mean the area within the impoundment for rainfall and the actual water surface area for evaporation. A

population
A group of interbreeding organisms of the same kind occupying a particular space. Generically, the number of humans or other living creatures in a designated area. N

population dose
The sum of radiation doses of individuals and is expressed in units of person-rem (e.g., if 1,000 people each received a radiation dose of 1 rem, their population dose would be 1,000 person-rem). U

population variability
The concept of differences in susceptibility of individuals within a population to toxicants due to variations such as genetic differences in metabolism and response of biological tissue to chemicals. N

porcelain enameling
The entire process of applying a fused vitreous enamel coating to a metal basis material. Usually this includes metal preparation and coating operations. A

portable air compressor
Any wheel, skid, truck, or railroad car mounted, but not self-propelled, equipment designed to activate pneumatic tools. This consists of an air compressor (air end); and a reciprocating rotary or turbine engine rigidly connected in permanent alignment and mounted on a common frame. Also included are all cooling, lubricating, regulating, starting, and fuel systems, and all equipment necessary to constitute a complete, self-contained unit with a rated capacity of 75 cfm or greater which delivers air at pressures greater than 50 psig, but does not include any pneumatic tools themselves. A

portable grinding
A grinding operation where the grinding machine is designed to be hand held and may be easily moved from one location to another. O

portable tank
A closed container having a liquid capacity more than 60 U.S. gallons, and not intended for fixed installation. O

portable x-ray
X-ray equipment designed to be hand-carried. O

portal of entry effects.
Biological response at the site of entry (e.g., the lungs, stomach) of a toxicant into the body. N

posing an exposure risk to food or feed
Being in any location where human food or animal feed products could be exposed to PCBs released from a PCB item. A PCB item poses an exposure risk to food or feed if PCBs released in any way from the PCB item have a potential pathway to human food or animal feed. EPA considers human food or animal feed to include items regulated by the U.S. Department of Agriculture or the Food and Drug

Administration as human food or animal feed; this includes direct additives. Food or feed is excluded from this definition if it is used or stored in private homes. A

positive crankcase ventilation (PCV) valves
The emission-critical parameter for a PCV valve is the volume of flow as a function of pressure differential across the valve. A

positive results in short-term tests
Positive results in assays for two or more of the following types of effect: (1) The induction of DNA damage and/or repair; (2) mutagenesis in bacteria, yeast, Neurospora or Drosophila melanogaster; (3) mutagenesis in mammalian somatic cells; (4) mutagenesis in mammalian germinal cells; or (5) neoplastic transformation of mammalian cells in culture. O

positive-pressure breathing apparatus
A self-contained breathing apparatus in which the pressure in the breathing zone is positive in relation to the immediate environment during inhalation and exhalation. O

positive-pressure fabric filter
A fabric filter with the fans on the upstream side of the filter bags. A

possession or control
In possession or control of the submitter, or of any subsidiary, partnership in which the submitter is a general partner, parent company, or any company or partnership which the parent company owns or controls, if the subsidiary, parent company, or other company or partnership is associated with the submitter in the research, development, test marketing, or commercial marketing of the chemical substance in question. (A parent company owns or controls another company if the parent owns or controls 50 percent or more of the other company's voting stock. A parent company owns or controls any partnership in which it is a general partner). Information is included within this definition if it is: (1) In the submitter's own files including files maintained by employees in the course of their employment. (2) In commercially available data bases to which the submitter has purchased access. (3) Maintained in the files in the course of employment by other agents of the submitter who are associated with research, development, test marketing, or commercial marketing of the chemical substance in question. A

post consumer waste
PCW. A material or product that has served its intended use and has been discarded for disposal after passing through the hands of a final user. PCW is a part of the broader category "recycled material." A

post emergency response
That portion of an emergency response performed after the immediate threat of a release has been stabilized or eliminated and clean-up of the site has begun. If post emergency response is performed by an employer's own employees who were part of the initial emergency response, it is considered to be part of the

initial response and not post emergency response. However, if a group of an employer's own employees, separate from the group providing initial response, performs the clean-up operation, then the separate group of employees would be considered to be performing post-emergency response. O

post-closure
The time period following the shutdown of a waste management or manufacturing facility. For monitoring purposes, this is often considered to be 30 years. N

post-closure plan
The plan for post-closure care prepared in accordance with the requirements of §§ 264.117 and 264.120 [of 40 CFR parts 260-299]. A

post-mining area
(1) A reclamation area or (2) the underground workings of an underground coal mine after the extraction, removal, or recovery of coal from its natural deposit has ceased and prior to bond release. A

postconsumer recovered paper
(1) Paper, paperboard and fibrous wastes from retail stores, office buildings, homes and so forth, after they have passed through their end-usage as a consumer item including: used corrugated boxes; old newspapers; old magazines; mixed waste paper; tabulating cards and used cordage.; and (2) All paper, paperboard and fibrous wastes that enter and are collected from municipal solid waste. A

potable water
(1) Water that is safe for drinking and cooking. N (2) Water which meets the quality standards prescribed in the U.S. Public Health Service Drinking Water Standards, published in 42 CFR part 72, or water which is approved for drinking purposes by the State or local authority having jurisdiction. O

potency
A comparative expression of chemical or drug activity measured in terms of the relationship between the incidence or intensity of a particular effect and the associated dose of a chemical, to a given or implied standard or reference. N

potential combustion concentration
[From a utility boiler] the theoretical emissions (ng/J, lb/million Btu net input) that would result from combustion of a fuel in an uncleaned state (without emission control systems) and: (a) For particulate matter is: (1) 3,000 ng/J (7.0 lb/million Btu) heat input for solid fuel; and (2) 75 ng/J (0.17 lb/million Btu) heat input for liquid fuels. (b) For sulfur dioxide is determined under [40 CFR] § 60.48a(b). (c) For nitrogen oxides is: (1) 290 ng/J (0.67 lb/million Btu) heat input for gaseous fuels; (2) 310 ng/J (0.72 lb/million Btu) heat input for liquid fuels; and (3) 990 ng/J (2.30 lb/million Btu) heat input for solid fuels. A

potential damage
Circumstances in which: (1) Friable ACBM is in an area regularly used by building occupants, including maintenance personnel, in the course

of their normal activities. (2) There are indications that there is a reasonable likelihood that the material or its covering will become damaged, deteriorated, or delaminated due to factors such as changes in building use, changes in operations and maintenance practices, changes in occupancy, or recurrent damage. A

potential electrical output capacity
Thirty-three (33) percent of the maximum design heat input capacity of the steam generating unit (e.g., a steam generating unit with a 100-MW (340 million Btu/hr) fossil-fuel heat input capacity would have a 33-MW potential electrical output capacity). For electric utility combined cycle gas turbines the potential electrical output capacity is determined on the basis of the fossil-fuel firing capacity of the steam generator exclusive of the heat input and electrical power contribution by the gas turbine. A

potential occupational carcinogen
Any substance, or combination or mixture of substances, which causes an increased incidence of benign and/or malignant neoplasms, or a substantial decrease in the latency period between exposure and onset of neoplasms in humans or in one or more experimental mammalian species as the result of any oral, respiratory or dermal exposure, or any other exposure which results in the induction of tumors at a site other than the site of administration. This definition also includes any substance which is metabolized into one or more potential occupational carcinogens by mammals. O

potential significant damage
Circumstances in which: (1) Friable ACBM is in an area regularly used by building occupants, including maintenance personnel, in the course of their normal activities. (2) There are indications that there is a reasonable likelihood that the material or its covering will become significantly damaged, deteriorated, or delaminated due to factors such as changes in building use, changes in operations and maintenance practices, changes in occupancy, or recurrent damage. (3) The material is subject to major or continuing disturbance, due to factors including, but not limited to, accessibility or, under certain circumstances, vibration or air erosion. A

potential sulfur dioxide emission rate
The theoretical sulfur dioxide emissions (ng/J, lb/million Btu heat input) that would result from combusting fuel in an uncleaned state and without using emission control systems. A

potential to emit
The capability at maximum design capacity to emit a pollutant after the application of air pollution control equipment. Annual potential shall be based on the larger of the maximum annual rated capacity of the stationary source assuming continuous operation, or on a projection of actual annual emissions. Enforceable permit conditions on the type of materials combusted or processed may be used in determining the annual potential. Fugitive emissions, to the extent quantifiable, will be considered in

determining annual potential for those stationary sources whose fugitive emissions are regulated by the applicable state implementation plan. A

potentially responsible party
PRP. Any individual or company--including owners, operators, transporters or generators--potentially responsible for, or contributing to, the contamination problems at a Superfund site. Whenever possible, EPA requires PRPs, through administrative and legal actions, to clean up hazardous waste sites they have contaminated. N

potroom
A building unit which houses a group of electrolytic cells in which aluminum is produced. A

POTW
Publicly owned treatment works. (1) A treatment works as defined by section 212(2) of the [Clean Water] Act, which is owned by a State, municipality, or intermunicipal or interstate agency. A (2) Any device or system used in the treatment (including recycling and reclamation) of municipal sewage or industrial wastes of a liquid nature which is owned by a "state" or "municipality" (as defined by Section 502(4) of the Clean Water Act). This definition includes sewers, pipes, or other conveyances only if they convey wastewater to a POTW providing treatment. A

pour point
The lowest temperature at which an oil will flow or can be poured under specified conditions of test. A

poured socket
The method of providing wire rope terminations in which the ends of the rope are held in a tapered socket by means of poured spelter or resins. O

powder coating
Any surface coating that is applied as a dry powder and is fused into a continuous coating film through the use of heat. A

powder or dry solid form
A state where all or part of the substance would have the potential to become fine, loose, solid particles. A

power and control tray cable
Type TC power and control tray cable is a factory assembly of two or more insulated conductors, with or without associated bare or covered grounding conductors under a nonmetallic sheath, approved for installation in cable trays, in raceways, or where supported by a messenger wire. O

power density
The intensity of electromagnetic radiation power per unit area expressed as watts/cm^2. U

power fuse
(Over 600 volts, nominal). See: fuse. O

power outlet
An enclosed assembly which may include receptacles, circuit breakers, fuseholders, fused switches, buses and watt-hour meter mounting means; intended to supply and control power to mobile homes, recreational vehicles

or boats, or to serve as a means for distributing power required to operate mobile or temporarily installed equipment. O

power sales agreement
A legally-binding document between a firm associated with a new independent power production facility (IPPF) or a new IPPF and a regulated electric utility that establishes the terms and conditions for the sale of power from a specific new IPPF to the utility. A

power setting
The power or thrust output of an engine in terms of kilonewtons thrust for turbojet and turbofan engines and shaft power in terms of kilowatts for turboprop engines. A

ppb
Abbreviation for parts per billion. U

PPETS
Pretreatment Permitting and Enforcement Tracking System under NPDES. U

ppm.
Abbreviation for parts per million by volume. A

PPSP
Power Plant Siting Program. N

PQL
Practical quantitation level. The lowest level that can be reliably achieved within specified limits of precision and accuracy during routine laboratory operating conditions. U

practicable
(1) Capable of being used consistent with: performance in accordance with applicable specifications, availability at a reasonable price, availability within a reasonable period of time, and maintenance of a satisfactory level of competition. A (2) Available and capable of being done after taking into consideration cost, existing technology, and logistics in light of overall project purposes. A (3) Capable of being done within existing constraints. The test of what is practicable depends upon the situation and includes consideration of the pertinent factors such as environment, community welfare, cost, or technology. A

practical knowledge
The possession of pertinent facts and comprehension together with the ability to use them in dealing with specific problems and situations. A

practice
The act of disposal of solid waste. A, O

pre-certification vehicle
An uncertified vehicle which a manufacturer employs in fleets from year to year in the ordinary course of business for product development, production method assessment, and market promotion purposes, but in a manner not involving lease or sale. A

pre-certification vehicle engine
An uncertified heavy duty engine owned by a manufacturer and used in a manner not involving lease or sale in a vehicle employed from year to

year in the ordinary course of business for product development, production method assessment and market promotion purposes. A

pre-discharge employee alarm
An alarm which will sound at a set time prior to actual discharge of an extinguishing system so that employees may evacuate the discharge area prior to system discharge. O

pre-verification exemption
A testing exemption which is applicable to products manufactured prior to product verification, and used by a manufacturer from year to year in the ordinary course of business, for product development, production method assessment, and market promotion purposes, but in a manner not involving lease or sale. A

precious metals
Gold, platinum, palladium and silver and their alloys. Any alloy containing 30 or greater percent by weight of precious metals is considered a precious metal. A

precipitate
A solid that separates from a solution because of some chemical or physical change. N

precipitation
Removal of solids from liquid waste so that the hazardous solid portion can be disposed of safely; removal of particles from airborne emissions. N

precipitation bath
The water, solvent, or other chemical bath into which the polymer or prepolymer (partially reacted material) solution is extruded, and that causes physical or chemical changes to occur in the extruded solution to result in a semihardened polymeric fiber. A

precipitation event, 1-year, 2-year, and 10-year, 24-hour
The maximum 24-hour precipitation event with a probable recurrence interval of once in one, two, and ten years respectively as defined by the National Weather Service and Technical Paper No. 40, "Rainfall Frequency Atlas of the U.S.," May 1961, or equivalent regional or rainfall probability information developed therefrom. A

precipitators
Air pollution control devices that collect particles from an emission by mechanical or electrical means. N

preconditioning
The operation of an automobile through one (1) EPA Urban Dynamometer Driving Schedule, described in 40 CFR Part 86. A

precontrolled vehicles
Light duty vehicles sold nationally (except in California) prior to the 1968 model-year and light-duty vehicles sold in California prior to the 1966 model year. A

precursor
(1) In photochemical terminology, a compound such as a volatile organic compound (VOC) that "precedes" an oxidant. Precursors react in sunlight to form ozone or other photochemical oxidants. N (2) A pollutant that takes

part in a chemical reaction resulting in the formation of one or more new pollutants. U

preferential bus/carpool lane
Any requirement for the setting aside of one or more lanes of a street or highway on a permanent or temporary basis for the exclusive use of buses or carpools, or both. B

preferential treatment
For any class of vehicles, means either the setting aside of one traffic lane for the exclusive use of such vehicles or other measures (for example, access metering or setting aside the entire street), which the EPA Administrator finds would be at least equal in VMT reduction effect to the establishment of such a lane. A

preliminary analysis
The engineering analysis performed by EPA prior to testing prescribed by the Administrator based on data and information submitted by a manufacturer or available from other sources. A

preliminary assessment
PA. Review of existing information and an off-site reconnaissance, if appropriate, to determine if a release may require additional investigation or action. A PA may include an on-site reconnaissance, if appropriate. A

premanufacture notice
PMN. Any notice submitted to EPA pursuant to [40 CFR] section 5(a)(1)(A) of the Clean Air Act in accordance with part 720. A

premanufacture notification
See PMN. U

preponderance of the evidence
Proof by information that, compared with that opposing it, leads to the conclusion that the fact at issue is more probably true than not. A

presence sensing device
A device designed, constructed and arranged to create a sensing field or area and to deactivate the clutch control of the press when an operator's hand or any other parts of his body is within such field or area. O

presiding officer
The official, without regard to whether he is designated as an administrative law judge or a hearing officer or examiner, who presides at the adversary adjudication. A

press
A mechanically powered machine that shears, punches, forms or assembles metal or other material by means of cutting, shaping, or combination dies attached to slides. A press consists of a stationary bed or anvil, and a slide (or slides) having a controlled reciprocating motion toward and away from the bed surface, the slide being guided in a definite path by the frame of the press. O

pressed and blown glass
Glass which is pressed, blown, or both, including textile fiberglass, noncontinuous flat glass, noncontainer glass, and other products listed in SIC 3229. It is separated into: (1) Glass

of borosilicate recipe. (2) Glass of soda-lime and lead recipes. (3) Glass of opal, fluoride, and other recipes. A

pressure
A force acting on a unit area. Usually shown as pounds per square inch (p.s.i.). A

pressure drop
A measure, in kilopascals, of the difference in static pressure measured immediately upstream and downstream of the air filter elements. A

pressure sewers
A system of pipes in which water, wastewater, or other liquid is transported to a higher elevation by use of pumping force. N

pressure vessel
A storage tank or vessel which has been designed to operate at pressures above 15 p.s.i.g. O

pressurized water reactor
PWR. A power reactor in which heat is transferred from the core to a heat exchanger by water kept under high pressure to achieve high temperature without boiling in the primary system. Steam is generated in a secondary circuit. Many reactors producing electric power are pressurized water reactors. U

pretreatment
The reduction of the amount of pollutants, the elimination of pollutants, or the alteration of the nature of pollutant properties in wastewater to a less harmful state prior to or in lieu of discharging or otherwise introducing such pollutants into a POTW. The reduction or alteration can be obtained by physical, chemical or biological processes, process changes or by other means. A

pretreatment control authority
(1) The POTW if the POTW's submission for its pretreatment program has been approved in accordance with the requirements of 40 CFR 403.11, or (2) The Approval Authority if the submission has not been approved. A

pretreatment requirements
Any substantive or procedural requirement related to pretreatment imposed on an industrial user. A

pretreatment standard
Any regulation containing pollutant discharge limits promulgated by the EPA in accordance with section 307(b) and (c) of the Federal Water Pollution Control Act, which applies to industrial users of a publicly owned treatment works. Further, any state or local pretreatment requirement applicable to a discharge and which is incorporated into a permit issued to a publicly owned treatment works under section 402 of the Federal Water Pollution Control Act. A

prevalence
The percentage of a population that is affected with a particular disease at a given time. N

prevention
Measures taken to minimize the release of wastes to the environment. N

prevention of significant deterioration

PSD. The policy incorporated in the CAA that limits increases in clean air areas to certain increments even though ambient air quality standards are being met. The policy is premised on the assumption that air quality better than ambient air quality standards is a valuable resource that should be protected, particularly around undeveloped areas of special importance such as national parks. U

preventive measures

Actions taken to reduce disturbance of ACBM or otherwise eliminate the reasonable likelihood of the material's becoming damaged or significantly damaged. A

primary aluminum reduction plant

Any facility manufacturing aluminum by electrolytic reduction. A

primary brake

A brake designed to be applied automatically whenever power to the prime mover is interrupted or discontinued. O

primary combustion air

The air admitted to a combustion system when the fuel is first oxidized. U

primary contact recreation

Activities where a person would have direct contact with water to the point of complete submergence, including but not limited to skin diving, swimming, and water skiing. A

primary control system

An air pollution control system designed to remove gaseous and particulate fluorides from exhaust gases which are captured at the cell. A

primary drinking water regulation

A regulation which--(A) applies to public water systems; (B) specifies contaminants which, in the judgment of the Administrator [of EPA], may have any adverse effect on the health of persons; (C) specifies for each such contaminant either--(i) a maximum contaminant level, if, in the judgment of the Administrator [of EPA], it is economically and technologically feasible to ascertain the level of such contaminant in water in public water systems, or (ii) if, in the judgment of the Administrator [of EPA], it is not economically or technologically feasible to so ascertain the level of such contaminant, each treatment technique known to the Administrator [of EPA] which leads to a reduction in the level of such contaminant sufficient to satisfy the requirements of [40 CFR § 1412; and (D) contains criteria and procedures to assure a supply of drinking water which dependably complies with such maximum contaminant levels; including quality control and testing procedures to insure compliance with such levels and to insure proper operation and maintenance of the system, and requirements as to (i) the minimum quality of water which may be taken into the system and (ii) siting for new facilities for public water systems. J

primary emission control system

The combination of equipment used for the capture and collection of

primary emissions (e.g., an open hood capture system used in conjunction with a particulate matter cleaning device such as an electrostatic precipitator or a closed hood capture system used in conjunction with a particulate matter cleaning device such as a scrubber). A

primary enforcement responsibility
The primary responsibility for administration and enforcement of primary drinking water regulations and related requirements applicable to public water systems within a State. A

primary industry category
Any industry category listed in the NRDC Settlement Agreement (*Natural Resources Defense Council v. Train*, 8 ERC 2120 [D.D.C. 1976], modified 12 ERC 1833 [D.D.C. 1979]). N Also listed in Appendix A of Part 122. A

primary intended service class
(a) The primary service application group for which a heavy-duty diesel engine is designed and marketed, as determined by the manufacturer. The primary intended service classes are designated as light, medium, and heavy heavy-duty diesel engines. The determination is based on factors such as vehicle GVW, vehicle usage and operating patterns, other vehicle design characteristics, engine horsepower, and other engine design and operating characteristics. A

primary metal cast
The metal that is poured in the greatest quantity at an individual plant. A

primary oxygen blow
The period in the steel production cycle of a Basic Oxygen Process Furnace (BOFP) during which a high volume of oxygen-rich gas is introduced to the bath of molten iron by means of a lance inserted from the top of the vessel. This definition does not include any additional, or secondary, oxygen blows made after the primary blow. A

primary panel
The surface that is considered to be the front surface or that surface which is intended for initial viewing at the point of ultimate sale or the point of distribution for use. A

primary pollutant
A pollutant emitted directly from a polluting source. U

primary processor of asbestos
A person who processes bulk asbestos to make an asbestos mixture or a product that contains asbestos. A primary processor who makes an asbestos mixture and then processes the asbestos mixture at the same site to make a different end product should report production of the final end product. Primary processing includes the mixing or repackaging of raw asbestos fiber. A

primary recipient
Any recipient which is authorized or required to extend Federal financial assistance to another recipient for the purpose of carrying out a program for which it receives Federal financial assistance. A

primary resistor
A device used in the primary circuit of an inductive ignition system to limit the flow of current. A

primary settling tank
The first settling tank for the removal of settleable solids through which wastewater is passed in a treatment works. U

primary standard
A national primary ambient air quality standard promulgated pursuant to section 109 of the [Clean Air] Act. A [ed. Intended to establish a level of air quality that, with an adequate margin of error, will protect public health].

primary standard attainment date
The date specified in the applicable implementation plan for the attainment of a national primary ambient air quality standard for any air pollutant. B

primary treatment
The first stage in wastewater treatment where substantially all floating or settleable solids, are removed by flotation and/or sedimentation. A

primary waste treatment
First steps in wastewater treatment; screen and sedimentation tanks are sued to remove most materials that floats or settle. Primary treatment results in the removal of about 30 percent of carbonaceous biochemical oxygen demand from domestic sewage. N

primary zinc smelter
Any installation engaged in the production, or any intermediate process in the production, of zinc or zinc oxide from the zinc sulfide ore concentrates through the use of pyrometallurgical techniques. A

prime coat operation
(1) The prime coat spray booth or dip tank, flash-off area, and bake oven(s) which are used to apply and dry or cure the initial coating on components of automobile or light-duty truck bodies. A (2) The coating application station, curing oven, and quench station used to apply and dry or cure the initial coating(s) on the surface of the metal coil. A

prime movers
Include steam, gas, oil, and air engines, motors, steam and hydraulic turbines, and other equipment used as a source of power. O

principal
Officer, director, owner, partner, key employee, or other person within a participant with primary management or supervisory responsibilities; or a person who has a critical influence on or substantive control over a covered transaction, whether or not employed by the participant. Persons who have a critical influence on or substantive control over a covered transaction are: (1) Principal investigators. (2) Bid and proposal estimators and preparers. A

principal importer
The first importer who, knowing that a new chemical substance will be imported rather than manufactured domestically, specifies the identity of

the chemical substance and the total amount to be imported. Only persons who are incorporated, licensed, or doing business in the United States may be principal importers. A

principal organic hazardous constituents
POHC. Constituents specified in an incinerator's facility permit from among those constituents listed in [40 CFR] Part 261, Appendix VIII, for each waste feed to be burned. This specification is based on degree of difficulty of incineration, of organic constituents in the waste, and on their concentration or mass in the waste feed. N

principal residence
Normally the voting residence, the habitation of the family or household which occupies the space for at least 51 percent of the time annually. Second homes, vacation, or recreation residences are not included in this definition. A commercial establishment with waste water flow equal to or smaller than one user equivalent (generally 300 gallons per day dry weather flows) is included. A

principal sponsor
An individual sponsor or the joint sponsor who assumes primary responsibility for the direction of a study and for oral and written communication with EPA. A

principally traded
The market place at which the greatest volume of trades normally occur. O

printing
The application of words, designs, and pictures to a substrate using ink. A

printing paper
Paper designed for printing, other than newsprint, such as offset and book paper. A

priority I regions
Any area with greater ambient concentrations of the following: (1) Sulfur dioxide--100 g/m^3 (0.04 ppm) annual arithmetic mean; 445 g/m^3 (0.17 ppm) 24-hour maximum. (2) Particulate matter--95 g/m^3 annual geometric mean; 325 g/m^3 24-hour maximum. (3) Carbon monoxide-- 55mg/m^3 (48 ppm) 1-hour maximum; 14mg/m^3 (12 ppm) 8-hour maximum. (4) Nitrogen dioxide--100 g/m^3 (0.06 ppm) annual arithmetic mean. (5) Ozone 195 g/m^3 (0.10 ppm) 1-hour maximum. A

priority IA region
Any area which is Priority I primarily because of emissions from a single point source. A

priority II region
Any area which is not a Priority I region and has ambient concentrations between the following: (1) Sulfur Dioxides--60-100 g/m^3 (0.02-0.04 ppm) annual arithmetic mean; 260-445 g/m^3 (0.10-0.17 ppm) 24-hour maximum; any concentration above 1,300 g/m^3 (0.50 ppm) three-hour average. (2) Particulate matter-- 60-95 g/m^3 annual geometric mean; 150-325 $/m^3$ 24-hour maximum. A

priority III region
Areas which do not meet the criteria for Priority I or II. A

priority water quality areas
For the purposes of [40 CFR] §35.2015, specific stream segments or bodies of water, as determined by the State, where municipal discharges have resulted in the impairment of a designated use or significant public health risks, and where the reduction of pollution from such discharges will substantially restore surface or groundwater uses. A

private applicator
A certified applicator who uses or supervises the use of any pesticide which is classified for restricted use for purposes of producing any agricultural commodity on property owned or rented by him or his employer or (if applied without compensation other than trading of personal services between producers of agricultural commodities) on the property of another person. C

private carrier of property by motor vehicle
Any person not included in terms "common carrier by motor vehicle" or "contract carrier by motor vehicle," who or which transports in interstate or foreign commerce by motor vehicle property of which such person is the owner, lessee, or bailee, when such transportation is for sale, lease, rent or bailment, or in furtherance of any commercial enterprise. A

private collection
The collecting of solid wastes for which citizens or firms, individually or in limited groups, pay collectors or private operating agencies. U

privately owned treatment works
Any device or system which is (a) used to treat wastes from any facility whose operator is not the operator of the treatment works and (b) not a "POTW" [publicly owned treatment work]. A, M

probit model
A dose-response model that can be derived under the assumption that individual tolerance is a random variable following log normal distribution. N

proceeding
Any rulemaking, adjudication, or licensing conducted by EPA under Federal environmental statutes or under regulations which implement those Acts. A

process
The preparation of a chemical substance or mixture, after its manufacture, for distribution in commerce (1) in the same form or physical state as, or in a different form or physical state from, that in which it was received by the person so preparing such substance or mixture, or (2) as part of a mixture or article containing the chemical substance or mixture. A, K

process emissions
Emissions that are captured directly at the source of generation. A

process for commercial purposes
The preparation of a chemical substance or mixture containing the chemical substance after manufacture of the substance, for distribution in commerce with the purpose of obtaining an immediate or eventual commercial advantage for the processor. Processing of any amount of a chemical substance or mixture is included in this definition. If a chemical substance or mixture containing impurities is processed for commercial purpose, then the impurities also are processed for commercial purposes. A

process fugitive emissions
Particulate matter emissions from an affected facility that are not collected by a capture system. A

process gas
Any gas generated by a petroleum refinery process unit, except fuel gas and process upset gas. A

process generated waste water
Water directly or indirectly used in the operation of a feedlot for any or all of the following: spillage or overflow from animal or poultry watering systems; washing, cleaning or flushing pens, barns, manure pits or other feedlot facilities; direct contact swimming, washing or spray cooling of animals; and dust control. A

process heater
A device that transfers heat liberated by burning fuel to fluids contained in tubes, except water that is heated to produce steam. A

process improvement
Routine changes made for safety and occupational health requirements, for energy savings, for better utility, for ease of maintenance and operation, for correction of design deficiencies, for bottleneck removal, for changing product requirements, or for environmental control. A

process solely for export
To process for commercial purposes solely for export from the United States under the following restriction on domestic activity: Processing must be performed at sites under the control of the processor; distribution in commerce is limited to purposes of export; and the processor may not use the chemical substance except in small quantities solely for research and development. A

process stream
All reasonably anticipated transfer, flow, or disposal of a chemical substance, regardless of physical state or concentration, through all intended operations of processing, including the cleaning of equipment. A

process unit shutdown
A work practice or operational procedure that stops production from a process unit or part of a process unit. An unscheduled work practice or operational procedure that stops production from a process unit or part of a process unit for less than 24 hours is not a process unit shutdown. The use of spare equipment and technically feasible bypassing of equipment without stopping production are not process unit shutdowns. A

process upset gas
Any gas generated by a petroleum refinery process unit as a result of start-up, shut-down, upset or malfunction. A

process wastes
Any designated toxic pollutant, whether in wastewater or otherwise present, which is inherent to or unavoidable resulting from any manufacturing process, including that which comes into direct contact with or results from the production or use of any raw material, intermediate product, finished product, byproduct or waste product and is discharged into the navigable waters. A

process wastewater
(1) Any water which, during manufacturing or processing, comes into direct contact with or results from the production use of any raw material, intermediate product, finished product, byproduct, or waste product. A (2) The term "process wastewater" does not include contaminated non-process wastewater. A (3) Also specifically excludes noncontact cooling water, material storage yard runoff (either raw material or processed wood storage), and boiler blowdown. For the dry process hardboard, veneer, finishing, particleboard, and sawmills and planing mills subcategories, fire control water is excluded from the definition. A (4) In the case of tire and inner tube plants constructed before 1959, discharges from the following: soapstone solution applications; steam cleaning operations; air pollution control equipment; unroofed process oil unloading areas; mold cleaning operations; latex applications; and air compressor receivers. Discharges from other areas of such plants shall not be classified as process waste water for the purposes of this section. A (5) Any process generated waste water and any precipitation (rain or snow) which comes into contact with any manure, litter or bedding, or any other raw material or intermediate or final material or product used in or resulting from the production of animals or poultry or direct products (e.g. milk, eggs). A (6) Water which comes in contact with benzene during manufacturing or processing operations conducted within a process unit. Process wastewater is not organic wastes, process fluids, product tank drawdown, cooling tower blowdown, steam trap condensate, or landfill leachate. A

process weight
The total weight of all materials and solid fuels introduced into any specific process. Liquid and gaseous fuels and combustion air will not be considered as part of the process weight unless they become part of the product. For a cyclical or batch operation, the process weight per hour will be derived by dividing the total process weight by the number of hours from the beginning of any given process to the completion thereof, excluding any time during which the equipment is idle. For a continuous operation, the process weight per hour will be derived by dividing the process weight for the number of hours in a given period of time by the number of hours in that period. For fluid catalytic cracking units, process weight shall

mean the total weight of material introduced as fresh feed to the cracking unit. For sulfuric acid production units, the nitrogen in the air feed shall not be included in the calculation of process weight. A

processing activities
All those activities which include (1) preparation of a substance identified in Subpart D [of 40 CFR parts 700-789] after its manufacture to make another substance for sale or use, (2) repackaging of the identified substance, or (3) purchasing and preparing the identified substance for use or distribution in commerce. A

processor
Any person who processes a chemical substance or mixture. K

procurement item
Any device, good, substance, material, product, or other item whether real or personal property which is the subject of any purchase, barter, or other exchange made to procure such an item. I

procuring agency
Any federal agency, or any state agency or agency of a political subdivision of a state which is using appropriated federal funds for such procurement, or any person contracting with any such agency with respect to work performed under such contract. A, I

produce
(1) To manufacture, process, formulate, or repackage. O (2) To manufacture, prepare, compound, propagate, or process any pesticide or device, or active ingredient used in producing a pesticide. The dilution by individuals of formulated pesticides for their own use and according to the directions on registered labels shall not of itself result in such individuals being included in the definition of "producer" for purposes of FIFRA. C

producer
Any person, as defined by the FIFRA Act, who produces [or imports] any pesticide, active ingredient, or device (including packaging, repackaging, labeling and relabeling). A

product
Any noise-producing or noise-reducing product for which regulations have been promulgated under Part 211; the term includes "test product." A

product accumulator vessel
Any distillate receiver, bottoms receiver, surge control vessel, or product separator in Volatile Hazardous Air Pollutant (VHAP) service that is vented to atmosphere either directly or through a vacuum-producing system. A product accumulator vessel is in VHAP service if the liquid or the vapor in the vessel is at least 10 percent by weight VHAP. A

product change
Any change in the composition of the furnace charge that would cause the electric submerged arc furnace to become subject to a different mass

standard applicable under this subpart. **A**

product frosted
That portion of the "furnace pull" associated with the fraction of finished incandescent lamp envelopes which is frosted; this quantity shall be calculated by multiplying "furnace pull" by the fraction of finished incandescent lamp envelopes which is frosted. **A**

product tank
A stationary unit that is designed to contain an accumulation of materials that are fed to or produced by a process unit, and is constructed primarily of non-earthen materials (e.g., wood, concrete, steel, plastic) which provide structural support. **A**

product tank drawdown
Any material or mixture of materials discharged from a product tank for the purpose of removing water or other contaminants from the product tank. **A**

product testing
Operations such as dye penetrant testing, hydrotesting, and ultrasonic testing. **A**

production
The manufacture of a substance from any raw material for feedstock chemical, but such terms do not include: (1) The manufacture of a substance that is used and entirely consumed (except for trace quantities) in the manufacture of other chemicals, or (2) The reuse or recycling of a substance. Production includes spilling or venting of controlled substances equal to or in excess of one hundred pounds per event; however, each production plant is allowed two spills or ventings of less than 1,000 pounds within a given control period. **A**

production allowances
The privileges granted to produce calculated levels of controlled substances. **A**

production area size
That area in which production facilities, loading facilities, and all buildings that house product processes are located. **A**

production verification vehicle
Any vehicle selected for testing, tested or verified pursuant to the production verification requirements of this subpart. **A**

production volume
(1) For a domestic manufacturer, the number of vehicle units domestically produced in a particular model year but not exported. (2) For a foreign manufacturer, the number of vehicle units of a particular model imported into the United States. **A** (3) The quantity of a chemical substance which is produced by a manufacturer, as measured in kilograms or pounds. **N**

production-weighted average
The manufacturer's production-weighted average particulate emission level, for certification purposes, of all of its diesel engine families included in the particulate averaging program. It is calculated at the end of the model year by multiplying each family particulate emission limit by its respective production, summing these

terms, and dividing the sum by the total production of the effected families. Those vehicles produced for sale in California or at high altitude shall be averaged separately from those produced for sale in any other area. A

production-weighted NO$_X$ average
The manufacturer's production-weighted average NO$_X$ emission level, for certification purposes, of all of its light-duty truck engine families included in the NO$_X$ averaging program. It is calculated at the end of the model year by multiplying each family No$_X$ emission limit by its respective production, summing those terms, and dividing the sum by the total production of the effected families. Those vehicles produced for sale in California or at high altitude shall each be averaged separately from those produced for sale in any other area. A

profit
The net proceeds obtained by deducting all allowable costs (direct and indirect) from the price. (Because this definition of profit is based on applicable federal cost principles, it may vary from many firms' definition of profit, and may correspond to those firms' definition of "fee.") A

program
Any program, project, or activity for the provision of services, financial assistance, or other benefits to individuals (including education or training, health, welfare, housing, rehabilitation, or other services, whether provided through employees of the recipient of Federal financial assistance or provided by others through contracts or other arrangements with the recipient, and including work opportunities or other assistance to individuals), or for the provisions of facilities for furnishing services, financial assistance, or other benefits to individuals. The services, financial assistance, or other benefits provided under a program receiving Federal financial assistance shall be deemed to include (1) any services, financial assistance, or other benefits provided with the aid of Federal financial assistance or with the aid of any nonfederal funds, property, or other resources required to be expended or made available for the program to meet matching requirements or other conditions which must be met in order to receive the Federal financial assistance, and (2) any services, financial assistance, or other benefits provided in or through a facility provided with the aid of Federal financial assistance or such non-Federal resources. A

program directive
Any formal written statement by the Administrator, the Deputy Administrator, the Assistant Administrator, a Staff Office Director, the General Counsel, a Deputy Assistant Administrator, an Associate General Counsel, or a division Director of an Operational Office that is intended to guide or direct Regional Offices in the implementation or enforcement of the provisions of the statute. A

program of requirements
A comprehensive document (booklet) describing program activities to be

accomplished in the new special purpose facility or improvement. It includes architectural, mechanical, structural, and space requirements. A

prohibit specification
To prevent the designation of an area as a present or future disposal site. A

project
The activities or tasks EPA identifies in the assistance agreement. A

project costs
All costs incurred by a grantee in accomplishing the objectives of a grant project, not limited to those costs which are allowable in computing the final EPA grant amount or total Federal assistance. U

project officer
The EPA official designated in the assistance agreement (as defined in EPA assistance) as EPA's program contact with the recipient; Project Officers are responsible for monitoring the project. A

project schedule
A timetable specifying the dates of key project events including public notices of proposed procurement actions, subagreement awards, issuance of notice to proceed with building, key milestones in the building schedule, completion of building, initiation of operation and certification of the project. A

properties
Characteristics by which a substance may be identified. Physical properties describe its state of matter, color, odor, and density; chemical properties describe its behavior in reaction with other materials. U

proportional sampling
Sampling at a rate that produces a constant ratio of sampling rate to stack gas flow rate. A

proposal
(1) That stage in the development of an action when an agency subject to the Act has a goal and is actively preparing to make a decision on one or more alternative means of accomplishing that goal and the effects can be meaningfully evaluated. Preparation of an environmental impact statement on a proposal should be timed so that the final statement may be completed in time for the statement to be included in any recommendation or report on the proposal. A proposal may exist in fact as well as by agency declaration that one exists. A (2) A solicited or unsolicited bid, application, request, invitation to consider or similar communication by or on behalf of a person seeking to participate or to receive a benefit, directly or indirectly, in or under a covered transaction. A

propose to manufacture or import
A person has made a firm management decision to commit financial resources for the manufacture or import of the specified chemical. A

propose to manufacture, process, or distribute
A person has made a management decision to commit financial resources

toward the manufacture, processing, or distribution of a chemical substance or mixture. A

proposed permit
A State NPDES permit prepared after the close of the public comment period (and, when applicable, any public hearing and administrative appeals) which is sent to EPA for review before final issuance by the State; not a draft permit. A

protect health and the environment
Protection against any unreasonable adverse effects on the environment. C

protective clothing
(1) At least a hat or other suitable head covering, a long sleeved shirt and long legged trousers or a coverall type garment (all of closely woven fabric covering the body, including arms and legs), shoes and socks. A (2) Clothing or any other materials or devices that shield against unintended exposure to pesticides. A (3) Clothing designed to protect an employee against contact with or exposure to a hazardous material. O

protective laboratory practices and equipment
Those laboratory procedures, practices and equipment accepted by laboratory health and safety experts as effective, or that the employer can show to be effective, in minimizing the potential for employee exposure to hazardous chemicals. O

protective shield or guard
A device or guard attached to the muzzle end of the tool, which is designed to confine flying particles. O

protocol
The plan and procedures which are to be followed in conducting a test. A

proven emission control systems
Emission control components or systems (and fuel metering systems) that have completed full durability testing evaluation over a vehicle's useful life in some other certified engine family, or have completed bench or road testing demonstrated to be equal or more severe than certification mileage accumulation requirements. Alternatively, proven components or systems are those that are determined by EPA to be of comparable functional quality and manufactured using comparable materials and production techniques as components or systems which have been durability demonstrated in some other certified engine family. In addition, the components or systems must be employed in an operating environment (e.g., temperature, exhaust flow, etc.,) similar to that experienced by the original or comparable components or systems in the original certified engine family. A

provide for
In the phrase "the plan shall (should) provide for" means explain, establish or set forth steps or courses of action. A

proximate analysis
The analysis of a solid fuel to

determine (on a percentage basis) how much moisture, volatile matter, fixed carbon, and ash the sample contains; usually the fuel's heat value is also established. U

PRP
Potentially responsible party (CERCLA). N

PS
Point source. U

PSD
Prevention of significant deterioration. U

PSD station
Any station operated for the purpose of establishing the effect on air quality of the emissions from a proposed source for purposes of prevention of significant deterioration as required by 40 CFR § 51.24(N). U

PSES
Pretreatment standards for existing sources, under section 307(b) of the [Federal Water Pollution Control] Act. A

PSI
Pollutant standard index. U

psi.
Pressure in pounds of force per square inch. U

psia.
Pounds per square inch absolute. U

psig.
Pounds per square inch gage. U

PSNS
Pretreatment standards for new sources, under section 307(c) of the [Federal Water Pollution Control] Act. A

PSM
Point source monitoring. U

PTA
Part throttle acceleration. A

PTC type choke heaters
A positive temperature coefficient resistant ceramic disc capable of providing heat to the thermostatic coil when electrically energized. A

PTD
Part throttle deceleration. A

PTE
Permanent total enclosure. A

PTM
Performance test method. U

PTS
Project tracking system. N

public, (the)
In the broadest sense, the people as a whole, the general populace. There are a number of identifiable "segments of the public" which may have a particular interest in a given program or decision. Interested and affected segments of the public may be affected directly by a decision, either beneficially or adversely; they may be affected indirectly; or they may have some other concern about the decision. In addition to private citizens, the public may include, among others,

representatives of consumer, environmental, and minority associations; trade, industrial, agricultural, and labor organizations; public health, scientific, and professional societies; civic associations; public officials; and governmental and educational associations. A

public vessel
A vessel owned or bareboat chartered and operated by the United States, by a State or political subdivision thereof, or by a foreign nation, except when such vessel is engaged in commerce. D

public water supplies
Water distributed from a public water system. A

public water system
A system for the provision to the public of piped water for human consumption, if such system has at least fifteen service connections or regularly serves an average of at least twenty-five individuals daily at least 60 days out of the year. Such term includes (1) any collection, treatment, storage, and distribution facilities under control of the operator of such system and used primarily in connection with such system, and, (2) any collection or pretreatment storage facilities not under such control which are used primarily in connection with such system. A public water system is either a community water system or a noncommunity water system. A, J

publication rotogravure printing press
Any number of rotogravure printing units capable of printing simultaneously on the same continuous web or substrate and includes any associated device for continuously cutting and folding the printed web, where the following saleable paper products are printed: catalogues, including mail order premium; direct mail advertisements, including circulars, letters, pamphlets, cards, and printed envelopes; display advertisements, including general posters, outdoor advertisements, car cards, window posters, counter and floor displays, point-of-purchase, and other printed display material; magazines; miscellaneous advertisements, including brochures, pamphlets, catalogue sheets, circular folders, announcements, package inserts, book jackets, market circulars, magazine inserts, and shopping news; newspapers, magazine and comic supplements for newspapers, and preprinted newspaper inserts, including hi-fi and spectacolor rolls and sections; periodicals; and telephone and other directories, including business reference services. A

publicly owned freshwater lake
A freshwater lake that offers public access to the lake through publicly owned contiguous land so that any person has the same opportunity to enjoy non-consumptive privileges and benefits of the lake as any other person. If user fees are charged for public use and access through State or substate operated facilities, the fees must be used for maintaining the public access and recreational facilities of this lake or other publicly owned freshwater lakes in the State, or for improving the quality of these lakes. A

publicly owned treatment works
POTW. A treatment works as defined by section 212 of the [Clean Water] Act, which is owned by State or municipality (as defined by 40 CFR section 212 of the [Clean Water] Act). This definition includes any sewers that convey wastewater to such a treatment works, but does not include pipes, sewers or other conveyances not connected to a facility providing treatment. The term also means the municipality as defined in section 502(4) of the Act, which has jurisdiction over the indirect discharges to and the discharges from such a treatment works. A

published exposure level
The exposure limits published in "NIOSH Recommendations for Occupational Health Standards" dated 1986 incorporated by reference, or if none is specified, the exposure limits published in the standards specified by the American Conference of Governmental Industrial Hygienists in their publication "Threshold Limit Values and Biological Exposure Indices for 1987-88" dated 1987 incorporated by reference. O

pull-out device
A mechanism attached to the operator's hands and connected to the upper die or slide of the press, that is designed, when properly adjusted, to withdraw the operator's hands as the dies close, if the operator's hands are inadvertently within the point of operation. O

pulling tension
The longitudinal force exerted on a cable during installation. O

pulmonary edema
An accumulation of an excessive amount of fluid in the lungs. U

pulmonary emphysema
An anatomic change in the lungs characterized by a breakdown of the walls of the alveoli, which can become enlarged, lose their resilience, and disintegrate. The disease is accompanied by increasingly severe shortness of breath. U

pulmonary function
The performance of the respiratory system in supplying oxygen to, and removing carbon dioxide from, the body (via the circulating blood). This requires that air move into and out of the alveoli at an adequate rate (ventilation), that blood circulate through pulmonary capillaries adjacent to alveoli at an adequate rate (perfusion), and that oxygen pass freely from alveoli to blood as carbon dioxide passes in the opposite direction (diffusion). Pulmonary function tests are used to try to identify and locate abnormalities in performance capability. U

pulp
Fiber material produced by chemical or mechanical means from such raw materials as virgin wood pulp, secondary fibers, and rags, and used in the manufacture of paper and paperboard. U

pulping system
The equipment used to convert fibrous raw materials into a homogeneous mixture suspended in water, which can be further processed into paper products. U

pulverization
The crushing or grinding of all material into small pieces. N

pumping station
Mechanical devices installed in sewer or water systems or other liquid-carrying pipelines that move the liquids to a higher level. N

purge
The coating material expelled from the spray system when clearing it. A

push pit
A waste storage system in which a hydraulically powered bulkhead that traverses the length of the pit periodically pushes the stored waste into the hopper of a compactor. It is sometimes used in stationary compactor transfer systems. U

push stick
A narrow strip of wood or other soft material with a notch cut into one end and which is used to push short pieces of material through saws. O

putlog
A scaffold member upon which the platform rests. O

putrescible
A substance that can rot quickly enough to cause odors and attract flies. U

putrescible waste
Any solid waste subject to putrefaction and capable of attracting or providing food for birds and vectors. U

PWR
Pressurized water reactor. A power reactor in which heat is transferred from the core to a heat exchanger by water kept under high pressure to achieve high temperature without boiling in the primary system. Steam is generated in a secondary circuit. Many reactors producing electric power are pressurized water reactors. U

PWS
Public water system. D

PWSS
Public water supply system. D

pyrolysis
The chemical decomposition of organic matter through the application of heat in an oxygen-deficient atmosphere. The products are water, carbon monoxide, hydrogen, and an inorganic residue. The gases may be collected and stored or used, and the residue may be further processed into such useful materials as carbon and sand or used as landfill. U

pyrolytic gas and oil
Gas or liquid products that possess usable heating value that is recovered from the heating of organic material (such as that found in solid waste), usually in an essentially oxygen-free atmosphere. A

pyrometer
An instrument for measuring or recording temperatures. U

pyrophoric
A chemical that will ignite spontaneously in air at a temperature of 130 degrees F (54.4 degrees C) or below. O

Q

QA
Quality assurance. U

QAPP
Quality Assurance Project Plan. A

QC
Quality control. U

QCW
Quality criteria for water. U

QNCR
Quarterly Non-compliance Action Plan. D

qualified
One who, by possession of a recognized degree, certificate, or professional standing, or who by extensive knowledge, training, and experience, has successfully demonstrated his ability to solve or resolve problems relating to the subject matter, the work, or the project. O

qualified ground water scientist
A scientist or engineer who has received a baccalaureate or post-graduate degree in the natural sciences or engineering, and has sufficient training and experience in ground water hydrology and related fields as may be demonstrated by state registration, professional certifications, or completion of accredited university courses that enable that individual to make sound professional judgments regarding ground water monitoring and contaminant fate and transport. A

qualified person
(1) A person who by reason of experience or training is familiar with the operation to be performed and the hazards involved. O (2) One with a recognized degree or professional certificate and extensive knowledge and experience in the subject field who is capable of design, analysis, evaluation and specifications in the subject work, project, or product. O (2) One familiar with the construction and operation of the equipment and the hazards involved. O

qualified testing laboratory
A properly equipped and staffed testing laboratory which has capabilities for and which provides the following services: (a) Experimental testing for safety of specified items of equipment and materials referred to in this standard to determine compliance with appropriate test standards or performance in a specified manner; (b) Inspecting the run of such items of equipment and materials at factories for product evaluation to assure compliance with the test standards; (c) Service-value determinations through field inspections to monitor the proper use of labels on products and with authority for recall of the label in the event a hazardous product is installed; (d) Employing a controlled procedure for identifying the listed and/or labeled equipment or materials tested; and (e) Rendering creditable reports or findings that are objective and without bias of the tests and test methods employed. O

Quality Assurance Program Plan
A formal document which describes an orderly assembly of management policies, objectives, principles, organizmarational responsibilities, and procedures by which an agency or laboratory specifies how it intends to: (a) produce data of documented quality, and (b) provide for the preparation of quality assurance project plans and standard operating procedures. A

Quality Assurance Project Plan
QAPP. A written document, associated with all remedial site sampling activities, which presents in specific terms the organization (where applicable), objectives, functional activities, and specific quality assurance (QA) and quality control (QC) activities designed to achieve the data quality objectives of a specific project(s) or continuing operation(s). The QAPP is prepared for each specific project or continuing operation (or group of similar projects or continuing operations). The QAPP will be prepared by the responsible program office, regional office, laboratory, contractor, recipient of an assistance agreement, or other organization. For an enforcement action, potentially responsible parties may prepare a QAPP subject to lead agency approval. A

quality assurance unit
Any person or organizational element, except the study director, designated by testing facility management to perform the duties relating to quality assurance of the studies. A

quality assurance/quality control
A system of procedures, checks, audits, and corrective actions to ensure that all EPA research design and performance, environmental monitoring and sampling, and other technical and reporting activities are of the highest achievable quality. N

quality factor
Q. The linear-energy-transfer-dependent factor by which absorbed doses are multiplied to obtain (for radiation protection purposes) a quantity that expresses--on a common

scale for all ionizing radiations--the effectiveness of the absorbed dose. U

quantitative fit test
The measurement of the effectiveness of a respirator seal in excluding the ambient atmosphere. The test is performed by dividing the measured concentration of challenge agent in a test chamber by the measured concentration of the challenge agent inside the respirator facepiece when the normal air purifying element has been replaced by an essentially perfect purifying element. A

quantum
The smallest indivisible quantity of radiant energy; a photon. U

quarry method
A variation of the sanitary landfilling area method in which the waste is spread and compacted in a depression; cover material is usually obtained elsewhere. B

quarter
A 3-month period; the first quarter concludes on the last day of the last full month during the 180 days following initial startup. A

quench station
That portion of the metal coil surface coating operation where the coated metal coil is cooled, usually by a water spray, after baking or curing. A

quench tank
A water-filled tank used to cool incinerator residues, or hot materials during industrial processes. N

quick disconnect valve
A device which starts the flow of air by inserting of the hose (which leads from the facepiece) into the regulator of self-contained breathing apparatus, and stops the flow of air by disconnection of the hose from the regulator. O

R

R.
Rankine. U

R&D
Research and development. U

RA
(1) See relative accuracy. U (2) See remedial action. U (3) Remedial action. N (4) Regional Administrator of a federal agency such as EPA or OSHA. N (5) Resource application. N (6) Risk assessment. N (7) Risk analysis. U

RAATS
RCRA Administrative Action Tracking System. N

RAC
Response action coordinator. N

raceway
A channel designed expressly for holding wires, cables, or busbars, with additional functions as permitted in this subpart. Raceways may be of metal or insulating material, and the term includes rigid metal conduit, rigid nonmetallic conduit, intermediate metal conduit, liquidtight flexible metal conduit, flexible metallic tubing, flexible metal conduit, electrical metallic tubing, underfloor raceways, cellular concrete floor raceways, cellular metal floor raceways, surface raceways, wireways, and busways. O

racial classifications
(1) American Indian or Alaskan native. A person having origins in any of the original peoples of North America, and who maintains cultural identification through tribal affiliation or community recognition. (2) Asian or Pacific Islander. A person having origins in any of the original peoples of the Far East, Southeast Asia, the Indian subcontinent, or the Pacific Islands. This area includes, for example, China, Japan, Korea, The Philippine Islands, and Samoa. (3) Black and not of Hispanic origin. A person having origins in any of the black racial groups of Africa. (4) Hispanic. A person of Mexican, Puerto Rican, Cuban, Central or South American or other Spanish culture or origin, regardless of race. (5) White,

not of Hispanic origin. A person having origins in any of the original peoples of Europe, North Africa, or the Middle East. A

rack dryer
Any equipment used to reduce the moisture content of grain in which the grain flows from the top to the bottom in a cascading flow around rows of baffles (racks). A

RACM
(1) Regulated asbestos-containing material. A (2) Reasonably available control measures. N

RACT
Reasonably available control technology. N

RAD
Radiation absorbed dose. (1) The special unit of absorbed dose of ionizing radiation. A dose of one rad equals the absorption of 100 ergs of radiation energy per gram of absorbing material. [See: absorbed dose]. (2) One RAD of absorbed dose is equal to .01 joules per kilogram. N

radiant energy
(1) Or radiation. The energy traveling as a wave unaccompanied by transfer of matter. Examples include x-rays, visible light, ultraviolet light, radio waves, etc. A (2) Energy that travels outward in all directions from its sources. O

radiation
(1) Any or all of the following: Alpha, beta, gamma, or X-rays; neutrons; and high-energy electrons, protons, or other atomic particles; but not sound or radio waves, nor visible, infrared, or ultraviolet light. A (2) Any form of energy propagated as rays, waves, or streams of energetic particles. The term is frequently used in relation to the emission of rays from the nucleus of an atom. N (3) See radiant energy. A

radiation absorbed dose
RAD. (1) The special unit of absorbed dose of ionizing radiation. A dose of one rad equals the absorption of 100 ergs of radiation energy per gram of absorbing material. [Compare: absorbed dose]. (2) One RAD of absorbed dose is equal to .01 joules per kilogram. N

radiation area
Any area, accessible to personnel, in which there exists radiation at such levels that a major portion of the body could receive in any 1 hour a dose in excess of 5 millirem, or in any 5 consecutive days a dose in excess of 100 millirem. O

radiation protection guide
Radiation level which should not be exceeded without careful consideration of the reasons for doing so. O

radiation standards
Regulations that govern exposure to permissible concentrations of and transportation of radioactive materials. N

radical
A group of atoms that takes part in a chemical reaction as a unit and is

normally incapable of existence except as part of a compound. So-called free radicals are formed as intermediate products in some reactions of organic compounds and play an important role in the reactions. U

radioactive
Substances that emit rays either naturally or as a result of scientific manipulation. N

radioactive decay
Disintegration of the nucleus of an unstable nuclide by spontaneous emission of charged particles and/or photons. U

radioactive materials
(1) As included within the definition of "pollutant" in section 502 of the [Federal Water Pollution Control] Act covers only radioactive materials which are not encompassed in the definitions of source, byproduct, or special nuclear materials as defined by the Atomic Energy Act of 1954, as amended, and regulated pursuant to the latter Act. Examples of radioactive materials not covered by the Atomic Energy Act and, therefore, included within the term "pollutant" are radium and accelerator produced isotopes. A (2) Any material which spontaneously emits radiation. A (3) Any material which emits, by spontaneous nuclear disintegration, corpuscular or electromagnetic emanations. O

radioactive waste
Any waste which contains radioactive material in concentrations which exceed those listed in 10 CFR Part 20, Appendix B, Table II, Column 2, or exceed the "Criteria for Identifying and Applying Characteristics of Hazardous Waste and for Listing Hazardous Waste" in 40 CFR Part 261, whichever is applicable. A

radiobiology
The study of the principles, mechanisms, and effects of radiation on living things. N

radioecology
The study of the effects of radiation on plants and animals in natural communities. N

radioisotopes
Radioactive forms of chemical compounds; such as cobalt-60, used in the treatment of diseases. N

radionuclide
(1) Any nuclide that emits radiation. (A nuclide is a species of atom characterized by the constitution of its nucleus and hence by the number of protons, the number of neutrons, and the energy content). A (2) A type of atom which spontaneously undergoes radioactive decay. A

radius of vulnerable zone
The maximum distance from the point of release of a hazardous substance in which the airborne concentration could reach the level of concern under specified weather conditions. N

radon
A colorless naturally occurring, radioactive, inert gaseous element formed by radioactive decay of radium atoms in soil or rocks. N

radon decay products
A term used to refer collectively to the immediate products of the radon decay chain. These include Po-218, Pb-214, Bi-214, and Po-214, which have an average combined half-life of about 30 minutes. N

rail ladder
A fixed ladder consisting of side rails joined at regular intervals by rungs or cleats and fastened in full length or in sections to a building, structure, or equipment. O

railcar loading station
That portion of a metallic mineral processing plant where metallic minerals or metallic mineral concentrates are loaded by a conveying system into railcars. A

railcar unloading station
That portion of a metallic mineral processing plant where metallic ore is unloaded from a railcar into a hopper, screen, or crusher. A

railing
A vertical barrier erected along exposed sides of stairways and platforms to prevent falls of persons. The top member of railing usually serves as a handrail. O

railroad
All the roads in use by any common carrier operating a railroad, whether owned or operated under a contract, agreement, or lease. A

ramp method
A variation of the sanitary landfilling area method in which a cover material is obtained by excavating in front of the working face. A variation of this method is called the progressive slope sanitary landfilling method. C

random incident field
A sound field in which the angle of arrival of sound at a given point in space is random in time. A

range
The minimum and maximum measurement limits. A

range of concentration
The highest concentration, the lowest concentration, and the average concentration of an additive in a fuel. A

RAP
Remedial action plan. U

rare earth metals
The elements scandium, yttrium, and lanthanum to lutetium, inclusive. A

rasp
A machine that grinds waste into a manageable material and helps prevent odor. N

rated incinerator capacity
The number of tons of solid waste that can be processed in an incinerator per 24-hour period when specified criteria prevail. U

rated load
The manufacturer's recommended maximum load. O

rated power
The maximum power/thrust available

for takeoff at standard day conditions as approved for the engine by the Federal Aviation Administration. A

rated pressure ratio
RPR. The ratio between the combustor inlet pressure and the engine inlet pressure achieved by an engine operating at rated output. A

rated speed
The speed at which the manufacturer specifies the maximum rated horsepower of an engine. A

rating
The rating of a jack is the maximum working load for which it is designed to lift safely that load throughout its specified amount of travel. Note: To raise the rated load of a jack, the point of application of the load, the applied force, and the length of level arm should be those designated by the manufacturer for the particular jack considered. O

raw data
Any laboratory worksheets, records, memoranda, notes, or exact copies thereof, that are the result of original observations and activities of a study and are necessary for the reconstruction and evaluation of the report of that study. In the event that exact transcripts of raw data have been prepared (e.g., tapes which have been transcribed verbatim, dated, and verified accurate by signature), the exact copy or exact transcript may be substituted for the original source as raw data. "Raw data" may include photographs, microfilm or microfiche copies, computer printouts, magnetic media, including dictated observations, and recorded data from automated instruments. A

raw ink
All purchased ink. A

raw material equivalent
Equal to the raw material usage multiplied by the volume of air scrubbed via wet scrubbers divided by the total volume of air scrubbed. A

raw sewage
Untreated wastewater. N

RCRA
The Resource Conservation and Recovery Act of 1976 (P.L. 94-580, as amended). A

RCRIS
RCRA Information System. I

RD
Remedial design. An engineering phase that follows the record of decision when technical drawings and specifications are developed for the subsequent remedial action at a site on the National Priorities List. (See: redmedial design). N

RD/RA
Remedial design/remedial action. L

RDA
Recommended daily allowance. N

RDF
Refuse derived fuel. U

rDNA
Recombinant DNA. The new DNA

that is formed by combining pieces of DNA from different organisms or cells. N

RE
Reportable event. N

re-refined oil
Used oil from which the physical and chemical contaminants acquired through previous use have been removed through a refining process. A, I

re-refining
The refining of petroleum products after they have been used in order to return them to their original uses (e.g., the re-refining of waste oil into lubricating oil). U

reactive
A substance that is normally unstable and readily undergoes violent change; or reacts violently with water; or generates toxic gases, vapors or fumes in a quantity sufficient to present danger to human health or the environment when mixed with water. N

reactivity
An Environmental Protection Agency characteristic of hazardous waste which identifies waste that under routine management, presents a hazard because of instability or extreme reactivity (e.g., the tendency to create vigorous reactions with air or water, tendency to explode, to exhibit thermal instability with regard to shock, ready reaction to generate toxic gases). U

reactor
(1) A vat, vessel, or other device in which chemical reactions take place. A (2) Any vessel in which vinyl chloride is partially or totally polymerized into polyvinyl chloride. A

reactor opening loss
The emissions of vinyl chloride occurring when a reactor is vented to the atmosphere for any purpose other than an emergency relief discharge as defined in [40 CFR] § 61.65(a). A

readily accessible
Capable of being reached quickly for operation, renewal, or inspections, without requiring those to whom ready access is requisite to climb over or remove obstacles or to resort to portable ladders, chairs, etc. O

readily water-soluble substances
Chemicals which are soluble in water at a concentration equal to or greater than 1,000 mg/l. A

real property
Except as otherwise defined by State law, land or any interest therein including land improvements, structures, fixtures and appurtenances thereto, but excluding movable machinery and equipment. A

real-ear protection at threshold
The mean value in decibels of the occluded threshold of audibility (hearing protector in place) minus the open threshold of audibility (ears open and uncovered) for all listeners on all trials under otherwise identical test conditions. A

REAP
Regional Enforcement Activities Plan. N

reasonable assistance
Providing timely and unobstructed access to test products or products and records, required by this part, and opportunity for copying such records or testing such test products. A

reasonable expense
Any expense incurred due to repair of a warranty failure caused by a non-original equipment certified part, including, but not limited to, all charges in any expense categories that would be considered payable by the involved vehicle manufacturer to its authorized dealer under a similar warranty situation where an original equipment part was the cause of the failure. Included in "reasonable expense" are any additional costs incurred specifically due to the processing of a claim involving a certified aftermarket part or parts as covered in these regulations. A

reasonable further progress
Annual incremental reductions in emissions of the applicable air pollutant (including substantial reductions in the early years following approval or promulgation of plan provisions under this part and section 110(a)(2)(I) [of the CAA] and regular reductions thereafter) which are sufficient in the judgment of the Administrator, to provide for attainment of the applicable national ambient air quality standard by the date required in section 172(a) [of the CAA]. B

reasonably available control measures
RACM. A broadly defined term referring to technologies and other measures that can be used to control pollution; includes Reasonably Available Control Technology and other measures. In the case of PM-10, it refers to approaches for controlling small or dispersed source categories such as road dust, woodstoves, and open burning. N

reasonably available control technology
RACT. (1) Devices, systems, process modifications, or other apparatus or techniques that are reasonably available taking into account (a) the necessity of imposing such controls in order to attain and maintain a national ambient air quality standard, (b) the social, environmental and economic impact of such controls, and (c) alternative means of providing for attainment and maintenance of such standard. (This provision defines RACT for the purposes of [40 CFR] §§ 51.110(c)(2) and 51.341(b) only). A
(2) The level of air pollutant emissions control required to be imposed on all existing sources in non-attainment areas, pursuant to §172 of CAA. (3) Devices, systems, process modifications, or other apparatus or techniques, the application of which will permit attainment of the emission limitations set forth in Appendix B, 40 CFR Part 51, provided that Appendix B is not intended, and shall not be construed, to require or encourage State agencies to adopt such emission limitations without due consideration of (a) the necessity of imposing such emission limitations in order to attain and maintain a national standard, (b) the social and economic impact of such emission limitations, and (c) alternative means of providing for

attainment and maintenance of such national standard. A

reasons of business confidentiality

Includes the concept of trade secrecy and other related legal concepts which give (or may give) a business the right to preserve the confidentiality of business information and to limit its use or disclosure by others in order that the business may obtain or retain business advantages it derives from its rights in the information. The definition is meant to encompass any concept which authorizes a federal agency to withhold business information under 5 U.S.C. 552(b)(4), as well as any concept which requires EPA to withhold information from the public for the benefit of a business under 18 U.S.C. 1905 or any of the various statutes cited in [40 CFR] § 2.301 through § 2.309. A

rebricking

Cold replacement of damaged or worn refractory parts of the glass melting furnace. Rebricking includes replacement of the refractories comprising the bottom, sidewalls, or roof of the melting vessel; replacement of refractory work in the heat exchanger; replacement of refractory portions of the glass conditioning and distribution system. A

rebuttable presumption against registration

An EPA regulatory policy which provides that the existence of certain types of scientific data indicating a pesticide causes harm to humans or the environment will justify the EPA refusing to register the pesticide unless the registrant provides more persuasive evidence to the contrary. U

receiving property

Any residential or commercial property that receives the sound from railroad facility operations, but that is not owned or operated by a railroad; except that occupied residences located on property owned or controlled by the railroad are included in the definition of "receiving property." For purposes of this definition, railroad crew sleeping quarters located on property owned or controlled by the railroad are not considered as residences. If, subsequent to the publication date of these regulations, the use of any property that is currently not applicable to this regulation changes, and it is newly classified as either residential or commercial, it is not receiving property until four years have elapsed from the date of the actual change in use. A

receiving property measurement location

A location on receiving property that is on or beyond the railroad facility boundary and that meets receiving property measurement location criteria. A

receiving waters

Any body of water where untreated wastes are dumped. N

receptacle

A contact device installed at the outlet for the connection of a single attachment plug. A single receptacle is a single contact device with no other contact device on the same yoke. A multiple receptacle is a single device containing two or more receptacles. O

recharge
A process, natural or artificial, by which water is added to the saturated zone of an aquifer. A

recharge area or zone
An area in which water reaches the zone of saturation (ground water) by surface infiltration; in addition, a "major recharge area" is an area where a major part of the recharge to an aquifer occurs. A

recipient
(1) Any person who purchases or otherwise obtains a chemical substance directly from a person who manufactures, imports, or processes the substance. A (2) Any State, or any political subdivision or instrumentality thereof, any public or private agency, institution, organization, or other entity, or any individual, in any State to which or whom Federal financial assistance is extended, directly or through another recipient, for any program, or who otherwise participates in carrying out such program, including any successor, assignee, or transferee thereof, but such term does not include any ultimate beneficiary under such program. A

reciprocal translocations
Chromosomal translocations resulting from reciprocal exchanges between two or more chromosomes. A

reciprocating-grate stoker
A stoker with a bed of bars or plates arranged so that alternate pieces, or rows of pieces, reciprocate slowly in a horizontal sliding mode and act to push the solid waste along the stoker surface. F

recirculated cooling water
Water which is passed through the main cooling condensers for the purpose of removing waste heat from the generating unit, passed through a cooling device for the purpose of removing such heat from the water and then passed again, except for blowdown, through the main cooling condensers. A

recirculation
Those cold rolling operations which include recirculation of rolling solutions at mill stands. A

reclaimed
If a material is processed to recover a usable product, or if it is regenerated. Examples are recovery of lead values from spent batteries and regeneration of spent solvents. A

reclamation
The restoration of land, water, or waste materials to usefulness through such methods as sanitary landfilling, wastewater treatment, and materials recovery. U

reclamation area
The surface area of a coal mine which has been returned to required contour and on which revegetation (specifically, seeding or planting) work has commenced. A

reclamation bond release
The time at which the appropriate regulatory authority returns a reclamation or performance bond based upon its determination that reclamation work (including, in the case of underground mines, mine sealing and abandonment procedures) has been satisfactorily completed. A

recombinant bacteria
A type of microorganism whose genetic makeup has been altered by deliberate introduction of new genetic elements. The offspring of these altered bacteria also contain these new genetic elements. N

recombinant DNA
rDNA. The new DNA that is formed by combining pieces of DNA from different organisms or cells. N

recommencing discharger
A source which recommences discharge after terminating operations. A

recommended decision
The recommended findings and conclusions of the Presiding Officer in an expedited hearing. A

recommended exposure limit
REL. The highest allowable airborne concentration established by OSHA that is not expected to injure a worker. Expressed as a ceiling limit or as a time-weighted average (TWA), usually for 10-hour work shifts. N

recommended maximum contaminant level
RMCL. The maximum level of a contaminant in drinking water at which no known or anticipated adverse affect on human health would occur, and which includes an adequate margin of safety. Recommended levels are nonenforceable health goals. (See: maximum contaminant level). N

reconfigured emission-data vehicle
An emission-data vehicle obtained by modifying a previously used emission-data vehicle to represent another emission-data vehicle. A

reconstructed source
An existing facility in which components are replaced to such an extent that the fixed capital cost of the new components exceed 50 percent of the capital cost that would be required to construct a comparable entirely new facility. New source performance standards may be applied to sources which are reconstructed after the proposal of the standard if it is technologically and economically feasible to meet the standard. N

reconstruction
Will be presumed to have taken place where the fixed capital cost of the new components exceed 50 percent of the fixed capital cost of a comparable entirely new facility or source. However, any final decision as to whether reconstruction has occurred shall be made in accordance with the provisions of 40 CFR 60.15(f)(1)-(3). A reconstructed source will be treated as a new source except that use of an alternative fuel or raw material by reason of an order in effect under Sections 2(a) and (b) of the Energy Supply and Environmental Coordination

Act of 1974 (or any superseding legislation), by reason of a natural gas curtailment plan in effect pursuant to the Federal Power Act, or by reason of an order or rule under Section 125 of the [Clean Air] Act, shall not be considered reconstruction. In determining best available control technology for a reconstructed source, the provisions of 40 CFR 60.15(f)(4) shall be taken into account in assessing whether a standard of performance under 40 CFR Part 60 is applicable to such source. A

record
Any item, collection, or grouping of information regardless of the form or process by which it is maintained (e.g., paper document, microfiche, microfilm, X-ray film, or automated data processing.) O

Record Of Decision
ROD. A public document that explains which cleanup alternative(s) will be used at a National Priorities List site. The record of decision is based on information and technical analysis generated during the remedial investigation/feasibility study and consideration of public comments and community concerns. N

recordable occupational injuries or illnesses
Any occupational injuries or illnesses which result in: (1) Fatalities, regardless of the time between the injury and death, or the length of the illness; or (2) Lost workday cases other than fatalities, that result in lost workdays; or (3) Nonfatal cases without lost workdays which result in transfer to another job or termination of employment, or require medical treatment (other than first aid) or involve: loss of consciousness or restriction of work or motion. This category also includes any diagnosed occupational illnesses which are reported to the employer but are not classified as fatalities or lost workday cases. O

recorded
Written or otherwise registered in some form for preserving information, including such forms as drawings, photographs, videotape, sound recordings, punched cards, and computer tape or disk. A

recoverable
The capability and likelihood of being recovered from solid waste for a commercial or industrial use. I

recoverable resources
Materials that still have useful physical, chemical, or biological properties after serving their original purpose and can, therefore, be reused or recycled for the same or other purposes. A

recovered material
Waste material and byproducts which have been recovered or diverted from solid waste, but such term does not include those materials and byproducts generated from, and commonly reused within, an original manufacturing process (P.L. 94-580, 90 Stat. 2800, 42 U.S.C. 6903, as amended by P.L. 96-482). A, I

recovered resources
Material or energy recovered from solid waste. I

recovered solvent
The solvent captured from liquid and gaseous process streams that is concentrated in a control device and that may be purified for reuse. A

recovery
The process of obtaining materials or energy resources from solid waste. A

recovery device
An individual unit of equipment, such as an absorber, carbon adsorber, or condenser, capable of and used for the purpose of recovering chemicals for use, reuse, or sale. A

recurrent expenditures
Those expenditures necessary for normal operations of the entity in the daily conduct of operations which would not be classed as unusual or extraordinary and would be expected to recur on a periodic basis. Recurrent expenditures would not include items such as procurement of real property, extraordinary equipment purchases, nor one time management studies. A

recycled
Used, reused, or reclaimed. A

recycled material
A material that is used in place of a primary, raw or virgin material in manufacturing a product and consists of materials derived from post consumer waste, industrial scrap, material derived from agricultural wastes and other items, all of which can be used in the manufacture of new products. A

recycled oil
Any used oil which is reused, following its original use, for any purpose (including the purpose for which the oil was originally used). Such term includes oil which is re-refined, reclaimed, burned or reprocessed. I

recycling
(1) Converting solid waste into new products by using the resources contained in discarded materials. N (2) The process by which recovered materials are transformed into new products. A

red border
An EPA document that is undergoing final review before being submitted for final management decision. N

red tide
A proliferation of ocean plankton that may kill large numbers of fish. This natural phenomenon may be stimulated by the addition of nutrients. N

reducing agent
In a reduction reaction (which always occurs simultaneously with an oxidation reaction) the reducing agent is the chemical or substance which (1) combines with oxygen or 92) loses electrons to the reaction. See: "oxidation." N

reduction control system
An emission control system which reduces emissions from sulfur recovery

plants by converting these emissions to hydrogen sulfide. A

reentry
The action of entering an area or site at, in, or on which a pesticide has been applied. A

reentry time
The period of time immediately following the application of a pesticide to a field when unprotected workers should not enter. A

reference day conditions
The reference ambient conditions to which the gaseous emissions (HC, CO, CO_2, and smoke) are to be corrected. The reference day conditions are as follows: Temperature = 15° C, specific humidity = 0.00629 kg H_2O/kg of dry air, and pressure = 101325 Pa. A

reference dose
RfD. An estimate (with uncertainty spanning perhaps an order of magnitude) of the daily exposure to the human population (including sensitive subpopulations) that is likely to be without deleterious effects during a lifetime. The RfD is reported in units of mg of substance/kg body weight/day for oral exposures, or mg of substance/m^3 of air breathed for inhalation exposures. N

reference method
Any method of sampling and analyzing for an air pollutant. A

reference substance
(1) Any chemical substance or mixture, or analytical standard, or material other than a test substance, feed, or water, that is administered to or used in analyzing the test system in the course of a study for the purposes of establishing a basis for comparison with the test substance for known chemical or biological measurements. A (2) A chemical used to access the constancy of response of a given species of test organisms to that chemical, usually by use of the acute LC_{50}. (It is assumed that any change in sensitivity to the reference substance will indicate the existence of some similar change in degree of sensitivity to other chemicals whose toxicity is to be determined). A

referring agency
The federal agency which has referred any matter to the Council (on Environmental Quality) after a determination that the matter is unsatisfactory from the standpoint of public health or welfare or environmental quality. A

refillable beverage container
A beverage container that when returned to a distributor or bottler is refilled with a beverage and reused. A

refiner
Any person who owns, leases, operates, controls, or supervises a refinery. A

refinery
(1) A plant in which flammable or combustible liquids are produced on a commercial scale from crude petroleum, natural gasoline, or other

hydrocarbon sources. O (2) A plant at which gasoline is produced. A

refinery process unit
Any segment of the petroleum refinery in which a specific processing operation is conducted. A

reformulated gasoline
Gasoline with a different composition from conventional gasoline (e.g., lower aromatics content) and that results in the production of lower levels of air pollutants. N

refractory erosion
The erosion of refractory surfaces by the washing action of moving liquids, such as molten slags or metals, or the action of moving gases. U

refractory expansion joint
An open joint left open so that refractories can expand thermally or permanently; also, small spaces or gaps built into a refractory structure to permit sections of masonry to expand and contract freely and to prevent the distortion or buckling of furnace structures under excessive expansion stresses. These joints are built in such a way that the masonry can move but that little or no air or gas can leak through. U

refractory material
Nonmetallic substances used to line furnaces because they can endure high temperatures and resist abrasion, spalling, and slagging. U

refractory wall
A wall made of heat-resistant material. U

refund
The sum, equal to the deposit, that is given to the consumer or the dealer or both in exchange for empty returnable beverage containers. A

refuse
A term generally used for all solid waste materials. [See solid waste]. U

Refuse Act
Section 13 of the River and Harbor Act of March 3, 1899. A

Refuse Act permit
Any permit issued under the Refuse Act. A [ed. Refuse Act permits were succeeded by NPDES permits]. U

refuse reclamation
Conversion of solid waste into useful products, e.g., composting organic wastes to make a soil conditioner. N

refuse-derived fuel
(1) RDF. The combustible, or organic, portion of municipal waste that has been separated out and processed for use as fuel. U (2) A type of MSW produced by processing MSW through shredding and size classification. A

regeneration
Manipulation of individual cells or masses of cells to cause them to develop into whole plants. N

region
(1) An air quality control region designated by the Secretary of Health, Education, and Welfare or the Administrator; (2) Any area· designated by a State agency as an air

quality control region and approved by the Administrator; or (3) Any area of a State not designated as an air quality control region under paragraph (m) (1) or (2) of this section. A (4) One of the ten Federal regions of the United States. U

Regional Administrator
(1) One of the ten Regional Administrators of the U.S. Environmental Protection Agency. A (2) The Administrator of any Regional Office of EPA or any officer or employee thereof to whom his authority is duly delegated. Where the Regional Administrator has authorized the Regional Judicial Officer to act, the term "Regional Administrator" shall include the Regional Judicial Officer. In a case where the complainant is the Assistant Administrator for Enforcement or his delegate, the term "Regional Administrator" as used in these rules shall mean the Administrator. A

regional hearing clerk
An individual duly authorized by the Regional Administrator to serve as hearing clerk for a given region. Correspondence may be addressed to the Regional Hearing Clerk, United States Environmental Protection Agency (address of Regional Office--see Appendix). In a case where the complainant is the Assistant Administrator for Enforcement or his delegate, the term "regional Hearing Clerk" as used in these rules shall mean the Hearing Clerk. A

regional judicial officer
A person designated by the Regional Administrator under 40 CFR § 22.04(b) to serve as a Regional Judicial Officer. A

regional limitation
The requirement that a source which is located in an air quality control region in which a national primary ambient air quality standard for an air pollutant is being exceeded in that region, may not emit such pollutant in amounts which exceed any emission limitation (and may not violate any other requirement) which applies to such source, under the applicable implementation plan for such pollutant. A

regional office
One of the ten EPA regional offices. A

regional response team
RRT. Is composed of representatives of Federal agencies and a representative from each State in the Federal region. During a response to a major hazardous materials incident involving transportation or a fixed facility, the On-Scene Coordinator (OSC), may request that the RRT be convened to provide advice or recommendations in specific issues requiring resolution. Under the NCP, RRTs may be convened by the chairman when a hazardous materials discharge or release exceeds the response capability available to the OSC in the place where it occurs; crosses regional boundaries; or may pose a substantial threat to the public health, welfare, or environment; or the regionally significant amounts of property. Regional contingency plans specify

detailed criteria for activation of RRTs. RRTs may review plans developed in compliance with Title III, if local emergency planning committee so requests. N

regional scale
Usually a rural area of reasonable homogeneous geography extending from tens to hundreds of kilometers. A

register
As applied to a motor vehicle, means the licensing of such motor vehicle for general operation on public roads or highways by the appropriate agency of the Federal government or by the Commonwealth. A

registered professional engineer
A person who has been duly and currently registered and licensed by an authority within the United States or its territories to practice the profession of engineering. A

registrant
A person who has registered any pesticide pursuant to the provisions of FIFRA. U

registration
Formal listing with EPA of a new pesticide before it can be sold or distributed in intra- or inter-state commerce. The product must be registered under the Federal Insecticide, Fungicide, and Rodenticide Act. EPA is responsible for registration (pre-market licensing) of pesticides on the basis of data demonstrating that they will not cause unreasonable adverse effects on human health or the environment when used according to approved label directions. N

registration division
The unit established within the Environmental Protection Agency charged with administration of the Pesticide Residue amendment to the Federal Food, Drug, and Cosmetic Act (section 408). A

regulated area
(1) An area where entry and exit is restricted and controlled. O (2) An area established by the employer to demarcate areas where airborne concentrations of asbestos exceed, or can reasonably be expected to exceed, the permissible exposure limit. O

regulated asbestos-containing material
RACM. (a) Friable asbestos material, (b) Category I nonfriable ACM that has become friable, (c) Category I nonfriable ACM that will be or has been subjected to sanding, grinding, cutting, or abrading, or (d) Category II nonfriable ACM that has a high probability of becoming or has become crumbled, pulverized, or reduced to powder by the forces expected to act on the material in the course of demolition or renovation operations regulated by this subpart. A

regulated chemical
Any chemical substance or mixture for which export notice is required under [40 CFR] § 707.60. A

regulated medical waste
Those medical wastes that have been listed in [40 CFR] § 259.30(a) and that

must be managed in accordance with the requirements of this part. A

regulated pest
A specific organism considered by a State or Federal agency to be a pest requiring regulatory restrictions, regulations, or control procedures in order to protect the host, man and/or his environment. A

regulated substance
(A) Any substance defined in section 101(14) of the Comprehensive Environmental Response, Compensation, and Liability Act of 1980 (but not including any substance regulated as a hazardous waste under subtitle C), and (B) petroleum, including crude oil or any fraction thereof which is liquid at standard conditions of temperature and pressure (60 degrees Fahrenheit and 14.7 pounds per square inch absolute). [ed. Could include other substances regulated by TSCA & FIFRA]. U

regulated waste (medical)
Liquid or semi-liquid blood or other potentially infectious materials; contaminated items that would release blood or other potentially infectious materials in a liquid or semi-liquid state if compressed; items that are caked with dried blood or other potentially infectious materials and are capable of releasing these materials during handling; contaminated sharps; and pathological and microbiological wastes containing blood or other potentially infectious materials. O

regulatory compliance
Meeting the requirements of federal or state regulations regarding facility design, construction, operation, performance, closure and post-closure care. N

Regulatory Interpretative Memoranda
RIMs. In 1980, EPA adopted a formal procedure for issuing binding interpretations of the hazardous waste regulations. These interpretations were called Regulatory Interpretative Memoranda (RIMs), and EPA also considered issuing Program Implementation Guidelines (PIGs) and Technical Amendment Regulations (TARs), 45 Fed. Reg. 55386 (August 19, 1980). The RIM program could have been very helpful, especially in applying the complex hazardous waste program to specific factual situations. However, EPA has largely abandoned this approach, preferring instead to explain and interpret its regulations by issuing regulatory amendments. Only a few RIMs have been issued by the agency. EPA has relied on technical guidance documents. U

Reid vapor pressure
RVP. The absolute vapor pressure of volatile crude oil and volatile non-viscous petroleum liquids, except liquified petroleum gases, as determined by ASTM D323-72. A

reimbursement period
A period that begins when the data from the last non-duplicative test to be completed under a test rule are submitted to EPA and ends after an amount of time equal to that which had been required to develop data or after five years, whichever is later. A

reinforced wheels
"Reinforced" as applied to grinding wheels shall define a class of organic wheels which contain strengthening fabric or filament. The term "reinforced" does not cover wheels using such mechanical additions as steel rings, steel cup backs or wire or tape winding. O

REL
Recommended exposure limit. U

related coatings
All non-ink purchased liquids and liquid-solid mixtures containing VOC solvent, usually referred to as extenders or varnishes, that are used at publication rotogravure printing presses. A

relative accuracy
RA. A comparison of the CEMS [continuous emission monitoring system] response to a value measured by a performance test method (PTM). The test is used to validate the calibration technique and verify the ability of the CEMS to provide representative and accurate measurements. A

relative percent of percutaneous absorption
100 times the ratio between total urinary excretion of compound following topical administration and total urinary excretion of compound following intravenous injection. A

release
As defined by section 101(22) of CERCLA. Any spilling, leaking, pumping, pouring, emitting, emptying, discharging, injecting, escaping, leaching, dumping, or disposing into the environment (including the abandonment or discarding of barrels, containers, and other closed receptacles containing any hazardous substance or pollutant or contaminant), but excludes: (A) Any release which results in exposure to persons solely within a workplace, with respect to a claim which such persons may assert against the employer of such persons; (B) emissions from the engine exhaust of a motor vehicle, rolling stock, aircraft, vessel, or pipeline pumping station engine; (C) release of source, byproduct, or special nuclear material from a nuclear incident, as those terms are defined in the Atomic Energy Act of 1954, if such release is subject to requirements with respect to financial protection established by the Nuclear Regulatory Commission under section 170 of such Act, or, for the purposes of section 104 of CERCLA or any other response action, any release of source, byproduct, or special nuclear material from any processing site designated under section 102(a)(1) or 302(a) of the Uranium Mill Tailings Radiation Control Act of 1978; (D) and the normal application of fertilizer. For purposes of the NCP, release also means threat of release. A

relevant and appropriate requirements
Those cleanup standards, standards of control, and other substantive requirements, criteria, or limitations promulgated under federal environmental or state environmental or facility siting laws that, while not "applicable" to a hazardous substance, pollutant, contaminant, remedial

action, location, or other circumstance at a CERCLA site, address problems or situations sufficiently similar to those encountered at the CERCLA site that their use is well suited to the particular site. Only those state standards that are identified in a timely manner and are more stringent than federal requirements may be relevant and appropriate. A

relief valve
Each pressure relief device including pressure relief valves, rupture disks and other pressure relief systems used to protect process components from over pressure conditions. "Relief valve" does not include polymerization shortstop systems, refrigerated water systems or control valves or other devices used to control flow to an incinerator or other air pollution control device. A

relief valve discharge
Any nonleak discharge through a relief valve. A

rem
Roentgen equivalent man. A measurement of radiation by biological effect on human tissue. N

remedial action
RA. Those actions consistent with permanent remedy taken instead of, or in addition to, removal action in the event of a release or threatened release of a hazardous substance into the environment, to prevent or minimize the release of hazardous substances so that they do not migrate to cause substantial danger to present or future public health or welfare or the environment. The term includes, but is not limited to, such actions at the location of the release as storage, confinement, perimeter protection using dikes, trenches, or ditches, clay cover, neutralization, cleanup of released hazardous substances and associated contaminated materials, recycling or reuse, diversion, destruction, segregation of reactive wastes, dredging or excavations, repair or replacement of leaking containers, collection of leachate and runoff, on-site treatment or incineration, provision of alternative water supplies, any monitoring reasonably required to assure that such actions protect the public health and welfare and the environment and, where appropriate, post-removal site control activities. The term includes the costs of permanent relocation of residents and businesses and community facilities (including the cost of providing "alternative land of equivalent value" to an Indian tribe pursuant to CERCLA section 126(b)) where EPA determines that, alone or in combination with other measures, such relocation is more cost-effective than, and environmentally preferable to, the transportation, storage, treatment, destruction, or secure disposition off-site of such hazardous substances, or may otherwise be necessary to protect the public health or welfare; the term includes off-site transport and off-site storage, treatment, destruction, or secure disposition of hazardous substances and associated contaminated materials. For the purpose of the NCP, the term also includes enforcement activities related thereto. A

remedial design
RD. The technical analysis and procedures which follow the selection of remedy for a site and result in a detailed set of plans and specifications for implementation of the remedial action. A

remedial investigation
A process undertaken by the lead agency (or responsible party if the responsible party will be developing a cleanup proposal) which emphasizes data collection and site characterization. The remedial investigation is generally performed concurrently and in an interdependent fashion with the feasibility study. However, in certain situations, the lead agency may require potentially responsible parties to conclude initial phases of the remedial investigation prior to initiation of the feasibility study. A remedial investigation is undertaken to determine the nature and extent of the problem presented by the release. This includes sampling and monitoring, as necessary, and includes the gathering of sufficient information to determine the necessity for and proposed extent of remedial action. Part of the remedial investigation involves assessing whether the threat can be mitigated or minimized by controlling the source of the contamination at or near the area where the hazardous substances or pollutants were originally located (source control remedial actions) or whether additional actions will be necessary because the hazardous substances or pollutants or contaminants have migrated from the area of their original location (management of migration). A

remedial investigation/feasibility study
RI/FS. Two distinct, but related studies, usually performed at the same time. The RI/FS is intended to: (1) gather the data necessary to determine the type and extent of contamination at a Superfund site; (2) identify and screen cleanup alternatives for remedial action; and (3) analyze in detail the technology and costs of the alternatives. N

Remedial Project Manager
RPM. The Federal official designated by EPA (or the USCG for vessels) to coordinate, monitor, or direct remedial or other response activities; or the Federal official DOD designates to coordinate and direct Federal remedial or other response actions resulting from releases of hazardous substances, pollutants, or contaminants from DOD facilities or vessels. A

remedial response
A long-term action that stops or substantially reduces a release or threat of a release of hazardous substances that is serious but not an immediate threat to public health. N

remedy or remedial action
Those actions consistent with permanent remedy taken instead of, or in addition to, removal action in the event of a release or threatened release of a hazardous substance into the environment, to prevent or minimize the release of hazardous substances so that they do not migrate to cause substantial danger to present or future public health or welfare or the environment. The term includes,

but is not limited to, such actions at the location of the release as storage, confinement, perimeter protection using dikes, trenches or ditches, clay cover, neutralization, cleanup of released hazardous substances or contaminated materials, recycling or reuse, diversion, destruction, segregation of reactive wastes, dredging or excavations, repair or replacement of leaking containers, collection of leachate and runoff, on-site treatment or incineration, provision of alternative water supplies, and any monitoring reasonably required to assure that such actions protect the public health and welfare and the environment. The term includes the costs of permanent relocation of residents and businesses and community facilities where the President determines that, alone or in combination with other measures, such relocation is more cost-effective than and environmentally preferable to the transportation, storage, treatment, destruction, or secured disposition off-site of such hazardous substances, or may otherwise be necessary to protect the public health or welfare. The term does not include off-site transport of hazardous substances or contaminated materials unless the President determines that such actions: are more cost-effective than other remedial actions; will create new capacity to manage in compliance with Subtitle C of the Solid Waste Disposal Act, hazardous substances in addition to those located at the affected facility; or are necessary to protect public health or welfare or the environment from a present or potential risk which may be created by further exposure to the continued presence of such substances or materials (as defined by section 101(24) of CERCLA). A, L

remote-control circuit
Any electric circuit that controls any other circuit through a relay or an equivalent device. O

removal
(1) As defined by section 311(a)(8) of the CWA. Removal of oil or hazardous substances from the water and shorelines or the taking of such other actions as may be necessary to minimize or mitigate damage to the public health or welfare or to the environment. As defined by section 101(23) of CERCLA, remove or removal means the cleanup or removal of released hazardous substances from the environment; such actions as may be necessary taken in the event of the threat of release of hazardous substances into the environment; such as may be necessary to monitor, assess, and evaluate the release or threat of release of hazardous substances; the disposal of removed material, or the taking of such other actions as may be necessary to prevent, minimize, or mitigate damage to the public health or welfare or to the environment, which may otherwise result from a release or threat of release. The term includes, in addition, without being limited to, security fencing or other measures to limit access, provision of alternative water supplies, temporary evacuation and housing of threatened individuals not otherwise provided for, action taken under section 104(b) of CERCLA, post-removal site control, where appropriate, and any emergency

assistance which may be provided under the Disaster Relief Act of 1974. For the purpose of the NCP, the term also includes enforcement activities related thereto. A (2) The taking out or the stripping of substantially all asbestos or materials from a damaged area, a functional space, or a homogeneous area in a school building. A

removal action
Short-term immediate actions taken to address releases of hazardous substances that require expedited response. (See: cleanup). N

remove
To take out RACM or facility components that contain or are covered with RACM from any facility. A

renal toxicity
Ability to damage kidney cells; kidney toxicity. N

renewal system
The technique in which test organisms are periodically transferred to fresh test solution of the same composition. A

renewal test
A test without continuous flow of solution, but with occasional renewal of test solutions after prolonged periods, e.g., 24 hours. A

renovation
Altering a facility or one or more facility components in any way, including the stripping or removal or RACM from a facility component. Operations in which load-supporting structural members are wrecked or taken out are demolitions. A

rent
Use of another's property in return for regular payment. N

rep
A measurement of radiation by energy development in human tissue. (Acronym for roentgen equivalent physical). N

repackager
A person who buys a substance identified in Subpart D of [40 CFR parts 700-789] or mixture, removes the substance or mixture from the container in which it was bought, and transfers this substance, as is, to another container for sale. A

repair
Overhauling, rebuilding, reconstructing, or reconditioning of structures or substrates where asbestos is present. A

replacement
Expenditures for obtaining and installing equipment, accessories, or appurtenances during the useful life of the treatment works necessary to maintain the capacity and performance for which such works are designed and constructed. D The term "operation and maintenance" includes replacement. A

replacement cost
The capital needed to purchase all the depreciable components in a facility. A

replicate
Two or more duplicate tests, samples, organisms, concentrations or exposure chambers. A

reportable quantity
RQ. (1) The quantity of a hazardous substance that triggers reports under CERCLA. If a substance is released in amounts exceeding its RQ, the release must be reported to the National Response Center, the SERC, and community emergency coordinators for areas likely to be affected. N (2) The quantity of material that when spilled must be reported to the DOT (Section 311 of the Clean Water Act). D (3) Quantities of hazardous substances that may be harmful as set forth in 40 CFR § 117.3, the discharge of which is a violation of section 311(b)(3) of the FWPCA and requires notice as set forth in 40 CFR § 117.21 or requires notice pursuant to § 304.7 CERCLA. A

reporting agency
The applicable State agency or, in metropolitan areas, a local air pollution control agency designated by the State to carry out the provisions of 40 CFR § 58.40. A

reporting area
The geographical area for which the daily index is representative for the reporting period. This area(s) may be the total urban area (or subpart thereof) or each of any number of distinct geographical subregions of the urban area deemed necessary by the reporting agency for adequate presentation of local air quality conditions. A

reporting day
The calendar day during which the daily report is given. A

reporting period
The time interval for which the daily report is representative. Normally, the reporting period is the 24-hour period immediately preceding the time of the report and should coincide to the extent practicable with the reporting day. In cases where the index will be forecasted the reporting period will include portions of the reporting day for which no monitoring data are available at the time of the report. A

reporting year
The most recent complete corporate fiscal year during which a person manufactures, imports, or processes the listed substance. A

repowering
The replacement of an existing coal-fired boiler with one or more clean coal technologies, in order to achieve significantly greater emission reduction relative to the performance of technology in widespread use as of the enactment of the Clean Air Act amendments. N

representative
Any person, including an authorized employee representative, authorized by a party or intervenor to represent him in a proceeding. O

representative exposure
Measurements of an employee's noise dose or 8-hour time-weighted average sound level that the employers deem

to be representative of the exposures of other employees in the workplace. O

representative of the news media
Any person actively gathering news for an entity that is organized and operated to publish or broadcast news to the public. The term "news" means information that is about current events or that would be of current interest to the public. Examples of news media entities include television or radio stations broadcasting to the public at large, and publishers of periodicals (but only in those instances when they can qualify as disseminators of "news") who make their products available for purchase and subscription by the general public. These examples are not intended to be all-inclusive. Moreover, as traditional methods of news delivery evolve (e.g., electronic dissemination of newspapers through telecommunications services), such alternative media would be included in this category. In the case of "freelance" journalists, they may be regarded as working for a news organization if they can demonstrate a solid basis for expecting publication through that organization, even though not actually employed by it. A publication contract would be the clearest proof, but EPA may also look to the past publication record of a requestor in making this determination. A

representative point
(a) A location in surface waters or ground waters at which specific conditions or parameters may be measured in such a manner as to characterize or approximate the quality or condition of the water body; or (b) A location in process or waste waters at which specific conditions or parameters are measured and will adequately reflect the actual condition of those waters or waste waters for which analysis was made. A

representative sample
(1) Any sample of the waste, which is equivalent to the total waste in composition, and physical and chemical properties. (2) A sample of a universe or whole (e.g., waste pile, lagoon, ground water) which can be expected to exhibit the average properties of the universe or whole. A

reprocessing
The action of changing the condition of a secondary material. U

reproductive health hazard
Any agent that has a harmful effect on the adult male or female reproductive system or the developing fetus or child. Such hazards affect people in several ways, including loss of sexual drive, mental disorders, impotence, infertility, sterility, mutagenic effects on germ cells, teratogenic effects on the fetus, and transplacental carcinogenesis. N

reproductive toxicity
Harmful effects on fertility, gestation, or offspring, caused by exposure of either parent to a substance. N

reproductive toxins
Chemicals which affect the reproductive capabilities including

chromosomal damage (mutations) and effects on fetuses (teratogenesis). O

requestor
An industrial user or a POTW or other interested person seeking a variance from the limits specified in a categorical pretreatment standard. A

reregistration
The reevaluation and relicensing of existing pesticides originally registered prior to current scientific and regulatory standards. EPA reregisters pesticides through its Registration Standards Program. N

rescission
Enacted legislation cancelling budget authority previously provided by the Congress. U

research
A systematic investigation, including research development, testing and evaluation, designed to develop or contribute to generalizable knowledge. A

research octane number
RON. A measurement of a gasoline's knock characteristics which is determined by American Society for Testing and Materials analytical method designated D-2699. A

research permits
Research permits may be issued for the dumping of any materials, other than materials specified in [40 CFR] § 227.5 or for any of the materials listed in [40 CFR] § 227.6 except as trace contaminants, unless subject to the exclusion of [40 CFR] § 227.6(g), into the ocean as part of a research project when it is determined that the scientific merit of the proposed project outweighs the potential environmental or other damage that may result from the dumping. Research permits shall specify an expiration date no later than 18 months from the date of issue. A

research subject to regulation
Similar terms are intended to encompass those research activities for which a federal department or agency has specific responsibility for regulating as a research activity, (for example, Investigational New Drug requirements administered by the Food and Drug Administration). It does not include research activities which are incidentally regulated by a federal department or agency solely as part of the department's or agency's broader responsibility to regulate certain types of activities whether research or nonresearch in nature (for example, Wage and Hour requirements administered by the Department of Labor). A

reseller
Any person who purchases gasoline identified by the corporate, trade, or brand name of a refiner from such refiner or a distributor and resells or transfers it to retailers or wholesale purchaser-consumers displaying the refiner's brand, and whose assets or facilities are not substantially owned, leased, or controlled by such refiner. A

reservoir
Any natural or artificial holding

area used to store, regulate, or control water. N

residence
Any home, house, apartment building, or other place of dwelling which is occupied during any portion of the relevant year. A

residence time
The length of time during which a hazardous waste is subjected to elevated temperatures during incineration. N

residential application
Application of a pesticide (other than application by a commercial applicator) directly to humans or pets or application of a pesticide in, on, or around all structures, vehicles or areas associated with the household or homelife or non-commercial areas where children spend time, including, but not limited to: (i) Gardens, non-commercial greenhouses, yards, patios, houses, pleasure marine craft, mobile homes, campers and recreational vehicles, non-commercial campsites, home swimming pools and kennels; (ii) Articles, objects, devices or surfaces handled or contacted by humans or pets in all structures, vehicles or areas listed above; and (iii) Educational, lounging and recreational areas of preschools, nurseries and day camps. A

residential property
Any property that is used for any of the purposes described in the following standard land use codes (ref. *Standard Land Use Coding Manual*. U.S. DOT/ FHWA Washington, D.C., reprinted March 1977): 1, Residential: 651, Medical and other Health Services; 68, Educational Services; 691, Religious Activities; and 711, Cultural Activities. A

residential solid waste
The wastes generated by the normal activities of households, including, but not limited to, food wastes, rubbish, ashes, and bulky wastes. A

residential tank
A tank located on property used primarily for dwelling purposes. A

residential use
Use of a pesticide directly: (1) On humans or pets; (2) In, on, or around any structure, vehicle, article, surface, or area associated with the household, including but not limited to areas such as non-agricultural outbuildings, non-commercial greenhouses, pleasure boats and recreational vehicles, or (3) In any preschool or day care facility. A

residential/commercial areas
Those areas where people live or reside, or where people work in other than manufacturing or farming industries. Residential areas include housing and the property on which housing is located, as well as playgrounds, roadways, sidewalks, parks, and other similar areas within a residential community. Commercial areas are typically accessible to both members of the general public and employees and include public assembly properties, institutional properties, stores, office buildings, and transportation centers. A

residual oil
A general term used to indicate a heavy viscous fuel oil. A

residual risk
The quantity of health risk remaining after application of the MACT (Maximum Achievable Control Technology). N

residual volume
The volume of air remaining in the lungs after a maximal forceful exhalation. N

residual waste control needs; land disposal needs
(1) An identification of the necessary controls to be established over the disposition of residual wastes which could affect water quality and a description of the proposed actions necessary to achieve such controls. (2) An identification of the necessary controls to be established over the disposal of pollutants on land or in subsurface excavations to protect ground and surface water quality and a description of the proposed actions necessary to achieve such controls. A

residual wastes
Those solid, liquid, or sludge substances from man's activities in the urban, agricultural, mining and industrial environment remaining after collection and necessary treatment. A

residue
(1) The material that remains after completion of a chemical or physical process, such as combustion, distillation, evaporation, or filtration.

(2) The active ingredient(s), metabolite(s) or degradation product(s) that can be detected in the crops, soil, water, or other component of the environment, including man, following the use of the pesticide. A

residue conveyor
Generally a drag or flight conveyor used to remove incinerator residue from a quench trough to a discharge point. U

resilient floor covering
Asbestos-containing floor tile, including asphalt and vinyl floor tile, and sheet vinyl floor covering containing more than 1 percent asbestos as determined using polarized light microscopy according to the method specified in appendix A, subpart F, 40 CFR Part 763, Section 1, Polarized Light Microscopy. A

resistance
For plants and animals, the ability to withstand poor environmental conditions and/or attacks by chemical or disease. The ability may be inborn or developed. N

resource conservation
Reduction of the amounts of solid waste that are generated, reduction of overall resource consumption, and utilization of recovered resources. I

resource recovery
(1) The recovery of material or energy from solid waste. I (2) A term describing the extraction and utilization of materials and energy from the waste stream. Materials are used in the manufacturing of new

products, or converted into some form of fuel or energy source. U

resource recovery facility
(1) Any facility at which solid waste is processed for the purpose of extracting, converting to energy, or otherwise separating and preparing solid waste for reuse. Energy conversion facilities must utilize solid waste to provide more than 50 percent of the heat input to be considered a resource recovery facility under this ruling. A (2) Any physical plant that processes residential, commercial, or institutional solid wastes biologically, chemically, or physically, and recovers useful products, such as shredded fuel, combustible oil or gas, steam, metal, glass, etc. for recycling. A

resource recovery system
A solid waste management system which provides for collection, separation, recycling, and recovery of solid wastes, including disposal of nonrecoverable waste residues. I

resource recovery unit
A facility that combusts more than 75 percent non-fossil fuel on a quarterly (calendar) heat input basis. A

respirable
Of a size small enough to be inhaled deep into the lung. U

respiratory protection
Devices that will protect the wearer's respiratory system from overexposure by inhalation to airborne contaminants. Respiratory protection is used when a worker must work in an area where he/she might be exposed to concentration in excess of the allowable exposure limit. N

respiratory rate
The frequency of a complete cycle of a breath (inhalation and exhalation). N

respond or response
Remove, removal, remedy and remedial action. L

respondent
Any person against whom a complaint has been issued. U

response action
(1) A method, including removal, encapsulation, enclosure, repair, operations and maintenance, that protects human health and the environment from friable ACBM. A (2) All activities undertaken to address the problems created by hazardous substances at a National Priorities List site. A (3) A CERCLA-authorized action involving either a short-term removal action or a long-term removal response that may include but is not limited to: removing hazardous materials from a site to an EPA-approved hazardous waste facility for treatment, containment, or destruction; containing the waste safely on-site; destroying or treating the waste on-site; and identifying and removing the source of ground-water contamination and halting further migration of contaminants. (See: cleanup). N

responsible agency
The organizational element that has the legal duty to ensure that owners,

operators, or users of facilities comply with these guidelines. A (2) The organizational element that has the legal duty to ensure that owners, operators or users of land disposal sites comply with these guidelines. U

responsible party
(1) Someone who can provide additional information on the hazardous chemical and appropriate emergency procedures, if necessary. O (2) [With regard to PCBs,] the owner of the PCB equipment, facility, or other source of PCBs or his/her designated agent (e.g., a facility manager or foreman). A

restoration
Measures taken to return a site to pre-violation conditions. N

restricted area
Any area access to which is controlled by the employer for purposes of protection of individuals from exposure to radiation or radioactive materials. O

restricted use
When a pesticide is registered, some or all of its uses may be classified (under FIFRA regulations) for restricted use if the pesticide requires special handling because of its toxicity. Restricted-use pesticides may be applied only by trained, certified applicators or those under their direct supervision. N

restriction enzymes
Enzymes that recognize certain specific regions of a long DNA molecule and then cut the DNA into smaller pieces. N

restrictive lung disease
Lung disease in which the expansion of the lung is restricted either because of alterations in the supportive structures of the lung (parenchyma) or because of disease of the pleura, the chest wall, or the neuromuscular apparatus. An example is fibrosis. N

retail outlet
Any establishment at which gasoline or diesel fuel is sold or offered for sale for use in motor vehicles. A

retailer
(1) Any person who owns, leases, operates, controls, or supervises a retail outlet. A (2) A person who distributes in commerce a chemical substance, mixture, or article to ultimate purchasers who are not commercial entities. A

retan-wet finish
The final processing steps performed on a tanned hide including, but not limited to, the following wet processes: retan, bleach, color, and fatliquor. A

retarder (active)
A device or system for decelerating rolling rail cars and controlling the degree of deceleration on a car by car basis. A

retarder sound
A sound which is heard and identified by the observer as that of a retarder, and that causes a sound level meter indicator at fast meter response [40 CFR § 201.1(l)] to register an increase of at least ten decibels above

the level observed immediately before hearing the sound. A

retention
The state of being held in a specific location. Used to refer to the amount of an inhaled material that remains in the lung (pulmonary retention) or to the amount of a toxicant dose that remains in the body or body compartment for a specified period of time. N

retention chamber
A structure within a flow-through test chamber which confines the test organisms, facilitating observation of test organisms and eliminating loss of organisms in outflow water. A

retort-type incinerator
A multiple-chamber incinerator in which the gases travel from the end of the ignition chamber, then pass through the mixing and combustion chamber. U

retread tire
A worn automobile, truck, or other motor vehicle tire whose tread has been replaced. A

retrofit
The addition or removal of an item of equipment, or a required adjustment, connection, or disconnection of an existing item of equipment, for the purpose of reducing emissions. A

retrofit device
Any component, equipment, or other device: (1) Which is designed to be installed in or on an automobile as an addition to, as a replacement for, or through alteration or modification of, any original component, equipment, or other device; and (2) Which any manufacturer, dealer, or distributor of such device represents will provide higher fuel economy than would have resulted with the automobile as originally equipped. The term also includes fuel and oil additives for use in an automobile. The term does not include fuel flow measuring instruments or other driving aids which will not be evaluated in this program. A

retrofitted configuration
The test configuration after adjustment of engine calibrations to the retrofit specifications and after all retrofit hardware has been installed. A

returnable beverage container
A beverage container for which a deposit is paid upon purchase and for which a refund of equal value is payable upon return. A

reuse
The reintroduction of a waste material or product into the economic stream without any chemical or physical change. An example is the empty soft drink bottle that is returned to the bottling company, sterilized, and refilled. U

reverberation time
The time that would be required for the mean-square sound pressure level, originally in a steady state, to fall 60 dB after the source is stopped. A

reverberatory furnace
Includes the following types of

reverberatory furnaces: stationary, rotating, rocking, and tilting. U

reverse osmosis
Method of waste treatment that uses a semi-permeable membrane to separate water from pollutants. N

review
Refers to the process of examining documents located in response to a request that is for a commercial use (see paragraph (e) of this section) to determine whether any portion of any document located is permitted to be withheld. It also includes processing any documents for disclosure, e.g., doing all that is necessary to excise them and otherwise prepare them for release. Review does not include time spent resolving legal or policy issues regarding the application of exemptions. (Documents must be reviewed in responding to all requests; however, review time may only be charged to Commercial Use Requesters). A

R_f
The furthest distance traveled by a test material on a thin-layer chromatography plate divided by the distance traveled by a solvent front (arbitrarily set at 10.0 cm in soil TLC studies). A

RfD
Reference dose. N

RFI
Remedial Field Investigation. N

RFP
(1) Request For Proposal. U (2) Reasonable further progress. N

RI
Remedial Investigation. U

RI/FS
Remedial Information/Feasibility Study. N

RIA
Regulatory Impact Assessment. N

ribonucleic acid
RNA. A molecule that carries the genetic message from DNA to a cell's protein-producing mechanisms; similar to, but chemically different from, DNA. N

RIMs
Regulatory Interpretative Memoranda. U

RIN
Regulation Identifier Number. U

ring rolls
A class for forging equipment used for shaping weldless rings from pierced discs or thick-walled, ring-shaped blanks between rolls which control wall thickness, ring diameter, height and contour. O

Ringelmann chart
Actually, a series of charts, numbered from 0 to 5, that simulate various smoke densities, by presenting different percentages of black. A Ringelmann No. 1 is equivalent to 20 percent black; a Ringelmann No. 5, to 100 percent. They are used for measuring the opacity of smoke arising from stacks and other sources by matching the actual emission with the various numbers, or densities,

indicated by the charts. Ringelmann numbers are sometimes used in setting emission standards.

RIP
RCRA Implementation Plan. U

riparian rights
Entitlement of a land owner to the water on or bordering his property, including the right to prevent diversion or misuse of upstream waters. Generally, a matter of state law. N

rise
The vertical distance from the top of a tread to the top of the next higher tread. O

rise time
The time required for the spark voltage to increase from 10 percent to 90 percent of its maximum value. A

riser
The upright member of a step situated at the back of a lower tread and near the leading edge of the next higher tread. O

riser height
The vertical distance from the top of a tread to the top of the next higher tread or platform/landing or the distance from the top of a platform/landing to the top of the next higher tread or platform/landing. O

rising current separator
A separator that uses a form of elutriation to sort mixed materials by a countercurrent flow of water or other fluid. U

risk
The potential for realization of unwanted negative consequences or events. N

risk assessment
A qualitative or quantitative evaluation of the environmental and/or health risk resulting from exposure to a chemical or physical agent (pollutant); combines exposure assessment results with toxicity assessment results to estimate risk. N

risk characterization
The final step of a risk assessment, which is a description of the nature and often the magnitude of human risk, including attendant uncertainty. N

risk communication
The exchange of information about health or environmental risks between risk assessors, risk managers, the general public, news media, interest groups, etc. N

risk estimate
A description of the probability that organisms exposed to a specified dose of chemical will develop an adverse response (e.g., cancer). N

risk factor
Characteristic (e.g., race, sex, age, obesity) or variable (e.g., smoking, occupational exposure level) associated with increased probability of a toxic effect. N

risk management
The process of evaluating alternative

regulatory and non-regulatory responses to risk and selecting among them. The selection process necessarily requires the consideration of legal, economic and social factors. N

risk-specific dose
The dose corresponding to a specified level of risk. N

river basin
The land area drained by a river and its tributaries. N

RMCL
Recommended maximum contaminant level. The maximum level of a contaminant in drinking water at which no known or anticipated adverse affect on human health would occur, and which includes an adequate margin of safety. Recommended levels are nonenforceable health goals. (See: maximum contaminant level.) N

roadways
Surfaces on which motor vehicles travel. This term includes highways, roads, streets, parking areas, and driveways. A

ROC
Record Of Communication. N

rocking-grate stoker
A stoker with a bed of bars or plates on axles. When the axles are rocked in a coordinated manner, the solid waste is lifted and advanced along the surface of the grate. G

ROD
Record Of Decision (CERCLA). N

rodenticide
A chemical or agent used to destroy rats or other rodent pests, or to prevent them from damaging food, crops, etc. N

rodenticides
All substances or mixtures of substances intended for preventing, destroying, repelling, or mitigating animals belonging to the Order Rodentia of the Class Mammalia, and closely related species, declared to be pests. Rodenticides include, but are not limited to: (i) Baits, tracking powders, and fumigants intended to kill or repel rodents; (ii) Repellents intended for use on plants, surfaces, in premises, or in or on packaging or other materials such as food containers, plastic pipe, telephone cables, and building materials, for the purpose of repelling rodents; and (iii) Reproductive inhibitors intended to reduce or otherwise alter the reproductive capacity or potential of rodents. A

Roentgen
R. The special unit of exposure. One roentgen equals 2.58×10^{-4} coulomb per kilogram of air. U

Roentgen Equivalent Man
REM. The unit of dose equivalent from ionizing radiation to the human body, used to measure the amount of radiation to which a person or a part of a human has been exposed. N

ROG
Reactive organic gases. N

rolling
The reduction in thickness or diameter of a workpiece by passing it between lubricated steel rollers. There are two subcategories based on the rolling process. In the rolling with neat oils subcategory, pure or neat oils are used as lubricants for the rolling process. In the rolling with emulsions subcategory, emulsions are used as lubricants for the rolling process. A

roof
The exterior surface on the top of a building. This does not include floors which, because a building has not been completely built, temporarily become the top surface of a building. O

roof monitor
That portion of the roof of a potroom where gases not captured at the cell exit from the potroom. A

roofing bracket
A bracket used in sloped roof construction, having provisions for fastening to the roof or supported by ropes fastened over the ridge and secured to some suitable object. O

root crops
Plants whose edible parts are grown below the surface of the soil. A

rotary kiln stoker
A cylindrical, inclined device that rotates, thus causing the solid waste to move in a slow cascading and forward motion. H

rotary screen
An inclined, meshed cylinder that rotates on its axis and screens material placed in its upper end. U

rotary spin
A process used to produce wool fiberglass insulation by forcing molten glass through numerous small orifices in the side wall of a spinner to form continuous glass fibers that are then broken into discrete lengths by high velocity air flow. A

rough fish
Those fish not prized for eating, such as gar and suckers. Most are more tolerant of changing environmental conditions than game species. N

rounded
A number shortened to the specific number of decimal places in accordance with the "Round Off Method" specified in ASTM E 29-67. A

route of exposure
The means by which toxic agents gain access to an organism (e.g., ingestion, inhalation, dermal exposure, intravenous, subcutaneous, intramuscular, intraperitoneal administration). N

routine maintenance
An area, such as a boiler room or mechanical room, that is not normally frequented by students and in which maintenance employees or contract workers regularly conduct maintenance activities. A

routine use
With respect to the disclosure of a record, the use of such record for a

purpose which is compatible with the purpose for which it was collected. O

RP
Responsible party. N

RPAR
Rebuttable Presumption Against Registration of a pesticide (FIFRA). N

RPM
(1) Remedial Project Manager. U (2) Revolutions per minute. U

RQ
Reportable quantity. The quantity of a hazardous substance or oil spilled that triggers reporting under CERCLA and section 311 of the Clean Water Act. If a substance is released in amounts exceeding its RQ, the release must be reported to the National Response Center, the SERC, and community emergency coordinators for areas likely to be affected. N

RQG
Reduced quantity generator. U

RRC
Regional Response Center. (EPA) N

RRT
Regional response team. Is composed of representatives of Federal agencies and a representative from each State in the Federal region. During a response to a major hazardous materials incident involving transportation or a fixed facility, the OSC may request that the RRT be convened to provide advice or recommendations in specific issues requiring resolution. Under the NCP, RRTs may be convened by the chairman when a hazardous materials discharge or release exceeds the response capability available to the OSC in the place where it occurs; crosses regional boundaries; or may pose a substantial threat to the public health, welfare, or environment; or the regionally significant amounts of property. Regional contingency plans specify detailed criteria for activation of RRTs. RRTs may review plans developed in compliance with Title III, if the local emergency planning committee so requests. N

RSD
Risk specific dose. U

RTECS
Registry of Toxic Effects of Chemical Substances. U

rubbish
A general term for solid waste, excluding food wastes and ashes, taken from residences, commercial establishments, and institutions. A

run
The net period of time during which an emission sample is collected. Unless otherwise specified, a run may be either intermittent or continuous within the limits of good engineering practice. A

run-on
Any rainwater, leachate, or other liquid that drains over land onto any part of a facility. A

rungs
Ladder crosspieces of circular or

oval cross-section on which a person may step in ascending or descending. O

runner
The lengthwise horizontal bracing or bearing members or both. O

running changes
Those changes in vehicle or engine configuration, equipment or calibration which are made by an OEM or ICI in the course of motor vehicle or motor vehicle engine production. A

running loss
Fuel evaporative emissions resulting from an average trip in an urban area or the simulation of such a trip. A

running sample
One obtained by lowering an unstoppered beaker or bottle from the top of the gasoline to the level of the bottom of the outlet connection or swing line, and returning it to the top of the top of the diesel fuel at a uniform rate of speed such that the beaker or bottle is about 3/4 full when withdrawn from the diesel fuel. A

runoff
(1) That portion of precipitation that flows over the ground surface and returns to streams. It can collect pollutants from air or land and carry them to the receiving waters. N (2) Any rainwater, leachate, or other liquid that drains over land from any part of a facility. A (3) (1) The flow of storm water resulting from precipitation coming into contact with petroleum refinery property. A (4) The portion of precipitation that drains from an area as surface flow. A

runoff coefficient
The fraction of total rainfall that will appear at a conveyance as runoff. A

runway
A passageway for persons, elevated above the surrounding floor or ground level, such as a footwalk along shafting or a walkway between buildings. O

RVP
Reid vapor pressure. U

RWS
Rural Water Survey. N

°R
Degree Rankine. U

S

S&A
Surveillance and analysis. U

SAB
Science Advisory Board. A

SAE
Society of Automotive Engineers. O

safe surface
A horizontal surface intended to be occupied by personnel, which is so protected by a fall protection system that it can be reasonably assured that said occupants will be protected against falls. O

safety belt
A device, usually worn around the waist which, by reason of its attachment to a lanyard and lifeline or a structure, will prevent a worker from falling. O

safety block
A prop that, when inserted between the upper and lower dies or between the bolster plate and the face of the slide, prevents the slide from falling of its own deadweight. O

safety can
An approved closed container, of not more than 5 gallons capacity, having a flash-arresting screen, spring-closing lid and spout cover and so designed that it will safely relieve internal pressure when subjected to fire exposure. O

safety factor
The ratio of the ultimate breaking strength of a member or piece of material or equipment to the actual working stress or safe load when in use. O

safety guard
An enclosure designed to restrain the pieces of the grinding wheel and furnish all possible protection in the event that the wheel is broken in operation. See paragraph (b) of [29 CFR] § 1910.215. O

safety screen
An air- and water-tight diaphragm

safety screen
An air- and water-tight diaphragm placed across the upper part of a compressed air tunnel between the face and bulkhead, in order to prevent flooding the crown of the tunnel between the safety screen and the bulkhead, thus providing a safe means of refuge and exit from flooding or flooded tunnel. O

safety system
The integrated total system, including the pertinent elements of the press, the controls, the safeguarding and any required supplemental safeguarding, and their interfaces with the operator, and the environment, designed, constructed and arranged to operate together as a unit, such that a single failure or single operating error will not cause injury to personnel due to point of operation hazards. O

safety-monitoring system
A safety system in which a competent person monitors the safety of all employees in a roofing crew, and warns them when it appears to the monitor that they are unaware of the hazard or are acting in an unsafe manner. The competent person must be on the same roof as and within visual sighting distance of the employees, and must be close enough to verbally communicate with the employees. O

saline estuarine waters
Those semi-enclosed coastal waters which have a free connection to the territorial sea, undergo net seaward exchange with ocean waters, and have salinities comparable to those of the ocean. Generally, these waters are near the mouth of estuaries and have cross-sectional annual mean salinities greater than twenty-five (25) parts per thousand. A

salinity
The degree of salt in water. N

salt water intrusion
The invasion of fresh surface or ground water by salt water. If the salt water comes from the ocean, it is called sea water intrusion. N

salvaging
The controlled removal of waste materials for utilization. A

sample system
The system which provides for the transportation of the gaseous emission sample from the sample probe to the inlet of the instrumentation system. A

sampler
A device used with or without flow measurement to obtain an adequate portion of water or waste for analytical purposes. May be designed for taking a single sample (grab), composite sample, continuous sample, or periodic sample. U

sampling area
Any area, whether contiguous or not, within a school building which contains friable material that is homogeneous in texture and appearance. A

sanctions
Actions taken against a State or local government by the federal government for failure to plan or to

implement a SIP. Examples include withholding of highway funds and a ban on construction of new sources. N

sand filters
Devices that remove some suspended solids from sewage. Air and bacteria decompose additional wastes filtering through the sand so that cleaner water drains from the bed. N

sanitary landfill
A disposal facility employing an engineered method of disposing of solid wastes on land in a manner which minimizes environmental hazards by spreading the solid wastes in thin layers, compacting the solid wastes to the smallest practical volume, and applying cover material at the end of each working day. Such facility complies with the [EPA] Agency Guidelines for the Land Disposal of Solid Wastes as prescribed in 40 CFR part 241. A

sanitary landfill density
Sanitary landfill density is the ratio of the combined weight of solid waste and the soil cover to the combined volume of the solid waste and the soil cover, $(W_{sw} + W_{soil}/V_{sw} + V_{soil})$. U

sanitary landfill liner
An impermeable barrier, manufactured, constructed, or existing in a natural condition, that is utilized to collect leachate. The component parts of a sanitary landfill liner consist of but are not limited to the natural subgrade which is the undisturbed in place earth upon which construction will commence, the sub-base, the impermeable membrane, the protective cover, and drainage facilities. U

sanitary landfilling methods
See area method, quarry method, ramp method, trench method, and wet area method. U

sanitary sewer
(1) Underground pipes that carry only domestic or commercial waste, not storm-water. N (2) A conduit intended to carry liquid and water-carried wastes from residences, commercial buildings, industrial plants and institutions together with minor quantities of ground, storm and surface waters that are not admitted intentionally. A

sanitary survey
An onsite review of the water source, facilities, equipment, operation and maintenance of a public water system for the purpose of evaluating the adequacy of such source, facilities, equipment, operation and maintenance for producing and distributing safe drinking water. A

sanitation
Control of physical factors in the human environment that can harm development, health, or survival. N

SARA
The Superfund Amendments and Reauthorization Act of 1986. In addition to certain free-standing provisions of law, it includes amendments to CERCLA, the Solid Waste Disposal Act, and the Internal

Revenue Code. Among the free-standing provisions of law is Title III of SARA, also known as the "Emergency Planning and Community Right-to-Know Act of 1986" and Title IV of SARA, also known as the Radon Gas and Indoor Air Quality Research Act of 1986." Title V of SARA amending the Internal Revenue Code is also known as the "Superfund Revenue Act of 1986." A

sarcoma
A malignant tumor arising in connective tissue and composed primarily of anaplastic cells resembling supportive tissue. N

SAROAD
Storage and retrieval of aerometric data. A

SAROAD site identification form
One of the several forms in the SAROAD system. It is the form which provides a complete description of the site (and its surroundings) of an ambient air quality monitoring station. A

satellite vehicle
A small collection vehicle that transfers its load into a larger vehicle operating in conjunction with it. A

saturated solution
A solution in which the dissolved solute is in equilibrium with an excess of undissolved solute; or a solution in equilibrium such that at a fixed temperature and pressure, the concentration of the solution is at its maximum value and will not change even in the presence of an excess of solute. A

saturator
The equipment in which asphalt is applied to felt to make asphalt roofing products. The term saturator includes the saturator, wet looper, and coater. A

sawing
Cutting a workpiece with a band, blade, or circular disc having teeth. A

scaffold
Any temporary elevated platform and its supporting structure used for supporting workmen or materials or both. O

SCAP
Superfund Comprehensive Accomplishments Plan. U

scavenging
The uncontrolled and unauthorized removal of materials at any point in the solid waste management system. A

SCE
Sister chromatid exchange. N

scf.
Standard cubic feet. U

scfh.
Standard cubic feet per hour. U

scfm.
Standard cubic feet per minute. U

schedule and timetable of compliance
A schedule of required measures including an enforceable sequence of

actions or operations leading to compliance with an emission limitation, other limitation, prohibition, or standard. B

schedule of compliance
(1) A schedule of remedial measures included in a "permit," including an enforceable sequence of interim requirements (for example, actions, operations, or milestone events) leading to compliance with the "appropriate Act and regulations"). A (2) A schedule of remedial measures including an enforceable sequence of actions or operations leading to compliance with an effluent limitation, other limitation prohibition, or standard. D

scheduled maintenance
Any adjustment, repair, removal, disassembly, cleaning, or replacement of facility or vehicle components or systems which is performed on a periodic basis to prevent part failure or malfunction, or anticipated as necessary to correct an overt indication of malfunction or failure for which periodic maintenance is not appropriate. A

school
(1) Any elementary or secondary school as defined in section 198 of the Elementary and Secondary Education Act of 1965 (20 U.S.C. 2854). (2) Any structure suitable for use as a classroom, including a school facility such as a laboratory, library, school eating facility, or facility used for the preparation of food. (3) Any gymnasium or other facility which is specially designed for athletic or recreational activities for an academic course in physical education. (4) Any other facility used for the instruction or housing of students or for the administration of educational or research programs. (5) Any maintenance, storage, or utility facility, including any hallway, essential to the operation of any facility described in this definition of "school building" under paragraphs (1) (2) (3), or (4). (6) Any portico or covered exterior hallway or walkway. (7) Any exterior portion of a mechanical system used to condition interior space. (7) Any structures used for the instruction of school children, including classrooms, laboratories, libraries, research facilities and administrative facilities. (8) School eating facilities, and school kitchens. A

scope of study
Absorption toxicokinetics refers to the bioavailability, i.e., the rate and extent of absorption of the test substance, and metabolism and excretion rates of the test substance after absorption. A

scope of work
A document similar in content to the program of requirements but substantially abbreviated. It is usually prepared for small-scale projects. A

scoping
A preliminary public discussion of the information to be developed, alternatives to be considered, and issues to be discussed in an EIS. U

scrap
Materials discarded from manufacturing operations that may be suitable for reprocessing. N

scrap metal
Is bits and pieces of metal parts (e.g.,) bars, turning, rods, sheets, wire) or metal pieces that may be combined together with bolts or soldering (e.g., radiators, scrap automobiles, railroad box cars), which when worn or superfluous can be recycled. A

screen
A device for separating material according to size by passing undersize material through one or more mesh surfaces (screens) in series and retaining oversize material on the mesh surfaces (screens). A

screw conveyor
A rotating helical shaft that moves material, such as incinerator siftings, along a trough or tube. U

scrubber
A device that uses a liquid spray to remove aerosol and gaseous pollutants from an air stream. The gases are removed either by absorption or chemical reaction. Solid and liquid particulates are removed through contact with the spray. Scrubbers are used for both the measurement and control of pollution. U

scrubbing
The washing of impurities from any process gas stream. A

SCUBA diving
A diving mode independent of surface supply in which the diver uses open circuit self-contained underwater breathing apparatus. O

scuppers
Openings around the deck of a vessel which allows water falling onto the deck to flow overboard. Should be plugged during fuel transfer. A

SD
Standard deviation. U

SDWA
Safe Drinking Water Act. U

SEA
State-EPA agreements. U

seafood
The raw material, including freshwater and saltwater fish and shellfish, to be processed, in the form in which it is received at the processing plant. A

sealable equipment
Equipment enclosed in a case or cabinet that is provided with a means of sealing or locking so that live parts cannot be made accessible without opening the enclosure. The equipment may or may not be operable without opening the enclosure. O

search
Includes all time spent looking for material that is responsive to a [FOIA] request, including page-by-page or line-by-line identification of material within documents. Searching for material must be done in the most

efficient and least expensive manner so as to minimize costs for both the EPA and the requestor. For example, EPA will not engage in line-by-line search when merely duplicating an entire document would prove the less expensive and quicker method of complying with a request. "Search" will be distinguished, moreover, from "review" of material in order to determine whether the material is exempt from disclosure. Searches may be done manually or by computer using existing programming. A

SEC
Securities and Exchange Commission. U

secator
A separating device that throws mixed material onto a rotating shaft; heavy and resilient materials bounce off one side of the shaft, whereas light and elastic materials land on the other and are cast in the opposite direction. U

secondary burner
A burner installed in the secondary combustion chamber of an incinerator to maintain a minimum temperature and to complete the combustion of incompletely burned gases. Compare: afterburner. U

secondary combustion air
The air introduced above or below a fuel bed by a natural, induced, or forced draft. See overfire air and underfire air. U

secondary contact recreation
Activities where a person's water contact would be limited to the extent that bacterial infections of eyes, ears, respiratory, or digestive systems or urogenital areas would normally be avoided (such as wading or fishing). A

secondary containment
Applies to containers and tanks. In container systems, secondary containment consists of a base (concrete or other impervious material) which must have the capacity to contain ten percent (10%) of the volume of containers or the volume of the largest container, whichever is greater. In tank systems, secondary containment includes one or more of the following: an external liner, a vault, a double-walled tank or equivalent device (approved by the Regional Administration). N

secondary control system
An air pollution control system designed to remove gaseous and particulate fluorides from gases which escape capture by the primary control system. A

secondary drinking water regulation
A regulation which applies to public water systems and which specifies the maximum contaminant levels which, in the judgment of the Administrator [of EPA], are requisite to protect the public welfare. Such regulations may apply to any contaminant in drinking water (A) which may adversely affect the odor or appearance of such water and consequently may cause a substantial number of the persons

served by the public water system providing such water to discontinue its use, or (B) which may otherwise adversely affect the public welfare. Such regulations may vary according to geographic and other circumstances. J

secondary emissions
(1) Emissions that escape capture by a primary emission control system. A (2) Emissions which would occur as a result of the construction or operation of a major stationary source or major modification, but do not come from the major stationary source or major modification itself. Secondary emissions include emissions from any off-site support facility which would not be constructed or increase its emissions except as a result of the construction or operation of the major stationary source or major modification. Secondary emissions do not include any emissions which come directly from a mobile source, such as emissions from the tailpipe of a motor vehicle, from a train, or from a vessel. A

secondary hood system
The equipment (including hoods, ducts, fans, and dampers) used to capture and transport secondary emissions. A

secondary industry category
Any industry category which is not a "primary industry category." A

secondary materials
Recovered resources that are used as raw materials in some manufacturing processes. U

secondary maximum contaminant levels
SMCLs which apply to public water systems and which, in the judgement of the Administrator, are requisite to protect the public welfare. The SMCL means the maximum permissible level of a contaminant in water which is delivered to the free flowing outlet of the ultimate user of public water system. Contaminants added to the water under circumstances controlled by the user, except those resulting from corrosion of piping and plumbing caused by water quality, are excluded from this definition. A

secondary pollutant
A pollutant formed in the atmosphere by chemical changes taking place between primary pollutants and sometimes other substances present in the air. U

secondary standard
A national secondary ambient air quality standard promulgated pursuant to section 109 of the [Clean Air] Act. A [ed. A secondary standard establishes that ambient concentration of the pollutant that, with an adequate margin of safety, will protect the public welfare (i.e. all parts of the environment other than human health) from adverse impacts]. U

secondary treatment
The second step in most publicly owned waste treatment systems in which bacteria consume the organic parts of the waste. It is accomplished by bringing together waste, bacteria, and oxygen in trickling filters or in the activated sludge process. This treatment removes floating and

settleable solids and about 90 percent of the oxygen-demanding substances and suspended solids. Disinfection is the final stage of secondary treatment. (See: primary, tertiary treatment). N

Section 208 plan
An areawide waste treatment management plan prepared under Section 208 of the Federal Water Pollution Control Act (FWPCA), as amended. See 40 CFR Part 126 and 40 CFR Part 35, Subpart F. A

Section 404 program
An "approved State Program" to regulate the "discharge of dredged material" and the "discharge of fill material" under section 404 of the Clean Water Act in "State regulated waters." A

Section 5 notice
Any [TSCA] PMN, consolidated PMN, intermediate PMN, significant new use notice, exemption notice, or exemption application. A

sectional ladder
A non-self-supporting portable ladder, nonadjustable in length, consisting of two or more sections of ladder so constructed that the sections may be combined to function as a single ladder. Its size is designated by the overall length of the assembled sections. O

sectionally supported wall
A furnace or boiler wall of special refractory blocks or shapes that are mounted on and supported at intervals of height by metallic hangers. U

secure maximum contaminant level
Maximum permissible level of a contaminant in water which is delivered to the free flowing outlet of the ultimate user of a water supply, the consumer, or of contamination resulting from corrosion of piping and plumbing caused by water quality. N

sediment(s)
The unconsolidated inorganic and organic material that is suspended in and being transported by surface water, or has settled out and has deposited into beds. A (2) Soil, sand, and minerals washed from land into water usually after rain. They pile up in reservoirs, rivers and harbors, destroying fish-nesting areas and holes of water animals, and clouding the water so that needed sunlight might not reach aquatic plants. Careless farming, mining, and building activities will expose sediment materials, contributing to their being washed off the land after rainfalls. N

sedimentation
A process for removal of solids before filtration by gravity or separation. A

sedimentation tanks
Holding areas for waste water where floating wastes are skimmed off and settled solids are pumped out for disposal. N

seeding
The sowing of seed and placement of seedlings to produce farm, ranch, or forest crops and includes the placement of soil beds for seeds or

seedlings on established farm and forest lands. A

seepage
The movement of liquids or gases through soil without the formation of definite channels. U

seeps
Small springs of discolored, malodorous leachate that are frequently formed along the lower edges of many landfills. U

segment
A portion of an approved planning area, the surface waters of which have common hydrologic characteristics (or flow regulation patterns); common natural physical, chemical and biological characteristics and processes; and common reactions to external stresses, such as the discharge of pollutants. Segments will be classified as either a water quality segment or an effluent limitation segment as follows: (1) Water quality segment. Any segment where it is known that water quality does not meet applicable water quality standards and/or is not expected to meet applicable water quality standards even after the application of the effluent limitations required by sections 301(b)(1)(B) and 301(b)(2)(A) of the [Clean Water] Act. (2) Effluent limitation segment. Any segment where it is known that water quality is meeting and will continue to meet applicable water quality standards or where there is adequate demonstration that water quality will meet applicable water quality standards after the application of the effluent limitations required by sections 301(b)(1)(B) and 301(b)(2)(A) of the [Clean Water] Act. A

segregated stormwater sewer system
A drain and collection system designed and operated for the sole purpose of collecting rainfall runoff at a facility, and which is segregated from all other individual drain systems. A

seismic activity
Earthquake activity (see also fault). U

select carcinogen
Any substance which meets one of the following criteria: (i) It is regulated by OSHA as a carcinogen; or (ii) It is listed under the category, "known to be carcinogens," in the Annual Report on Carcinogens published by the National Toxicology Program (NTP) (latest edition); or (iii) It is listed under Group 1 ("carcinogenic to humans") by the International Agency for Research on Cancer Monographs (IARC) (latest editions); or (iv) It is listed in either Group 2A or 2B by IARC or under the category, "reasonably anticipated to be carcinogens" by NTP, and causes statistically significant tumor incidence in experimental animals in accordance with any of the following criteria: (A) After inhalation exposure of 6-7 hours per day, 5 days per week, for a significant portion of a lifetime to dosages of less than 10 mg/m^3; (B) After repeated skin application of less than 300 (mg/kg of body weight) per week; or (C) After oral dosages of less than 50 mg/kg of body weight per day. O

selective pesticide
A chemical designed to affect only certain types of pests leaving other plants and animals unharmed. N

self-contained breathing apparatus
A respiratory protection device that consists of a supply or means of respirable air, oxygen, or oxygen-generating material, carried by the wearer. N

self-purification
The natural processes occurring in a stream or other body of water that result in the reduction of bacteria, satisfaction of the BOD, stabilization of organic constituents, replacement of depleted dissolved oxygen, and the return of the stream biota to normal. Also called natural purification. U

semi-confined aquifer
An aquifer that is partially confined by a soil layer (or layers) of low permeability through which recharge and discharge can occur. N

semi-wet
Those steelmaking air cleaning systems that use water for the sole purpose of conditioning the temperature and humidity of furnace gases such that the gases may be cleaned in dry air pollution control systems. A

semiannual
A 6-month period; the first semiannual period concludes on the last day of the last month during the 180 days following initial startup for new sources; and the first semiannual period concludes on the last day of the last full month during the 180 days after the effective date of a specific subpart that references this subpart for existing sources. A

semiautomatic feeding
Feeding wherein the material or part being processed is placed within or removed from the point of operation by an auxiliary means controlled by operator on each stroke of the press. O

semiconductors
Solid state electrical devices which perform functions such as information processing and display, power handling, and interconversion between light energy and electrical energy. A

semipermeable membrane
A barrier, usually thin, that permits passage of particles up to a certain size or of special nature. Often used to separate colloids from their suspending liquid, as in dialysis. U

senescence
Term for the aging process. Sometimes used to describe lakes or other bodies of water in advanced stages of eutrophication. N

sensitivity
The slope of the analytical curve, i.e. functional relationship between emission intensity and concentration. A

sensitization
An allergic condition that usually affects the skin or lungs. Once exposure to a substance has caused a reaction, the individual may be

sensitized to that substance and further exposure even at low levels may elicit an adverse reaction. N

sensitizer
A chemical that causes a substantial proportion of exposed people or animals to develop an allergic reaction in normal tissue after repeated exposure to the chemical. O

sensor
A device that measures a physical quantity or the change in a physical quantity, such as temperature, pressure, flow rate, pH, or liquid level. A

separate collection
Collecting recyclable materials which have been separated at the point of generation and keeping those materials separate from other collected solid waste in separate compartments of a single collection vehicle or through the use of separate collection vehicles. A

separate storm sewer
A conveyance or system of conveyances (including but not limited to pipes, conduits, and channels) located in an urbanized area and primarily operated for the purpose of collecting and conveying storm water runoff. It does not include any conveyance which discharges process waste water or storm water runoff contaminated by contact with aggregations of wastes, raw materials, or pollutant-contaminated soil, from lands or facilities used for industrial or commercial activities, into navigable waters or into another conveyance or system of conveyances defined as a separate storm sewer. A

separately derived system
A premises wiring system whose power is derived from generator, transformer, or converter winding and has no direct electrical connection, including a solidly connected grounded circuit conductor, to supply conductors originating in another system. O

separation
The process of dividing solid waste into designated categories, which may be as general as paper from metals from glass or as specific as clear glass from colored glass. Also called segregation. U

separator
A mechanical device or system for the separation of solid waste. U

septage
The liquid and solid material pumped from a septic tank, cesspool, or similar domestic sewage treatment system, or a holding tank when the system is cleaned or maintained. A

septic tank
A water-tight covered receptacle designed to receive or process, through liquid separation or biological digestion, the sewage discharge from a building sewer. The effluent from such a receptacle is distributed for disposal through the soil and settled solids and scum from the tank are pumped out periodically and hauled to a treatment facility. A

SERC
State Emergency Response Commission. U

serial number
The identification number assigned by the manufacturer to a specific production unit. A

series resistance
The sum of resistances from the condenser plates to the condenser's external connections. A

serious acute effects
Human injury or human disease processes that have a short latency period for development, result from short-term exposure to a chemical substance, or are a combination of these factors and which are likely to result in death or severe or prolonged incapacitation. A

serious chronic effects
Human disease processes or other adverse effects that have a long latency period for development, result from long-term exposure, are long-term illnesses, or are a combination of these factors and that are likely to result in death, severe or prolonged incapacitation, disfigurement, or severe or prolonged loss of the ability to use a normal bodily or intellectual function with a consequent impairment of normal activities. A

serious hazard
Any condition or practice which would be classified as a serious violation of applicable federal or state statutes, regulations or standards, based on criteria contained in the current *OSHA Field Operations Manual* or an approved state plan counterpart, except that the element of employer knowledge shall not be considered. O

serosa
A membrane producing a serous secretion, or containing serum or a serumlike substance. N

seven-day average
The arithmetic mean of pollutant parameter values for samples collected in a period of 7 consecutive days. A

service
The conductors and equipment for delivering energy from the electricity supply system to the wiring system of the premises served. O

service cable
Service conductors made up in the form of a cable. O

service conductors
The supply conductors that extend from the street main or from transformers to the service equipment of the premises supplied. O

service connector
The pipe that carries tap water from the public water main to a building. N

service drop
The overhead service conductors from the last pole or other aerial support to and including the splices, if any, connecting to the service-entrance conductors at the building or other structure. O

service equipment
The necessary equipment, usually consisting of a circuit breaker or switch and fuses, and their accessories, located near the point of entrance of supply conductors to a building or other structure, or an otherwise defined area, and intended to constitute the main control and means of cutoff of the supply. O

service life
The period of time during which a component of a waste treatment management system will be capable of performing a function. A

service-entrance cable
A single conductor or multiconductor assembly provided with or without an overall covering, primarily used for services. O

services
A contractor's labor, time, or efforts which do not involve the delivery of a specific end item, other than documents (e.g., reports, design drawing, specifications). This term does not include employment agreements or collective bargaining agreements. A

servicing
Workplace activities such as constructing, installing, setting up, adjusting, inspecting, modifying, and maintaining and/or servicing machines or equipment. These activities include lubrication, cleaning or unjamming of machines or equipment and making adjustments or tool changes, where the employee may be exposed to the unexpected energization or startup of the equipment or release of hazardous energy. O

SETS
Site Enforcement Tracking System. N

setting up
Any work performed to prepare a machine or equipment to perform its normal production operation. O

settleable solids
(1) That matter in wastewater which will not stay in suspension during a preselected period, such as one hour, but either settles to the bottom or floats to the top. (2) In the Imhoff cone test, the volume of matter that settles to the bottom of the cone in one hour. U

settlement
The sinking of the surface of a sanitary landfill because of such factors as decomposition, consolidation, drainage, and underground failures. The degree and uniformity of settlement depends on the kind of refuse and how thoroughly it was compacted. U

settling chamber
(1) Any chamber designed to reduce the velocity of the products of combustion and thus to promote the settling of fly ash from the gas stream before it is discharged into the environment. Also called expansion, separation, or subsidence chamber. (2) A series of screens placed in the way of flue gases to slow the stream of air, thus helping gravity to pull particles out of the emission into a collection area. N

settling tank
(1) A container that gravimetrically separates oils, grease, and dirt from petroleum solvent, together with the piping and ductwork used in the installation of this device. A (2) A holding area for waste water, where heavier particles sink to the bottom and can be siphoned off. N

settling velocity
The velocity at which a given dust will fall out of dust-laden gas under the influence of gravity only. Also called terminal velocity. U

severe property damage
Substantial physical damage to property, damage to the treatment facilities which causes them to become inoperable, or substantial and permanent loss of natural resources which can reasonably be expected to occur in the absence of a bypass. Severe property damage does not mean economic loss caused by delays in production. A

sewage
(1) The waste and wastewater produced by residential and commercial establishments and discharged into sewers. N (2) Human body wastes and the wastes from toilets and other receptacles intended to receive or retain body wastes except that, with respect to commercial vessels on the Great Lakes such term shall include graywater. D

sewage collection system
Common lateral sewers, within a publicly-owned treatment system, which are primarily installed to receive wastewaters directly from facilities which convey wastewater from individual structures or from private property, and which include service connection "Y" fittings designed for connection with those facilities. The facilities which convey wastewater from individual structures or from private property to the public lateral sewer, or its equivalent, are specifically excluded from the definition, with the exception of pumping units, and pressurized lines, for individual structures or groups of structures when such units are cost effective and are owned and maintained by the grantee. A

sewage from vessels (NPDES)
Human body wastes and the wastes from toilets and other receptacles intended to receive or retain body wastes that are discharged from vessels and regulated under section 312 of CWA, except that with respect to commercial vessels on the Great Lakes this term includes graywater. For the purposes of this definition, "graywater" means galley, bath, and shower water. A

sewage sludge
(1) The solids, residues, and precipitate separated from or created in sewage by the unit processes of a "publicly owned treatment works." "Sewage" as used in this definition means any wastes, including wastes from humans, households, commercial establishments, industries, and storm water runoff, that are discharged to or otherwise enter a publicly owned

treatment works. A (2) Any solid, semisolid or liquid waste generated by a municipal wastewater treatment plant the ocean dumping of which may unreasonably degrade or endanger human health, welfare, or amenities, or the marine environment, ecological systems, and economic potentialities. A, E (3) Any solid, semi-solid, or liquid residue removed during the treatment of municipal waste water or domestic sewage. Sewage sludge includes, but is not limited to, solids removed during primary, secondary, or advanced waste water treatment, scum, septage, portable toilet dumpings, type III marine sanitation device pumpings (33 CFR part 159), and sewage sludge products. Sewage sludge does not include grit or screenings, or ash generated during the incineration of sewage sludge. A

sewage treatment works
Municipal or domestic waste treatment facilities of any type which are publicly owned or regulated to the extent that feasible compliance schedules are determined by the availability of funding provided by Federal, State, or local governments. A

sewer
A channel that carries waste water and stormwater runoff from the source to a treatment plant or receiving stream. Sanitary sewers carry household and commercial waste. Storm sewers carry runoff from rain or snow. Combined sewers are used for both purposes. N

sewer line
A lateral, trunk line, branch line, or other enclosed conduit used to convey waste to a downstream waste management unit. A

sewerage
The entire system of sewage collection, treatment, and disposal. Also applies to all effluent carried by sewers. N

shake
A separation along the grain, most of which occurs between the rings of annual growth. O

shall
Mandatory. O

shear shredder
A shredder that cuts material between two large blades or between a blade and a stationary edge. U

sheaves
Grooved pulleys, and shall be so classified unless used as flywheels. O

sheen
An iridescent appearance on the surface of water; a quantity of oil that creates a sheen is a harmful quantity subject to regulation under section 311 of the Clean Water Act. A

shell deposition
The measured length of shell growth that occurs between the time the shell is ground at test initiation and test termination 96 hours later. A

shift
The regular production work period for one group of workers. A

shipped liquid ammonia
Liquid ammonia commercially shipped for which the Department of Transportation requires 0.2 percent minimum water content. A

shipping losses
Discharges resulting from loading tank cars or tank trucks; discharges resulting from cleaning tank cars or tank trucks; and discharges from air pollution control scrubbers designed to control emissions from loading or cleaning tank cars or tank trucks. A

shore
A supporting member that resists a compressive force imposed by a load. O

short-term exposure limit
STEL. A time-weighted average OEL that the American Conference of Government and Industrial Hygienists (ACGIH) indicates should not be exceeded any time during the work day. Exposures at the STEL should not be longer than 15 minutes and should not be repeated more than 4 times per day. There should be at least 60 minutes between successive exposure at the STEL. N

short-term test indicative of carcinogenic potential
Either any limited bioassay that measures tumor or preneoplastic induction, or any test indicative of interaction of a chemical substance with DNA (i.e., positive response in assays for gene mutation, chromosomal aberrations, DNA damage and repair, or cellular transformation). A

short-term test indicative of the potential to cause a developmentally toxic effect
Any *in vivo* preliminary development toxicity screen conducted in a mammalian species, or any *in vitro* developmental toxicity screen, including any test system other than the intact pregnant mammal, that has been extensively evaluated and judged reliable for its ability to predict the potential to cause developmentally toxic effects in intact systems across a broad range of chemicals or within a class of chemicals that includes the substance of concern. A

shotgun
Non-scientific term for the process of breaking up the DNA derived from an organism and then moving each separate and unidentified DNA fragment into a bacterium. N

should
Recommended. O

show window
Any window used or designed to be used for the display of goods or advertising material, whether it is fully or partly enclosed or entirely open at the rear and whether or not it has a platform raised higher than the street floor level. O

SHP
Shaft horsepower. A

shredder
A machine used to break up waste materials into smaller pieces by cutting or tearing. U

shutdown
The cessation of operation of an affected facility for any purpose. A

SI
(1) Site Inspection. U (2) Surface impoundments. N (2) Spark ignition. N

SIC
The *Standard Industrial Classification Manual*, published by the Office of Management and Budget in the Executive Office of the President, defines industries in accordance with the composition and structure of the economy and covers the entire field of economic activities. The Calendar of Federal Regulations uses SIC terminology whenever possible throughout the "Sectors Affected" sections. U

SICEA
Steel Industry Compliance Extension Act. N

sick building syndrome
A set of symptoms that affect a number of building occupants during the time they spend in the building and diminish or go away during periods when they leave the building. Cannot be traced to specific pollutants or sources within the building. (Compare to: "building-related illness"). N

side-rolling ladder
A semifixed ladder, nonadjustable in length, supported by attachments to a guide rail, which is generally fastened to shelving, the plane of the ladder being also its plane of motion. O

side-step ladder
One from which a man getting off at the top must step sideways from the ladder in order to reach the landing. O

siftings
The fine materials that fall from a fuel bed through its grate openings during incineration. U

signal word
(1) That portion of a tag's inscription that contains the word or words that are intended to capture the employee's immediate attention. O (2) The word(s) used on a pesticide label --Danger, Warning, Caution--to indicate the level of toxicity of the chemicals. N

signaling circuit
Any electric circuit that energizes signaling equipment. O

signals
Moving signs, provided by workers, such as flagmen, or by devices, such as flashing lights, to warn of possible or existing hazards. O

significant
(1) In reference to a net emissions increase or the potential of a source to emit any of the following pollutants, a rate of emissions that would equal or exceed any of the rates listed in 40 CFR § 52.21 paragraph (b)(23)(i). (2) In reference to a net emissions increase or the potential of a source to emit a pollutant subject to regulation under the Clean Air Act that paragraph (b)(23)(i) of 40 CFR § 52.21 does not

list any emissions rate. (3) Notwithstanding paragraph 40 CFR § paragraph (b)(23)(i), significant means any emissions rate or any net emissions increase associated with a major stationary source or major modification, which would be constructed within 10 kilometers of a Class I area, and have an impact on such area equal to or greater than 1 g/m^3, (24-hour average). A

significant adverse environmental effects
When injury to the environment by a chemical substance which reduces or adversely affects the productivity, utility, value, or function of biological, commercial, or agricultural resources, or which may adversely affect a threatened or endangered species. A substance will be considered to have the potential for significant adverse environmental effects if it has one of the following: (1) An acute aquatic EC$_{50}$ of 1 mg/L or less. (2) An acute aquatic EC$_{50}$ of 20 mg/L or less where the ratio of aquatic vertebrate 24-hour to 48-hour EC$_{50}$ is greater than or equal to 2.0. (3) A Maximum Acceptable Toxicant Concentration (MATC) of less than or equal to 100 parts per billion (100 ppb). (4) An acute aquatic EC$_{50}$ of 20 mg/L or less coupled with either a measured bioconcentration factor (BCF) equal to or greater than 1,000x or in the absence of bioconcentration data a log P value equal to or greater than 4.3. A

significant adverse reactions
Reactions that may indicate a substantial impairment of normal activities or long-lasting or irreversible damage to health or the environment. A

significant biological treatment
The use of an aerobic or anaerobic biological treatment process in a treatment works to consistently achieve a 30-day average of at least 65 percent removal of BOD. A

significant deterioration
Pollution from a new source in previously "clean" areas. N [ed. An increase in air pollution in an area meeting a national ambient air quality standards, when the increase equals or exceeds allowable increments for that pollutant established by the Congress or EPA]. U

significant discharge
Any point source discharge for which timely management action must be taken in order to meet the water quality objectives within the period of the operative water quality management plan. The significant nature of the discharge is to be determined by the State, but must include any discharge which is causing or will cause water quality problems. A

significant economic loss
Under emergency conditions, for a productive activity, the profitability would be substantially below the exected profitability for that activity; or, for other types of activities, where profits cannot be calculated, the value of public or private fixed assets would be substantially below the

expected value for those assets. Only losses caused by the emergency conditions, specific to the impacted site, and specific to the geographic area affected by the emergency conditions are included. The contribution of obvious mismanagement to the loss will not be considered in determining loss. In evaluating the significant of an economic loss for productive activities, the Agency will consider whether the expected reduction in profitability exceeds what would be expected as a result of normal fluctuations over a number of years, and whether the loss would affect the long-term financial viability expected from the productive activity. In evaluating the significance of an economic loss for situations other than productive activities, the Agency will consider reasonable measures of expected loss. A

significant environmental effects
(i) Any irreversible damage to biological, commercial, or agricultural resources of importance to society; (ii) Any reversible damage to biological, commercial, or agricultural resources of importance to society if the damage persists beyond a single generation of the damaged resource or beyond a single year, or (iii) Any known or reasonably anticipated loss of members of an endangered or threatened species. "Endangered" or "threatened" species are those species identified as such by the Secretary of the Interior. A

significant hazard to public health
Any level of contaminant which causes or may cause the aquifer to exceed any maximum contaminant level set forth in any promulgated National Primary Drinking Water Standard at any point where the water may be used for drinking purposes or which may otherwise adversely affect the health of persons, or which may require a public water system to install additional treatment to prevent such adverse effect. A

significant impairment
Visibility impairment which, in the judgment of the Administrator, interferes with the management, protection, preservation or enjoyment of the visitor's visual experience of the mandatory Class I Federal area. This determination must be made on a case-by-case basis taking into account the geographic extent, intensity, duration, frequency and time of the visibility impairment, and how these factors correlate with (1) times of visitor use of the mandatory Class I Federal area, and (2) the frequency and timing of natural conditions that reduce visibility. A

significant industrial user
(1) Except as provided in paragraph (2) below, the term Significant Industrial User means: (i) All industrial users subject to Categorical Pretreatment Standards under 40 CFR 403.6 and 40 CFR chapter I, subchapter N; and (ii) Any other industrial user that: discharges an average of 25,000 gallons per day or more of process wastewater to the POTW (excluding sanitary, noncontact cooling and boiler blowdown wastewater); contributes a process wastestream which makes up 5 percent or more of the average dry weather

hydraulic or organic capacity of the POTW treatment plant; or is designated as such by the Control Authority as defined in 40 CFR 403.12(a) on the basis that the industrial user has a reasonable potential for adversely affecting the POTW's operation or for violating any pretreatment standard or requirement (in accordance with 40 CFR 403.8(f)(6)). (2) Upon a finding that an industrial user meeting the criteria in paragraph (1)(ii) above has no reasonable potential for adversely affecting the POTW's operation or for violating any pretreatment standard or requirement, the Control Authority (as defined in 40 CFR 403.12(a)) may at any time, on its own initiative or in response to a petition received from an industrial user or POTW, and in accordance with 40 CFR 403.8(f)(6), determine that such industrial user is not a significant industrial user. A

significant materials
Includes, but is not limited to: raw materials; fuels; materials such as solvents, detergents, and plastic pellets; finished materials such as metallic products; raw materials used in food processing or production; hazardous substances designated under section 101(14) of CERCLA; any chemical the facility is required to report pursuant to section 313 of title III of SARA; fertilizers; pesticides; and waste products such as ashes, slag and sludge that have the potential to be released with storm water discharges. A

significant municipal facilities
Those publicly owned sewage treatment plants that discharge a million gallons per day or more and are therefore considered by states to have the potential for substantial effect on the quality of receiving waters. N

significant source of ground water
(1) An aquifer that: (i) Is saturated with water having less than 10,000 milligrams per liter of total dissolved solids; (ii) is within 2,500 feet of the land surface; (iii) has a transmissivity greater than 200 gallons per day per foot, Provided, That any formation or part of a formation included within the source of ground water has a hydraulic conductivity greater than 2 gallons per day per square foot; and (iv) is capable of continuously yielding at least 10,000 gallons per day to a pumped or flowing well for a period of at least a year; or (2) an aquifer that provides the primary source of water for a community water system. A

significantly affects the environment
An action that does significant harm to the environment even though on balance the action may be beneficial to the environment. To the extent applicable, the responsible official shall address the considerations set forth in the CEQ Regulations under 40 CFR 1508.27 in determining significant effect. A

significantly more stringent limitation
BOD_5 and SS limitations necessary to meet the percent removal requirements of at least 5 mg/l more stringent than the otherwise applicable concentration-based limitations (e.g.,

less than 25 mg/l in the case of the secondary treatment limits for BOD_5 and SS) or the percent removal limitations in 40 CFR § 133.102 and 133.105, if such limits would, by themselves, force significant construction or other significant capital expenditure. A

signs
The warnings of a hazard, temporarily or permanently affixed or placed, at locations where hazards exist. O

silica
$SiO2$. Silicon dioxide, which is a major constituent of fireclay refractory materials either alone or in chemical combinations. U

silicomanganese zirconium
That alloy containing 60 to 65 percent by weight silicon, 1.5 to 2.5 percent by weight calcium, 5 to 7 percent by weight zirconium, 0.75 to 1.25 percent by weight aluminum, 5 to 7 percent by weight manganese, and 2 to 3 percent by weight barium. A

silicon metal
Any silicon alloy containing more than 96 percent silicon by weight. A

silt
Fine particles of soil or rock that can be picked up by air or water and deposited as sediment. N

silviculture
Management of forest land for timber. Sometimes contributes to water pollution, as in clear-cutting. N

silviculture point source
Any discernible, confined and discrete conveyance related to rock crushing, gravel washing, log sorting or log storage facilities which are operated in connection with silvicultural activities and from which pollutants are discharged into navigable waters. This term does not include nonpoint source activities inherent to silviculture such as nursery operations, site preparation, reforestation and subsequent cultural treatment, thinning, prescribed burning, pest and fire control, harvesting operations, surface drainage, and road construction and maintenance from which runoff results from precipitation events. N

similar composition
A pesticide product which contains only the same active ingredient(s), or combination of active ingredients, and which is in the same category of toxicity, as a federally registered pesticide product. A

similar product
A pesticide product which, when compared to a federally registered product, has a similar composition and a similar use pattern. A

similar systems
Engine, fuel metering and emission control system combinations which use the same fuel (e.g., gasoline, diesel, etc.), combustion cycle (i.e., two or four stroke), general type of fuel system (i.e., carburetor or fuel injection), catalyst system (e.g., none, oxidization, three-way plus oxidization, three-way only, etc.), fuel control

system (i.e., feedback or non-feedback), secondary air system (i.e., equipped or not equipped) and EGR (i.e., equipped or not equipped). A

similar use pattern
Use of a pesticide product which, when compared to a federally registered use of a product with a similar composition, does not require a change in precautionary labeling under 40 CFR § 162.10(h), and which is substantially the same as the federally registered use. Registrations involving changed use patterns are not included in this term. A

simple cycle gas turbine
Any stationary gas turbine which does not recover heat from the gas turbine exhaust gases to preheat the inlet combustion air to the gas turbine, or which does not recover heat from the gas turbine exhaust gases to heat water or generate steam. A

simple leachate collection
This system consists of a gravity flow drainfield installed under the waste disposal facility liner. This design is recommended for use when semi-solid or leachable solid wastes are placed in a lined pit excavated into a relatively thick, unsaturated, homogeneous layer of low permeability soil. A

SIMS
Secondary ion-mass spectometry. N

single cleat ladder
One which consists of a pair of side rails, usually parallel, but with flared side rails permissible, connected together with cleats that are joined to the side rails at regular intervals. O

single ladder
A single ladder is a non-self-supporting portable ladder, nonadjustable in length, consisting of but one section. Its size is designated by the overall length of the side rail. O

single stroke
One complete stroke of the slide, usually initiated from a full open (or up) position, followed by closing (or down), and then a return to the full open position. O

single stroke mechanism
An arrangement used on a full revolution clutch to limit the travel of the slide to one complete stroke at each engagement of the clutch. O

single-point adjustable suspension scaffold
A manually or power-operated unit designed for light duty use, supported by a single wire rope from an overhead support so arranged and operated as to permit the raising or lowering of platform to desired working positions. O

single-pole scaffold
Platforms resting on putlogs or cross beams, the outside ends of which are supported on ledgers secured to a single row of posts or uprights, and the inner ends of which are supported on or in a wall. O

sinking
Controlling oil spills by using an agent to trap the oil. Both sink to the bottom of the body of water and biograde there. N

sinking agents
Those materials which are applied to oil and hazardous substance spills to sink floating pollutants below the water surface. A

sintering
A heat treatment that causes adjacent particles of a material to cohere below a temperature that would cause them to melt. U

sintering machine
Any furnace in which a lead sulfide ore concentrate charge is heated in the presence of air to eliminate sulfur contained in the charge and to agglomerate the charge into a hard porous mass called "sinter." A

sintering machine discharge end
Any apparatus which receives sinter as it is discharged from the conveying grate of a sintering machine. A

SIP
State Implementation Plans. EPA-approved state plans for the establishment, regulation, and enforcement of air pollution standards. N

sister chromatid exchanges
SCE. Reciprocal interchanges of the two chromatid arms within a single chromosome. These exchanges are visualized during the metaphase portion of the cell cycle and presumably require enzymatic incision, translocation and ligation of at least two DNA helices. A

site
(1) The land or water area where any "facility or activity" is physically located or conducted, including adjacent land used in connection with the facility or activity. A (2) A contiguous property unit. Property divided only by a public right-of-way shall be considered one site. There may be more than one manufacturing plant on a single site. A (3) A contiguous property unit. Property divided only by a public right-of-way shall be considered one site. There may be more than one plant on a single site. The site for a person who imports a substance is the site of the operating unit within the person's organization which is directly responsible for importing the substance and which controls the import transaction and may in some cases be the organization's headquarters office in the United States. A

SITE
Superfund Innovative Technology Evaluation, EPA-supported research, development and demonstration projects designed to develop new remediation technologies. U

site buffer zone
The area of land between the active portion of a hazardous waste treatment, storage, or disposal facility and its property boundary line. Its purpose is to protect human health and the environment. U

site inspection
SI. An on-site investigation to determine whether there is a release or potential release and the nature of the associated threats. The purpose is to augment the data collected in the preliminary assessment and to generate, if necessary, sampling and other field data to determine if further action or investigation is appropriate. A

site lease
A legally-binding document signed between a firm associated with a new independent power production facility (IPPF) and a site owner that establishes the term and conditions under which the firm associated with the new IPPE has the binding right to utilize a specific site for the purposes of operating or constructing the new IPPF. A

site of construction
The general physical location of any building, highway, or other change or improvement to real property which is undergoing construction, rehabilitation, alteration, conversion, extension, demolition, and repair and any temporary location or facility at which a contractor, subcontractor, or other participating party meets a demand or performs a function relating to the contract or subcontract. A

site quality assurance and sampling plan
A written document, associated with site sampling activities, which presents in specific terms the organization (where applicable), objectives, functional activities, and specific quality assurance (QA) and quality control (QC) activities designed to achieve the data quality goals of a specific project(s) or continuing operation(s). The QA Project Plan is prepared for each specific project or continuing operation (or group of similar projects of continuing operations). The QA Project Plan will be prepared by the responsible program office, regional office, laboratory, contractor, recipient of an assistance agreement, or other organization. A

site safety and health supervisor
The individual located on a hazardous waste site who is responsible to the employer and has the authority and knowledge necessary to implement the site safety and health plan and verify compliance with applicable safety and health requirements. O

site-limited
A chemical substance is manufactured and processed only within a site and is not distributed for commercial purposes as a substance or as part of a mixture or article outside the site. Imported substances are never site-limited. A

site-limited intermediate
An intermediate manufactured, processed, and used only within a site and not distributed in commerce other than as an impurity or for disposal. Imported intermediates cannot be "site-limited." A

siting
The process of choosing a location for a facility. N

six-minute period
Any one of the 10 equal parts of a one-hour period. A

size classes of discharges
The following sizes of oil discharges which are provided as guidance to the On-Site Coordinator (OSC), and serve as the criteria for the actions delineated in Subpart E. They are not meant to imply associated degrees of hazard to public health or welfare, nor are they a measure of environmental damage. Any oil discharge that poses a substantial threat to the public health or welfare or results in critical public concern shall be classified as a major discharge regardless of the following quantitative measures. (a) Minor Discharge. A discharge to the inland waters of less than 1,000 gallons of oil or a discharge to the coastal waters of less than 10,000 gallons of oil. (b) Medium Discharge. A discharge of 1,000 to 10,000 gallons of oil in the inland waters or a discharge of 10,000 to 100,000 gallons of oil to the coastal waters. (c) Major Discharge. A discharge of more than 10,000 gallons of oil to the inland waters or more than 100,000 gallons of oil to the coastal waters. A

size classes of releases
Refers to the following size classifications which are provided as guidance to the OSC for meeting pollution reporting requirements. The final determination of the appropriate classification of a release will be made by the OSC based on consideration of the particular release (e.g., size, location, impact, etc.): (a) Minor release means a release of a quantity of hazardous substance(s), pollutant(s), or contaminant(s) that poses minimal threat to public health or welfare or the environment. (b) Medium release means a release not meeting the criteria for classification as a minor or major release. (c) Major release means a release of any quantity of hazardous substance(s), pollutant(s), or contaminant(s) that poses a substantial threat to public health or welfare or the environment or results in significant public concern. A

skimming
(1) The removal of slag from the molten converter bath. A (2) Using a machine to remove oil or scum from the surface of the water. N

skimming tank
A tank so designed that floating matter will rise and remain on the surface of the wastewater until removed, while the liquid discharges continuously under curtain walls or scum boards. U

skyshine
Radiation emitted through the roof of the shield (or unshielded roof) that scatters back to the ground level due to its deviation by the atmosphere. U

slag
The more or less completely fused and vitrified matter separated during the reduction of a metal from its ore. A

slagging of refractory materials
Destructive chemical action that forms slag on refractory materials subjected to high temperatures; or, a molten or viscous coating produced on refractory materials by ash particles. U

SLAMS
State or Local Air Monitoring Station(s). The SLAMS make up the ambient air quality monitoring network which is required by 40 CFR § 58.20 to be provided for in the State's implementation plan. This definition places no restrictions on the use of the physical structure or facility housing the SLAMS. Any combination of SLAMS and any other monitors (Special Purpose, NAMS, PSD) may occupy the same facility or structure without affecting the respective definitions of those monitoring station. A

slide
The main reciprocating press member. A slide is also called a ram, plunger, or platen. O

slimicides
All substances or mixtures of substances intended for use in preventing or inhibiting the growth of, or destroying biological slimes composed of combinations of algae, bacteria or fungi declared to be pests. Slimicides include, but are not limited to, slime control agents for use in industrial water cooling systems and in pulp and paper mill wet end systems. A

slope
A term of measurement in percent and means the increase in height over the distance measured. An increase of 1 foot over a distance of 5 feet is expressed as a 20 percent slope. O

slough
A wet or marshy area. U

slow meter response
The slow response of the sound level meter shall be used. The slow dynamic response shall comply with the meter dynamic characteristics in paragraph 5.4 of the *American National Standard Specification for Sound Level Meters*. ANSI S1.4-1971. This publication is available from the American National Standards Institute Inc., 1430 Broadway, New York, New York 10018. A

slow sand filtration
A process involving passage of raw water through a bed of sand at low velocity (generally less than 0.4 m/h) resulting in substantial particulate removal by physical and biological mechanisms. A

sludge
(1) Any solid, semisolid or liquid waste generated from a municipal, commercial, or industrial wastewater treatment plant, water supply treatment plant, or air pollution control facility exclusive of the treated effluent from a wastewater treatment plant. A (2) The accumulated semiliquid suspension of settled solids deposited from wastewaters or other fluids in tanks

or basins. It does not include solids or dissolved material in domestic sewage or other significant pollutants in water resources, such as silt, dissolved or suspended solids in industrial wastewater effluents, dissolved materials in irrigation return flows or other common water pollutants. A (3) An aggregate of oil and other matter of any kind in any form other than dredged spoil having a combined specific gravity equivalent to or greater than water. A

sludge digestion
The process by which organic or volatile matter in sludge is gasified, liquified, mineralized, or converted into more stable organic matter through the activities of either anaerobic or aerobic organisms. U

sludge oil
Muddy impurities and acid which have settled from a mineral oil. A

slurry
A watery mixture of insoluble matter that results from some pollution control techniques. N

slurry wall
An underground vertical wall made of relatively impermeable material that significantly retards leachate and ground water migration. N

sm^3
Standard cubic meters. A

small business concern
Any person whose total annual sales in the person's fiscal year preceding the date of the submission of the applicable [TSCA] section 5 notice, when combined with those of the parent company (if any), are less than $40 million. A (Ed: See small manufacturer).

small commercial establishments
For purposes of [40 CFR] § 35.2034 private establishments such as restaurants, hotels, stores, filling stations, or recreational facilities and private, non-profit entities such as churches, schools, hospitals, or charitable organizations with dry weather wastewater flows less than 25,000 gallons per day. A

small community
For the purposes of [40 CFR] §§ 35.2020(b) and 35.2032, any municipality with a population of 3,500 or less or highly dispersed sections of larger municipalities, as determined by the Regional Administrator. A

small manufacturer or importer
A manufacturer or importer that meets either of the following standards: (1) First standard. A manufacturer or importer of a substance is small if its total annual sales, when combined with those of its parent company (if any), are less than $40 million. However, if the annual production or importation volume of a particular substance at any individual site owned or controlled by the manufacturer or importer is greater than 45,400 kilograms (100,000 pounds), the manufacturer or importer shall not qualify as small for purposes of reporting on the production or importation of that substance at that site, unless the manufacturer or importer qualifies as small under

standard (2) of this definition. (2) Second standard. A manufacturer or importer of a substance is small if its total annual sales, when combined with those of its parent company (if any), are less than $4 million, regardless of the quantity of substances produced or imported by that manufacturer or importer. (3) Inflation index. EPA shall make use of the Producer Price Index for Chemicals and Allied Products, as compiled by the U.S. Bureau of Labor Statistics, for purposes of determining the need to adjust the total annual sales values and for determining new sales values when adjustments are made. EPA may adjust the total annual sales values whenever the Agency deems it necessary to do so, provided that the Producer Price Index for Chemicals and Allied Products has changed more than 20 percent since either the most recent previous change in sales values or the date of promulgation of this rule, whichever is later. EPA shall provide *Federal Register* notification when changing the total annual sales values. A

small manufacturer, processor, or importer
(1) A manufacturer or importer whose total annual sales are less than $500,000, based upon the manufacturer's or importer's latest complete fiscal year, except that no manufacturer or importer is a small manufacturer or importer with respect to PBBs or Tris which such person manufactured at one site or imported in quantities greater than 10,000 pounds during the latest calendar year. In the case or a company which is owned or controlled by another company, total annual sales shall be based on the total annual sales of the owned or controlled company, the parent company, and all companies owned or controlled by the parent company taken together. A

small quantities for research and development
(1) Quantities of a chemical substance manufactured, imported, processed or proposed to be manufactured, imported, or processed that (a) are no greater than reasonably necessary for such purposes and (b) after the publication of the revised inventory, are used by, or directly under the supervision of, a technically qualified individual(s). Any chemical substances manufactured, imported or processed in quantities less than 1,000 pounds annually shall be presumed to be manufactured, imported or processed for research and development purposes. No person may report for the inventory any chemical substance in such quantities unless that person can certify, that the substance was not manufactured, imported, or processed solely in small quantities for research and development, as defined in this section. A (2) PCB's. Any quantity of PCBs (a) that is originally packaged in one or more hermetically sealed containers of a volume of no more than five (5.0) milliliters, and (b) that is used only for purposes of scientific experimentation or analysis, or chemical research on, or analysis of, PCBs, but not for research or

analysis for the development of a PCB product. A (3) Quantities of a chemical substance manufactured, imported, or processed or proposed to be manufactured, imported, or processed solely for research and development that are not greater than reasonably necessary for such purposes. A

small quantity generator
A generator of hazardous wastes who in any calendar month generates no more than 1,000 kilograms (2,205 pounds) of hazardous waste in that month. O

small refinery
A domestic diesel fuel refinery (1) which has a crude oil or bonafide feedstock capacity of 50,000 barrels per day or less, and (2) which is not owned or controlled by any refiner with a total combined crude oil or bonafide feedstock capacity greater than 137,500 barrels per day. The above capacities shall be measured in terms of the average of the actual daily utilization rates of the affected refiners or refineries during the period January 1, 1988 to December 31, 1990. These averages will be calculated as barrels per calendar day. A

small-sized plants
Plants which process less than 3,720 kg/day (8,200 lbs/day) of raw materials. A

SMCL
Secondary maximum contaminant levels. The maximum permissible level of contaminant in water which is delivered to the free flowing outlet of the ultimate user of public water system. Contaminants added to the water under circumstances controlled by the user, except those resulting from corrosion of piping and plumbing caused by water quality, are excluded from this definition. A

smelting
The treatment of an ore by heat to separate out the desired metal. U

smelting furnace
Any vessel in which the smelting of copper sulfide ore concentrates or calcines is performed and in which the heat necessary for smelting is provided by an electric current, rapid oxidation of a portion of the sulfur contained in the concentrate as it passes through an oxidizing atmosphere, or the combustion of a fossil fuel. A

SMOA
Superfund Memorandum of Agreement. U

smog
(1) The irritating haze resulting from the sun's effect on certain pollutants in the air, notably those from automobile exhaust. (See: photochemical process). U (2) Also a mixture of fog and smoke. U

smoke
(1) Solid or liquid particles under 1 micron in diameter. (2) Particles suspended in air after incomplete combustion of materials containing carbon. N (3) The matter in the exhaust emissions which obscures the transmission of light. A

smoke density
The amount of solid matter contained in smoke. It is often measured by systems that relate the grayness of the smoke to an established standard. (See: Ringelmann chart). U

smoke number
SN. The dimensionless term quantifying smoke emissions. A

SMSA
Standard Metropolitan Statistical Area. N

SNAAQS
Secondary National Ambient Air Quality Standards. N

snagging
Grinding which removes relatively large amounts of material without regard to close tolerances or surface finish requirements. O

SNAP
Significant Non-compliance Action Plan. D

SNARL
Suggested no adverse response level. N

SNC
Significant noncompliance. U

SNUR
Significant New Use Rule (TSCA). N

SO₂
Sulfur dioxide. U

SO₃
Sulfur trioxide. U

SOCMA
Synthetic Organic Chemical Manufacturers Association. U

SOCs
Synthetic organic chemicals. Man-made organic chemicals. Some SOCs are volatile, others tend to stay dissolved in water rather than evaporate out of it. N

soda-lime recipe
Glass product composition of the following ranges of weight proportions: 60 to 75 percent silicon dioxide, 10 to 17 percent total R_2O (e.g., Na_2O and K_2O), 8 to 20 percent total RO but not to include any PbO (e.g., CaO, and MgO), 0 to 8 percent total R_2O_3 (e.g., Al_2O_3), and 1 to 5 percent other oxides. A

soft water
Any water that is not "hard", i.e., does not contain a significant amount of dissolved minerals such as salts containing calcium or magnesium. N

soil
(1) The unconsolidated mineral material on the immediate surface of the earth that serves as a natural medium for the growth of land plants; its formation and properties are determined by various factors such as parent material, climate, macro- and microorganisms, topography, and time. A (2) A mixture of mineral and organic chemical constituents, the latter containing compounds of high

carbon and nitrogen content and of high molecular weights, animated by small (mostly micro-) organisms. Soil may be handled in two states: (a) Undisturbed, as it has grown with time, in characteristic layers of a variety of soil types. (b) Disturbed, as it is usually sampled by digging and used in the test described here. A (3) All vegetation, soils and other ground media, including but not limited to, sand, grass, gravel, and oyster shells. It does not include concrete and asphalt. A

soil adsorption field
A sub-surface area containing a trench or bed with clean stones and a system of distribution piping through which treated sewage may seep into the surrounding soil for further treatment and disposal. N

soil aggregate
The combination or arrangement of soil separates (sand, silt, clay) into secondary units. These units may be arranged in the profile in a distinctive characteristic pattern that can be classified on the basis of size, shape, and degree of distinctness into classes, type, and grades. A

soil classification
The systematic arrangement of soils into groups or categories. Broad groupings are made on the basis of general characteristics, subdivisions, on the basis of more detailed differences in specific properties. The soil classification system used today in the United States is the 7th Approximation Comprehensive System. The ranking of subdivisions under the system is: order, suborder, great group, family and series. A

soil cohesion
The mutual attraction exerted between soil particles by molecular forces and moisture films. U

soil conditioner
An organic material like humus or compost that helps soil absorb water, build a bacterial community, and distribute nutrients and minerals. N

soil flushing
The process of site restoration by flooding the area of contamination and collecting the seepage with a series of shallow well points. It is a practical approach only when contamination is fairly shallow and confined to a fairly small area. U

soil gas
Gaseous elements and compounds that occur in the small spaces between particles of the earth and soil. Such gases can move through or leave the soil or rock, depending on changes in pressure. N

soil horizon
A layer of soil approximately parallel to the land surface. Adjacent layers differ in physical, chemical, and biological properties or characteristics such as color, structure, texture, consistency, kinds, and numbers of organisms present, and degree of acidity or alkalinity. A

soil injection
The emplacement of pesticides by

ordinary tillage practices within the plow layer of a soil. A

soil matrix
The portion of a given soil having the dominant color; in most cases, the matrix will be the portion of the soil having more than 50 percent of the same color. N

soil order
The broadest category of soil classification and is based on general similarities of physical/chemical properties. The formation by similar genetic processes causes these similarities. The soil orders found in the United States are: Alfisol, Aridisol, Entisol, Histosol, Inceptisol, Mollisol, Oxisol, Spodosol, Ultisol, and Vertisol. A

soil organic matter
The organic fraction of the soil; it includes plant and animal residues at various stages of decomposition, cells and tissues of soil organisms, and substances synthesized by the microbial population. A

soil permeability
The ease with which gases, liquids, or plant roots penetrate or pass through a layer of soil. N

soil pH
(1) The value obtained by sampling the soil to the depth of cultivation or solid waste placement, whichever is greater, and analyzing by the electrometric method. ("Methods of Soil Analysis, Agronomy Monograph No. 9," C.A. Black, ed., American Society of Agronomy, Madison, Wisconsin, pp. 914-926, 1965). A (2) The negative logarithm to the base 10 of the hydrogen ion activity of a soil as determined by means of a suitable sensing electrode coupled with a suitable reference electrode at a 1:1 soil: water ratio. A

soil phase
A subdivision of a soil series having features (e.g. slope, surface texture, and stoniness) that affect the use and management of the soil, but which do not vary sufficiently to differentiate it as a separate series. N

soil plasticity
The property of a soil that allows it to be deformed or molded while moist without cracking or falling apart. U

soil pore
An area within soil occupied by either air or water, resulting from the arrangement of individual soil particles or peds. N

soil profile
A vertical section of the soil through all its horizons and extending into the parent material. N

soil, renovating soil
Soil material that exists or is placed beneath a landfill that will provide the natural renovation of leachate emanating from the landfill. U

soil sealant
A chemical or physical agent used to plug porous soils to prevent leaching or percolation. U

soil series

(1) The basic unit of soil classification and is a subdivision of a family. A series consists of soils that were developed under comparable climatic and vegetational conditions. The soils comprising a series are essentially alike in all major profile characteristics except for the texture of the "A" horizon (i.e., the surface layer of soil). A (2) A group of soils having horizons similar in differentiating characteristics and arrangements in the soil profile, except for texture of the surface layer. N

soil structure

The combination or arrangement of primary soil particles into secondary particles, units, or peds. N

soil surface

The upper limits of the soil profile; for mineral soils, the upper limits of the highest mineral horizon (A-horizon); for organic soils, the upper limit of undecomposed organic matter. N

soil texture

(1) The relative proportions of the various sizes of particles (silt, and sand clay) in a soil. N (2) The classification of soils based on the relative proportions of the various soil separates present. The soil textural classes are: clay, sandy clay, silty clay, clay loam, silty clay loam, sandy clay loam, loam, silt loam, silt, sandy loam, loamy sand, and sand. A

sold or distributed

The aggregate amount of a pesticidal product released for shipment by the establishment in which the pesticidal product was produced. A

sole or principal source aquifer

(1) An aquifer which has been designated by the Administrator pursuant to sections 1424 (a) or (e) of the SDWA. A (2) An aquifer that is the sole source of drinking water for an area. Upon designation by the Administrator of EPA, development around a sole source aquifer that could contaminate the drinking water can be curtailed. U

solid waste

(1) Any garbage, refuse, sludge from a waste treatment plant, water supply treatment plant, or air pollution control facility and other discarded material, including solid, liquid, semisolid, or contained gaseous material resulting from industrial, commercial, mining, and agricultural operations, and from community activities, but does not include solid or dissolved material in domestic sewage, or solid or dissolved materials in irrigation return flows or industrial discharges which are point sources subject to permits under section 402 of the Federal Water Pollution Control Act, as amended (86 Stat. 880), or source, special nuclear, or byproduct material as defined by the Atomic Energy Act of 1954, as amended (68 Stat. 923). I (2) Any discarded material that is not excluded by § 261.4(a) or that is not excluded by variance granted under §§ 260.30 and 260.31 [or 40 CFR parts 260-299]. A (3) See 40 CFR § 261.2. A

solid waste boundary
The outermost perimeter of the solid waste (projected in the horizontal plane) as it would exist at completion of the disposal activity. A

solid waste disposal
The final placement of refuse that cannot be salvaged or recycled. N

Solid Waste Disposal Act of 1965
Predecessor of RCRA. U

solid waste management
The systematic administration of activities which provide for the collection, source separation, storage, transportation, transfer, processing, treatment, and disposal of solid waste. I

solid waste management facility
Includes--(A) any resource recovery system or component thereof, (B) any system, program, or facility for resource conservation, and (C) any facility for the collection, source separation, storage, transportation, transfer, processing, treatment or disposal of solid wastes, including hazardous wastes, whether such facility is associated with facilities generating such wastes or otherwise. I

solid waste product charge
A Federal, virgin materials tax built into an article's original purchase price in order to finance municipal collection and disposal of the article after it is discarded and becomes solid waste. Also called product disposal charge and solid waste disposal charge. U

solid waste storage container
A receptacle used for the temporary storage of solid waste while awaiting collection. A

solid-derived fuel
Any solid, liquid, or gaseous fuel derived from solid fuel for the purpose of creating useful heat and includes, but is not limited to, solvent refined coal, liquified coal, and gasified coal. A

solid-waste-derived fuel
A fuel that is produced from solid waste that can be used as a primary or supplementary fuel in conjunction with or in place of fossil fuels. The solid-waste-derived fuel can be in the form of raw (unprocessed) solid waste, shredded (or pulped) and classified solid waste, gas or oil derived from pyrolyzed solid waste, or gas derived from the biodegradation of solid waste. A

solidification and stabilization
Removal of wastewater from a waste or changing it chemically to make the waste less permeable and susceptible to transport by water. N

solution
A homogeneous mixture of two or more substances constituting a single phase. A

solution heat treatment
The process introducing a workpiece into a quench bath for the purpose of heat treatment following rolling, drawing or extrusion. A

solvent

(1) Substance (usually liquid) capable of dissolving or dispersing one or more other substances. N (2) A mixture that can dissolve other materials to form a uniform mixture. N (3) A substance (e.g., acetone) which is combined with the test substance to facilitate introduction of the test substance into the dilution water. A

solvent (industrial organic)

Any organic volatile liquid or compound, or any combination of these substances which are used to dissolve or suspend a nonvolatile or slightly volatile substance for industrial utilization. It shall also apply to such substances when used as detergents or cleansing agents. It shall not apply to petroleum products when such products are used as fuel. O

solvent feed

The solvent introduced into the spinning solution preparation system or precipitation bath. This feed stream includes the combination of recovered solvent and makeup solvent. A

solvent filter

A discrete solvent filter unit containing a porous medium that traps and removes contaminants from petroleum solvent, together with the piping and ductwork used in the installation of this device. A

solvent inventory variation

The normal changes in the total amount of solvent contained in the affected facility. A

solvent of high photochemical reactivity

Any solvent with an aggregate of more than 20 percent of its total volume composed of the chemical compounds classified below or which exceeds any of the following individual percentage composition limitations in reference to the total volume of solvent: (i) A combination of hydrocarbons, alcohols, aldehydes, esters, ethers, or ketones having an olefinic or cycloolefinic type of unsaturation: 5 percent; (ii) A combination of aromatic compounds with eight or more carbon atoms to the molecule except ethylbenzene: 8 percent; (iii) A combination of ethylbenzene, ketones having branched hydrocarbon structures, trichloroethylene or toluene: 20 percent. Whenever any organic solvent or any constituent of an organic solvent may be classified from its chemical structure into more than one of the above groups of organic compounds, it shall be considered as a member of the most reactive chemical group, that is, that group having the least allowable percentage of total volume of solvents. A

solvent recovery dryer

A class of dry cleaning dryers that employs a condenser to condense and recover solvent vapors evaporated in a closed-loop stream of heated air, together with the piping and ductwork used in the installation of this device. A

solvent recovery system

(1) The equipment associated with capture, transportation, collection,

concentration, and purification of organic solvents. It may include enclosures, hoods, ducting, piping, scrubbers, condensers, carbon adsorbers, distillation equipment, and associated storage vessels. A (2) An air pollution control system by which VOC solvent vapors in air or other gases are captured and directed through a condenser(s) or a vessel(s) containing beds of activated carbon or other adsorbents. For the condensation method, the solvent is recovered directly from the condenser. For the adsorption method, the vapors are adsorbed, then desorbed by steam or other media, and finally condensed and recovered. A

solvent-borne
A coating which contains five percent or less water by weight in its volatile fraction. A

solvent-borne ink systems
Ink and related coating mixtures whose volatile portion consists essentially of VOC solvent with not more than five weight percent water, as applied to the gravure cylinder. A

solvent-spun synthetic fiber
Any synthetic fiber produced by a process that uses an organic solvent in the spinning solution, the precipitation bath, or processing of the sun fiber. A

solvent-spun synthetic fiber process
The total of all equipment having a common spinning solution preparation system or a common solvent recovery system, and that is used in the manufacture of solvent-spun synthetic fiber. It includes spinning solution preparation, spinning, fiber processing and solvent recovery, but does not include the polymer production equipment. A

somatic cells
All cells other than germ cells or gametes. N

sonic boom
The thunderous noise made when shock waves reach the ground from a jet airplane exceeding the speed of sound. N

soot
Carbon dust formed by incomplete combustion. N

sorbents
Essentially inert and insoluble materials which are used to remove oil and hazardous substances from water through a variety of sorption mechanisms. Examples include: straw, expanded perlite, polyurethane foams, reclaimed paper fibers, peat moss. A

sorption
The action of soaking up or attracting substances; used in many pollution control processes. N

sound exposure level
The level in decibels calculated as ten times the common logarithm of time integral of squared A-weighted sound pressure over a given time period or event divided by the square of the standard reference sound pressure of 20 micropascals and a reference duration of one second. A

sound level
(1) The level in decibels measured by instrumentation which satisfies the requirements of *American National Standards Specification for Sound Level Meters* S1.4-1971 Type 1 or (S1A) or Type 2 if adjusted as shown in Table 1 (40 CFR § 201.1). This publication is available from the American National Standards Institute, Inc., 1430 Broadway, New York, New York 10018. For the purpose of these procedures the sound level is to be measured using the A-weighting of spectrum and either the FAST or SLOW dynamic averaging characteristics, as designated. It is abbreviated as L_A. A (2) Twenty times the logarithm to base 10 of the ratio of pressure of a sound to the reference pressure. The reference pressure is 20 micropascals (20 micronewtons per square meter). Note: Unless otherwise explicitly stated, it is to be understood that the sound pressure is the effect (rms) sound pressure, per American National Standards Institute, Inc., 1430 Broadway, New York, New York 10018. A (3) Ten times the common logarithm of the ratio of the square of the measured A-weighted sound pressure to the square of the standard reference pressure of 20 micropascals. Unit: decibels (dB). For use with this regulation, SLOW time response, in accordance with ANSI S1.4-1971 (R1976), is required. O

sound pressure level
In decibels, 20 times the logarithm to the base ten of the ratio of a sound pressure to the reference sound pressure of 20 micropascals (20 micronewtons per square meter). In the absence of any modifier, the level is understood to be that of a root-mean-square pressure. A

source
(1) Any building, structure, facility, or installation from which there is or may be the discharge of pollutants. D (2) Any building, structure, pile, impoundment or area used for interim storage or disposal that is or contains waste material containing radium in sufficient concentration to emit radon-222 in excess of this standard prior to remedial action. A

source control action
The construction or installation and start-up of those actions necessary to prevent the continued release of hazardous substances or pollutants or contaminants (primarily from a source on top of or within the ground, or in buildings or other structures) into the environment. A

source control remedial action
Measures that are intended to contain the hazardous substances or pollutants or contaminants where they are located or eliminate potential contamination by transporting the hazardous substances or pollutants or contaminants to a new location. Source control remedial actions may be appropriate if a substantial concentration or amount of hazardous substances or pollutants or contaminants remains at or near the area where they are originally located and inadequate barriers exist to retard migration of hazardous substances or pollutants or contaminants into the

environment. Source control remedial actions may not be appropriate if most hazardous substances or pollutants or contaminants have migrated from the area where originally located or if the lead agency determines that the hazardous substances or pollutants or contaminants are adequately contained. A

source individual
Any individual, living or dead, whose blood or other potentially infectious materials may be a source of occupational exposure to the employee. Examples include, but are not limited to, hospital and clinic patients; clients in institutions for the developmentally disabled; trauma victims; clients of drug and alcohol treatment facilities; residents of hospices and nursing homes; human remains; and individuals who donate or sell blood or blood components. O

source material
Any material except special nuclear material, which contains 0.05 percent or more of uranium, thorium, or any combination of the two. U

source operation
The last operation preceding the emission of an air contaminant, which operation (a) results in the separation of the air contaminant from process materials or in the conversion of the process materials into air contaminants, as in the case of combustion of fuel; and (b) is not primarily an air pollution abatement operation. A

source separation
The separation of individual recyclable components of solid waste at their point of generation for segregated collection and transport to specialized waste-processing sites or final manufacturing markets. U

source/receptor area
For each episode occurrence based on air monitoring, geographical, and meteorological factors: Source area is that area in which contaminants are discharged and a receptor area is that area in which the contaminants accumulate and are measured. A

SO$_x$
Sulfur oxide. U

spalling of refractory materials
The breaking or crushing of refractory materials due to thermal, mechanical, or structural decomposition. U

span drift
The change in instrument output over a stated time period, usually 24 hours, of unadjusted continuous operation, when the input concentration is a stated upscale value; usually expressed as percent full scale, e.g., span drift (maximum)-Not to exceed 1 percent/24 hours. A

span gas
A gas of known concentration which is used routinely to set the output level of an analyzer. A

spandex fiber
A manufactured fiber in which the

fiber-forming substance is a long chain synthetic polymer comprised of at least 85 percent of a segmented polyurethane. A

spare flue gas desulfurization system module
A separate system of sulfur dioxide emission control equipment capable of treating an amount of flue gas equal to the total amount of flue gas generated by an affected facility when operated cat maximum capacity divided by the total number of nonspare flue gas desulfurization modules in the system. A

spark plug
A device to suitably deliver high tension electrical ignition voltage to the spark gap in the engine combustion chamber. The emission critical parameters for spark plugs are: (A) Heat Rating; (B) Gap Spacing; (C) Gap Location; (D) Flashover, and (E) Dielectric Strength. A

SPCC
Spill prevention, containment, and countermeasure. U

special aquatic sites
Geographic areas, large or small, possessing special ecological characteristics of productivity, habitat, wildlife protection, or other important and easily disrupted ecological values. These areas are generally recognized as significantly influencing or positively contributing to the general overall environmental health or vitality of the entire ecosystem of a region. A

special decompression chamber
A chamber to provide greater comfort of employees when the total decompression time exceeds 75 minutes. O

special features enabling off-street or off-highway operation and use
(1) That has 4-wheel drive; and (2) That has at least four of the following characteristics calculated when the automobile is at curb weight, on a level surface, with the front wheels parallel to the vehicle's longitudinal centerline and the tires inflated to the manufacturer's recommended pressure: (i) Approach angle of not less than 28 degrees. (ii) Breakover angle of not less than 14 degrees. (iii) Departure angle of not less than 20 degrees. (iv) Running clearance of not less than 8 inches. (v) Front and rear axle clearances of not less than 7 inches each. A

special local need
An existing or imminent pest problem within a state for which the state lead agency, based upon satisfactory supporting information, has determined that an appropriate federally registered pesticide product is not sufficiently available. A

special nuclear material
This term refers to plutonium-239, uranium-233, uranium containing more than the natural abundance of uranium-235, or any material artificially enriched in any of these substances. U

special packaging
Packaging that is designed and constructed to be significantly difficult

for children under five years of age to open or obtain a toxic or harmful amount of the substance contained therein within a reasonable time, and that is not difficult for normal adults to use properly. A

special permission
The written consent of the authority having jurisdiction. O

special permits
Special permits may be issued for the dumping of materials which satisfy the Criteria and shall specify an expiration date no later than three years from the date of issue. A

special purpose equipment
Maintenance-of-way equipment which may be located on or operated from rail cars including: ballast cribbing machines, ballast regulators, conditioners and scarifiers, bolt machines, brush cutters, compactors, concrete mixers, cranes and derricks, earth boring machines, electric welding machines, grinders, grouters, pile drivers, rail heaters, rail layers, sandblasters, snow plows, spike drivers, sprayers and other types of such maintenance-of-way equipment. A

special purpose facility
A building or space, including land incidental to its use, which is wholly or predominantly utilized for the special purpose of an agency and not generally suitable for other uses, as determined by the General Services Administration. A

special review
(1) Formerly known as Rebuttable Presumption Against Registration (RPAR), this is the regulatory process through which existing pesticides suspected of posing unreasonable risks to human health, non-target organisms, or the environment are referred to for review by EPA. The review requires an intensive risk/benefit analysis with opportunity for public comment. If the risk of any use of a pesticide is found to outweigh social and economic benefits, regulatory actions--ranging from label revisions and use-restriction to cancellation or suspended registration--can be initiated. N (2) Refers to any interim administrative review of the risks and benefits of the use of a pesticide conducted pursuant to the provisions of EPA's Rebuttable Presumption Against Registration rules, 40 CFR 162.11(a), or any subsequent version of those rules. A

special source of ground water
Those Class I ground waters identified in accordance with the Agency's Ground-Water Protection Strategy published in August 1984 that: (1) Are within the controlled area encompassing a disposal system or are less than five kilometers beyond the controlled area; (2) are supplying drinking water for thousands of persons as of the date that the Department chooses a location within that area for detailed characterization as a potential site for a disposal system (e.g., in accordance with section 112(b)(1)(B) of the NWPA); and (3) are irreplaceable in that no reasonable alternative source of

drinking water is available to that population. A

special track work
Track other than normal tie and ballast bolted or welded rail or containing devices such as retarders or switching mechanisms. A

special waste
(1) Waste materials that require different management than other hazardous wastes because they occur in very large volumes but the potential hazard posed by the materials is relatively low and thus the materials are generally not amenable to the management techniques developed for hazardous waste. The waste includes cement kiln dust, utility waste (fly ash, bottom ash, scrubber sludge), phosphate mining and processing waste, uranium and other mining waste, and gas and oil drilling muds and oil production brines. (2) Nonhazardous solid wastes requiring handling other than that normally used for municipal solid waste. A

specially designated landfill
A landfill at which complete long term protection is provided for the quality of surface and subsurface waters from pesticides, pesticide containers, and pesticide-related wastes deposited therein, and against hazard to public health and the environment. Such sites should be located and engineered to avoid direct hydraulic continuity with surface and subsurface waters, and any leachate or subsurface flow into the disposal area should be contained within the site unless treatment is provided. Monitoring wells should be established and a sampling and analysis program conducted. The location of the disposal site should be permanently recorded in the appropriate local office of legal jurisdiction. Such facility complies with the Agency Guidelines for the Land Disposal of Solid Wastes as prescribed in 40 CFR Part 241. A

specialty steel
Those steel products containing alloying elements which are added to enhance the properties of the steel product when individual alloying elements (e.g., aluminum, chromium, cobalt, columbium, molybdenum, nickel, titanium, tungsten, vanadium, zirconium) exceed 3% or the total of all alloying elements exceed 5%. A

species
A reproductively isolated aggregate of interbreeding populations of organisms. N

specific chemical identity
The chemical name, Chemical Abstracts Service (CAS) Registry Number, or any other information that reveals the precise chemical designation of the substance. O

specific gravity
The ratio of the weight of a given volume of the material at a stated temperature to the weight of an equal volume of distilled water at a stated temperature. A

specification
A clear and accurate description of the technical requirement for

materials, products or services, which specifies the minimum requirement for quality and construction of materials and equipment necessary for an acceptable product. In general, specifications are in the form of written descriptions, drawings, prints, commercial designations, industry standards, and other descriptive references. A

specified work object
The specific process, method, machine, manufacture or composition of matter (including relatively minor modifications thereof) which is the subject of the experimental, developmental, research or demonstration work performed under an EPA grant. A

specimens
Any material derived from a test system for examination or analysis. A

spectral uncertainty
Possible variation in exposure to the noise spectra in the workplace. (To avoid the underprotection that would result from these variations relative to the assumed "Pink Noise" used to determine the NRR, an extra three decibel reduction is included when computing the NRR). A

spent lubricant
Water or an oil-water mixture which is used in forming operations to reduce friction, heat and wear and ultimately discharged. A

spent material
Any material that has been used and as a result of contamination can no longer serve the purpose for which it was produced without processing. A

spent nuclear fuel
Fuel that has been withdrawn from a nuclear reactor following irradiation, the constituent elements of which have not been separated by reprocessing. A

spill
(1) Any unplanned discharge or release of hazardous waste onto or into the land, air, or water. (2) The accidental spilling, leaking, pumping, emitting, emptying, or dumping of hazardous wastes or materials which, when spilled, become hazardous wastes into or on any land or water. A

spill (PCBs)
Both intentional and unintentional spills, leaks, and other uncontrolled discharges where the release results in any quantity of PCBs running off or about to run off the external surface of the equipment or other PCB source, as well as the contamination resulting from those releases. This policy applies to spills of 50 ppm or greater PCBs. The concentration of PCBs spilled is determined by the PCB concentration in the material spilled as opposed to the concentration of PCBs in the material onto which the PCBs were spilled. Where a spill of untested mineral oil occurs, the oil is presumed to contain greater than 50 ppm, but less than 500 ppm PCBs and is subject to the relevant requirements of this policy. A

spill event
A discharge of oil into or upon the navigable waters of the United States or adjoining shorelines in harmful quantities, as defined in 40 CFR Part 110. A

spill prevention control and countermeasure plan
A plan required to be developed and implemented by onshore facilities that includes physical structures and other measures to respond to and prevent spills of oil or hazardous substances from reaching navigable waters. U

spinning reserve
The sum of the unutilized net generating capability of all units of the electric utility company that are synchronized to the power distribution system and that are capable of immediately accepting additional load. The electric generating capability of equipment under multiple ownership is prorated based on ownership unless the proportional entitlement to electric output is otherwise established by contractual arrangement. A

spinning solution
The mixture of polymer, prepolymer, or copolymer and additives dissolved in solvent. The solution is prepared at a viscosity and solvent-to-polymer ratio that is suitable for extrusion into fibers. A

spiral classifier
A mechanical device for performing two types of wet separation of fine solids: same-density solids according to size and same-size solids according to density. The larger or denser solids are delivered up the spiral, somewhat drained. U

spirometer
An instrument that measures the flow and volume of air in and out of the lungs. U

SPMS
(1) Strategic Planning Management Strategy. B (2) Special purpose monitoring stations. U

spoil
Dirt or rock that has been removed from its original location, destroying the composition of the soil in the process, as with strip-mining or dredging. N

sponsor
(1) a person who initiates and supports, by provision of financial or other resources, a study; (2) a person who submits a study to the EPA in support of an application for a research or marketing permit; or (3) a testing facility, if it both initiates and actually conducts the study. A (4) The person or persons who design, direct and finance the testing of a substance or mixture. A

spontaneous ignition temperature
SIT. The temperature at which an oil ignites of its own accord in the presence of air oxygen under standard conditions. A

spot allowance
An allowance that may be used for purposes of compliance with a unit's sulfur dioxide emissions limitations requirements beginning in the year in

which the allowance is offered for sale. A

spot auction
An auction of a spot allowance. A

spot sample
One obtained at some specific location in the tank by means of a thief bottle, or beaker. A

sprawl
Unplanned development of open land. N

spray chamber
A chamber equipped with water sprays that cool and clean the combustion products passing through it. U

spraying area
Any area in which dangerous quantities of flammable vapors or mists, or combustible residues, dusts, or deposits are present due to the operation of spraying processes. O

sprinkler alarm
An approved device installed so that any waterflow from a sprinkler system equal to or greater than that from single automatic sprinkler will result in an audible alarm signal on the premises. O

sprinkler system
A system of piping designed in accordance with fire protection engineering standards and installed to control or extinguish fires. The system includes an adequate and reliable water supply, and a network of specially sized piping and sprinklers which are interconnected. The system also includes a control valve and a device for actuating an alarm when the system is in operation. O

sq. ft.
Square feet. U

SQG
Small quantity generator. U

squamous cell carcinoma
A malignant neoplasm derived from squamous epithelium. N

SRF
(1) State Revolving Funds. N (2) State Water Pollution Control Revolving Fund. A

SS
The pollutant parameter total suspended solids. A

SSA
Sole or principal source aquifer. A

SSCD
Stationary Source Compliance Division. U

SSUR
Stop, Sales, Use or Restriction. C

SSURO
Stop, Sale, Use and Removal Order. U

stability
The atmospheric condition existing when the temperature of the air rises rather than falls with altitude. It

allows for little or no vertical air movement. U

stabilization
To convert the active organic matter in sludge into inert, harmless material. N

stabilization (reduction)
Processes aimed at converting raw (untreated) sludges into a less offensive form with regard to odor, putrescibility rate, and pathogenic organism content. Major types of processes are: anaerobic digestion, aerobic digestion, lime treatment, chlorine oxidation. U

stabilization pond
A large shallow basin (usually 2 to 4 feet) for purifying many types of industrial wastes by allowing climatic conditions which favor the growth of bacteria and algae to convert organic materials into nontoxic organic substances. This method has been used extensively in the treatment of industrial waste-waters when a high degree of purification is not required. They have also proven successful in treating steel mill wastes. U

stable air
An air mass that remains in the same position rather than moving in its normal horizontal and vertical directions. Stable air does not disperse pollutants and can lead to high buildups of air pollution. U

stack
(1) Any chimney, flue, vent, roof monitor, conduit or duct arranged to vent emissions to the ambient air. A

(2) Any point in a source designed to emit solids, liquids, or gases into the air, including a pipe or duct but not including flares. A

stack effect
Used air, as in a chimney, that moves upward because it is warmer than the surrounding atmosphere. N

stack emissions
The particulate matter captured and released to the atmosphere through a stack, chimney, or flue. A

stack gas
See flue gas. U

stack in existence
That the owner or operator had (1) begun, or caused to begin, a continuous program of physical on-site construction of the stack or (2) entered into binding agreements or contractual obligations, which could not be cancelled or modified without substantial loss to the owner or operator, to undertake a program of construction of the stack to be completed within a reasonable time. A

stack sampling
The collecting of representative samples of gaseous and particulate matter that flows through a duct or stack. U

stage II controls
Systems placed on service station gasoline pumps to control and capture gasoline vapors during automobile refueling. N

stagnation
Lack of wind in an air mass or lack of motion in water. Both cases tend to entrap and concentrate pollutants. U

stair platform
An extended step or landing breaking a continuous run of stairs. O

stair railing
A vertical barrier erected along exposed sides of a stairway to prevent fall of persons. O

stairs, stairways
A series of steps leading from one level or floor to another, or leading to platforms, pits, boiler rooms, crossovers, or around machinery, tanks, and other equipment that are used more or less continuously or routinely by employees or only occasionally by specific individuals. For the purpose of this subpart, a series of steps and landings having three or more rises constitutes stairs or stairway. O

STALAPCO
State and local air pollution control officials. N

standard
(1) A national emission standard including a design, equipment, work practice or operational standard for a hazardous air pollutant proposed or promulgated. A (2) A standard which requires conditions, or the adoption or use of one or more practices, means, methods, operations, or processes, reasonably necessary or appropriate to provide safe or healthful employment and places of employment. O

standard conditions
(1) A temperature of 70°F and a pressure of 14.7 psia. A (2) A temperature of 293 K (68 degrees F) and a pressure of 101.3 kilopascals (29.92 in Hg). A

standard day conditions
Standard ambient conditions as described in the United States Standard Atmosphere, 1976, (i.e., temperature = 15° C, specific humidity = 0.00 kg/H_2O/kg dry air, and pressure = 101325 Pa). A

standard equipment
Those features or equipment which are marketed on a vehicle over which the purchaser can exercise no choice. A

Standard Industrial Classification Manual
The *Standard Industrial Classification Manual*, Superintendent of Documents, U.S. Government Printing Office, Washington, D.C. 20402 (incorporated by reference as specified in 40 CFR 52.742). A

standard metropolitan statistical areas
SMSA. Such areas as designated by the U.S. Bureau of the Budget in the following publication: "Standard Metropolitan Statistical Area," issued in 1967, with subsequent amendments. A

standard of performance
(1) (A) With respect to any air

pollutant emitted from a category of fossil fuel fired stationary sources to which subsection (b) applies, a standard--(B) With respect to any air pollutant emitted from a category of stationary sources (other than fossil fuel fired sources) to which [§ 111] subsection (b) [of the CAA] applies, a standard such as that referred to in subparagraph (A)(i); and (C) With respect to any air pollutant emitted from a particular source to which [§ 111] subsection (d) [of the CAA] applies, a standard which the State (or the Administrator [of EPA]) under the conditions specified in subsection (d)(2) determines is applicable to that source and which reflects the degree of emission reduction achievable through the application of the best system of continuous emission reduction which (taking into consideration the cost of achieving such emission reduction, and any nonair quality health and environmental impact and energy requirements) the Administrator [of EPA] determines has been adequately demonstrated for that category of sources. B (2) A standard for the control of the discharge of pollutants which reflects the greatest degree of effluent reduction which the Administrator [of EPA] determines to be achievable through application of the best available demonstrated control technology, processes, operating methods, or other alternatives, including, where practicable, a standard permitting no discharge of pollutants. D (3) Any restriction established by the Administrator on quantities, rates, and concentrations of chemical, physical, biological, and other constituents which are or may be discharged from new sources into navigable waters, the waters of the contiguous zone or the ocean. A

standard operating procedure
(1) A document which describes in detail an operation, analysis, or action which is commonly accepted as the preferred method for performing certain routine or repetitive tasks. A (2) A formal written procedure officially adopted by the plant owner or operator and available on a routine basis to those persons responsible for carrying out the procedure. A

standard pressure
A pressure of 760 mm of Hg (29.92 in. of Hg). [ed. See also standard conditions]. A

standard railing
A vertical barrier erected along exposed edges of a floor opening, wall opening, ramp, platform, or runway to prevent falls of persons. O

standard sample
The aliquot of finished drinking water that is examined for the presence of coliform bacteria. A

standard strength and construction
Any construction of railings, covers, or other guards that meets the requirements of this subpart. O

standard temperature
A temperature of 20 degrees C (69 degrees F). [ed. See also standard conditions]. A

standard wipe test (PCBs)

For spills of high-concentration PCBs on solid surfaces, a cleanup to numerical surface standards and sampling by a standard wipe test to verify that the numerical standards have been met. This definition constitutes the minimum requirements for an appropriate wipe testing protocol. A standard-size template (10 centimeters (cm) x 10 cm) will be used to delineate the area of cleanup; the wiping medium will be a gauze pad or glass wool of known size which has been saturated with hexane. It is important that the wipe be performed very quickly after the hexane is exposed to air. EPA strongly recommends that the gauze (or glass wool) be prepared with hexane in the laboratory and that the wiping medium be stored in sealed glass vials until it is used for the wipe test. Further, EPA requires the collection and testing of field blanks and replicates. A

standardized mortality ratio

The number of deaths, either total or cause-specific, in a given group expressed as a percentage of the number of deaths that could have been expected if the group has the same age and sex specific rates as the general population. Used in epidemiologic studies to adjust mortality rates to a common standard so that comparisons can be made among groups. N

standards for sewage sludge use or disposal

The regulations promulgated at 40 CFR Part 503 pursuant to section 405(d) of the CWA which govern minimum requirements for sludge quality, management practices, and monitoring and reporting applicable to the generation or treatment of sewage sludge from a treatment works treating domestic sewage or use or disposal of that sewage sludge by any person. A

standards for the development of test data

A prescription of (A) the (i) health and environmental effects, and (ii) information relating to toxicity, persistence, and other characteristics which affect health and the environment, for which test data for a chemical substance or mixture are to be developed and any analysis that is to be performed on such data, and (B) to the extent necessary to assure that data respecting such effects and characteristics are reliable and adequate (i) the manner in which such data are to be developed, (ii) the specification of any test protocol or methodology to be employed in the development of such data, and (iii) such other requirements as are necessary to provide such assurance. K

standby trust fund

A trust fund which must be established by an owner or operator who obtains a letter of credit or surety bond as specified in these regulations. The institution issuing the letter of credit or surety bond will deposit into the standby trust fund any drawings by the Regional Administrator on the credit or bond. A

STAPPA
State and Territorial Air Pollution Program Administrators. N

starting material
A substance used to synthesize or purify a technical grade of active ingredient (or the practical equivalent of the technical grade ingredient if the technical grade cannot be isolated) by chemical reaction. A

startup
The setting in operation of a source for any purpose. A

state
For most environmental statutes, the term state includes any one of the states of the United States as well as the District of Columbia, the Commonwealth of Puerto Rico, the Virgin Islands, Guam, American Samoa, the Trust Territory of the Pacific Islands (except in the case of RCRA), and the Commonwealth of the Northern Mariana Islands (except in the case of CWA). A, C, D, G, H, J, K

state 404 program
A state program which has been approved by EPA under section 404 of the Act to regulate the discharge of dredge or fill material into certain waters as defined in [40 CFR] § 232.2(p). A

state agency
The air pollution control agency primarily responsible for development and implementation of a state implementation plan under the Clean Air Act. A

state air pollution control agency
A single state agency designated by the governor of that state as the official state air pollution control agency for purposes of the Clean Air Act. A

state certifying authority
(1) For water pollution control facilities, the state pollution control agency as defined in section 502 of the Act. (2) For air pollution control facilities, the air pollution control agency designated pursuant to section 302(b)(1) of the Act; or (3) For both air and water pollution control facilities, any interstate agency authorized to act in place of the certifying agency of a state. A

state continuing planning process
The continuing planning process required by Section 303(e) of the [Clean Water] Act, as developed and approved pursuant to 40 CFR Part 130. A

state director
The chief administrative officer of any State or interstate agency operating an approved program, or the delegated representative of the State Director. If responsibility is divided among two or more State or interstate agencies, "State Director" is the chief administrative officer of the State or interstate agency authorized to perform the particular procedure or function to which reference is made. A

State Emergency Response Commission
SERC. Commission appointed by each state governor according to the requirements of SARA Title III. The

SERCs designate emergency planning districts, appoint local emergency planning committees, and supervise and coordinate their activities. N

state hazardous waste plan
A plan generated at the State level to deal with the management of hazardous waste generated, treated, stored or disposed of within the State or transported outside the State. N

State Implementation Plan
(1) SIP. EPA-approved state plan for the establishment, regulation, and enforcement of air pollution standards. N (2) The plan, including the most recent revision thereof, which has been approved or promulgated by the Administrator under section 110 of the Clean Air Act, and which implements the requirements of section 110. A

state lead agency
The state agency designated by the state to be responsible for registering pesticides to meet special local needs under sec. 24(c) of the FIFRA Act. A

state planning agency
That state agency designated to prepare a state water planning process pursuant to section 208(a)(6) of the Federal Water Pollution Control Act. A

state planning area
That area of the state that is not designated pursuant to section 208(a) (2), (3), or (4) of the Clean Water Act. State planning areas are to be identified in the planning process description that is submitted by the state for approval by the Regional Administrator. Depending upon the requirement being considered, the state planning area may be subdivided into "approved planning areas" that may include the entire state or portions of the state defined by hydrologic, political, or other boundaries. A

state primary drinking water regulation
A drinking water regulation of a state which is comparable to a national primary drinking water regulation. A

state program grant
The amount of federal assistance awarded to a state or interstate agency to assist in administering approved programs for the prevention, reduction and elimination of pollution. A

state regulated waters
"Waters of the United States" in which the Corps of Engineers suspends the issuance of section 404 [of CWA] permits upon approval of a state's section 404 permit program by the Administrator under section 404(h). These waters shall be identified in the program description as required by 40 CFR § 233.22(h)(1). The Secretary of Defense shall retain jurisdiction over the following waters (see CWA section 404(g)(1)): (a) Waters which are subject to the ebb and flow of the tide; (b) Waters which are presently used, or are susceptible to use in their natural condition or by reasonable improvement as a means to transport interstate or foreign commerce shoreward to their ordinary high water

mark; and (c) "Wetlands" adjacent to waters in paragraphs (a) and (b). A

state sewage sludge management agency
The agency designated by the Governor as having the lead responsibility for managing or coordinating the approved State program under this part. A

state water pollution control agency
The state agency designated by the governor having responsibility for enforcing state laws relating to the abatement of pollution. D

State/EPA Agreement
An agreement between the regional administrator and the state which coordinates EPA and state activities, responsibilities and programs. A

Statement Of Work
SOW. The portion of the Cooperative Agreement application and/or Superfund State Contract that describes the purpose and scope of activities and tasks to be carried out as a part of the proposed project. A

static
The test solution is not renewed during the period of the test. A

static loaded radius arc
A portion of a circle whose center is the center of a standard tire-rim combination of an automobile and whose radius is the distance from that center to the level surface on which the automobile is standing, measured with the automobile at curb weight, the wheel parallel to the vehicle's longitudinal centerline, and the tire inflated to the manufacturer's recommended pressure. A

static system
A test system in which the test solution and test organisms are placed in the test chamber and kept there for the duration of the test without renewal of the test solution. A

static test
A toxicity test with aquatic organisms in which no flow of test solution occurs. Solutions may remain unchanged throughout the duration of the test. A

static-replacement test
A test method in which the test solution is periodically replaced at specific intervals during the test. A

station wagon
A passenger automobile with an extended roof line to increase cargo or passenger capacity, cargo compartment open to the passenger compartment, a tailgate and one or more rear seats readily removed or folded to facilitate cargo carrying. A

stationary casting
The pouring of molten aluminum into molds and allowing the metal to air cool. A

stationary compactor
A powered machine which is designed to compact solid waste or recyclable materials, and which remains stationary when in operation. A

stationary emission source
An emission source which is not self-propelled. A

stationary gas turbine
Any simple cycle gas turbine, regenerative cycle gas turbine or any gas turbine portion of a combined cycle steam/electric generating system that is not self propelled. It may, however, be mounted on a vehicle for portability. A

stationary source
(1) Any building, structure, facility, or installation which emits or may emit an air pollutant for which a national standard is in effect. (2) Any building, structure, facility, or installation which emits or may emit any air pollutant subject to regulation under the Clean Air Act. A (3) Any building, structure, facility, or installation which emits or may emit any air pollutant which has been designated as hazardous by the Administrator. A (4) Any stationary building, facility, equipment, installation or operation (or combination thereof) which is located on one or more contiguous or adjacent properties and which is owned or operated by the same person (or by persons under common control), and which emits an air pollutant for which a national ambient air quality standards promulgated under section 109 of the Act is in effect or which has been designated a hazardous waste in § 112 of the Act. O

stationary source fuel or emission limitation
Any emission limitation, schedule or timetable of compliance, or other requirement, which is prescribed under the Clean Air Act (other than section 112 or section 303 of the Act) or contained in any applicable implementation plan (other than a requirement imposed pursuant to section 110(a)(2)(F)(v) of the Act), and which limits, or is designed to limit, stationary source emissions resulting from combustion of fuels, including a prohibition on, or specification of, the use of any fuel of any type, grade or pollution characteristic. A

stationery
Writing paper suitable for pen and ink, pencil, or typing. Matching envelopes are included in this definition. A

statistical significance
The statistical significance determined by using appropriate standard techniques of multivariate analysis with results interpreted at the 95 percent confidence level and based on data relating species which are present in sufficient numbers at control areas to permit a valid statistical comparison with the areas being tested. A

statistical sound level
The level in decibels that is exceeded in a stated percentage (x) of the duration of the measurement period. It is abbreviated as L_x. A

statistically significant effect
In statistical analysis of data, a health effect that exhibits differences between a study population and a control group that are unlikely to

control group that are unlikely to have arisen by chance alone. N

statute
The law as passed by Congress and signed by the President. N

steady-state
The time period during which the amounts of test substance being taken up and depurated by the test organisms are equal, i.e., equilibrium. A

steady-state bioconcentration factor
The mean concentration of the test substance in test organisms during steady-state divided by the mean concentration in the test solution during the same period. A

steam generating unit
(1) Any enclosed combustion device that uses fuel energy in the form of steam. A (2) A device that combusts any fuel or byproduct/waste to produce steam or to heat water or any other heat transfer medium. This term includes any municipal-type solid waste incinerator with a heat recovery steam generating unit or any steam generating unit that combusts fuel and is part of a cogeneration system or a combined cycle system. This term does not include process heaters as they are defined in this subpart. A

steam hammers
A type of drop hammer where the ram is raised for each stroke by a double-action steam cylinder and the energy delivered to the workpiece is supplied by the velocity and weight of the ram and attached upper die driven downward by steam pressure. Energy delivered during each stroke may be varied. O

steam sales agreement
A legally-binding document between a firm associated with a new independent power production facility (IPPF) or a new IPPF and an industrial or commercial establishment requiring steam that sets the terms and conditions under which a specific new IPPF will provide steam to the establishment. A

steel
An iron-base alloy containing carbon, manganese, and often other alloying elements. Steel is defined here to include only those iron-carbon alloys containing less than 1.2 percent carbon by weight. A

steel basis material
Cold rolled steel, hot rolled steel, and chrome, nickel and tin coated steel which are processed in coil coating. A

steel production cycle
The operations required to produce each batch of steel and includes the following major functions: Scrap charging, preheating (when used), hot metal charging, primary oxygen blowing, additional oxygen blowing (when used), and tapping. A

STEL
Short-term exposure limit. N

step 1 facilities planning
Preparation of a plan for facilities as described in 40 CFR Part 35, Subpart E or I. A

step 1 grant
A Federal grant for preparation of a waste water treatment facilities plan as described in 40 CFR § 35.930-1. A

step 2
A project to prepare design drawings and specifications as described in 40 CFR Part 35, Subpart E or I. A

step 2 + 3
A project which combines preparation of design drawings and specifications as described in [40 CFR] 6.501(b) and building as described in § 6.501(c). A

step 2 grant
A Federal grant for preparation of construction drawings and specifications for a waste water treatment facility as described in 40 CFR § 35.930-1. A

step 2 plus step 3 grant
Grant assistance for a project which combines grants as described in 40 CFR 35.930-1(a)(4). A

step 3
A project to build a publicly owned treatment works as described in 40 CFR Part 35, Subpart E or I. A

step 3 grant
A federal grant for fabrication and building of a publicly owned treatment works as described in 40 CFR 35.930-1. A

stepladder
A self-supporting portable ladder, nonadjustable in length, having flat steps and a hinged back. Its size is designated by the overall length of the ladder measured along the front edge of the side rails. O

steps
The flat crosspieces of a ladder on which a person may step in ascending or descending. O

sterilization
(1) In pest control, the use of radiation and chemicals to damage body cells needed for reproduction. (2) The destruction of all living organisms in water or on the surface of various materials. In contrast, disinfection is the destruction of most living organisms in water or on surfaces. N

still
(1) A device used to volatilize, separate, and recover petroleum solvent from contaminated solvent, together with the piping and ductwork used in the installation of this device. A (2) A closed chamber in which heat is applied to vaporize a substance; chemical decomposition may or may not take place. U

sterilize
The use of a physical or chemical procedure to destroy all microbial life including highly resistant bacterial endospores. O

stochastic
Based on the assumption that the actions of a chemical substance result from probabilistic events. N

stock configuration
When no modifications have been

made to the original equipment motorcycle that would affect the noise emissions of the vehicle when measured according to the acceleration test procedure. A

stock solution
The source of the test solution prepared by dissolving the test substance in dilution water or a carrier which is then added to dilution water at a specified, selected concentration by means of the test substance delivery system. A

stoke
The unit of kinematic viscosity. A

stoker
A mechanical device to feed solid fuel or solid waste to a furnace. U

stone feed
Limestone feedstock and millscale or other iron oxide additives that become part of the product. A

stone setters' adjustable multiple-point suspension scaffold
A swinging type scaffold having a platform supported by hangers suspended at four points so as to permit the raising or lowering of the platform to the desired working position by the use of hoisting machines. O

stop control
An operator control designed to immediately deactivate the clutch control and activate the brake to stop slide motion. O

storage
(1) Temporary holding of waste pending treatment or disposal. Storage methods include containers, tanks, waste piles, and surface impoundments. N (2) Retention of spent nuclear fuel or radioactive wastes with the intent and capability to readily retrieve such fuel or waste for subsequent use, processing, or disposal. A (3) The interim containment of solid waste after generation and prior to collection for ultimate recovery or disposal. A (4) The holding of hazardous waste for a temporary period, at the end of which the hazardous waste is treated, disposed, or stored elsewhere. A

storage and retrieval of aerometric data
SAROAD. A computerized system which stores and reports information relating to ambient air quality. A

storage bin
A facility for storage (including surge bins and hoppers) for metallic minerals prior to further processing or loading. A

storage for disposal
Temporary storage of PCBs that have been designated for disposal. A

storage of hazardous waste
The containment of hazardous waste, either on a temporary basis or for a period of years, in such a manner as not to constitute disposal of such hazardous waste. A

storage pit
A hole in the ground in which solid waste is held prior to processing. U

storage vessel
Each tank, reservoir, or container used for the storage of petroleum liquids, but does not include: (1) Pressure vessels which are designed to operate in excess of 204.9 kPa (15 psig) without emissions to the atmosphere except under emergency conditions, (2) Subsurface caverns or porous rock reservoirs, or (3) Underground tanks if the total volume of petroleum liquids added to and taken from a tank annually does not exceed twice the volume of the tank. A

STORET
Storage and retrieval of water-related data. N

storm sewer
A sewer designed to carry only storm waters, surface runoff, street wash waters, and drainage. A

storm water
Storm water runoff, snow melt runoff, and surface runoff and drainage. A

storm water discharge associated with industrial activity
The discharge from any conveyance which is used for collecting and conveying storm water and which is directly related to manufacturing, processing or raw materials storage areas at an industrial plant; does not include discharges from facilities or activities excluded from the NPDES program under 40 CFR part 122. A

storm water runoff
Water discharged as a result of rain, snow, or other precipitation. N

stormwater sewer system
A drain and collection system designed and operated for the sole purpose of collecting stormwater and which is segregated from the process wastewater collection system. A

stratification
(1) A condition identified by a difference in excess of 10 percent between the average concentration in the duct or stack and concentration at any point more than 1.0 meter from the duct or stack wall. A (2) Separating into layers. N

stratosphere
The portion of the atmosphere that is 10-to-25 miles above the earth's surface. N

stratum (plural strata)
A single sedimentary bed or layer, regardless of thickness, that consists of generally the same kind of rock material. A

street motorcycle
(1) Any motorcycle that: (a) With an 80 kg (176 lb) driver, is capable of achieving a maximum speed of at least 40 km/h (25 mph) over a level paved surface; and (b) Is equipped with features customarily associated with practical street or highway use, such features including but not limited to

any of the following: stoplight, horn, rear view mirror, turn signals; or (2) Any motorcycle that: (a) Has an engine displacement less than 50 cubic centimeters; (b) Produces no more than two brake horse power; (c) With an 80 kg (176 lb) driver, cannot exceed 48 km/h (30 mph) over a level paved surface. A

street refuse
Solid waste picked up when streets and sidewalks are swept manually and mechanically. U

street wastes
Materials picked up by manual or mechanical sweepings of alleys, streets, and sidewalks; wastes from public waste receptacles; and material removed from catch basins. A

stressed waters
Those receiving environments in which an applicant can demonstrate, to the satisfaction of the Administrator, that the absence of a balanced, indigenous population is caused solely by human perturbations other than the applicant's modified discharge. A

strip
To take off friable asbestos materials from any part of a facility. A

strip, sheet, and miscellaneous products
Steel products other than wire products and fasteners. A

strip-mining
A process that uses machines to scrape soil or rock away from mineral deposits just under the earth's surface. N

stripcropping
Growing crops in a systematic arrangement of strips or bands which serve as barriers to wind and water erosion. N

stripper
(1) A mechanism or die part for removing the parts or material from the punch. O (2) Any vessel in which residual vinyl chloride is removed from polyvinyl chloride resin, except bulk resin, in the slurry form by the use of heat and/or vacuum. In the case of bulk resin, stripper includes any vessel which is used to remove residual vinyl chloride from polyvinyl chloride resin immediately following the polymerization step in the plant process flow. A

stroking selector
The part of the clutch/brake control that determines the type of stroking when the operating means is actuated. The stroking selector generally includes positions for "Off" (Clutch Control), "Inch," "Single Stroke," and "Continuous" (when Continuous is furnished). O

structural member
Any load-supporting member of a facility, such as beams and load supporting walls; or any nonload-supporting member, such as ceilings and nonload-supporting walls. A

structure-activity relationship
Relationships of biological activity

or toxicity of a chemical to its chemical structure or substructure. N

stud, pin, or fastener
A fastening device specifically designed and manufactured for use in explosive-actuated fastening tools. O

study
Any experiment at one or more test sites, in which a test substance is studied in a test system under laboratory conditions or in the environment to determine or help predict its effects, metabolism, product performance (efficacy studies only as required by 40 CFR 158.640), environmental and chemical fate, persistence and residue, or other characteristics in humans, other living organisms, or media. The term "study" does not include basic exploratory studies carried out to determine whether a test substance or a test method has any potential utility. A

study completion date
The date the final report is signed by the study director. A

study director
The individual responsible for the overall conduct of a study. A

study initiation date
The date the protocol is signed by the study director. A

stuffing box pressure
The fluid (liquid or gas) pressure inside the casing or housing of a piece of equipment, on the process side of the inboard seal. A

subacute dietary LC_{50}
A concentration of a substance, expressed as parts per million in food that is lethal to 50 percent of the test population of animals under test conditions. A

subacute toxicity
The property of a substance or mixture of substances to cause adverse effects in an organism upon repeated or continuous exposure within less than one-half the lifetime of that organism. A

subagreement
A written agreement between an EPA recipient and another party (other than another public agency) and any lower tier agreement for services, supplies, or construction necessary to complete the project. Subagreements include contracts and subcontracts for personal and professional services, agreements with consultants, and purchase orders. A

subbituminous coal
Coal that is classified as subbituminous A, B, or C according to the American Society of Testing and Materials (ASTM) Standard Specification for Classification of Coals by Rank D388-77. A

subchronic
Of intermediate duration, usually used to describe studies or levels of exposure between five and 90 days. N

subchronic exposure
Exposure to a substance spanning

approximately 10% of the lifetime of an organism. N

subchronic oral toxicity
The adverse effects occurring as a result of the repeated daily exposure of experimental animals to a chemical for a part (approximately 10 percent for rats) of a life span. A

subclass
A classification of heavy-duty engines of heavy-duty vehicles based on such factors as gross vehicle weight rating, fuel usage (gasoline-, diesel-, and methanol-fueled), vehicle usage, engine horsepower or additional criteria that the Administrator shall apply. A

subconfiguration
A unique combination, within a vehicle configuration of equivalent test weight, road-load horsepower, and any other operational characteristics or parameters which the Administrator determines may significantly affect fuel economy within a vehicle configuration. A

subcutaneous
A method of exposure where the substance is injected beneath the skin. N

subgrant
An award of financial assistance in the form of money, or property in lieu of money, made under a grant by a grantee to an eligible subgrantee. The term includes financial assistance when provided by contractual legal agreement, but does not include procurement purchases, nor does it include any form of assistance which is excluded from the definition of grant in 40 CFR parts 1-51. A

subject invention
Any invention, discovery, improvement or development (whether or not patentable) made in the course of or under a grant or any subagreement (at any tier) thereunder. A

subject to the jurisdiction of the United States
Subject to the jurisdiction of the United States by virtue of United States citizenship, United States vessel documentation or numbering, or as provided for by international agreement to which the United States is a party. N

submission
(1) A request by a POTW for approval of a Pretreatment Program to the EPA or a Director; (2) a request by a POTW to the EPA or a Director for authority to revise the discharge limits in categorical Pretreatment Standards to reflect POTW pollutant removals; or (3) a request to the EPA by an NPDES state for approval of its state pretreatment program. A

subsidence
The lowering of the natural land surface in response to: Earth movements; lowering of fluid pressure; removal of underlying supporting material by mining or solution of solids, either artificially or from natural causes; compaction due to wetting (hydrocompaction); oxidation of organic matter in soils; or added load on the land surface. A

subsoil
The layer of earth beneath the topsoil, which is usually lacking in appreciable quantities of organic matter. U

substance
A chemical substance or mixture unless otherwise indicated. A

substantial business relationship
The extent of a business relationship necessary under applicable State law to make a guarantee contract issued incident to that relationship valid and enforceable. A "substantial business relationship" must arise from a pattern of recent or ongoing business transactions, in addition to the guarantee itself, such that a currently existing business relationship between the guarantor and the owner or operator is demonstrated to the satisfaction of the applicable EPA Regional Administrator. A

substate
Any public regional, local, county, municipal, or inter-municipal agency, or regional or local public (including interstate) solid or hazardous waste management authority, or other public agency below the State level. A

subsurface soil injection
A special method of landfarming hazardous waste with vapor pressures exceeding 78 millimeters of mercury. See deep-well disposal. U

suction manometers
This system consists of a network of porous "stones" connected by hoses/tubing to a vacuum pump. The porous "stones" or suction manometers are installed along the sides and under the bottom of the waste disposal facility liner. This type of system works best when installed in relatively permeable unsaturated soil immediately adjacent to the disposal facility's bottom and/or sides. A

sudden accident
An unforeseen and unexpected occurrence which is not continuous or repeated in nature. A

sudden accidental occurrence
An occurrence which is not continuous or repeated in nature. A

suitable
That which fits, and has the qualities or qualifications to meet a given purpose, occasion, condition, function, or circumstance. O

sulfate
A compound in which the hydrogen of sulfuric acid is replaced by either a metal or by an organic radical, to become a sulfate salt or sulfate ester, respectively. U

sulfide
Total sulfide as measured by the potassium ferricyanide titration method described in Appendix A or the Modified Monier-Williams method described in Appendix B. A

sulfite
A compound in which the hydrogen of sulfurous acid is replaced by either a metal or by an organic radical, to

become a sulfite salt or sulfite ester, respectively. U

sulfur dioxide
SO2. A heavy, pungent, colorless gas formed primarily by the combustion of fossil fuels. This major air pollutant is unhealthy for plants, animals, and people. N

sulfur oxide/particulate complex
The primary pollutant emissions of sulfur dioxide and the secondary particulate compounds that are formed from them in the atmosphere. Abbreviated SPC. U

sulfur percentage
The percentage of sulfur as determined by ASTM standard test method D 2622-87, entitled "Standard Test Method for Sulfur in Petroleum Products by X-Ray Spectrometry". A

sulfur recovery plant
Any plant that recovers elemental sulfur from any gas stream. A

sulfuric acid pickling
Those operations in which steel products are immersed in sulfuric acid solutions to chemically remove oxides and scale, and those rinsing operations associated with such immersions. A

sulfuric acid plant
Any facility producing sulfuric acid by the contact process by burning elemental sulfur, alkylation acid, hydrogen sulfide, or acid sludge, but does not include facilities where conversion to sulfuric acid is utilized primarily as a means of preventing emissions to the atmosphere of sulfur dioxide or other sulfur compounds. A

sulfuric acid production unit
Any facility producing sulfuric acid by the contact process by burning elemental sulfur, alkylation acid, hydrogen sulfide, organic sulfides and mercaptans, or acid sludge, but does not include facilities where conversion to sulfuric acid is utilized primarily as a means of preventing emissions to the atmosphere of sulfur dioxide or other sulfur compounds. A

sump
(1) A depression or tank that catches liquid runoff for drainage or disposal, like a cesspool. N (2) A pit or reservoir that meets the definition of tank and those troughs/trenches connected to it that serve to collect hazardous waste for transport to hazardous waste storage, treatment, or disposal facilities; except that as used in the landfill, surface impoundment, and waste pile rules, "sump" means any lined pit or reservoir that serves to collect liquids drained from a leachate collection and removal system or leak detection system for subsequent removal from the system. A

Superfund
The program operated under the legislative authority of CERCLA and SARA that funds and carries out the EPA solid waste emergency and long-term removal remedial activities. These activities include establishing the National Priorities List investigating sites for inclusion on the list, determining their priority level on the list, and conducting and/or

supervising the ultimately determined cleanup and other remedial actions. N

Superfund Memorandum of Agreement
SMOA. A nonbinding, written document executed by an EPA Regional Administrator and the head of a state agency that may establish the nature and extent of EPA and state interaction during the removal, pre-remedial, remedial, and/or enforcement response process. The SMOA is not a site-specific document although attachments may address specific sites. The SMOA generally defines the role and responsibilities of both the lead and the support agencies. A

Superfund State Contract
SSC. A joint, legally binding agreement between EPA and another party(s) to obtain the necessary assurances before an EPA-lead remedial action or any political subdivision-lead activities can begin at a site, and to ensure State or Indian Tribe involvement as required under CERCLA section 121(f). A

supernatant
The liquid remaining above a layer of settleable solids after the solids collected at the bottom of a vessel. U

supersaturated solution
See oversaturated solution. A

supplemental appropriation
An appropriation enacted as an addition to a regular annual appropriation act. Supplemental appropriations acts provide additional budget authority beyond original estimates for programs or activities (including new programs authorized after the date of the original appropriation act) for which the need for funds is too urgent to be postponed until the next regular appropriation. U

supplementary control system
Any technique for limiting the concentration of a pollutant in the ambient air by varying the emissions of that pollutant according to atmospheric conditions, particularly when the conditions are conducive to ground level concentrations in excess of natural ambient standards. The term supplementary control system may not include any dispersion technique based solely on the use of a stack the height of which exceeds good engineering practice (as determined under regulations implementing section 123 of the CAA). A

supplier of water
Any person who owns or operates a public water system. A, J

support media
The quartz sand or glass beads used to support the plant. A

support system
A structure such as underpinning, bracing, or shoring, which provides support to an adjacent structure, underground installation, or sides of an excavation. O

suppressed combustion
Those basic oxygen furnace

steelmaking wet air cleaning systems which are designed to limit or suppress the combustion of carbon monoxide in furnace gases by restricting the amount of excess air entering the air pollution control system. A

surface casing
The first string of well casing to be installed in the well. A

surface coating
The process of coating a copper workpiece as well as the associated surface finishing and flattening. A

surface coating operation
(1) Any prime coat, guide coat, or topcoat operation on an automobile or light-duty truck surface coating line. A (2) The system on a metal furniture or on a large appliance surface coating line used to apply and dry or cure an organic coating on the surface of the metal furniture part or product. The surface coating operation may be a prime coat or a top coat operation and includes the coating application station(s), flash-off area, and curing oven. A

surface collecting agents
Those chemical agents that form a surface film to control the layer thickness of oil. A

surface cracking
Discontinuities that develop in the cover material of a sanitary landfill due to the surface drying or settlement of the solid waste. These discontinuities may result in the exposure of solid waste and thus lead to the entrance or egress of vectors, intrusion of water, and venting of decomposition gases. U

surface feet per minute
sfpm. The distance in feet any one abrasive grain on the peripheral surface of a grinding wheel travels in 1 minute. O

surface impoundment
SI. A facility or part of a facility which is a natural topographic depression, man-made excavation, or diked area formed primarily of earthen materials (although it may be lined with man-made materials), which is designed to hold an accumulation of liquid wastes or wastes containing free liquids, and which is not an injection well. Examples of surface impoundments are holding, storage, settling, and aeration pits, ponds, and lagoons. A

surface moisture
Water that is not chemically bound to a metallic mineral or metallic mineral concentrate. A

surface treatment
A chemical or electrochemical treatment applied to the surface of a metal. Such treatments include pickling, etching, conversion coating, phosphating, and chromating. Surface treatment baths are usually followed by a water rinse. The rinse may consist of single or multiple stage rinsing. For the purposes of this part, a surface treatment operation is defined as a bath followed by a rinse, regardless of the number of stages. Each surface treatment bath, rinse

combination is entitled to discharge allowance. A

surface water
Water above the surface of the ground, including but not limited to lakes, ponds, reservoirs, artificial impoundments, streams, rivers, springs, seeps and wetlands. A

surfacing material
Material in a school building that is sprayed-on, troweled-on, or otherwise applied to surfaces such as acoustical plaster on ceilings and fireproofing materials on structural members, or other materials on surfaces for acoustical, fireproofing, or other purposes. A

surfactant
(1) A surface active chemical agent, usually made up of phosphates, used in detergents to cause lathering. U (2) Those methylene blue active substances amendable to measurement by the method described in "Methods for Chemical Analysis of Water and Wastes," 1971, Environmental Protection Agency, Analytical Quality Control Laboratory, page 131. A

surgical waste
The waste generated by surgical techniques in the treatment of disease, injury, or deformity. U

surveillance system
(1) A series of monitoring devices designed to determine environmental quality. (2) A required part of state implementation plans, established to monitor all aspects of progress toward attainment of air quality standards and to identify potential episodes of high pollutant concentrations in time to take prevention action. U

SUS
Saybolt Universal Seconds as determined by the Standard Method of Test for Saybolt Viscosity (ASTM D-88-56), and may be determined by use of the SUS conversion tables specified in ASTM Method D2161-66 following determination of viscosity in accordance with the procedures specified in the Standard Method of Test for Viscosity of Transparent and Opaque Liquids (ASTM D445-65). O

susceptibility
The degree to which an organism is affected by a pesticide at a particular level of exposure. A

suspended solids
Small particles of solid pollutants that float on the surface of, or are suspended in, sewage or other liquids. They resist removal by conventional means. (See: total suspended solids). N

suspension
(1) The act of suspending the use of a pesticide when EPA deems it necessary to do so in order to prevent an imminent hazard resulting from continued use of the pesticide. An emergency suspension takes effect immediately; under an ordinary suspension, a registrant can request a hearing before the suspension goes into effect. Such hearing process might take six months. N (2)

Depending on the context, either (a) temporary withdrawal of the authority to obligate grant funds pending corrective action by the grantee or subgrantee or a decision to terminate the grant, or (b) an action taken by a suspending official in accordance with agency regulations implementing E.O. 12549 to immediately exclude a person from participating in grant transactions for a period, pending completion of an investigation and such legal or debarment proceedings as may ensue. A

suspension culture
Individual cells or small clumps of cells growing in a liquid nutrient medium. N

swamp
A type of wetland that is dominated by woody vegetation and does not accumulate appreciable peat deposits. Swamps may be fresh or salt water and tidal or non-tidal. N

SWC
Settlement with conditions. U

SWDA
Solid Waste Disposal Act of 1980 (P.L. 96-482). N

sweep device
A single or double arm (rod) attached to the upper die or slide of the press and designed to move the operator's hands to a safe position as the dies close, if the operator's hands are inadvertently within the point of operation. O

sweet water
The solution of 8-10 percent crude glycerine and 90-22 percent water that is a by-product of saponification or fat splitting. A

switch
A device for opening and closing or changing the connection of a circuit. O

switchboard
A large single panel, frame, or assembly of panels which have switches, buses, instruments, overcurrent and other protective devices mounted on the face or back or both. Switchboards are generally accessible from the rear as well as from the front and are not intended to be installed in cabinets. O

switcher locomotive
Any locomotive designated as a switcher by the builder or reported to the ICC as a switcher by the operator-owning-railroad and including, but not limited to, all locomotives of the builder/model designations listed in Appendix A to this subpart. A

SWMU
Solid Waste Management Unit. U

SWU
Standard Work Units. U

synergism
The cooperative action of separate substances such that the total effect is greater than the sum of the effects of the substances acting independently. U

synthetic fiber
Any fiber composed partially or

entirely of materials made by chemical synthesis, or made partially or entirely from chemically-modified naturally-occurring materials. A

synthetic organic chemicals
SOCs. Man-made organic chemicals. Some SOCs are volatile, others tend to stay dissolved in water rather than evaporate out of it. N

synthetic organic chemicals manufacturing industry
The industry that produces, as intermediates or final products, one or more of the chemicals listed in 40 CFR § 60.489. A

system
Any motor vehicle modification which controls or causes the reduction of substances emitted from motor vehicles. A

system emergency reserves
An amount of electric generating capacity equivalent to the rated capacity of the single largest electric generating unit in the electric utility company (including steam generating units, internal combustion engines, gas turbines, nuclear units, hydroelectric units, and all other electric generating equipment) which is interconnected with the affected facility that has the malfunctioning flue gas desulfurization system. The electric generating capability of equipment under multiple ownership is prorated based on ownership unless the proportional entitlement to electric output is otherwise established by contractual arrangement. A

system load
The entire electric demand of an electric utility company's service area interconnected with the affected facility that has the malfunctioning flue gas desulfurization system plus firm contractual sales to other electric utility companies. Sales to other electric utility companies (e.g., emergency power) not on a firm contractual basis may also be included in the system load when no available system capacity exists in the electric utility company to which the power is supplied for sale. A

system of records
A group of any records under the control of any agency from which information is retrieved by the name of the individual or by some identifying number, symbol, or other identifying particular assigned to the individual. O

system response
The time interval from a step change in opacity in the stack at the input to the continuous monitoring system to the time at which 95 percent of the corresponding final value is reached as displayed on the continuous monitoring system data recorder. A

systemic
Relating to the whole body, rather than its individual parts. N

systemic pesticide
A chemical that is taken up from the ground or absorbed through the surface and carried through the

systems of the organism being protected, making it toxic to pests. **U**

T

2-year, 24-hour precipitation event
The maximum 24-hour precipitation event with a probable recurrence interval of once in two years as defined by the National Weather Service and Technical Paper No. 40, "Rainfall Frequency Atlas of the U.S.," May 1961, or equivalent regional or rainfall probability information developed therefrom. A

24-hour period
The period of time between 12:01 a.m. and 12:00 midnight. A

30-day average
The arithmetic mean of pollutant parameter values of samples collected in a period of 30 consecutive days. A

T
Temperature, degrees Fahrenheit or Kelvin. U

t1/2
First-order half-life. The time required for the concentration of the chemical to be reduced to one-half its initial value. A

table Z
OSHA's Toxic and Hazardous Substances Tables Z-1, Z-2, and Z-3 of air contaminants, found in 29 CFR 1910.1000. These tables record PELs, TWAs, and ceiling concentrations for the materials listed. N

tabulating cards
Cards used in automatic tabulating machines; "tabulating paper" is paper used in tabulating forms for use on automatic data processing equipment. A

tag
(1) Stiff paper, metal or other hard material that is tied or otherwise affixed to the packaging of a protector. A (2) Temporary signs, usually attached to a piece of equipment or part of a structure, to warn of existing or immediate hazards. A (3) A device usually made of card, paper, pasteboard, plastic or other material used to identify a hazardous condition. O

tail-end techniques
Methods for controlling air pollution

554

by treating the polluted air stream after the pollutants have been formed. U

tagout
The placement of a tagout device on an energy isolating device, in accordance with an established procedure, to indicate that the energy isolating device and the equipment being controlled may not be operated until the tagout device is removed. O

tagout device
A prominent warning device, such as a tag and a means of attachment, which can be securely fastened to an energy isolating device in accordance with an established procedure, to indicate that the energy isolating device and the equipment being controlled may not be operated until the tagout device is removed. O

tailings
Residue of raw materials or waste separated out during the processing of crops or mineral ores. N

tallow
A product made from beef cattle or sheep fat that has a melting point of 40 degrees C or greater. A

tampering
The removal or rendering inoperative by any person, other than for purposes of maintenance, repair, or replacement, of any device or element of design incorporated into any product in compliance with regulations under Section 6 of the Noise Control Act, prior to its sale or delivery to the ultimate purchaser or while it is in use; or the use of a product after such device or element of design has been removed or rendered inoperative by any person. A

tangible net worth
Tangible assets that remain after deducting liabilities; such assets would not include intangibles such as goodwill and rights to patents or royalties. A

tank
A stationary device, designed to contain an accumulation of hazardous waste which is constructed primarily of non-earthen materials (e.g., wood, concrete, steel, plastic) which provide structural support. A

tank fuel volume
The volume of fuel in the fuel tank(s), which is determined by taking the manufacturer's nominal fuel tank(s) capacity and multiplying by 0.40, the result rounded using ASTM E 29-67 to the nearest tenth of a U.S. gallon. A

tank system
A hazardous waste storage or treatment tank and its associated ancillary equipment and containment system. A

tape sampler
A device used in the measurement of both gases and fine particulates. It allows air sampling to be made automatically at predetermined times. U

tankage
Dried animal by-product residues used in feedstuffs. A

tapping
The removal of slag or product from the electric submerged arc furnace under normal operating conditions such as removal of metal under normal pressure and movement by gravity down the spout into the ladle. A

tapping period
The time duration from initiation of the process of opening the tap hole until plugging of the tap hole is complete. A

target abatement dates
Target abatement dates or schedules of compliance for all significant dischargers, nonpoint source control measures, residual and land disposal controls, and stormwater system needs, including major interim and final completion dates, and requirements that are necessary to assure an adequate tracking of progress toward compliance. A

target organ effects
The following is a target organ categorization of effects which may occur, including examples of signs and symptoms and chemicals which have been found to cause such effects. These examples illustrate the range and diversity of effects and hazards found in the workplace, and the broad scope employers must consider in this area, but are not intended to be all inclusive.
  a. Hepatoxins - Chemicals which produce liver damage.
  Signs and Symptoms - Jaundice; liver enlargement.
  Chemicals - Carbon tetrachloride; nitrosamines.
  b. Nephrotoxins - Chemicals which produce kidney damage.
  Signs and Symptoms - Edema; proteinuria.
  Chemicals - Halogenated hydrocarbons; uranium.
  c. Neurotoxins -Chemicals which produce their primary toxic effects on the nervous system.
  Signs and Symptoms - Narcosis, behavioral changes; decrease in motor functions.
  Chemicals - Mercury, carbon disulfide.
  d. Agents which act on blood hematopoietic system -Decrease hemoglobin function; deprive the body tissues of oxygen.
  Signs and Symptoms - Cyanosis; loss of consciousness.
  Chemicals - Carbon monoxide; cyanides.
  e. Agents which damage the lung- Chemicals which irritate or damage the pulmonary tissue.
  Signs and Symptoms - Cough, tightness of chest, shortness of breath.
  Chemicals - Silica; asbestos.
  f. Reproductive toxins - Chemicals which affect the reproductive capabilities including chromosomal damage (mutations) and effects on fetuses (teratogenesis).
  Signs and Symptoms - Birth defects; sterility.
  Chemicals - Lead; DBCP.
  g. Cutaneous hazards - Chemicals which affect the dermal layer of the body.
  Signs and Symptoms - Defatting of he skin; rashes; irritation.
  Chemicals - Ketones; chlorinated compounds.

h. Eye hazards - Chemicals which affect the eye or visual capacity.
Signs and Symptoms - Conjunctivitis; corneal damage.
Chemicals - Organic solvents; acids. N

target organ toxin
A toxic substance that attacks a specific organ of the body. For example, overexposure to carbon tetrachloride can cause liver damage. N

target organ/system
An organ or functional system (e.g., respiratory, immune, excretory, reproductive systems) which demonstrates toxicity to a specific chemical; not necessarily the organ/system with the highest accumulation of the chemical, but rather that which elicits a toxic response(s) of concern. N

TARs
Technical amendment regulations. See regulatory interpretative memoranda for description. U

TAT
Technical Assistance Team. N

TB
Trial burn. U

TCA
1,1,1-trichloroethane. N

TCAA
Trichloroacetic acid. N

TCDD
2,3,7,8-Tetrachlorodibenzo-p-dioxin. A

TCE
Trichloroethylene. A stable, low-boiling colorless liquid, toxic by inhalation. TCE is used as a solvent, metal degreasing agent, and in other industrial applications. N

TCL
Target cleanup levels. U

TC$_{Lo}$
Toxic concentration low. U

TCLP
Toxicity characteristic leaching procedure. U

TCM
Transportation control measure. A

TCP
Transportation Control Plan. U

TD
Toxic dose. U

TD$_{Lo}$
Lowest dose of a substance. The lowest dose of a substance introduced by any route other than inhalation over any given period of time and reported to produce any toxic effect in humans or to produce tumorigenic or reproductive effects in animals or humans. N

TDS
Total dissolved solids. A

Technical Assistance Team
TAT. N

technical grade of active ingredient
A material containing an active

ingredient: (1) Which contains no inert ingredient, other than one used for purification of the active ingredient; and (2) Which is produced on a commercial or pilot-plant production scale (whether or not it is ever held for sale). A

technical review criteria
TRC. D

technically qualified individual
A person or persons (1) who, because of training, or experience, or a combination of these factors, is capable of understanding the health and environmental risks associated with the chemical substance which is used under his or her supervision, (2) who is responsible for enforcing appropriate methods of conducting scientific experimentation, analysis, or chemical research to minimize such risks, and (3) who is responsible for the safety assessments and clearances related to the procurement, storage, use, and disposal of the chemical substance as may be appropriate or required within the scope of conducting a research and development activity. A

technologically enhanced natural radioactivity
TENR. Naturally radioactive nuclides whose relationship to the location of persons has been altered through man's activities such as by the activities of mining, tunneling, development of underground caverns, development of wells, and travel in space or at high altitudes. U

technology-based standards
Effluent limitations applicable to direct and indirect sources which are developed on a category-by-category basis using statutory factors, not including water-quality effects. N

TEGD
Technical Enforcement Guidance Document. U

TEL
Tetraethyl lead. U

telecommunications center
An installation of communication equipment under the exclusive control of an organization providing telecommunications service, that is located outdoors or in a vault, chamber, or a building space used primarily for such installations. O

telecommunication service
The furnishing of a capability to signal or communicate at a distance by means such as telephone, telegraph, police and fire alarm, community antenna television, or similar system, using wire, conventional cable, coaxial cable, wave guides, microwave transmission, or other similar means. O

tempering
The process whereby glass is heated near the melting point and then rapidly cooled to increase its mechanical and thermal endurance. A

ten-year 24-hour precipitation event
The maximum 24-hour precipitation event with a probable recurrence interval of once in 10 years as defined by: (1) The National Weather Service and Technical Paper No. 40, "Rainfall Frequency Atlas of the U.S.," May

1961, or equivalent regional or rainfall probability information developed therefrom. (2) The U.S. Department of Commerce, National Oceanic and Atmospheric Administration, National Weather Service, or equivalent regional or rainfall probability information. A

ten-year 24-hour rainfall event
The maximum precipitation event with a probable recurrence interval of once in 10 years as defined by the National Weather Service in technical paper no. 40, "Rainfall Frequency Atlas of the U.S.," May 1961, and subsequent amendments or equivalent regional or State rainfall probability information developed therefrom. A

teratogenic
Substances that are suspected of causing malformations or serious deviations from the normal type, which can not be inherited in or on animal embryos or fetuses. N

teratogenicity
The capacity of a physical or chemical agent to cause non-hereditary congenital malformations (birth defects) in offspring. N

termination
Permanent withdrawal of the authority to obligate previously-awarded grant funds before that authority would otherwise expire. It also means the voluntary relinquishment of that authority by the grantee or subgrantee. Termination does not include: (1) Withdrawal of funds awarded on the basis of the grantee's underestimate of the unobligated balance in a prior period; (2) Withdrawal of the unobligated balance as of the expiration of a grant; (3) Refusal to extend a grant or award additional funds, to make a competing or noncompeting continuation, renewal, extension, or supplemental award; or (4) Voiding of a grant upon determination that the award was obtained fraudulently, or was otherwise illegal or invalid from inception. A

terms and conditions of registration
The terms and conditions governing lawful sale, distribution, and use approved in conjunction with registration including labeling, use classification, composition, and packaging. A

terne coating
Coating steel products with terne metal by the hot dip process including the immersion of the steel product in a molten bath of lead and tin metals, and the related operations preceding and subsequent to the immersion phase. A

terracing
Dikes built along the contour of agricultural land to hold runoff and sediment, thus reducing erosion. N

terrestrial radiation
Radiation emitted by naturally occurring radionuclides such as potassium-40; the natural decay chains uranium-238, uranium-235, or thorium-232; or from cosmic-ray induced radionuclides in the soil. U

territorial seas
The belt of the seas measured from

the line of ordinary low water along that portion of the coast which is in direct contact with the open sea and the line marking the seaward limit of inland waters, and extending seaward a distance of three miles. A, D

tertiary treatment
Advanced cleaning of waste water that goes beyond the secondary or biological stage. It removes nutrients such as phosphorus and nitrogen and most suspended solids. U

test chamber
The individual containers in which test organisms are maintained during exposure to test solution. A

test compressor
A compressor used to demonstrate compliance with the applicable noise emissions standard. A

test data
Data from a formal or informal test or experiment, including information concerning the objectives, experimental methods and materials, protocols, results, data analyses (including risk assessments), recorded observations, monitoring data, measurements, and conclusions from a study, test or experiment, recorded observation, monitoring, or measurement. A

test engine
An engine in a test sample. A

test exhaust system
An exhaust system in selective enforcement audit test sample. A

test facility
A laboratory that has been set up and calibrated to conduct ANSI Std S3.19-1974 tests on hearing protective devices. A

test hearing protector
A hearing protector that has been selected for testing to verify the value to be put on the label, or which has been designated for testing to determine compliance of the protector with the labeled value. A

test marketing
The distribution in commerce of no more than a predetermined amount of a chemical substance, mixture, article containing that chemical substance or mixture, or a mixture containing that substance, by a manufacturer or processor, to no more than a defined number of potential customers to explore market capability in a competitive situation during a predetermined testing period prior to the broader distribution of that chemical substance, mixture, or article in commerce. A

test period
The combination of the exposure period and the post-exposure period; or, the entire duration of the test. A

test request
A request submitted to the manufacturer by the Administrator that will specify the hearing protector category, and test sample size to be tested according to [40 CFR] § 211.212-1, and other information regarding the audit. A

test sample
(1) The collection of vehicles of the same configuration which have been drawn from the population of vehicles of that configuration and which will receive exhaust emission testing. (2) The collection of light-duty trucks or heavy-duty engines of the same configuration which have been selected to receive exhaust emission testing. A

test sample size
The number of vehicles of the same category or configuration in a test sample. U

test solution
(1) The test substance and the dilution water in which the test substance is dissolved or suspended. A (2) Dilution water containing the dissolved test substance to which test organisms are exposed. A

test subject
The person wearing the respirator for quantitative fit testing. A

test substance
(1) The form of chemical substance or mixture that is specified for use in testing. A (2) A substance or mixture administered or added to a test system in a study, which substance or mixture: (a) is the subject of an application for a research or marketing permit supported by the study, or is the contemplated subject of such an application; or (b) is an ingredient, impurity, degradation product, metabolite, or radioactive isotope of a substance described by paragraph (a) of this definition, or some other substance related to a substance described by that paragraph, which is used in the study to assist in characterizing the toxicity, metabolism, or other characteristics of a substance described by that paragraph. A

test system
Any animal, plant, microorganism, chemical or physical matrix, including but not limited to soil or water, or subparts thereof, to which the test, control, or reference substance is administered or added for study. "Test system" also includes appropriate groups or components of the system not treated with the test, control, or reference substance. A

test vehicle
A vehicle in a test sample or a production verification vehicle. A

test weight
The weight, within an inertia weight class, which is used in the dynamometer testing of a vehicle, and which is based on its loaded vehicle weight in accordance with the provisions of [40 CFR] Part 86. A

test weight basis
The basis on which equivalent test weight is determined in accordance with § 86.129-94 of subpart B of this 40 CFR parts 86-99. A

testing agent
Any person who develops test data on a retrofit device. A

testing exemption
(1) An exemption from the prohibitions of Section 10(a)(1), (2), (3), and (5) of FIFRA, which may be

granted under Section 10(b)(1) of the Act for research, investigations, studies, demonstrations, or training, but not for national security. A (2) An exemption which may be granted under section 203(b)(1) for the purpose of research investigations, studies, demonstrations or training, but not including national security. A

testing facility
A person who actually conducts a study, i.e., actually uses the test substance in a test system. "Testing facility" encompasses only those operational units that are being or have been used to conduct studies. A

tetrachloroethylene
(Or priority pollutant No. 85). The value obtained by the standard method Number 610 specified in 44 FR 69464, 69571 (December 3, 1979). A

textile fiberglass
Fibrous glass in the form of continuous strands having uniform thickness. A

TH
Total hardness. N

theoretical air
The quantity of air, calculated from the chemical composition of a waste, required to burn the waste completely. Also referred to as theoretical combustion air and stoichiometric air. U

therapeutic index
The ratio of the dose required to produce toxic or lethal effect to dose required to produce non-adverse or therapeutic response. N

thermal conductivity
The specific rate of heat flow per hour through refractory materials or other substances expressed in British thermal units per square feet of area for a temperature difference of 1° F and for a thickness of 1 foot (30.48 centimeters) expressed as British thermal units per square feet per hour per degree Fahrenheit per foot. U

thermal deflection rate
The angular degrees of rotation per degree of temperature change of the thermostatic coil. A

thermal dryer
A unit in which the surface moisture content of a metallic mineral or a metallic mineral concentrate is reduced by direct or indirect contact with a heated gas stream. A

thermal efficiency
The ratio of heat used to total heat generated. U

thermal pollution
Discharge of heated water from industrial processes that can affect the life processes of aquatic plants and animals. N

thermal processing
Processing of waste material by means of heat. A

thermal shock resistance
The ability of a material to withstand sudden heating or cooling, or both, without cracking or spalling. U

thermal system insulation
Material in a school building applied to pipes, fittings, boilers, breeching, tanks, ducts, or other interior structural components to prevent heat loss or gain, or water condensation, or for other purposes. A

thermal treatment
The treatment of hazardous waste in a device which uses elevated temperatures as the primary means to change the chemical, physical, or biological character or composition of the hazardous waste. Examples of thermal treatment processes are incineration, molten salt, pyrolysis, calcination, wet air oxidation, and microwave discharge. U

thermal turbulence
Air movement and mixing caused by convection. U

thermocouple
Two lengths of wire, made from different kinds of homogeneous metals, that are connected to form a complete electric circuit; they develop an electromotive force when one junction is at a different temperature from the other. U

thermostat
A temperature-actuated device. A

thermostatic coil
A spiral-wound coil of thermally-sensitive material which provides rotary force (torque) and/or displacement as a function of applied temperature. A

thermostatic switch
An element of thermally-sensitive material which acts to open or close an electrical circuit as a function of temperature. A

third party
A method for preparing EPA's environmental impact statement whereby the applicant retains a consultant, the responsible official exercises a concurrence review, and then the responsible official supervises the approved consultant in the preparation of the EIS. This method is optional and requires approval of both the new source applicant and the responsible official prior to the execution of an agreement to prepare the EIS. Generally, the preparation of the EIS under the third party method would be initiated prior to the preparation of the environmental impact assessment by the applicant and would thereby serve the purpose of any such environmental assessment analyses. A

thixotropic
Describes a material which appears and acts as a solid when undisturbed but will change to a semi-liquid when agitated; describes a material whose viscosity is a function of shear rate. U

THM
Trihalomethane. A

THMFP
Trihalomethanes formation potential. N

threshold dose
The minimum application of a given

substance required to produce a measurable effect. F

threshold limit value
TLV. Represents the air concentrations of chemical substances to which it is believed that workers may be daily exposed without adverse effect. N

threshold planning quantity
A quantity designated for each chemical on the list of extremely hazardous substances that triggers notification by facilities to the state emergency response commission that such facilities are subject to emergency planning under SARA Title III. N

threshold toxicant
A substance showing an apparent level of effect that is a minimally effective dose, above which a response occurs; below that dose no response is expected. N

throttle
The mechanical linkage which either directly or indirectly controls the fuel flow to the engine. A

tidal
A situation in which the water level periodically fluctuates due to the action of lunar (moon) and solar (sun) forces upon the rotating earth. N

tidal marsh
Low, flat marshlands traversed by interlaced channels and tidal sloughs and subject to tidal inundation; normally, the only vegetation present is salt-tolerant bushes and grasses. N

tidal volume
The volume of air that is inspired or expired in a single breath during regular breathing. The symbol is VT. U

tiering
The coverage of general matters in broader environmental impact statements (such as national program or policy statements) with subsequent narrower statements or environmental analyses (such as regional or basinwide program statements or ultimately site-specific statements) incorporating by reference the general discussions and concentrating solely on the issues specific to the statement subsequently prepared. Tiering is appropriate when the sequence of statements or analyses is: (a) From a program, plan, or policy environmental impact statement to a program, plan, or policy statement or analysis of lesser scope or to a site-specific statement or analysis. (b) From an environmental impact statement on a specific action at an early stage (such as need and site selection) to a supplement (which is preferred) or a subsequent statement or analysis at a later stage (such as environmental mitigation). Tiering in such cases is appropriate when it helps the lead agency to focus on the issues which are ripe for decision and exclude from consideration issues already decided or not yet ripe. A

TIM
Time in mode. A

time to 90 percent response
The time interval from a step

change in the input concentration at the instrument inlet to a reading of 90 percent of the ultimate recorded concentration. A

time-response curve
The curve relating cumulative percentage response of a test batch of organisms, exposed to a single dose or single concentration of a chemical, to a period of exposure. A

time-weighted average
TWA exposure is the airborne concentration of a material to which a person is exposed, averaged over the total exposure time--generally the total workday (8 to 12 hours). Also see "TLV." N

timed delay
A delayed diaphragm displacement controlled to occur within a given time period. A

TIP
Transportation Improvement Program. A

tipping
The unloading of refuse from a collection truck. U

tipping fee
A fee for the unloading or dumping of waste at a landfill, transfer station or waste-to-energy facility, usually stated in dollars per ton. U

tipping floor
The unloading area for vehicles that are delivering solid waste to an incinerator or other processing plant. U

tire
(1) The following types of tires: passenger car tires, light- and heavy-duty truck tires, high speed industrial tires, bus tires, and special service tires (including military, agricultural, off-the-road, and slow speed industrial). A
(2) Any agricultural airplane, industrial, mobile home, light-duty truck and/or passenger vehicle tire that has a bead diameter less than or equal to 0.5 meter (m) (19.7 inches) and a cross section dimension less than or equal to 0.325 m (12.8 in.), and that is mass produced in an assembly line fashion. A

TI/RE
Toxicity Identification/Reduction Evaluation. N

tissue
A group of similar cells. N

titration
The determination of a constituent in a known volume of solution by the measured addition of a solution of known strength to completion of the reaction as signaled by observation of an end point. U

TLV
Threshold limit value. U

TMDL
Total maximum daily load. A

TME
Test marketing exemption. U

TML
Tetramethyl lead. U

to chamber
To fit properly without the use of excess force, the case being duly supported. O

to commence construction
To engage in a continuous program of on-site construction including site clearance, grading, dredging, or land filling specifically designed for an indirect source in preparation for the fabrication, erection, or installation of the building components of the indirect source. For the purpose of this paragraph, interruptions resulting from acts of God, strikes, litigation, or other matters beyond the control of the owner shall be disregarded in determining whether a construction or modification program is continuous. A

to commence modification
To engage in a continuous program of on-site modification, including site clearance, grading, dredging, or land filling in preparation for a specific modification of the indirect source. A

to use any registered pesticide in a manner inconsistent with its labeling
To use any registered pesticide in a manner not permitted by the labeling: Provided, That the term shall not include (1) applying a pesticide at any dosage, concentration, or frequency less than that specified on the labeling, (2) applying a pesticide against any target pest not specified on the labeling if the application is to the crop, animal, or site specified on the labeling, unless the Administrator [of EPA] has required that the labeling specifically state that the pesticide may be used only for the pests specified on the labeling after the Administrator [of EPA] has determined that the use of the pesticide against other pests would cause an unreasonable adverse effect on the environment, (3) employing any method of application not prohibited by the labeling, or (4) mixing a pesticide or pesticides with a fertilizer when such mixture is not prohibited by the labeling: Provided further, That the term also shall not include any use of a pesticide in conformance with section 5, 18, or 24 of this Act [FIFRA], or any use of a pesticide in a manner that the Administrator [of EPA] determines to be consistent with the purposes of this Act: And provided further, That after March 31, 1979, the term shall not include the use of a pesticide for agricultural or forestry purposes at a dilution less than label dosage unless before or after that date the Administrator [of EPA] issues a regulation or advisory opinion consistent with the study provided for in section 27(b) of the Federal Pesticide Act of 1978, which regulation or advisory opinion specifically requires the use of definite amounts of dilution. C

TOC
Total organic carbon. A, N, U

toe
The bottom of the working face of a sanitary landfill, where deposited solid waste is in contact with virgin ground or previous lift. U

toeboard
(1) A vertical barrier at floor level erected along exposed edges of a floor opening, wall opening platform, runway, or ramp to prevent falls of materials. O
(2) A barrier secured along the sides and ends of a platform to guard against the falling of material. O

toilet tissue
A sanitary tissue paper. The principal characteristics are softness, absorbency, cleanliness, and adequate strength (considering easy disposability). It is marketed in rolls of varying sizes or in interleaved packages. A

tolerance
(1) The ability of an organism to cope with changes in its environment. (2) The safe level of any chemical applied to crops that will be used as food or feed. N (3) The permissible residue levels for pesticides in raw agricultural produce and processed foods. Whenever a pesticide is registered for use on a food or a feed crop, a tolerance (or exemption from the tolerance requirement) must be established. EPA establishes the tolerance levels, which are enforced by the Food and Drug Administration and the Department of Agriculture. N (3) The amount of a pesticide residue that legally may be present in or on a raw agricultural commodity under the terms of a tolerance under FFDCA section 408 or a processed food under the terms of a food additive regulation under FFDCA section 409. Tolerances are usually expressed in terms of parts of the pesticide residue per million parts of the food (ppm), by weight. A

tons per day
Annual tonnage divided by 260 days. A

tool
An explosive-actuated fastening tool, unless otherwise indicated, and all accessories pertaining thereto. O

top sample
A spot sample obtained 6 inches (150 mm) below the top surface of the liquid. A

topcoat operation
The topcoat spray booth, flash-off area, and bake oven(s) which are used to apply and dry or cure the final coating(s) on components of automobile and light-duty truck bodies. A

topographic map
A map indicating surface elevations of an area through the use of contour lines. It also shows population centers and other cultural and land-use features, surface water drainage patterns and forests. These maps enable quick identification of areas of slopes that are more suitable for sanitary landfills. U

topography
The physical features of a surface area including relative elevations and the position of natural and man-made features. N

topsoil
The surface layer of soil, which usually refers to soil that contains humus and is capable of supporting good plant growth. U

torr
A unit of pressure which equals 133.3 pascals or 1mm Hg at 0 degrees C. A

total annual sales
The total annual revenue (in dollars) generated by the sale of all products of a company. Total annual sales must include the total annual sales revenue of all sites owned or controlled by that company and the total annual sales revenue of that company's subsidiaries and foreign or domestic parent company, if any. A

total dissolved solids
(1) TDS. The total dissolved (filterable) solids as determined by use of the method specified in 40 CFR Part 136. A (2) The total filterable residue that passes through a standard glass fiber filter disk and remains after evaporation and drying to a constant weight at 180 degrees C. It is considered to be a measure of the dissolved salt content of the water. A

total fluorides
Elemental fluorine and all fluoride compounds as measured by reference methods specified 40 CFR § 60.195 or by equivalent or alternative methods (See: § 60.8(b)). A

total maximum daily load (TMDL)
(1) The sum of the individual waste load allocations (WLAs) for point sources and load allocations (LAs) for nonpoint sources and natural background. If a receiving water has only one point source discharger, the TMDL is the sum of that point source WLA plus the LAs for any nonpoint sources of pollution and natural background sources, tributaries, or adjacent segments. TMDLs can be expressed in terms of either mass per time, toxicity, or other appropriate measure. A (Also see: waste load allocation). (2) For each water quality segment, or appropriate portion thereof, the total allowable maximum daily load of relevant pollutants during critical flow conditions for each specific water quality criterion being violated or expected to be violated. (i) Such total maximum daily loads shall be established at levels necessary to achieve compliance with applicable water quality standards. (ii) Such loads shall take into account: (A) Provision for seasonal variation; and (B) Provision of a margin of safety which takes into account any lack of knowledge concerning the relationship between effluent limitations and water quality. (3) For each water quality segment where thermal water quality criteria are being violated or expected to be violated, the total daily thermal load during critical flow conditions allowable in each segment. (i) Such loads shall be established at a level necessary to assure the protection and propagation of a balanced, indigenous population of fish, shellfish, and wildlife. (ii) Such loads shall take into account: (A) Normal water temperature; (B) Flow rates; (C) Seasonal variations; (D) Existing

sources of heat input; and (E) The dissipative capacity of the waters within the identified segment. (iii) Each estimate shall include an estimate of the maximum heat input that can be made into the waters of each segment where temperature is one of the criteria being violated or expected to be violated and shall include a margin of safety which takes into account lack of knowledge concerning the development of thermal water quality criteria for protection and propagation of fish, shellfish and wildlife in the waters of the identified segments. (4) For each water quality segment, a total allocation for point sources of pollutants and a gross allotment for nonpoint sources of pollutants. (i) A specific allowance for growth shall be included in the allocation for point sources and the gross allotment for nonpoint sources. (ii) The total of the allocation for point sources and the gross allotment for nonpoint sources shall not exceed the total maximum daily load. (5) Where predictive mathematical models are used in the determination of total maximum daily loads, an identification and brief description of the model, and the specific use of the model. (Note: Total maximum daily loads shall not be determined by designated areawide planning agencies except where the State has delegated such responsibility to the designated agency. In those cases where the responsibility has not been delegated, the State shall determine total maximum daily loads for a designated areawide planning area). (6) No point source load allocation developed pursuant to this section shall be less stringent than effluent limitations standards, or prohibitions required to be established pursuant to Sections 301, 302, 304, 306, 307, 311, and 316 of the [Clean Water] Act. A

total organic active ingredients
The sum of all organic active ingredients covered by [40 CFR] § 455.20(a) which are manufactured at a facility subject to this subpart. A

total organic compounds
TOC. Those compounds measured according to the procedures in [40 CFR] § 60.614. For the purposes of measuring molar composition and hourly emissions rate as required in this section, and TOC concentration as required in section 60.615, those compounds which the Administrator has determined do not contribute appreciably to the formation of ozone are to be excluded. The compounds to be excluded are identified in Environmental Protection Agency's statements on ozone abatement policy for SIP revisions. A

total phenols
Total phenolic compounds as measured by the procedure listed in 40 CFR Part 136 (distillation followed by colorimetric--4AAP). A

total project cost
The sum of the direct and indirect costs allocable to the project incurred or to be incurred, less allocable credits. U

total rated capacity
The sum of the rated capacities of all fuel-burning equipment connected

to a common stack. The rated capacity shall be the maximum guaranteed by the equipment manufacturer or the maximum normally achieved during use as determined by the Administrator, whichever is greater. A

total residual chlorine
(Or total residual oxidants for intake water with bromides). The value obtained using the amperometric method for total residual chlorine described in 40 CFR part 136. U

total resource effectiveness (TRE) index value
A measure of the supplemental total resource requirement per unit reduction of TOC associated with an individual air oxidation vent stream, based on vent stream flow rate, emission rate of TOC, net heating value, and corrosion properties (whether or not the vent stream is halogenated), as quantified by the equation given under [40 CFR] § 60.614. A

total solids
The sum of dissolved and undissolved constituents in water or wastewater, usually stated in milligrams per liter. U

total suspended nonfilterable solids
TSNS as measured by the technique utilizing glass fiber disks as specified in "Standard Methods for the Examination of Water and Wastewater" (13th Edition). A

total suspended particulate
Particulate matter as measured by the method described in appendix B of part 50 [40 CFR]. A

total suspended solids
TSS. A measure of the suspended solids in wastewater, effluent, or water bodies, determined by using tests for "total suspended non-filterable solids." (See: suspended solids). N

total test distance
Defined for each class of motorcycles in [40 CFR] § 86.427-78. A

total toxic organics
TTO. The sum of the concentrations for each of the following toxic organic compounds which is found in the discharge at a concentration greater than ten (10) micrograms per liter: 1,1,1 chloroform, trichloroethane, methylene chloride, bis (2-ethylhexyl) phthlate, toluene, trichloroethylene. A

total trihalomethanes
TTHM. The sum of the concentration in milligrams per liter of the trihalomethane compounds (trichloromethane [chloroform], dibromochloromethane, bromodichloromethane and tribromomethane [bromoform]), rounded to two significant figures. A

totally enclosed manner
Any manner that will ensure no exposure of human beings or the environment to any concentration of PCBs. A

totally enclosed treatment facility
A facility for the treatment of hazardous waste which is directly connected to an industrial production process and which is constructed and

operated in a manner which prevents the release of any hazardous waste or any constituent thereof into the environment during treatment. An example is a pipe in which waste acid is neutralized. A

totally-encapsulated chemical protective (TECP) suit
A full body garment which is constructed of protective clothing materials; covers the wearer's torso, head, arms, legs and respirator; may cover the wearer's hands and feet with tightly attached gloves and boots; completely encloses the wearer and respirator by itself or in combination with the wearer's gloves or boots. O

TOX
Total organic halide. N

toxaphene
A material consisting of technical grade chlorinated camphene having the approximate formula of $C_{10}H_{10}Cl_8$ and normally containing 67-69 percent chlorine by weight. A

toxaphene formulator
A person who produces, prepares or processes a formulated product comprising a mixture of toxaphene and inert materials or other diluents into a product intended for application in any use registered under the Federal Insecticide, Fungicide and Rodenticide Act, as amended (7 U.S.C. 135, et seq.). A

toxaphene manufacturer
A manufacturer, excluding any source which is exclusively a toxaphene formulator, who produces, prepares or processes toxaphene or who uses toxaphene as a material in the production, preparation or processing of another synthetic organic substance. A

toxic
A chemical falling within any of the following categories:
(a) A chemical that has a median lethal dose (LD_{50}) of more than 50 milligrams per kilogram but not more than 500 milligrams per kilogram of body weight when administered orally to albino rats weighing between 200 and 300 grams each. (b) A chemical that has a median lethal dose (LD_{50}) of more than 200 milligrams per kilogram but not more than 1,000 milligrams per kilogram of body weight when administered by continuous contact for 24 hours (or less if death occurs within 24 hours) with the bare skin of albino rabbits weighing between two and three kilograms each. (c) A chemical that has a median lethal concentration (LC_{50}) in air of more than 200 parts per million but not more than 2,000 parts per million by volume of gas or vapor, or more than two milligrams per liter but not more than 20 milligrams per liter of mist, fume, or dust, when administered by continuous inhalation for one hour (or less if death occurs within one hour) to albino rats weighing between 200 and 300 grams each. O

toxic chemical release form
Information form required to be submitted by facilities that manufacture, process, or use (in quantities above a specific amount)

chemicals listed under SARA Title III. N

toxic cloud
Airborne mass of gases, vapors, fumes, or aerosols containing toxic materials. N

toxic concentration low
TC_{Lo}. The lowest concentration of a substance in air to which humans or animals have been exposed for any given period of time that has produced any toxic effect in humans or produced a tumorigenic or reproductive effect in animals or humans. N

toxic effect
An adverse change in the structure or function of an experimental animal as a result of exposure to a chemical substance. A

toxic material
A material in concentration or amount which exceeds the applicable limit established by a standard, such as [40 CFR] §§ 1910.1000 and 1910.1001 or, in the absence of an applicable standard, which is of such toxicity so as to constitute a recognized hazard that is causing or is likely to cause death or serious physical harm. O

toxic pollutant
(1) Those pollutants, or combinations of pollutants, including disease-causing agents, which after discharge and upon exposure, ingestion, inhalation or assimilation into any organism, either directly from the environment or indirectly by ingestion through food chains, will, on the basis of information available to the Administrator of EPA, cause death, disease, behavioral abnormalities, cancer, genetic mutations, physiological malfunctions (including malfunctions in reproduction) or physical deformations, in such organisms or their offspring. D (2) Any pollutant listed as toxic under section 307(a)(1) of 40 CFR 100-149 or, in the case of sludge use or disposal practices, any pollutant identified in regulations implementing section 405(d) of the Clean Water Act. A

toxic substance
(1) A chemical or mixture that may present an unreasonable risk of injury to health or the environment. N (2) Any chemical substance, biological agent (bacteria, virus, fungus, etc.), or physical stress (noise, heat, cold, vibration, repetitive motion, ionizing and non-ionizing radiation hypo--or hyperbaric pressure, etc.) which: (i) is listed in the last printed edition of the National Institute for Occupational Safety and Health (NIOSH) Registry of Toxic Effects of Chemical Substances (RTECS); or (ii) has yielded positive evidence of an acute or chronic health hazard in testing conducted by, or known to, the employer; or (iii) is the subject of a material safety data sheet kept by or known to the employer indicating that the material may pose a hazard to human health. O

toxicant
(1) A chemical that controls pests by killing rather than repelling them. (2) A harmful substance or agent that may injure an exposed organism. N

toxicity
(1) Acute and/or chronic toxicity. A (2) The property of a substance to cause any adverse physiological effects. A (2) The quality or degree of being poisonous or harmful to plant, animal or human life. N

toxicity curve
The curve produced from toxicity tests when LC_{50} values are plotted against duration of exposure. (This term is also used in aquatic toxicology, but in a less precise sense, to describe the curve produced when the median period of survival is plotted against test concentrations). A

toxicology
The study of the nature, effects, and detection of poisons in living organisms. N

TPQ
Threshold planning quantity. U

traceable
A local standard that has been compared and certified, either directly or via not more than one intermediate standard, to a primary standard such as a National Bureau of Standards Standard Reference Material (NBS SRM) or a USEP/NBS-approved Certified Reference Material (CRM). A

tracer
(1) A foreign substance mixed with or attached to a given substance for the determination of the location or distribution of the substance. (2) An element or compound that has been made radioactive so that it can be easily followed (traced) in biological and industrial processes. Radiation emitted by the radioisotope pinpoints its location. U

tracking form
The Federal Medical Waste Tracking Form that must accompany all applicable shipments of regulated medical wastes generated within one of the Covered States. A

tractor
Any two or three wheeled vehicle used exclusively for agricultural purposes, or for snow plowing, including self-propelled machines used exclusively in growing, harvesting or handling farm produce. A

trade name
The trademark name or commercial trade name for a material or product. N

trade secret
Any confidential formula, pattern, process, device, or information or compilation of information that is used in an employer's business and that gives the employer an opportunity to obtain an advantage over competitors who do not know or use it. O

traditional pollutant
Biochemical oxygen demand (BOD), suspended solids (SS) and pH. A

traffic flow measure
Any measure, such as signal light synchronization, freeway metering and curbside parking restrictions, that is taken for the purpose of improving the flow of traffic and thereby

reducing emissions of air pollutants from motor vehicles. A

training
(1) The planned and organized activity of a consultant to impart skills, techniques and methodologies to employers and their employees to assist them in establishing and maintaining employment and a place of employment which is safe and healthful. O (2) The process of making proficient through instruction and hands-on practice in the operation of equipment, including respiratory protection equipment, that is expected to be used and in the performance of assigned duties. O

transfer and loading system
Any facility used to transfer and load coal for shipment. A

transfer efficiency
The ratio of the amount of coating solids transferred onto the surface of a part or product to the total amount of coating solids used. A

transfer facility
(1) Any transportation related facility including loading docks, parking areas, storage areas and other similar areas where shipments of hazardous waste are held during the normal course of transportation. A (2) PCBS. Any transportation-related facility including loading docks, parking areas, and other similar areas where shipments of PCB waste are held during the normal course of transportation. Transport vehicles are not transfer facilities under this definition, unless they are used for the storage of PCB waste, rather than for actual transport activities. Storage areas for PCB waste at transfer facilities are subject to the storage facility standards of [40 CFR] § 761.65, but such storage areas are exempt from the approval requirements of § 761.65(d) and the recordkeeping requirements [40 CFR] § 761.180, unless the same PCB waste is stored there for a period of more than 10 consecutive days between destinations. A

transfer station
A site at which solid wastes are concentrated for transport to a processing facility or land disposal site. A transfer station may be fixed or mobile. A

transformation
(1) A resource recovery method including the collection and physical treatment of a waste product for use as raw material in the manufacture of a different product (e.g., glass that is collected, ground, and then used to make bricks). (2) The process of placing new genes into a host cell, thereby inducing the host cell to exhibit functions encoded by the DNA. N

transit incentive program
A mix of incentive or disincentive provisions most likely to obtain maximum use of carpooling and mass transit so as to reduce vehicle miles traveled (VMT). Some incentive examples are: subsidies to employees using mass transit, preferential parking or other benefits for those who travel in carpools, provision of vanpooling services, provision of special charter or employer buses to and from mass

transit stops and formal information systems so that employees can select optimum carpool arrangements. Some examples of disincentive provisions are: reduction in employee parking spaces, surcharges on use of parking spaces for single passenger drivers and non-preferential parking for single passenger drivers. A

translocation
(1) The transfer of matter from one location to another within the soil. N
(2) The transference or transport of chemical from the site of uptake to other plant components. A

transmission class
A group of transmissions having the following common features: basic transmission type (manual, automatic, or semi-automatic), number of forward speeds (e.g., manual, four speed, three speed automatic, two speed semiautomatic), and other characteristics determined to be significant by the Administrator (e.g., "creeper" first gear, overdrive final gear ratio, or overdrive unit) considering factors such as the manufacturer's recommendation for use and/or the numerical gear ratios. A

transmission configuration
A unique combination, within a transmission class, of the number of forward gears, and, if applicable, overdrive. The Administrator may further subdivide a transmission configuration (based on such criteria as gear ratios, torque converter multiplication ratio, stall speed, shift calibration, etc.) if he determines that significant fuel economy differences exist within that transmission configuration. A

transmissive fault
A fault or fracture that has sufficient permeability and vertical extent to allow fluids to move between formations. A

transmissivity
The hydraulic conductivity integrated over the saturated thickness of an underground formation. The transmissivity of a series of formations is the sum of the individual transmissivities of each formation comprising the series. A

transpiration
The process by which water vapor is lost to the atmosphere from living plants. The term can also be applied to the quantity of water thus dissipated. N

transport or transportation
The carriage and related handling of any material by a vessel, or by any other vehicle, including aircraft. E

transport or transportation of hazardous substances
The movement of a hazardous substance by any mode, including pipeline (as defined in the Pipeline Safety Act), and in the case of a hazardous substance which has been accepted for transportation by a common or contract carrier, the term "transport" or "transportation" shall include any stoppage in transit which is temporary, incidental to the transportation movement, and at the ordinary operating convenience of a

common or contract carrier, and any such stoppage shall be considered as a continuity of movement and not as the storage of a hazardous substance. L

transport vehicle
A motor vehicle or rail car used for the transportation of cargo by any mode. Each cargo-carrying body (e.g., trailer, railroad freight car) is a separate transport vehicle. A

transportation control measure
(1) TCM. Any measure that is directed toward reducing emissions of air pollutants from transportation sources. Such measures include, but are not limited to, those listed in section 108(f) of the Clean Air Act. A (2) Any measure, such as reducing vehicle use, changing traffic flow patterns, decreasing emissions from individual motor vehicles, or altering existing modal split patterns that is directed toward reducing emissions of air pollutants from transportation sources. A

transportation improvement program
TIP. The staged multiyear program of transportation improvements including an annual (or biennial) element which is required in 23 CFR part 450. A

transportation-related onshore and offshore facilities
(A) Onshore and offshore terminal facilities including transfer hoses, loading arms and other equipment and appurtenances used for the purpose of handling or transferring oil in bulk to or from a vessel as well as storage tanks and appurtenances for the reception of oily ballast water or tank washings from vessels, but excluding terminal waste treatment facilities and terminal oil storage facilities. (B) Transfer hoses, loading arms and other equipment appurtenant to a nontransportation-related facility which is used to transfer oil in bulk to or from a vessel. (C) Interstate and intrastate onshore and offshore pipeline systems including pumps and appurtenances related thereto as well as in-line or breakout storage tanks needed for the continuous operation of a pipeline system, and pipelines from onshore and offshore oil production facilities, but excluding onshore and offshore piping from wellheads to oil separators and pipelines which are used for the transport of oil exclusively within the confines of a nontransportation-related facility or terminal facility and which are not intended to transport oil in interstate or intrastate commerce or to transfer oil in bulk to or from a vessel. (D) Highway vehicles and railroad cars which are used for the transport of oil in interstate or intrastate commerce and the equipment and appurtenances related thereto, and equipment used for the fueling of locomotive units, as well as the rights-of-way on which they operate. Excluded are highway vehicles and railroad cars and motive power used exclusively within the confines of a nontransportation-related facility or terminal facility and which are not intended for use in interstate or intrastate commerce. A

transporter
(1) (In the RCRA program) A person

engaged in the off-site transportation of hazardous waste by air, rail, highway, or water. N (2) PFB. Any person engaged in the transportation of regulated PCB waste by air, rail, highway, or water for purposes other than consolidation by a generator. A

transuranic radioactive waste
Waste containing more than 100 nanocuries of alpha-emitting transuranic isotopes, with half-lives greater than twenty years, per gram of waste, except for: (1) High-level radioactive wastes; (2) wastes that the Department has determined, with the concurrence of the Administrator, do not need the degree of isolation required by this part; or (3) wastes that the Commission has approved for disposal on a case-by-case basis in accordance with 10 CFR Part 61. A

transuranium
Nuclides having an atomic number greater than that of uranium (i.e., greater than 92). U

trash-to-energy plan
Plan for putting waste back to work by burning trash to produce energy. N

traveling-grate stoker
A stoker that is essentially a moving chain belt carried on sprockets and covered with separated, small, metal pieces called keys. The entire top surface can act as a grate while moving through the furnace but can flex over the sprocket wheels at the end of the furnace, return under the furnace, and reenter the furnace over sprocket wheels at the front. U

TRC
(1) Technical Review Criteria (under NPDES). D (2) Total residual chlorine. The value obtained by the iodometric titration with an amperometric endpoint method specified in 40 CFR 136.3. A

TRE
(1) Total resource effectiveness. U (2) Toxicity Reduction Evaluation. N

tread
The horizontal member of a step. O

tread run
The horizontal distance from the leading edge of a tread to the leading edge of an adjacent tread. O

tread width
The horizontal distance from front to back of tread including nosing when used. O

treatability study
A study in which a hazardous waste is subjected to a treatment process to determine: (1) whether the waste is amenable to the treatment process, (2) what pre-treatment (if any) is required, (3) the optimal process conditions needed to achieve the desired treatment, (4) the efficiency of a treatment process for a specific waste or wastes, or (5) the characteristics and volumes of residuals from a particular treatment process. Also included in this definition for the purpose of the [40 CFR] § 261.4 (e) and (f) exemptions are liner compatibility, corrosion, and other material compatibility studies and toxicological and health effects

studies. A "treatability study" is not a means to commercially treat or dispose of hazardous waste. A

treated regulated medical waste
Regulated medical waste that has been treated to substantially reduce or eliminate its potential for causing disease, but has not yet been destroyed. A

treatment
When used in connection with hazardous waste, any method, technique, or process, including neutralization, designed to change the physical, chemical, or biological character or composition of any hazardous waste so as to neutralize such waste or so as to recover energy or material resources from the waste, or so as to render such waste nonhazardous, or less hazardous; safer to transport, store, or dispose of; or amenable for recovery, amenable for storage, or reduced in volume. A

treatment facility
All structures which contain, convey, and as necessary, chemically or physically treat coal rine drainage, coal preparation plant process wastewater, or drainage from coal preparation plant associated areas, which remove pollutants regulated by this Part from such waters. This includes all pipes, channels, ponds, basins, tanks and all other equipment serving such structures. A

treatment, storage, and disposal facility
TSD or TSDF. Site where a hazardous substance is treated, stored, or disposed. TSD facilities are regulated by EPA and states under RCRA. N

treatment system
See treatment facility. A

treatment technique requirement
A requirement of the national primary drinking water regulations which specifies for a contaminant a specific treatment technique(s) known to the EPA administrator which leads to a reduction in the level of such contaminant sufficient to comply with the requirements of 40 CFR part 141. A

treatment technology
Any unit operation or series of unit operations that alters the composition of a hazardous substance or pollutant or contaminant through chemical, biological, or physical means so as to reduce toxicity, mobility, or volume of the contaminated materials being treated. Treatment technologies are an alternative to land disposal of hazardous wastes without treatment. A

treatment works
(A) Any devices and systems used in the storage, treatment, recycling, and reclamation of municipal sewage, domestic sewage, or industrial wastes of a liquid nature to implement section 201 of the [FWPCA], or necessary to recycle or reuse water at the most economical cost over the estimated or useful life of the works, including intercepting sewers, outfall sewers, sewage collection systems, individual systems, pumping power, and other equipment, and their appurtenances;

extensions, improvements, remodeling, additions, and alterations thereof; elements essential to provide a reliable recycled supply such as standby treatment units and clear well facilities; and any works, including site acquisition of the land that will be an integral part of the treatment process (including land use for the storage of treated wastewater in land treatment systems prior to land application) or is used for ultimate disposal of residues resulting from such treatment (including land for composting sludge, temporary storage of such compost and land used for the storage of treated wastewater in land treatment systems before land application). (B) Also, any other method or system for preventing, abating, reducing, storing, treating, separating, or disposing of municipal waste, including storm water runoff, or industrial waste, including waste in combined storm water and sanitary sewer systems. Any application for construction grants which includes wholly or in part such methods or systems shall, in accordance with guidelines published by the pursuant to subparagraph (C) of this paragraph, contain adequate data and analysis demonstrating such proposal to be, over the life of such works, the most cost efficient alternative to comply with section 301 or 302 of the Clean Water Act, or the requirements of section 201 of the Clean Water Act. (C) For the purposes of subparagraph (B) of this paragraph, the Administrator shall, within one hundred and eighty days after the date of enactment of this title, publish and thereafter revise no less often than annually, guidelines for the evaluation of methods, including cost-effective analysis, described in subparagraph (B) of this paragraph. A, D

treatment works phase or segment
Any cost-effective portion of a complete waste treatment system described in a facilities plan under 40 CFR § 35.2030, which can be identified as a contract or discrete subitem or subcontract. Completion of building of a treatment works phase or segment may, but need not in and of itself, result in an operable treatment works. A

treatment works treating domestic sewage
A POTW or any other sewage sludge or wastewater treatment devices or systems, regardless of ownership (including Federal facilities), used in the storage, treatment, recycling, and reclamation of municipal or domestic sewage, including land dedicated for the disposal of sewage sludge. This definition does not include septic tanks or similar devices. For purposes of this definition, "domestic sewage" includes waste and waste water from humans or household operations that are discharged to or otherwise enter a treatment works. A

treatment zone
A soil area of the unsaturated zone of a land treatment unit within which hazardous constituents are degraded, transformed, or immobilized. A

trench
A narrow excavation (in relation to its length) made below the surface of the ground. In general, the depth is

greater than the width, but the width of a trench (measured at the bottom) is not greater than 15 feet (4.6 m). If forms or other structures are installed or constructed in an excavation so as to reduce the dimension measured from the forms or structure to the side of the excavation to 15 feet (4.6 m) or less (measured at the bottom of the excavation), the excavation is also considered to be a trench. O

trench method
Sanitary landfilling method in which the waste is spread and compacted in a trench. The excavated spoil is spread and compacted over the waste to form a basic cell structure. U

trend assessment survey
See baseline assessment survey. A

trestle ladder
A trestle ladder is a self-supporting portable ladder, non-adjustable in length, consisting of two sections hinged at the top to form equal angles with the base. The size is designated by the length of the side rails measured along the front edge. O

trial burn
A trial incineration of hazardous waste that tests an incinerator's destruction efficiency. N

trichloroethylene
TCE. A stable, low-boiling colorless liquid, toxic by inhalation. TCE is used as a solvent, metal degreasing agent, and in other industrial applications. N

trickling filter
A biological treatment device; wastewater is trickled over a bed of stones covered with bacterial growth, the bacteria break down the organic wastes in the sewage and produce cleaner water. N

trigger date
(a) In the case of particulate matter and sulfur dioxide, August 7, 1977, and (b) in the case of nitrogen dioxide, February 8, 1988. A

trihalomethane
THM. One of the family of organic compounds, named as derivatives of methane, wherein three of the four hydrogen atoms in methane are each substituted by a halogen atom in the molecular structure. A

trimming presses
A class of auxiliary forging equipment which removes flash or excess metal from a forging. This trimming operation can also be done cold, as can coining, a product sizing operation. O

trip or tripping
Activation of the clutch to "run" the press. O

trip type
Any class of vehicle trips possessing one or more characteristics (e.g., work, nonwork; peak, off-peak; freeway, nonfreeway) that distinguish vehicle trips in the class from vehicle trips not in the class. A

triple rinse
The flushing of containers three

times, each time using a volume of the normal diluent equal to approximately ten percent of the container's capacity, and adding the rinse liquid to the spray mixture or disposing of it by a method prescribed for disposing of the pesticide. A

trippage
The number of round trips the average refillable bottle makes between the filler and the consumer. U

tris
Tris (2,3-dibromopropyl) phosphate (also commonly named DBPP, TBPP, and Tris-BP). A

trolley ladder
A semifixed ladder, nonadjustable in length, supported by attachments to an overhead track, the plane of the ladder being at right angles to the plane of motion. O

trommel
A perforated, rotating, horizontal cylinder that may be used in resource recovery facilities to break open trash bags, to remove glass and such small items as stones and dirt, and to remove cans from incinerator residue. U

trophic condition
A relative description of a lake's biological productivity based on the availability of plant nutrients. The range of trophic conditions is characterized by the terms of oligotrophic for the least biologically productive, to eutrophic for the most biologically productive. A

troposphere
The portion of the atmosphere between seven and ten miles from the Earth's surface, where clouds form. U

truck loading station
That portion of a metallic mineral processing plant where metallic minerals or metallic mineral concentrates are loaded by a conveying system into trucks. A

truck unloading station
That portion of a metallic mineral processing plant where metallic ore is unloaded from a truck into a hopper, screen, or crusher. A

trucked batteries
Batteries moved into or out of the plant by truck when the truck is actually washed in the plant to remove residues left in the truck from the batteries. A

true vapor pressure
The equilibrium partial pressure exerted by a petroleum liquid as determined in accordance with methods described in American Petroleum Institute Bulletin 2517, Evaporation Loss from External Floating Roof Tanks, Second Edition, February 1980. A

trust fund
The Hazardous Substance Response Fund established by section 221 of CERCLA or, in the case of a hazardous waste disposal facility for which liability has been transferred under section 107(k) of this Act [CERCLA], the Post-closure Liability Fund established by section 232. L

trustee
An official of a federal natural resources management agency designated in subpart G of the NCP or a designated state official or Indian tribe who may pursue claims for damages under section 107(f) of CERCLA. A

TSCA
The Toxic Substances Control Act, 15 U.S.C. 2601 *et seq.* A

TSD
(1) Treatment, storage, or disposal [facility]. U (2) Technical Support Document. U

TSP
Total suspended particulates. U

TSS
Total suspended solids. A measure of the suspended solids in wastewater, effluent, or water bodies, determined by using tests for "total suspended non-filterable solids". (See: suspended solids). N

TTHM
Total trihalomethane. D

TTO
Total toxic organics. A

tube and coupler scaffold
An assembly consisting of tubing which serves as posts, bearers, braces, ties, and runners, a base supporting the posts, and special couplers which serve to connect the uprights and to join the various members. O

tubular welded frame scaffold
A sectional panel or frame metal scaffold substantially built up of prefabricated welded sections which consists of posts and horizontal bearer with intermediate members. O

tubular welded sectional folding scaffold
A sectional, folding metal scaffold either of ladder frame or inside stairway design, substantially built of prefabricated welded sections, which consist of end frames, platform frame, inside inclined stairway frame and braces, or hinged connected diagonal and horizontal braces, capable of being folded into a flat package when the scaffold is not in use. O

tuck pointing
Removal, by grinding, of cement, mortar, or other nonmetallic jointing material. O

tuck pointing wheels
Tuck pointing wheels, usually Type 1, reinforced organic bonded wheels have diameter, thickness and hole size dimension. They are subject to the same limitations of use and mounting as Type 1 wheels. O

tumbling
The process of polishing, deburring, removing sharp corners, and generally smoothing parts for both cosmetic and functional purposes, as well as the process of washing the finished parts and cleaning the abrasion media. A

tundra
A type of ecosystem dominated by lichens, mosses, grasses, and woody plants. Tundra is found at high latitudes (arctic tundra) and high altitudes (alpine tundra). Arctic tundra is underlain by permafrost and is usually very wet. (See: wetlands). N

turbidimeter
A device that measures the amount of suspended solids in a liquid. N

turbidity
Hazy air due to the presence of particles and pollutants; a similar cloudy condition in water due to suspended silt or organic matter. N

turbine
An engine that forces a stream of gas or liquid through jets at high pressure against the curved blades of a wheel, thus forcing the blades to turn. U

turbines employed in oil/gas production or oil/gas transportation
Any stationary gas turbine used to provide power to extract crude oil/natural gas from the earth or to move crude oil/natural gas, or products refined from these substances through pipelines. A

turnover bar
A bar used in die setting to manually turn the crankshaft of the press. O

tuyeres
Openings or ports in a grate through which air can be directed to improve combustion. U

TVOC
Total volatile organic compound. U

TWA
Time-weighted average exposure is the airborne concentration of a material to which a person is exposed, averaged over the total exposure time generally the total workday (8 to 12 hours). Also see "TLV." N

twenty-five-year 24-hour rainfall event
The maximum precipitation event with a probable recurrence interval of once in 25 years as defined by the National Weather Service in technical paper no. 40, "Rainfall Frequency Atlas of the United States," May, 1961, and subsequent amendments or equivalent regional or State rainfall probability information developed therefrom. A [ed. Similar events are established for 10-year, 50-year, 100-year and 500-year rainfall events]. U

two hand control device
A two hand trip that further requires concurrent pressure from both hands of the operator during a substantial part of the die-closing portion of the stroke of the press. O

two hand trip
A clutch actuating means requiring the concurrent use of both hands of the operator to trip the press. O

TWPL
Total weighted pollutant load. U

type A packaging
Containers designed to maintain their integrity, i.e., not allow any radioactive material to be released and

to keep the shielding properties intact, under normal transportation conditions. The test conditions which must be met are defined in 49 CFR 173, 398b and include heat, cold, reduced air pressure, vibration, water spray endurance, free drop, penetration, and compression standards. U

type B packaging
Containers designed to meet the standards established for hypothetical transportation accident conditions, as well as meeting the Type A packaging standards, without reducing the effectiveness of the shielding or allowing releases in excess of those enumerated in 49 CFR 173.398c(1). The standards to be met by Type B packages, in addition to the Type A standards, are defined in 49 CFR 173.398c(2) and include puncture, thermal, water immersion, and higher free drop tests. U

type I sound level meter
A sound level meter which meets the Type I requirements of American National Standard Specification S1.4-1971 for sound level meters. This publication is available from the American National Standards Institute, Inc., 1430 Broadway, New York, New York 10018. A

type of pesticidal product
Each individual product as identified by: the produce name; EPA Registration Number (or EPA File Symbol, if any, for planned products, or Experimental Permit Number, if the pesticide is produced under an Experimental Use Permit); active ingredients; production type (technical, formulation, repackaging, etc.); and, market for which the product was produced (domestic, foreign, etc.). In cases where a pesticide is not registered, registration is not applied for, or the pesticide is not produced under an Experimental Use Permit, the term shall also include the chemical formulations. A

type of resin
The broad classification of resin referring to the basic manufacturing process for producing that resin, including, but not limited to, the suspension, dispersion, latex, bulk, and solution processes. A

type SE
Having a flame-retardant, moisture-resistant covering, but not required to have inherent protection against mechanical abuse. O

type USE
Recognized for underground use, having a moisture-resistant covering, but not required to have a flame-retardant covering or inherent protection against mechanical abuse. Single-conductor cables having an insulation specifically approved for the purpose do not require an outer covering. O

U

U (uranium)
Measured by the procedure discussed in 40 CFR 141.25(b)(2), or an equivalent method. A

U.S. Environmental Protection Agency
EPA. Established in 1970 by Presidential Executive Order, bringing together parts of various government agencies involved with the control of pollution. N

U-235
Uranium-235. Naturally occurring Uranium. A radioactive heavy metal element used in nuclear reactors and the production of nuclear weapons. N

U-238
Uranium-238. A radioactive heavy metal element used in nuclear reactors and the production of nuclear weapons. The most abundant radium isotope. N

UAQI
Uniform Air Quality Index. N

UCATA
Uniform Contribution Among (Joint) Tortfeasors Act. U

UCC
Ultra clean coal. Coal that has been washed, ground into fine particles, then chemically treated to remove sulfur, ash, silicone, and other substances; usually briquetted and coated with a sealant made from coal. N

UCFA
Uniform Comparative Fault Act (Section 6, Superfund). U

UCR
Unit cancer risk. N

UDDS
Urban dynamometer driving schedule. U

UEL
Upper explosive limit. U

585

UFL
Upper flammable limit. U

Ug/m³
Microgram per cubic meter. U

UIAs
Urban impact analyses. U

UIC
Underground Injection Control. Program under Part C of the Safe Drinking Water Act, including an "approved program." A

ultimate analysis
The chemical analysis of a solid, liquid, or gaseous fuel. In the case of coal, coke, or solid waste, the amounts of carbon, hydrogen, sulfur, nitrogen, oxygen, and ash are determined. U

ultimate consumer
The first person who purchases an automobile for purposes other than resale, or leases an automobile. A

ultimate purchaser
With respect to any new motor vehicle or new motor vehicle engine, the first person who in good faith purchases such new motor vehicle or new engine for purposes other than resale. B, G

ultra clean coal
UCC. Coal that has been washed, ground into fine particles, then chemically treated to remove sulfur, ash, silicone, and other substances; usually briquetted and coated with a sealant made from coal. N

ultraviolet rays
Radiation from the sun that can be useful or potentially harmful. UV rays from one part of the spectrum enhance plant life and are useful in some medical and dental procedures; UV rays from other parts of the spectrum to which humans are exposed (e.g., while getting a sun tan) can cause skin cancer or other tissue damage. The ozone layer in the atmosphere provides a protective shield that limits the amount of ultraviolet rays that reach the Earth's surface. N

umbo
The narrow end (apex) of the oyster shell. A

unacceptable adverse effect
Impact on an aquatic or wetland ecosystem which is likely to result in significant degradation of municipal water supplies (including surface or ground water) or significant loss of or damage to fisheries, shell-fishing, or wildlife habitat or recreation areas. In evaluating the unacceptability of such impacts, consideration should be given to the relevant portions of the section 404(b)(1) guidelines (40 CFR part 230). A

unauthorized dispersion technique
Any dispersion technique which, under section 123 of the CAA and the regulations promulgated pursuant to that section, may not be used to reduce the degree of emission limitation otherwise required in the applicable SIP. A

unbleached papers
Papers made of pulp that have not been treated with bleaching agents. A

uncertainty
In the conduct of risk assessment (hazard identification, dose-response assessment, exposure assessment, risk characterization) the need to make assumptions or best judgments in the absence of precise scientific data creates uncertainties. These uncertainties, expressed qualitatively and sometimes quantitatively, attempt to define the usefulness of a particular evaluation in making a decision based upon the available data. N

uncertainty factor
UF. One of several, generally 10-fold factors, applied to a NOAEL or a LOAEL to derive a reference dose (RfD) from experimental data. UFs are intended to account for (a) the variation in the sensitivity among the members of the human population; (b) the uncertainty in extrapolating animal data to humans; (c) the uncertainty in extrapolating from data obtained in a less-than-lifetime exposure study to chronic exposure; and (d) the uncertainty in using a LOAEL rather than a NOAEL for estimating the threshold region. N (Also see: NOAEL and LOAEL).

unconfined aquifer
An aquifer that contains water under atmospheric pressure. Not overlain by impermeable stratum, the water level in the aquifer may rise or fall according to the volume of water stored, a variable dependent upon seasonal cycles of natural recharge. U

uncontrolled hazardous waste site
An area identified as an uncontrolled hazardous waste site by a governmental body, whether Federal, state, local or other where an accumulation of hazardous substances creates a threat to the health and safety of individuals or the environment or both. Some sites are found on public lands such as those created by former municipal, county, or state landfills where illegal or poorly managed waste disposal has taken place. Other sites are found on private property, often belonging to generators or former generators of hazardous substance wastes. Examples of such sites include, but are not limited to, surface impoundments, landfills, dumps, and tank or drum farms. Normal operations at TSD sites are not covered by this definition. O

under the direct supervision of [a certified applicator]
The act or process whereby the application of a pesticide is made by a competent person acting under the instructions and control of a certified applicator who is responsible for the actions of that person and who is available if and when needed, even though such certified applicator is not physically present at the time and place the pesticide is applied. A

underground drinking water source
(i) an aquifer supplying drinking water for human consumption, or (ii) an aquifer in which the ground water

contains less than 10,000 mg/1 total dissolved solids. A Also see underground source of drinking water. U

underground injection
The subsurface emplacement of fluids through a bored, drilled or driven well; or through a dug well, where the depth of the dug well is greater than the largest surface dimension. (See also "injection well.") A

underground injection control
UIC. The program under the Safe Drinking Water Act that regulates the use of wells to pump fluids into the ground. N

underground source of drinking water
(1) USDW. As defined in the UIC program, this term refers to aquifers that are currently being used as a source of drinking water, and those that are capable of supplying a public water system. They have a total dissolved solids content of 10,000 milligrams per liter or less, and are not "exempted aquifers." (See: exempted aquifer.) N (2) An aquifer or its portion: (a)(1) Which supplies any public water system; or (2) Which contains a sufficient quantity of ground water to supply a public water system; and (i) Currently supplies drinking water for human consumption; or(ii) Contains fewer than 10,000 mg/l total dissolved solids; and (b) Which is not an exempted aquifer. A

underground storage tank
UST. Any one or combination of tanks (including underground pipes connected thereto) which is used to contain an accumulation of regulated substances, and the volume of which (including the volume of the underground pipes connected thereto) is 10 percent or more beneath the surface of the ground. Such term does not include any--(A) farm or residential tank of 1,100 gallons or less capacity used for storing motor fuel for noncommercial purposes; (B) tank used for storing heating oil for consumptive use on the premises where stored; (C) septic tank; (D) pipeline facility (including gathering lines) regulated under--(i) the Natural Gas Pipeline Safety Act of 1968, (49 U.S.C.App. 1671, et seq.), (ii) the Hazardous Liquid Pipeline Safety Act of 1979 (49 U.S.C.App. 2001, et seq.), or (iii) which is an intrastate pipeline facility regulated under state laws comparable to the provisions of law referred to in clause (i) or (ii) of this subparagraph; (E) surface impoundment, pit, pond, or lagoon; (F) storm water or waste water collection system; (G) flow-through process tank; (H) liquid trap or associated gathering lines directly related to oil or gas production and gathering operations; or; (I) storage tank situated in an underground area (such as a basement, cellar, mineworking, drift, shaft, or tunnel) if the storage tank is situated upon or above the surface of the floor. The term "underground storage tank" shall not include any pipes connected to any tank which is described in subparagraphs (A) through (I). I

underground tank
A device meeting the definition of

"tank" in § 260.10 whose entire surface area is totally below the surface of and covered by the ground. A

underground uranium mine
A man-made underground excavation made for the purpose of removing material containing uranium for the principal purpose of recovering uranium. A

undisturbed performance
The predicted behavior of a radiation disposal system, including consideration of the uncertainties in predicted behavior, if the disposal system is not disrupted by human intrusion or the occurrence of unlikely natural events. A

UNEP
United Nations Environment Programme. N

unexpended consumption allowances
Consumption allowances that have not been used. At any time in any control period, a person's unexpended consumption allowances are the total of the calculated level of consumption allowances he has authorization to hold at that time for that control period, minus the calculated level of controlled substances that the person has produced and imported in that control period until that time. A

uniquely military equipment, systems, and operations
Excludes from the scope of the order the design of Department of Defense equipment and systems that are unique to the national defense mission, such as military aircraft, ships, submarines, missiles, and missile sites, early warning systems, military space systems, artillery, tanks, and tactical vehicles; and excludes operations that are uniquely military such as field maneuvers, naval operations, military flight operations, associated research test and development activities, and actions required under emergency conditions. The term includes within the scope of the Order Department of Defense workplaces and operations comparable to those of industry in the private sector such as: vessel, aircraft, and vehicle repair, overhaul, and modification (except for equipment trials); construction; supply services; civil engineering or public works; medical services; and office work. O

unit cancer risk
A measure of the probability of an individual's developing cancer as a result of exposure to a specified unit ambient concentration. For example, an inhalation unit cancer risk of 3.0 x 10^{-4} near a point source implies that if 10,000 people breathe a given concentration of a carcinogenic agent (e.g., u^1 g/m^3) for 70 years, three of the 10,000 will develop cancer as a result of this exposure. In water the exposure unit is usually 1 ug/l, while in air it is 1 ug/m^3. N

unit package
A package that is labeled with directions to use the entire contents of the package in a single application. A

unitized tooling
A type of die in which the upper and lower members are incorporated into a self-contained unit so arranged as to hold the die members in alignment. O

units
All concentrations are given in weight per volume (e.g., in mg/liter). A

universal biohazard symbol
The symbol design that conforms to the design shown in 29 CFR 1910.145(f)(8)(ii). A

universal precautions
An approach to infection control. According to the concept of Universal Precautions, all human blood and certain human body fluids are treated as if known to be infectious for HIV, HBV, and other bloodborne pathogens. O

unleaded gasoline
Gasoline containing not more than 0.05 gram of lead per gallon and not more than 0.005 gram of phosphorus per gallon. A

unliquidated obligations
Reports prepared on a cash basis mean the amount of obligations incurred by the grantee that has not been paid. For reports prepared on an accrued expenditure basis, they represent the amount of obligations incurred by the grantee for which an outlay has not been recorded. A

unloading leg
A device which includes a bucket-type elevator which is used to remove grain from a barge or ship. A

unobligated balance
The portion of the funds authorized by the federal agency that has not been obligated by the grantee and is determined by deducting the cumulative obligations from the cumulative funds authorized. A

unprotected side or edge
Any side or edge of a roof perimeter where there is no wall three feet (.9 meters) or more in height. O

unproven emission control systems
Emission control components or systems (and fuel metering systems) that do not qualify as proven emission control systems. A

unreasonable adverse effects on the environment
Any unreasonable risk to man or the environment, taking into account the economic, social, and environmental costs and benefits of the use of any pesticide. A, C

unreasonable degradation of the marine environment
(1) Significant adverse changes in ecosystem diversity, productivity and stability of the biological community within the area of discharge and surrounding biological communities, (2) Threat to human health through direct exposure to pollutants or through consumption of exposed aquatic organisms, or (3) Loss of esthetic, recreational, scientific or economic values which is unreasonable in

relation to the benefit derived from the discharge. A

unreclaimable residues
Residual materials of little or no value remaining after incineration. A

unsaturated zone
The zone between the land surface and the water table. A

UNSCEAR
United Nations Scientific Committee on the Effects of Atomic Radiation. U

unscheduled maintenance
Any inspection, adjustment, repair, removal, disassembly, cleaning, or replacement of vehicle components or systems which is performed to correct a part failure or vehicle (if the engine were installed in a vehicle) malfunction. A

unsolicited proposal
An informal written offer to perform funded work for which the government did not publish a solicitation. A

unstable
Tending toward decomposition or other unwanted chemical change during normal handling or storage. N

unstable (reactive) liquid
A liquid which in the pure state or as commercially produced or transported will vigorously polymerize, decompose, condense, or will become self-reactive under conditions of shocks, pressure, or temperature. O

unstable material
Earth material, other than running, that because of its nature or the influence of related conditions, cannot be depended upon to remain in place without extra support, such as would be furnished by a system of shoring. O

unstable reactive
A chemical that, in the pure state, or as produced or transported, will vigorously polymerize, decompose, condense, or become self-reactive under conditions of shocks, pressure, or temperature. N

untreated regulated medical waste
Regulated medical waste that has not been treated to substantially reduce or eliminate its potential for causing disease. A

upland
Any area that does not qualify as a wetland because the associated hydrologic regime is not sufficiently wet to elicit development of vegetation, soils, and/or hydrologic characteristics associated with wetlands. Such areas occurring in floodplains are more appropriately termed nonwetlands. N

upper bound cancer risk-assessment
A qualifying statement indicating that the cancer risk estimate is not a true value in that the dose-response modeling used provides a value which is not likely to be an underestimate of the true value. The true value may be lower than the upper bound cancer risk estimate and it may even be close to zero. This results from the use of

a statistical upper confidence limit and from the use of conservative assumptions in deriving the cancer risk estimate. N

upper explosive limit or upper flammable limit
UEL, or UFL of a vapor or gas; the highest concentration (highest percentage of the substance in air) that will produce a flash of fire when an ignition source (heat, arc, or flame) is present. At higher concentrations, the mixture is too "rich" to burn. Also see "LEL." N

upper limit
The emission level for a specific pollutant above which a certificate of conformity may not be issued or may be suspended or revoked. A

upper respiratory tract
The structures that conduct air into the lungs, including the nasal cavity, mouth, pharynx, and larynx. N

upper sample
A spot sample taken at the mid-point of the upper third of the tank contents. A

uppermost aquifer
The geologic formation nearest the natural ground surface that is an aquifer, as well as lower aquifers that are hydraulically interconnected with this aquifer within the facility's property boundary. A

uprights
The vertical members of a trench shoring system placed in contact with the earth and usually positioned so that individual members do not contact each other. Uprights placed so that individual members are closely spaced, in contact with or interconnected to each other, are often called "sheeting." O

upset
An exceptional incident in which there is unintentional and temporary noncompliance with technology-based permit effluent limitations because of factors beyond the reasonable control of the permittee. An upset does not include noncompliance to the extent caused by operational error, improperly designed treatment facilities, inadequate treatment facilities, lack of preventive maintenance, or careless or improper operation. N

uptake
The sorption of a test substance into and onto aquatic organisms during exposure. A

uptake phase
The initial portion of a bioconcentration test during which the organisms are exposed to the test solution. A

uranium
A radioactive heavy metal element used in nuclear reactors and the production of nuclear weapons. Term refers usually to U-238, the most abundant radium isotope, although a small percentage of naturally-occurring uranium is U-235. N

uranium byproduct material (tailings)
The wastes produced by the

extraction or concentration of uranium from any ore processed primarily for its source material content. Ore bodies depleted by uranium solution extractions and which remain underground do not constitute byproduct material. A

uranium fuel cycle
The operations of milling of uranium ore, chemical conversion of uranium, isotopic enrichment of uranium, fabrication of uranium fuel, generation of electricity by a light-water-cooled nuclear power plant using uranium fuel, and reprocessing of spent uranium fuel, to the extent that these directly support the production of electrical power for public use utilizing nuclear energy, but excludes mining operations, operations at waste disposal sites, transportation of any radioactive material in support of these operations, and the reuse of recovered non-uranium special nuclear and by-product materials from the cycle. A

urban and industrial stormwater systems needs
(1) An identification of the required improvements to existing urban and industrial stormwater systems, including combined sewer overflows, that are necessary to attain and maintain applicable water quality standards. (2) An identification of the needed urban and industrial stormwater systems for areas not presently served over at least a 20-year planning period (in 5-year increments) that are necessary to attain and maintain applicable water quality standards, emphasizing appropriate land management and other nonstructural techniques for control of urban and industrial stormwater runoff. (3) the reduction in capital construction costs brought about by nonstructural control measures, and any capital and annual operating costs of such facilities and practices. A

urban area population
(1) The population defined in the most recent decennial U.S. Census of Population Report. A (2) The population defined in "1970 Census of Population; Supplementary Report: Population of Urbanized Areas Established Since the 1970 Census, for the United States; 1970." U.S. Bureau of Census, PC(S)-106, U.S. Government Printing Office, Washington, D.C., October 1976. A

urban bus
A heavy-duty diesel-powered passenger-carrying vehicle with a load capacity of fifteen or more passengers and intended primarily for intra-city operation, i.e., within the confines of a city or greater metropolitan area. Urban bus operation is characterized by short rides and frequent stops. To facilitate this type of operation, more than one set of quick-opening entrance and exit doors would normally be installed. Since fares are usually paid in cash or tokens rather than purchased in advance in the form of tickets, urban buses would normally have equipment installed for collection of fares. Urban buses are also typically characterized by the absence of equipment and facilities for long distance travel, e.g., rest rooms, large luggage compartments, and

facilities for stowing carry-on luggage. A

urban runoff
Storm water from city streets, usually carrying litter and organic wastes. N

urban scale
The overall, citywide conditions with dimensions on the order of 4 to 50 kilometers. This scale would usually require more than one site for definition. A

USC
United States Code. It contains a consolidation and codification of all laws of the United States. The USC is divided into 50 titles which represent broad areas subject to Federal law. U

USCA
United States Code Annotated. U

USCG
United States Coast Guard. U

USDA
United States Department of Agriculture. U

USDW
Underground Source of Drinking Water. A

use
Any act of handling or release of a pesticide, or exposure of man or the environment to a pesticide through acts, including but not limited to: (1) Application of a pesticide, including mixing and loading and any required supervisory action in or near the area of application; (2) Storage actions for pesticides and pesticide containers; and (3) Disposal actions for pesticides and pesticide containers. [ed. "Use" as defined here incorporates application. However, the certification requirement for certain restricted use pesticides only applies with respect to applications of such pesticides. Many aspects of use do not include application (e.g., storage, transportation), and hence are outside the requirement for certification]. A

use of asbestos
The presence of asbestos-containing material in school buildings. A

use stream
All reasonably anticipated transfer, flow, or disposal of a chemical substance, regardless of physical state or concentration, through all intended operations of industrial, commercial, or consumer use. A

use-dilution
A dilution specified on the label or labeling which produces the concentration of the pesticide for a particular purpose or effect. A

used oil
Any oil which has been (A) refined from crude oil, (B) used, and (C) as a result of such use, contaminated by physical or chemical impurities. I

use-pattern
The manner in which a pesticide is applied and includes the following parameters of pesticide application: (1) Target pest; (2) Crop or animals treated; (3) Application site; and (4)

Application technique, rate and frequency. A

used or reused
A material is "used" or "reused" if it is either: (i) Employed as an ingredient (including use as an intermediate) in an industrial process to make a product (for example, distillation bottoms from one process used as feedstock in another process). However, a material will not satisfy this condition if distinct components of the material are recovered as separate end products (as when metals are recovered from metal-containing secondary materials); or (ii) Employed in a particular function or application as an effective substitute for a commercial product (for example, spent pickle liquor used as phosphorous precipitant and sludge conditioner in wastewater treatment). A

useful life
(1) The period during which a treatment works operates. (Not "design life" which is the period during which a treatment works is planned and designed to be operated). A (2) A period of time/mileage as specified in [40 CFR] Part 86 for a nonconforming vehicle which begins at the time of resale (for a motor vehicle or motor vehicle engine owned by the ICI at the time of importation) or release to the owner (for a motor vehicle or motor vehicle engine not owned by the ICI at the time of importation) of the motor vehicle or motor vehicle engine by the ICI after modification and/or test pursuant to [40 CFR] § 85.1505 or § 85.1509. A (3) (a) For light-duty vehicles a period of use of 5 years or 50,000 miles, whichever first occurs. (b)(1) For a light-duty truck engine family or heavy-duty engine family, the average period of use up to engine retirement, or rebuild, whichever occurs first, as determined by the manufacturer under § 86.084-21(b)(4)(ii)(B). (2) For a specific light-duty truck or heavy-duty engine, the period of use represented by the first occurring of the following: (i) The engine reaches the point of needing to be rebuilt, according to the criteria established by the manufacturer under § 86.084-21(b)(4)(ii)(C), or (ii) The engine reaches its engine family's useful life. (3) If the useful life of a specific light-duty truck or heavy-duty engine is found to be less than 5 years or 50,000 miles (or the equivalent), the useful life shall be a period of use of 5 years or 50,000 miles (or the equivalent), whichever occurs first, as required by section 202(d)(2) of the Clean Air Act. (4) For purpose of identification this option shall be known as the average useful-life period. A (5) Estimated period during which a facility or piece of equipment will be operated. A

user charge
A charge levied on users of a treatment works, or that portion of the ad valorem taxes paid by a user, for the user's proportionate share of the cost of operation and maintenance (including replacement) of such works under sections 204(b)(1)(A) and 201(h)(2) of the Clean Water Act. A

USFWS
United States Fish and Wildlife Service.N

USGS
United States Geological Survey. N

UST
Underground storage tank. Any one or combination of tanks (including underground pipes connected thereto) which is used to contain an accumulation of regulated substances, and the volume of which (including the volume of the underground pipes connected thereto) is 10 percent or more beneath the surface of the ground. Such term does not include any--(A) farm or residential tank of 1,100 gallons or less capacity used for storing motor fuel for noncommercial purposes; (B) tank used for storing heating oil for consumptive use on the premises where stored; (C) septic tank; (D) pipeline facility (including gathering lines) regulated under--(i) the Natural Gas Pipeline Safety Act of 1968, (49 U.S.C. App. 1671, et seq.), (ii) the Hazardous Liquid Pipeline Safety Act of 1979 (49 U.S.C.App. 2001, et seq.), or (iii) which is an intrastate pipeline facility regulated under state laws comparable to the provisions of law referred to in clause (i) or (ii) of this subparagraph; (E) surface impoundment, pit, pond, or lagoon; (F) storm water or waste water collection system; (G) flow-through process tank; (H) liquid trap or associated gathering lines directly related to oil or gas production and gathering operations; or; (I) storage tank situated in an underground area (such as a basement, cellar, mineworking, drift, shaft, or tunnel) if the storage tank is situated upon or above the surface of the floor. The term "underground storage tank" shall not include any pipes connected to any tank which is described in subparagraphs (A) through (I). I

UST program
A program under RCRA (Subtitle I) that regulates underground tanks storing petroleum products and any substances defined as hazardous under Superfund (CERCLA) and RCRA. The UST program does not require permits for underground tanks but instead mandates that owner-operators meet specific notification and technical requirements. N

UST system
An underground storage tank, connected underground piping, underground ancillary equipment, and containment system, if any. A

utility competitive bid solicitation
A public request from a regulated electric utility for offers to the utility for meeting future capacity needs. A new independent power production facility (IPPF) may be regarded as having been "selected" in such solicitation pursuant to 40 CFR section 405(g)(6)(A)(iv) if the utility has named the IPPF as a project with which it intends to negotiate a power sales agreement. A

utilization equipment
Equipment which utilizes electric energy for mechanical, chemical, heating, lighting, or similar purpose. O

utilization system
A system which provides electric power and light for employee workplaces; includes the premises wiring system and utilization equipment. O

UZM
Unsaturated zone monitoring. N

V

V
 Volt(s). U

v/v
 Volume per volume. U

vaccine
 Dead or partial or modified antigen used to induce immunity to certain infectious diseases. N

vacuum break
 A vacuum-operated device to open the carburetor choke plate a predetermined amount on cold start. A

vacuum leakage
 Leakage into the vacuum cavity of a vacuum break. A

vacuum purge system
 A vacuum system with a controlled air flow to purge the vacuum system of undesirable manifold vapors. A

vacuum spark advance disconnect retrofit
 A device or system installed on a motor vehicle that prevents the ignition vacuum advance from operating either when the vehicle's transmission is in the lower gears, or when the vehicle is traveling below a predetermined speed, so as to achieve reduction in exhaust emissions of hydrocarbon and carbon monoxide from 1967 and earlier light-duty vehicles of at least 25 and 9 percent, respectively. A

valid emission performance warranty claim
 A claim in which there is no evidence that the vehicle had not been properly maintained and operated in accordance with manufacturer instructions, the vehicle failed to conform to applicable emission standards as measured by an Office Director-approved type of emission warranty test during its useful life and the owner is subject to sanction as a result of the test failure. A

valid study
 A study that has been conducted in

598

accordance with the Good Laboratory Practice standards of 40 CFR Part 160 or generally accepted scientific methodology and that EPA has not determined to be invalid. A

validated test
A test determined by the Environmental Protection Agency to have been conducted and evaluated in a manner consistent with accepted scientific procedures. A

valuable commercial and recreational species
Those [animal or fish] species for which catch statistics are compiled on a routine basis by the Federal or State agency responsible for compiling such statistics for the general geographical area impacted, or which are under current study by such Federal or State agencies for potential development for commercial or recreational use. A

value engineering
VE. A specialized cost control technique based on a systematic and creative approach which identifies and focuses on unnecessarily high cost in a project in order to arrive at a cost saving without sacrificing the reliability or efficiency of the project. A

value for pesticide purposes
That characteristic of a substance or mixture of substances which produces an efficacious action on a pest. A

valve height
The greatest linear dimension of the oyster as measured from the umbo to the ventral edge of the valves (the farthest distance from the umbo). A

van
A light-duty truck having an integral enclosure, fully enclosing the driver compartment and load carrying device, and having no body sections protruding more than 30 inches ahead of the leading edge of the windshield. A

vapor
The gaseous phase of substances that are liquid or solid at atmospheric temperature and pressure, such as steam. N

vapor barrier
That material used to prevent or substantially inhibit the transfer of water, corrosive liquids and steam or other hot vapors from the outside of a garment to the wearer's body. O

vapor density
The weight of a vapor or gas compared to the weight of an equal volume of air is an expression of the density of the vapor or gas. Materials lighter than air have vapor densities less than 1.0 (examples: acetylene, methane, hydrogen). Materials heavier than air (examples: propane, hydrogen, sulfide, ethane, butane, chlorine, sulfur dioxide) have vapor densities greater than 1.0. All vapors and gases will mix with air, but the lighter materials will tend to rise and dissipate (unless confined). Heavier vapors and gases are likely to concentrate in low places--along or under floors, in sumps, sewers, and manholes, in trenches and ditches-- where they may create fire or health hazards. N

vapor dispersion
The movement of vapor clouds in air due to wind, gravity spreading, and mixing. N

vapor incinerator
Any enclosed combustion device that is used for destroying organic compounds and does not necessarily extract energy in the form of steam or process heat. A

vapor pressure
The pressure at which a liquid or solid is in equilibrium with its vapor at a given temperature. A

vapor recovery disposal system
A system of processing vapors and gases of organic compounds discharged during gasoline loading or unloading operations. This system shall consist of one of the following: (i) A refrigeration-condensation system, adsorption-absorption system, or the equivalent that processes all vapors and gases and ultimately converts no less than 90 percent by weight of the processed vapors and gases back to the liquid product, or (ii) A vapor handling system that directs all vapors and gases to a fuel gas system, which will dispose of no less than 90 percent by weight of the processed vapors and gases, or (iii) Other equipment of an efficiency equal to or greater than paragraphs (i) and (ii), if approved by the Administrator. A

vapor recovery system
(1) A closed system of pipes, valves, and compressor in which vapors that might otherwise escape into the atmosphere are compressed to liquid form and returned to their source. (2) A vapor gathering system capable of collecting all hydrocarbon vapors discharged from the storage vessel and a vapor disposal system capable of processing such hydrocarbon vapors and gases so as to prevent their emission to the atmosphere. A

vapor-mounted seal
A foam-filled primary seal mounted continuously around the circumference of the tank so there is an annular vapor space underneath the seal. The annular vapor space is bounded by the bottom of the primary seal, the tank wall, the liquid surface, and the floating roof. A

vapor-tight marine vessel
A marine vessel with a benzene product tank that has been demonstrated within the preceding 12 months to have no leaks. A

vapor-tight tank truck
A tank truck or railcar for which it has been demonstrated within the preceding 12 months that its product tank will sustain a pressure change of not more than 750 pascals within 5 minutes after it is pressurized to a minimum of 4,500 pascals. A

vaporization
The change of a substance from the liquid to the gaseous state. One of the three basic contributing processes of air pollution, the others being attrition and combustion. U

variance
(1) Government permission for a delay or exception in the application

of a given law, ordinance, or regulation. N (2) (NPDES) Any mechanism or provision under section 301 or 316 of CWA or under 40 CFR part 125, or in the applicable "effluent limitations guidelines" which allows modification to or waiver of the generally applicable effluent limitation requirements or time deadlines of CWA. This includes provisions which allow the establishment of alternative limitations based on fundamentally different factors or on sections 301(c), 301(g), 301(h), 301(i), or 316(a) of CWA. A (3) The temporary deferral of a final compliance date for an individual source subject to an approved regulation, or a temporary change to an approved regulation as it applies to an individual source. A

variation

A divergency in the developing organism beyond the usual range of structural constitution that may not adversely affect survival or health. A specific category in the evaluation of developmental effects. N

vault

An enclosure above or below ground which personnel may enter and is used for the purpose of installing, operating, and/or maintaining equipment and/or cable. O

VE

Value engineering. U

vector

(1) An organism, often an insect or rodent, that carries disease. (2) An object that is used to transport genes into a host cell (vectors can be plasmids viruses, or other bacteria). A gene is placed in the vector; the vector infects the bacterium. N

vegetable tan

The process of converting hides into leather using chemicals either derived form vegetable matter or synthesized to produce effects similar to those chemicals. A

vehicle

(1) Any agent which facilitates the mixture, dispersion or solubilization of a test substance with a carrier. A (2) Any new production light-duty vehicle as defined in Subpart A of 40 CFR parts 86-99. A (3) Any motor vehicle, machine, or tractor, which is propelled by mechanical power and capable of transportation of property on a street or highway and which has a gross vehicle weight rating in excess of 10,000 pounds and a partially or fully enclosed operator's compartment. A

vehicle configuration

A unique combination of basic engine, engine code, inertia weight class, transmission configuration, and axle ratio. A

vehicle curb weight

The actual or the manufacturer's estimated weight of the vehicle in operational status and all standard equipment, and weight of fuel at nominal tank capacity, and the weight of optional equipment computed in accordance with 40 CFR § 86.078-24; incomplete light duty trucks shall have vehicle curb weight specified by the manufacturer. A

vehicle for hire
Any chauffeur-driven, spark-ignition-powered motor vehicle used for the purpose of providing transportation for a fee or charge, such as taxicabs and limousine services. A

vehicle or engine configuration
The specific subclassification unit of an engine family or certified part application group as determined by engine displacement, fuel system, engine code, transmission and inertia weight class, as applicable. A

vehicle trip
Any movement of a motor vehicle from one location to another that results in the emission of air pollutants by the motor vehicle. A

vehicle type
Any class of motor vehicles (e.g., precontrolled, heavy duty vehicles, gasoline powered trucks) whose emissions characteristics are significantly different from the emissions characteristics of motor vehicles not in the class. A

vehicle useful life
(1) For light-duty vehicles and light-duty trucks a period of use of 5 years or 50,000 miles, whichever first occurs. (2) For gasoline-fueled heavy-duty engines a period of use of 5 years or 50,000 miles of vehicle operation or 1,500 hours of engine operation (or an equivalent period of 1,500 hours of dynamometer operation), whichever first occurs. (3) For diesel heavy-duty engines a period of use of 5 years or 100,000 miles of vehicle operation or 3,000 hours of engine operation (or an equivalent period of 1,000 hours of dynamometer operation), whichever first occurs. A

vent
An opening through which there is mechanically induced air flow for the purpose of exhausting from a building air carrying particulate matter emissions from one or more affected facilities. A

ventilated
Provided with a means to permit circulation of air sufficient to remove an excess of heat, fumes, or vapors. O

ventilated cell composting
A method in which the compost is mixed and aerated by being dropped through a vertical series of ventilated cells. U

ventilation/suction
The act of admitting fresh air into a space in order to replace stale or contaminated air; achieved by blowing air into the space. Similarly, suction represents the admission of fresh air into an interior space by lowering the pressure outside of the space, thereby drawing the contaminated air outward. N

verified
Accepted by design, evaluation, or inspection by a registered professional engineer. O

vertical slip forms
Forms which are jacked vertically and continuously during placing of the concrete. O

vessel
Every description of watercraft or other artificial contrivance used, or capable of being used, as a means of transportation on water. A, L

VHAP
Volatile hazardous air pollutant. A

VHS
Vertical and horizontal spread. A term used in relation to the transport of landfill wastes to nearby receptors. U

viable embryos (fertility)
Eggs in which fertilization has occurred and embryonic development has begun. This is determined by candling the eggs 11 days after incubation has begun. It is difficult to distinguish between the absence of fertilization and early embryonic death. The distinction can be made by breaking out eggs that appear infertile and examining further. This distinction is especially important when a test compound induces early embryo mortality. Values are expressed as a percentage of eggs set. A

vibration
The periodic motion of friable ACBM which may result in the release of asbestos fibers. A

vinyl chloride
A chemical compound used in producing some plastics. Excessive exposure to this substance may cause cancer. N [ed. Vinyl chloride has been designated a hazardous air pollutant under § 112 of the CAA]. U

violating facility
Any facility that is owned, leased, or supervised by an applicant, recipient, contractor, or subcontractor that EPA lists under 40 CFR Part 15 as not in compliance with federal, state, or local requirements under the Clean Air Act or Clean Water Act. A facility includes any building, plant, installation, structure, mine, vessel, or other floating craft. A

violation
Any incident of excess emissions, regardless of the circumstances of the occurrence. A

virgin material
A raw material, including previously unused copper, aluminum, lead, zinc, iron, or other metal or metal ore, any undeveloped resource that is, or with new technology will become, a source of raw materials. I

virus
The smallest form of microorganisms capable of causing disease. N

viscose process
The fiber forming process where cellulose and concentrated caustic soda are reacted to form soda or alkali cellulose. This reacts with carbon disulfide to form sodium cellulose xanthate, which is then dissolved in a solution of caustic soda. After ripening, the solution is spun into an acid coagulating bath. This precipitates the cellulose in the form of a regenerated cellulose filament. A

viscosity
The property of liquids which causes

them to resist instantaneous change of shape, or instantaneous rearrangement of their parts, due to internal friction. The resistance which the particles of a liquid offer to a force tending to move them in relation to each other. Viscosity of oils is usually expressed as the number of seconds at a definite temperature required for a standard quality of oil to flow through a standard apparatus. A

viscous
(1) Thick, resistant to flow, having a high viscosity. A (2) A viscosity of 45 SUS or more. O

visibility impairment and impairment of visibility
Any humanly perceptible change in visibility (visual range, contrast, coloration) from that which would have existed under natural conditions. A

visible emissions
Any emissions which are visually detectable without the aid of instruments, coming from [regulated asbestos-containing material] (RACM) or asbestos-containing waste material, or from any asbestos milling, manufacturing, or fabricating operation. This does not include condensed, uncombined water vapor. A

vital capacity
The maximal volume of air exhaled after the deepest inspiration without forced or rapid effort. In adult humans, generally 5 liters. N

vitrification
A process whereby high temperatures effect permanent chemical and physical changes in a ceramic body, most of which is transformed into glass. U

VMT
Vehicle miles traveled. N

VOC
Volatile organic compounds. U

VOC content
All volatile organic compounds that are in a coating expressed as kilograms of VOC per liter of coating solids. A

VOC emission control device
Equipment that destroys or recovers VOC. A

VOC emission reduction system
A system composed of an enclosure, hood, or other device for containment and capture of VOC emissions and a VOC emission control device. A

VOC emissions
The mass of volatile organic compounds (VOC's), expressed as kilograms of VOC's per liter of applied coating solids, emitted from a surface coating operation. A

VOC solvent
An organic liquid or liquid mixture consisting of VOC components. A

VOL
Volatile organic liquid. A

volatile
Any substance that evaporates at a low temperature. N

volatile hazardous air pollutant
VHAP. A substance regulated under the Clean Air Act for which a standard for equipment leaks of the substance has been proposed and promulgated. Benzene and vinyl chloride are VHAPs. A

volatile organic compounds
(1) VOC. (1) Any compound containing carbon and hydrogen or containing carbon and hydrogen in combination with any other element which has a vapor pressure of 1.5 pounds per square inch absolute (77.6mm Hg) or greater under actual storage conditions. A (2) Any organic compounds that participate in atmospheric photochemical reactions or that are measured by Method 18, 24, 25, or 25A or an equivalent or alternative method as defined in 40 CFR § 60.2. A (3) Any compound of carbon, excluding carbon monoxide, carbon dioxide, carbonic acid, metallic carbides or carbonates, and ammonium carbonate, which participates in atmospheric photochemical reactions. A.

volatile synthetic organic chemicals
Chemicals that tend to volatilize or evaporate from water. N

volatility
The property of a substance or substances to convert into vapor or gas without chemical change. A

volatilization
The loss of a substance to the air from a surface or from solution by evaporation. A

volt
V. The unit of electromotive force (1 volt = 1 watt/1 ampere). U

volume reduction
The processing of waste materials so as to decrease the amount of space the materials occupy. Reduction is accomplished by mechanical, thermal or biological processes. U

voluntarily submitted information
Business information in EPA's possession--(1) The submission of which EPA had no statutory or contractual authority to require; and (2) The submission of which was not prescribed by state or regulation as a condition of obtaining some benefit (or avoiding some disadvantage) under a regulatory program of general applicability, including such regulatory programs as permit, licensing, registration, or certification programs, but excluding programs concerned solely or primarily with the award or administration by EPA of contracts or grants. A

voluntary emissions recall
A repair, adjustment, or modification program voluntarily initiated and conducted by a manufacturer to remedy any emission-related defect for which direct notification of vehicle or engine owners has been provided. A

VOM
Volatile organic materials. A

vulnerability analysis
Assessment of elements in the community that are susceptible to

damage should a release of hazardous materials occur. N

vulnerable zone
An area over which the airborne concentration of a chemical involved in an accidental release could reach the level of concern. N

W

W
Watt(s). U

wall hole
An opening less than 30 inches but more than 1 inch high, of unrestricted width, in any wall or partition; such as a ventilation hole or drainage scupper. O

wall opening
An opening at least 30 inches high and 18 inches wide, in any wall or partition, through which persons may fall, such as a yard-arm doorway or chute opening. O

wane
Bark, or the lack of wood from any cause, on the corner of a piece. O

warning
For air quality contingency plans, the warning level indicates that air quality is continuing to degrade and that additional control actions are necessary. A warning will be declared when any one of the following levels is reached at any monitoring site: (1) SO_2--1,600 ug/m^3 (0.6 ppm), 24-hour average. (2) particulate--625 ug/m^3, 24-hour average. (3) SO_2 and particulate combined--product of SO_2 ug/m^3, 24-hour average and particulate AG2 ug/m^3, 24-hour average equal to 261 x 10^3. (4) CO--34 mg/m^3 (30 ppm), 8-hour average. (5) Ozone (O_3)--800 ug/m^3 (0.4 ppm), 1-hour average. (6) NO_2--2,260 ug/m^3 (1.2 ppm), 1-hour average; 565 ug/m^3 (0.3 ppm), 24-hour average and meteorological conditions are such that pollutant concentrations can be expected to remain at the above levels for 12 or more hours or increase, or in the case of ozone, the situation is likely to reoccur within the next 24 hours unless control actions are taken. A

warning device
A sound emitting device used to alert and warn people of the presence of railroad equipment. A

wash-oil circulation tank
Any vessel that functions to hold the wash oil used in light-oil recovery operations or the wash oil used in the wash-oil final cooler. A

wash-oil decanter
Any vessel that functions to separate, by gravity, the condensed water from the wash oil received from a wash-oil final cooler or from a light-oil scrubber. A

washer
A machine which agitates fabric articles in a petroleum solvent bath and spins the articles to remove the solvent, together with the piping and ductwork used in the installation of this device. A

washout
The carrying away of solid waste by waters of the base flood. A

waste
(1) Unwanted materials left over from manufacturing processes, refuse from places of human or animal habitation. N (2) Any spent nuclear fuel or radioactive waste isolated in a disposal system. A (3) Any material resulting from industrial, commercial, mining or agricultural operations, or from community activities that is discarded or is being accumulated, stored, or physically, chemically, thermally, or biologically treated prior to being discarded, recycled, or discharged. A

waste form
The materials comprising the radioactive components of waste and any encapsulating or stabilizing matrix. A

waste generator
Any owner or operator of a source covered by this subpart whose act or process produces asbestos-containing waste material. A

waste load allocation
The maximum load of pollutants each discharger of waste is allowed to release into a particular waterway. Discharge limits are usually required for each specific water quality criterion being, or expected to be, violated. N

waste material containing TCDD or waste(s) containing TCDD
Any waste material or waste(s) resulting from manufacture or processing of 2,4,5-Trichlorophenol or its pesticide derivatives, or any waste(s) resulting from manufacturing processes using equipment that was at some time used in the manufacture of 2,4,5-Trichlorophenol or its pesticide derivatives. A

waste management practices
Refers to aspects of a facility's design, operation and closure that ensure protection of human health and the environment while treating, storing or disposing of hazardous waste. N

waste management unit
A piece of equipment, structure, or transport mechanism used in handling, storage, treatment, or disposal of waste. Examples of a waste

management unit include a tank, surface impoundment, container, oil-water separator, individual drain system, steam stripping unit, thin-film evaporation unit, waste incinerator, and landfill. A

waste management unit boundary
A vertical surface located at the hydraulically downgradient limit of the unit. This vertical surface extends down into the uppermost aquifer. A

waste material or waste
Any garbage, refuse, sludge from a waste treatment plant or water supply facility and other discarded material including solid, liquid, semisolid, or contained gaseous material resulting from industrial, commercial, mining and agricultural operations. A

waste oil
Used products primarily derived from petroleum, which include, but are not limited to, fuel oils, motor oils, gear oils, cutting oils, transmission fluids, hydraulic fluids, and dielectric fluids. A

waste paper
Any of the following "recovered materials": (1) Postconsumer materials such as: (i) Paper, paperboard, and fibrous wastes from retail stores, office buildings, homes, and so forth, after they have passed through their end usage as a consumer item, including: Used corrugated boxes, old newspapers, old magazines, mixed waste paper, tabulating cards, and used cordage, and (ii) All paper, paperboard, and fibrous wastes that enter and are collected from municipal solid waste; and (2) Manufacturing, forest residues, and other wastes such as: (i) Dry paper and paperboard waste generated after completion of the papermaking process (that is, those manufacturing operations up to and including the cutting and trimming of the paper machine reel into smaller rolls or rough sheets) including: Envelope cuttings, bindery trimmings, and other paper and paperboard waste resulting from printing, cutting, forming, and other converting operations; bag, box, and carton manufacturing wastes; and butt rolls, mill wrappers, and rejected unused stock; and; (ii) Finished paper and paperboard from obsolete inventories of paper and paperboard manufacturers, merchants, wholesalers, dealers, printers, converters, and others. A

waste pile
Any noncontainerized accumulation of solid, nonflowing waste that is used for treatment or storage. A

waste reduction
The prevention or restriction of waste generation at its source by redesigning products or the patterns of production and consumption. U

waste shipment record
The shipping document, required to be originated and signed by the waste generator, used to track and substantiate the disposition of asbestos-containing waste material. A

waste stabilization ponds
Large, shallow basins used to purify wastewaters by storage under climatic conditions that favor the growth of microorganisms, and thus promote the stabilization of organic waste. U

waste stream
(1) A general term for the total waste output of an area, location, or facility. U (2) The waste generated by a particular process unit, product tank, or waste management unit. The characteristics of the waste stream (e.g., flow rate, benzene concentration, water content) are determined at the point of waste generation. Examples of a waste stream include process wastewater, product tank drawdown, sludge and slop oil removed from waste management units, and landfill leachate. A

waste water
Water carrying dissolved or suspended solids from homes, farms, businesses, and industries. N

wasteload allocation
WLA. The portion of a receiving water's loading capacity that is allocated to one of its existing or future point sources of pollution. WLAs constitute a type of water quality-based effluent limitation. A

wastewater treatment process
(1) Includes any process which modifies characteristics such as BOD, COD, TSS, and pH, usually for the purpose of meeting effluent guidelines and standards. B, K (2) Any process which modifies characteristics such as BOD, COD, TSS, and pH, usually for the purpose of meeting effluent guidelines and standards; it does not include any process where the purpose of which is to remove vinyl chloride from water. A (3) Any component, piece of equipment, or installation that receives, manages, or treats process wastewater, product tank drawdown, or landfill leachate prior to direct or indirect discharge in accordance with the National Pollutant Discharge Elimination System permit regulations under 40 CFR part 122. These systems typically include individual drain systems, oil-water separators, air flotation units, equalization tanks, and biological treatment units. A

wastewater treatment tank
A tank that is designed to receive and treat an influent wastewater through physical, chemical, or biological methods. A

wastewater treatment unit
A device which (a) is part of a wastewater treatment facility which is subject to regulation under either Section 402 or Section 307(b) of the Clean Water Act; and (b) receives and treats or stores an influent wastewater which is a hazardous waste as defined in 40 CFR § 261.3; or generates and accumulates a wastewater treatment sludge which is a hazardous waste as defined in 40 CFR § 261.3, or treats or stores a wastewater treatment sludge which is a hazardous waste as defined in 40 CFR § 261.3 and (c) meets the definition of tank in 40 CFR § 260.10. A

water management division director
One of the Directors of the Water Management Divisions within the Regional offices of the Environmental Protection Agency or this person's delegated representative. A

water pollution
The addition of harmful or objectionable material causing an alteration of water quality. N

water quality assessment and segment classifications
(1) An assessment of existing and potential water quality problems within the approved planning area or designated areawide planning area, including an identification of the types and degree of problems and the sources of pollutants (both point and nonpoint sources) contributing to the problems. The results of this assessment should be reflected in the state's report required under section 305(b) of the [Federal Water Pollution Control] Act. (2) The classification of each segment as either water quality or effluent limitation as defined in § 130.2(O) of this chapter. (i) Segments shall include the surrounding land areas that contribute or may contribute to alterations in the physical, chemical, or biological characteristics of the surface waters. (ii) Water quality problems generally shall be described in terms of existing or potential violations of water quality standards. (iii) Each water quality segment classification shall include the specific water quality parameters requiring consideration in the total maximum daily load allocation process. (iv) In the segment classification process, upstream sources that contribute or may contribute to such alterations should be considered when identifying boundaries of each segment. (v) The classification of segments shall be based on measurements of instream water quality, where available. A

water quality criteria
Specific levels of water quality which, if reached, are expected to render a body of water suitable for its designated use. The criteria are based on specific levels of pollutants that would make the water harmful if used for drinking, swimming, farming, fish production, or industrial processes. N

water quality limited segment
Any segment where it is known that water quality does not meet applicable water quality standards, and/or is not expected to meet applicable water quality standards, even after the application of the technology-based effluent limitations required by 301(b) and 306 of the Clean Water Act. A

water quality limited stream segment
A stretch of navigable waters where effluent limitations in NPDES permits for direct discharges are determined by water quality standards rather than technology-based effluent standards. U

water quality management
The plan for managing the water quality, including consideration of the relationship of water quality to land

and water resources and uses, on an area wide basis, for each EPA/state approved planning area and for those areas designated pursuant to section 208a(2), (3), or (4) of the [Federal Water Pollution Control] Act within a state. A

water quality management plan
WQM. A state or areawide waste treatment management plan developed and updated in accordance with the provisions of sections 205(j), 208 and 303 of the Clean Water Act and 40 CFR § 130.3. A

water quality standard
(1) A management plan that considers (a) what water will be used for, (b) setting water quality criteria levels to protect those uses, (c) implementing and enforcing the water treatment plans, and (d) protecting existing high quality waters, and establish regulations designating standards for all stream and river segments. N (2) Standards established pursuant to section 10(c) of the Federal Water Pollution Control Act, and State-adopted water quality standards for navigable waters which are not interstate waters. A

water seal controls
A seal pot, p-leg trap, or other type of trap filled with water that has a design capability to create a water barrier between the sewer line and the atmosphere. A

water solubility
The maximum concentration of a chemical compound which can result when it is dissolved in water. If a substance is water soluble, it can very readily disperse through the environment. N

water supplier
A person who owns or operates a public water system. N

water supply system
The collection, treatment, storage and distribution of potable water from source to consumer. N

water table
(1) The level of ground water. N (2) The upper limit of the part of the soil or underlying rock material that is wholly saturated with water; (3) the upper surface of the zone of saturation in ground waters in which the hydrostatic pressure is equal to atmospheric pressure. N

water used in agricultural or wildlife propagation
Produced water of good enough quality to be used for wildlife or livestock watering or other agricultural uses and actually put to such use during periods of discharge. A

water-reactive
A chemical that reacts with water to release a gas that is either flammable or presents a health hazard. O

waterborne ink systems
Ink and related coating mixtures

whose volatile portion consists of a mixture of VOC solvent and more than five weight percent water, as applied to the gravure cylinder. A

waterborne or water reducible
A coating which contains more than five weight percent water in its volatile fraction. A

waters of the United States
(a) All waters which are currently used, were used in the past, or may be susceptible to use in interstate or foreign commerce, including all waters which are subject to the ebb and flow of the tide; (b) All interstate waters, including interstate wetlands; (c) All other waters such as intrastate lakes, rivers, streams (including intermittent streams), mudflats, sandflats, wetlands, sloughs, prairie potholes, wet meadows, playa lakes, or natural ponds the use, degradation, or destruction of which would affect or could affect interstate or foreign commerce including any such waters: (1) Which are or could be used by interstate or foreign travelers for recreational or other purposes; (2) From which fish or shellfish are or could be taken and sold in interstate or foreign commerce; or (3) Which are used or could be used for industrial purposes by industries in interstate commerce; (d) All impoundments of waters otherwise defined as waters of the United States under this definition; (e) Tributaries of waters identified in paragraphs (a) through (d) of this definition; (f) The territorial sea; and (g) Wetlands adjacent to waters (other than waters that are themselves wetlands) identified in paragraphs (a) through (f) of this definition. A

watershed
The land area that drains into a stream. N

watertight
So constructed that moisture will not enter the enclosure. O

waterwall furnace
A furnace constructed with walls of welded steel tubes through which water is circulated to absorb the heat of combustion. It can be used as an incinerator, and the stream or hot water generated may be recycled. U

waterwall incinerator
An incinerator whose furnace walls consist of vertically arranged metal tubes through which water passes and absorbs the radiant energy from burning solid waste. Additional boiler packages in the flue control the conversion of water to stream of a specified temperature and pressure. U

weak nitric acid
Acid which is 30 to 70 percent in strength. A

weatherproof
So constructed or protected that exposure to the weather will not interfere with successful operation. Rainproof, raintight, or watertight equipment can fulfill the requirements for weatherproof where varying weather conditions other than

wetness, such as snow, ice, dust, or temperature extremes, are not a factor. O

weed
Any plant which grows where not wanted. C

Weibull model
A dose-response model of the form:
$$P(d) = 1 - \exp(-bd^m)$$
where P(d) is the probability of cancer due to a continuous dose rate d, and b and m are constants. N

weight-of-evidence
The extent to which the available biomedical data support the hypothesis that a substance causes an effect in humans. For example, the following factors increase the weight-of-evidence that a chemical poses a hazard to humans; an increase in the number of tissue sites affected by the agent; an increase in the number of animal species, strains, sexes, and a number of experiments and doses showing a response; the occurrence of a clear-cut dose-response relationship as well as a high level of statistical significance in the occurrence of the adverse effect in treated subjects compared with untreated controls; a dose related shortening of the time of occurrence of the adverse effect; etc. N

welder and welding operator
Any operator of electric or gas welding and cutting equipment. O

well
(1) Any shaft or pit dug or bored into the earth, generally of a cylindrical form, and often walled with bricks or tubing to prevent the earth from caving in. A (2) A well is a permanent complete enclosure around a fixed ladder, which is attached to the walls of the well. Proper clearances for a well will give the person who must climb the ladder the same protection as a cage. O

well (UIC)
A bored, drilled or driven shaft, or a dug hole, whose depth is greater than the largest surface dimension. A

well injection
(1) Disposal of liquid wastes through a hole or shaft to a subsurface stratum. A (2) The subsurface emplacement of "fluids" through a bored, drilled, or driven "well" or through a dug well, where the depth of the dug well is greater than the largest surface dimension. A

well log
A log obtained from a well, showing such information as resistivity, radioactivity, spontaneous potential, and acoustic velocity as a function of depth. A

well monitoring
The measurement, by on-site instruments or laboratory methods, of the quality of water in a well. A

well plug
A watertight and gastight seal installed in a borehole or well to prevent movement of fluids. A

well record

A concise statement of the available data regarding a well, such as a scout ticket, etc. A

well stimulation

Several processes used to clean the well bore, enlarge channels, and increase pore space in the interval to be injected thus making it possible for wastewater to move more readily into the formation, and includes (1) surging, (2) jetting, (3) blasting, (4) acidizing, (5) hydraulic fracturing. A

well workover

Any reentry of an injection well; including, but not limited to, the pulling of tubular goods, cementing or casing repairs; and excluding any routine maintenance (e.g. reseating the packer at the same depth, or repairs to surface equipment). A

wells, Class II

Wells which inject fluids: (a) which are brought to the surface in connection with conventional oil or natural gas production and may be commingled with waste waters from gas plants which are an integral part of production operations, unless those waters would be classified as a hazardous waste at the time of injection; (b) for enhanced recovery of oil or natural gas; and (c) for storage of hydrocarbons which are liquid at standard temperature and pressure. A

wet

Those steelmaking air cleaning systems that primarily use water for furnace gas cleaning. A

wet air pollution control scrubbers

Air pollution control devices used to remove particulates and fumes from air by entraining the pollutants in a water spray. A

wet barking operations

Includes hydraulic barking operations and wet drum barking operations which are those drum barking operations that use substantial quantities of water in either water sprays in the barking drums or in a partial submersion of the drums in a "tub" of water. A

wet desulfurization system

Those systems which remove sulfur compounds from coke oven gases and produce a contaminated process wastewater. A

wet process

Any process or operation in a workroom which normally results in surfaces upon which employees may walk or stand becoming wet. O

wet scrubber system

Any emission control device that mixes an aqueous stream or slurry with the exhaust gases from a steam generating unit to control emissions of particulate matter or sulfur dioxide. A

wet scrubbers

Air pollution control devices used to remove particulates and fumes from air by entraining the pollutants in a water spray. A

wetland hydrology
In general terms, permanent or periodic inundation or prolonged soil saturation sufficient to create anaerobic conditions in the soil. N

wetlands
Those areas that are inundated or saturated by surface or ground water at a frequency or duration sufficient to support, and that under normal circumstances do support, a prevalence of vegetation typically adapted for life in saturated soil conditions. Wetlands generally include playa lakes, swamps, marshes, bogs and similar areas such as sloughs, prairie potholes, wet meadows, prairie river overflows, mudflats, and natural ponds. A

wetting agent
A chemical that reduces the surface tension of water and enables it to soak into porous material more readily. U

WF
Weighting factor. U

wheel
That portion of a rim wheel which provides the method of attachment of the assembly to the axle of a vehicle and also provides the means to contain the inflated portion of the assembly (i.e., the tire and/or tube). O

white goods
Large appliances such as refrigerators, washers and dryers. The terminology was derived from the standard white color of these appliances that existed until recent years. N

WHO
World Health Organization. U

whole body
All human organs or tissue exclusive of the integumentary system (skin) and the cornea. A

whole body dose
The radiation dose to the entire body. U

whole body irradiation
Pertains to the case in which the entire body is exposed to the incident electromagnetic energy or in which the cross section of the body is smaller than the cross section of the incident radiation beam. O

wholesale purchaser-consumer
Any organization that is an ultimate consumer of gasoline and which purchases or obtains gasoline from a supplier for use in motor vehicles and receives delivery of that product into a storage tank of at least 550-gallon capacity substantially under the control of that organization. A

wildlife habitat
Waters and surrounding land areas used by fish, other aquatic life, and wildlife at any stage of their life history or activity. A

wildlife refuge
An area designated for the

protection of wild animals, within which hunting and fishing are either prohibited or strictly controlled. N

wind
The natural, horizontal movement of air. U

window jack scaffold
A scaffold, the platform of which is supported by a bracket or jack which projects through a window opening. O

windrow composting
An open-air method in which compostable material is sorted, shredded, placed in long rows or piles, and turned for aeration. Modified windrowing involves blowing controlled amounts of air through the material in ventilated bins, which is a quicker and more efficient method. The process may be aerobic or anaerobic. U

wire products and fasteners
Steel wire, products manufactured from steel wire, and steel fasteners manufactured from steel wire or other steel shapes. A

wireways
Sheet metal troughs with hinged or removable covers for housing and protecting electric wires and cable and in which conductors are laid in place after the wireway has been installed as a complete system. O

with modified-processes
Using any technique designed to minimize emissions without the use of add-on pollution controls. A

withdraw specification
To remove from designation any area already specified as a disposal site by the U.S. Army Corps of Engineers or by a state which has assumed the section 404 program, or any portion of such area. A

within the impoundment
When used for purposes of calculating the volume of process wastewater which may be discharged, shall mean the surface area within the impoundment at the maximum capacity plus the area of the inside and outside slopes of the impoundment dam and the surface area between the outside edge of the impoundment dam and seepage ditches upon which rain falls and is returned to the impoundment. For the purpose of such calculations, the surface area allowance for external appurtenances to the impoundment shall not be more than 30 percent of the water surface area within the impoundment dam at maximum capacity. A

WL
Working level. U

WLA
Wasteload allocation. A

WLM
Working level month. U

women's business enterprise
A women's business enterprise is a business which is certified as such by a state or federal agency, or which meets the following definition: A

women's business enterprise is an independent business concern which is at least 51 percent owned by a woman or women who also control and operate it. Determination of whether a business is at least 51 percent owned by a woman or women shall be made without regard to community property laws. For example, an otherwise qualified WBE which is 51 percent owned by a married woman in a community property state will not be disqualified because her husband has a 50 percent interest in her share. Similarly, a business which is 51 percent owned by a married man and 49 percent owned by an unmarried woman will not become a qualified WBE by virtue of his wife's 50 percent interest in his share of the business. A

wood characteristics
Distinguishing features which by their extent and number determine the quality of a piece of wood. O

wood fiber furnish subdivision mills
Those mills where cotton fibers are not used in the production of fine papers. A

wood irregularities
Natural characteristics in or on wood that may lower its durability, strength, or utility. O

wood pulp
The mixture of pulverized wood fibers and water that is used to make cellulose derivatives (e.g., paper, rayon). U

wood pulp waste
Fiber residue generated by a manufacturing process. U

wood residue
Bark, sawdust, slabs, chips, shavings, mill trim, and other wood products derived from wood processing and forest management operations. A

wool
The dry raw wool as it is received by the wool scouring mill. A

wool fiberglass
Fibrous glass of random texture, including fiberglass insulation, and other products listed in SIC 3296. N

wool fiberglass insulation
A thermal insulation material composed of glass fibers and made from glass produced or melted at the same facility where the manufacturing line is located. A

work area
A room or defined space in a workplace where a chemical substance is manufactured, processed, or used and where employees are present. A

work practice controls
Controls that reduce the likelihood of exposure by altering the manner in which a task is performed (e.g., prohibiting recapping of needles by a two handed technique). O

working chamber
The space or compartment under air

pressure in which the work is being done. O

working day
(1) Any day on which federal government offices are open for normal business. Saturdays, Sundays, and official federal holidays are not working days; all other days are. A (2) Working days. Mondays through Fridays but shall not include Saturdays, Sundays, or federal holidays. In computing 15 working days, the day of receipt of any notice shall not be included, and the last day of the 15 working days shall be included. O

working face
That portion of the land disposal site where solid wastes are discharged and are spread and compacted prior to the placement of cover material. A

working level
(1) WL. Any combination of short-lived radon decay products in one liter of air that will result in the ultimate emission of alpha particles with a total energy of 130 billion electron volts. A (2) A unit of measure for documenting exposure to radon decay products. One working level is equal to approximately 200 picocuries per liter. N

working level month
WLM. A unit of measure used to determine cumulative exposure to radon. N

working load
Load imposed by men, materials, and equipment. O

workplace
(1) An establishment at one geographic location containing one or more work areas. A (2) An establishment, job site, or project, at one geographical location containing one or more work areas. O

WOT
Wide open throttle. A

WQA
Water Quality Act of 1987. U

WQC
(1) Water quality criteria. U (2) Water quality management. A

WQM
Water Quality Management Plan. A

WQS
Water Quality Standards. A

writing paper
A paper suitable for pen and ink, pencil, typewriter or printing. A

written instructions for proper maintenance and use
Those maintenance and operation instructions specified in the owner's manual as being necessary to assure compliance of a vehicle with applicable emission standards for the useful life of the vehicle that are: (i) In accordance with the instructions specified for performance on the

manufacturer's prototype vehicle used in certification (including those specified for vehicles used under special circumstances), and (ii) In compliance with the requirements of [40 CFR] § 86.XXX-38 (as appropriate for the applicable model year vehicle/engine classification), and (iii) In compliance with any other regulations promulgated by the Office Director governing maintenance and use instructions. A

WSRA
Wild and Scenic Rivers Act. U

wt.
Weight. U

WWEMA
Waste and Wastewater Equipment Manufacturers' Association. N

WWTP
Wastewater treatment plant. N

XYZ

xenobiotic
Term for non-naturally occurring man-made substances found in the environment (i.e., synthetic material solvents, plastics). N

xerographic/copy paper
Any grade of paper suitable for copying by the xerographic process (a dry method of reproduction). A

YTD
Year to date. N

ZBB
Zero base budgeting. N

zero device-miles
The period of time between retrofit installation and the accumulation of 100 miles of automobile operation after installation. A

zero drift
The change in measurement system output over a stated period, usually 24 hours, of unadjusted continuous operation when the input concentration is zero; usually expressed as percent full scale. A

zero gas
A gas containing less than 1 ppm sulfur dioxide. A

zero grade air
Artificial "air" consisting of a blend of nitrogen and oxygen with oxygen concentrations between 18 and 21 mole percent. A

zero hours
That point after normal assembly line operations and adjustments are completed and before ten (10) additional operating hours have been accumulated, including emission testing, if performed. A

zero kilometers
That point after normal assembly line operations and adjustments, after normal dealer setup and preride inspection operations have been completed, and before 100 kilometers of vehicle operation of three hours of

engine operation have been accumulated, including emission testing if performed. A

zero miles
That point after initial engine starting (not to exceed 100 miles of vehicle operation, or three hours of engine operation) at which normal assembly line operations and adjustments are completed, and including emission testing, if performed. A

zero tolerance
No amount of pesticide chemical may remain on the raw agricultural commodity when it is offered for shipment. A zero tolerance for a pesticide chemical in or on a raw agricultural commodity may be established because, among other reasons: (a) A safe level of the pesticide chemical in the diet of two different species of warm-blooded animals has not been reliably determined. (b) The chemical is carcinogenic to or has other alarming physiological effects upon one or more of the species of the test animals used, when fed in the diet of such animals. (c) The pesticide chemical is toxic, but is normally used at times when, or in such manner that, fruit, vegetables, or other raw agricultural commodities will not bear or contain it. (d) All residue of the pesticide chemical is normally removed through good agricultural practice such as washing or brushing through weathering or other changes in the chemical itself, prior to introduction of the raw agricultural commodity into interstate commerce. A

zero-based budgeting
ZBB. A process that emphasizes management's responsibility for planning, budgeting and evaluation. ZBB provides for analysis of alternative methods of operation and various levels of effort. It places new programs on an equal footing with existing programs by requiring ranking of program priorities and thereby provides a systematic basis for allocating resources. U

zero-order reaction
A reaction in which the rate of disappearance of a chemical is independent of the concentration of the chemical or the concentration of any other chemical present in the reaction mixture. A

ZHE
Zero headspace extractor. N

zinc
Total zinc and is determined by the method specified in 40 CFR § 136.3. A

ZOI
Zone of incorporation. N

zone of aeration
The zone between the land surface and the water table. A

zone of influence
The area contiguous to a ditch, channel, or other drainage structure that is directly affected by it. N

zone of initial dilution
ZID. The region of initial mixing surrounding or adjacent to the end of the outfall pipe or diffuser ports,

provided that the ZID may not be larger than allowed by mixing zone restrictions in applicable water quality standards. A

zone of saturation
That part of the earth's crust in which all voids are filled with water. U

zooplankton
Tiny aquatic animals that fish feed on. N

ZRL
Zero risk level. N

Other Related Products by Government Institutes...

BOOKS
For more information on these books and others, please call our Publications Department at (301) 921-2355. Note: prices are subject to change without prior notice.

Book of Lists for Regulated Hazardous Substances, 1993 Edition
Edited by Government Institutes' Staff
Softcover, 345 Pages, May '93, $67 ISBN: 0-86587-337-2

Clean Air Handbook
By F. William Brownell and Lee B. Zeugin
Softcover, 336 pages, Mar '91, $79 ISBN: 0-86587-239-2

Clean Water Handbook
By J. Gordon Arbuckle et al
Softcover, 446 Pages, June '90, $85 ISBN: 0-86587-210-4

Directory of Environmental Information Sources, 4th Edition
Edited by Thomas F. P. Sullivan
Softcover, 322 Pages, Nov '92, $74 ISBN: 0-86587-326-7

Emergency Planning and Community Right-to-Know Act Handbook, 4th Edition
By J. Gordon Arbuckle et al
Softcover, 192 Pages, Jan '92, $67 ISBN: 0-86587-272-4

Environmental Audits, 6th Edition
By Lawrence Cahill and Raymond Kane
Softcover, 592 Pages, Nov '89, $75 ISBN: 0-86587-776-9

Environmental Engineering Dictionary, 2nd Edition
By C.C. Lee, Ph.D.
Hardcover, 630 Pages, Oct '92, $88 ISBN: 0-86587-328-3

Environmental Law Handbook, 12th Edition
By J. Gordon Arbuckle et al
Hardcover, 550 Pages, Apr '93, $68 ISBN: 0-86587-350-X

Environmental Statutes, 1993 Edition
Hardcover, 1,165 Pages, Mar '93, $59 ISBN: 0-86587-352-6

Fundamentals of Environmental Science and Technology
Edited by Porter-C. Knowles
Softcover, 140 pages, Sep '92, $24.95 ISBN: 0-86587-302-X

Greening of American Business: Making Bottom-Line Sense of Environmental Responsibility
Edited by Thomas F. P. Sullivan
Softcover, 350 pages, Sep '92, $24.95 ISBN: 0-86587-295-3

Ground Water Handbook, 2nd Edition
By U.S. Environmental Protection Agency
Softcover, 295 Pages, Mar '92, $69 ISBN: 0-86587-279-1

Health and Safety Audits
By John W. Spencer
Softcover, 336 pages, Apr '92, $65 ISBN: 0-86587-297-X

OSHA Compliance Handbook
By W. Scott Railton
Softcover, 448 Pages, May '92, $79 ISBN: 0-86587-290-2

RCRA Hazardous Wastes Handbook, 9th Edition
By Ridgway M. Hall Jr.
Softcover, 547 Pages, Sep '91, $98 ISBN: 0-86587-270-8

State Environmental Law Handbooks
These comprehensive handbooks are written by respected attorneys from each state, with hands-on experience in dealing daily with the maze of state and federal environmental regulations. For more information on available and forthcoming State Environmental Law Handbooks, please call our Publications Department at (301) 921-2355.

Superfund Manual: Legal and Management Strategies, 5th Edition
By Ridgway M. Hall, Jr. et al
Softcover, 468 Pages, May '93, $95 ISBN: 0-86587-344-5

TSCA Handbook, 2nd Edition
By John D. Conner, Jr. et al
Softcover, 490 Pages, Nov '89, $89 ISBN: 0-86587-791-2

Underground Storage Tank Management: A Practical Guide, 4th Edition
By Joyce A. Rizzo
Softcover, 420 Pages, Nov '91, $79 ISBN: 0-86587-271-9

SUBSCRIPTIONS

Environmental, Health & Safety CFR Update Service
Published Monthly, Code 7200, U.S. $225/year, Outside U.S. $252/year
ISBN: 0-86587-700-9

Environmental Management Review
Edited by Government Institutes' Staff
Published Quarterly, Code 6000, U.S. $188/year, Outside U.S. $252/year
ISSN: 1041-8182

Waste Minimization and Recycling Report
Published monthly, Code 7000, ISSN: 0889-5509 U.S. $198/year; Outside U.S. $252/yr.

COURSES

Our courses reach tens of thousands of professionals each year. Combining the legal, regulatory, technical, management and financial aspects of today's key environmental, health and safety issues — such as environmental laws and regulations, RCRA, CERCLA, UST, TSCA, environmental management, OSHA, pollution prevention, clean air, clean water, and many other topics — we bring together the leading authorities from industry, business and government to shed light on the problems and challenges you face each day. For more information on these and other courses, please call our Education Department at (301) 921-2345.

IN-PLANT TRAINING

These customized training courses ensure effective, relevant, and focused training by tailoring the training program and materials to satisfy the unique requirements of your organization and the specific training needs of your audience. For more information on in-plant training, call our Training Department at (301) 921-2366 to discuss your environmental training needs.

VIDEOS

For more information on these and other videos, please call our Publications Department at (301) 921-2355. Note: prices are subject to change without prior notice.

**Emergency Planning and Community Right-to-Know Act:
What it Means to You**
VHS/15 min./Code 115/1990 $98

Environmental Liability
VHS/18 min./Code 136 $495

Essentials of an Environmental Site Assessment
VHS/50 min./Code 114/1989 $198

Hazard Communication: Employee Introduction
VHS/19 min./Code 117/1985 $495

Hazwoper Awareness Level Training: Your Role as a First Responder
VHS/15 min./Code 139/1991 $495

MSDS: Cornerstone of Chemical Safety
VHS/19 min./Code 116/1986 $495

Our Environment: The Law and You
VHS/23 min./Code 119/1989 $495

Pollution Prevention: The Bottom Line
VHS/24 min./Code 125/1990 $295

To receive a free catalog of our books, courses and videos, please call: (301) 921-2355

or write:
Government Institutes, Inc.
4 Research Place, Suite 200
Rockville, MD 20850